PRENTICE HALL

WORLD EXPLORER

PEOPLE, PLACES, AND CULTURES

James B. Kracht

PEARSON

Prentice Hall

IN ASSOCIATION WITH DK Publishing

Needham, Massachusetts
Upper Saddle River, New Jersey

is a registered trademark of Dorling Kindersley Limited.

Acknowledgments appear on pp. 706–708, which constitutes an extension of this copyright page.

Pearson Prentice Hall™ is a trademark of Pearson Education, Inc.
Pearson® is a registered trademark of Pearson plc.
Prentice Hall® is a registered trademark of Pearson Education, Inc.

ISBN 0-13-166800-5

3 4 5 6 7 8 9 10   08 07 06 05

Author

In 1995, **James B. Kracht** was named Director of the writing team for the Texas Essential Knowledge and Skills for Social Studies and in 1996 was selected as Director of the Social Studies Center for Educator Development. Dr. Kracht is currently Associate Dean for Undergraduate Programs and Teacher Education in the College of Education at Texas A&M University. He has been a faculty member in the Department of Geography and the Department of Teaching, Learning, and Culture at Texas A&M University since 1974. He is also a professional development specialist for the Texas Social Studies Center and co-director of a national demonstration project for interdisciplinary curriculum development at the middle grades.

In 1995, Dr. Kracht was named Director of the writing team for the Texas Essential Knowledge and Skills for Social Studies and in 1996 was selected as Director of the Social Studies Center for Educator Development. Dr. Kracht is currently Associate Dean for Undergraduate programs and Teacher Education in the College of Education at Texas A&M University. He has been a faculty member in the Department of Geography and the Department of Teaching, Learning, and Culture at Texas A&M University since 1974. He is also a professional development specialist for the Texas Social Studies Center and co-director of a national demonstration project for interdisciplinary curriculum development at the middle grades.

Dorling Kindersley is an international publishing company specialising in the creation of high quality reference content for books, CD-ROMs, online, and video. The hallmark of DK content is its unique combination of educational value and strong visual style. This combination allows DK to deliver appealing, accessible, and engaging educational content that delights children, parents, and teachers around the world.

Teacher Reviewers

Betty Adair
Cameron Middle School
Nashville, Tennessee

Marietta Clark
Northview Middle School
Kodak, Tennessee

Nan Elmore
Beardon Middle School
Knoxville, Tennessee

Kristi Karis
West Ottawa Middle School
Holland, Michigan

Deborah J. Miller
Detroit Public Schools
Detroit, Michigan

Nancy Myers
Carter Middle School
Strawberry Plains, Tennessee

Rebecca Revis
Sylvan Hills Junior High School
Sherwood, Arkansas

Flossie Ware
Bellevue Junior High School
Memphis, Tennessee

Program Reviewers

Reading Specialist

Bonnie Armbruster, Ph.D.
Professor of Education
University of Illinois at Urbana-Champaign
Champaign, Illinois

Curriculum and Assessment Specialist

Jan Moberley
Dallas, Texas

Special Program Consultant

Landon Risteen
Chicago, Illinois

Program Advisors

Michal Howden
Social Studies Consultant
Zionsville, Indiana

Kathy Lewis
Social Studies Consultant
Fort Worth, Texas

Joe Wieczorek
Social Studies Consultant
Baltimore, Maryland

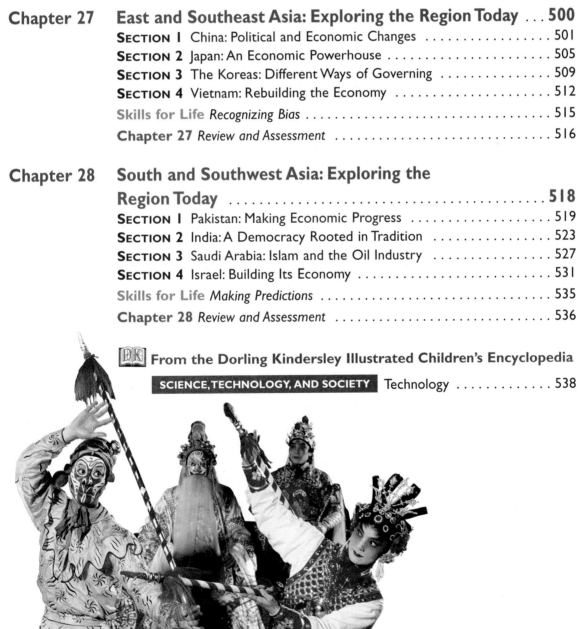

UNIT 7

The Pacific Realm 540

Special Features

Adapted from the Dorling Kindersley Illustrated Children's Encyclopedia

Explore the world through the fascinating images and content of Dorling Kindersley.

Country and Regional Profiles

Examine countries and regions in-depth through special maps, charts, and data.

Skills for Life

Master the essential social studies skills that you will use all your life.

Links to . . .

See how social studies links to other subjects you study in school.

**China
Labor Force**

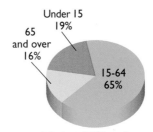

**United Kingdom
Age Structure
(in years)**

Connections

Investigate the connections among social studies topics.

Regional Database

Find data, including statistics, locator maps, and flags, for every country in a region.

Charts, Graphs, and Tables

SIZE OF CONTINENTS

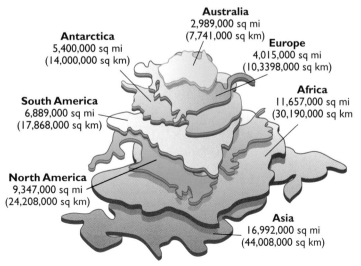

Australia
2,989,000 sq mi
(7,741,000 sq km)

Antarctica
5,400,000 sq mi
(14,000,000 sq km)

Europe
4,015,000 sq mi
(10,3398,000 sq km)

South America
6,889,000 sq mi
(17,868,000 sq km)

Africa
11,657,000 sq mi
(30,190,000 sq km

North America
9,347,000 sq mi
(24,208,000 sq km)

Asia
16,992,000 sq mi
(44,008,000 sq km)

Maps

Chapter Maps

How Latitude and Longitude Form the Global Grid

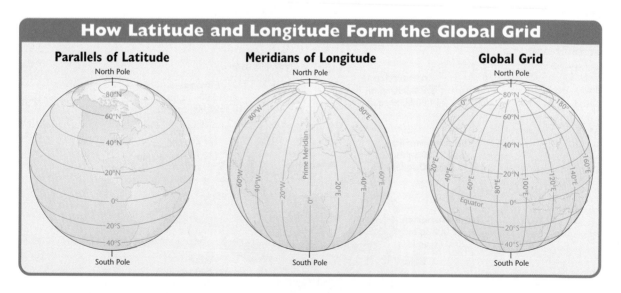

Parallels of Latitude

Meridians of Longitude

Global Grid

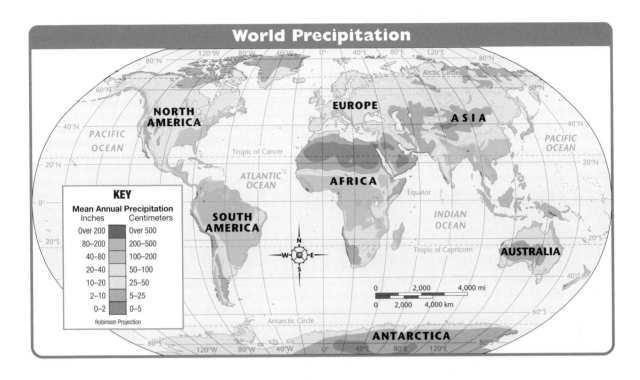

World Precipitation

KEY
Mean Annual Precipitation

Inches	Centimeters
Over 200	Over 500
80–200	200–500
40–80	100–200
20–40	50–100
10–20	25–50
2–10	5–25
0–2	0–5

Robinson Projection

Atlas

Success in social studies comes from doing three things well—reading, testing, and writing. The following pages present strategies to help you read for meaning, understand test questions, and write well.

Reading for Meaning

Do you have trouble remembering what you read? Here are some tips from experts that will improve your ability to recall and understand what you read:

BEFORE YOU READ

Preview the text to identify important information.
Like watching the coming attractions at a movie theater, previewing the text helps you know what to expect. Study the questions and strategies below to learn how to preview what you read.

Ask yourself these questions:	Use these strategies to find the answers:
• What is the text about?	Read the headings, subheadings, and captions. Study the photos, maps, tables, or graphs.
• What do I already know about the topic?	Read the questions at the end of the text to see if you can answer any of them.
• What is the purpose of the text?	Turn the headings into *who, what, when, where, why,* or *how* questions. This will help you decide if the text compares things, tells a chain of events, or explains causes and effects.

Organize information in a way that helps you see meaningful connections or relationships.

Taking notes as you read will improve your understanding. Use graphic organizers like the ones below to record the information you read. Study these descriptions and examples to learn how to create each type of organizer.

Sequencing

A **flowchart** helps you see how one event led to another. It can also display the steps in a process.

Use a flowchart if the text—
- tells about a chain of events.
- explains a method of doing something.

TIP▶ List the events or steps in order.

Comparing and Contrasting

A **Venn diagram** displays similarities and differences.

Use a Venn diagram if the text—
- compares and contrasts two individuals, groups, places, things, or events.

TIP▶ Label the outside section of each circle and list differences.
Label the shared section and list similarities.

Student Success Handbook

AS YOU READ

(continued)

Categorizing Information

A **chart** organizes information in categories.

Use a chart if the text—
- lists similar facts about several places or things.
- presents characteristics of different groups.

TIP▶ Write an appropriate heading for each column in the chart to identify its category.

COUNTRY	FORM OF GOVERNMENT	ECONOMY
Cuba	communist dictatorship	command economy
Puerto Rico	democracy	free enterprise system

Identifying Main Ideas and Details

A **concept web** helps you understand relationships among ideas.

Use a concept web if the text—
- provides examples to support a main idea.
- links several ideas to a main topic.

TIP▶ Write the main idea in the largest circle. Write details in smaller circles and draw lines to show relationships.

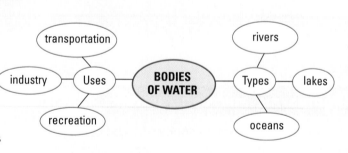

Organizing Information

An **outline** provides an overview, or a kind of blueprint for reading.

Use an outline to organize ideas—
- according to their importance.
- according to the order in which they are presented.

TIP▶ Use Roman numerals for main ideas, capital letters for secondary ideas, and Arabic numerals for supporting details.

> **I. Differences Between the North and the South**
>   **A.** Views on slavery
>   **1.** Northern abolitionists
>   **2.** Southern slave owners
>   **B.** Economies
>   **1.** Northern manufacturing
>   **2.** Southern agriculture

Identifying Cause and Effect

A **cause-and-effect** diagram shows the relationship between what happened (effect) and the reason why it happened (cause).

Use a cause-and-effect chart if the text—
- lists one or more causes for an event.
- lists one or more results of an event.

TIP▶ Label causes and effects. Draw arrows to indicate how ideas are related.

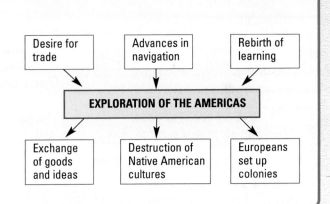

AFTER YOU READ

Test yourself to find out what you learned from reading the text.

Go back to the questions you asked yourself before you read the text. You should be able to give more complete answers to these questions:
- What is the text about?
- What is the purpose of the text?

You should also be able to make connections between the new information you learned from the text and what you already knew about the topic.

Study your graphic organizer. Use this information as the *answers*. Make up a meaningful *question* about each piece of information.

Student *Success* Handbook

Taking Tests

Do you panic at the thought of taking a standardized test? Here are some tips that most test developers recommend to help you achieve good scores.

MULTIPLE-CHOICE QUESTIONS

Read each part of a multiple-choice question to make sure you understand what is being asked.

Many tests are made up of multiple-choice questions. Some multiple-choice items are **direct questions.** They are complete sentences followed by possible answers, called distractors.

Direct Question	What is a narrow strip of land that has water on both sides and joins two larger bodies of land called?
The **distractors** list the possible answers.	**A** a bay **B** an isthmus **C** a lake **D** an island
Try each distractor as an answer to your question. Rule out the ones that don't work.	You can rule out A and C because they are bodies of water, not land. You can rule out D because an island is completely surrounded by water.

Other multiple-choice questions are **incomplete sentences** that you are to finish. They are followed by possible answers.

The **stem** tells you what the question is looking for	A narrow strip of land that has water on both sides and joins two larger bodies of land is called
Distractors	**A** a bay **B** an isthmus **C** a lake **D** an island
Turn the stem into a direct question, using *who, what, when, where,* or *why.*	What is a narrow strip of land that has water on both sides and joins two larger bodies of land called?

WHAT'S BEING TESTED?

Identify the type of question you are being asked.

Social studies tests often ask questions that involve reading comprehension. Other questions may require you to gather or interpret information from a map, graph, or chart. The following strategies will help you answer different kinds of questions.

Reading Comprehension Questions

What to do:

How to do it:

1. Determine the content and organization of the selection.

Read the **title.** Skim the selection. Look for key words that indicate time, cause-and-effect, or comparison.

2. Analyze the questions.
Do they ask you to *recall facts?*

Look for **key words** in the stem:
According to the selection . . .
The selection states that . . .

Do they ask you to *make judgments?*

The main idea of the selection is . . .
The author would likely agree that . . .

3. Read the selection.

Read quickly. Keep the questions in mind.

4. Answer the questions.

Try out each distractor and choose the best answer. Refer back to the selection if necessary.

Example:
A Region of Diversity The Khmer empire was one of many kingdoms in Southeast Asia. Unlike the Khmer empire, however, the other kingdoms were small because Southeast Asia's mountains kept people protected and apart. People had little contact with those who lived outside their own valley.

Why were most kingdoms in Southeast Asia small?
A disease killed many people
B lack of food
C climate was too hot
D mountains kept people apart

TIP▶ The key word because tells why the kingdoms were small.
(The correct answer is D.)

Student *Success* Handbook

Map Questions

What to do:	How to do it:
1. Determine what kind of information is presented on the map.	Read the map **title.** It will indicate the purpose of the map. Study the **map key.** It will explain the symbols used on the map. Look at the **scale.** It will help you calculate distance between places on the map.
2. Read the question. Determine which component on the map will help you find the answer.	Look for **key words** in the stem. About <u>how far</u> . . . [use the scale] <u>What crops</u> were grown in . . . [use the map key]
3. Look at the map and answer the question in your own words.	Do not read the distractors yet.
4. Choose the best answer.	Decide which distractor agrees with the answer you determined from the map.

Example

In which of these countries are Thraco-Illyrian languages spoken?

A Romania
B Albania
C Hungary
D Lithuania

TIP▶ Read the labels and the key to understand the map.
(The correct answer is B.)

Graph Questions

What to do:

1. Determine the purpose of the graph.

2. Determine what information on the graph will help you find the answer.

3. Choose the best answer.

How to do it:

Read the graph **title.** It indicates what the graph represents.

Read the **labels** on the graph or on the key. They tell the units of measurement used by the graph.

Decide which distractor agrees with the answer you determined from the graph.

Example

Religious Persuasion in France

A **circle graph** shows the relationship of parts to the whole in terms of percentages.

After Roman Catholics, the next largest religious population in France is
A Buddhist   **C** Jewish
B Protestant   **D** Muslim

TIP▶ Compare the percentages listed in the labels.
(The correct answer is D.)

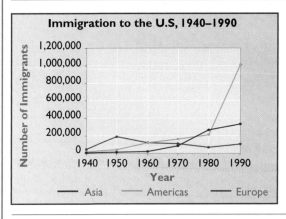

A **line graph** shows a pattern or change over time by the direction of the line.

Between 1980 and 1990, immigration to the U.S. from the Americas
A decreased a little   **C** stayed about the same
B increased greatly   **D** increased a little

TIP▶ Compare the vertical distance between the two correct points on the line graph.
(The correct answer is B.)

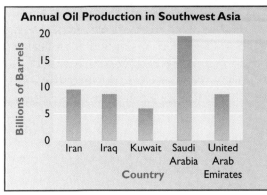

A **bar graph** compares differences in quantity by showing bars of different lengths.

Saudi Arabia produces about how many more billions of barrels of oil a year than Iran?
A 5 billion   **C** 15 billion
B 10 billion   **D** 20 billion

TIP▶ Compare the heights of the bars to find the difference.
(The correct answer is B.)

Writing for Social Studies

When you face a writing assignment, do you think, "How will I ever get through this?" Here are some tips to guide you through any writing project from start to finish.

THE WRITING PROCESS

Follow each step of the writing process to communicate effectively.

Step 1. Prewrite

- Establish the purpose.
- Define the topic.
- Determine the audience.
- Gather details.

Step 2. Draft

- Organize information logically in an outline or graphic organizer.
- Write an introduction, body, and conclusion.
- State main ideas clearly.
- Include relevant details to support your ideas.

Step 3. Revise

- Edit for clarity of ideas and elaboration.

Step 4. Proofread

- Correct any errors in spelling, grammar, and punctuation.

Step 5. Publish and Present

- Copy text neatly by hand, or use a typewriter or word processor.
- Illustrate as needed.
- Create a cover, if appropriate.

TYPES OF WRITING FOR SOCIAL STUDIES

Identify the purpose for your writing.

Each type of writing assignment has a specific purpose, and each purpose needs a different plan for development. The following descriptions and examples will help you identify the three purposes for social studies writing. The lists of steps will help you plan your writing.

Writing to Inform

Purpose: to present facts or ideas

Example

During the 1960s, research indicated the dangers of the insecticide DDT. It killed insects but also had long-term effects. When birds and fish ate poisoned insects, DDT built up in their fatty tissue. The poison also showed up in human beings who ate birds and fish contaminated by DDT.

TIP▶ Look for these **key terms** in the assignment: <u>explain</u>, <u>describe</u>, <u>report</u>, <u>narrate</u>

How to get started:
- Determine the topic you will write about.
- Write a topic sentence that tells the main idea.
- List all the ideas you can think of that are related to the topic.
- Arrange the ideas in logical order.

Writing to Persuade

Purpose: to influence someone

Example

Teaching computer skills in the classroom uses time that could be spent teaching students how to think for themselves or how to interact with others. Students who can reason well, express themselves clearly, and get along with other people will be better prepared for life than those who can use a computer.

TIP▶ Look for these **key terms** in the assignment: <u>convince</u>, <u>argue</u>, <u>request</u>

How to get started:
- Make sure you understand the problem or issue clearly.
- Determine your position.
- List evidence to support your arguments.
- Predict opposing views.
- List evidence you can use to overcome the opposing arguments.

Writing to Provide Historical Interpretations

Purpose: to present the perspective of someone in a different era

Example

The crossing took a week, but the steamship voyage was hard. We were cramped in steerage with hundreds of others. At last we saw the huge statue of the lady with the torch. In the reception center, my mother held my hand while the doctor examined me. Then, my father showed our papers to the official, and we collected our bags. I was scared as we headed off to find a home in our new country.

TIP▶ Look for these **key terms** in the assignment: <u>go back in time</u>, <u>create</u>, <u>suppose that</u>, <u>if you were</u>

How to get started:
- Study the events or issues of the time period you will write about.
- Consider how these events or issues might have affected different people at the time.
- Choose a person whose views you would like to present.
- Identify the thoughts and feelings this person might have experienced.

*Student **Success** Handbook*

RESEARCH FOR WRITING

Follow each step of the writing process to communicate effectively.

After you have identified the purpose for your writing, you may need to do research. The following steps will help you plan, gather, organize, and present information.

Step 1. Ask Questions

| **Ask yourself questions to help guide your research.** | What do I already know about the topic?
What do I want to find out about the topic? |

Step 2. Acquire Information

| **Locate and use appropriate sources of information about the topic.** | Library
Internet search
Interviews |
| **Take notes.** | Follow accepted format for listing sources. |

Step 3. Analyze Information

| **Evaluate the information you find.** | Is it relevant to the topic?
Is it up-to-date?
Is it accurate?
Is the writer an authority on the topic?
Is there any bias? |

Step 4. Use Information

| **Answer your research questions with the information you have found. (You may find that you need to do more research.)** | Do I have all the information I need? |
| **Organize your information into the main points you want to make. Identify supporting details.** | Arrange ideas in outline form or in a graphic organizer. |

Step 5. Communicate What You've Learned

Review the purpose for your writing and choose an appropriate way to present the information.	**Purpose**	**Presentation**
	inform	formal paper, documentary, multimedia
	persuade	essay, letter to the editor, speech
	interpret	journal, newspaper account, drama
Draft and revise your writing, and then evaluate it.	Use a rubric for self-evaluation.	

EVALUATING YOUR WRITING

Use the following rubric to help you evaluate your writing.

	Excellent	Good	Acceptable	Unacceptable
Purpose	Achieves purpose—to inform, persuade, or provide historical interpretation—very well	Informs, persuades, or provides historical interpretation reasonably well	Reader cannot easily tell if the purpose is to inform, persuade, or provide historical interpretation	Lacks purpose
Organization	Develops ideas in a very clear and logical way	Presents ideas in a reasonably well-organized way	Reader has difficulty following the organization	Lacks organization
Elaboration	Explains all ideas with facts and details	Explains most ideas with facts and details	Includes some supporting facts and details	Lacks supporting details
Use of Language	Uses excellent vocabulary and sentence structure with no errors in spelling, grammar, or punctuation	Uses good vocabulary and sentence structure with very few errors in spelling, grammar, or punctuation	Includes some errors in grammar, punctuation, and spelling	Includes many errors in grammar, punctuation, and spelling

Geography: Tools and Concepts

GOVERNMENT

Learn about different forms of government . . .

SCIENCE, TECHNOLOGY, AND SOCIETY

See how people change their environment . . .

HISTORY

Discover who helped build America . . .

What do you want to learn?

CULTURE
Examine differences among cultures . . .

ECONOMICS
Follow workers as they earn a living . . .

GEOGRAPHY
Learn where people live, and why they live there . . .

CITIZENSHIP
Recognize our rights and duties . . .

A journal can be your personal record of discovery. As you learn about the tools and concepts of geography, you can include journal entries about what you read, write, think, and create. For your first entry, write about how geography affects you. How does it affect where you live, what you wear, what you eat, and when you sleep?

EXPLORER'S JOURNAL

Guiding Questions

What questions do I need to ask to understand the tools and concepts of geography?

Asking questions is an important part of learning. Think about what information you would want to know if you were visiting a new place, and what questions you might ask to find the answers. The questions on these pages can help guide your study. You might want to try adding a few of your own!

GEOGRAPHY

Many physical processes have shaped our planet. Some of these processes are violent. Earthquakes and volcanoes can change the landscape in a matter of minutes. Other processes are slow, and almost unnoticeable. Wind slowly wears down rocks and rain carries soil into rivers. Gradually the Earth changes. Mountains, rivers, valleys, and even whole continents are created and changed.

❶ What are some features of the Earth's geography?

HISTORY

People have been living on the Earth for a long time. Geography has played an important role in their history. People move from place to place, seeking better ways of life. Sometimes, they move because of environmental disasters. Other times, they are driven to a new place by war or uncaring governments. The study of geography includes the histories of people and places.

❷ How can knowing a people's history help to better understand them?

CULTURE

Every group of people has a special way of doing things. They have a particular set of beliefs and values. All of these things are affected by geography. Culture can unite people, and it can separate them from other people. The physical landscape of an area gives every group a special set of challenges to meet in order to survive. As people learn to meet these challenges, they develop culture.

❸ Are the world's many cultures more alike or more different?

GOVERNMENT

In order to live together, people need a government. It organizes the way people live and protects them. Yet there are many forms of government, and people must make important choices. Around the world, wherever you go, you will find many examples of the choices they have made.

4 Under what kinds of government do people live?

ECONOMICS

People around the world find many ways to make a living. Some raise crops, herd sheep, or mine for metals. Some labor in steel mills or automobile factories. Others work in medicine or law. Everyone, in fact, takes part in the economy. Learning about the economic choices people make will help you better understand and succeed in the world of work.

5 How do people use the world's resources?

CITIZENSHIP

No matter where they live, people have duties and responsibilities as citizens. These duties, however, depend on the kind of government they have. In some countries, such as the United States, people enjoy many rights, but they must also accept many responsibilities.

6 How do people fulfill their responsibilities as citizens?

SCIENCE, TECHNOLOGY, AND SOCIETY

Science and technology have changed both the face of the Earth and the societies that people have created. People have the ability to change their environment. They can build houses to protect themselves from the weather and climate. They can change the course of rivers and cut down forests.

7 What are the benefits and challenges created by science and technology?

 Take It to the NET

For more information on geography, visit the World Explorer: People, Places, and Cultures companion Web site at **phschool.com.**

ACTIVITY ATLAS

Geography: Tools and Concepts

◆ ◆

Learning about geography tools and concepts requires you to be an explorer, and no explorer would start out without first checking some facts. Begin by exploring the maps and answering the questions on the following pages.

▲ Why do people in this place wear this type of clothing?

▶ Why do visitors to this area become short of breath easily?

Take It to the NET

Items marked with this logo are periodically updated on the Internet. To get current information about geography, go to **phschool.com**.

World: Physical

ALASKA (U.S.)

NORTH AMERICA

Tropic of Cancer

Equator

SOUTH AMERICA

ANDES MOUNTAINS

Tropic of Capricorn

Antarctic Circle

▲ Why did ancient people in this area become expert sailors?

▲ Why do relatively few people live in this area?

EUROPE

ITALY

SAHARA

AFRICA

ASIA

AUSTRALIA

ANTARCTICA

Arctic Circle

Tropic of Cancer

Equator

Tropic of Capricorn

20°W 0° 20°E 40°E 60°E 80°E 100°E 120°E 140°E 160°E 180°

80°N

60°N

40°N

20°N

0°

20°S

20°W 0° 20°E 40°E 60°E 80°E 100°E 120°E 140°E 160°E 80°

| 0 | 1,500 | 3,000 mi |
| 0 | 1,500 | 3,000 km |

KEY

Elevation

Feet		Meters
Over 13,000		Over 3,960
6,500–13,000		1,980–3,960
1,600–6,500		480–1,980
650–1,600		200–480
0–650		0–200
Below sea level		Below sea level

Robinson Projection

I. PLACE
Analyze the Meaning and Purpose of Geography Think about the word *geography*. The word part *geo* comes from a Greek word meaning "earth." *Graphy* means "science of," from an earlier word that meant "to write." How would you define *geography*?

People who are interested in geography are very curious about our world. Look at the pictures on these two pages. The question that accompanies each picture is the type of question that geographers ask. For each picture, write another question a geographer might ask.

ACTIVITY ATLAS

The World: Continents, Oceans, and Seas

2. LOCATION

Locate the Continents and Oceans Study the map above to learn the locations of the continents and oceans. The United States is on the continent of North America. What ocean lies between North America and Africa? Which continent is south of North America? Which ocean lies north of Europe? What two continents share borders with Asia?

3. LOCATION

Compare the Continents This map shows the relative sizes and shapes of the continents because it is a flat map. Look closely. Is Africa smaller, larger, or about the same size as North America? How much larger is Asia than North America? Is Europe larger or smaller than South America? Which continent is the smallest?

4. MOVEMENT

Explore Transportation Corridors Seventy-five percent of the world is covered by water, most of it in the oceans. Ships follow regular trade routes from country to country. This map shows some of the trade routes in the Pacific Ocean.

A. Imagine that a manufacturer is shipping goods from Jakarta, Indonesia, to Vancouver, Canada. At what cities would the ship stop?

B. Which trip covers more distance: Wellington, New Zealand to Tokyo, Japan or Lima, Peru to Los Angeles?

C. Having a good ocean port allows a nation to send and receive goods from other countries. What other benefits do countries gain from being on a trade route?

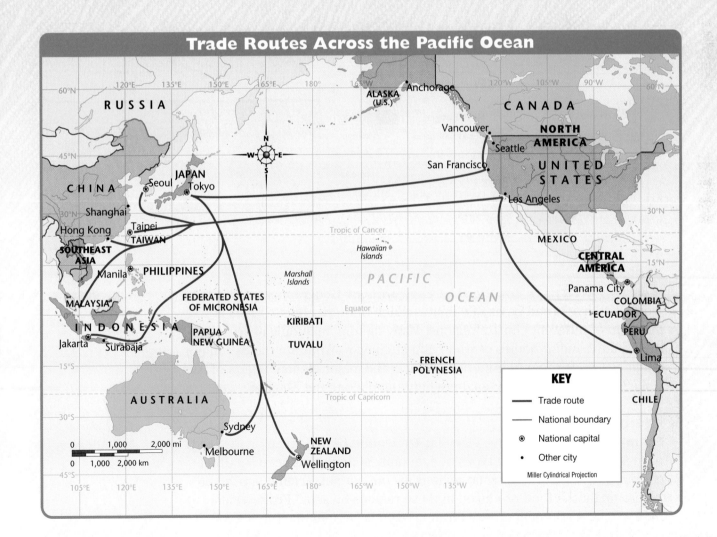

Trade Routes Across the Pacific Ocean

KEY
— Trade route
— National boundary
⊛ National capital
• Other city
Miller Cylindrical Projection

The World: Climate Regions

KEY

Tropical
- Tropical wet
- Tropical wet and dry

Dry
- Semiarid
- Arid

Mild
- Mediterranean
- Humid subtropical
- Marine west coast

Continental
- Humid continental
- Subarctic

Polar
- Tundra
- Ice cap
- Highlands
- Ice pack

Robinson Projection

5. REGIONS

Identify Patterns in the Physical Environment Geographers divide the world into five broad types of climates. Each of these climate types is made up of different climate regions. Many factors, including nearness to the Equator and to bodies of water, affect climate. What are the two major climate regions of South America? What is the major climate region of Australia? What is the major climate region found along the Equator?

6. REGIONS

Examine the Effect of the Physical Environment The map on the next page shows the important types of economic activity that occur in different parts of the world. In what regions is commercial farming important? Where might the food produced in these regions be sent? From which parts of the world might these farming regions get manufactured goods?

World Economic Activity

KEY

- Nomadic herding
- Hunting and gathering
- Forestry
- Livestock raising
- Commercial farming
- Subsistence farming
- Manufacturing and trade
- Commercial fishing
- Little or no activity

Robinson Projection

Take It to the NET

Going to Extremes

7. PLACE

Compare Geographic Factors The diagram below gives information about the highest and lowest recorded temperatures around the world. What place has the world's highest recorded temperature? What place has the world's lowest recorded temperature? What is the hottest temperature recorded in North America? How many degrees (in Fahrenheit) higher is the hottest place than the coldest place, according to the diagram?

 Take It to the NET

LOWEST TEMPERATURE	HIGHEST TEMPERATURE
North America	**North America**
-81° F (-63° C) Snag, Yukon, Canada	134° F (57° C) Death Valley, California, USA
South America	**South America**
-27° F (-33° C) Sarmiento, Argentina	120° F (49° C) Rivadavia, Argentina
Asia	**Asia**
-90° F (-68° C) Verkhoyansk/Oimekon	129° F (54° C) Tirat, Tsvi, Israel
Europe	**Europe**
-67° F (-55° C) Ust `Schugor, Russia	122° F (50° C) Seville, Spain
Africa	**Africa**
-11° F (-24° C) Ifrane, Morocco	136° F (58° C) El Azizia, Libya
Australia	**Australia**
-9° F (-22° C) Charlotte Pass, Australia	128° F (53° C) Cloncurry, Australia
Antarctica	**Antarctica**
-129° F (-89° C) Vostok	59° F (15° C) Vanda Station

Using Geography Skills

Historical Map

USING MAPS

A map is a drawing that shows the distribution and arrangement of features on the Earth. There are many different kinds of maps, and people have been creating and using them ever since they began to explore the world around them. The map above is from 1589. Looking at older maps can tell us a great deal about how earlier peoples thought the world looked.

Comparing Maps
Look at the map on this page and compare it with the map of the world in the Activity Atlas on page 6. What differences do you see? What are some reasons for these differences?

Making a Map
Maps can show anything from a specific place to the entire world. Create a map of your neighborhood, including any important features. Display your map in the classroom.

Understanding the Earth

READING FOCUS

1. How does the movement of the Earth around the sun affect our environment?

2. What is the effect of latitude on climate?

KEY TERMS

environment	latitude
orbit	low latitudes
revolution	high latitudes
axis	middle latitudes
rotation	

KEY PLACES

Equator	Arctic Circle
Tropic of Cancer	Antarctic Circle
Tropic of Capricorn	

MAIN IDEA

The relationship between the Earth and the sun creates our days, seasons, and climate, and influences our environment.

NOTE TAKING

Copy the concept web shown here. As you read the section, fill in the blank ovals with information about the Earth. Add as many ovals as you need.

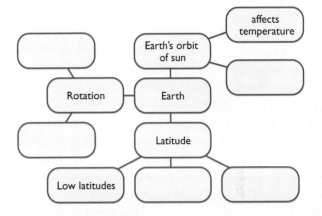

Setting the Scene

"The Sky Father opened his hand. Within every crease there lay innumerable grains of shining maize [corn]. In his thumb and forefinger he took some of the shining grains and placed them in the sky as brilliant stars to be a guide to humans when the bright sun was hidden."

This is part of an ancient myth of the Pueblos, who live in what today is the southwestern United States. They used the story to explain the appearance of the night sky.

The Earth, the Sun, and Our Environment

The Earth, the sun, the planets, and most of the stars we see in the night sky are part of a galaxy, or family of stars. We call our galaxy the Milky Way because the lights from its billions of stars look like a milky band across the night sky. There are other galaxies, but they are so distant that they are only specks of light. Our sun is a star in the Milky Way. The sun provides light and the energy needed for life on the Earth. It affects our **environment,** or surroundings, in countless ways.

The Surface of the Sun

SCIENCE AND TECHNOLOGY

The sun is the largest object in our solar system and accounts for more than 99% of the total mass of the solar system.

Critical Thinking What are some of the ways that the sun affects life on the Earth?

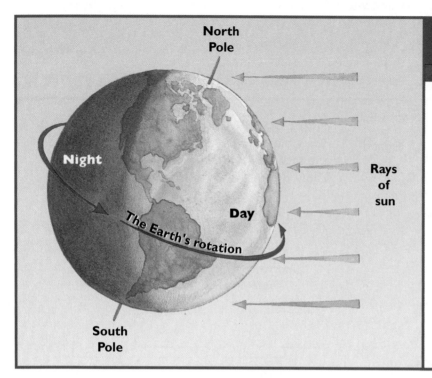

North Pole

Night

The Earth's rotation

Day

Rays of sun

South Pole

How Night Changes Into Day

GEOGRAPHY This diagram shows how places on the Earth move from night into day. Today, it takes almost 24 hours for the Earth to make one complete rotation. One-half of the Earth is always lighted by the sun, while the other half is in darkness. **Chart Study** As time passes, the Earth spins more and more slowly. What will eventually happen to the length of a day? Find North America on the globe. Which coast receives daylight first?

Understanding Days and Nights The sun may be about 93 million miles (150 million km) away, but it still provides the Earth with heat and light. The Earth travels around the sun in an oval-shaped path called an **orbit.** It takes 365 ¼ days, or just a little more than one year, for the Earth to complete one **revolution,** or journey, around the sun.

As the Earth revolves around the sun, it is also spinning in space. The Earth turns around its **axis**—an imaginary line running through it between the North and South poles. Each complete turn, which takes about 24 hours, is called a **rotation.** As the Earth rotates, it is daytime on the side facing the sun, and it is night on the side away from the sun.

Understanding Seasons At certain times of the year and in certain places, days are longer than nights, and at other times, nights are longer than days. This happens, in part, because the Earth's axis is at an angle. At some points in the Earth's orbit, the tilt causes a region to face toward the sun for more hours than it faces away from the sun. Days are longer. At other times, the region faces away from the sun for more hours than it faces toward the sun. Days are shorter.

The Earth's tilt and orbit also cause changes in temperatures. The warmth you feel depends on how directly the sunlight falls on the region in which you live. Some regions receive much fairly direct sunlight, while other regions receive no direct sunlight.

The amount of sunlight also partly determines how much food we produce and where people live. For example, fewer crops grow in regions that receive little direct sunlight, so fewer people live there. Regions that get more sunlight, like the United States, can grow more food to feed large populations.

The Effect of Latitude

Imaginary lines, called lines of **latitude,** are east-west circles around the globe. Some of these lines of latitude have special names. They divide the Earth into regions according to the amount of sunlight they receive.

Look at the diagram below. The **Equator** is a latitude line that circles the Earth exactly halfway between the North Pole and the South Pole. On about March 21 and September 23, the sun is directly over the Equator. At those times, days are almost exactly as long as nights. These days are the spring and fall equinoxes.

Two other lines of latitude are the **Tropic of Cancer** and the **Tropic of Capricorn.** On June 21 or 22, the sun shines directly above the Tropic of Cancer. This day is the summer solstice (SOHL stiss), in the Northern Hemisphere. On December 21 or 22, the sun shines directly above the Tropic of Capricorn. This day marks the winter solstice in the Northern Hemisphere. The seasons are reversed in the Southern Hemisphere. When would the summer solstice occur there?

The area between the Tropic of Cancer and the Tropic of Capricorn is called the **low latitudes,** or the tropics. Any location in the

Midnight Sun The Earth's axis is at an angle, which makes the Earth seem to lean. When the North Pole leans toward the sun, the sun never sets. At the same time, the South Pole leans away from the sun, so at the South Pole, the sun never rises. This lasts for six months. When the South Pole leans toward the sun, this pole has six months of continuous sunlight.

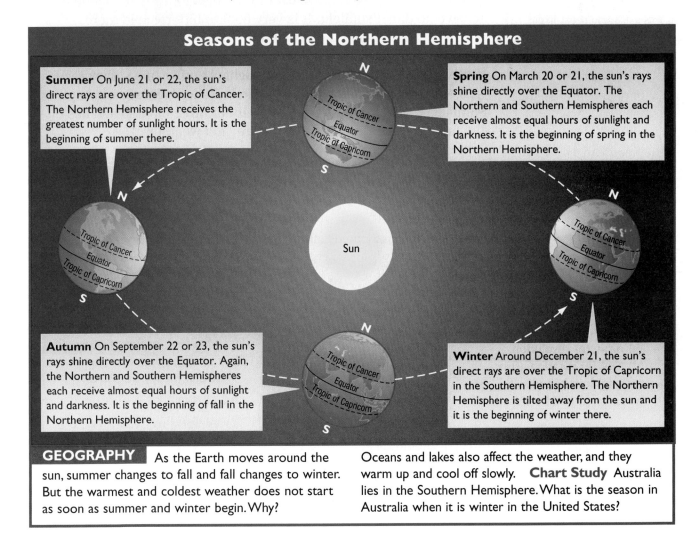

Seasons of the Northern Hemisphere

Summer On June 21 or 22, the sun's direct rays are over the Tropic of Cancer. The Northern Hemisphere receives the greatest number of sunlight hours. It is the beginning of summer there.

Spring On March 20 or 21, the sun's rays shine directly over the Equator. The Northern and Southern Hemispheres each receive almost equal hours of sunlight and darkness. It is the beginning of spring in the Northern Hemisphere.

Sun

Autumn On September 22 or 23, the sun's rays shine directly over the Equator. Again, the Northern and Southern Hemispheres each receive almost equal hours of sunlight and darkness. It is the beginning of fall in the Northern Hemisphere.

Winter Around December 21, the sun's direct rays are over the Tropic of Capricorn in the Southern Hemisphere. The Northern Hemisphere is tilted away from the sun and it is the beginning of winter there.

GEOGRAPHY As the Earth moves around the sun, summer changes to fall and fall changes to winter. But the warmest and coldest weather does not start as soon as summer and winter begin. Why? Oceans and lakes also affect the weather, and they warm up and cool off slowly. **Chart Study** Australia lies in the Southern Hemisphere. What is the season in Australia when it is winter in the United States?

GEOGRAPHY This field of icebergs creates a beautiful, if eerie landscape. Icebergs are large, floating masses of ice that have broken away from glaciers. **Critical Thinking** In what regions are you most likely to find icebergs?

low latitudes receives direct sunlight at some time during the year. In this region, it is almost always hot.

Two other latitude lines set off distinct regions. To the north of the Equator, at 66°N, is the **Arctic Circle.** To the south of the Equator, at 66°S, is the **Antarctic Circle.** The regions between these circles and the poles are the **high latitudes,** or the polar zones. The high latitudes receive no direct sunlight. It is very cool to bitterly cold there.

Two areas remain: the **middle latitudes** of the northern and southern hemispheres, or the temperate zones. At some times of the year, these areas receive fairly direct sunlight. At other times, they receive fairly indirect sunlight. So, the middle latitudes have seasons: spring, summer, winter, and fall. Each lasts about three months and has distinct patterns of daylight, temperature, and weather.

SECTION I ASSESSMENT

AFTER YOU READ

RECALL

1. Identify: (a) Equator, (b) Tropic of Cancer, (c) Tropic of Capricorn, (d) Arctic Circle, (e) Antarctic Circle

2. Define: (a) environment, (b) orbit, (c) revolution, (d) axis, (e) rotation, (f) latitude, (g) low latitudes, (h) high latitudes, (i) middle latitudes

COMPREHENSION

3. How do the Earth's rotation, its tilt, and its orbit around the sun affect our environment?

4. How does latitude affect the climate of various regions of the Earth?

CRITICAL THINKING AND WRITING

5. **Exploring the Main Idea** Review the Main Idea statement at the beginning of this section. Then, write a paragraph describing what might happen to plant and animal life on the Earth if the Earth did not tilt on its axis, and why.

6. **Drawing Conclusions** It is June 21st. You are traveling from the middle latitudes of North America to the middle latitudes of Africa. Write a journal entry that describes what kind of temperature differences you might expect between these two places.

ACTIVITY

7. **Writing to Learn** Write a storybook for a young child explaining the relationship between the Earth and the sun.

The Five Themes of Geography

Setting the Scene

Michael Collins, an astronaut who went to the moon, described Earth as he saw it from his spaceship in July 1969, about 200 miles above the Earth.

"The Indian Ocean flashes incredible colors of emerald jade and opal in the shallow water surrounding the Maldive Islands…. Now the sun glints in unusual fashion off the ocean near Formosa [Taiwan]. There are intersecting surface ripples just south of the island, patterns which are clearly visible and which, I think, must be useful to fishermen who need to know about these currents."

The Study of Geography

From his high perch, Michael Collins was looking at the world as a geographer does. **Geography** is the study of the Earth. Geographers analyze the Earth from many points of view. They discuss how far one place is from another. They study oceans, plant life, landforms, and people. Geographers study how the Earth and its people affect each other.

GEOGRAPHY Huge clouds drift over the Indian Ocean while the nearby land remains clearly visible. **Critical Thinking** What features of the land can you identify?

How Latitude and Longitude Form the Global Grid

Parallels of Latitude

Meridians of Longitude

Global Grid

GEOGRAPHY

Latitude and longitude lines can help you find the absolute location, or geographic address, of a place. You can give the address as, for example, 20°S, 140°E. **Map Study** Find 20°S, 140°E on the Global Grid. What continent is found at this location?

The Themes of Geography: Five Ways to Look at the Earth

In their work, geographers are guided by two basic questions: (1) Where are things located? and (2) Why are they there? The answers can be organized according to five themes: location, place, human-environment interaction, movement, and regions.

Location Geographers begin a study of a place by describing its location. They identify the absolute location by using two kinds of imaginary lines around the Earth: latitude and longitude.

Lines of latitude are the imaginary east-west circles around the globe. They are also called **parallels,** because they are parallel to one another. These circles divide the globe into units called **degrees.** In the middle of the globe is the parallel called the Equator, which is 0° latitude. Geographers measure locations north and south of the Equator. The farthest latitude north of the Equator is 90° north, the location of the North Pole. The farthest latitude south of the Equator is 90° south, the location of the South Pole.

Geographers also must pinpoint a place from east to west. For this they use lines of **longitude.** These lines, also called **meridians**, circle the globe from north to south. All meridians begin and end at the North and South poles. The **Prime Meridian**, which runs through Greenwich, England, is 0° longitude. Geographers describe locations as east or west of the Prime Meridian. The maximum longitude is 180°, halfway around the world from the Prime Meridian.

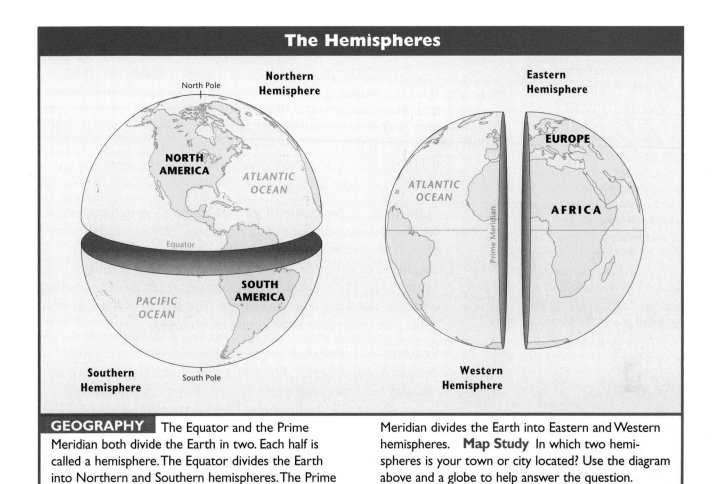

The Hemispheres

Northern Hemisphere

North Pole

NORTH AMERICA

ATLANTIC OCEAN

Equator

PACIFIC OCEAN

SOUTH AMERICA

Southern Hemisphere

South Pole

Eastern Hemisphere

ATLANTIC OCEAN

EUROPE

AFRICA

Western Hemisphere

GEOGRAPHY The Equator and the Prime Meridian both divide the Earth in two. Each half is called a hemisphere. The Equator divides the Earth into Northern and Southern hemispheres. The Prime Meridian divides the Earth into Eastern and Western hemispheres. **Map Study** In which two hemispheres is your town or city located? Use the diagram above and a globe to help answer the question.

Geographers also discuss relative location. This explains where a place is by describing places near it. Suppose you live in Victoria, Texas. Victoria's relative location is about 120 miles southeast of Austin, the capital city.

Place Geographers also study place. This includes a location's physical and human features. To describe physical features, you might say the climate is hot or that the land is hilly. Human features include how many people live in a place and the work they do.

On maps, geographers use color or special symbols to show regions. A place can be part of several regions at the same time. For example, Houston, Texas, is in both a plains region and an oil-producing region.

LINKS TO

Math

Using Latitude Latitude can be used to measure distance north or south. One degree of latitude is equal to about 69 miles. For example, Wichita Falls, Texas, is located about 5 degrees north of San Antonio. Therefore, we can determine that Wichita Falls is about 345 miles north of San Antonio (5 x 69 = 345).

GOVERNMENT

The government plays an important role in balancing the interaction of humans with the environment. For example, the Missouri River once supported some of the most abundant fish and wildlife in North America. However, the river often flooded and barges could not always navigate it. People wanted to tame the river. As a result, in the late 1800s the United States government began building a series of huge dams. The river channel was also straightened and deepened to make it easier for barges to travel the river. As a result of the changes, the river could no longer support fish and wildlife. In the late twentieth century, the government recognized this and took some steps to restore parts of the river.

Critical Thinking Why do you think the government wanted to control the river? Do you think governments should try to change the natural environment?

Human-Environment Interaction The theme of interaction stresses how people affect their environment, the physical characteristics of their natural surroundings, and how their environment affects them. For instance, because farms in Turkey receive little rain, farmers irrigate the land. As a result, people have more food. However, irrigation causes salt to build up in the soil. Farmers must then treat to soil to get rid of the salt. As a result, food could become more expensive.

Movement The theme of movement helps geographers understand the relationship among places. Movement helps explain how people, goods, and ideas get from one place to another. For example, when people from other countries came to the United States, they brought traditional foods that enriched the American way of life. The theme of movement helps you understand such cultural changes.

Regions Geographers use the theme of regions to make comparisons. A region has a unifying characteristic such as climate, land, population, or history. For example, the Nile Valley region is a snake shaped region on either side of the Nile River. The region runs through several countries. Life in the valley is much different from life in the regions alongside the valley. There, the landscape is mostly desert.

SECTION 2 ASSESSMENT

AFTER YOU READ

RECALL

1. Define (a) geography, (b) parallel, (c) degree, (d) longitude, (e) meridian, (f) Prime Meridian

COMPREHENSION

2. Why do people study geography?

3. What are the five themes of geography?

CRITICAL THINKING AND WRITING

4. **Exploring the Main Idea** Review the Main Idea statement at the beginning of this section. Then, write a paragraph explaining why it is important to study the geography of the earth.

5. **Drawing Conclusions** The city of Buenos Aires is at approximately 34° S latitude and 58° W longitude. From this information, how can you tell in which hemispheres this city is located?

ACTIVITY

 Take It to the NET

6. **Measuring Latitude and Longitude** Measure the degrees of latitude and longitude that show your location on the Earth. Draw a map that includes lines of latitude and longitude, and indicate your location on the map. Visit the World Explorer: People, Places, and Cultures section of **phschool.com** for help in completing this activity.

Using the Tools of Geography

BEFORE YOU READ

READING FOCUS

1. What are the advantages and disadvantages of globes and maps in showing the Earth's surface?

2. How did Mercator try to create an accurate map?

3. What are the parts of a map?

KEY TERMS

globe
scale
distortion
projection

compass rose
cardinal direction
key
grid

KEY PEOPLE

Gerhardus Mercator
Arthur Robinson

MAIN IDEA

Representing the Earth as a globe and as a flat map present different problems.

NOTE TAKING

Copy the concept web shown here. As you read the section, fill in the ovals with information about the tools of geography. Add as many ovals as you need.

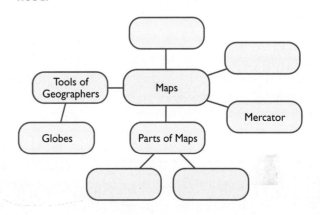

Setting the Scene

You might expect a map to be printed on a piece of paper. But hundreds of years ago, people made maps out of whatever was available. The Inuit (IN oo it) people carved detailed, accurate maps on pieces of wood. They needed maps that were portable, durable, and waterproof.

Globes and Maps

In those days, people knew very little about the land and water beyond their own homes. Their maps showed only the areas they traveled.

As people explored the Earth, they collected information about the shapes and sizes of islands, continents, and bodies of water. Mapmakers wanted to present this information accurately. The best way was to put it on a **globe,** a round model of the Earth itself. By using the same shape, mapmakers could show the continents and oceans of the Earth much as they really are. The only difference would be the **scale,** or size.

CULTURE The Marshall Islanders made wood maps of the southwest Pacific Ocean. Palm sticks show wave patterns and ocean currents and shells show islands. **Critical Thinking** Why do you think the people made their maps out of these materials? Why was it important to show ocean currents on their maps?

The World: A Mercator Projection

GEOGRAPHY Mercator maps make areas near the poles look bigger than they are. This is because on a globe, the lines of longitude meet at the poles, but on a flat Mercator map, they are parallel. Mercator maps are useful to navigators because the longitude and latitude lines appear straight. Navigators can use these lines and a compass to plot a ship's route. **Map Study** Here Greenland looks bigger than it really is. What other areas do you think might look larger than they should? Why?

But there is a problem with globes. A globe cannot be detailed enough to be useful and at the same time be small enough to be convenient. People, therefore, also need flat maps.

Flat maps, however, present another problem. Because the Earth is round it is impossible to show the Earth on a flat surface without some **distortion,** or change in the accuracy of its shapes and distances. Something is going to look larger or smaller than it really is.

AS YOU READ

Monitor Your Reading
What question would you ask Gerhardus Mercator about the map he made in 1569?

Making Maps

In 1569, a geographer named **Gerhardus Mercator** (juh RAHR duhs muhr KAYT uhr) created a flat map to help sailors navigate long journeys around the globe. To make his map flat, Mercator expanded the area between longitudes near the poles. Mercator's map was very useful to sailors. They made careful notes about the distortions they found on their journeys. More than 400 years later, those notes and the Mercator **projection,** or method of putting a map of the Earth onto a flat piece of paper, are used by nearly all deep-sea navigators.

When Mercator made his map, he made sure that the shape of the landmasses and ocean areas was similar to the shapes on a globe. But he had to stretch the spaces between the longitudes. This distorted the sizes of some of the land. Land near the Equator was about right, but land near the poles became much larger. For example, on Mercator's map, Greenland looks bigger than South America when it is only one eighth the size.

The World: Interrupted and Robinson Projections

Interrupted Projection

ARCTIC OCEAN

NORTH AMERICA
EUROPE
ASIA
60°N
30°N
PACIFIC OCEAN
ATLANTIC OCEAN
AFRICA
0°
Equator
INDIAN OCEAN
SOUTH AMERICA
AUSTRALIA
30°S
60°S
180° 150°W 120°W 90°W 60°W 30°W 0° 30°E 60°E 90°E 120°E 150°E
ANTARCTICA

Robinson Projection

ARCTIC OCEAN

NORTH AMERICA
EUROPE
ASIA
60°N
30°N
PACIFIC OCEAN
ATLANTIC OCEAN
AFRICA
0°
Equator
SOUTH AMERICA
INDIAN OCEAN
AUSTRALIA
30°S
180° 150°W 120°W 90°W 60°W 30°W 0° 30°E 60°E 90°E 120°E 150°E
60°S
ANTARCTICA

Mapmakers have tried other techniques. The interrupted projection is like the ripped peel of an orange. By creating gaps in the picture of the world, mapmakers showed the size and shape of land accurately. The gaps make it impossible to figure distances correctly. You could not use this projection to chart a course across an ocean.

Today, many geographers believe **Arthur Robinson's** projection is the best world map available. This projection shows the size and shape of the land quite accurately. Sizes of the oceans and distances are also fairly accurate. However, even a Robinson projection has distortions, especially in areas around the edges of the map.

There are many other types of projections. Each has advantages and drawbacks. It all depends on how you want to use each one.

The Parts of a Map

Geographers use symbols and tools on maps. One of the most important is a **compass rose,** which is a model of a compass. It tells the **cardinal directions,** which are north, south, east, and west.

Maps also have an indicator for scale that tells what a certain distance on the map stands for on the surface of the Earth. Scales vary

GEOGRAPHY There are many ways to show a globe on a flat map. The interrupted projection map, on the left, shows the real sizes and shapes of continents. While the Robinson projection does distort the globe a little, it shows the sizes and shapes of countries most accurately. **Critical Thinking** Do you think the Robinson projection would be as useful to a navigator as the Mercator projection? Why or why not?

A Road Map

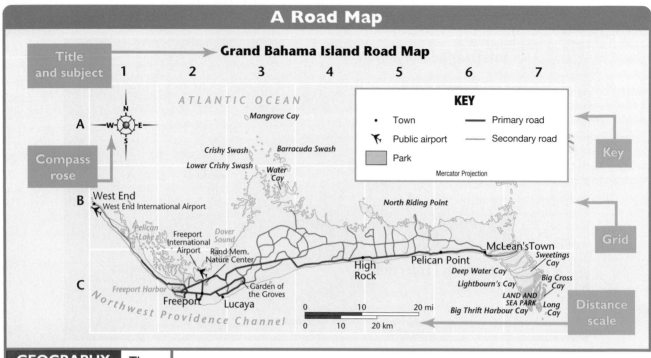

Grand Bahama Island Road Map

Title and subject

Compass rose

Key

Grid

Distance scale

GEOGRAPHY The road map above has a grid of numbers and letters to help locate places. **Map Study** What airport is located at B-1? Where can you find Freeport?

depending on the map. On the map 1 inch might equal 1 mile or 100 miles on the ground.

Mapmakers use symbols to indicate landmarks, such as roads or towns. These symbols are explained in the **key,** or legend.

Maps often include a **grid.** Some maps use a grid of latitude and longitude lines. Other maps use a grid of letters and numbers.

SECTION 3 ASSESSMENT

AFTER YOU READ

RECALL
1. Identify the people:
  (a) Gerhardus Mercator,
  (b) Arthur Robinson

2. Define: (a) globe, (b) scale, (c) distortion, (d) projection, (e) compass rose, (f) cardinal direction, (g) key, (h) grid

COMPREHENSION
3. Compare the use of maps and globes for showing the Earth.

4. What is the main problem with the interrupted projection?

5. Why are the different parts of a map important?

CRITICAL THINKING AND WRITING
6. Exploring the Main Idea Review the Main Idea statement at the beginning of this section. Then list some of the obstacles faced by mapmakers.

7. Making Comparisons You are planning a hiking trip to a nearby state park. You have two maps: a road map and a map of the park. What advantages does each map have?

ACTIVITY
8. Writing to Learn Think of a place you like to visit. How would you tell a friend to get there? Make some notes about directions and landmarks you could include in a map. Then, make a map that shows how to get there.

Studying Distribution Maps

Mexico: Population Distribution

UNITED STATES

Gulf of Mexico

MEXICO

Tropic of Cancer

KEY
• One dot represents 200,000 people

Lambert Azimuthal Equal-Area Projection

0   200   400 mi

0   200   400 km

Learn the Skill

A distribution map is a specialized map that shows how something—people, forests, volcanoes—is distributed, or scattered, over land. A population distribution map, for example, shows how a population is distributed in a particular area. To study a distribution map, follow these steps:

A. Read the title of the map. The title will tell you the topic of the map.

B. Read the key. The key will give you important information you need to understand the map. Often, it will show a symbol and tell you what the symbol stands for.

C. Use the information from the key to read the map.

Practice the Skill

Now that you know how to read a distribution map, study the population distribution map of Mexico. Look at the key to get a sense of what the map is about. How is population represented on the map? How many people does each symbol stand for? Where do most of the people of Mexico live? Why do you think the population is distributed the way it is? Think about physical factors such as climate and landforms.

Apply the Skill

See the Chapter Review and Assessment at the end of this chapter for more questions on distribution maps.

Review and Assessment

Chapter Summary

The following ideas are important to remember about Chapter 1:

GEOGRAPHY: TOOLS AND CONCEPTS

Section 1
The Earth revolves around the sun while rotating on its axis. It is tilted on this axis. The combination of these elements creates our days and nights and our seasons.

Section 2
Geographers organize their study of the Earth by organizing it into five themes: location, place, human-environment interaction, movement, and regions.

Section 3
Geographers have created various tools, including globes and maps, to make the study of the Earth both accurate and easy. These include a variety of map projections. They use the map key, compass rose, scale, and grid to give information about a map.

Reviewing Key Terms

Match the following geography terms with their definitions.

Column I
1. globe
2. latitude
3. scale
4. geography
5. longitude
6. Prime Meridian
7. Equator
8. cardinal direction

Column II
a. model of the Earth
b. imaginary line that circles the globe halfway between the North and South poles
c. imaginary lines that circle the Earth from east to west
d. imaginary lines circling the globe from north to south
e. a line of longitude that runs through Greenwich, England
f. the study of the Earth
g. the size of an area on a map as compared to the area's actual size
h. north, south, east, or west

Reviewing the Main Ideas

1. How does the physical relationship between the Earth and the sun create our days, seasons, and climate? (Section 1)
2. What is the difference between the geographic themes of place and location? (Section 2)
3. What is the human-environment interaction theme of geography? (Section 2)
4. Use the theme of regions to compare your region to another. (Section 2)
5. Why have geographers created so many different types of maps? (Section 3)
6. What is the difference between a globe and a map? (Section 3)
7. Why does "distortion" matter? (Section 3)
8. How do you use the term *grid* in geography? (Section 3)

Map Activity

The Globe

For each place listed below, write the letter from the globe that shows its location on your own paper.

1. Prime Meridian
2. Equator
3. North Pole
4. South Pole
5. Europe
6. Africa
7. South America
8. North America

 Take It to the NET

Enrichment For more map activities using geography skills, visit the Social Studies section of **phschool.com.**

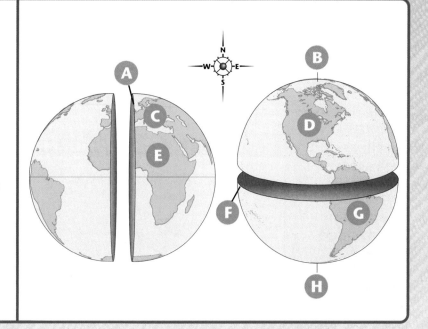

Writing Activity

Writing a Paragraph

1. Write a paragraph describing ways that you have seen people use maps. You may include such things as road maps, maps for seats in a sports arena or areas in a museum, or even hand-drawn maps to a friend's house.

Writing a Report

2. Write a brief report explaining why spring arrives earlier in some parts of the United States than in other parts. You may include illustrations showing the tilt of the Earth in relation to the sun, or maps showing the different regions of the United States and when spring arrives in those regions.

Applying Your Skills

Turn to the Skills for Life activity on p. 23 to help you complete the following activity.

Find a distribution map in the library or on the Internet. Write a series of questions that test an understanding of how to read and use the map. Trade your map and questions with a partner and answer each other's questions.

Critical Thinking

1. **Making Inferences** If the sun is directly over the Tropic of Capricorn, how many months will it be before spring arrives in the United States?
2. **Generalizing** All maps of the Earth that are drawn on a flat piece of paper include distortions. Are there also distortions on maps of small areas, such as your town? Explain your answer.

 Take It to the NET

Activity Create a map of your city or town and include a legend or key. Visit the World Explorer: People, Places, and Cultures section of **pschool.com** for help in completing this activity.

Chapter 1 Self-Test As a final review activity, take the Chapter 1 Self-Test and get instant feedback on your answers. To take the test, visit the Social Studies section of **phschool.com.**

Earth's Physical Geography

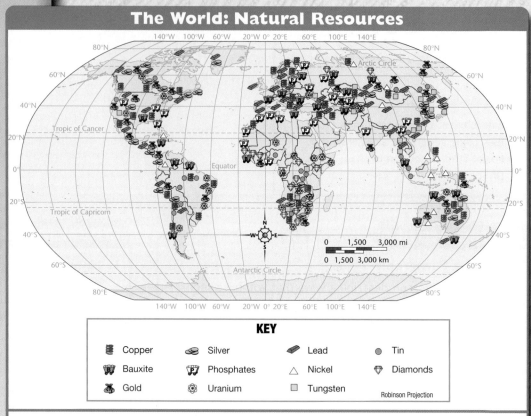

The World: Natural Resources

KEY

Copper	Silver	Lead	Tin	
Bauxite	Phosphates	Nickel	Diamonds	
Gold	Uranium	Tungsten		

Robinson Projection

USING MAPS

Study the natural resources map. Then, complete the following activities.

Learning About Resources

Visit the library or the Internet to learn about the uses of the natural resources listed in the map key. Organize the information you find in a brief report, making sure to explain why these resources are important.

Drawing Conclusions

Many countries have a wealth of natural resources. Yet not all of these countries have prospered from these resources. Work with a partner to make a list of reasons as to why this might be so.

Physical Features and Processes

READING FOCUS QUESTIONS

1. What physical processes occur within the Earth?
2. What physical processes occur on the Earth's surface?
3. Describe air and water—two of the most important natural resources needed for life on Earth.

KEY TERMS

landform	plate tectonics
mountain	plate
hill	weathering
plateau	erosion
plain	atmosphere

KEY PLACES

Pangaea

MAIN IDEA

Physical processes both within the Earth and on its surface are constantly changing and renewing its physical features: its land, air, and water.

NOTE TAKING

Copy the outline shown here. As you read the section, fill in the outline with information about Earth. Add headings and details to make the outline more complete.

> I. **Physical features and processes inside Earth**
>   A. Earth's structure
>   1. 75 percent water
>   2.
>   B. Pangaea
> II. **Physical features and processes on Earth's surface**
>   A. Weathering
>   B.
> III. **Natural resources**
>   A. Air
>   B.

Setting the Scene

Earthquakes and volcanic eruptions are two forces that shape and reshape the Earth. They provide clues about the Earth's structure and are one reason why the Earth's surface constantly changes.

Physical Processes Inside the Earth

To understand events like volcanic eruptions and earthquakes, geographers study the Earth's structure. Pictures of the Earth show a great deal of water and some land. The water covers about 75 percent of the Earth's surface in lakes, rivers, seas, and oceans. Only 25 percent of the Earth's surface is land.

In part, continents are unique because of their **landforms,** or shapes and types of land. **Mountains** are landforms that rise usually more than 2,000 feet (610 m) above sea level. They are wide at the bottom and rise steeply to a narrow peak or ridge. **Hills** are lower and less steep than mountains. A **plateau** is a large, elevated piece of flat land. **Plains** are large areas of flat or gently rolling land. Many are along coasts, while others are in the interior.

CULTURE Hawaii Island has the largest active volcano in the world. Molten lava formed the islands one at a time. Eventually, plants and animals arrived. About 2,000 years ago, the first humans settled on the islands. **Critical Thinking** What kinds of challenges might the first settlers have faced? How might these people have changed the land they found?

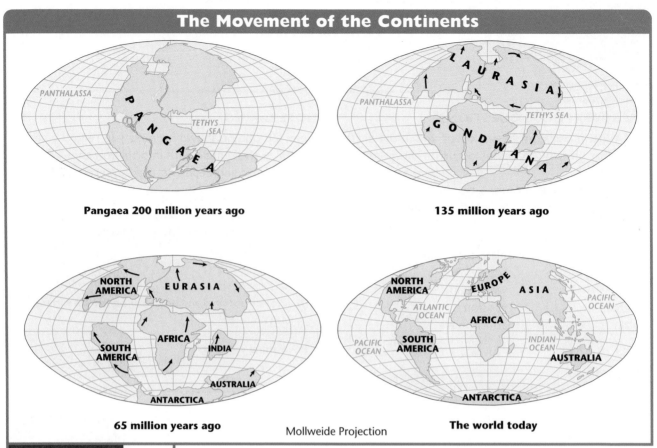

The Movement of the Continents

PANTHALASSA
P A N G A E A
TETHYS SEA

Pangaea 200 million years ago

L A U R A S I A
PANTHALASSA
TETHYS SEA
G O N D W A N A

135 million years ago

NORTH AMERICA
EURASIA
SOUTH AMERICA
AFRICA
INDIA
AUSTRALIA
ANTARCTICA

65 million years ago

Mollweide Projection

NORTH AMERICA
EUROPE
ASIA
ATLANTIC OCEAN
PACIFIC OCEAN
AFRICA
PACIFIC OCEAN
SOUTH AMERICA
INDIAN OCEAN
AUSTRALIA
ANTARCTICA

The world today

GEOGRAPHY

These diagrams, based on the theory of plate tectonics, show how Pangaea broke apart and formed the continents we know today. **Map Study** If you were a scientist trying to prove the theory of plate tectonics, what clues would you look for?

Pangaea: The Supercontinent   Geographers theorize that at one time the Earth had only one huge landmass, called **Pangaea** (pan JEE uh). They think that Pangaea split into pieces and began to pull apart, with the pieces forming our continents.

Geographers explain the movement of continents with a theory called **plate tectonics.** According to this theory, the outer skin of the Earth, called the crust, is broken into huge pieces called **plates.** The continents and oceans are the top of the crust. Below the plates is a layer of rock called magma, which is hot enough to be fairly soft. The plates float on the magma. Over time, the plates move about, taking the continents with them. This movement is very slow. A plate that moves quickly might shift just 2 inches (5 cm) a year.

Volcanoes, Earthquakes, and Shifting Plates   The vast plates move in different directions. Some ocean plates move apart, and magma leaks through cracks in the crust. Over time, the cooling rock builds up to form lines of underwater mountains called ridges. In other places, the plates push against one another, forcing one plate under the other. Tremendous pressure and heat build up. Molten rock moves upward, sometimes exploding onto the surface and producing a volcano.

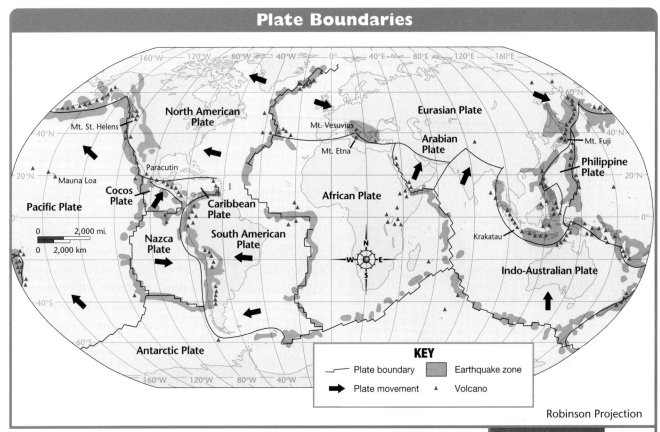

Plate Boundaries

KEY

Plate boundary	Earthquake zone
Plate movement	▲ Volcano

Robinson Projection

Along plate boundaries, there are many weak places in the Earth's crust. When plates push against one another, the crust cracks and splinters from the pressure. The cracks are called faults. When the crust moves along faults, it releases great amounts of energy in the form of earthquakes. These movements can cause dramatic changes.

Physical Processes on the Earth's Surface

Forces like volcanoes slowly build up the Earth; other forces slowly break it down. Often, the forces that break the Earth down are not as dramatic as volcanoes, but the results can last just as long.

Weathering is a process that breaks rocks down into tiny pieces. Three things cause weathering: wind, rain, and ice. Slowly but surely, they wear away the Earth's landforms. Hills and low, rounded mountains show what weathering can do. The Appalachian Mountains in the eastern United States once were as high as the Rocky Mountains of the western United States. Wind and rain have weathered them into much lower peaks. Weathering helps create soil, too. Tiny pieces of rock combine with decayed animal and plant material to form soil.

Once this breaking down has taken place, small pieces of rock may be carried to new places by a process called **erosion.** Weathering and erosion slowly create new landforms.

GEOGRAPHY

The Earth's plates move very slowly—a fast moving plate moves even slower than your hair grows. When plates move away from each other, they create oceans and valleys. When they push into one other, they create mountains and volcanoes. **Movement** Based on the direction the plates are moving, name the areas where you think oceans are getting bigger.

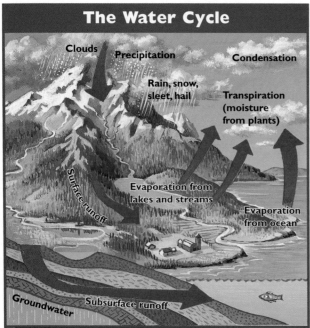

The Water Cycle

Clouds

Precipitation

Condensation

Rain, snow,
sleet, hail

Transpiration
(moisture
from plants)

Surface runoff

Evaporation from
lakes and streams

Evaporation
from ocean

Groundwater   Subsurface runoff

SCIENCE AND TECHNOLOGY Ocean water is too salty to drink or to irrigate crops. However, the oceans are a source of fresh water. How does this happen? When water evaporates from the ocean's surface, salt is left behind. The water vapor rises and forms clouds. The rain that falls to the Earth is fresh. **Chart Study** Once rain has fallen, how does water return to the ocean?

Air and Water: Natural Resources Needed for Life

The Earth is surrounded by a thick layer of special gases called the **atmosphere.** It provides life-giving oxygen for people and animals and life-giving carbon dioxide for plants. The atmosphere also acts like a blanket. It holds in the right amount of heat from the sun, making life possible. Without this blanket, solar heat would rise out back into space, making the Earth too cold to support life. Winds help to distribute this heat around the globe.

About 97 percent of the Earth's water is found in its oceans. This water is salty. Fresh water, or water without salt, makes up only a tiny percentage of all the Earth's water. Most fresh water is frozen at the North and South Poles. Fresh water comes from lakes, rivers, and rain. Also, fresh water, called groundwater, is stored in the soil and in rock layers below the surface of the Earth. This diagram shows the movement of all the water on the Earth's surface, in the ground, and in the air. The Earth does have enough water for people. However, some places have too much water and other places have too little.

SECTION 1 ASSESSMENT

AFTER YOU READ

RECALL

1. Identify: (a) Pangaea

2. Define: (a) landform, (b) mountain, (c) hill, (d) plateau, (e) plain, (f) plate tectonics, (g) plate, (h) weathering, (i) erosion, (j) atmosphere

COMPREHENSION

3. What are some physical processes that occur inside of the Earth, and what has been their effect?

4. What are some physical processes that occur on the Earth's surface, and what has been their effect?

5. What should people know about air and water and how they affect life on the Earth?

CRITICAL THINKING AND WRITING

6. **Exploring the Main Idea** Review the Main Idea statement at the beginning of this section. Write a paragraph responding to the following questions. (a) What physical processes can you see in your neighborhood? (b) How are they changing the features of the land?

7. **Recognizing Cause and Effect** List reasons why it is helpful for people to understand the causes of earthquakes and volcanoes.

ACTIVITY

8. **Writing to Learn** Suppose you were able to see the region you live in 10,000 years from now. Describe how the landforms might look. Explain what might have caused those changes.

SECTION 2

Geographic Factors and Natural Resources

BEFORE YOU READ

READING FOCUS QUESTIONS

1. What are natural resources?
2. Why is energy a scarce natural resource?

KEY TERMS

natural resource
raw material
recyclable resource
renewable resource
nonrenewable resource
fossil fuel

MAIN IDEA

The Earth has many natural resources; some can be recycled, some can be renewed, while others are nonrenewable.

NOTE TAKING

Copy the concept web shown here. As you read the section, fill in the ovals with information about geographic factors and natural resources. Add as many ovals as you need.

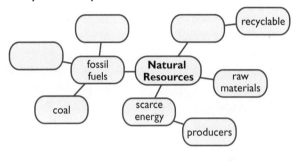

Setting the Scene

What can we do with the garbage we create? People are searching for answers. In 1995, architect Kate Warner built a house in Martha's Vineyard, Massachusetts. She used materials most people call trash. The builders mixed concrete with ash left over from furnaces that burn trash. Then they used the mixture to make the foundation of the house. Warner wanted glass tiles in the bathroom. So she had glassmakers create them out of old car windshields. "By making use of waste materials, the manufacturers of these new building materials are creating exciting new markets and completing a loop," Warner said. In this loop, materials are used over and over again.

Natural Resources

Like many people, Kate Warner wants to use the Earth's natural resources wisely. She believes this is the only way for humans to survive. A **natural resource** is anything from the Earth that people use in meeting their needs for food, clothing, and shelter. Examples of these resources include soil, water, minerals, and vegetation.

ECONOMICS Factories make new steel for bicycles and buildings by combining iron and other natural resources with recycled "scrap" steel. **Critical Thinking** What might happen if people did not recycle scrap steel?

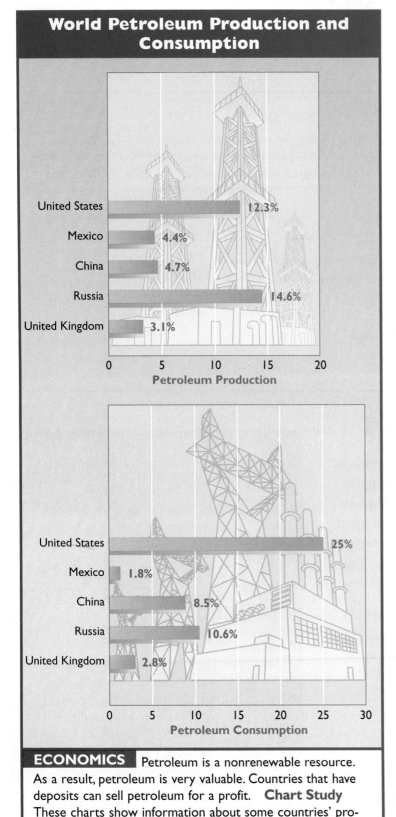

World Petroleum Production and Consumption

Petroleum Production

United States	12.3%
Mexico	4.4%
China	4.7%
Russia	14.6%
United Kingdom	3.1%

(Scale: 0, 5, 10, 15, 20)

Petroleum Consumption

United States	25%
Mexico	1.8%
China	8.5%
Russia	10.6%
United Kingdom	2.8%

(Scale: 0, 5, 10, 15, 20, 25, 30)

ECONOMICS Petroleum is a nonrenewable resource. As a result, petroleum is very valuable. Countries that have deposits can sell petroleum for a profit. **Chart Study** These charts show information about some countries' production and consumption of petroleum. Which of these countries produces the most petroleum? Which country consumes the most?

People use some resources just the way they come from nature. Water is one example. But most resources must be changed in some way to make them useful. These resources are called raw materials. Trees, for example, are a **raw material**. They must be processed to make them into useful materials such as paper and lumber.

Three Kinds of Resources Geographers divide the Earth's natural resources into three groups. The first group is **recyclable resources**. Water, nitrogen, and carbon are examples of recyclable resources. These resources recycle through our environment naturally. The water cycle, for instance, naturally recycles our fresh water supply.

A second group of resources is called **renewable resources**. Examples include trees and other living things on the Earth. These resources are different from recyclable resources because they can be replaced. For instance, a timber company may harvest all the trees in an area. If the company plants new trees to replace them, however, they are renewing the resource.

The third group of resources is called **nonrenewable resources**. When they are used up, they cannot be replaced. Most nonliving things, such as minerals, coal, natural gas, and petroleum, are nonrenewable resources.

Ancient Energy: Fossil Fuel Often people take some things for granted. Lights turn on when a switch is flicked. The house is warm in winter or cool in summer. The car runs. All of these things require **fossil fuels,** which include coal, natural gas, and petroleum. Fossil fuels were created over millions of years from the remains of prehistoric plants and animals. These fuels are no longer being created. As a result, fossil fuels are nonrenewable resources.

Energy Resources

Everyone in the world needs energy. Much of these energy needs are filled by fossil fuels like petroleum, natural gas, and coal. But these energy resources are not evenly spread around the world. Certain areas are rich in some energy resources, while others have very few.

Countries like Saudi Arabia and Mexico have huge amounts of oil. Others, like the United States and China, have coal and natural gas. Countries with many rivers, such as the countries of northwestern Europe, can use water energy to create electricity. Others, such as Japan, have very few energy sources.

Growing Needs and the Search for New Supplies   In 1973, members of the Organization of Petroleum Exporting Countries (OPEC) raised their oil prices. In addition, some members decided to produce less oil. In the United States, this caused a shortage of gasoline, which is made from oil. When there is a shortage of something, it is more expensive. In this case, the price of gas more than doubled. Companies that used oil to make electricity asked people to use as little electricity as possible.

Just because a country uses large amounts of energy does not mean that country has its own large energy resources. The biggest users of energy are industrial countries like the United States and the nations of Western Europe. Japan, which has few petroleum resources of its own, uses over twice as much energy as all of Africa. If a country does not have enough energy resources of its own, it must buy them from other countries. The oil shortages of the 1970s made people see they needed more sources of energy, including petroleum.

AS YOU READ

Use Prior Knowledge What things can you and your family do to use less fossil fuel in your everyday life?

SECTION 2 ASSESSMENT

AFTER YOU READ

RECALL

1. Define: (a) natural resource, (b) raw material, (c) recyclable resource, (d) renewable resource, (e) nonrenewable resource, (f) fossil fuel

COMPREHENSION

2. What are the different types of natural resources?

3. What factors have made energy scarce?

CRITICAL THINKING AND WRITING

4. **Exploring the Main Idea** Review the Main Idea statement at the beginning of this section. Make a list of reasons why people must be careful about how they use nonrenewable resources.

5. **Drawing Inferences** What do you think might happen to the United States if it could no longer buy petroleum from other countries?

ACTIVITY

6. **Finding Solutions** Work with a partner and choose a specific natural resource, such as wood, petroleum, or steel. Then brainstorm a list of ways to protect our supply of that resource. You might consider ways to limit use, to recycle, or to replace it when used. List your five best ideas and share them with your class.

Climate and Vegetation

BEFORE YOU READ

READING FOCUS QUESTIONS

1. What is the difference between weather and climate?
2. What role do wind and water play in creating our climate?
3. What are the five major climate regions and what kinds of vegetation grow in each region?

KEY TERMS

weather
temperature
precipitation
climate
vegetation

MAIN IDEA

The climate of an area affects the vegetation that will grow there, as well as the ways in which people and animals live.

NOTE TAKING

Copy the cause-and-effect chart shown here. As you read the section, fill in the chart with causes and effects of climate and vegetation. Add more topics to the chart with information from the section.

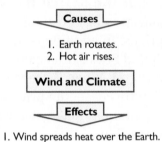

Causes
1. Earth rotates.
2. Hot air rises.

Wind and Climate

Effects
1. Wind spreads heat over the Earth.

GEOGRAPHY Tornadoes can easily flatten buildings. Tornado winds are the most powerful and violent winds on the Earth. **Critical Thinking** How can people protect themselves from the dangers of tornadoes? What is the economic effect of tornadoes and other severe weather?

Setting the Scene

In late May 1996, a tornado's furious winds tore down the movie screen of a drive-in theater in St. Catherine's, Ontario, Canada. Ironically, the week's feature movie was *Twister*, a film about tornadoes.

The Difference between Weather and Climate

Weather is the day-to-day changes in the air. It is measured primarily by temperature and precipitation. **Temperature** is how hot or cold the air feels. **Precipitation** is water that falls to the ground as rain, sleet, hail, or snow.

Climate is the average weather of a place over many years. Weather, on the other hand, is what people see from day to day. The Earth has many climate regions. Climate varies among different latitudes and is also greatly affected by wind, water, and landforms.

The World: Precipitation

NORTH AMERICA
EUROPE
ASIA
PACIFIC OCEAN
AFRICA
ATLANTIC OCEAN
SOUTH AMERICA
INDIAN OCEAN
AUSTRALIA
ANTARCTICA

Arctic Circle
Tropic of Cancer
Equator
Tropic of Capricorn
Antarctic Circle

KEY

Mean Annual Precipitation

Inches	Centimeters
Over 200	Over 500
80–200	200–500
40–80	100–200
20–40	50–100
10–20	25–50
2–10	5–25
0–2	0–5

0   2,000   4,000 mi
0   2,000   4,000 km

Robinson Projection

The Impact of Wind and Water

Without wind and water, the Earth would overheat. Together, wind and water moderate the effect of the sun's heat. Heat causes air to rise, especially near the Equator and over warm ocean water. Cold air sinks toward the surface away from the Equator. Wind blows from places where air is sinking toward places where air is rising. The Earth's rotation bends this flow to create circular wind patterns. So, depending on where you are in a circling weather system, the wind may be blowing north, south, east, or west.

The Earth's rotation also creates ocean currents, which are like rivers in the oceans. Some currents carry warm water from near the Equator toward the north and the south. Other currents carry cold water from the poles toward the Equator. Oceans also moderate the climate of nearby land just by their presence. Water takes longer to heat and cool than land. As a result, when the land has warmed during the summer, the nearby ocean remains cooler. Air blowing over the ocean becomes cool and then cools the land. In the winter, the opposite occurs.

Raging Storms   Wind and water can make climates milder, but they also create storms. Hurricanes are storms that form over the ocean in the tropics. Hurricanes rotate in a counter-clockwise direction around an "eye." They have winds of at least 74 miles (124 km) per hour and usually involve heavy rainfall. Tornadoes are just as dangerous, but they affect smaller areas. Their wind can range from 40 miles (67 km) per hour to over 300 miles (501 km) per hour and wreck anything in their path.

GEOGRAPHY   The mean annual precipitation is the amount of rain or snow that falls in a region in an average year.   **Map Study** Which areas get the most precipitation? Which get the least?

LINKS TO

Science

Smog Normally, air is cooler at higher altitudes. During a temperature inversion, however, a layer of warm air sits on top of the cooler air. The warm air traps pollution near the ground. This mixture of dangerous smoke and fog is called *smog*. The brown air seen in cities such as Los Angeles and Denver is smog caused by car exhaust.

Desert Vegetation

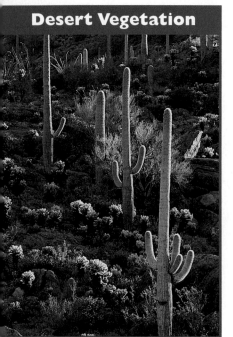

GEOGRAPHY Cacti have waxy skins that hold moisture in. Prickly spines protect a cactus from being eaten by animals. **Critical Thinking** Why do you think cacti have developed these distinct features?

Climate and Vegetation

Every climate region has its own special characteristics, such as amount of rain and sunlight, temperature, and nutrients, or elements, that plants use as food. Plants adapt, or adjust, to the characteristics of a climate. Geographers discuss five broad types of climates. Each has its unique **vegetation,** or plants that grow there naturally.

Tropical   Found in the low latitudes, this climate is hot, wet, and sunny. The vegetation is tropical rain forest with thousands of kinds of plants. Trees grow to 130 feet (40 meters). Other trees, vines, and ferns grow in their shade.

Dry   A dry, hot climate with little rain and sandy, gravelly soil. Vegetation is sparse and plant roots are shallow to absorb water before it evaporates. Some plants have small leaves, which lose little moisture.

Moderate *wetline* Found in the middle latitudes, this climate has moderate rainfall, temperatures that rarely fall below freezing, and varied vegetation. Forests include deciduous trees (trees that lose their leaves in fall), shrubs, low bushes, wildflowers, and a variety of grasses.

Continental   Summer temperatures are moderate to hot; winters are cold. Vegetation includes grasslands and forests. Large deciduous forests occur where temperatures are moderate, while colder regions have coniferous trees (trees with needles and cones).

Polar   This climate is found in the high latitudes and is cold all year. Vegetation includes low shrubs, mosses, and lichens (plants that grow on rocks). There are no trees and few flowering plants.

SECTION 3 ASSESSMENT

AFTER YOU READ

RECALL

1. Define: (a) weather, (b) temperature, (c) precipitation, (d) climate, (e) vegetation

COMPREHENSION

2. Compare weather and climate and give an example of each.

3. How do wind and water influence climate?

4. Name the five major climate regions of the world and describe the vegetation in each.

CRITICAL THINKING AND WRITING

5. **Exploring the Main Idea** Review the Main Idea statement at the beginning of this section. Then make a chart. In the first column, identify the climate region. In the second column, tell what factors help create that climate. In the third column, describe the vegetation that grows there.

6. **Predicting** How can understanding the differences in climate regions help you better understand differences among

civilizations and cultures? Write a paragraph to explain.

ACTIVITY

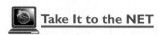 Take It to the NET

7. **Making a Climate Map** Create a map showing the Earth's climate zones. Use a different color to indicate each zone. Visit the World Explorer: People, Places and Cultures section at **phschool.com** for help in completing this activity.

Understanding Charts

The World's Highest Active Volcanoes		
Peak	Country	Elevation (in feet)
San Pedro	Chile	20,161
Arácar	Argentina	19,954
Guallatiri	Chile	19,918
Tupungatito	Chile/Argentina	19,685
Sabancaya	Peru	19,577

Learn the Skill

Charts are helpful because they organize information in a way that makes it easy to read and understand. To understand and use charts, follow these steps:

A. Read the title to identify the topic of the chart. This chart's title tells you that it contains information about the highest active volcanoes in the world.

B. Read the chart. Use the column heads to understand the information in each row of the chart. The column heads in this chart provide information about the volcano peak, the country in which it is located, and its elevation measure in feet. Using this information, you can tell that the San Pedro Peak in Chile is 20,161 feet and that the Sabancaya Peak in Peru is 19,577 feet.

C. Pose and answer questions about the chart. First, write two questions about geographic distributions shown in the chart data. For example, you might ask, "In which world region are all of the world's highest active volcanoes located?" Then, write the answers to your questions.

Practice the Skill

Study the chart about temperature and precipitation in Charleston, South Carolina. How much precipitation does Charleston get in January? In April? During which month does Charleston get the most precipitation? During which month is the average temperature 67 degrees? Which month is the hottest? Which month is the coldest?

Temperature and Precipitation in Charleston		
Month	Temperature (Fahrenheit)	Precipitation (inches)
January	48	3.5
February	51	3.5
March	58	4.5
April	65	3.0
May	73	4.0
June	78	6.5
July	82	7.0
August	81	7.0
September	76	5.0
October	67	3.0
November	58	2.5
December	51	3.0

Apply the Skill

See the Chapter Review and Assessment at the end of this chapter for more questions about charts.

CHAPTER 2 Review and Assessment

Creating a Chapter Summary

On a separate piece of paper, copy this web. Then, add more ovals and fill them in with information summarizing what you have learned about each topic.

Physical Features

Earth's Physical Geography

Natural Resources

Climate and Vegetation

Reviewing Key Terms

Write a definition for each of the following words.

1. landform
2. plate tectonics
3. atmosphere
4. erosion
5. natural resource
6. fossil fuel
7. climate
8. vegetation

Reviewing the Main Ideas

1. How do the Earth's physical processes change and renew the physical features of our planet?
(Section 1)

2. How do plate tectonics shape the Earth?
(Section 1)

3. What are the three groups that geographers divide the Earth's natural resources into? Give examples of each. (Section 2)

4. What is the difference between renewable and nonrenewable resources? Give an example of each. (Section 2)

5. Explain the difference between climate and weather. (Section 3)

6. What are the Earth's major climate regions? Give an example of the kinds of vegetation that grow in each of the climate regions. (Section 3)

Map Activity

Geography

For each place listed below, write the letter on the map that shows its location. Use the Atlas at the back of the book to complete the exercise.

1. Australia

2. North Pole

3. Equator

4. Atlantic Ocean

5. Tropic of Capricorn

 Take It to the NET

Enrichment For more map activities using geography skills, visit the social studies section of **phschool.com**.

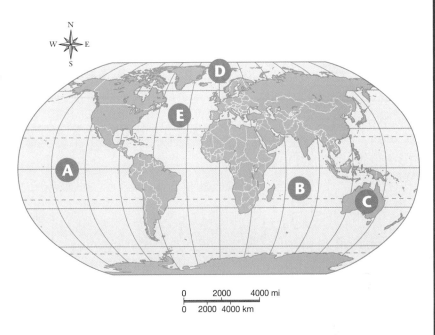

```
0        2000      4000 mi
0    2000  4000 km
```

Writing Activity

1. Writing a News Report   Choose a well-known natural disaster such as Hurricane Mitch or the eruption of Mount St. Helens. Find out where it happened, why it happened, and what the immediate and long-term effects were. Then, write a news report that describes the natural disaster in geographic terms.

2. Predicting Events   Write a paragraph about the possibility of predicting earthquakes, volcanoes, and other natural events. Do you think scientists can make these predictions? Why or why not?

Applying Your Skills

Turn to the Skills for Life activity on p.37 to help you complete the following activity.

Scan a recent newspaper or magazine for a chart. Write four or five statements based on the information in the chart.

Critical Thinking

1. Identifying Central Issues How does water affect a region's landforms and climate?

2. Recognizing Cause and Effect   Why is the Earth continually changing its form?

 Take It to the NET

Activity What are the physical features of the region in which you live? Click on each link to learn about the different biomes and ecosystems of the world. Visit the World Explorer: People, Places, and Cultures section of **phschool.com** for help in completing this activity.

Chapter 2 Self-Test As a final review activity, take the Chapter 2 Self-Test and get instant feedback on your answers. To take the test, visit the Social Studies section of **phschool.com**.

Earth's Human and Cultural Geography

World Time Zones

KEY

Non-standard time

Miller Projection

USING MAPS

When it is 6 a.m. in Houston, it is 3 p.m. in Moscow. That is because the world has been divided into 24 Standard time zones—one for each hour of the day. Without world time zones, every place would have to determine its own time. There would be so many different local times that it would cause confusion. Use the World Time Zones map to complete these activities.

Interpreting Maps

Study the map and try to figure out how to read it. Then, write three questions that can be answered by studying the map. Exchange questions with a classmate and try to find the answers using the map.

Problem Solving

Think about what the world would be like without 24 Standard time zones. Write a brief report on whether these 24 zones are a good idea or whether they should be changed. If you think they should be changed, present a new system that you think should replace the old one.

Population Patterns in Places and Regions

BEFORE YOU READ

READING FOCUS QUESTIONS

1. What accounts for the distribution of the Earth's population?
2. What is population density?
3. What are the causes of population growth?

KEY TERMS

population
population distribution
demographer
population density
birthrate

death rate
life expectancy
Green Revolution

MAIN IDEA

The Earth's population is growing rapidly, due to modern technology and scientific developments, and is concentrated in areas where it is easiest to live.

NOTE TAKING

Copy the cause-and-effect chart shown here. As you read the section, fill in the chart with information about population patterns. Add more topics and cause-and-effect sequences to the chart.

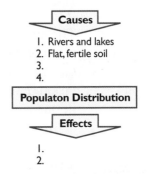

Causes
1. Rivers and lakes
2. Flat, fertile soil
3.
4.

Populaton Distribution

Effects
1.
2.

Setting the Scene

Imagine that you go to school in Tokyo, the capital of Japan. Every day you ride a train to school. People jam the train. Most people must stand. Often, special station guards push people inside so the doors can close behind them.

This is not an exaggeration. Japan is smaller than California, but it is home to 125 million people and extremely crowded.

What Is Population Distribution?

The world's **population,** or total number of people, is spread unevenly over the Earth's surface. **Population distribution** describes how the population is spread out across the world.

Demographers, scientists who study population, know that many factors affect where people live. Most major civilizations began along bodies of water. Rivers and lakes form transportation corridors for trade and travel and are a source of water for drinking and farming. Most people chose places with flat, fertile soil, adequate rainfall, a suitable climate, and ample natural resources. Many of these factors still influence where people live. Consider the population distribution of the different continents.

CULTURE At rush hour in Tokyo, white-gloved guards jam two more passengers onto an already full train. **Critical Thinking** Compare the crowded conditions in Japan with crowding you've experienced. How do very crowded situations make you feel?

More than 81 percent of Earth's population lives in Asia, Europe, and North America. These continents total about 53 percent of the world's land. However, these continents have large areas of fertile soil, favorable landforms, ample fresh water, rich natural resources, and good climates.

Other continents have smaller populations partly because it is harder to live there. For example, about 309 million people live in South America. Many live along the Atlantic coast. Other regions have mountains, dry plains, and rain forests. Fewer people live there.

What Is Population Density?

The average number of people who live in a square mile (or square kilometer) is called **population density.** In a country with a high density, people are crowded together. Japan has one of the highest population densities in the world. In Tokyo, more than 25,000 people live in one square mile (9,664 people per sq km).

In contrast, Canada has a lower population density. It has about eight persons per square mile (about three persons per sq km). Many factors affect Canada's population. For instance, its cool climate has a short growing season, which limits farming.

Studying Population Density   Demographers measure population density by dividing the number of people living in a place by the number of square miles (or sq km) of that place. Remember that population density is an *average*. People are not evenly distributed over the land. New York City, for example, has a very dense population. However, New York state has many fewer people per square mile. Even in the city, some areas are more densely populated than others.

GEOGRAPHY

For hundreds of years the world's population rose very slowly. Recently, however, the rate of growth has skyrocketed. **Critical Thinking** How does the graph show the change in the growth of the world's population?

World Population Growth, A.D. 1200–2000

Population in Billions (y-axis: 0, 1, 2, 3, 4, 5, 6, 7, 8)

Year (x-axis: 1200, 1300, 1400, 1500, 1600, 1700, 1800, 1900, 2000)

Population Growth

Today, the Earth's population is growing steadily. Population growth depends on the birthrate and the death rate. The **birthrate** is the number of live births each year per 1,000 people. The **death rate** is the number of deaths each year per 1,000 people. By comparing these numbers, demographers can figure out population growth.

For centuries, the world population grew slowly. Without modern technology, food was often scarce. Also, many people died of disease. Although the birthrate was high, so was the death rate. **Life expectancy,** the average number of years that people live, was short.

Reasons for Population Growth Today Population growth occurs because the birth rate is higher than the death rate. In the United States, for example, the average life expectancy for women is about 80 years and for men about 73 years.

Two scientific developments have made this possible. First, new farming methods have greatly increased the world's food supply. Scientists have developed new varieties of food crops and new ways to protect crops from insects. New fertilizers can enrich the soil, and scientists have also discovered ways to raise crops with less water. These changes in agriculture are called the **Green Revolution.**

Scientists have also made advancements in medicine and health. Doctors can now treat people who once died of illnesses and injuries. As a result, people live longer lives.

SECTION 1 ASSESSMENT

AFTER YOU READ

RECALL

1. Define: (a) population, (b) population distribution, (c) demographer, (d) population density, (e) birthrate, (f) death rate, (g) life expectancy, (h) Green Revolution

COMPREHENSION

2. Why is the Earth's population unevenly distributed around the world?

3. Explain population density and give examples.

4. Why is the Earth's population growing faster now than in the past?

CRITICAL THINKING AND WRITING

5. **Exploring the Main Idea** Review the Main Idea statement at the beginning of this section. Write a paragraph explaining how population distribution adds to the challenge of dealing with our rapid population growth.

6. **Making Predictions** What can we do to improve health care for children around the world? If scientists discover ways to stop diseases from spreading, how might this affect societies around the world?

ACTIVITY

7. **Writing to Learn** You are a demographer studying the population of your community. Make a list of questions to ask and possible sources for answers.

The Influences of Human Migration

BEFORE YOU READ

READING FOCUS QUESTIONS

1. Why do people migrate?
2. What effect is migration having on cities?

KEY TERMS
migration
immigrant
"push-pull" theory
urbanization
rural area
urban area

KEY PLACES
Cuba
Jakarta
São Paulo

NOTE TAKING
Copy the chart shown here. As you read the section, fill in the chart with information about migration. Add more bulleted points to the chart.

Reasons People Migrate	Effects of Urbanization
• Poverty	• Overcrowded cities
• Unable to find work	• Lack of adequate housing
•	•
•	•

MAIN IDEA
The world's population is on the move.

Fleeing Cuba

HISTORY These men are preparing to leave Cuba on a makeshift raft, hoping to arrive in Florida. They are fleeing the regime of the dictator Fidel Castro. **Critical Thinking** What conflicts do you know about that have resulted in migration? What effect might migration have on the countries that take in refugees?

Setting the Scene

Roberto Goizueta (goy zoo AY tuh) was the former head of Coca-Cola, one of the largest companies in the world. Yet, when he came to the United States from **Cuba** in 1960, he had nothing. This is how he described his escape from the largest island nation in the Caribbean Sea:

"When my family and I came to this country [the United States], we had to leave everything behind…our photographs hung on the wall, our wedding gifts sat on the shelves."

Like millions of others who came to the United States, Roberto Goizueta helped the nation become a land of prosperity.

Migration: The Movement of People

Humans have always been on the move. When they move from one place to another, it is called **migration. Immigrants** are people who leave one country and move to another. For centuries, hundreds of thousands of people have migrated to the United States. Since the late 1970s, more than 700,000 people migrated here from Vietnam, 800,000 from Central America, 900,000 from Caribbean islands.

Demographers use the **"push-pull" theory** to explain immigration. It says that people migrate because certain things "push" them to leave. Often, the reasons are economic. People may be poor, unable to find work or buy land. Sometimes people are pushed to move by war or other conflict, or by the actions of a government.

For instance, in 1959 there was a revolution in Cuba led by Fidel Castro. He established a Communist government where the people have little say in that government. Some Cubans who opposed the Communists fled to America to find safety, freedom, and better opportunities.

What about the "pull" part of the theory? The hope for better living conditions "pulls" people to a country. Cubans settled in Florida because it was near their former home. It had a large Spanish-speaking population and a climate and vegetation similar to Cuba's. In addition, the United States has a limited government, which means that the government's power over citizens is limited. People enjoy freedom and have a right to vote for their leaders. All these factors "pulled" many Cubans to America.

Other Kinds of Immigration Sometimes, people are forced to migrate. Australia was colonized by English immigrants. Some were convicts who served their sentences in Australia and stayed when their sentences were done. War also forces people to migrate. In the mid-1990s, war broke out among three ethnic groups in the former Yugoslavia, in Eastern Europe. Many refugees fled to escape the warfare. Also, victorious soldiers of one group often forced entire communities of other groups to leave. Millions of immigrants flooded into other countries in Eastern and Western Europe.

Cuba and Florida: Climate Regions

KEY

Tropical Climates

Tropical wet and dry

Mild Climates

Humid subtropical

⊛ National capital

• Other city

Lambert Azimuthal Equal-Area Projection

GEOGRAPHY Since 1959, about one million Cubans have fled their communist-ruled country to find a new life in the United States. Many have settled in Florida. **Map Study** Use the map scale to determine about how far Cuba lies from the mainland of Florida. How are the climates of southern Florida and Cuba similar?

The World Becomes More Urban

One of the biggest challenges to today's nations is people migrating to cities from farms and small villages. In recent years, the population of major cities has grown tremendously. The movement of people to cities and the growth of cities is called **urbanization.**

What pushes people from rural areas and pulls them to cities?

Growing Cities, Growing Challenges
Cities in Indonesia are an example of urbanization. In the past, most Indonesians were farmers, fishers, and hunters. They lived in **rural areas,** or villages in the countryside. Recently more and more Indonesians have moved to **urban areas,** or cities and nearby towns. The urban population is increasing rapidly. For example, in 1978, about 4.5 million people lived in the capital of **Jakarta.** Today over 10 million people live there.

In South America, too, vast numbers of people are moving from rural to urban areas. **São Paulo, Brazil** is now the largest city in South America. In 1995, its population was nearly 16 million, and by 2015, it is expected to be 21 million.

The problem of urbanization is complex. Cities suffer because too many people are coming too fast. Cities are overcrowded and cannot provide adequate housing, jobs, schools, hospitals, and other services. Rural areas suffer because of lack of people. Fewer people mean fewer farmers. Less food is produced, and everybody suffers.

With so many daily problems, why do immigrants flock to São Paulo and other big cities? Most are seeking a better life for their families. They are looking for jobs, decent houses, and good schools. Above all, most want more opportunities for their children.

ECONOMICS

Across the world, growing cities face special challenges. Sometimes, there is not enough housing for newcomers to the cities. Sometimes, newcomers cannot afford the housing that is available. Until they find better housing, many newcomers build whatever shelters they can.
Critical Thinking What kinds of factors do you think would push people to a city like Cairo, seen above, despite inadequate housing?

SECTION 2 ASSESSMENT

AFTER YOU READ

RECALL

1. Identify: (a) Cuba, (b) Jakarta, (c) São Paulo

2. Define: (a) migration, (b) immigrant, (c) "push-pull" theory, (d) urbanization, (e) rural area, (f) urban area

COMPREHENSION

3. What "pushes" people from one country to another?

4. What "pulls" people to one country from another?

5. How is migration changing the world's cities?

CRITICAL THINKING AND WRITING

6. **Exploring the Main Idea** Review the Main Idea statement at the beginning of this section. Write a paragraph predicting what effect increasing urbanization might have on the world.

7. **Making Inferences** Think about how population movement affects the community you live in, then make a list of examples that show the ways your community is affected.

ACTIVITY

8. **Writing to Learn** When people migrate from rural to urban areas, they may face hardships and challenges. Imagine that you are considering whether or not to move from a rural area to a city. Make a two-column chart listing the benefits of moving to the city in one column, and the drawbacks in the other. Use the list to help you decide whether or not to move.

SECTION 3
Culture and Cultural Institutions

BEFORE YOU READ

READING FOCUS QUESTIONS

1. How is culture a total way of life?
2. What institutions are basic to all societies?
3. How is language part of culture?
4. What is the relationship among philosophy, religion, and culture?

KEY TERMS

culture   institution
cultural trait   social structure
culture region   nuclear family
technology   extended family
cultural landscape   ethics

MAIN IDEA

Culture affects everything a group of people does, what they believe, how they behave, and how they organize their society.

NOTE TAKING

Copy the outline shown here. As you read the section, fill in the outline with information about culture. Add headings and details to make the outline more complete.

> **I. Culture: A Total Way of Life**
>   A. Elements of culture
>   I. Cultural traits
>   2.
>   B. How land affects culture
> **II. Institutions Basic to all Societies**
>   A. Family
> **III. Language as Culture**
> **IV. Religion and Culture**

Setting the Scene

"All right, students," your teacher says, "time to clean the room. Kaitlyn—I'd like you to sweep the floor today. Guy and Keisha, please dust the shelves and windowsills. Eric and Bobby, you do the lunch dishes."

Would you be surprised if this happened in your classroom? There are many differences between Japanese and American schools. In Japan, students are expected to help keep their classrooms clean. Japanese students generally spend more time studying than American students do. They go to school five and one-half days a week.

Of course, Japanese schools are also very much like American schools. In both places, students study math, science, literature, and history. They enjoy sports, music, art, and drama.

CULTURE These students in Japan are listening closely as their classmate speaks. **Critical Thinking** How is your classroom like a classroom in Japan? How is it different?

Culture: A Total Way of Life

If you met students from Japan, you might have many questions. What do you eat for lunch? What kinds of music do you like? What makes you laugh?

CULTURE How people live is part of their culture. Different cultures sometimes interact with their environment in similar ways. In mountainous Japan, farmers build terraces on the hillsides to increase the amount of land available for farming. Terrace farming is also used in other cultures, including those in South America and South Asia. **Critical Thinking** How else do you think different cultures interact with their environments in similar ways?

Answers to these questions will tell you something about the culture of Japan. **Culture** is the way of life of a group of people who share similar beliefs and customs. The language Japanese students speak, how they dress, what they study, and what they do after school are part of their culture.

Elements of Culture   Culture includes the work people do, their behaviors, their beliefs, their ways of doing things, and their creative expressions. A particular group's distinct skills, customs, and ways of doing things are called **cultural traits.** Over time, cultural traits may change, but cultures change very slowly.

The people of Japan have a unique culture. So do the people of the United States. Each of these groups of people live in a **culture region,** an area in which people share the same cultural traits. These traits are influenced by the issues in the society in which people live. American music is an example. Slavery and the experiences of African Americans led them to develop blues and jazz. This music expressed their feelings about their experiences.

Although every culture region has its own culture traits, some aspects of culture are shared. For example, Shakespeare wrote plays that are part of the English culture. However, he wrote about universal themes—ideas that are of interest to all people. His work has been translated into other languages for people of many cultures to read and appreciate.

People and Their Land   Geographers study culture in relation to the environment. They want to know how landforms, climate, vegetation, and resources affect culture.

Geographers are also interested in the effect people have on their environment. Often the effect is linked to a culture's **technology,** or tools and the skills people need to use them. Technology helps people use natural resources and change the environment, and includes computers and the Internet as well as other tools and the skills needed to make them.

A group's **cultural landscape** includes any changes to its environment. It also includes technology used to make the changes. For example, Bali, in Indonesia, has many mountains. Therefore, people carved terraces in them to make flat farmland. Central India, on the other hand, has much level land. Farmers there would probably not develop technology to create terraces.

Culture and Political Boundaries   Culture changes slowly but political boundaries sometimes change rapidly. War and changes in political leadership can divide culture regions, but the culture often survives. For example, Austria and Germany are part of the same culture region. Austria has been long separated from Germany. And following World War II, Germany itself was divided into two countries, a separation that lasted more than 40 years. Through all this, the culture of Austria, East Germany, and West Germany remained closely linked.

Institutions Basic to All Societies

Every culture has basic institutions that help people organize their lives together. An **institution** is an important practice, relationship, or organization in a society or culture. Among these are government, economic, educational, religious, and family institutions. These are all part of a culture's **social structure.** This is a way of organizing people into smaller groups. Each smaller group has certain tasks. Some groups gather food, others protect the community, while others raise children. Social structure helps people work together to meet the basic needs of individuals, families, and communities.

The family is the basic social unit of any culture. Families teach customs and traditions of the culture. They teach children how to grow up, behave, treat others, and learn.

Kinds of Families

In some cultures, the basic family unit is the **nuclear family.** It is made up of a mother, a father, and their children.

Another type of family is the **extended family.** It includes parents and their children. It may also include grandparents, aunts, uncles, cousins, and other relatives. These family members may live in the same house or close by.

Language and Culture

All cultures have language. In fact, every culture is based on language. It lets people communicate everything they need to share in their culture. Without language, people could not pass on what they know or believe to their children.

A culture's language reflects the things that its people think are important. For example, English has the word *snow* for the white stuff that falls in some places in winter. But the Inuits of North America have over 13 words for snow. Why? Where the Inuits live, snow covers the ground for a good part of the year. Snow is a more important part of their environment than it is to people of other cultures. The Inuits, therefore, have created words to meet their needs.

In some countries, people speak different languages. For example, the official language of Egypt is Arabic. It is spoken by most Egyptians. But some Egyptians speak Italian, Greek, or Armenian. Canada has two official languages, French and English, and Native Americans there speak a number of other languages. People who speak these languages are culturally different in some ways from other people in their country. They may celebrate different festivals, wear different clothes, or have different customs for such things as dating or education.

LINKS TO
Language Arts

Cultural Borrowing The Phoenicians were ancient traders along the Mediterranean Sea. Their alphabet had 22 letters, and they wrote from right to left. The Greeks saw this writing system and based their own alphabet on it—with one difference. The Greeks, like us, wrote from left to right. We owe our alphabet, in part, to these two ancient cultures.

CULTURE The end of Ramadan, a month-long period of spiritual reflection, means a joyous celebration for these Egyptian Muslims. **Critical Thinking** What important religious or cultural events do you and your family observe?

Religions of the World						
	Christianity	Buddhism	Islam	Hinduism	Judaism	Confucianism
Deity	God	Various gods	God (Allah)	Brahman	God (Yahweh)	None
Founder	Jesus Christ	The Buddha	Muhammad	No single founder	Abraham	Confucius
Holy Book	Bible	Tripitika	Quran	Numerous sacred writings	Hebrew Bible, Torah	Writings of Confucius
Clergy	Ministers, priests	Monks and ministers	Imam	Guru, Holy Man, Brahman	Rabbis	None
Members	1.9 billion	300 million	1 billion	793 million	14 million	5 million

CULTURE This chart lists major religions of the world. **Chart Study** Which of the religions on the chart has the greatest number of members?

Religion and Culture

Religion is basic to every culture. Religion helps answer questions about the meaning and purpose of life. It helps define the values that people believe are important. Religion can also guide people in **ethics,** or standards of accepted behavior.

Religious beliefs vary, but most believers expect people to treat one another well and to behave properly. The chart above lists major religions of the world. Every religion celebrates important people and events in its history. Muslims celebrate Ramadan. Christians celebrate Christmas. Buddhists celebrate the birth and death of Buddha. These celebrations remind believers of the sacrifices others have made and of the joy of their faith.

SECTION 3 ASSESSMENT

AFTER YOU READ

RECALL

1. Define: (a) culture, (b) cultural trait, (c) culture region, (d) technology, (e) cultural landscape, (f) institution, (g) social structure, (h) nuclear family, (i) extended family, (j) ethics

COMPREHENSION

2. How does culture affect all aspects of a person's life?

3. What institutions would you find in every society?

4. How does language influence culture?

5. Explain the relationship between religion and culture.

CRITICAL THINKING AND WRITING

6. Exploring the Main Idea Review the Main Idea statement at the beginning of this section. Then, list cultural traits that are characteristic of your culture.

ACTIVITY

 Take It to the NET

7. Identifying Regional Characteristics Create a chart showing the characteristics of the region in which you live. Model your chart on the information and data included on the Web site. Visit the World Explorer: People, Places, and Cultures section of **phschool.com** for help in completing this activity.

SECTION 4

Economic and Political Systems

BEFORE YOU READ

READING FOCUS QUESTIONS

1. What are the categories of industry and what do they produce?
2. What are the basic economic systems in use around the world?
3. What are the important types of government?

KEY TERMS

economy
producer
goods
services
consumer
primary industry
secondary industry
tertiary industry
quaternary industry
traditional economy

market economy
capitalism
free enterprise
command economy
government
direct democracy
monarchy
constitution
representative
  government
dictatorship

NOTE TAKING

Copy the concept web shown here. As you read the section, fill in the circles with information about economic and political systems. Add more circles to make the web more complete.

MAIN IDEA

Societies make various choices in how to organize their economies and governments in order to provide for the needs of their people.

Setting the Scene

Muhammad Yunnus was a professor of economics in the country of Bangladesh (bahng gluh DESH), a poor nation in South Asia. Yunnus wanted to help poor Bangladeshis improve their lives.

In the early 1970s, Yunnus met Sufiya Khatun. She made bamboo stools but earned only two cents a day because she could only make a few stools. If she had more money for supplies, she could have made more, but Sufiya had no way to borrow money. Forty-two other people in her village also needed money to build their businesses. They needed an average of just $26 each, but banks wouldn't bother making loans for just $26.

In 1976, Yunnus opened a bank to loan small amounts of money only to poor people. Yunnus's bank has loaned money to 2 million customers.

ECONOMICS Most of Muhammad Yunnus's customers are women seeking to open small businesses. This woman used her loan to start a weaving shop. **Critical Thinking** List some ways that the loans improved the lives of the people. How do you think these loans improved the economy of Bangladesh?

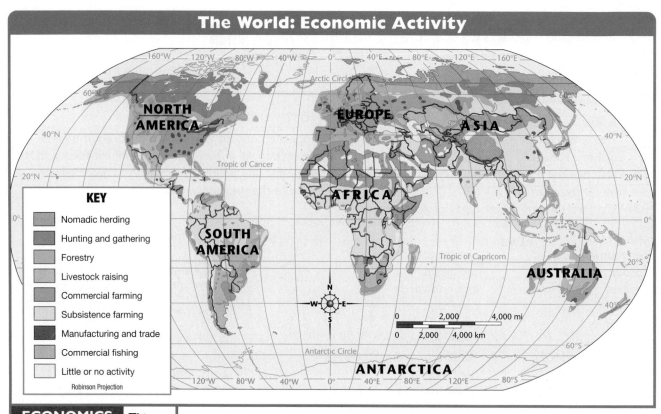

The World: Economic Activity

KEY

- Nomadic herding
- Hunting and gathering
- Forestry
- Livestock raising
- Commercial farming
- Subsistence farming
- Manufacturing and trade
- Commercial fishing
- Little or no activity

Robinson Projection

ECONOMICS This map uses a color-coded key to show the most common economic activities that take place across the world. Use the key to make comparisons among the continents. **Map Study** After you read the paragraphs on developed and developing countries on page 54, look at the map and identify the continents where you think the most developed countries might be located. Explain your answer.

AS YOU READ

Use Prior Knowledge Think about each member of your family and what he or she does. Is each a consumer, a producer, or both? Explain why.

Categories of Industry

Banks like the one Yunnus started help people become productive members of their nation's economy. An **economy** is a system for producing, distributing, and consuming goods and services. Owners and workers are **producers.** They make products, such as bamboo baskets or automobiles. Those products are called **goods.** Some products are really **services** that producers perform for other people. They may style hair, edit books, or heal diseases. **Consumers** are people who buy the goods and use the services.

There are four categories of economic activities or industries. **Primary industry** is the part of the economy that produces raw materials. Examples include agriculture, fishing, mining, and forestry. **Secondary industry** refers to manufacturing businesses. They take materials from primary industries and other secondary industries and make them into goods. **Tertiary industry** refers to service companies. Examples include banking, transportation, health care, and police protection. **Quaternary industry** refers to information technologies. Quaternary industries provide Internet services, computer software, and cable and telephone service.

Economic Systems

Cultures choose the way they organize their economies. There are three basic systems: traditional, market, and command economies. In a **traditional economy,** the customs, traditions, and habits of the group influence the producing, buying, and selling of goods. The Tuareg of the Sahara in northern Africa are an example. These people are nomadic herders who travel about the region in search of food and water for their animals. They produce most of the things they need and trade with others for what they need and cannot produce.

The American economic system is often called the **free enterprise system.** This system is characterized by private or corporate ownership of capital goods; investments that are determined by private decisions rather than by state control; and determined in a free market. The free enterprise system is often called **capitalism** or a **market economy.** When a company sells its products in a free market, it earns a profit, or money. A company may produce goods, but consumers may not buy them at the price at which they are offered. Prices will then have to be lowered.

In a **command economy,** economic decisions are made by the central government. The government decides what products are made, how much is produced, and what the goods cost. Consumers and businesses have little control of the goods. There are two major types of command economies—socialism and communism.

In a socialist system, the government owns most basic industries. The government decides how much to pay workers and how much to charge for goods. It uses profits to pay for services such as health care and education. In this system, other industries and services follow the capitalist model.

Capitalism Replaces Communism

ECONOMICS This photograph was taken in Berlin shortly after communist East Germany united with capitalist West Germany. These East German children had never seen so many different school supplies before. **Critical Thinking** Why would these children not be used to seeing so many different school supplies for sale?

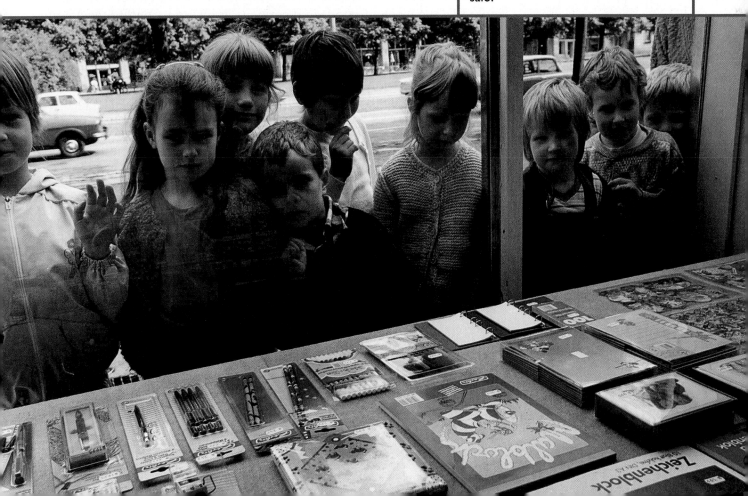

Chinese citizens mark the 22nd anniversary of Communist rule in their country at Beijing's Gate of Heavenly Peace Square. **Critical Thinking** How does your community mark important events in America's history?

The Chinese National Day Parade

无产阶级文化大革命万岁

They are privately owned and consumers decide which products to buy. A few countries follow socialism or have socialist programs. These countries include Spain, Portugal, and Italy.

In a communist system, the central government owns all property, such as farms and factories. It controls all aspects of citizens' lives, including the price of goods and services, how much is produced, and how much workers are paid. Today, only a few of the world's nations practice communism. They include Cuba, China, and North Korea.

Developed and Developing Countries   Cultures can also be described by how many industries they have. About one quarter of the people of the world live in developed nations. These are countries such as the United States, Canada, Japan, and most Western European countries. They have many industries and machinery and technology are in wide use. Most citizens can get a good education and health care. Large commercial farms use modern technology. They need fewer workers but produce large amounts of food.

The majority of the world's population lives in developing countries. These nations have few industries and most are poor. People often suffer from disease, food shortages, unsafe water, poor education and health services, and changing governments.

Types of Government

Government is the system that sets up and enforces a society's laws and institutions. Some governments are controlled by a few people. Others are controlled by many.

Direct Democracy   A democracy is a type of government in which supreme political authority rests with the people. The people hold power and government is carried out only with the consent of the people. A democracy can either be direct or indirect. In a direct democracy, citizens participate directly in decision-making. One example of a direct democracy is a New England town meeting. In town meetings, every adult citizen can vote on laws, budget items, and town officers.

Monarchy   Until about 100 years ago, one of the most common forms of government was a **monarchy.** In this system, a king or queen rules the government. The ruler inherits the throne by birth. At one time, many monarchies were forms of unlimited, or nearly unlimited government. The only limits that were placed on the monarch were custom, church law, or oaths of obligation. Citizens had little say in the affairs of their country.

　　Monarchies still exist today. Sweden, Denmark, Great Britain, Spain, and Switzerland are examples. However, these monarchies do not have unlimited power. The power of the rulers and the government is limited. These countries have **constitutions,** or sets of laws that define and often limit the government's power.

Representative Government   In a **representative government,** also known as a republic, the people hold the power to govern and rule. They elect representatives who create laws. If the people do not like what a representative does, they can refuse to re-elect that person. They can also work to change laws they do not like because the citizens have a responsibility to participate in government. They should keep informed about issues affecting the country, and know about the leaders who serve them, and accept responsibility for voting. The United States and Canada are examples of representative government.

CULTURE   In Great Britain's constitutional monarachy, the monarch has little authority. The real power is wielded by Parliament, an elected body like our Congress. **Critical Thinking** If the monarchy has little authority in Great Britain, why do you think it still exists?

Josef Stalin was one of the world's cruelest dictators. He ruled the former Soviet Union from the 1920s until 1953. He controlled every aspect of Soviet life and jailed or executed anybody who opposed him.
Critical Thinking How do you think dictators gain control of their countries' governments?

Representative government developed from direct democracy. However, it took many centuries for modern representative government to develop. Gradually citizens began demanding more personal freedoms. They demanded protection from actions of their own government, and wanted a voice in the decisions made by government. The republic established in the United States provided these rights and freedoms.

Dictatorship A **dictatorship** is a form of government in which one person, the dictator, holds almost total power to govern. It is another type of unlimited government. Dictators decide what happens in their countries. They make the laws and decide if there will be elections. Citizens have few rights. When dictators take over, they often make promises that sound good, like ending crime or providing better social services. Sometimes they keep their promises, but more often, they do not. Either way, people lose the right to make their own decisions.

SECTION 4 ASSESSMENT

AFTER YOU READ

RECALL

1. Define: (a) economy, (b) producer, (c) goods, (d) services, (e) consumer, (f) primary industry, (g) secondary industry, (h) tertiary industry, (i) quaternary industry, (j) traditional economy, (k) market economy, (l) capitalism, (m) free enterprise, (n) command economy, (o) government, (p) direct democracy, (q) monarchy, (r) constitution, (s) representative government, (t) dictatorship

COMPREHENSION

2. Describe the basic types of economic activities and give examples of each.

3. What types of economic systems do nations use?

4. What are the differences in the types of government?

CRITICAL THINKING AND WRITING

5. **Exploring the Main Idea** Review the Main Idea statement at the beginning of this section. Which economic and government systems do you think are best? List reasons for your choices.

6. **Comparing** Compare the role of citizens in the United States, a representative government, with the role of citizens living in a nondemocratic contemporary society such as North Korea or Cuba. How are they different?

ACTIVITY

7. **Writing to Learn** Imagine that you have begun a project to increase voting in your community. A statewide election is approaching. Write a letter to a newspaper. Describe two reasons why people should vote in the election.

Using Special Purpose Maps

Learn the Skill

Language is a part of culture. People who study languages have divided all of the world's different languages into several groups. English is a part of the Indo-European language family. Languages in the same group may have several things in common, including the same or a similar alphabet. Japanese and Korean alphabets, for example, are completely different from the English alphabet. Spanish and English, on the other hand, have a similar alphabet as well as many similar words.

Language groups can be shown on a special purpose map. This map shows major language groups throughout the world. To read a special purpose map, do the following:

A. Locate the title. This tells you what the map is about. What is the subject of this map?

B. Study the key. This map is color-coded. A different color is used on the map for each of the world's language groups. Count the number of language groups. How many are there? What group includes English and Spanish? What color is it?

C. Check the map itself. Notice that is it a world map. Find North America and South America on the left side of the map. Find Europe, Asia, Africa, Australia, and Antarctica. Are all areas of the world shown on this map?

Practice the Skill

Use the map to answer these questions: What language group can be found in Northern Africa? What are the two main language groups of South America? Where are the Ural-Altaic language groups spoken? What language group can be found in Southern India? Which language group covers the greatest area on the map? Which language group is spoken more in Europe—Ural-Altaic or Indo-European? On how many continents does the Indo-European language group exist?

Apply the Skill

See the Chapter Review and Assessment at the end of this chapter for more questions on special purpose maps.

Major Language Groups

KEY

- Amerindian
- Indo-European
- Afro-Asiatic
- African
- Ural-Altaic
- Dravidian
- Sino-Tibetan
- Malayo-Polynesian
- Japanese and Korean
- Other

Robinson Projection

Review and Assessment

Creating a Chapter Summary

On a sheet of paper, draw a chart like this one. Include the information that has already been completed. Then, complete the remaining boxes with details summarizing what you have learned.

Population	Migration	Culture	Economic and Political Institutions
	People migrate for many reasons. Sometimes, certain things, such as war, "push" them to leave. Other times they leave because hope for better conditions "pulls" them to another place. One effect of migration is rapid urbanization.		

Reviewing Key Terms

Match the definitions in Column I with the key terms in Column II.

Column I

1. growth of city populations caused by the movement of people to cities

2. products that are made to be sold

3. the average number of people living in an area

4. economic system in which businesses are privately owned

5. area in which most of the people share the same cultural traits

Column II

a. culture region

b. urbanization

c. goods

d. population density

e. market economy

Reviewing the Main Ideas

1. How does the Earth's physical geography affect where people settle? (Section 1)

2. What factors are causing a rapid increase in human population? (Section 1)

3. What are some conditions that push people to leave their country and pull them to migrate to another country? (Section 2)

4. Why are people in many parts of the world moving from rural to urban areas? (Section 2)

5. How does culture affect what a group does and believes? (Section 3)

6. What are three institutions that are basic to all cultures? (Section 3)

7. Compare the traditional, market, and command economic systems. (Section 4)

8. What systems have societies developed for organizing their governments? (Section 4)

Map Activity

Continents

For each place listed below, write the letter from the map that shows its location.

1. Asia
2. Antarctica
3. Africa
4. South America
5. North America
6. Europe
7. Australia

 Take It to the NET

Enrichment For more map activities using geography skills, visit the social studies section of **phschool.com.**

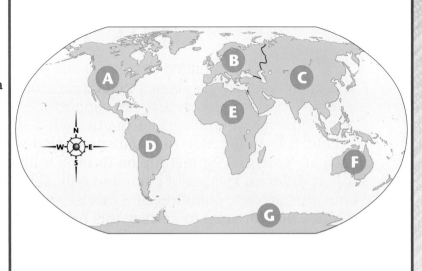

Writing Activity

1. **Writing a Report** Visit your school or local library and gather information to learn how the population of your state has changed in the past fifty years. Write a brief report explaining why people migrated to or from your state.

2. **Writing a Public Service Message** Imagine that your town is having a "culture fair." The fair will introduce people to cultures from other countries. It will also introduce people to different cultures within the United States. Write a public service message for the fair for the local radio station. A public service message includes the time, place, and purpose of the event. It should also tell people how and why they should get involved with the fair.

Applying Your Skills

Turn to the Skills for Life activity on p. 57 to help you complete the following activity.

Use your school or local library or the Internet to find information on a cultural topic such as distribution of ethnic groups, religions, or types of music in the United States. Using this information, draw a special purpose map of the United States that shows this information. Then, write a series of questions to test an understanding of the map. Trade your map and questions with a partner and answer each other's questions.

Critical Thinking

1. **Recognizing Cause and Effect** How have Africa's landforms and climate affected its population distribution?

2. **Drawing Conclusions** Explain the meaning of this statement: "Today, many countries of the world are becoming more urban." What does this statement tell you about the movement of people?

 Take It to the NET

Activity Patterns of human migration have shaped cultures and regions around the world. What impact has migration had on the region in which you live? Visit the World Explorer: People, Places, and Cultures section of **phschool.com** for help in completing this activity.

Chapter 3 Self-Test As a final review activity, take the Chapter 3 Self-Test and get instant feedback on your answers. To take the test, visit the Social Studies section of **phschool.com.**

THE EARTH

A large round rock spinning through space is our home in the universe. The Earth is one of the nine planets that circle around the sun, and it is the only planet in our solar system that can support life. Unlike the other planets, the Earth is just the right distance from the sun so that it is not too hot and not too cold. It has oxygen in the atmosphere and water in the oceans, both of which are essential for life. Alpine forests, rolling prairies, and vast deserts all support different species of plant and animal life in a fragile balance of nature. Population growth, pollution, and misuse of natural resources are human activities that threaten to destroy this balance.

? How do geographic features influence population centers around the globe? What can people do to preserve the balance of nature that is critical to the future of the planet?

Clouds containing tiny drops of water float low in the atmosphere, carrying water from the seas and land that falls as rain.

Atmosphere

Crust

Mantle

Outer core

Inner core

The Earth is made of layers of air, water, iron, nickel, and rock around a core of iron and nickel.

OCEANS
The oceans are large water-filled hollows in the Earth's crust. Their average depth is 2.2 miles (3.5 km).

CRUST
The top layer of rock at the Earth's surface is called the crust. It can be 44 miles (70 km) deep below the continents but only 4 miles (6 km) deep below the ocean floor. The temperature at the bottom of the crust is about 1,900°F (1,050°C).

MANTLE
Under the Earth's crust is the mantle. It is a layer of rock about 1,800 miles (2,900 km) thick. At the base of the mantle, the temperature can be as high as 6,700°F (3,700°C). The high pressure pushing against the mantle keeps it from turning into a liquid.

OUTER CORE
The center of the Earth has an outer core. It is about 1,240 miles (2,000 km) thick and is made of liquid iron. Its temperature is about 4,000°F (2,200°C).

INNER CORE
The center of the Earth is a ball of solid iron and nickel. It is about 1,712 miles (2,740 km) across. Its temperature is about 8,100°F (4,500°C).

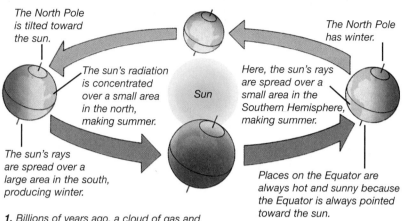

The North Pole is tilted toward the sun.

The sun's radiation is concentrated over a small area in the north, making summer.

Sun

The North Pole has winter.

Here, the sun's rays are spread over a small area in the Southern Hemisphere, making summer.

The sun's rays are spread over a large area in the south, producing winter.

Places on the Equator are always hot and sunny because the Equator is always pointed toward the sun.

SEASONS

North and south of the Equator, seasons change as the Earth moves around the sun. The Earth is tilted at an angle of 23.5° compared to its orbit. This angle makes the poles point toward or away from the sun at different times of the year.

1. *Billions of years ago, a cloud of gas and dust contracted (shrank) to form the sun. The rest of the cloud then contracted even more. It broke up into large clumps made up of particles of ice and rock. After a short time, the particles stuck to each other and began to form the planets.*

2. *When the Earth was forming, rock particles crashing into each other made the planet very hot. The surface was liquid and gave off a red-hot glow. It took the Earth about 100 million years to form into a ball of rock.*

3. *Radioactivity in the rock particles produced heat. The whole planet melted. Liquid iron sank to the center of the Earth to form the core. Lighter rocks floated above the iron. The surface cooled to form the crust. Volcanoes erupted and poured out gases. These gases formed the atmosphere. Steam from the volcanoes turned to a liquid and filled the world's oceans with water.*

4. *About 3.5 billion years ago, tiny living things began to grow. About 2.5 billion years ago, some of these organisms produced oxygen. The oxygen began to build up in the atmosphere. Parts of the crust broke up and slowly moved to create the world's landforms as they are today.*

FORMATION OF THE EARTH

Scientists have calculated that the Earth is billions of years old. Some moon rocks and meteorites (pieces of rock that fall to the Earth from space) are the same age, which suggests that the whole solar system formed at the same time. The sun, the Earth, and the other planets were formed from a huge cloud of gas and dust in space.

THEORIES OF THE EARTH

People once believed that the Earth was flat. About 2,500 years ago, the Greeks found out that the Earth is round. In 260 B.C., a Greek scientist named Aristarchus suggested that the Earth moves around the sun. It was not until 1543 that Polish astronomer Nicolaus Copernicus (1473–1543) proved that Aristarchus was right.

Welcome to
The United States and Canada

ECONOMICS *Learn about the growth of industry in our nation's cities ...*

SCIENCE, TECHNOLOGY, AND SOCIETY *Learn how technology helped people settle the West ...*

CULTURE *Study the creative arts of Canada's native people ...*

What do you want to learn?

CITIZENSHIP

Understand the roles and responsibilities of American citizens ...

GOVERNMENT

Witness Quebec's vote on independence ...

GEOGRAPHY

Climb one of the region's tallest mountains ...

HISTORY

Sail with explorers of new lands ...

A journal can be your personal record of discovery. As you learn about the United States and Canada, you can include journal entries about what you read, write, think, and create. For your first entry, write your thoughts on where in the United States and Canada you would like to go and what you would want to see there.

EXPLORER'S JOURNAL

Guiding Questions

What questions do I need to ask to understand the United States and Canada?

Asking questions is a good way to learn. Think about what information you would want to know if you were visiting a new place, and what questions you might ask to find the answers. The questions on these pages can help guide your study of the United States and Canada. You might want to try adding a few of your own!

GEOGRAPHY

The United States and Canada offer a rich variety of physical features that have affected the history and settlement patterns of these two nations. Vast regions of desert and tundra, rich farming plains, and natural harbors and waterways have greatly affected where and how people live. As people have learned to adapt to and modify the physical environment, they have used these geographic factors to build prosperous nations.

① **How has physical geography affected the settlement patterns and the economies of the United States and Canada?**

HISTORY

The early history of the United States and Canada is full of challenges, victories, and conflicts. Europeans arriving in the Americas struggled with native peoples for control of the land, and later, England and France fought for control of territories. The American colonies fought for, and won, their independence from Britain, and went on to build a powerful nation. In both Canada and the United States, citizens have worked to maintain their freedom and unity as a people.

② **How have historical events affected the cultures of the United States and Canada?**

CULTURE

When European settlers arrived in what is now the United States and Canada, they brought elements of their own cultures with them, and also adopted the ways of the native people. As the nations grew and welcomed immigrants from around the world, these citizens contributed to what would become new, uniquely diverse cultures.

③ **How has cultural diversity benefited and challenged these two nations?**

GOVERNMENT

The governments of the United States and Canada have evolved from colonial rule to democratic forms of government in which the people have a strong voice. In its early history, not all citizens of the United States had a voice in government. Today, however, people in both countries are working to ensure equal representation of all citizens.

4 **How have the United States and Canada developed the strong, democratic forms of government they have today?**

ECONOMICS

The United States and Canada are rich in fertile lands that have made both countries important agricultural producers. Natural resources such as minerals and lumber have contributed to the economies of both nations. With the development of industry, the two nations have grown into world economic powers.

5 **How did the United States and Canada become two of the wealthiest nations in the world?**

CITIZENSHIP

In both the United States and Canada, citizens are encouraged to participate in the political process through voting, running for public office, and speaking out about important issues. In both countries, individual citizens are free to voice their opinions, and to work to guarantee individual rights and equal justice for all people within the nation.

6 **How have ordinary citizens in the United States and Canada worked to achieve justice and equality for all?**

SCIENCE, TECHNOLOGY, AND SOCIETY

Since the 1800s, technology has been used to improve farming, manufacturing, and health care in the United States and Canada. Today, the economies of both nations rely heavily on technology in industry, and are using new methods to help improve and protect the environment. In addition, both countries are world leaders in scientific research.

7 **How has modern technology both benefited and created challenges for the United States and Canada?**

 Take It to the NET

For more information on the United States and Canada, visit the World Explorer: People, Places, and Cultures companion Web site at **phschool.com.**

ACTIVITY ATLAS

The United States and Canada

◆ ◆

To learn about Canada and the United States, start by checking some facts. Begin by exploring the maps of the United States and Canada and answering the questions on the following pages.

Relative Location

CANADA

Arctic Circle

N W E S

UNITED STATES

PACIFIC OCEAN

ATLANTIC OCEAN

Tropic of Cancer

Relative Size

UNITED STATES

CANADA

I. LOCATION

Locate the United States and Canada Look at the map at the left. In this unit, you will read about the United States, which is colored orange on the map, and Canada, which is green. Which country extends farther north? If you were on the east coast of the United States, which direction would you travel to get to the Pacific Ocean?

2. REGIONS

Compare the United States and Canada Look at the map to the left. Compare it to the map above. Notice that not all of the United States is shown on the second map. Which country do you think is bigger, the United States mainland or Canada?

 Take It to the NET

Items marked with this logo are periodically updated on the Internet. To get current information about the geography of the United States and Canada, go to **phschool.com**.

United States and Canada: Political

KEY

—— National boundary

⊛ National capital

• Other city

Lambert Azimuthal Equal-Area Projection

0   500   800 mi

0   500   800 km

HAWAII (U.S.)

PACIFIC OCEAN

0 100 200 mi

0 100 200 km

3. LOCATION

Identify Places in the United States and Canada The United States and Canada together take up most of the continent of North America. Look at the map. What other country is on the same continent? What country borders Canada? What countries border the United States? Name the cities that are the national capitals of the United States and Canada. What two states in the United States do not share a border with any other state? Which of the Canadian cities on the map is the farthest south? North?

4. PLACE

Locate Bodies of Water in the United States and Canada Rivers, lakes, and oceans are vital to a nation's development. Look at the map. What three oceans border the United States and Canada? Find the Great Lakes on the map. How many are there? Which one lies entirely within the United States? What river connects the Great Lakes to the Atlantic Ocean? The largest bay in the world is located in Canada. What is its name? Would you enter the bay from the Pacific Ocean or from the Atlantic Ocean?

Take It to the NET

United States and Canada: Land Use

KEY
- Nomadic herding
- Hunting and gathering
- Forestry
- Livestock raising
- Commercial farming
- Subsistence farming
- Manufacturing and trade
- Commercial fishing
- Little or no activity

Lambert Azimuthal Equal-Area Projection

5. HUMAN-ENVIRONMENT INTERACTION

Compare Land Use in the United States and Canada How many different types of land use are identified on this map? Which is the most common use of the land in Canada? In the United States? Why do you think hunting and gathering is the most common use of land in northern Canada?

6. REGIONS

Compare Land Use to Physical Features Look at the physical map on the next page. Compare it to the land use map above. What physical feature is close to most manufacturing areas? Why do you think manufacturing areas are located near these features?

7. LOCATION

Identify Relative Location A friend is traveling around North America. She sends you postcards with clues to her whereabouts. Use her clues and the map below to identify her relative location in the United States and Canada.

A. Whew! I've been hiking through the Rocky Mountains! Right now I'm heading south. I just crossed the Colorado River. What country am I in?

B. Today, I crossed the northern border of the United States, and I'm flying to Vancouver Island in Canada. In which direction am I traveling?

C. Now I'm on a ship. We're heading from the Gulf of St. Lawrence to the Great Lakes. What river will we travel on?

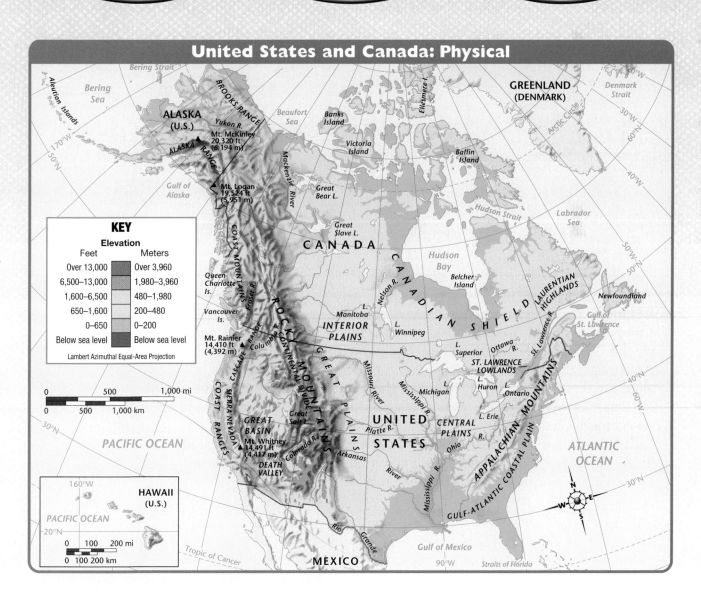

United States and Canada: Physical

KEY

Elevation

Feet	Meters
Over 13,000	Over 3,960
6,500–13,000	1,980–3,960
1,600–6,500	480–1,980
650–1,600	200–480
0–650	0–200
Below sea level	Below sea level

Lambert Azimuthal Equal-Area Projection

ACTIVITY ATLAS

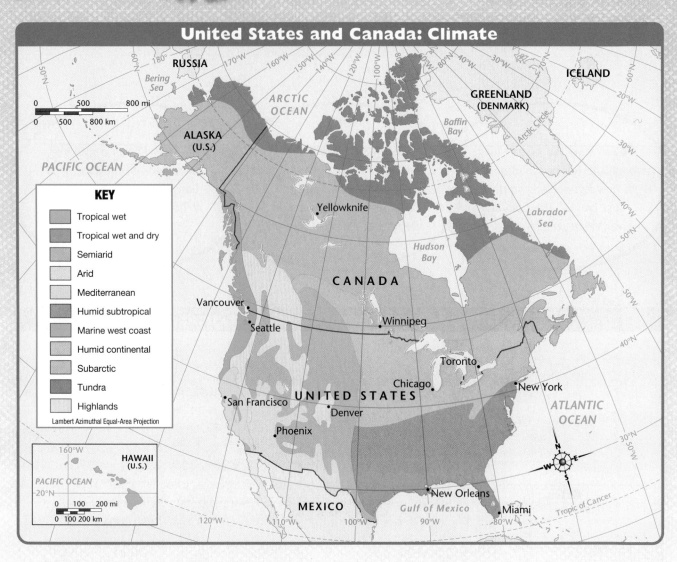

United States and Canada: Climate

KEY

- Tropical wet
- Tropical wet and dry
- Semiarid
- Arid
- Mediterranean
- Humid subtropical
- Marine west coast
- Humid continental
- Subarctic
- Tundra
- Highlands

Lambert Azimuthal Equal-Area Projection

8. REGIONS

Compare Climates You already know that climate affects the way people live. For example, you don't find snowplows on the beach or skis in the desert! Look at this map. How many different types of climate regions are there in the United States and Canada? Do the climates seem to change more from east to west or from north to south? Which of the two countries has a region of humid subtropical climate? Which country has the biggest area of subarctic climate? The city of Winnipeg is located in what climate region? Which cities in the United States and Canada are located in the marine west coast climate region?

The Tallest, Longest, Largest, and Deepest...

THE TALLEST MOUNTAINS OF THE UNITED STATES AND CANADA

Mt. McKinley	**Mt. Logan**	**Mt. Whitney**	**Mt. Rainier**
20,320 ft./ 6,194m	19,524 ft./ 5,951m	14,491 ft./ 4,417m	14,410 ft./ 4,392m
Alaska	Yukon Territory	California	Washington

THE LONGEST RIVERS OF THE UNITED STATES AND CANADA

River	Mouth	Length
Mackenzie	Beaufort Sea	2,635 mi/4,241 km
Mississippi	Gulf of Mexico	2,348 mi/3,779 km
Missouri	Mississippi River	2,315 mi/3,726 km
Yukon	Bering Sea	1,979 mi/3,185 km
St. Lawrence	Gulf of St. Lawrence	1,900 mi/3,058 km
Rio Grande	Gulf of Mexico	1,885 mi/3,034 km
Arkansas	Mississippi River	1,459 mi/2,348 km

THE LARGEST LAKES OF THE UNITED STATES AND CANADA

Winnipeg 9,094 sq mi 23,553 sq km

Erie 9,930 sq mi 25,719 sq km

Great Slave 11,170 sq mi 28,930 sq km

Great Bear 12,000 sq mi 31,080 sq km

Michigan 22,400 sq mi 58,016 sq km

Huron 23,919 sq mi 59,586 sq km

Superior 31,820 sq mi 82,414 sq km

9. PLACE

Compare Physical Features The United States and Canada have many different types of landforms. Study the charts, graphs, and diagrams on this page. Locate each of the landforms on the maps in this Activity Atlas. How much deeper is Great Slave Lake than Lake Superior? Which river is almost twice as long as the Arkansas River? How much bigger is Lake Huron than Lake Winnipeg? Which rivers have their mouths, or end, in other rivers? Where would you go to climb the highest mountain in the United States and Canada?

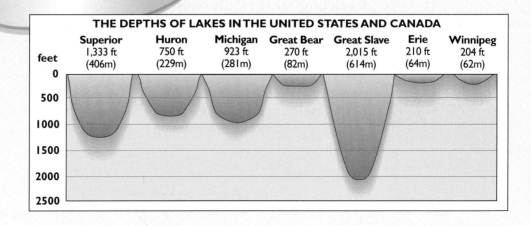

THE DEPTHS OF LAKES IN THE UNITED STATES AND CANADA

	Superior	Huron	Michigan	Great Bear	Great Slave	Erie	Winnipeg
feet	1,333 ft (406m)	750 ft (229m)	923 ft (281m)	270 ft (82m)	2,015 ft (614m)	210 ft (64m)	204 ft (62m)

CHAPTER

4

THE UNITED STATES AND CANADA:
Physical Geography

SECTION I
Physical Features

SECTION 2
Humans and the Physical Environment

SECTION 3
Geographic Factors and Natural Resources

United States and Canada: Natural Resources

KEY

- Hydroelectric power
- Iron
- Copper
- Bauxite
- Gold
- Silver
- Phosphates
- Uranium
- Lead
- Nickel
- Tungsten
- Coal
- Petroleum

Lambert Azimuthal Equal-Area Projection

USING MAPS

The United States and Canada are rich in natural resources. Both countries have used their resources to build a variety of industries. Study the map and the map key. Then, complete the following activities.

Locating Natural Resources

Make lists to answer the following questions: Which resources are not found in Canada? Which resources are found along the Gulf of Mexico? Which resources are found just north of the Great Lakes? If you are unfamiliar with some of the resources, look them up in a dictionary.

Conserving Resources

Some resources, such as gold or petroleum, are not renewable and could someday be used up. What do you think governments should do to conserve their resources? What would you suggest to conserve some of the resources shown on the map?

Physical Features

READING FOCUS

1. Where in the world are the United States and Canada located?
2. What are the main landforms of the United States and Canada?
3. What are the major bodies of water in the United States and Canada?

KEY TERMS

Continental Divide
glacier
transportation corridors
tributary

KEY PLACES

Rocky Mountains
Appalachian Mountains
Death Valley
Great Lakes
St. Lawrence River
Mississippi River

NOTE TAKING

Copy the chart below. As you read the section, fill in the chart with information about the physical features of the United States and Canada.

	United States	Canada
Land Forms		
Bodies of Water		

MAIN IDEA

The United States and Canada have a wide variety of unique physical features, including mountains, farmlands, great lakes, and mighty rivers.

Setting The Scene

Alaska's Mount McKinley is the highest mountain in North America and attracts thousands of visitors every year. In 1992, Ruth Kocour joined a team of climbers to scale the 20,320-foot (6,194-m) peak. After the team had set up camp at 9,500 feet (2,896 m), the first storm arrived. The team quickly built walls of packed snow to shield their tents from the wind. They dug a snow cave to house their kitchen and waited for the storm to blow itself out. Kocour recalls, "Someone on another team went outside for a few minutes, came back, and had a hot drink. His teeth cracked."

Maybe camping in the cold mountains is not for you. Perhaps you would prefer the sunny beaches of the South or the giant forests of the Northwest. Maybe you would like to see the Arizona desert or the vast plains of central Canada. The landscape of the United States and Canada varies greatly.

Climbing Mount McKinley

GEOGRAPHY

Dressed for warmth and carrying heavy backpacks, hikers stride across Mount McKinley's Kahiltna Glacier.
Critical Thinking Why might hiking on this mountain be dangerous?

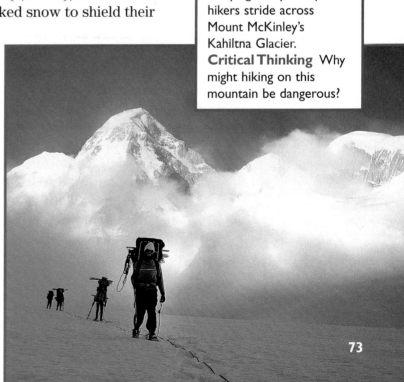

Where in the World Are We?

The United States and Canada are located in North America. To the east is the Atlantic Ocean, to the west, the Pacific. To the north, Canada borders the Arctic Ocean, while to the south, the United States borders Mexico and the Gulf of Mexico. The United States also includes Alaska and Hawaii.

Canada is larger than the United States and is the second-largest country in the world. The United States is the fourth largest country. But the United States has almost 10 times as many people as Canada.

Landforms of the United States and Canada

From outer space, the United States and Canada appear as one land-mass, with mountain ranges and vast plains running from north to south. Locate the following land forms on the physical map in the Activity Atlas on page 69.

Extending about 3,000 miles (4,830 km) along the western section of the continent, the **Rocky Mountains** are the largest mountain system in North America. Along the spine of the Rockies runs the **Continental Divide,** the boundary that separates the flow of rivers to the oceans. On the east side of the Rockies, rivers flow to the Atlantic Ocean, the Arctic Ocean, and the Gulf of Mexico. On the west side, they flow to the Pacific Ocean.

The second largest mountain system, the **Appalachian Mountains,** lies in the east. The Appalachians stretch about 1,600 miles (2,570 km), becoming the Laurentian Highlands in Canada.

Between the Rockies and the Appalachians lies a huge plains area. In Canada, these lowlands are called the Interior Plains. In the United States, they are called the Great Plains and the Central Plains. Much of this region has rich soil. In the wetter eastern area, farmers grow crops like corn and soybeans, while in the drier western area, farmers grow wheat, and ranchers raise livestock.

Special Features of the United States   The United States has several unique features. A plains area runs along its eastern and southern coasts. In the Northeast, this plain is narrow; it broadens as it spreads south and west. Flat, fertile land and access to the sea attracted many settlers to this area, and large cities developed.

West of the Rockies lies a region of plateaus and basins. The largest of these basins, the Great Basin, is the site of the Great Salt Lake in the west and **Death Valley,** the hottest place in North America, in the southwest. Farther west lie two more mountain ranges, the Sierra Nevada in California and the Cascades in Washington and Oregon.

Far to the north, snow and ice cover Alaska's many mountains. **Glaciers,** huge, slow-moving sheets of ice, fill many of the valleys between these mountains. Most of Alaska's people live along the warmer southern coast.

> **AS YOU READ**
>
> Summarize What are the major landforms of the United States and Canada?

Special Features of Canada   Canada, too, has a number of unique features. East of Alaska lies the Yukon (YOO kahn) Territory of Canada. Mount Logan, Canada's highest peak, is here. It is part of the Coast Mountains, which stretch south along the Pacific almost to the United States border.

East of the Interior Plains lies the Canadian Shield, a region of ancient rock covered by a thin layer of soil that covers about half of Canada, where few people live. Southeast of the shield are the St. Lawrence Lowlands, home to more than half of the country's population. While these fertile lowlands produce about one third of the country's crops, the region is also Canada's manufacturing center.

Major Bodies of Water

Both the United States and Canada have important lakes and rivers. Many American and Canadian cities developed near these bodies of water. As you read, find these water bodies on the physical map in the Activity Atlas on page 69.

Lakes Superior, Michigan, Huron, Erie, and Ontario make up the **Great Lakes,** the world's largest group of freshwater lakes. Only Lake Michigan lies entirely in the United States. The other four lakes are part of the border between the United States and Canada.

Melting ice from ancient glaciers formed the Great Lakes. Today, the Great Lakes are important waterways in both the United States and Canada. Shipping on the Great Lakes helped industry to develop in the two countries.

A Ship on the St. Lawrence Seaway

GEOGRAPHY   This picture shows a ship passing through the Welland Canal on the St. Lawrence Seaway. The canal, which connects Lakes Erie and Ontario, is 27.6 miles (44.4 km) long.   **Critical Thinking**   Why do you think that people sometimes call the St. Lawrence Seaway "Canada's highway to the sea"? Where does it start and end?

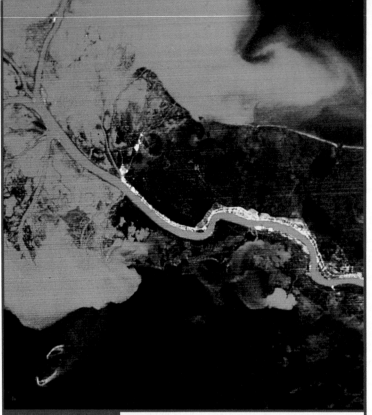

GEOGRAPHY As the Mississippi River flows into the Gulf of Mexico, it dumps silt, forming a huge triangular plain called a delta. This satellite image shows the shape of the delta. The waters of the Mississippi are shown as light blue, and the land is shown in shades of black. **Critical Thinking** Do you think a delta would be a good place to raise crops? Why?

Mighty Rivers Canada has two major rivers. The Mackenzie River, the country's longest, forms in the Rockies and flows north into the Arctic Ocean. The **St. Lawrence River** connects the Great Lakes to the Atlantic Ocean. People have modified their environment by building a system of locks and canals that enable large ships to navigate the river. As a result, the St. Lawrence is one of North America's most important **transportation corridors.**

In Canada, the St. Lawrence is called the "Mother of Canada." In the United States, America's largest river has an equally grand title. Native Americans call the **Mississippi River** the "Father of Waters." It begins in Minnesota and flows through the Central Plains to the Gulf of Mexico. Two other major rivers, the Ohio and the Missouri, are tributaries of the Mississippi. A **tributary** (TRIB yoo ter ee) is a stream that flows into a larger river.

SECTION 1 ASSESSMENT

AFTER YOU READ

RECALL
1. Identify: (a) Rocky Mountains, (b) Appalachian Mountains, (c) Death Valley, (d) Great Lakes, (e) St. Lawrence River, (f) Mississippi River

2. Define: (a) Continental Divide, (b) glacier, (c) transportation corridors, (d) tributary

COMPREHENSION
3. Describe the locations of the United States and Canada in relation to other countries and major bodies of water.

4. Describe two ways in which the physical features have affected life in the United States and Canada.

5. How do people of the United States and Canada use the major bodies of water in these two countries?

CRITICAL THINKING AND WRITING
6. **Exploring the Main Idea** Review the Main Idea statement at the beginning of this section. Then list five unique physical features found in the United States and Canada.

7. **Making Inferences** Hundreds of years ago, many people coming to the United States and Canada settled along coastal plains and rivers. Why do you think these areas attracted settlers?

ACTIVITY
8. **Writing a Paragraph** Suppose that you are planning a vacation. If you had your choice, what physical features of the United States and Canada would you like to see? Write a paragraph describing the places you would like to visit and why.

Humans and the Physical Environment

READING FOCUS

1. What types of climate zones can be found in the United States and Canada?

2. What are the four types of natural vegetation zones that can be found in the United States and Canada?

KEY TERMS

rain shadow   permafrost

tropics   prairie

tundra

MAIN IDEA

The wide range of climate and vegetation zones found in the United States and Canada is caused by a variety of factors.

NOTE TAKING

Copy the concept web shown below. As you read the section, fill in the web with information about the climate of each type of vegetation zone and where each zone is located.

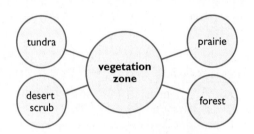

Setting the Scene

On a hot and sunny February morning, a reporter left his home in Miami Beach, Florida, and headed for the airport. Wearing lightweight trousers and a short-sleeved shirt, he boarded a plane to snowy Toronto. Was he forgetting something? Surely he knew that the temperature would be below freezing in Toronto.

He did, indeed, know all about the bitter cold that would greet him when he got off the plane. But he was going to do research for an article on Toronto's tunnels and underground malls. He wanted to find out whether people could really visit hotels, restaurants, and shops without having to go outside.

Climate Zones

Climate zones in the United States and Canada range from the polar climate of northern Canada to the desert climate of the southwestern United States. Factors such as the size of a region, latitude, mountains, and oceans affect the kinds of climates found in a region.

Canada's Climates—Braving the Cold   Generally, the farther a location is from the Equator, the colder its climate. Since Canada lies well to the north of the Equator, much of it is very cold!

Coping with the Climate

GEOGRAPHY

Whatever the weather might be outside, it is always pleasant in climate-controlled Eaton Center, a shopping mall in Toronto, Ontario.

Critical Thinking What are some of the ways that you modify your environment to cope with the climate in your region?

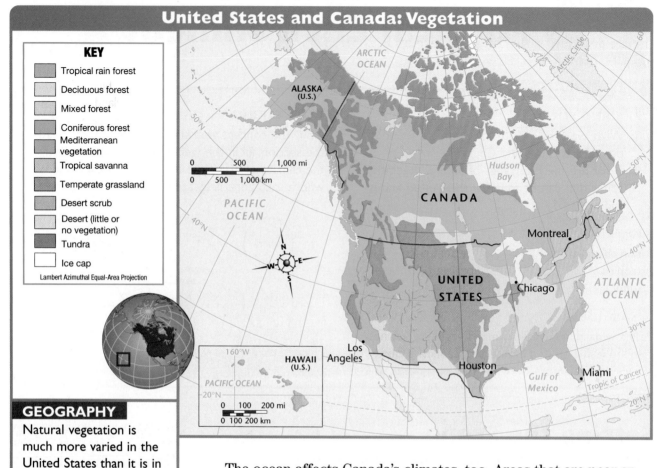

KEY

Tropical rain forest

Deciduous forest

Mixed forest

Coniferous forest

Mediterranean vegetation

Tropical savanna

Temperate grassland

Desert scrub

Desert (little or no vegetation)

Tundra

Ice cap

Lambert Azimuthal Equal-Area Projection

GEOGRAPHY

Natural vegetation is much more varied in the United States than it is in Canada. **Map Study** In terms of natural vegetation, what part of the United States has the most in common with Canada?

The ocean affects Canada's climates, too. Areas that are near an ocean may have milder climates than areas inland. The waters of the Pacific Ocean help make the climate of the northwestern coast of Canada mild all year, while inland areas often have climate extremes.

Finally, mountains influence climate, especially rainfall. Winds blowing from the Pacific Ocean rise as they meet the mountains in the west, cooling and dropping their moisture. The air is dry when it reaches the other side of the mountains. This area of **rain shadow** is on the dry, sheltered side of a mountain that receives little rainfall.

Climates of the United States   Latitude also influences climate in the United States. On the climate map in the Activity Atlas on page 70, you will see that Alaska lies far from the Equator and is cold for a good part of the year. The southern tip of Florida and Hawaii lie near or within the **tropics,** the area between the 23°N and 23°S lines of latitude. Here, it is almost always warm.

As in Canada, wet winds from the Pacific Ocean drop their moisture before they cross the western mountains, leaving the eastern sections of California and the states of Nevada, Utah, and Arizona semiarid or desert.

East of the Great Plains, the country has continental climates. In the north, summers are warm and winters are cold and snowy. In the south, summers tend to be long and hot, while winters are mild.

Natural Vegetation Zones

Climate determines the different vegetation zones. There are four major kinds of natural vegetation or plant life.

Northern Tundras   The **tundra** is a cold, dry region in the far north that is covered with snow for more than half the year. The Arctic tundra contains **permafrost,** or permanently frozen soil. During the short, cool summer, the surface of the permafrost thaws. Mosses, grasses, and bright wildflowers grow there.

Prairies   **Prairies,** also known as grasslands, are regions of flat or rolling land covered with grasses. The world's largest prairie covers much of the American central states and stretches into the provinces of Alberta, Saskatchewan (suh SKACH uh wun), and Manitoba in Canada.

Desert Scrub   With little rainfall, desert and semiarid regions have few plants. The Great Basin is a large, very dry region between the Rocky Mountains and the Sierras in the United States.

Forests   Forests cover nearly one third of the United States and almost one half of Canada. The mild climate of the northern Pacific Coast, for example, encourages great forests of trees.

Cattle Raising in the West

GEOGRAPHY   Many people in the plains and other lowland areas of western North America make a living by raising cattle. These cowhands in Texas are rounding up cattle and bringing them into a fenced area.
Critical Thinking Why do you think that areas of flat or rolling land are better for raising cattle than mountainous areas?

SECTION 2 ASSESSMENT

AFTER YOU READ

RECALL
1. Define: (a) rain shadow, (b) tropics, (c) tundra, (d) permafrost, (e) prairie

COMPREHENSION
2. How do the climate zones of the United States differ from those of Canada?
3. List the four types of natural vegetation zones found in the United States and Canada.

CRITICAL THINKING AND WRITING
4. **Exploring the Main Idea** Review the Main Idea statement at the beginning of this section. Then create a chart showing the types of climate zones mentioned in this section and the causes for each type of climate zone.
5. **Comparing and Contrasting** Write a paragraph that compares and contrasts the climate and vegetation of the tundra with that of the area around the Great Lakes. Use the climate map in the Activity Atlas to help you.

ACTIVITY
6. **Creating a Travel Brochure** Create a short travel brochure, inviting tourists to visit one of the climate zones described in this section. Use words and illustrations to describe the area and why tourists would find it appealing.

SECTION 3

Geographic Factors and Natural Resources

BEFORE YOU READ

READING FOCUS

1. What are the important natural resources of the United States, and how do they contribute to the economy?
2. What are the important natural resources of Canada, and how do they contribute to the economy?

KEY TERMS

alluvial
hydroelectricity

KEY PLACES

Grand Coulee Dam
St. Lawrence Lowlands

NOTE TAKING

Copy the chart shown here. As you read the section, fill in locations of where you can find each type of natural resource in the United States and Canada.

Type of Resource	United States	Canada
soil/farmland		
water/hydroelectric power		
oil		
forests		

MAIN IDEA

The rich natural resources of the United States and Canada have helped to build two of the leading economies in the world.

Setting the Scene

Surrounded by redwood forests, Carlotta, California, has little more than a gas station and a general store. Yet on one day in September 1996, police arrested more than 1,000 people here. It was the scene of a showdown. A logging company wanted to cut down some of the oldest redwood trees in the world. Protesters wanted to preserve the forest and the animals that live there. Both sides believed in the importance of natural resources. But they disagreed about how to use them.

Natural Resources of the United States

Native Americans, pioneers, and explorers knew North America was a land of abundant fertile soil, water, forests, and minerals.

Soil   The Midwest and the South have rich, dark soils called **alluvial** (uh LOO vee ul) soils, the fertile topsoil left by rivers after a flood. Areas that have good soil are suitable for farming.

Water   Water is a vital resource for drinking, growing crops, industries, and transportation. Some rivers, such as the Mississippi, Ohio, and Missouri Rivers, also serve as important shipping routes.

Preserving the Forest

GEOGRAPHY

These redwood trees are part of Muir Woods National Monument, a national park just northwest of San Francisco, California.   **Critical Thinking** Is it important to preserve our natural resources? Why?

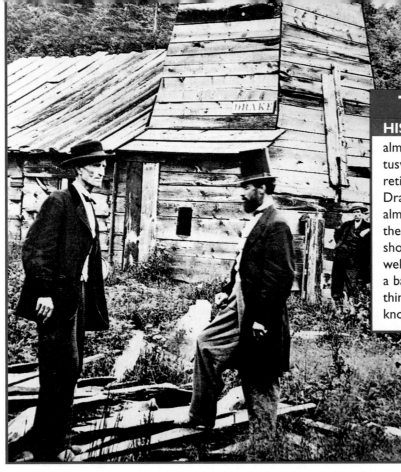

Water is used for other purposes, too. Dams along many rivers generate **hydroelectricity** (hy dro ee lek TRIS ih tee), or power generated by moving water. The **Grand Coulee** (KOO lee) **Dam** on the Columbia River in the state of Washington produces more hydroelectricity than any other U.S. dam.

Abundant Energy and Mineral Resources The United States is the second-largest producer of coal, petroleum, and natural gas in the world. Abundant energy resources have fueled industrial expansion and have helped to provide Americans with one of the world's highest standards of living.

The United States also has valuable deposits of copper, gold, granite, iron ore, and lead and these minerals are very important to many industries.

A Wealth of Trees America's forests are an important resource. In the Pacific Northwest, the South, the Appalachians, and areas around the Great Lakes, forests produce lumber, wood pulp for paper, and fine hardwoods for furniture.

Natural Resources of Canada

Canada's first European settlers earned their living as fur trappers, loggers, fishers, and farmers. Today, less than 5 percent of Canada's workers earn their living in these ways.

Farmland About 12 percent of Canada's land is suitable for farming. Most is located in the Prairie Provinces, and produces most of Canada's wheat and beef. The **St. Lawrence Lowlands** are another major agricultural region and produce grains, milk, vegetables, and fruit.

Minerals and Energy Resources About 85 percent of the nation's iron ore comes from mines near the Quebec-Newfoundland border. The region also has large deposits of gold, silver, zinc, copper, and uranium. The Prairie Provinces, particularly Alberta, have large oil and natural gas deposits.

Canada harnesses the rivers of Quebec Province to make hydroelectricity. These rivers generate enough hydroelectric power so that some can be exported to the northeastern United States.

Forests With almost half its land covered in forests, Canada is a leading producer of timber products. These products include lumber, paper, plywood, and wood pulp. The major timber-producing provinces include British Columbia, Quebec, and Ontario.

ECONOMICS Powerful tugboats tow huge booms of logs harvested from Canada's forests.
Critical Thinking
What wood products do you use in your daily life? How important are these products to you?

SECTION 3 ASSESSMENT

AFTER YOU READ

RECALL
1. Identify: (a) Grand Coulee Dam, (b) St. Lawrence Lowlands
2. Define: (a) alluvial, (b) hydroelectricity

COMPREHENSION
3. Why is water an important resource in the United States and how is it used?
4. Describe the major natural resources in Canada.

CRITICAL THINKING AND WRITING
5. Exploring the Main Idea Review the Main Idea statement at the beginning of this section. Then write a paragraph describing the natural resources of the United States and Canada, and explain how they benefit the economies of the two nations.
6. Comparing and Contrasting Based on what you know about the physical geography of the two countries, why do you think their resources are similar?

ACTIVITY

 Take It to the NET

7. Protecting Natural Resources Think of a natural resource in your community that needs to be protected, such as a forest or wetland. As a class, develop a plan to protect this resource. Visit the World Explorer: People, Places, and Cultures section of **phschool.com** for help in completing this activity.

Using Graphic Organizers

What You Need
▶ paper
▶ pencil

Learn the Skill

Knowing how to organize can help you keep track of the information you read. One good way to organize information is to use a graphic organizer. Graphic organizers can help you visually sort and understand information that you read. One helpful kind of graphic organizer is the concept map or web. With this type of graphic organizer, the subject or main topic is written in an oval in the center of the map. Features and details about this topic are written in ovals around the center. Read the following passage and then follow the steps below to help you organize the information into a concept map.

Bodies of Water

Water is one of the most important resources on the Earth. There are many different types of bodies of water found around the world, and they are used for a variety of purposes.

Types Some of the largest bodies of water include oceans, which contain salt water. Seas are also large bodies of salt water, but they are smaller than oceans. Lakes are smaller bodies of water, usually containing fresh water and surrounded by land. Rivers are large streams that usually flow into lakes and other large bodies of water.

Uses Water is used for many different things. People require water for nourishment, and they also enjoy rivers, lakes, and oceans for recreation. In addition, many industries rely on water to create electricity and help run factories. Finally, water is an important means of transportation of both people and goods.

A. Gather the materials you need.

B. Draw an oval in the middle of a sheet of paper. Write the topic for the map inside the oval. The topic for this map is "Bodies of Water."

C. Think about the different features of the topic. Look for headings and subheadings in the text to help you determine the features to include in the map. For example, two features for the topic "Bodies of Water" include the different types of bodies of water and the uses of bodies of water. Note how the features have been added to the map.

D. Add details from the text to each feature. Look at the map to see how details from the text about each of the features have been added.

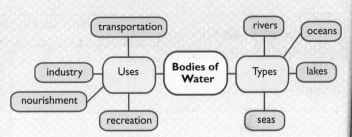

Practice the Skill

Read the text about the natural resources of the United States on pp. 80–81. Follow the steps you learned to create a concept map to organize this information.

Apply the Skill

See the Chapter Review and Assessment at the end of this chapter for more questions on using graphic organizers.

CHAPTER 4

Review and Assessment

Creating a Chapter Summary

On a separate piece of paper draw a chart like this one, and include the information that summarizes the physical features of the United States. Then, fill in the remaining boxes with summaries of the information you learned in this chapter.

	United States	Canada
Physical Features		
Physical Enviroment	The United States has a wide variety of physical features ranging from the glaciers of northern Alaska, to Death Valley in the Great Basin. There are mountain ranges, vast plains, and important rivers and lakes.	
Natural Resources		

Reviewing Key Terms

Choose the correct word(s) for each of the definitions below.

1. an area that receives little rainfall on the dry, sheltered side of a mountain

   A tributary   **C** rain shadow

   B tundra   **D** river

2. a large mass of ice that flows slowly over land

   A glacier   **C** tundra

   B prairie   **D** mountain

3. a cold dry region that is covered with snow for more than half the year

   A summit   **C** prairie

   B alluvial   **D** tundra

4. a stream that flows into a larger river

   A tributary   **C** alluvial

   B glacier   **D** lake

5. relating to fertile soil deposited by a river or stream

   A tundra   **C** tributary

   B alluvial   **D** prairie

Reviewing the Main Ideas

1. Describe two major landforms and bodies of water in the United States. (Section 1)

2. Describe two major landforms and bodies of water in Canada. (Section 1)

3. What factors influence the types of climate and vegetation found in the United States and Canada? (Section 2)

4. What are the four major types of natural vegetation found in the United States and Canada? (Section 2)

5. List two natural resources for the United States and describe their importance to the nation's economy. (Section 3)

6. List two natural resources for Canada and describe their importance to the nation's economy. (Section 3)

Map Activity

United States and Canada

For each place listed below, write the letter from the map that shows its location. Use the maps in the Activity Atlas to help you.

1. Canadian Shield
2. Great Basin
3. Great Plains
4. Rocky Mountains
5. Appalachian Mountains
6. Pacific Ocean
7. Atlantic Ocean
8. Great Lakes

 Take It to the NET

Enrichment For more map activities using geography skills, visit the social studies section of **phschool.com**.

Writing Activity

1. **Writing a Poem** Write a poem describing some aspect of the geography of the region where you live. Choose from landforms, bodies of water, climate, vegetation, or other natural resources.

2. **Writing a Travel Postcard** Imagine that you are vacationing in one of the regions described in this chapter. Write a postcard to a friend at home describing some of the physical features and vegetation that you've seen, and what the weather is like.

3. **Creating a Chart** What are the similarities and differences between the natural resources of the United States and Canada? Create a chart that shows these similarities and differences.

Applying Your Skills

Turn to the Skills for Life activity on p. 83 to help you complete the following activity.

Visit the library or the Internet to learn more about the Rocky Mountains. Create a concept web to organize the information you learned about these mountains.

Critical Thinking

1. **Drawing Conclusions** If you were going to build a new city in the United States or Canada, where would you locate it? What geographic features would influence your decision?

2. **Recognizing Cause and Effect** How does climate affect the growth of vegetation in the United States and Canada? Give two examples.

 Take It to the NET

Activity Create a shaded relief map showing the major physical features of Canada. Visit the World Explorer: People, Places, and Cultures section of **phschool.com** for help in completing this activity.

Chapter 4 Self-Test As a final review activity, take the Chapter 4 Self-Test and get instant feedback on your answers. To take the test, visit the Social Studies section of **phschool.com**.

THE UNITED STATES AND CANADA:
Shaped by History

An Astronaut's Answers: An Interview with John Glenn

On February 20, 1962, American John Glenn orbited the Earth three times in the spacecraft Friendship 7. He was the first American to travel around the Earth in space. He recently answered the question about why space exploration is necessary by saying in an interview:

"The crucial hands-on experience of my flight in the Mercury program helped make the Gemini flights possible. The Gemini flights then helped make the Apollo missions to the moon a reality. Apollo gave us valuable information for the Shuttle missions, and the Shuttle/Mir program prepares us for the International Space Station. This is the nature of progress. Each of the missions has built on the knowledge gained from the previous flights.

We are a curious, questing people and our research in this new laboratory of space represents an opportunity to benefit people right here on Earth and to increase our understanding of the universe. The potential scientific, medical, and economic benefits from space are beyond our wildest dreams. That's why astronauts went to the moon, and that's why we continue to pursue our dreams of space exploration."

USING PRIMARY SOURCES

When reading a text, especially for the purposes of gathering information, it is important to distinguish between primary and secondary sources. A primary source is an original document, such as a speech, novel, poem, diary, eyewitness account, or interview. A secondary source is a commentary on a primary source, such as a book review.

Using Interviews
Working with a partner, make a list of the ways that John Glenn says his flight strengthened the position of the United States as a world power. Then, summarize your ideas and share them with the rest of the class. Be sure to give details from Glenn's interview to support your conclusions.

Writing an Essay
Write an essay about the future of space exploration in the United States. Answer these questions in your essay:

1. How do you think John Glenn's flight prepared the way for future space exploration in the United States?
2. Predict possible reasons for space exploration in the future.

SECTION 1

Exploration in the Americas

BEFORE YOU READ

READING FOCUS

1. Who were the first Americans?
2. What effect did the arrival of Europeans have on Native Americans?
3. How did the United States win its independence from Great Britain?

KEY TERMS

indentured servant
plantation
boycott
Revolutionary War
Declaration of
   Independence
Constitution

KEY PEOPLE AND PLACES

Christopher Columbus
Jamestown
William Penn
Pennsylvania Colony
Thomas Jefferson
George Washington

NOTE TAKING

Copy the flow chart below. As you read the section, fill in the events that occurred in the Americas up to the time the British colonies gained independence.

30,000 years ago   Hunters and gatherers reach North America

↓

1400s   Christopher Columbus reaches lands in the Caribbean

1500s

↓

1600s

↓

1700ss

MAIN IDEA

European settlers and colonizers spread out across the Americas, took control of Native American lands, and eventually gained their independence.

Setting the Scene

Perhaps as early as 30,000 years ago, small family groups of hunters and food gatherers reached North America from Asia. This human migration took place during the last ice age. Some scientist think that, at that time, so much water froze into thick ice sheets that the sea level dropped, exposing a land bridge between Siberia and Alaska. Hunters followed herds of bison and mammoths across this land bridge. Other migrating people may have paddled boats and fished along the coasts.

Who Were the First Americans?

In the novel *The Crown of Columbus*, Louise Erdrich, an American writer, describes the variety of Native American cultures before the Europeans arrived:

   "[They] had hundreds of societies, millions of people, whose experience had told them that the world was a pretty diverse place. Walk for a day in any direction and what do you find: A tribe with a whole new set of gods, a language as distinct from your own as Tibetan is from Dutch—very little, in fact, that's even slightly familiar."

The Europeans Arrive

Native Americans' ways of life began to change forever after 1492 when **Christopher Columbus** explored islands in the Caribbean Sea.

Early Tools

HISTORY This bone tool was found near the area where scientists think a land bridge once connected Asia and North America. **Critical Thinking** Why do you think the first Americans used bone as a material for making tools?

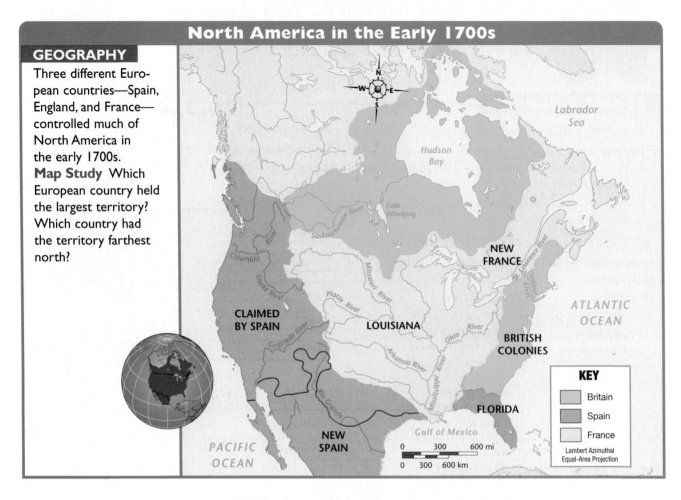

North America in the Early 1700s

Spanish and French Claims to the Americas During the 1500s, Spanish settlers spread out across the Americas. They often enslaved native peoples, forcing them to work in mines or on farms under harsh conditions.

Spain gained great wealth from her American colonies, and soon other countries wanted colonies in the Americas. France, for example, sent explorers to claim land along the St. Lawrence and Mississippi rivers.

The English Colonists Grow Powerful English settlers established 13 colonies along the Atlantic Coast where they came to start new lives, be free from debt, own land, and practice their religion freely.

The first permanent English settlement was **Jamestown,** Virginia, founded in 1607 and, by 1619, it had the beginnings of self-government. In the same year, the first Africans arrived here as **indentured servants,** people who had to work for a period of years to gain freedom. Later, about 1640, Africans were brought as slaves. Many were forced to work on the **plantations,** large farms in the South.

In 1620, the Pilgrims arrived in Massachusetts from England. They wanted to worship God in their own way and to govern themselves. They named their settlement Plymouth. About 60 years later, **William Penn** founded the **Pennsylvania Colony.**

Problems developed between France and Britain, and in 1754, they went to war over land in North America. Americans call this war the French and Indian War. With the colonists' help, the British were victorious.

The Break With Britain

To help pay the cost of war with France, Great Britain imposed many kinds of taxes on the colonies, and goods bought from Britain were also taxed. Since no one represented the colonists in the British Parliament, the colonists demanded, "no taxation without representation." They also **boycotted,** or refused to buy, British goods.

Patriots such as Samuel Adams, Thomas Paine, and Patrick Henry encouraged colonists to rebel against British rule, and the **Revolutionary War** began in 1775. **Thomas Jefferson** wrote the official **Declaration of Independence,** and in July 1776, representatives from each colony voted for independence. **George Washington** led the American forces to victory in 1781. The Treaty of Paris, signed in 1783, made American independence official for the 13 new states.

To form a strong central government, state representatives met in Philadelphia in 1787 and wrote the **Constitution.** The Constitution, approved in 1789, established a government of three branches in which the government's powers are limited and citizens have rights that the government cannot take away.

SECTION I ASSESSMENT

AFTER YOU READ

RECALL

1. Identify: (a) Christopher Columbus, (b) Jamestown, (c) William Penn, (d) Pennsylvania Colony, (e) Thomas Jefferson, (f) George Washington

2. Define: (a) indentured servant, (b) plantation, (c) boycott, (d) Revolutionary War, (e) Declaration of Independence, (f) Constitution

COMPREHENSION

3. Where do many scholars think the first Americans came from?

4. Identify and explain causes for a major conflict between Native Americans and the European colonists.

5. What did American colonists do to resist British rule in the American colonies?

CRITICAL THINKING AND WRITING

6. **Exploring the Main Idea** Review the Main Idea statement at the beginning of this section. Write a paragraph describing how the Spanish and the French treated the Native Americans.

7. **Recognizing Cause and Effect** Why did the colonists object to the taxes placed on them by the British?

ACTIVITY

 Take It to the NET

8. **Plymouth** Learn about the lives and history of the Pilgrims of Plymouth, Massachusetts. Write and perform a skit depicting the daily lives of Pilgrims or one significant event such as the first Thanksgiving. Visit the World Explorer: People, Places, and Cultures section of **phschool.com** for help in completing this activity.

Growth and Conflict in the United States

READING FOCUS

1. How was President Jefferson responsible for doubling the size of the United States?
2. How did the United States begin to grow and prosper?
3. What were the causes and effects of the United States Civil War?

KEY TERMS

Louisiana Purchase
immigrant
Industrial Revolution
abolitionist
Confederacy
Civil War
Reconstruction
segregate

KEY PEOPLE

Meriwether Lewis
William Clark
Andrew Jackson
Abraham Lincoln

NOTE TAKING

Copy the chart shown below. As you read the section, fill in information about the ways in which the United States grew, and the conflicts the United States faced.

Growth	Conflicts
Louisiana Purchase	War with Mexico

MAIN IDEA

After growing to include land from the Atlantic to the Pacific Oceans, the United States was torn apart by the Civil War in the 1860s.

The Lewis and Clark Expedition

HISTORY It took Meriwether Lewis (left) and William Clark (right) three years to complete their exploration of the lands west of the Mississippi River. **Critical Thinking** Why do you think the information gathered by Lewis and Clark was so valuable to America?

Setting the Scene

In 1803, President Thomas Jefferson sent **Meriwether Lewis** and **William Clark** to explore land west of the Mississippi River. As they journeyed all the way to the Pacific Coast, Lewis and Clark found plants and animals completely new to them. With this new information, Lewis and Clark created accurate, highly valuable maps of the region. They also met Native American groups along the way. During these meetings, the two men tried to learn about the region and set up trading alliances. Few of those Native Americans had any idea how this visit would change their way of life.

A Growing Nation

In 1803, President Jefferson bought all the land between the Mississippi River and the eastern slopes of the Rocky Mountains from France for only $15 million. This sale of land, called the **Louisiana Purchase,** doubled the size of the United States. Since little was known about this land, Lewis and Clark were sent to explore it.

The Nation Prospers

As the country grew, so did the meaning of democracy. In the 13 original states, only white males who owned property could vote. New states passed laws giving the vote to all white men 21 years old or older, whether they owned property or not. Soon, all states gave every adult white male the right to vote. Women and African Americans, however, could not vote.

In 1828, voters elected **Andrew Jackson** as president. He supported the interests of poor farmers, laborers, and settlers who wanted Native American lands in the Southeast.

More Room to Grow   The United States also continued to gain land. In 1836, American settlers in the Mexican territory of Texas rebelled against Mexican authority. With a force of more than 4,000 men, Antonio López de Santa Anna, Mexico's new leader, marched towards San Antonio to personally put down the rebellion. Although Santa Anna would defeat the Texans at the Alamo and Goliad, he would lose decisively to Sam Houston, the leader of the Texas volunteers, and his men at the Battle of San Jacinto on April 21, 1836. The territory was named the Lone Star Republic of Texas. In 1845, Texas became part of the United States. Only a year later, the United States went to war with Mexico and gained much of what is now the Southwest region. In the 1840s, American wagon trains began to cross the continent heading for the West as Americans started to settle this new land.

The Industrial Revolution   At the same time, thousands of people were pouring into cities in the Northeast. Many were **immigrants,** or people who moved from one country to another. This movement was spurred by the **Industrial Revolution,** or the change from making goods by hand to making them by machine.

The first industry to change was clothmaking, or textiles. New spinning machines and power looms enabled people to make cloth more quickly than they could by hand. Other inventions, such as the steam engine, made travel easier and faster. Steamboats and steam locomotives moved people and goods rapidly. By 1860, railroads linked most major Northeastern and Southeastern cities.

The Civil War and Reconstruction

In the late 1700s, a new machine called the cotton gin was invented. It quickly removed seeds from cotton, which made the crop more profitable. Cotton wore out the soil, though, and plantation owners wanted to expand into new western lands. Growing cotton still required many laborers for planting and harvesting. Since plantation owners relied on enslaved Africans, that meant that slavery would spread into the new territories. Some people did not want this and a debate began. Should the states or the federal government decide about slavery in the new territories?

HISTORY   In the 1820s, a Cherokee leader named Sequoyah developed a system of writing that enabled his people to read and write in their own language. **Critical Thinking** What do you think were some of the benefits of this system of writing?

AS YOU READ

Monitor Your Reading How did the cotton gin and new land affect slavery in the United States?

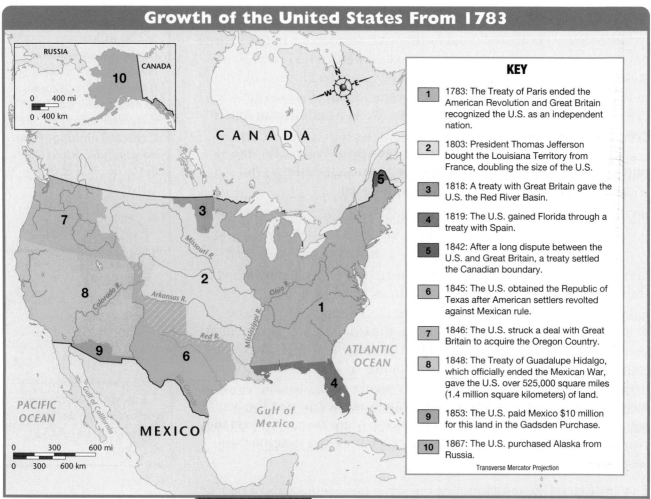

Growth of the United States From 1783

KEY

1 1783: The Treaty of Paris ended the American Revolution and Great Britain recognized the U.S. as an independent nation.

2 1803: President Thomas Jefferson bought the Louisiana Territory from France, doubling the size of the U.S.

3 1818: A treaty with Great Britain gave the U.S. the Red River Basin.

4 1819: The U.S. gained Florida through a treaty with Spain.

5 1842: After a long dispute between the U.S. and Great Britain, a treaty settled the Canadian boundary.

6 1845: The U.S. obtained the Republic of Texas after American settlers revolted against Mexican rule.

7 1846: The U.S. struck a deal with Great Britain to acquire the Oregon Country.

8 1848: The Treaty of Guadalupe Hidalgo, which officially ended the Mexican War, gave the U.S. over 525,000 square miles (1.4 million square kilometers) of land.

9 1853: The U.S. paid Mexico $10 million for this land in the Gadsden Purchase.

10 1867: The U.S. purchased Alaska from Russia.

Transverse Mercator Projection

GEOGRAPHY The region known as the United States grew to its present size over a period of about 100 years. As you can see, the United States made agreements with many countries in order to gain land.
Map Study What parts of the United States were once claimed by Great Britain? How did the United States acquire the Louisiana Territory? How did the United States acquire Alaska?

Causes of Conflict Until 1850, there were equal numbers of slave and free states in the United States. Then, California was admitted to the union as a free state. When the Southern states objected, Congress passed the Fugitive Slave Act. It said people anywhere in the country must return enslaved Africans who had escaped to their owners. Before this law, an enslaved African who could make the journey safely into a free state was considered free. The Fugitive Slave Act only increased the argument over slavery.

Thousands of Northerners became **abolitionists** (ab uh LISH un ists), people who wanted to end slavery. Many helped slaves escape to Canada where slavery was illegal. Most Southerners, however, felt that abolitionists were robbing them of their property.

When **Abraham Lincoln,** a Northerner, was elected president in 1860, many Southerners feared they would have little say in government. Some Southern states seceded, or withdrew, from the United States. They founded the Confederate States of America, or the **Confederacy.**

Conflict Erupts Into War

In 1861, the **Civil War** between the North and the South erupted and lasted four years. The North, known as the Union, had more industry, wealth, and soldiers; the Confederacy had experienced military officers and cotton. Southerners hoped that the foreign countries that bought cotton would help supply the Confederacy with the materials necessary to fight the war.

In 1863, Lincoln issued the Emancipation Proclamation which freed enslaved Africans in areas loyal to the Confederacy. After this, thousands of African Americans joined the fight against the South.

The Civil War ended with a Union victory in 1865. Lincoln wanted the Southern states to return willingly to the Union. This was the first step for the **Reconstruction,** or rebuilding, of the nation.

Reconstructing the Union

Less than a week after the end of the war, Lincoln was assassinated and Congress took control of Reconstruction. The Union Army governed the South until new state officials were elected. But as soon as the Union Army withdrew, Southern lawmakers voted to **segregate,** or separate, blacks from whites. The conflict between North and South ended with preserving the United States, but segregation affected all aspects of life for nearly a hundred years. The long struggle to guarantee equality to all Americans still lay ahead.

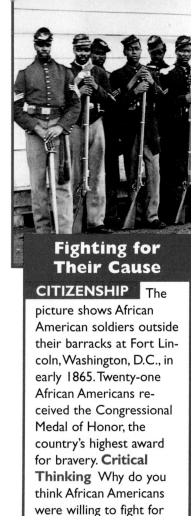

Fighting for Their Cause

CITIZENSHIP The picture shows African American soldiers outside their barracks at Fort Lincoln, Washington, D.C., in early 1865. Twenty-one African Americans received the Congressional Medal of Honor, the country's highest award for bravery. **Critical Thinking** Why do you think African Americans were willing to fight for the Union?

SECTION 2 ASSESSMENT

AFTER YOU READ

RECALL

1. Identify: (a) Meriwether Lewis, (b) William Clark, (c) Andrew Jackson, (d) Abraham Lincoln

2. Define: (a) Louisiana Purchase, (b) immigrant, (c) Industrial Revolution, (d) abolitionist, (e) Civil War, (f) Reconstruction, (g) segregate, (h) Confederacy

COMPREHENSION

3. What land did the United States gain as a result of the Louisiana Purchase?

4. What region did the United States gain through war with Mexico in 1846?

5. Why did the Southern states withdraw from the Union?

CRITICAL THINKING AND WRITING

6. **Exploring the Main Idea** Review the Main Idea statement at the beginning of this section. Then, write three paragraphs explaining how the westward expansion of the United States affected Native Americans, enslaved Africans, and citizens of the Southern states.

7. **Identifying Cause and Effect** How did the issue of slavery become a cause of the Civil War?

ACTIVITY

8. **Making a Chart** The Native Americans had a different attitude about the land than the white settlers had. Find out more about the Native Americans who were forced to leave the southeastern states and move to Oklahoma. Make a chart that compares and contrasts how these attitudes toward the land separated the Native American culture and the white settlers' culture.

SECTION 3

The Emergence of a World Power

BEFORE YOU READ

READING FOCUS

1. What events were taking place in the United States from 1865 to 1914?
2. What events led to United States involvement in World War I and World War II?
3. How did the United States change after World War II?

KEY TERMS

labor force
settlement house
Homestead Act
Holocaust
communism
Cold War
civil rights movement

KEY PEOPLE

Jacob Riis
Jane Addams
Franklin D. Roosevelt
Harry S. Truman
Martin Luther King, Jr.

NOTE TAKING

Copy the web diagram shown here. As you read the section, fill in the empty ovals with forces that made the United States a world power.

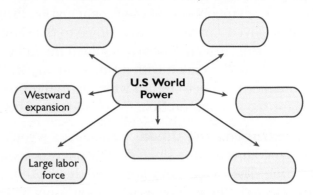

MAIN IDEA

As the United States expanded and its economy grew, it began to play a more important role in world affairs.

Setting the Scene

Jacob Riis was an angry man. In his book *How the Other Half Lives,* he took his readers on tours of tenement life in the late 1800s. He wanted other people to be angry, too—angry enough to change things.

"Come over here. Step carefully over this baby—it is a baby, in spite of its rags and dirt—under these iron bridges called fire escapes, but loaded down…with broken household goods, with washtubs and barrels, over which no man could climb from a fire…. That baby's parents live in the rear tenement here…. There are plenty of houses with half a hundred such in."

Riis himself had experienced these conditions first hand. Like many immigrants before him, Riis had suffered in the years following his arrival in the United States. Though he overcame the obstacles to become a journalist, Riis never forgot his past and worked hard for reform.

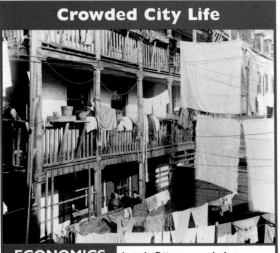

Crowded City Life

ECONOMICS Jacob Riis argued that tenements like these in New York City, which crowded as many as 10 people to a room, bred misery, disease, and crime. **Critical Thinking** What do you think Jacob Riis wanted "the other half" of the people to do about tenements and poverty?

Life in the West

SCIENCE, TECHNOLOGY, AND SOCIETY

New technology helped settlers turn vast areas of the West into productive farmland. Above, a huge combine harvester cuts wheat on a farm in Washington State. **Critical Thinking** Why was the development of new farming technology important to the settling of the Plains region?

The United States From 1865 to 1914

The Industrial Revolution made life easier for the rich and the middle class, but life did not improve for many of the poor. City slums were crowded with poor immigrants, many of whom could not speak English. These newcomers were a huge **labor force,** or supply of workers. But employers paid them very little, and even small children had to work so that families could make ends meet.

Reformers like Jacob Riis began to protest such poverty. In Chicago, **Jane Addams** set up a **settlement house,** or community center, for poor immigrants. Mary Harris Jones traveled across the country to help miners organize for better wages. Because of her work to end child labor, people called her "Mother Jones."

To escape poverty, many people moved to the open plains and prairies of the Midwest. When the United States government passed the **Homestead Act** in 1862, it gave 160 acres (65 hectares) of land to any adult willing to farm it and live on it for five years. Railroads helped connect the East and West coasts, which speeded up settlement. But life on the plains was not easy because trees and water were often in short supply, and settlers faced swarms of insects, wild prairie fires, and temperatures that were very hot in summer and cold in winter. Still, most homesteaders held on for the five years.

The United States Expands Beyond Its Shores   The United States also expanded beyond its immediate borders. In 1867, Secretary of State William Seward arranged for the United States to buy the territory of Alaska from Russia. In 1898, the United States took control of Hawaii, another territory. In the same year, the United States fought and won the Spanish-American War, gaining control of the Spanish lands of Cuba, Puerto Rico, Guam, and the Philippines. Because America had a strong economy and military strength, it was able to gain overseas territory.

The World at War

As a player in world affairs, the United States was drawn into international conflicts. In 1914, World War I broke out in Europe. The United States joined the Allied Powers of Great Britain and France three years later. They fought against the Central Powers, which included Germany, Austria-Hungary, and Turkey. With American help, the Allies won the war in 1918.

In the United States, the economy boomed during the 1920s. Women enjoyed new freedoms and the hard-won right to vote. More and more people bought cars, refrigerators, radios, and other modern marvels.

In 1929, however, the world faced an economic disaster called the Great Depression. In America, factories closed, people lost their jobs, and farmers lost their farms. Many banks closed, and people lost their life savings. In 1933, President **Franklin D. Roosevelt** took office. He created a plan called the New Deal. This was a series of government programs to help people get jobs and to restore the economy. Some of these programs, like Social Security, are still in place today.

The Great Depression was very hard on Germany and its people lost hope. In 1933, they responded by turning to Adolf Hitler who became dictator of Germany. Hitler convinced Germans they were a superior ethnic group and should take over Europe. In 1939, Hitler's armies invaded Poland, starting World War II. The allied powers of Great Britain, France, and Russia fought against the Axis Powers of Germany, Italy, and Japan.

Hitler forced countless Jews, Gypsies, Slavs, and others into brutal prison camps murdering millions of people, including some six million Jews. This horrible mass murder is called the **Holocaust** (HAHL uh kawst).

Up to this point, however, the United States did not get involved in the war. But in 1941, Japan attacked a United States naval base at Pearl Harbor, Hawaii. The Japanese were allied with the Germans, so the United States declared war on both nations and sent armed forces to fight in Europe and in the Pacific. President Roosevelt, who led the nation in war, died in April 1945, and Vice President **Harry S. Truman** became president.

In May 1945, the Allies defeated the Germans. During the summer, President Truman decided to drop two atomic bombs on Japan, which convinced Japan to give up. Finally, World War II was over.

GOVERNMENT

During World War I, the United States government paid for the war effort by selling bonds. These were certificates that included a promise to pay back the face amount plus interest. Posters like this urged Americans to buy bonds to win the war.
Critical Thinking Why do you think many people felt it was their duty as citizens of a democratic society to participate in buying bonds?

Postwar Responsibilities

After World War II, the United States took on new international responsibilities. The Soviet Union had been created in 1922. It adopted a form of government called **communism** where the state owns all property, such as farms and factories. After World War II, the communist Soviet Union took control of many Eastern European countries and imposed communism on them. The leader of the Soviet Union, Joseph Stalin, was a dictator who had complete control over the government and over the lives of the people. Unlike the United States, where officials are elected by the people and have to answer to them, Stalin answered to no one.

The United States feared that the Soviets were trying to spread communism throughout the world. As a result, the United States and the Soviet Union entered the **Cold War.** This was a period of great tension which lasted more than 40 years, although the two countries never faced each other in an actual war. Two wars grew out of this tension—the Korean War and the Vietnam War.

The economy of the United States boomed after World War II. But not all citizens shared in the benefits. In many areas, segregation was a way of life. People like **Martin Luther King, Jr.,** led the **civil rights movement** to end segregation and win rights for African Americans. This success inspired others who felt they were treated unequally.

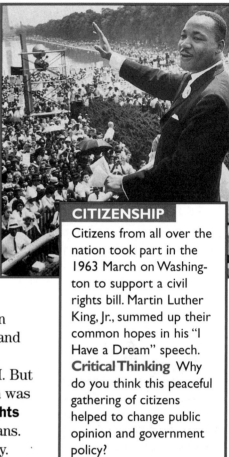

CITIZENSHIP

Citizens from all over the nation took part in the 1963 March on Washington to support a civil rights bill. Martin Luther King, Jr., summed up their common hopes in his "I Have a Dream" speech. **Critical Thinking** Why do you think this peaceful gathering of citizens helped to change public opinion and government policy?

SECTION 3 ASSESSMENT

AFTER YOU READ

RECALL

1. Identify: (a) Jacob Riis, (b) Jane Addams, (c) Franklin D. Roosevelt, (d) Harry S. Truman, (e) Martin Luther King, Jr.

2. Define: (a) labor force, (b) settlement house, (c) Homestead Act, (d) Holocaust, (e) communism, (f) Cold War, (g) civil rights movement

COMPREHENSION

3. How did the Industrial Revolution affect economic conditions in the United States?

4. What effect did the Great Depression have on the United States and Germany?

5. What were some of the challenges faced by the United States after World War II?

CRITICAL THINKING AND WRITING

6. **Exploring the Main Idea** Review the Main Idea statement at the beginning of this section. Then, write a paragraph describing how the United States carried out its responsibilities as a world power.

7. **Recognizing Cause and Effect** How did the Homestead Act help settle the Plains?

ACTIVITY

8. **Using Primary Sources** People who stay home during a war also find ways to help their country. Interview family and friends who remember the period of time during World War II. Ask questions about such things as rationing, volunteer work, and the employment of women during the war. Then, write a report about what life was like at home during the war.

Settlement, Trade, and Independence in Canada

BEFORE YOU READ

READING FOCUS

1. Why were France and Britain rivals in Canada?
2. How did Canada become an independent nation?
3. How did Canada become a world power?

KEY TERMS

dominion
bilingual

KEY PEOPLE AND PLACES

Ontario
Quebec
Louis Papineau
William Mackenzie

NOTE TAKING

Copy the flowchart shown below. As you read the section, fill in the important events that led to Canada becoming a strong and independent industrial power.

1713 Treaty gives Great Britain the Hudson Bay and Acadia
1754
1867
World War I & II
1982

MAIN IDEA

Canada won independence from Great Britain, grew industrially, and established close relations with the United States, but the tensions between the French and British cultures in Canada remain.

The Fur Trade in Canada

ECONOMICS The trade in beaver furs is an example of a primary economic activity which supplied the raw materials for beaver hats, like the one shown here. These hats were the height of fashion in Europe during the 1700s and 1800s, making the trade in beaver furs highly profitable.

Critical Thinking
What do you think happened to the demand for beaver hats when fashions changed in Europe?

Setting the Scene

The Haida are one of Canada's First Nations, living on the Queen Charlotte Islands off the coast of British Columbia. Haida mythology is very rich and complex. As in many Native American folktales, animals play an important role in Haida mythology. The Haida believe, for example, that the Raven created the Earth when he became tired of flying over a world covered with water. The Beaver is another important figure in Haida mythology. Imagine how the Haida felt when European trappers killed almost all of the beavers to make fur hats.

The French and the British in Canada

The profitable fur trade in Canada brought two European powers—France and Great Britain—into conflict. In 1713, they signed a peace treaty, giving Great Britain the Hudson Bay region and southeastern Canada, called Acadia. But this peace was uneasy. Against their will, French Catholics in Acadia came under the rule of British Protestants. The French controlled the lowlands south of Hudson Bay and around the St. Lawrence River, and both countries wanted to control the Ohio River Valley, farther to the south. The French wanted beavers for furs; the British wanted land for settlement.

The contest for this region was so intense that in 1754, it erupted into the Seven Years' War, called the French and Indian War in the United States. The British won the decisive Battle of Quebec in 1759 and gained complete control over Canada. Some French settlers returned to France and those who stayed resisted English culture. The Quebec Act gave the French people there the right to speak their own language, practice their own religion, and follow their own customs.

During the American Revolution, Americans who did not want independence were called British Loyalists. After the war, many Loyalists moved to Canada. But most did not want to live in a French culture. Great Britain divided the land into two colonies, Upper and Lower Canada. Most Loyalists moved into Upper Canada, now called **Ontario**. French Canadians remained in Lower Canada, now **Quebec.**

Canada Seeks Self-Rule

Both French Canadians and British Canadians hated British rule, but the two groups did not join in rebellion. In 1837, a French Canadian named **Louis Papineau** (pah pee NOH) organized a revolt in Lower Canada. His goal was to establish the region as a separate country. In Upper Canada, **William Mackenzie** led the people against British rule. The British easily defeated the rebels in both cases.

British leaders, afraid more trouble was coming, agreed to give Canadians more control of their government by uniting Upper and Lower Canada to form the Province of Canada. Because the British feared the Canadians might make a successful rebellion, not all the provinces were included in the union.

But Canadians felt that all provinces should be represented for their government to be effective. In 1864, leaders from every province met and worked out a plan to form a union. On July 1, 1867, the British Parliament accepted the plan and passed the British North American Act. This made Canada "one Dominion under the name of Canada." A **dominion** is a self-governing area but still subject to Great Britain. But now a central government would run the country. Canada had won its "peaceful revolution."

Canada Takes Its Place in the World
When Britain entered World War I, Canadians were still British subjects. Canada, therefore, entered the war, too. Canada contributed so much in resources and soldiers to the Allied victory that the young country became a world power. Great Britain recognized Canada's new strength and granted it more independence. During the Great Depression, Canada focused on solving problems at home, but when World War II began in 1939, Canada took part. Once again, Canadian efforts helped win the war.

The Battle of Quebec, 1759

HISTORY The Battle of Quebec was a turning point in the French and Indian War. This painting illustrates how British troops found a path through the cliffs that protected Quebec. **Critical Thinking** Do you think that Quebec would have fallen to the British if troops had not found a path in? Why or why not?

Canada: Postwar to the Present

During the war, Canadians built factories. They made war supplies and goods like clothes and shoes. Because of the war, people could not get such products from Europe. After the war, Canadian goods found a ready market in Europe.

Also during the postwar years, immigrants poured into Canada. They came from Asia, Europe, Africa, and the Caribbean. The newcomers filled jobs in new factories and other businesses. Soon, Canada became the world's fourth-largest industrial nation.

Canada and the United States–Trading Partners and Friends

As Canada grew in industrial power, Canada and the United States became cooperative neighbors. They worked together to clean up industrial pollution in Lake Erie. They signed an agreement to control air pollution. Trade between Canada and the United States also became increasingly important to both countries.

Old Conflicts Arise

Industrialization brought not only new friends but old conflicts. British Canadians built new factories in Quebec, alarming French Canadians. By 1976, some French Canadians were tired of being part of Canada. Quebec, they argued, should be independent. Instead, new laws made Canada a **bilingual** country. That is, Canada had two official languages—English and French. In addition Canadians could now change their constitution without Great Britain's permission. Canada was completely independent.

SECTION 4 ASSESSMENT

AFTER YOU READ

RECALL

1. Identify: (a) Ontario, (b) Quebec, (c) Louis Papineau, (d) William Mackenzie

2. Define: (a) dominion, (b) bilingual

COMPREHENSION

3. Explain why the Ohio River Valley was important to both the French and the English.

4. Describe Canada's "peaceful revolution."

5. How did Canada become an industrial power after World War II?

CRITICAL THINKING AND WRITING

6. **Exploring the Main Idea** Review the Main Idea statement at the beginning of this section. Then, write an editorial supporting either the French or English point of view regarding the problems in Canada.

ACTIVITY

7. **Drawing a Political Cartoon** French Canadians have argued that Quebec should be separate and independent from Canada. Draw a political cartoon that might have appeared in a French Canadian newspaper favoring independence for Quebec.

Sequencing Events on a Timeline

What You Need
You can make your own timeline. You will need:
▶ a sheet of paper
▶ a ruler
▶ a pencil or pen

Learn the Skill

A timeline is an easy way to make sense of dates and events of the past. It is a simple diagram that shows how dates and events relate to one another. To sequence events on a timeline, follow these steps to create a timeline of your life:

A. Gather the materials you need.

B. Use the ruler to draw a straight line across the sheet of paper. Draw a big dot on the left end of the line.

C. Mark the years. Next to the first dot, write the year you were born. Measure 1/2 inch down from the first dot, mark the spot with another dot, and write the next year under the dot. Continue until you reach the current year. Then write "Present" under the last dot.

D. Add the events. Above the first dot, write "Born in (write the name of the town where you were born.)" Now write several other important events in your life next to other dates on the timeline. Connect each label to the right place on the timeline by drawing a line.

E. Give your timeline a title.

Practice the Skill

Read the following paragraph about Canada's road to self-rule. Sequence the events in the paragraph on a timeline.

France and Great Britain signed a peace treaty in 1713, giving Great Britain the Hudson Bay region and the southeastern corner of Canada. However, 41 years later both countries would enter the French and Indian War over the issue of land. In 1763, the Treaty of Paris gave Great Britain control over all of Canada. Twenty years later, British loyalists from the United States began to move to upper Canada after the end of the American Revolution. At this time, French Canadians lived in Quebec in lower Canada. Soon, the French and British would align to defend themselves in Canada against the United States during the War of 1812. In 1837, citizens across Canada organized revolts against Great Britain, but were defeated. Thirty years later, the British North America Act made Canada a self-governing area.

Apply the Skill

See the Chapter Review and Assessment at the end of this chapter for more questions on timelines.

Creating a Chapter Summary

On a separate sheet of paper, draw a diagram like this one, and include the information that summarizes Section 1. Then, create three other timelines to summarize the events you read about in Sections 2, 3, and 4.

Exploration in the Americas

Pennsylvania colony founded

Pilgrims arrive

Revolutionary War starts

Treaty of Paris

Columbus explores the Caribbean

Jamestown founded

Africans brought as slaves

French and Indian War

Colonies win war

Constitution approved

1492   1607 1620   1640 1680   1754 1775   1781 1783   1789

Reviewing Key Terms

Complete each sentence with a word or words from the list below.

Reconstruction   boycott
abolitionist   American Revolution
Cold War

1. The American colonies won their independence from Great Britain in the _____.

2. An _____ is a person who believed slavery was wrong and wanted to end the practice.

3. The plan to rebuild the United States after the Civil War was known as _____.

4. A _____ is a refusal to buy goods from a company or country.

5. The _____ was a period of great tension between the United States and the Soviet Union.

Reviewing the Main Ideas

1. How did the first people get to North America? (Section 1)

2. How did Europeans change Native American ways of life? (Section 1)

3. Why did early colonists want to break away from Great Britain? (Section 2)

4. How did the United States expand its territory? (Section 2)

5. Name one cause of the Civil War. (Section 2)

6. Besides African Americans, which groups campaigned for civil rights after the 1950s? (Section 3)

7. Why did Canada become more independent from Britain after World War I? (Section 4)

8. After World War II, Canada's influence on the rest of the world increased. Why? (Section 4)

Map Activity

Canada

For each place listed below, write the letter from the map that shows its location.

1. Ontario

2. Quebec

3. Lake Erie

4. St. Lawrence Seaway

 Take It to the NET

> **Enrichment** For more map activities using geography skills, visit the social studies section of **phschool.com.**

Writing Activity

1. Writing a Summary Think about ways in which the United States and Canada are similar. How are they different? Write a summary comparing the two countries.

2. Using Primary Sources Some of the events described in this chapter were written about first-hand. Choose one event from the chapter to research. Visit your school or local library and use primary sources such as autobiographies, journals, or letters written by someone who participated in the event. You might also use additional information about the event, such as current books or articles describing the events, or information from the Internet. When you are done collecting information, write a brief report using direct quotations from your primary source to make your report more lively.

Applying Your Skills

Turn to the Skills for Life activity on p. 101 to help you complete the following activity.

Interview a family member and gather information about important events in their life, and the years in which these events occurred. Use this information to create a timeline of that person's life.

Critical Thinking

1. Identifying Central Issues Explain why Southern colonists thought that they needed slaves.

2. Making Comparisons Compare the ways in which the United States and Canada gained their independence from Great Britain.

3. Drawing Conclusions Why do you think many French Canadians want to be independent from English-speaking Canadians?

 Take It to the NET

Activity Create a timeline of significant events of one of the historic periods you read about. Visit the World Explorer: People, Places, and Cultures section of **phschool.com** for help in completing this activity.

Chapter 5 Self-Test As a final review activity, take the Chapter 5 Self-Test and get instant feedback on your answers. To take the test, visit the Social Studies section of **phschool.com** for help in completing this activity.

THE UNITED STATES AND CANADA:
Rich in Culture

Toronto and the CN Tower

UNDERSTANDING ARCHITECTURE

The photograph above shows the skyline in Toronto, Ontario. The distinct building topped with a needle-like structure is the CN Tower, a communications and observation tower in downtown Toronto.

Studying Landmark Buildings

If you were asked to paint a picture of a landmark building in your community, which one would you choose? Why? Choose a landmark building and take a photograph of it. Then, paint a picture that shows the unique features of that particular building, such as the materials it is made from, the shape or size of the building, or the style of architecture.

Using Primary and Secondary Sources

Visit your local library or historical society and find information about the landmark building you chose to paint, including the style of architecture it represents, and the time period in which it was built. If possible, interview people in your community who might have first-hand information about the building and its history. Present your findings to the rest of the class in a brief oral report.

Cultural Diversity in the United States and Canada

BEFORE YOU READ

READING FOCUS

1. What led to cultural diversity in North America?
2. How did various ethnic groups affect the culture of the United States and Canada?
3. What led to religious diversity in the United States and Canada?

KEY TERMS

cultural diversity   ethnic group
cultural exchange   religious diversity

MAIN IDEA

People from all over the world have immigrated to North America, making the United States and Canada culturally and religiously diverse countries.

NOTE TAKING

Copy the web diagram below. As you read the section, fill in the ovals with the items, including religion, which various cultures have exchanged or brought to North America.

Native Americans — Groups in North America — Africans — Asians — French

Setting the Scene

This view of **cultural diversity,** or a wide variety of cultures, comes from Tito, a teenager from Mexico.

"My parents say, 'you have to learn the American culture.' I listen to them, but then I think about an ideal society where there's a little bit of every culture and it goes together just right. Different ideas would come together and make everything a whole lot better."

Diverse Cultures in North America

North America has always been culturally diverse. When the first Europeans arrived, they found many different Native American groups. These groups spoke different languages and had different ways of life. The cultures of the first Americans reflected their different environments. Native American people living near the ocean ate a great deal of fish and told stories about the sea. People living in the forest hunted and trapped forest animals. These groups traded with one another and when groups trade, they also share ideas and ways of doing things. This process is called **cultural exchange.**

When Europeans began to explore and colonize North America, they changed Native American life in a number of ways.

Chinese New Year

CULTURE Chinese American Boy Scouts in San Francisco proudly show off a dragon, which symbolizes Chinese New Year. **Critical Thinking** What elements of cultural exchange can you identify from this photo?

105

For example, early Spanish explorers brought horses with them. Native Americans had never before seen horses, but these animals soon became an important part of their culture. Native Americans also learned to use the rifle brought by later European settlers.

Native Americans contributed many things to European culture as well. They taught the French how to trap and survive in the forest. They taught English families how to grow local foods such as corn and pumpkins.

Cultural exchange also took place between enslaved Africans and their owners. The Africans learned English and used European tools. African music and foods often entered the daily lives of slave owners.

AS YOU READ

Summarize What kinds of things did the Europeans learn from Native Americans?

Immigration and Cultural Exchange

Over the centuries, more and more Europeans and people from other areas flocked to North America. The immigrants made up different **ethnic groups**—people who share a language, history, and culture. When these groups settled in Canada and the United States, hoping for a better life, they made important contributions. For example, when Russian settlers came to the Great Plains, they brought a kind of hardy wheat that grew well in the cold climate of their home country. Farmers soon learned that this tough wheat grew well in the Great Plains climate. These immigrants helped the Great Plains become the leading wheat-growing area in the United States today.

For the first two hundred years, mainly European immigrants came to North America. By the mid-1800s Asian immigrants began arriving. Waves of Asian immigrants from China, Japan, and later from

Canada: Ethnic Groups

1.5%
11.5%
20%
40%
27%

■ British
■ French
■ German, Italian, Ukrainian, Scandinavian, Dutch, Polish, and other European
■ Native American (including Inuit)
■ Other

CULTURE Like the United States, Canada is very ethnically diverse.
Chart Study Hundreds of years ago, Native Americans were the largest ethnic group in Canada. What group is the largest today? What percentage of Canada's people are of European descent?

Thailand, Vietnam, Cambodia, and other nations have settled in the United States and Canada. In recent years there has also been an increase in immigrants coming from South Asian countries, such as India and Pakistan. All these immigrants have brought with them their special foods, holidays such as the Chinese New Year, martial arts such as the Japanese *judo* and Korean *tae kwan do*, and acupuncture, an ancient Chinese method of treating disease. In return, these immigrants have absorbed many things from U.S. and Canadian culture.

When immigrants move from one country to another, they must make difficult decisions. For instance, what parts of their original culture should they keep and what should they change? They must learn the language, laws, and manners of the people in the new country without losing the traditions of their former cultures.

Almost all immigrants cling to things that remind them of their former homes. Think about your family or your friends' families. Does someone play a musical instrument special to their heritage? Do they use special phrases from the language they learned from their parents or grandparents? These customs give people a sense of identity. They also help to enrich life in North America.

Religious Diversity in North America

Just as there has always been cultural diversity in North America, there has always been **religious diversity** as well. When European explorers and colonists first arrived in the Americas, they found Native Americans practicing a wide variety of religions. Different tribes held different philosophical beliefs, but common to most tribes was the belief in a powerful and mysterious spirit force. This powerful spirit lived in nature and could be contacted by certain people or through certain ceremonies. Many Native Americans in the United States and Canada continue to hold their ancient beliefs and practice some of the ceremonies.

The earliest European settlers of North America were Christian. Many, such as the pilgrims of Plymouth Colony, came to escape religious persecution in England. As more colonies were established, a

LINKS TO
Math

Using Your Fingers and Toes Native Americans created the first number systems north of the Mexican border. The San Gabrielino in California used "all my hand finished" to mean 10. "All my hand finished and one foot" was 15. The Chukchee used their fingers to count. Their word for "five" is *hand*, for "ten" *both hands*, and for "twenty" *man*—meaning both hands and both feet.

Major Religious Holidays		
Christian	Jewish	Islamic
Christmas–Commemorates the birth of Jesus Christ	**Rosh Hashanah**–The Jewish New Year	**Ramadan**–The Islamic holy month commemorating when God first revealed Himself to the prophet Muhammad
Easter–Commemorates the resurrection of Jesus Christ	**Yom Kippur**–Day of Atonement	

CULTURE This chart highlights some of the major religious holidays celebrated in North America. **Chart Study** Who is the focus of both Christian holidays? Which holidays are celebrated in your community?

Freedom of Religion

CULTURE This image shows the Puritans arriving in North America in the 1600s. They left Great Britain in search of religious freedom. **Critical Thinking** Do you think that the freedom to practice religion is important to people? Why?

spirit of toleration for different religions spread. When the United States Constitution was written, it guaranteed that no one would have to pay taxes to support religion. It also guaranteed that people could practice any religion they chose.

Religious tolerance attracted many immigrants to the United States and Canada. Jews fled religious persecution in Europe in the 1800s and 1900s to settle here. In the later 1900s, many people who practice the religion of Islam immigrated here. Today, people of Christian, Jewish, Islamic, and other religions practice their faith freely in the United States and Canada.

SECTION I ASSESSMENT

AFTER YOU READ

RECALL
1. Define: (a) cultural diversity, (b) cultural exchange, (c) ethnic group, (d) religious diversity

COMPREHENSION
2. Describe the cultural exchange that occurred between Native Americans and Europeans.

3. How is freedom of religion protected in the United States?

CRITICAL THINKING AND WRITING
4. **Exploring the Main Idea** Review the Main Idea statement at the beginning of this section. Then, list as many ways as you can think of that immigrants from various ethnic groups have contributed to culture in the United States and Canada.

5. **Drawing Conclusions** Write a paragraph describing how development in North America might have been different if Native Americans had not shared their cultural knowledge.

ACTIVITY

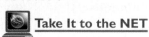 **Take It to the NET**

6. **Creating a Cultural Scrapbook** Create a cultural scrapbook with stories and illustrations showing the cultural diversity of your state or community. Model your scrapbook on the one shown on the web site. Visit the World Explorer: People, Places, and Cultures section of **phschool.com** for help in completing this activity.

Creative Expression and Artistic Traditions

BEFORE YOU READ

READING FOCUS

1. How do the literature and music of the United States and Canada reflect diverse cultures?
2. How do the art and architecture of the United States and Canada reflect the history and landscape of the nations?

KEY TERMS

Quebecois literature
improvisation
Group of Seven

KEY PEOPLE

Langston Hughes
Andrew Wyeth

NOTE TAKING

Copy the chart shown here. As you read the section, fill in the chart with information in each category.

	Literature	Music	Art	Architecture
United States				
Canada				

MAIN IDEA

The literature, music, art, and architecture of the United States and Canada reflect the history, landscape, and cultural diversity of the two countries.

Setting the Scene

As immigrants settled into life in the United States and Canada, they began to create their own unique cultures. Their art, literature, and music reflected their experiences in the new land. This excerpt is from a short story by American author Willa Cather, about a Czech immigrant who built a life on the American plains.

"When Rosicky went out to his wagon, it was beginning to snow—the first snow of the season, and he was glad to see it. He rattled out of town and along the highway through a wonderfully rich stretch of country, the finest farms in the county. He admired this High Prairie, as it was called, and always liked to drive through it. His own place lay in a rougher territory, where there was some clay in the soil and it was not so productive. When he bought his land, he hadn't the money to buy on High Prairie; so he told his boys, when they grumbled, that if their land hadn't some clay in it, they wouldn't own it at all. All the same, he enjoyed looking at these fine farms, as he enjoyed looking at a prize bull."

Literature and Music

Like Willa Cather, other American authors often wrote about the lives of common people. In John Steinbeck's novel, *The Grapes of Wrath*, a poor farm family escapes dust storms in the Southern Great Plains in the 1930s. African American poet **Langston**

The American Experience

CULTURE The work of U.S. and Canadian authors and artists, such as Willa Cather (pictured below), draws on the unique character of the North American landscape and the history and experience of its inhabitants. **Critical Thinking** Was the physical geography of the land important in the work of American authors? Why?

109

Hughes describes life in Harlem, New York City, in the early 1900s. Although Hughes was writing from his experience as an African American, his work was appreciated by people from a variety of backgrounds, and his poetry created a link among different cultures. Hughes' work helped many white people understand the African American experience.

Unique Voices in Literature

The novels and stories of many American authors reflect the wide range of American culture. Herman Melville wrote New England whaling stories, including the classic novel *Moby Dick*. Mark Twain wrote about life on the Mississippi River, as well as "tall tales" that expressed a uniquely American humor. In the second half of the 1800s, Walt Whitman wrote poetry full of vivid images and energetic language. His work expressed the growing self-confidence of American writers.

Canadian writers achieved fame for their work as well. Mark Twain highly praised Lucy Maud Montgomery's coming-of-age stories that began with the book, *Anne of Green Gables*. The heroine, Anne, was "the dearest and most moving and delightful child since Alice in Wonderland," Twain said. Today, Canadian writers such as Margaret Atwood and Alice Munro receive high praise for their work.

Canadian literature is often written in both French and English. French Canadian literature is called **Quebecois** (keh beh KWAH) **literature,** after the province of Quebec whose citizens speak French as their primary language. *Quebecois* literature is an example of how issues and conflicts in society influence creative expression. Until the 1830s, no French-Canadian poets or novelists had any of their work published in Canada. In the 1960s Quebec poets worked to create a French-Canadian identity. Paul Chamberland, in his book called *Terre Quebec*, which means "the land of Quebec," encourages readers to take pride in their French roots.

CULTURE In the picture below, Louis Armstrong poses with his band, the Hot Five. With his brilliant trumpet playing and his inventive musical mind, Louis Armstrong was one of the most influential figures in jazz history. **Critical Thinking** What does this picture tell you about the musical style of jazz? How does jazz relate to the American spirit?

Musical Traditions

Have you ever listened to music at a Caribbean carnival, heard Cajun Zydeco music from Louisiana, or bluegrass music from the Southeast? These are just a few of the different musical styles in American culture.

One of the most important American musical styles is jazz. An important element in jazz is **improvisation,** in which musicians do not follow music written down, but spontaneously create their own. This has allowed jazz to grow to include a variety of cultural influences.

Jazz began with black American music and African rhythms. It later included elements of folk and classical music from Africa, Europe, Asia, and other places. Jazz is a uniquely American blend of sounds from many cultures. It has become popular throughout the world as a style of music that goes beyond the boundaries of society.

One of the most important jazz musicians of all time was Louis "Satchmo" Armstrong. In the 1920s and 1930s Armstrong became known as the world's greatest jazz trumpet and cornet player. He was also a singer whose rough, gravelly voice was recognized around the world. Armstrong introduced the "swing" style of jazz and popularized a kind of jazz singing without words called *scat*. Through his immense popularity as an entertainer, Armstrong brought American jazz to the whole world.

Art and Architecture

As in literature, the art and architecture of the United States and Canada have been influenced by history and by the landscape.

Art   Painter **Andrew Wyeth** is one of America's most popular artists. His works focus on rural scenes that are reminders of a way of life long gone—old buildings, abandoned boats, deserted beaches. Other American landscape artists include Fitz Hugh Lane, who painted the seacoasts of New England, and Georgia O'Keeffe, known for her landscape paintings of the desert Southwest.

CULTURE   An Inuit artist uses a drill to put the finishing touches on a soapstone carving. Creating such traditional artwork is one way the Inuit retain their identity.   **Critical Thinking** What figures are shown in this sculpture? What universal themes are conveyed in this piece of art?

Native Americans have a long artistic tradition. From ancient times gifted artists have created beautiful pottery, baskets, woven cloth and rugs, beadwork, and metal jewelry. Many Native American artists continue this tradition today. Native groups such as the Haida of Canada's northwest coast produce fine woodcarvings. These artists express the close relationship that exists between their lives and their art.

In Canada, several painters formed the **"Group of Seven"** in the 1920s and 1930s. These artists developed bold new techniques for their paintings of Canada's landscapes. The group inspired other Canadian artists to experiment. Some ethnic artists followed other paths. Inuit printmakers and sculptors give new life to the images and ideas of their ancestors.

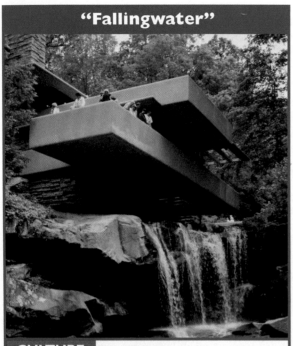

"Fallingwater"

CULTURE The "Fallingwater" house is located in Mill Run, Pennsylvania, and was designed by the American architect, Frank Lloyd Wright. Built for Edgar J. Kaufmann and his family in 1935 as a weekend retreat, "Fallingwater" is one of the most influential works of twentieth-century architecture. **Critical Thinking** What about this house is special? What does it say about architecture and nature?

Architecture The very diverse landscapes of the United States and Canada have influenced architecture in both countries. In the United States, architect Frank Lloyd Wright became famous for designing homes in the prairie style that blended with the landscape of the Midwest. The cool white and pastel stucco homes of the Southwest reflect the hot climate of the region. The Canadian architect Arthur Erickson designed buildings in Vancouver, British Columbia that are in harmony with the landscape.

In the 1900s, architects began to design new kinds of commercial buildings. A famous "race for the sky" took place in New York City. In the summer of 1929, an automobile tycoon, Walter Chrysler, battled Wall Street's Manhattan Trust Company for the title of the world's tallest building. Work on the buildings proceeded at break-neck speed, and just as it appeared that the bank would take the title in the spring of 1930, a crew atop the Chrysler Building put up a thin spire on the building to claim the title of world's tallest building at 1,046 feet. However, the title would be short-lived. Only four months later, the Empire State Building was completed.

In this new era, skyscrapers reflected the new wealth and power of the United States and Canada.

SECTION 2 ASSESSMENT

AFTER YOU READ

RECALL

1. Identify: (a) Langston Hughes, (b) Andrew Wyeth

2. Define: (a) *Quebecois* literature, (b) improvisation, (c) Group of Seven

COMPREHENSION

3. How have the different cultures of the United States influenced American music and literature?

4. How has the physical geography of Canada influenced Canadian art and architecture?

CRITICAL THINKING AND WRITING

5. **Exploring the Main Idea** Review the Main Idea statement at the beginning of this section and the chart you completed as you read. Then, write a paragraph that explains how art, literature, and music reflect the history, the physical landscape, and the cultural diversity of the United States and Canada.

6. **Drawing Conclusions** Write a paragraph explaining why you think that jazz is both uniquely American, and also appealing to people from all over the world.

ACTIVITY

7. **Reading Poetry** Read a poem by Langston Hughes or Walt Whitman. Write a paragraph explaining in what ways the poem reflects American life.

Conflict and Cooperation Among Cultures

BEFORE YOU READ

READING FOCUS

1. How were conflicts settled between the indigenous peoples and the governments of Canada and the United States?
2. What conflicts have ethnic groups faced in Canada and the United States?

KEY TERMS

reservation
indigenous
quota

KEY PEOPLE AND PLACES

Chippewa
Nunavut

NOTE TAKING

Copy the chart shown below. As you read the section, fill in information about conflicts and their solutions that culture groups faced in the United States and Canada.

	Conflicts	Solutions
United States		
Canada		

MAIN IDEA

Conflicts among groups within Canada and the United States have, at times, been resolved peacefully, though some continue.

Setting the Scene

During World War II, the Canadian army took over the land of the **Chippewa** tribe for a military base. The Chippewa were sent to a **reservation,** or area that the government set aside for them. The government said it would return the land after the war. Although the war ended in 1945, the land was not returned until 1994. Chippewa chief Thomas M. Bressette felt that his people deserved better treatment from the government:

"While our people were giving their lives [in the war] in Europe, the Government here in Canada was taking their land away from them and putting us on postage-stamp [size] reserves. We're asking for a share in the resources. We don't want to appear as beggars dependent on the government handouts, but we are now being denied the resources that we so willingly gave up to support this nation."

Government and Native Peoples: Conflict and Cooperation

From the time the first European explorers arrived in North America, there was both conflict and cooperation between the Europeans and the native peoples. Early European settlers in North America took

113

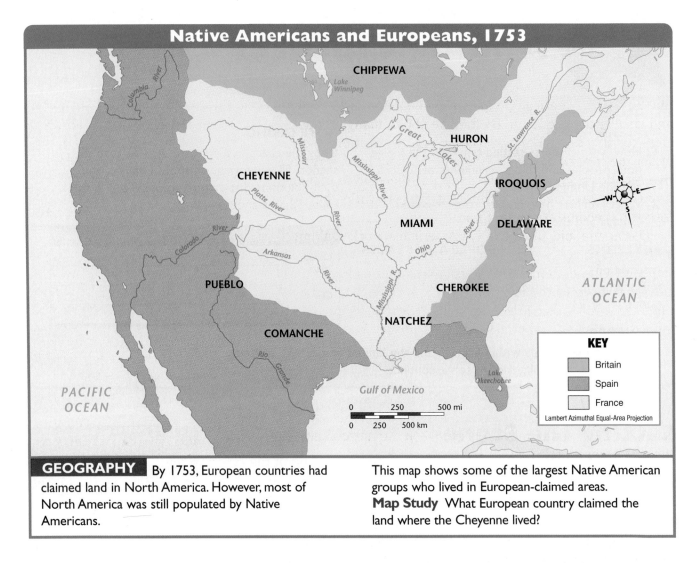

Native Americans and Europeans, 1753

CHIPPEWA

Lake Winnipeg

Columbia River

Missouri

CHEYENNE

Platte River

River

Colorado River

PUEBLO

Arkansas

Rio Grande

COMANCHE

PACIFIC OCEAN

Great Lakes

HURON

St. Lawrence R.

Mississippi River

MIAMI

Ohio

River

IROQUOIS

DELAWARE

CHEROKEE

NATCHEZ

Gulf of Mexico

Lake Okeechobee

ATLANTIC OCEAN

KEY
- Britain
- Spain
- France

Lambert Azimuthal Equal-Area Projection

0   250   500 mi
0   250   500 km

GEOGRAPHY By 1753, European countries had claimed land in North America. However, most of North America was still populated by Native Americans.

This map shows some of the largest Native American groups who lived in European-claimed areas.
Map Study What European country claimed the land where the Cheyenne lived?

over the land of **indigenous** peoples, the people who were natives of North America. Many indigenous people were sent to reservations, while others were denied equal rights and facilities.

AS YOU READ

Monitor Your Reading
How is the history of Canada's indigenous peoples similar to that of Native Americans in the United States?

Indigenous People in Canada

Despite being forced off of their land, indigenous people in Canada worked hard to hold onto their cultural identity and to regain their rights. Today, new laws in Canada allow indigenous peoples to use their own languages in their schools, and native people are working to have their own languages on street signs in their communities.

For centuries, the Inuit, nomadic hunters, lived in the Arctic. They had great survival skills and were fine craftsmen and artists. As times changed however, many Inuit lost their traditional artistic skills and feared that they would slowly lose their identity as Inuit people as well. In the early 1990s, the Inuit people convinced the Canadian government to grant them a vast section of land, once part of the Northwest Territory. On April 1, 1999, they moved to this new homeland, and called it **Nunavut** (NOO nah voot), or "Our Land."

Native Americans and the United States Government

In the 1700s, as more and more settlers came to the United States, Native American peoples were squeezed into smaller and smaller areas of land. By the late 1800s, many groups were forcibly moved to and confined on reservation land under the control of the government. Without land, these Native Americans could no longer support themselves in their traditional ways, such as by hunting. Little by little, they were forced to become dependent upon government assistance.

During the mid 1900s, Native Americans worked along with other groups in the United States to gain civil rights. By the late 1900s, conflicts between Native Americans and the United States government were being settled peacefully by the courts. Native leaders won back important rights including fishing, forest, and mineral rights on tribal lands.

Citizens and Immigrants in Conflict

For centuries people from all over the world have flocked to the rich lands of North America. As waves of immigrants arrived, conflicts sometimes arose between the newcomers and those already established.

The Quebec Question

From the beginning, Canada's leaders made immigration easy. At first they preferred European settlers and laws set limits on immigrants who were Jews, Asians, or Africans. But that has changed. Today, people of all ethnic groups may move to Canada as long as they can financially support themselves.

French Canadians are the focus of one of the greatest conflicts. These are mainly descendants of people who stayed after the British won control of Canada from France. The French Canadians of Quebec are very concerned about preserving their heritage. The Canadian government attempts to cooperate with the needs of French Canadians. For example, both English and French are official languages. In Quebec special laws promote French culture and language, but many French Canadians want more. They want Quebec to become a separate country, while the Canadian government wants Canada to remain one country. This conflict between French Canadians and English-speaking Canadians still remains unresolved.

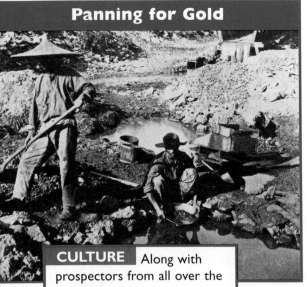

Panning for Gold

CULTURE Along with prospectors from all over the United States and its territories, the California Gold Rush of the mid-nineteenth century brought many immigrants to the state searching for work and a new life on the frontier. In the picture above, Chinese immigrants pan for gold in a California creek. **Critical Thinking** Besides work-related accidents, what other risks might immigrants have encountered when working in a new land?

Citizens and Immigrants in the United States

Poverty, political problems, and famine caused thousands of Europeans to come to the United States during the 1800s. At first the newcomers were welcome. The land was big, and there was plenty of work to do. But conflicts soon arose between new immigrants and U.S. citizens. During the 1850s, thousands of Chinese came to the United States to work in the California gold mines and to build the railroads. As their numbers grew, many other groups felt the Chinese were taking too many jobs. In 1882 the United States passed the Chinese Exclusion Act, which stopped Chinese workers from coming to the United States. Americans began to worry about the large number of immigrants from certain European countries, too. After World War I, the United States established **quotas,** certain numbers allowed, for various countries.

During the 1900s, many Spanish-speaking people immigrated to the United States from Mexico and Central and South America. Conflicts have arisen over whether public school classes should be taught in Spanish as well as English. Some people have tried to pass a law making English the official language of the United States.

Today, conflicts between cultural groups within the United States continue to exist. However, most Americans attempt to find peaceful solutions to these problems, and ways to cooperate with one another.

SECTION 3 ASSESSMENT

AFTER YOU READ

RECALL

1. Identify: (a) Chippewa, (b) *Nunavut*

2. Define: (a) reservation, (b) indigenous, (c) quota

COMPREHENSION

3. How has the Canadian government cooperated with the Inuit people to help them preserve their culture?

4. As Native Americans became confined on reservations in the United States, why did they become more dependent on government assistance?

5. Describe the main conflict between French Canadians and the Canadian government.

CRITICAL THINKING AND WRITING

6. **Exploring the Main Idea** Review the Main Idea statement at the beginning of this section. Then, write a paragraph comparing how the gov-

ernments of the United States and Canada each handled conflicts with native peoples in those two countries.

ACTIVITY

7. **Making Predictions** Write a paragraph explaining why you think returning homelands to indigenous peoples will create more conflict or will ease conflict. List at least two reasons for your opinion.

Identifying Primary and Secondary Sources

What You Need

To figure out the differences between primary and secondary sources, you will need:
▶ Several sources including magazines, newspapers, nonfiction books, a textbook, an encyclopedia, and a copy of the Constitution of the United States, which can be found in an encyclopedia.
▶ Paper
▶ A pen or pencil

Learn the Skill

You must use sources in order to do research. The best sources of information are often primary sources. Primary sources are written by people who experienced a particular event or time period firsthand. They are writing from their own experience. Examples of primary sources are:

letters, journals, autobiographies, government documents, such as declarations or laws, speeches, interviews, and home videos.

Secondary sources are written by people who did not experience a particular event or time period firsthand. These people are reporting what they have heard or read about an event. Examples of secondary sources are:

nonfiction books, textbooks, most magazine and newspaper articles

You can learn to identify primary and secondary sources by doing the following:

A. Gather the materials you need.

B. Make a two-column chart. Label the first column "Primary Sources." Label the second column "Secondary Sources."

C. Decide whether each source is a primary source or a secondary source. If you need help, reread the definitions above.

D. Write the names of your sources into the correct column of your chart.

E. When finished, compare your chart with a partner.

Practice the Skill

Below are two articles about the Gourd Dance. A Gourd Dance is a traditional Native American dance performed by the Kiowa people. One article is written by N. Scott Momaday, a Kiowa author and poet. The other article is written by a sixth grade student. Which article is a primary source? Which article is a secondary source? How do you know?

> It's in Oklahoma in July. It's apt to be very humid and very hot and we wear blankets. But once the movement starts and the drum starts gathering momentum, reaching a certain pitch, you get deep into the motion of the dance, and that feeling is indescribable. It's wonderful…I know why those warriors danced before they went out on raiding expeditions. It is a great way to gather yourself up, and you feel very much alive.
> —N. Scott Momaday

Source: Bolton, Jonathan, and Claire Wilson. *Scholars, Writers, and Professionals (American Indian Lives)*, New York: Facts on File, 1994. p. 113

> The Gourd Dance is a dance of the Kiowa Indians. The men of this Native American tribe dance it while wearing blankets. They are accompanied by the drum. The dancers wear blankets, even in hot, humid weather. The dance prepares them for raiding expeditions.
> —Jonathan Smith, Sixth Grader

Apply the Skill

See the Chapter Review and Assessment at the end of this chapter for more questions on interpreting primary sources.

Creating a Chapter Summary

On a separate sheet of paper, draw a diagram like this one, and include the information that summarizes Sections 1. Then fill in the second and third box with a summary of Sections 2 and 3.

THE UNITED STATES AND CANADA: RICH IN CULTURE

Section 1
Europeans arriving in North America encountered different cultural and religious beliefs among Native Americans. Different ethnic groups immigrating to North America made the United States and Canada culturally diverse.

Section 2

Section 3

Reviewing Key Terms

Match the definitions in Column I with the key terms in Column II.

Column I

1. the exchange of customs, ideas, or things between two cultures

2. a wide variety of cultures

3. an area set aside for native peoples

4. people who share a language, history, and culture

5. a certain number allowed

6. the act of spontaneously creating something

7. native to a certain area

8. work by French Canadian authors

9. a wide variety of religions

Column II

a. cultural diversity

b. cultural exchange

c. ethnic group

d. reserve

e. indigenous

f. religious diversity

g. *Quebecois* literature

h. quota

i. improvisation

Reviewing the Main Ideas

1. What contributions have Native Americans made to American culture? (Section 1)

2. What are some important contributions that immigrants have made to American culture? (Section 1)

3. How are history and landscape reflected in the art and literature of Canada and the United States? (Section 2)

4. How has cultural diversity helped shape American music? (Section 2)

5. How have conflicts between Native American groups and the U. S. Government begun to be resolved? (Section 3)

6. Why has there been conflict between U.S. citizens and new immigrants in the past and in more recent times? (Section 3)

Map Activity

Native American Groups

For each Native American group listed below, write the letter from the map that shows its location.

1. Miami
2. Chippewa
3. Cherokee
4. Iroquois
5. Pueblo
6. Cheyenne
7. Comanche
8. Huron

 Take It to the NET

Enrichment For more map activities using geography skills, visit the social studies section of **phschool.com**.

Writing Activity

1. **Writing a Poem** Much of the literature of America has been influenced by the history, landscape, and cultural diversity of the country. Write a short poem that shows one or more of these influences. The poem might be about your own family history, or that of your neighbors or classmates. It might be about the history of the place where you live, or about an historical event. Or it might be about the landscape where you live, or of places you have visited.

2. **Writing a Journal** Imagine that your family has just immigrated to the United States from another country. (You choose the country!) Write three journal entries describing your experiences and feelings on your first day of school in America, during your first trip to the grocery store, and watching an American television program or movie.

Applying Your Skills

For each of the following, decide whether it is a primary or secondary source. Make sure to explain your answers.

1. an encyclopedia entry about architecture in the United States
2. a journal entry
3. a research report about the Inuit
4. an interview with Willa Cather in a literary journal

Critical Thinking

1. **Drawing Conclusions** What are some advantages of having many different cultures influence your own culture? What are some disadvantages?

2. **Making Predictions** Think about the Inuit people moving to *Nunavut*, their new homeland. What do you think might happen to their culture in this new place? How will their lives be changed?

 Take It to the NET

Activity Canada's history and cultural identity have been shaped by a variety of cultural groups. Compare and contrast different cultural groups on the "Canadian Museum of Civilization" Web site. Visit the World Explorer: People, Places, and Cultures section of **phschool.com** for help in completing this activity.

Chapter 6 Self-Test As a final review activity, take the Chapter 6 Self-Test and get instant feedback on your answers. To take the test, visit the Social Studies section of **phschool.com**.

THE UNITED STATES: Exploring the Region Today

America the Beautiful

O beautiful for spacious skies,
For amber waves of grain,
For purple mountain majesties
Above the fruited plain!
America! America!
God shed His grace on thee,
and crown thy good with brotherhood,
From sea to shining sea.

Words by Katherine Lee Bates
Music by Samuel A. Ward

UNDERSTANDING SONG

Katherine Lee Bates wrote the words to "America the Beautiful" in 1893. Bates was a Massachusetts poet and a teacher. She attended Wellesley College, where she also taught. Later, Samuel A. Ward set her poem to music. The song has become a popular American hymn. First read the words, then listen to a recording of the song. Think about how Ward's music adds to Bates's poem.

Analyzing Song Lyrics

The song, "America the Beautiful" describes several different geographic regions in America. Read the lyrics to the song and then make a list of the places that the song describes. Study a map of the United States and try to figure out where you might find the places described. What kinds of words and images does the song's writer use to describe each place? How do you think the writer felt about America, based on the lyrics of the song?

Writing Song Lyrics

Writing song lyrics is a lot like writing poetry. Think about a place or a landscape that you know and love. Make a list of words that you think best describe that place. Be as specific as possible, and think about the images that your words will convey to someone. Share your lyrics with a partner, and discuss for which kind of music your lyrics would be best suited.

The Northeast
An Urban Center

Setting the Scene

For at least a century, the streets of New York City have been crowded. One hundred years ago, horse-drawn carriages caused traffic jams. Now, 3 million riders squeeze into New York's subway cars every day. Others travel the 1,745 miles (2,807 km) of bus lines, catch one of the city's 12,000 taxis, or ride the ferry boat. And many people drive their own cars through the city's busy streets.

New York is not unique. Washington, D.C., Philadelphia, and Boston are also crowded. In these big cities, millions of people **commute**, or travel to work, each day. Many drive to the city from the suburbs, but many who live in the city travel from one area to another in order to work.

A Region of Cities

Did you ever hear of Bowash? That is what some people call the chain of cities from Boston to New York to Washington, D.C. This coastal region of the Northeast is a **megalopolis** (meg uh LAHP uh lis), a type of region where cities and suburbs have grown so close together they form one big urban area. Look at the map on page 123 to see how large this area is.

City Streets

GEOGRAPHY

During rush hour, New York City's streets fill with cars. If you are in a hurry, try walking or grabbing a subway train instead of driving.
Critical Thinking What does this traffic tell you about where and how people live in this region?

The Northeast

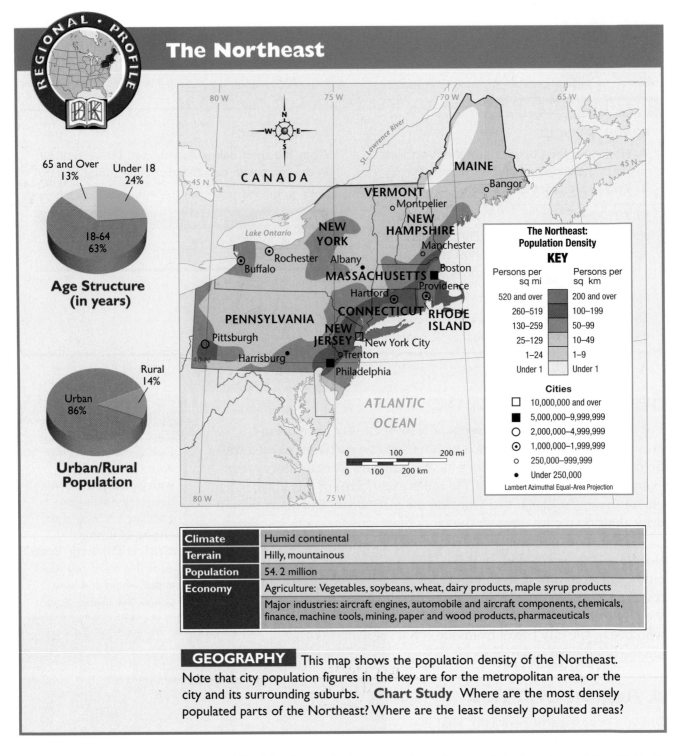

Age Structure (in years)

- 65 and Over 13%
- Under 18 24%
- 18-64 63%

Urban/Rural Population

- Rural 14%
- Urban 86%

The Northeast: Population Density

KEY

Persons per sq mi	Persons per sq km
520 and over	200 and over
260–519	100–199
130–259	50–99
25–129	10–49
1–24	1–9
Under 1	Under 1

Cities

□	10,000,000 and over
■	5,000,000–9,999,999
○	2,000,000–4,999,999
◉	1,000,000–1,999,999
○	250,000–999,999
•	Under 250,000

Lambert Azimuthal Equal-Area Projection

Climate	Humid continental
Terrain	Hilly, mountainous
Population	54. 2 million
Economy	Agriculture: Vegetables, soybeans, wheat, dairy products, maple syrup products
	Major industries: aircraft engines, automobile and aircraft components, chemicals, finance, machine tools, mining, paper and wood products, pharmaceuticals

GEOGRAPHY This map shows the population density of the Northeast. Note that city population figures in the key are for the metropolitan area, or the city and its surrounding suburbs. **Chart Study** Where are the most densely populated parts of the Northeast? Where are the least densely populated areas?

The Northeast is the most densely populated region of the United States. A region's population density is the average number of people per square mile (or square kilometer). The population is denser in parts of New Jersey than in crowded countries like India or Japan!

The Northeast's economy is based on cities, many founded in colonial times, along rivers or near the ocean as transportation and trade centers. Today, manufacturing, finance, communications, and government employ millions of urban Northeasterners.

An Urban Megalopolis

KEY
- Metropolitan area
- Freeway
- Tollway
- ⊛ National capital
- • Other city

Lambert Azimuthal Equal-Area Projection

GEOGRAPHY You can drive from Washington, D.C., to Boston, Massachusetts, almost entirely within urban areas. **Map Study** Compare this map with the one in the Regional Profile. What similarities are there between the two maps?

Philadelphia and Boston   Philadelphia and Boston were important in our nation's early history. In Philadelphia, America's founders adopted the Declaration of Independence and the Constitution. Some early struggles against the British took place in Boston.

Today, **Philadelphia** is an industrial powerhouse located near the mouth of the Delaware River. Important land and water transportation routes pass through here as ships, trucks, and trains bring in raw materials from all over the world. Thousands of factories process food, refine petroleum, and manufacture chemicals. Hundreds of products are then shipped out for sale.

The **Boston** area is home to more than 20 colleges and universities. Cambridge (KAYM brij), a Boston suburb, is the home of Harvard, the oldest university in the United States. The city is also famous for its science and technology centers. Boston's universities and scientific companies often work together to design new products and to carry out medical research.

AS YOU READ

Find Main Ideas   In what ways are Philadelphia and Boston important to the United States?

Good-bye City Life In 1845, Henry David Thoreau moved to Walden Pond in Massachusetts. His life there was an experiment in living alone and with only the essentials. He cut down trees and built a one-room house. He planted a vegetable garden and gathered wild fruit. There he wrote *Walden*, a classic of American literature.

New York City Visitors are often surprised by how big New York City is. More than 8 million people live there. The city covers an area of about 320 square miles (830 sq km) on islands and the mainland around the mouth of the Hudson River. The various parts of the city are connected by tunnels and bridges.

New York City is our nation's "money capital" and about 350,000 New Yorkers work for banks and other financial institutions. The famous New York Stock Exchange is on Wall Street.

Unfortunately, New York City was also the site of devastating terrorist attacks on September 11, 2001. Terrorists used passenger planes to kill thousands of people and destroy the World Trade Center towers, buildings that symbolized the importance of New York City. However, New York and the people living there recovered from the attack and the city continues to be a center of culture and business.

A Gateway for Immigrants

On January 1, 1892, 15-year-old Annie Moore who had sailed from Ireland by steamship stepped into the registry room of the Ellis Island Immigrant Station. Here she received a $10 gold piece for being the first immigrant to arrive at the new station.

From 1892 to 1943, the first stop for millions of immigrants to the United States was Ellis Island. From here, immigrants could see the Statue of Liberty, half a mile away in New York Harbor.

New York and other port cities of the Northeast have been important gateways for immigrants. In the 1800s, many Irish, Germans, and Scandinavians immigrated to the United States. Later, immigrants poured in from Southern and Eastern Europe. During the 1900s, people also came from the Caribbean, Asia, and Africa.

SECTION 1 ASSESSMENT

AFTER YOU READ

RECALL

1. Identify: (a) Philadelphia, (b) Boston, (c) New York City

2. Define: (a) commute, (b) megalopolis

COMPREHENSION

3. How does the population density of the Northeast affect the ways people live and work?

4. How have immigrants affected the culture of the Northeast?

CRITICAL THINKING AND WRITING

5. **Exploring the Main Idea** Review the Main Idea statement at the beginning of this section. Then, make a list of reasons why the cities of Philadelphia, Boston, and New York are so important to the economy of the United States.

6. **Making Comparisons** Think about the histories of, and major industries in, Philadelphia and Boston. Construct a Venn diagram to show how the two cities are similar and different.

ACTIVITY

7. **Writing a Journal Entry** Imagine you are a young immigrant arriving at Ellis Island. Write a journal expressing your feelings about coming to a new land.

SECTION 2

The South
Growth in Population and Industry

BEFORE YOU READ

READING FOCUS

1. How are the South's land and water important to its economy?
2. How has the growth of industry changed the South?

KEY TERMS

petrochemical
industrialization
Sun Belt

KEY PLACES

Atlanta
Washington, D.C.

NOTE TAKING

Copy the table below. As you read the section, fill in the table with information about the South's agriculture, natural resources, and industry, and the locations of each.

Agriculture	Natural Resources	Industries

MAIN IDEA

While the South produces a wide variety of agricultural products and natural resources, in the past fifty years, it has become industrialized as well.

Setting the Scene

From July 19 to August 4, 1996, the city of **Atlanta,** Georgia, was the center of the world. More than two million people from 172 countries visited the city during that time to see a very special event. It was the 1996 Summer Olympic Games.

Atlanta today is a center of trade, transportation, and communication. It is located in one of the fastest-growing regions of the United States—the South.

The Varied Land of the South

The South's geography makes many different types of jobs possible. The South is warmer than regions farther north, it receives plenty of rain, and the plains along the Atlantic Ocean and the Gulf of Mexico have rich soil. Together, these features make much of the South a great place for growing crops and raising animals.

Farming in the South Farming has always been important to the South's economy and farmers once depended on cotton as their only source of income. Today, cotton still brings a lot of money to the South, especially to Alabama, Mississippi, and Texas, but "King Cotton" no longer rules this region. Most southern farmers produce a wide variety of crops and farm animals.

Atlanta Hosts the Olympics

ECONOMICS

Famous boxer Muhammad Ali lights the Olympic torch at the 1996 Summer Olympic Games in Atlanta, Georgia. **Critical Thinking** In what ways do you think hosting the Olympics benefited the city of Atlanta?

The South

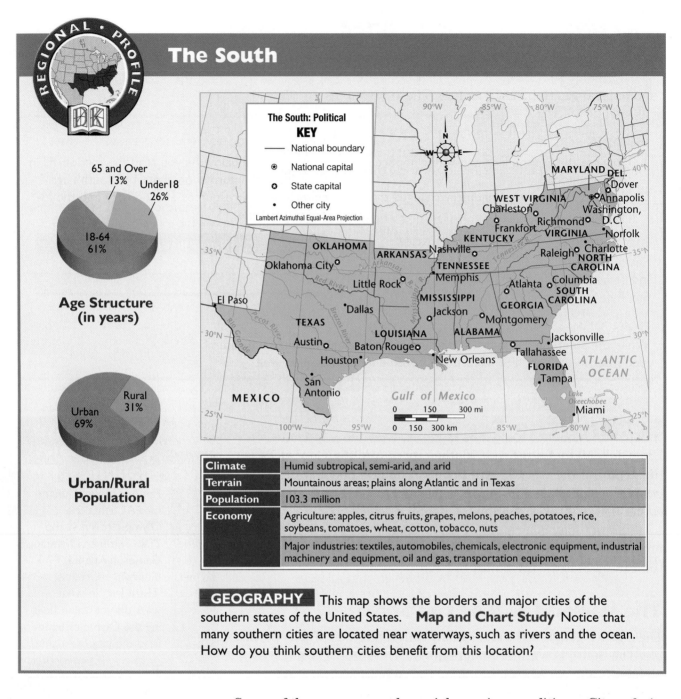

Age Structure (in years)

65 and Over 13%
Under 18 26%
18-64 61%

Urban/Rural Population

Rural 31%
Urban 69%

The South: Political
KEY

— National boundary
⊛ National capital
⊙ State capital
• Other city

Lambert Azimuthal Equal-Area Projection

Climate	Humid subtropical, semi-arid, and arid
Terrain	Mountainous areas; plains along Atlantic and in Texas
Population	103.3 million
Economy	Agriculture: apples, citrus fruits, grapes, melons, peaches, potatoes, rice, soybeans, tomatoes, wheat, cotton, tobacco, nuts
	Major industries: textiles, automobiles, chemicals, electronic equipment, industrial machinery and equipment, oil and gas, transportation equipment

GEOGRAPHY This map shows the borders and major cities of the southern states of the United States. **Map and Chart Study** Notice that many southern cities are located near waterways, such as rivers and the ocean. How do you think southern cities benefit from this location?

Some of these crops need special growing conditions. Citrus fruits require year-round warmth and sunshine. Florida has plenty of both and more oranges, tangerines, grapefruits, and limes are grown here than in any other state. Rice needs the warm moist growing conditions found in Arkansas, Louisiana, and Mississippi, so it is grown along the coast of the Gulf of Mexico and also in the Mississippi River valley.

Some areas of the South have become famous for their agricultural products. Georgia is known as the Peach State and is famous for its peanuts and pecans. Texas raises more cattle than any other state. Arkansas raises the most chickens and turkeys. These items are just a sample of what is produced.

Drilling and Mining in the South In some parts of the South, what is under the soil is as important as what grows in it. In Louisiana, Oklahoma, and Texas, companies drill for oil and natural gas to be used as fuel. These resources are also made into **petrochemicals,** such as plastics and paint. In Alabama, Kentucky, West Virginia, and Tennessee, miners dig for coal. Southern states are also leading producers of salt, sulfur, lead, zinc, and bauxite—a mineral used to make aluminum.

Southern Fish and Forests People in the South can also make a living in fishing and forestry. The Chesapeake Bay area near Maryland and Virginia is famous for its shellfish. However, the South's fishing industry is strongest in Louisiana and Texas. The timber industry is found in nearly every southern state. Softwood trees are used for building or for paper, and hardwood trees for furniture.

Southern Cities and Industries

Over the past 50 years, the South has gone through many changes. Though the South's rural areas are important, most people in the South today live in cities. They work in factories, high-technology firms, tourism, or in one of the other industries in this region's growing economy. This change from an agriculture-based economy to an industry-based economy is called **industrialization.**

Textiles and Technology One of the most important industries in the South is the textile industry, which makes cloth.

Textile mills were first built in this region to use the South's cotton and many still make cotton cloth today. Many others now make cloth from synthetic, or human-made, materials. The textile industry is strongest in Georgia, the Carolinas, and Virginia.

Promoting Trade

Since it went into effect in 1994, the North American Free Trade Agreement (NAFTA) has had a big impact on the economy of the South and the United States as a whole. This agreement between the United States, Canada, and Mexico has phased out tariffs, or taxes on trade, and other trade barriers between these countries. The agreement has sharply increased trade, since each country can now sell goods to its neighbors more cheaply. NAFTA has had an especially strong impact on Texas and on other states that border Mexico or Canada.

Critical Thinking How has NAFTA affected the economies of these countries?

New industries are growing all across the South. One is the high-technology industry, which makes computers and other electronic products. Some centers of high technology are Raleigh, North Carolina, and Austin, Texas. In Florida, Texas, and Alabama, people work for the National Aeronautics and Space Administration (NASA) running the nation's space exploration program.

Transportation and Tourism Some of the South's largest cities play big roles in the transportation industry. Miami, Florida, is a gateway to Central and South America. New Orleans, Louisiana, connects the Gulf of Mexico to the Mississippi River system. The South is part of the **Sun Belt,** a broad area of the United States stretching from the southern Atlantic Coast to the coast of California. It is known for its warm weather. Some arrivals are older adults who want to retire to places without cold winters. Others come for both the weather and the jobs that the Sun Belt offers. Still others come to the South as tourists.

Our Nation's Capital The city of Washington is not in any state. Instead, it is in the District of Columbia, which lies between the states of Maryland and Virginia. This area was chosen as the site for the nation's capital in 1790. **Washington, D.C.,** is home to the nation's leaders and to hundreds of foreign diplomats.

SECTION 2 ASSESSMENT

AFTER YOU READ

RECALL

1. Identify: (a) Atlanta, (b) Washington, D.C.

2. Define: (a) petrochemical, (b) industrialization, (c) Sun Belt

COMPREHENSION

3. How do the geography and climate of the South help make it an important agricultural region?

4. Why have many people in the South moved from rural areas to urban areas?

CRITICAL THINKING AND WRITING

5. **Exploring the Main Idea** Review the Main Idea statement at the beginning of this section. Then, make a list of some of the most important economic activities of the South.

6. **Recognizing Cause and Effect** In this section you have learned that the population of the South is growing. Write a paragraph explaining how the South's geography and economy were affected by this growth.

ACTIVITY

7. **Writing an Advertisement** Imagine you work in an advertising firm in Atlanta, Georgia, in Houston, Texas, or in Miami, Florida. Create an advertisement to persuade people to move to your city or state. The advertisement can be designed for a newspaper or a magazine, or for radio, television, or the Internet.

The Midwest
Technology Brings Change

BEFORE YOU READ

READING FOCUS

1. How is technology changing agriculture in the Midwest?
2. How is the change in agriculture affecting the growth of cities?

KEY TERMS

mixed-crop farm
recession
corporate farm
capital

KEY PLACES

Chicago
Detroit
St. Louis

MAIN IDEA

Along with the growth of large corporate farms, many people have moved from family farms to the growing cities in the Midwest.

NOTE TAKING

Copy the cause-and-effect chart below. As you read the section, fill in the chart with the causes and effects of technological changes in agriculture.

Causes
1.
2.

Changes in agriculture bring growth to cities

Effects
1.
2.

Setting the Scene

Camille LeFevre grew up in Black River Falls, Wisconsin. Her family included generation after generation of farmers, and she spent her childhood on her parents' sheep farm.

Camille remembers her childhood with deep affection. Yet, like thousands of farm children who grew up in the 1980s and 1990s, she did not follow in her parents' footsteps. Farming in the Midwest changed, and Camille chose a different path for herself.

Technology Brings Changes to the Midwest

The Midwest is often called "the heartland" because it is the agricultural center of our nation. The soil is rich, and the climate is suitable for producing corn, soybeans, and livestock. Technology helped make farms productive. Inventions like the steel plow, the windmill, and barbed wire helped settlers carve out farms on the plains. Today, technological innovations continue to shape the world of agriculture and the way people farm the land.

ECONOMICS On most farms, sheep-shearing takes place once a year. The wool from this breed of sheep—the Suffolk—is used to make industrial and upholstery fabrics. **Critical Thinking** Raising sheep for wool is an example of a primary industry. Industries that turn wool into thread and fabrics are secondary industries. What do you think happens to the fabrics made from the wool of these sheep?

The Midwest

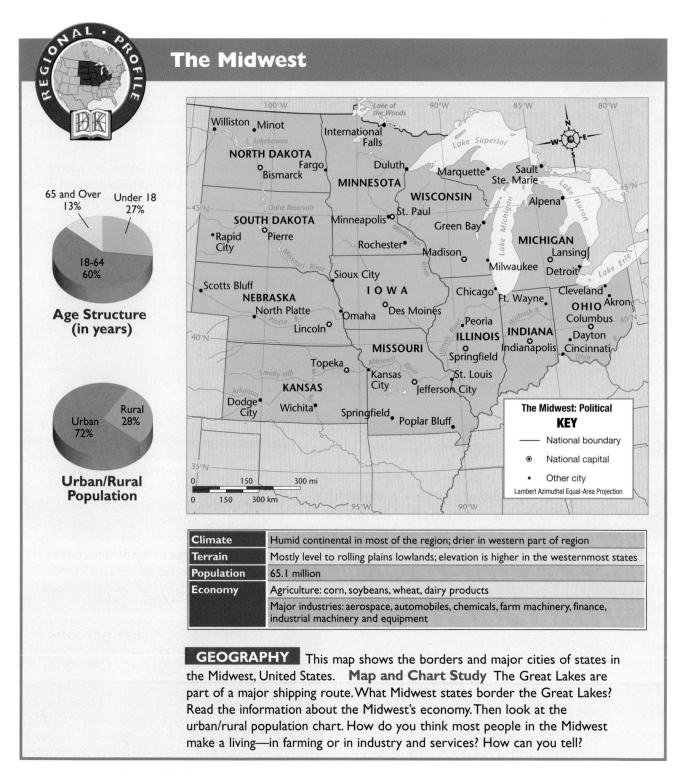

65 and Over
13%

Under 18
27%

18-64
60%

**Age Structure
(in years)**

Urban
72%

Rural
28%

**Urban/Rural
Population**

Climate	Humid continental in most of the region; drier in western part of region
Terrain	Mostly level to rolling plains lowlands; elevation is higher in the westernmost states
Population	65.1 million
Economy	Agriculture: corn, soybeans, wheat, dairy products
	Major industries: aerospace, automobiles, chemicals, farm machinery, finance, industrial machinery and equipment

GEOGRAPHY This map shows the borders and major cities of states in the Midwest, United States. **Map and Chart Study** The Great Lakes are part of a major shipping route. What Midwest states border the Great Lakes? Read the information about the Midwest's economy. Then look at the urban/rural population chart. How do you think most people in the Midwest make a living—in farming or in industry and services? How can you tell?

Family Farms Dwindle Until the 1980s, small family farms operated in this region, and many were **mixed-crop farms.** That is, they grew several different crops, so, if one crop failed, the farm had others.

In the 1960s and 1970s, family farms prospered. The world population was rising, and demand for American farm products was high. Farmers felt that they could increase their business if they enlarged their farms. To build bigger farms, many farmers bought more land and equipment, borrowing money from local banks.

In the early 1980s, there was a country-wide **recession** (rih SESH un), or a downturn in business activity. The demand for farm products dropped at the same time interest rates on loans increased. As a result, many farmers were not able to make enough money to pay their loans. Some families sold or left their farms. In fact, over one million American farmers have left their land since 1980.

Corporate Farms Expand

Some of the farms that were sold were bought by agricultural companies that combined small farms to form large ones called **corporate farms.** Large agricultural companies had more **capital,** or money used to expand a business. They could afford to buy the expensive land and equipment that modern farming requires. These large farms could be run more efficiently.

Corporate farmers rely on machines and computers to do much of the work. Kansas offers a good example of corporate farming—having fewer workers and larger farms. In Kansas, 90 percent of the land is farmland or ranchland, but less than 10 percent of the people are farmers or ranchers.

Not every farm in the Midwest is a corporate farm. But most small farms do not earn enough money to support a family so family farmers usually have another job as well. Young adults often leave the farm and move to the cities where there are more opportunities.

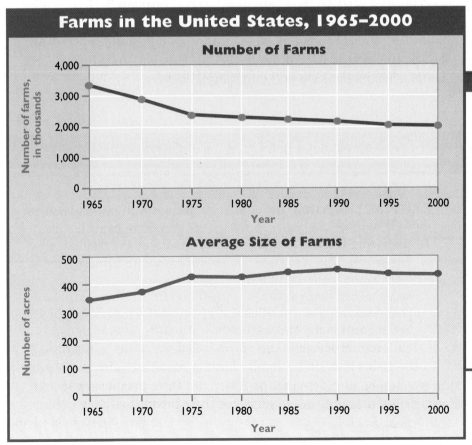

Farms in the United States, 1965–2000

Number of Farms

Number of farms, in thousands

Average Size of Farms

Number of acres

Year

ECONOMICS As this graph shows, the number of farms has decreased, while the size of farms has grown. These changes came about because many owners of small family farms could not make enough money to cover their expenses. As a result, they sold their farms and left the land. **Chart Study** When was there the greatest change in the number of farms and farm size in the United States—between 1965 and 1975 or between 1980 and 2000?

The Midwest Grows Cities

Most people in the Midwest today live in towns and cities. Yet many of these cities got their start as places to process and ship farm products.

Chicago: At the Center of Things   **Chicago,** Illinois, is a good example. Located on Lake Michigan, it was surrounded by prairies and farms in the mid-1800s. Farmers sent their corn, wheat, cattle, and hogs to Chicago. Mills and meat-packing plants turned these products into foods and shipped them east on the Great Lakes. When railroads were built, Chicago really boomed. By the late 1800s, it had become a steel-making and manufacturing center. Farm equipment was one of the most important manufactured products made in Chicago.

Today, Chicago is the biggest city in the heartland. It is known for its ethnic diversity and lively culture. It is the hub of major transportation routes—highways, railroads, airlines, and shipping routes. Chicago is also the home of the first skyscraper to be built in the Midwest.

Other Cities   The Midwest has other large cities. Two of them—**Detroit** and **St. Louis**—have played an important role in the country's history. Detroit, Michigan, is called "the Motor City." Here, you will find the headquarters of the American automobile industry.

Covered wagons, not cars, used to roll through St. Louis, Missouri. Located on the Mississippi River, this city was the starting point for pioneers heading west. Today, a huge stainless steel arch beside the river marks St. Louis as the "Gateway to the West." St. Louis is also a banking and commercial center.

ECONOMICS

This view from the shores of Lake Michigan shows the many skyscrapers in Chicago's downtown area. The Sears Tower, to the left, is the tallest building in the United States **Critical Thinking** What do the skyscrapers of Chicago tell you about the economic importance of that city?

SECTION 3 ASSESSMENT

AFTER YOU READ

RECALL

1. Identify: (a) Chicago, (b) Detroit, (c) St. Louis

2. Define: (a) mixed-crop farm, (b) recession, (c) corporate farm, (d) capital

COMPREHENSION

3. Why did family farmers face hard times in the 1980s?

4. What caused Chicago to boom during the 1800s?

CRITICAL THINKING AND WRITING

5. **Exploring the Main Idea** Review the Main Idea statement at the beginning of this section. Then, write a paragraph explaining why the number of farms in the Midwest has declined while the size of farms has increased.

6. **Identifying Central Issues** Think of how farming has changed with the development of corporate farms. List the advantages and disadvantages of corporate farming.

ACTIVITY

7. **Writing a Letter** Suppose you are a farmer and you have decided to sell your farm and move to a city. Write a letter to a friend explaining your decision.

The West
Land of Precious Resources

BEFORE YOU READ

READING FOCUS

1. What are the resources of the West?
2. How are people working to balance conservation with the need to use natural resources?

KEY TERMS

forty-niner
mass transit

KEY PLACES

Sierra Nevada
Pacific Northwest
Portland
San Jose

NOTE TAKING

Copy the chart below. As you read the section, fill in the table with information about the resources of the West, where they are found, and what concerns there are over conserving each resource.

Resource	Where Found	Concerns

MAIN IDEA

The West has many natural resources, but as the population grows, protecting the environment and using resources wisely is becoming a challenge.

Setting the Scene

An American president stood before Congress and made the following statement:

"The conservation of our natural resources and their proper use constitute the fundamental problem which underlies almost every other problem of our national life. . . . But there must be . . . a realization . . . that to waste, to destroy our natural resources, to skin and exhaust the land instead of using it so as to increase its usefulness, will result in undermining . . . the very prosperity which we ought by right to hand down to [our children]."

President Theodore Roosevelt made this statement nearly one hundred years ago. He understood that the vast resources of the West would not last without proper care.

A Wealth of Resources

An incredible wealth of natural resources has drawn people to the West for well over 400 years. The Spanish were well established on the West Coast even before the Pilgrims settled in New England in the 1620s. Then, after Lewis and Clark's exploration of the Louisiana Territory in the early 1800s, more people began to move westward.

Preserving the Physical Environment

GEOGRAPHY

Congress declared Yosemite a national park in 1890. Yosemite Falls, which drops some 2,425 feet (740 m), is higher than any big-city skyscraper. **Critical Thinking** Why do you think so many people visit national parks like Yosemite?

The West

Age Structure (in years)
- 65 and Over 11%
- Under 18 28%
- 18-64 61%

Urban/Rural Population
- Rural 14%
- Urban 86%

The West: Natural Resources
KEY

Hydroelectric power	Uranium	Nickel
Copper	Coal	Tungsten
Gold	Petroleum	Sugar cane
Silver	Lead	Fruits
Phosphates		

Transverse Mercator Projection

Climate	Semiarid southwest; highlands in the mountains; marine along the northern Pacific Coast
Terrain	Plains from eastern area to mountain ranges in the west
Population	65.6 million
Economy	Agriculture: wheat, greenhouse/nursery products, ranching/cattle
	Major industries: aerospace and aircraft products, chemicals, machinery, mining for minerals and petroleum, wood and paper products

GEOGRAPHY   This map shows the natural resources of the western states of the United States.   **Map and Chart Study** What states have deposits of petroleum? What state's resources are mostly agricultural? What states do you think were most likely to have been part of the Gold Rush in the 1800s?

Resources and Population   With the California Gold Rush in 1849, the population of the region exploded. The sleepy port of San Francisco boomed into a prosperous city as hopeful miners arrived there, bought supplies, and headed off to the **Sierra Nevada** expecting to strike it rich.

Further discoveries of valuable minerals drew more and more people westward. New settlers needed timber to build homes and after the Civil War, logging camps, sawmills, and paper mills sprang up in the **Pacific Northwest.**

At first, the resources of the West seemed unlimited. The use of these resources did create wealth and many jobs. However, it also created new challenges.

Managing Resources in the Sierras   For many years, people searching for gold treated the Sierra Nevada carelessly. The **forty-niners,** the first miners of the Gold Rush, washed small bits of gold from the streams, but to get at larger deposits, big mining companies used water cannons to blast away entire hillsides. They left behind huge, ugly piles of rock.

After the Gold Rush, California's population soared. To meet the demand for new houses, loggers cleared many forests and engineers built dams to send water through pipes to coastal cities. Next to the dams, they built hydroelectric (hy droh ee LEK trik) plants. Cities like San Francisco got water and power this way, but the dams flooded whole valleys of the Sierras.

To save parts of the West as natural wilderness, Congress created several national parks and forests. Yet these, too, have developed problems. Yosemite (yoh SEM ut ee) National Park now gets so many visitors that it has traffic jams and air pollution in the summer, and must limit the number of campers in the park. Dam-building has

A Black Bear in its Natural Habitat

GEOGRAPHY

Many westerners are working to preserve the land areas where black bears and other wild animals live. Parts of the West have been made into national parks, forests, and wilderness areas. In addition, logging companies are working to preserve the environment by planting new trees to replace the ones that have been cut down.

Critical Thinking
Does conservation of natural resources in a certain region affect the wildlife that lives in that region? In other regions?

stopped. Laws protect the habitats of certain animals. In addition, logging companies are limited in the amount of timber they can cut down.

Using and Preserving Resources

Most westerners today are not miners, farmers, or loggers. Rather, they work and live in cities. Their challenge is to figure out how to use natural resources wisely.

Portland, Oregon   **Portland** was founded in 1845 near the junction of the Willamette and Columbia rivers. Portland became a trade center for lumber, furs, grain, salmon, and wool. In the 1930s, new dams produced cheap electricity and Portland attracted many manufacturing industries. Over time, the factories polluted the Willamette River. Federal, state, and local governments—and industries—have worked to clean up this valuable resource.

San Jose, California   Urban sprawl is a problem in **San Jose.** The area around San Jose was known as "Valley of the Heart's Delight" for its beautiful orchards and farms. Now it is called "Silicon Valley," because it is the heart of the computer industry.

San Jose's most valuable resource is its people and they come from all parts of the world. The greater population density has created crowded freeways and air pollution. To counter these problems, San Jose has built a light-rail mass transit system. **Mass transit** replaces individual cars with energy-saving buses or trains.

SECTION 4 ASSESSMENT

AFTER YOU READ

RECALL

1. Identify: (a) Sierra Nevada, (b) Pacific Northwest, (c) Portland, (d) San Jose

2. Define: (a) forty-niner, (b) mass transit

COMPREHENSION

3. How have people used the resources of the West?

4. How are these resources being protected today?

CRITICAL THINKING AND WRITING

5. **Exploring the Main Idea** Review the Main Idea statement at the beginning of this section. Then, list some of the challenges people of the West face in preserving and protecting their natural resources.

6. **Recognizing Cause and Effect** Write a paragraph explaining how rapid urban growth has affected the natural resources of the West.

ACTIVITY

 Take It to the NET

7. **Developing a Conservation Plan** California's forests are one of its most valuable natural resources. Think about the importance of conservation as you read about California's forests. Develop a conservation plan for one of the natural resources in your region. Visit the World Explorer: People, Places, and Cultures section of **phschool.com** for help in completing this activity.

Understanding Special Purpose Maps

United States: Railroad Routes of the Late 1800s

KEY

— Railroads 1865–1900

Albers Equal-Area Conic Projection

Learn the Skill

As you explore the world, you will encounter many different kinds of special purpose maps. You have already encountered some special purpose maps in previous chapters. To help you learn more about how to understand and use special purpose maps, follow these steps:

A. Read the title of the map. The title will tell you the purpose and content of the map. The title of the map above tells you that it is about railroad routes in the United States from the late 1800s.

B. Read the information in the map key. Even though a special purpose map shows only one kind of information, it may present many pieces of data. The map key above shows railroad lines from 1865 to 1900 in red.

C. Study the map to identify its main ideas and try to draw conclusions based on the information.

Practice the Skill

Use the map to answer these questions:

- How many states did the Pennsylvania Railroad run through?

- How many states did not have railroad routes running through them?

- If you were traveling from Baltimore to St. Louis, which railway line would you take?

Apply the Skill

See the Chapter Review and Assessment at the end of this chapter for more questions on understanding special purpose maps.

Review and Assessment

Creating a Chapter Summary

On a separate piece of paper, draw a web like this one, and include the information about the Northeast. Continue completing the web by adding important details about each of the regions in the United States.

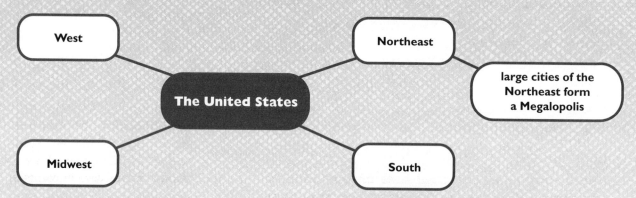

West

Northeast

large cities of the
Northeast form
a Megalopolis

The United States

Midwest

South

Reviewing Key Terms

Write a definition for each of the key terms. Then, use each term in a sentence.

1. commute (p.121)
2. megalopolis (p.121)
3. industrialization (p.127)
4. mixed-crop farm (p.130)
5. recession (p.131)
6. capital (p.131)
7. forty-niner (p.135)
8. mass transit (p.136)

Reviewing the Main Ideas

1. What are some of the large cities of the Northeast? (Section 1)
2. How does the Northeast serve as a gateway to the country? (Section 1)
3. How do people in the South make a living? (Section 2)
4. How does warm weather affect the economy of the South? (Section 2)
5. What major changes have occurred in the Midwest since the 1980s? (Section 3)
6. Describe the differences between family farms and corporate farms. (Section 3)
7. What are the main natural resources of the West? (Section 4)
8. How has life in the West changed since the days of the California Gold Rush? (Section 4)

Map Activity

United States

For each place listed below, write the letter from the map that shows its location.

1. Boston
2. New York City
3. Washington, D.C.
4. Atlanta
5. Chicago
6. Dallas
7. Portland
8. San Jose

 Take It to the NET

Enrichment For more map activities using geography skills, visit the social studies section of **phschool.com**.

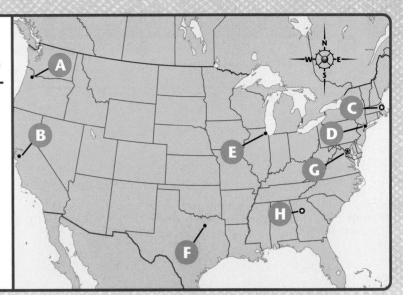

Writing Activity

1. **Writing a Travel Guide** If you had friends who were visiting the United States for the first time, what information would you want to share with them? Which cities would you tell them to visit? Write a brief travel guide for your friends that takes them to all four regions. Suggest activities for each region. Provide background information to help your friends understand the history and culture of each region.

2. **Using Primary Sources** Miners and other people in the gold rush towns left letters and journals that give us a picture of life during the gold rush. Use your local or school library, or the Internet, to find some of these primary sources. Then, using the information you find, write a brief report on some aspect of the gold rush.

Applying Your Skills

Turn to the Skills for Life activity on p. 137 to help you complete the following actvity.

Look at the map on p. 134. Write a series of questions that can be answered by studying the map. Exchange your questions with a classmate and answer each other's questions.

Critical Thinking

1. **Making Comparisons** Identify at least one major trend that two or more regions of the United States have in common.

2. **Compare and Contrast** Create a chart that shows the similarities and differences between the Northeast and the South.

3. **Drawing Conclusions** If the use of resources continues in the West as it has, what are some likely results?

 Take It to the NET

Activity Read an overview of the United States economy. How do the location, population, and resources of a region impact its economy? How do these factors impact the economy in your region? Visit the World Explorer: People, Places, and Cultures section of **phschool.com** for help in completing this activity.

Chapter 7 Self-Test As a final review activity, take the Chapter 7 Self-Test and get instant feedback on your answers. To take the test, visit the Social Studies section of **phschool.com**.

CANADA: Exploring the Region Today

Using Photographs

This train is taking on a load of wheat from the nearby grain elevator. The train takes the wheat west to the Pacific Coast or east to the Great Lakes. The wheat then is loaded on ships for export. Canada is the world's second leading grain exporter and the United States is the first.

UNDERSTANDING ECONOMICS

Study the photo. Make a list of all of the steps you think might be involved in growing wheat and transporting it to mills to be made into flour. Start with a farmer planting a seed. End with a loaf of bread on the table. Which steps may be represented in this photograph?

Jobs in Agriculture

Think about the many different kinds of jobs that the agricultural industry provides. Which job would you want? Would you enjoy being a farmer? Or would you rather work on a train or ship that hauls grain? Visit your school or local library or the Internet and research different jobs in agriculture. Then, find someone with such a job and interview them about the work they do. Write a report using the information you gather and share it with the rest of the class.

SECTION
1

Quebec
A Quiet Revolution

BEFORE YOU READ

READING FOCUS

1. Why is the French culture so strong in Quebec?

2. What are some of the concerns of Quebec's citizens?

3. What have French Canadians in Quebec done to preserve their culture?

KEY TERMS

Francophone
separatist
Quiet Revolution
referendum

KEY PEOPLE AND PLACES

Jacques Cartier
Quebec City
Montreal

NOTE TAKING

Copy the web diagram below. As you read the section, fill in the diagram with information about how the people of Quebec are preserving French culture.

Preserving French Culture

immigrants required to learn French

MAIN IDEA

Many of Quebec's citizens work hard to preserve their French culture, and some want Quebec to become independent from the rest of Canada.

Setting the Scene

In 1977, a new law in the province of Quebec said that all street signs must be in French only. That pleased the majority of Quebeckers who speak French, but it upset other Quebeckers. In 1993, a change in the law allowed English on signs as well. But French is the only language used in Quebec government, commerce, and education.

Canadian law states that the country has two official languages—English and French. French-speaking people live in every province. In Quebec, however, the first language of 83 percent of the people is French. English is the first language of 12 percent and the remaining 5 percent speak 35 different languages! Still, until the 1960s, government and business in Quebec were conducted in English, just as they were in the rest of Canada. It took a long political battle to change things in Quebec.

The French Influence in Quebec

Canada's history explains why Quebec is so French. In the 1530s, **Jacques Cartier** (ZHAHK kahr TYAY), a French explorer, sailed up the St. Lawrence River near today's **Quebec City.**

One Country, Two Languages

CULTURE

In Quebec, traffic signs say "STOP" in Canada's two official languages, French and English. **Critical Thinking** Why do you think it is important to the people of Quebec to have signs appear in two languages?

Quebec

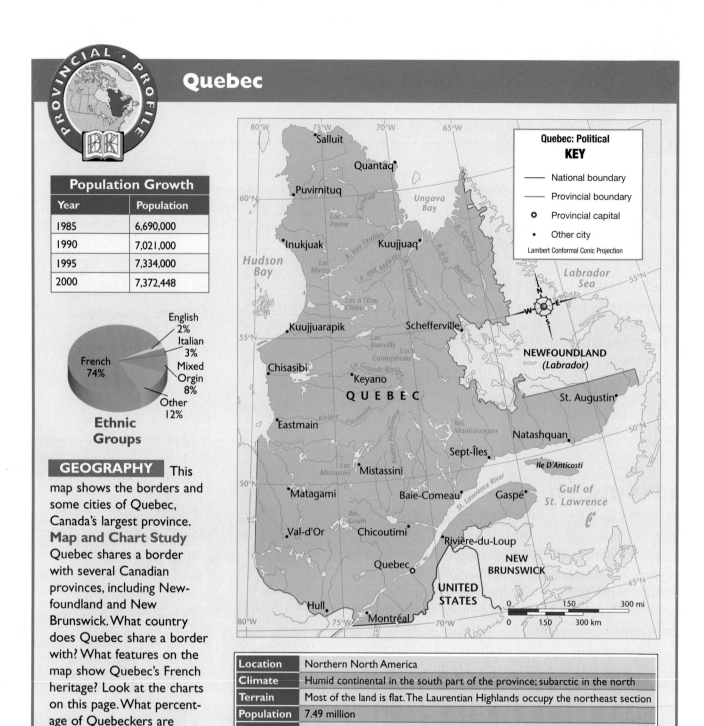

Population Growth

Year	Population
1985	6,690,000
1990	7,021,000
1995	7,334,000
2000	7,372,448

Ethnic Groups

- French 74%
- English 2%
- Italian 3%
- Mixed Orgin 8%
- Other 12%

GEOGRAPHY This map shows the borders and some cities of Quebec, Canada's largest province. **Map and Chart Study** Quebec shares a border with several Canadian provinces, including Newfoundland and New Brunswick. What country does Quebec share a border with? What features on the map show Quebec's French heritage? Look at the charts on this page. What percentage of Quebeckers are French? About how much has Quebec's population grown since 1985?

Quebec: Political
KEY
— National boundary
— Provincial boundary
⊙ Provincial capital
• Other city
Lambert Conformal Conic Projection

Location	Northern North America
Climate	Humid continental in the south part of the province; subarctic in the north
Terrain	Most of the land is flat. The Laurentian Highlands occupy the northeast section
Population	7.49 million
Economy	Agriculture: fish, dairy products, hay, hogs, cattle, tobacco
	Major industries: wood, wood products, aircraft, railway locomotives, chemical and pharmaceutical products, copper, asbestos, iron, gold, titanium, aluminum

Cartier and his men became friends with the Stadacona (stad uh KOH nuh), the native people of the area. Some places in Quebec and elsewhere in Canada have Stadacona names. Cartier and later explorers gave other places French names. **Montreal,** for instance, is French for "Mount Royal."

Cartier claimed the region we now know as Quebec for France. But England also claimed the region. The two countries eventually fought over it. France lost, and in 1763 the territory went to the British. However, tens of thousands of French colonists lived in the region. Today, their descendants make up the majority of Quebec's population. They are **Francophones** (FRANG koh fohnz), or people who speak French as their first language.

Quebec: A Distinct Society within Canada

In the 1960s, some Francophones began to demand independence from the rest of Canada. They opposed using English as the only official language, and worried that their language and culture might die. They also believed that they were contributing much to Canada but getting little back. For the most part, Francophones held only low-paying jobs. They faced prejudice because they were French speakers.

Francophones who wanted independence were called **separatists.** They wanted Quebec to separate, or break away, from Canada. Separatists formed a political party, which won control of the Quebec provincial legislature in 1976. This peaceful change in Quebec's government is called the **Quiet Revolution.**

French became the official language, to be used in education, government, and commerce. Immigrants were required to learn French. Still, Quebec remained a province of Canada.

In 1980, the provincial government held a **referendum.** In a referendum, voters cast ballots for or against an issue. This referendum asked voters whether Quebec should become a separate nation. A majority voted no.

The Canadian government feared separatists could force the nation to separate, so they tried to meet their demands. Quebeckers wanted their province to be a "distinct society" within Canada with its own special way of life. If this was guaranteed, they would stay part of Canada. There was only one way to do this—change Canada's constitution. In 1990 and 1992, the government held referendums

143

Winter Carnival

about the issue. Quebeckers voted to change the constitution but Canadians in other provinces voted not to. The referendums failed.

In 1995, Quebec held another referendum. Again, Quebeckers voted to remain part of Canada. But the margin was very slim. Canada's Prime Minister promised to try to change the constitution again. But Quebec's separatist leader warned, "The battle for a country is not over. And it will not be until we have one." The close vote on election day guaranteed that the issue will continue to be discussed.

Preserving Quebec's Culture

One of the ways in which Quebeckers celebrate their culture is through festivals. The Fête des Neiges (FET day NEZH), or winter festival, lasts 17 days. It even includes canoe races along the St. Lawrence River.

Another festival honors Jean Baptiste (ZHAHN bah TEEST), the patron saint, or special guardian, of French Canadians. The festival is held June 24. All over the province, people celebrate with bonfires, firecrackers, and street dances.

French style and cooking are alive in Quebec—with Quebec variations. Sugar pie, for example, uses maple sugar from the province's forests. Quebec has French architecture—with Quebec variations. All in all, Quebeckers have a lively culture to preserve and protect.

SECTION 1 ASSESSMENT

AFTER YOU READ

RECALL

1. Identify: (a) Jacques Cartier, (b) Quebec City, (c) Montreal

2. Define: (a) Francophone, (b) separatist, (c) Quiet Revolution, (d) referendum

COMPREHENSION

3. Explain the early history of French influence in Quebec.

4. What has the Canadian government done to try to meet the demands of the separatists?

5. Describe some of the ways Quebeckers celebrate their French culture today.

CRITICAL THINKING AND WRITING

6. **Exploring the Main Idea** Review the Main Idea statement at the beginning of this section. Then, make a list of reasons why many people in Quebec want to separate from Canada.

7. **Supporting a Point of View** Quebeckers are split almost evenly on the issue of independence from Canada. Write a paragraph giving your opinion on whether Quebec should become independent or not. Give reasons for your point of view.

ACTIVITY

8. **Asking Good Questions** Make a list of questions that ask about some of the features of Quebec culture that you would like to know more about. Visit the library and try to find the answers to your questions. Write a brief report on the information you find.

Ontario
A Thriving Economy

READING FOCUS

1. Why is Ontario considered the industrial heartland of Canada?
2. What resources contribute to Ontario's wealth?

KEY TERMS
United Empire Loyalists
Golden Horseshoe

KEY PLACES
Ottawa
Toronto

MAIN IDEA

Ontario's industrial and agricultural production and its abundance of natural resources make it the wealthiest Canadian province.

NOTE TAKING

Copy the chart below. As you read the section, fill in the chart with details about Ontario's major industries.

ONTARIO'S INDUSTRIES			
Service Industries	Manufacturing	Agriculture	Mining
Banking			
Tourism			

Setting the Scene

"Which is better—to be ruled by one tyrant three thousand miles away or by three thousand tyrants one mile away?" These words of Rev. Mather Byles reflected the attitude of thousands of people in the United States who remained loyal to Great Britain during the American Revolution.

In 1784, the American Revolution had ended with a British defeat, and thousands of colonists loyal to Great Britain had lost their wealth and their homes. Even their lives were threatened. Canada welcomed these **United Empire Loyalists,** as they were called. By 1785, about 6,000 of these Loyalists settled west of the Ottawa River in what is now Ontario. They brought their English heritage into a land that had been dominated by French culture. Their loyalty to Great Britain contributed to the establishment of the province of Ontario and helped shape modern-day Canada.

The Industrial Heartland of Canada

Ontario is not only the wealthiest province in Canada, it also has the largest population. About one-third of Canada's population lives there and nearly half of them have some English ancestry. Ontario is a center of manufacturing, service industries, and agriculture with almost half of Canada's industrial workers employed in the province.

British Influence in Ontario

CITIZENSHIP

This Latin motto on the Ontario coat of arms means "Loyal She Began, Loyal She Remains." It reflects the influence of the United Empire Loyalists in Ontario. **Critical Thinking** Why do you think the British government helped the United Empire Loyalists settle in Canada?

Ontario

CHAPTER 8   CANADA: EXPLORING THE REGION TODAY   145

Ontario

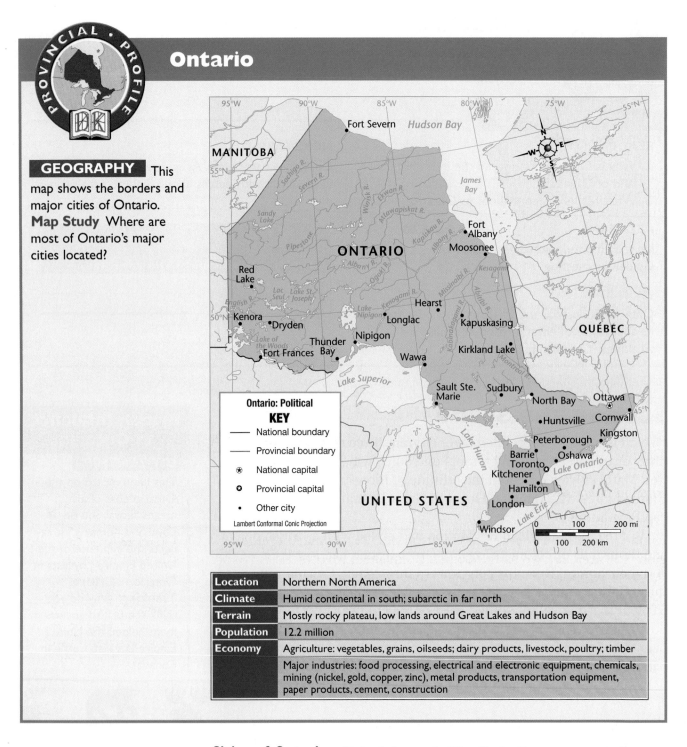

GEOGRAPHY This map shows the borders and major cities of Ontario. **Map Study** Where are most of Ontario's major cities located?

Location	Northern North America
Climate	Humid continental in south; subarctic in far north
Terrain	Mostly rocky plateau, low lands around Great Lakes and Hudson Bay
Population	12.2 million
Economy	Agriculture: vegetables, grains, oilseeds; dairy products, livestock, poultry; timber
	Major industries: food processing, electrical and electronic equipment, chemicals, mining (nickel, gold, copper, zinc), metal products, transportation equipment, paper products, cement, construction

Cities of Ontario Ontario's great cities lie in the warmer southern portion of the province, where about 90 percent of the population lives. Although there are rich agricultural lands in this region, most of the people live in cities and make up Ontario's large skilled labor force. Service industries such as banking, education, health care, legal services, and data processing employ nearly three-fourths of Ontario's workers.

Ottawa is the national capital of Canada. It lies on the south bank of the Ottawa River, which forms the border between the provinces of Ontario and Quebec. Canada's three Parliament buildings sit on Parliament Hill overlooking the Ottawa River. Ottawa's most important employer is the Canadian government, which employs more than 100,000 of the Ottawa area's residents.

Toronto is Ontario's capital, as well as Canada's largest urban area. It is the commercial, cultural, and financial center of Canada. Headquarters for Canada's largest banks and insurance companies are located in Toronto. Three of the world's 50 tallest buildings are located in downtown Toronto.

Toronto: Canada's Largest City

ECONOMICS The tall tower to the right in this photo is the CN (Canadian National) tower, the tallest free-standing structure in the world. **Critical Thinking** How do you think the tower is used?

The Golden Horseshoe The sprawling metropolitan area that includes Toronto is the center of Ontario's richest manufacturing region. The area, known as the **Golden Horseshoe,** follows the curve of the western shore of Lake Ontario. Most of Ontario's automobile plants are located here in the cities that cluster around the lakeshores. Manufacturing automobiles is Ontario's major industry, but other important industries include electrical equipment, meat-packing, chemicals, textiles, industrial machinery, and furniture.

Resources and Trade

Ontario is rich in natural resources such as timber, minerals, and fertile soils. It is also close to large population centers in North America. This is a great advantage for Ontario's economy because big cities provide markets for goods and services. The North American Free Trade Agreement (NAFTA) has greatly expanded trade between Canadian provinces such as Ontario and their neighbor to the south, the United States.

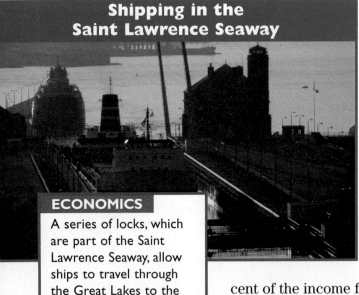

Shipping in the Saint Lawrence Seaway

Major transportation corridors such as the St. Lawrence Seaway, and Great Lakes, allow shipment of goods to ports in the United States and overseas, giving Ontario another great advantage. Thunder Bay on Lake Superior is a major port where ships pick up loads of grain from western provinces, or bring in goods from other areas.

Agriculture Ontario is Canada's leading producer of fruits and vegetables, as well as eggs and poultry products. Tobacco is an important cash crop, but most farms produce beef and dairy cattle in the rich pasturelands between Lake Ontario and Lake Huron. About 55 percent of the income from agriculture comes from livestock and livestock products. Milk is the most important product, followed by beef and pork.

Mining The rocky ground of the Canadian Shield in the central and northern regions of Ontario contains a variety of minerals. Nickel is the most important metal produced. Ontario mines provide a large percentage of the world's nickel. Copper is the second most important metal. Others include zinc, gold, uranium, iron ore, and silver.

Other riches mined from the earth include natural gas, petroleum, sand, and gravel. Limestone, marble, and granite mined in Ontario are used in buildings around the world.

SECTION 2 ASSESSMENT

AFTER YOU READ

RECALL

1. Identify: (a) Ottawa, (b) Toronto

2. Define: (a) United Empire Loyalists, (b) Golden Horseshoe

COMPREHENSION

3. What is Ontario's most important manufacturing industry?

4. How does being close to large population centers benefit Ontario's economy?

CRITICAL THINKING AND WRITING

5. **Exploring the Main Idea** Review the Main Idea statement at the beginning of this section. Then, list three ways that Ontario's access to transportation helps contribute to its thriving economy.

6. **Drawing Conclusions** Write a paragraph explaining why most of Ontario's population is located in the southern portion of the province, and why most of those people live in cities.

ACTIVITY

 Take It to the NET

7. **Understanding Natural Resources and the Economy** Lanark County in Ontario, Canada enjoys a thriving economy. Write a short report describing how a region's natural resources can help shape the economy. Use what you learn on the Web site as a basis for your report. Visit the World Explorer: People, Places, and Cultures section of **phschool.com** for help in completing this activity.

The Plains and British Columbia

Cultural and Economic Changes

Setting the Scene

One August day in 1821, after a long, difficult journey, about 195 Swiss immigrants reached their new land. It was summertime, but it was chilly on the Hudson Bay in northern Canada. The settlers had come to this land to become Canadian farmers. They had heard that these vast plains had good land and an excellent climate. However, they soon discovered that no shelter, food, or supplies were waiting for them and they survived only with the help of the native people. The settlers stayed on, enduring harsh winters and summers during which they fought drought, floods, and swarms of grasshoppers.

Over 180 years later and hundreds of miles west in the city of **Vancouver,** people are speaking Dutch, Japanese, Spanish, German, and English. On the city's streets, signs are written in English, Chinese, and other languages, restaurants serve the food of many different countries, and people practice the customs of many different cultures.

In both of these regions—the Canadian Plains and British Columbia—native people once practiced a unique culture. Today, these regions have undergone dramatic changes in both their cultures and in their economies.

Settling the Plains

HISTORY This photograph, taken in 1928, shows a group of young men on board the ship *Montcalm.* They are on their way from Great Britain to Canada to start a new life in the Prairie Provinces. **Critical Thinking** Why do you think these young men were so eager to settle in Canada?

Y.M.C.A.
CONDUCTED PARTY
OF
BRITISH MINERS'
SONS
UNDER CARE OF THE
UNITED
FROM
PIT TO PRAIRIE
MONTCALM

Religious Diversity in Saskatchewan

CULTURE

The onion-shaped domes of St. Julien's Greek Orthodox Church pierce the blue sky of Alvena. This small town is located in central Saskatchewan. Other Christian churches include Roman Catholic, Ukrainian Orthodox, and various Protestant denominations. **Critical Thinking** Why do you think that immigrant groups maintain the traditions and ways of life of the countries they came from?

LINKS TO

Science

Sanctuary Visitors to Saskatchewan's Grasslands National Park see some of North America's last untouched prairies. Ancient grasses called wheat grass, snowberry, and silver sage blow in the wind. The park is also home to 12 endangered and threatened species. They include certain kinds of hawks, burrowing owls, and short-horned lizards.

The Canadian Plains

Throughout the 1800s, European settlers trickled into the Canadian Plains, bringing changes to the cultures of the **indigenous** peoples. These are people descended from the people who first lived in the region. Settlers brought trade goods, such as pots, needles, and guns but they also brought European diseases such as measles. Europeans had **immunity,** or natural resistance to the diseases. But the indigenous peoples did not and as many as 75 percent of them died.

By the late 1870s, the ways of life of many native peoples living in the Plains region had ended. They had depended upon the buffalo for their way of life. They suffered greatly when most of the buffalo herds were killed off by European settlers. New immigrants from northern and eastern Europe moved to the Plains region, bringing a variety of languages and cultures with them. By the turn of the century, the Canadian Plains were a checkerboard of different ethnic settlements.

Maintaining Traditions

About one quarter of Canada's farmland is in the province of **Saskatchewan.** Most European immigrants became wheat farmers. Two thirds of Saskatchewan's farmland is still devoted to wheat. For this reason, the province is sometimes called "Canada's Breadbasket."

Today, immigrants still come to the Canadian prairies. Each year, prairie cities celebrate Ukrainian, Icelandic, and German festivals that include traditional dancing, art, and music. In some small towns, people still maintain the European languages and customs of their ancestors.

British Columbia

The first people who lived in what is now British Columbia belonged to several ethnic groups. Each group spoke its own language and had its own customs and complex society. Along the coast, people caught fish, whales, and shellfish. They also carved giant **totem poles,** which were symbols for a group, a clan, or a family. Other groups hunted game in dense inland forests.

In the late 1500s, Spanish, British, and Russian traders began to arrive in the area. Trade did not change the native peoples' lives a great deal, but in 1858, gold was discovered along the **Fraser River.** Within

PROVINCIAL · PROFILE

British Columbia

Ethnic Groups

- Chinese 5%
- English 18%
- Other 37%
- Mixed origin 40%

Population Growth

Year	Population
1985	2,990,000
1990	3,300,000
1995	3,766,000
2000	4,063,760

GEOGRAPHY

This map shows the borders and major cities of British Columbia. **Map and Chart Study** Look at the charts and the economic information on this page. Is any one ethnic group much larger than the others? About how much has the population grown since 1985? How does British Columbia's growing population make a living?

British Columbia: Political

KEY

- —— National boundary
- —— Provincial boundary
- ⊙ Provincial capital
- • Other city

Lambert Conformal Conic Projection

Location	Northern North America
Climate	Marine west coast along the Pacific Coast; highland climates in the east
Terrain	Mountainous, bordered by coastal regions in the west, along the Pacific Coast; a high plateau region lies between two main mountain ranges
Population	4.1 million
Economy	Agriculture: dairy products, fish, cattle, apples and other tree fruit, wheat
	Major industries: wood and wood products, paper, food and beverages, petroleum and coal products, tourism, copper, natural gas, coal, zinc, lead, gold, silver

weeks, tens of thousands of people had arrived in the town of Victoria on Vancouver Island. When gold was discovered in the Cariboo Mountains, more miners came, and **boomtowns** sprang up. A boomtown is a settlement that quickly springs up to serve the needs of miners.

Native people soon became the smallest minority of the population and were pushed onto small land areas, called reserves. Many of their customs, religions, and languages were banned.

AS YOU READ

Draw Inferences
How did the discovery of gold affect life in British Columbia?

In 1881, Canadians began to build a railroad to link Vancouver to the eastern part of Canada. The railroad project brought more change, as immigrants from all over the world came to work on the railroad. In a few short years, British Columbia became a well-settled region.

British Columbia Today

The Canadian Pacific Railroad did unite all of Canada, but the mountains have remained a barrier between British Columbia and the rest of the country. Today, about two thirds of British Columbians live along the coast, west of the mountains. Many feel that their future lies with the **Pacific Rim** countries—those that border the Pacific Ocean—not with the rest of Canada.

Another link between British Columbia and the Pacific Rim is a diversity of cultures. About 11 percent of people living in the region are of Asian descent.

Trade is yet another link between British Columbia and the Pacific Rim. Forty percent of the province's trade is with Asian countries, and British Columbia is eager to maintain good relationships with her trading partners. As a result, in many of the region's schools, students learn Asian languages, including Japanese, Cantonese Chinese, or Mandarin Chinese. Some even learn Punjabi (pun JAH bee), a language of India and Pakistan.

SECTION 3 ASSESSMENT

AFTER YOU READ

RECALL

1. Identify: (a) Vancouver, (b) Saskatchewan, (c) Fraser River, (d) Pacific Rim

2. Define: (a) indigenous, (b) immunity, (c) totem pole, (d) boomtown

COMPREHENSION

3. How did European immigrants change the culture of the Canadian Plains?

4. What ties exist between the people of British Columbia and the Pacific Rim?

CRITICAL THINKING AND WRITING

5. **Exploring the Main Idea** Review the Main Idea statement at the beginning of this section. Then, make an outline of a speech a leader of an indigenous tribe might give to Canadian government officials, explaining how government policies have affected his tribe's way of life.

6. **Identifying Central Issues** In the late 1800s, the Canadian Pacific Railroad connected the eastern provinces to British Columbia. Write a paragraph explaining the importance of the completion of the Canadian Pacific Railroad.

ACTIVITY

7. **Writing an Advertisement** Suppose that the year is 1900. You want to encourage people to come and start farms in Saskatchewan. The government will give 160 acres of land to anyone willing to try. Make a poster advertising free land. You may show weather, soil, scenery, or settler communities. Describe conditions so many will want to come.

Summarizing Information

What You Need

You can summarize information. You will need:
- ▶ book or textbook lesson
- ▶ paper or notebook
- ▶ pencil or pen

Learn the Skill

You probably read many things in one day. It's not possible to remember everything you read. Summarizing information will help you pick out the main points of what you read, and can even help you study for tests. More importantly, it will help you make sense of the ideas you read or hear about. To learn the skill of summarizing, think about your activities yesterday. Your goal will be to describe the main points of your day from when you woke up to when you went to sleep.

A. Work from start to finish. When you summarize, it's best to start at the beginning and work through to the end. When summarizing your day, start with when you woke up.

B. List the main points. Remember that a summary describes the main points, not the small details.

C. Add a few details to the list. Although you do not want to list too many details, it helps to list a few that may help jog your memory. For example, you might write, "ate breakfast" as a main point. You can add the details of what you ate if the meal was special in some way. As you make your list, add details after some of the main points.

D. Turn your list into a summary. Summaries are usually in paragraph form. Once you have made your list, you can add transitions to make it into a paragraph. Transitions are words that connect one idea to the next by showing how the ideas are related to each other. For example, if your

list reads: 1) woke up, 2) got dressed, 3) ate breakfast, you might write, "First I woke up. Then, after I got dressed, I ate breakfast."

Summary

After I woke up yesterday morning, I got dressed and put on my new sweater. Then I ate blueberry pancakes for breakfast. My first class at school was math, and we did fractions. Then I went to gym class. After an assembly, I ate lunch. We had a field trip to the town hall in the afternoon. After school, I went to my Grandpa's house for dinner. Then I did homework and went to bed.

Practice the Skill

Summarizing a day is good for journal writing, but not much help in your schoolwork. However, the steps you just took will help you in school when you apply them to what you read or hear.

Practice by writing a summary of this chapter. Follow the four steps you took when summarizing your day. The headings in the chapter will help you pick the main points to list. Topic sentences in paragraphs will also help you find main points and interesting details. Remember to turn your list into a written summary, different from the diagram summary in the chapter review.

Apply the Skill

See the Chapter Review and Assessment at the end of this chapter for more questions about summarizing information.

CHAPTER 8 Review and Assessment

Creating a Chapter Summary

On a separate piece of paper, draw a diagram like this one, and include the information that summarizes Section 1. Then, fill in the remaining two boxes with summaries of Sections 2 and 3.

CANADA: EXPLORING THE REGION TODAY

Section 1
Quebec is a distinct society within Canada. Many people living in Quebec speak French and are of French descent. They are working to preserve their French cultural heritage, and many want Quebec to separate from Canada and become independent.

Section 2

Section 3

Reviewing Key Terms

Match the key terms in Column I with the definitions in Column II.

Column I
1. Francophone
2. separatist
3. Quiet Revolution
4. referendum
5. Golden Horseshoe
6. immunity
7. totem pole

Column II
a. a ballot or vote in which voters decide for or against a certain issue
b. a natural resistance to disease
c. a person who speaks French as his or her first language
d. a peaceful change in the government of Quebec, making French the official language
e. a tall, carved wooden pole containing symbols
f. the sprawling metropolitan area that includes Toronto
g. someone who wants Quebec to break away

Reviewing the Main Ideas

1. What is the largest cultural group in Quebec? (Section 1)
2. What is the main political aim of many French Canadians? (Section 1)
3. Why does Ontario need a large skilled labor force? (Section 2)
4. Why does most agricultural activity take place in the southern part of Ontario? (Section 2)
5. What is Saskatchewan's main contribution to Canada's economy? (Section 3)
6. Identify different groups of people who have shaped British Columbia's culture. (Section 3)

Map Activity

Canada

For each place listed below, write the letter from the map that shows its location.

1. Quebec
2. Montreal
3. Ontario
4. Ottawa
5. Toronto
6. British Columbia
7. Vancouver

 Take It to the NET

Enrichment For more map activities using geography skills, visit the social studies section of **phschool.com.**

Writing Activity

1. **Recognizing Bias** The slogans "Masters in Our Own House" and "United From Sea to Sea" are from the dispute over Quebec. Determine which side of the issue each slogan supports.

2. **Drawing Conclusions** Many immigrants came to Ontario in the late 1700s. What advantages and disadvantages do you think this move had for them?

3. **Recognizing Cause and Effect** Identify several different events in western Canada that led to the decline of the native peoples' cultures.

Critical Thinking

1. **Writing a Paragraph** Make a list of the distinguishing characteristics of Quebec, Saskatchewan, and British Columbia. Then pick one province. Write a letter to a friend, trying to convince your friend to move to the province.

2. **Writing a Report** The native peoples of British Columbia had close ties to their natural environment. Visit the library and gather information on one of the tribes of native peoples living in British Columbia. Write a report detailing the ways that they used their natural resources for food, shelter, and cultural traditions.

 Take It to the NET

Activity Read about the industries that fuel Canada's economy. How would your life be different without the products and industries you read about? Visit the World Explorer: People, Places, and Cultures section of **phschool.com** for help in completing this activity.

Chapter 8 Self-Test As a final review activity, take the Chapter 8 Self-Test and get instant feedback on your answers. To take the test, visit the Social Studies section of **phschool.com.**

Applying Your Skills

Turn to the Skills for Life Activity on p. 153 to help you complete the following activity.

Find a newspaper or magazine article on a topic that interests you. Read the article and then follow the steps for writing a summary in order to summarize the information you have read.

IMMIGRATION

From the arrival of the first colonists in the 1600s, the United States and Canada have both been nations of immigrants. People from all over the world have come to the U.S. and Canada, contributing to the rich ethnic heritage of these countries. Some immigrants hoped to escape poverty, war, or discrimination in their native lands, while others came to find adventure, a fresh start, and new opportunities.

? How has the ethnic diversity created by a nation of immigrants influenced the cultures of the United States and Canada?

THE FIRST IMMIGRANTS
Most of the early colonists who settled in what became the United States came from England in the 17th and 18th centuries. Some of these early immigrants could not afford the travel costs and came as indentured servants. These people agreed to work for a fixed number of years to pay for their passage. Others were African slaves who were brought to the colonies against their will.

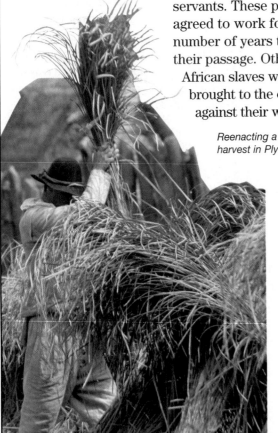

Reenacting a Pilgrim harvest in Plymouth, MA

FLEEING FAMINE AND POVERTY
More than seven million people entered the U.S. from 1820 to 1870, mostly from Northern and Western Europe. About a third were Irish, seeking escape from a famine brought on by potato crop failures in the 1840s. Another third were from Germany, where political unrest forced thousands to flee. While most new immigrants settled on the East Coast, many Germans traveled to the rich farmlands in the middle of the country.

THE GREAT WAVE
From the early 1900s to the Great Depression of the 1930s, a huge wave of immigrants—more than 30 million people— poured into the United States from every part of the world. Many came to escape the economic troubles, political changes, and strict religious laws of Europe.

RELIGIOUS FREEDOM
Many people came to America seeking the freedom to practice their chosen religion, a right that would be later guaranteed by the First Amendment to the Constitution. In colonial times, religious groups such as the Quakers and the Puritans fled from harsh treatment in England. More that two and a half million Jews from Eastern Europe emigrated to the United States between 1880 and 1920 to escape cultural and religious persecution.

CHINESE IMMIGRATION

In the mid-1800s, many Chinese people crossed the Pacific Ocean. They came to California in search of gold. Instead, they found violent anti-Chinese protests, unfair taxes, and laws to prevent their families from joining them. Labor shortages led companies to hire Chinese workers to help build transcontinental railroads in both the U.S. and in Canada.

VANCOUVER
Vancouver is located in southwestern British Columbia. It is Canada's leading Pacific port and reflects the great cultural diversity of the province. Many of its citizens are descended from the Chinese immigrants who helped to build the Canadian west.

PRESERVING HERITAGE
Many immigrants choose to settle in communities made up of people from their native lands. Most American cities contain ethnic neighborhoods, where residents continue to speak their native language as well as English. These neighborhoods have ethnic shops, places of worship, and businesses. They are also the site of many traditional festivals.

An immigrant family arrives in New York in 1910.

IMMIGRATION LIMITS

By 1910, most immigrants were coming from Southern and Eastern Europe. Some native-born Americans felt threatened by their large numbers. Consequently, Congress passed the first quota laws limiting the number of people allowed into the country.

Welcome to Latin America

CULTURE

Visit a remote village in the Andes ...

HISTORY

Explore the ruins of an ancient city ...

GEOGRAPHY

Search for plant life in Mexico's Sonoran Desert ...

What do you want to learn?

ECONOMICS

Visit an open-air market in Lima ...

SCIENCE, TECHNOLOGY, AND SOCIETY

Build a television on an assembly line ...

GOVERNMENT

See the "Pink House," the home of Argentina's government in Buenos Aires ...

CITIZENSHIP

Celebrate the return of a democratic president ...

A journal can be your personal record of discovery. As you learn about Latin America, you can create journal entries about what you read, write, think, and create. For your first entry, think about the geography of Latin America. How have Latin America's physical features influenced life in this region of the world? How is life in rural areas different from life in urban areas?

EXPLORER'S JOURNAL

Guiding Questions

What questions do I need to ask to understand Latin America?

Asking questions is a good way to learn. Think about what information you would want to know if you were visiting a new place, and what questions you might ask to find out. The questions on these pages can help guide your study of Latin America. You might want to try adding a few of your own!

GEOGRAPHY

Latin America is a region of variety, contrast, and extremes. Its rugged mountains, dense tropical rain forests, and rushing rivers are valuable natural resources but can make travel and communication difficult. Volcanoes along the Pacific Coast produce fertile soil, yet limited types of crops are produced. While vast arid regions remain sparsely populated, wet tropical areas produce sugar, bananas, and cotton. Today, Latin Americans are working together to develop their natural resources.

❶ How has geography influenced the social and economic development of Latin America?

HISTORY

When explorers from Europe arrived in Latin America in the 1500s, Native American civilizations had already flourished there for hundreds of years. Groups such as the Mayas, Aztecs, and Incas had built great cities and established rich cultures. Rather than live peaceably with the indigenous people, the Europeans claimed their land and treasures as their own. Many Native Americans perished, while others were enslaved. The history of Latin America tells of conquests, political struggles, and a blending of cultures from around the world.

❷ How has Latin America's history influenced modern day Latin American societies?

CULTURE

The different regions in which Latin Americans live together define Latin American culture. Many people in Latin America are mestizos of Spanish and Native American descent. Others maintain indigenous cultures or cultural traditions that come from Africa, Europe, or Asia. Their customs and religions are as diverse and varied as those found in other parts of the world, including the United States.

❸ How are Latin American cultures alike? How are they different?

GOVERNMENT

Political rivalries and military government control have played a major role in Latin America's history. Often the Latin American people are caught in the middle and must struggle for their civil and human rights. Today, however, countries in Latin America are slowly moving toward democratic governments similar to that in the United States, with two or more political parties and peaceful transfers of power.

4 How have the governments of Latin America changed over time, and how are they organized today?

ECONOMICS

Traditionally, agriculture has been the basis for Latin America's economy. But not all Latin American countries have fertile farmland. Instead of farming, some countries have relied on one or two products to support their economies, which made them weak when these products were not in demand. Now, however, many Latin American countries are developing new resources to diversify and improve their sources of income and to boost their economies.

5 What economic activities support the people of Latin America?

CITIZENSHIP

Since first breaking ties with European rulers to gain independence, citizens of Latin America have worked to have a voice in their governments. Yet, difficult economic conditions, illiteracy, and ruthless political leaders have hindered their efforts. As Latin American countries move toward democracy and free elections, the people of Latin American are finding more opportunities to voice their opinions.

6 What opportunities do citizens of Latin America have to participate in the political process?

SCIENCE, TECHNOLOGY, AND SOCIETY

Ancient scientists developed the astrolabe, a tool used by Spanish explorers to help guide their ships. Had these sailors not reached the shores of Latin America, the history of that region would have been written differently. The development of science and technology in Latin America has been slow but is growing steadily. Latin American countries are becoming more industrialized as they build their economies for the global marketplace.

7 How have technology and science helped shape Latin America today?

 Take It to the NET

For more information on Latin America, visit the World Explorer: People, Places, and Cultures companion Web site at **phschool.com.**

ACTIVITY ATLAS

Latin America

◆◆◆◆◆◆◆◆◆◆◆◆◆◆◆◆◆◆◆◆◆◆◆◆◆◆◆◆◆◆

Being an explorer and a geographer means first checking some facts.
Begin by exploring the maps of Latin America on the following pages.

Relative Location

UNITED STATES

ATLANTIC OCEAN

LATIN AMERICA

Equator

PACIFIC OCEAN

Relative Size

LATIN AMERICA

UNITED STATES

I. LOCATION

Locate Latin America and the United States   Notice where the United States and Latin America are located relative to the Equator. On the other side of the Equator, seasons come at the opposite time of year. When it's summer here, it's winter there. In what season does your birthday fall? In what season would it fall if you lived below the Equator in Latin America?

2. REGIONS

Estimate Latin America's Size   How long is Latin America's west coast? To get an idea, roughly measure the length of the west coast of the United States. Then, measure the length of the west coast of Latin America. Begin at the edge of the Pacific Ocean where Mexico borders California. Finish at the southern tip of South America. About how many times longer is Latin America's Pacific coast than that of the United States?

 Take It to the NET

Items marked with this logo are periodically updated on the Internet. To get current information about the geography of Latin America, go to **phschool.com.**

Latin America: Political

KEY

— National boundary

⊛ National capital

• Other city

Lambert Azimuthal Equal-Area Projection

3. LOCATION

Compare the Size of Countries The map above shows the countries that make up Latin America. Which two countries are the biggest in land area?

4. MOVEMENT

Analyze the Migration of People by Their Languages Long ago, settlers from other countries took control of Latin America. Where were they from? Clues: Portuguese is the official language of Brazil, and Spanish is spoken in most other Latin American countries.

ACTIVITY ATLAS

Latin America: Physical

KEY

Elevation

Feet	Meters
Over 13,000	Over 3,960
6,500–13,000	1,980–3,960
1,600–6,500	480–1,980
650–1,600	200–480
0–650	0–200
Below sea level	Below sea level

⊛ National capital

• Other city

Lambert Azimuthal Equal-Area Projection

5. PLACE

Explore the Physical Features of Latin America Volcanoes created many of Latin America's dramatic features. Long ago, they formed the Andes Mountains and others became a chain of islands called the Lesser Antilles. Central America has volcanic mountains, too. Some are still active! Trace the Andes Mountains, the Lesser Antilles, and the mountains in Central America with your finger. Which of these areas has the highest altitude? Which is largest?

6. REGIONS

Locate Latin America's Physical Features   Your favorite aunt has once again taken off on an adventure. This time, she is traveling around Latin America by ship. Occasionally, she takes time to write you a postcard. Each contains a clue about her location. Use the map below and the map on the opposite page to answer her questions.

A. *Our ship is on the south side of the island of Hispaniola. A dense rain forest covers the island's mountain slopes. Which way will we sail to reach the Panama Canal?*

B. *We are sailing south past one of the Earth's driest deserts. It is in a long, skinny South American country that extends north and south along the continent's west coast. Where are we?*

C. *From the Falkland Islands, we traveled north and sailed past desert scrub for days. Finally, we saw tropical rain forest along the coast. What two major cities will we come to next?*

  Take It to the NET

Latin America: Natural Vegetation

KEY

- Tropical rain forest
- Mixed forest
- Coniferous forest
- Mediterranean vegetation
- Tropical savanna
- Temperate grassland
- Desert scrub
- Desert (little or no vegetation)
- Highlands (vegetation varies with elevation)

Lambert Azimuthal Equal-Area Projection

Latin America: Major Hydroelectric Plants

KEY

— National boundary

■ Hydroelectric Plants

Lambert Azimuthal Equal-Area Projection

7. HUMAN-ENVIRONMENT INTERACTION

Examine Ways People Have Modified Latin America's Physical Environment Hydroelectricity is electric power that is made by harnessing the power of water. One way is to build a dam across a river. The dam creates a large lake, lake water runs into the river, and turns a wheel, which creates electricity. What do you think are some advantages of building a dam across a river? What are some disadvantages?

Latin America's Longest and Highest ...

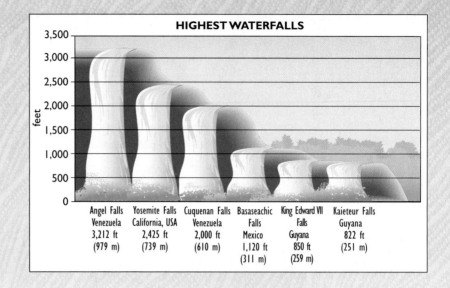

HIGHEST WATERFALLS

feet

| Angel Falls Venezuela 3,212 ft (979 m) | Yosemite Falls California, USA 2,425 ft (739 m) | Cuquenan Falls Venezuela 2,000 ft (610 m) | Basaseachic Falls Mexico 1,120 ft (311 m) | King Edward VII Falls Guyana 850 ft (259 m) | Kaieteur Falls Guyana 822 ft (251 m) |

THE LONGEST RIVERS

Amazon River — 4,000 mi (6,437 km)

Mississippi-Missouri River (U.S.) — 3,870 mi (6,019 km)

Rio de la Plata — 2,795 mi (4,700 km)

Orinoco River — 2,200 mi (2,500 km)

São Francisco River — 1,900 mi (2,900 km)

0   1,000   2,000   3,000   4,000 miles

Take It to the NET

VOLUME OF WATER IN RIVERS

River	Volume of Water (cubic meters per second)
Amazon River	180,000
Orinoco River	28,000
Rio de la Plata	19,500
Mississippi-Missouri River U.S.	17,545
São Francisco River	3,300

10,000 cubic meters per second

VOLCANOES OF LATIN AMERICA

Mexico	38
Guatemala	21
El Salvador	20
Honduras	4
Nicaragua	19
Costa Rica	11
Panama	2
Colombia	14
Ecuador	32
Peru	13
Chile	109
Bolivia	17
Argentina	15

▲ 2 volcanos

8. PLACE

Compare Physical Features Latin America's Angel Falls waterfall is the highest in the world. The Amazon River is the second longest river in the world and carries more water than any other...by far! Latin America is also one of the most active volcanic regions in the world. Study these charts and diagrams. What country would you visit to see the world's highest waterfall? How much higher is this waterfall than the second highest in Latin America? Which is the second longest river in Latin America? How many times more water does the Amazon carry than does the Mississippi? Which Latin American country has the most volcanoes? How many?

CHAPTER 9

LATIN AMERICA: Physical Geography

SECTION 1
Physical Features

SECTION 2
Humans and the Physical Environment

SECTION 3
Geographic Factors and Natural Resources

Looking at the Land

USING PICTURES

These rugged mountains are the Andes (AN deez). They stretch along the entire length of South America.

Comparing Geographic Regions

Think about where you live. Do you live in an area with mountains, or at a lower elevation? What do you think it would be like to live in or near the Andes? Brainstorm a list of adjectives that describe the landscape in this picture, then brainstorm another list that describes the landscape where you live. Write the two lists side by side so that you can compare them. How are the two different? How are they similar?

Understanding Climate

Have you ever been mountain climbing? How did the temperature change as you climbed higher? Based on your experience, do you think the climate is the same at the top of the Andes as at the bottom? Where would it be colder? Where would it be warmer? Would these changes affect the vegetation? The wild life? Where people live? How they live?

Physical Features

BEFORE YOU READ

READING FOCUS

1. What are some major landforms and regions in Latin America?
2. What are some major rivers in Latin America, and how do they affect the lives of the people living in the region?

KEY TERMS

plateau
isthmus
coral
tributary

KEY PLACES

Mexico
Central America
Caribbean
South America

MAIN IDEA

Latin America's geographic features make it a region of variety and contrast.

NOTE TAKING

Copy the chart below. As you read the section, fill in the chart with information about Latin America's geographic features, including its landforms and bodies of water.

Physical Features	Important Landforms	Important Bodies of Water	Other Water Resources
The Caribbean			
Mexico and Central America			
South America			

Setting the Scene

Latin America is located in the Western Hemisphere south of the United States. Latin America includes all the nations from Mexico to the tip of the continent of South America. It also includes the islands that dot the Caribbean (ka ruh BEE un) Sea. Geographic features divide Latin America into three smaller regions. They are (1) Mexico and Central America, (2) the Caribbean, and (3) South America.

The Amazon River's Many Uses

GEOGRAPHY The people who live near the Amazon River in Brazil rely on it for transportation, fish, and water. Families also wash their laundry right at the river bank.
Critical Thinking What are some of the ways that your life is affected by the physical features of the region where you live? Make a list.

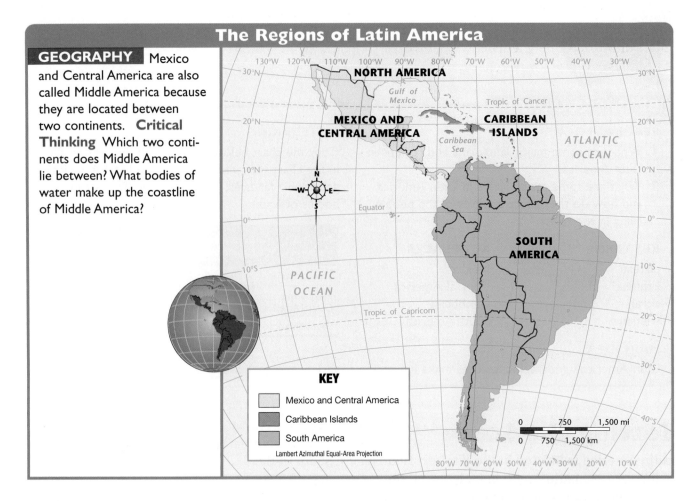

The Regions of Latin America

GEOGRAPHY Mexico and Central America are also called Middle America because they are located between two continents. **Critical Thinking** Which two continents does Middle America lie between? What bodies of water make up the coastline of Middle America?

About 500 years ago, Europeans sailed to Latin America and brought their own languages and ways of life with them. Since most came from Spain and Portugal, almost all Latin Americans today speak Spanish or Portuguese. These languages have their roots in the ancient language of Latin and as a result, the region is known as Latin America.

Latin America's Major Landforms and Regions

AS YOU READ

Monitor Your Reading How do you think the physical features of Latin America might be like those of the United States?

Imagine mountains that pierce the clouds and grassy plains that never seem to end. Picture wet rain forests, sunbaked deserts, and broad rivers. This is Latin America, a region of variety and contrast.

Mexico and Central America **Mexico** and **Central America** stretch 2,500 miles (4,023 km) from the U.S. border to South America. It is a distance that is almost equal to the width of the mainland United States. Mountains dominate this region and are a part of a huge system of mountain ranges that extends from Canada through the United States all the way to the tip of South America.

Between the mountains in Mexico lies Mexico's Central Plateau. A **plateau** (pla TOH) is a large raised area of mostly level land. Mexico's

Central Plateau makes up more than half of the country's area and most of Mexico's people live here. However, the surrounding mountains make it hard for people to travel to and from the Central Plateau.

Central America, located south of Mexico, is an isthmus. An **isthmus** is a narrow strip of land that has water on both sides and joins two larger bodies of land. Find Central America on the map in the Activity Atlas on page 163. What two large bodies of land does the isthmus of Central America connect? As in Mexico, narrow plains run along Central America's coasts. Between these coastal plains are rugged, steep mountains. More than a dozen of these mountains are active volcanoes. Volcanic ash has made the soil good for farming.

The Caribbean Imagine islands made of skeletons, or others that are the tips of underwater mountains. The **Caribbean** is made up of these two types of islands. The smaller islands were formed from the skeletons of tiny sea animals. Over hundreds of years, the skeletons formed a rocklike substance called **coral.**

The larger islands of the Caribbean are the tops of huge underwater mountains. Most people on the islands make a living farming.

South America **South America** contains many types of landforms, which you can see on the map in the Activity Atlas on page 164. Perhaps the most impressive landform is the Andes Mountains which run some 4,500 miles (7,250 km) along the western coast of South America. In some places, the Andes rise to heights of more than 20,000 feet (6,100 m).

The Andes are steep and difficult to cross. But their rich soil has drawn farmers to the region. East of the Andes are rolling highlands. These highlands spread across parts of Brazil, Venezuela (ven uh ZWAY luh), Guyana (gy AN uh), and other South American countries. Farther south are the Pampas (PAHM puz), a large plains area that stretches through Argentina (ar jun TEE nuh) and Uruguay (YOOR uh gway).

Herding Cattle on the Pampas
GEOGRAPHY
Grasslands known as the Pampas can also be found in Brazil. These grasslands are perfect for raising cattle. **Critical Thinking** How are these grasslands similar to the Great Plains in the United States?

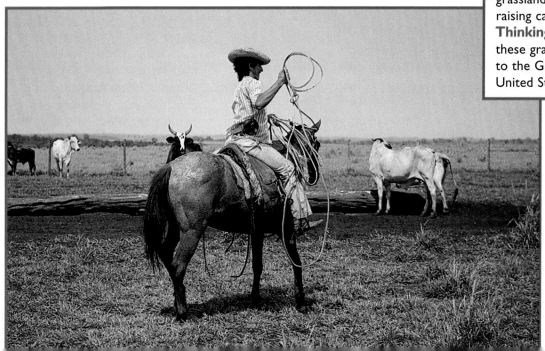

The plains areas, the eastern highlands, and the Andes frame the Amazon River Basin. The Amazon River Basin contains the largest tropical rain forest in the world. This dense forest covers more than a third of the continent.

The Rivers of Latin America

Latin America's rivers and lakes are some of the longest and largest bodies of water in the world. Rivers serve as transportation corridors in places where it is hard to build roads. The fish that swim the waters of Latin America provide food, and rushing water from large rivers provides power for electricity.

Amazon: The Ocean River   Latin America's Amazon (AM uh zahn) River is the second-longest river in the world, flowing 4,000 miles (6,437 km) from Peru across Brazil into the Atlantic Ocean. Only the Nile River in Africa is longer.

The Amazon River also carries more water than any other river in the world. In fact, it contains about 20 percent of all the fresh river water on the Earth. The Amazon River gathers power from the more than 1,000 **tributaries** (TRIB yoo tehr eez) that spill into it. Tributaries are the rivers and streams that flow into a larger river. With its tributaries, the Amazon drains an area of more than two million square miles

Other Rivers and Lakes   Latin America has many other bodies of water besides the Amazon. The Paraná (pah rah NAH), Paraguay, and Uruguay rivers form the Río de la Plata system. The Río de la Plata separates Argentina and Uruguay. Lake Titicaca is the highest lake in the world on which ships can travel. It lies high in the Andes Mountains on the border between Peru and Bolivia.

SECTION I ASSESSMENT

AFTER YOU READ

RECALL

1. Identify: (a) Mexico, (b) Central America, (c) Caribbean, (d) South America

2. Define: (a) plateau, (b) isthmus, (c) coral, (d) tributary

COMPREHENSION

3. Describe the major landforms of the three regions that make up Latin America.

4. Describe how Latin America's rivers affect the lives of people in the region.

CRITICAL THINKING AND WRITING

5. Exploring the Main Idea Review the Main Idea statement at the beginning of this section. Then, list two ways the physical features of Latin America show that it is a region of variety and contrast.

6. Making Comparisons Describe two ways in which the three regions of Latin America are different.

ACTIVITY

7. Expressing a Point of View Suppose that your family was planning to move to Latin America. If you had your choice, in which of the three regions of Latin America would you live? Explain why.

Humans and the Physical Environment

Setting the Scene

What's the climate like where you live? Is it hot? Cold? Rainy? Dry? If you lived in Latin America, the climate might be any of these. Climate in Latin America can vary greatly even within the same country.

In parts of the **Andes,** below-zero temperatures would set your teeth chattering. Travel down to the Amazon Basin, and you may be sweating in 90°F (32°C) heat. If you prefer dry weather, visit the **Atacama** (ah tah KAH mah) **Desert** in Chile or the Sonoran Desert in Mexico. These are two of the driest places on the Earth.

Climate: Hot, Cold, and Mild

The climate of the Caribbean is usually sunny and warm. From June to November, however, the region is often hit with fierce hurricanes. Winds from hurricanes can blow at over 180 miles per hour (300 km/hr) causing waves nearly 20 feet (6 m) high to smash into the coast. The storms tear roofs off houses, shatter windows, and yank huge trees from the ground.

Hurricanes are a part of life for people living in the Caribbean. But climate affects the people of Latin America in other ways,

GEOGRAPHY

Mexico's Sonoran Desert shows that even a hot, dry desert can be full of plant life. **Critical Thinking** What kinds of plants might you find growing in a desert? Why?

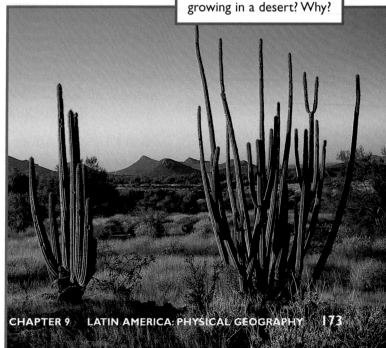

CHAPTER 9   LATIN AMERICA: PHYSICAL GEOGRAPHY   **173**

GEOGRAPHY If you climb high enough on a mountain, you will reach a place where the temperature never warms up. This chart shows how the temperature near the equator can vary with elevation. **Chart Study** Based on this chart, above what elevation will snow not melt? What grows beneath the tree line?

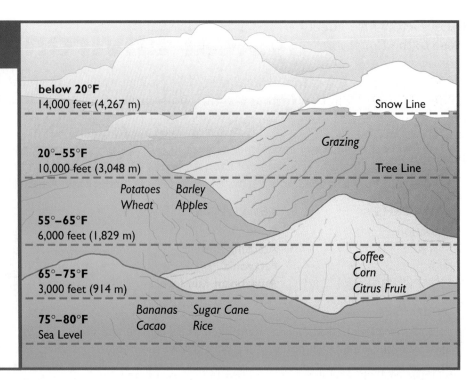

below 20°F
14,000 feet (4,267 m)

Snow Line

Grazing

20°–55°F
10,000 feet (3,048 m)

Tree Line

Potatoes   Barley
Wheat   Apples

55°–65°F
6,000 feet (1,829 m)

Coffee
Corn
Citrus Fruit

65°–75°F
3,000 feet (914 m)

Bananas   Sugar Cane
Cacao   Rice

75°–80°F
Sea Level

too. For example, people who live in the mountains need warm clothing and shelter to protect them against cool temperatures. The higher up the mountains you go, the cooler it gets.

Climate Regions of Latin America   Many parts of Latin America have a tropical wet climate. A tropical wet climate means hot, humid, rainy weather all year round. Rain forests thrive in this type of climate.

Other parts of Latin America have a tropical wet and dry climate. These areas are equally hot, but the rainy season does not last all year long. Parts of Mexico and Brazil and most of the Caribbean have a tropical wet and dry climate.

Much of Argentina, Uruguay, and Paraguay has a humid subtropical climate, similar to that of parts of the southern United States. People living in this climate usually have hot, wet summers and cool winters. Farmers in these areas can raise such crops as wheat and apples, which need a cold season to grow well. Farther south, the climate turns arid. Farmers raise sheep on the plains of this colder, drier area, called **Patagonia** (pat uh GOH nee uh).

What Factors Affect Climate?   **Elevation,** the height of land above sea level, is a key factor in the climate of mountainous Latin America. The higher the elevation, the colder the temperature. Suppose it is a warm 80°F (27°C) at sea level. Continue up to 6,000 feet (1,829 m), and the temperature may now be only about 60°F (16°C). Above 10,000 feet (3,048 m), the temperature may remain below freezing—too cold for people to live permanently.

AS YOU READ

Summarize Suppose that you were climbing a mountain. How would the vegetation you see change as you climb higher?

Other factors also affect Latin America's climate. Regions close to the Equator are generally warmer than those farther away.

Wind patterns affect the climate too. Winds move colder, drier air from the North and South Poles toward the Equator. They also move warmer, moister air from the Equator toward the Poles. In the Caribbean, sea breezes blowing toward shore help keep temperatures moderate. More rain falls on the sides of islands facing the wind than on sides facing away.

Natural Vegetation and Climate

Imagine a forest so dense and lush that almost no sunlight reaches the ground. Broad, green leaves, tangled vines, and thousands of species of trees and plants surround you. The air is hot and heavy with moisture. Welcome to the **Amazonian rain forest.**

Now, suppose you have traveled to the coast of northern Chile. You're in the Atacama Desert. There is very little moisture to this barren land, and there is little sign of life. The Andes shield this dry region from rain. Because winds move from east to west in this region, rain falls only on the eastern slope of the Andes at this latitude. This leaves the western side dry.

Elevation also affects vegetation. To grow at higher elevations, plants must be able to withstand cooler temperatures, chill winds, and irregular rainfall.

Tree Dwellers

GEOGRAPHY Tree sloths live in the rain forest trees of South America. They rarely descend from the trees. **Critical Thinking** Look carefully at the photograph. How do you think the sloth is well adapted to living in the trees?

SECTION 2 ASSESSMENT

AFTER YOU READ

RECALL

1. Identify: (a) Andes, (b) Atacama Desert, (c) Patagonia, (d) Amazonian rain forest

2. Define: (a) elevation

COMPREHENSION

3. Analyze how the people of Latin America adapt to their physical environments, including different climates.

4. How does climate affect the natural vegetation of Latin America?

CRITICAL THINKING AND WRITING

5. **Exploring the Main Idea** Review the Main Idea statement at the beginning of this section. Then, list three examples that support the statement: "The physical environment of Latin America varies greatly."

6. **Drawing Conclusions** In what ways would the life of a family living on a Caribbean island be different from a family living high in the Andes?

ACTIVITY

7. **Expressing an Opinion** Latin America has been called a land of extremes. Do you agree or disagree? Write a paragraph or more telling why. Support your opinion with examples.

Geographic Factors and Natural Resources

BEFORE YOU READ

READING FOCUS

1. What are Latin America's important natural resources?
2. Why is it important for Latin American nations not to rely too much on one resource?

KEY TERMS
hydroelectricity
diversify

KEY PLACES
Jamaica
Venezuela
Brazil
Colombia

NOTE TAKING

Copy the chart below. As you read the section, fill in the chart with information about factors that cause incomes from natural resources to decrease.

Lower Income from Natural Resources

MAIN IDEA

The distribution and use of natural resources in Latin America influence the economies of countries there.

An Agricultural Economy

ECONOMICS Many Latin American economies are based on agriculture. Half of Colombia's exports are coffee. **Critical Thinking** What problems do you think the economy of a country like Colombia might face?

Setting the Scene

Bolivia has always depended on mineral resources for wealth. At first, silver helped to bring money into Bolivia's treasury. Soon, however, another metal became even more important than silver. That metal was tin.

For many years, Bolivia enjoyed the good times that wealth from tin brought. Then, in the 1920s and 1930s, a world-wide economic crisis hit. Industries stopped buying tin, as well as other natural resources, and Bolivia suffered as its main resource failed to bring money into the economy. This economic crisis hit all of Latin America hard. It brought home a problem many Latin American nations have: They rely too much on one resource.

Latin America's Natural Resources

Fish, petroleum, water, silver, and forests are all natural resources of Latin America and are as varied as its physical features and climate.

Mexico and Central America: Riches of Land and Sea Mexico is a treasure chest of minerals. The country has deposits of silver, gold,copper, coal, iron ore, and just about any other mineral you can name. Mexico also has huge amounts of oil and natural gas.

In addition, trees cover nearly a quarter of Mexico's land. Wood from these trees is turned into lumber and paper products.

Central America's climate and rich soil are good for farming. The people grow coffee, cotton, sugar cane, and bananas. They also plant cacao trees. Cacao seeds are made into chocolate and cocoa.

Not all of Central America's resources are on land. People catch fish and shellfish in the region's waters. Central Americans use the energy of flowing water to produce power. This type of power is called **hydroelectricity** (hy droh ee lek TRIS ih tee) and is produced by huge dams that harness and control the energy.

The Caribbean: Farming Resources Caribbean countries also have rich soil and a good climate for farming. Farmers grow sugar cane, coffee, bananas, cacao, citrus fruits, and other crops. The Caribbean has other resources as well. **Jamaica** is one of the world's main producers of bauxite—a mineral used to make aluminum. Cuba and the Dominican Republic have nickel deposits, while Trinidad is rich in oil.

South America: A Wealth of Resources Like Mexico, South America is rich in minerals. Businesses drill for oil in many South American countries, but much of the oil is found in **Venezuela.**

South America's plants and fish are natural resources, too. Forests cover about half the continent and trees from these forests provide everything from wood for building to coconuts for eating. People harvest many rain forest plants to make medicines. Tuna, anchovies, and other fish are plentiful.

Like other parts of Latin America, South America has rich soil so farmers can grow many different crops there. Coffee is a key crop in **Brazil** and **Colombia.** Many South American economies rely on the production of sugar cane, cotton, and rice.

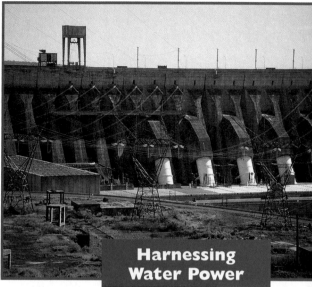

Harnessing Water Power

ECONOMICS The hydroelectric power plant at Itaipú Dam is the largest in the world. It harnesses the energy of the Paraná River to provide electric power to Paraguay and Brazil. **Critical Thinking** What detail in this picture is a clue that the dam is used to produce electricity?

Natural Resources and Economy

Not every country shares in the wealth of Latin America's resources. Some Latin American countries have many resources, while others have few. Some countries do not have the money they need to develop all of their resources.

Economic Factors and Weather Depending on one resource or crop can lead to problems. Many people in Latin America make their living by farming. Some Latin American countries depend on one or two crops, such as coffee, bananas, or sugar. When the price of a crop goes down, exports of that crop bring less money into the country. As a result, workers' wages may drop, and some workers may lose their jobs.

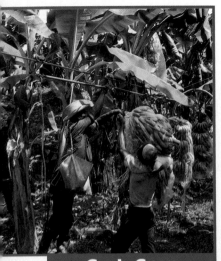

Cash Crop Farming

ECONOMICS Many Latin American economies are based on agriculture. For example, one third of Honduras's exports are bananas. **Critical Thinking** What problems do you think one-crop economies face?

Weather and disease also cause people and businesses to lose money. Hurricanes, droughts, and plant disease can damage crops, and weather can also hurt the fishing industry.

Depending on Oil Oil is one of Latin America's most valuable resources. But it is risky to depend on oil because oil prices increase and decrease, sometimes suddenly. Mexico, like Venezuela, is a major oil producer. In the mid-1980s, oil companies produced more oil than the world needed. As a result of this decrease in demand, prices dropped and Mexico earned much less income than it had expected. The same thing happened to Trinidad.

There are other problems as well. In the 1960s, oil was discovered in Ecuador. Soon, oil became the country's main export. But in 1987, earthquakes destroyed Ecuador's major oil pipeline and the country's income was slashed.

Avoiding the Problems of a One-Resource Country Latin American nations know the risks of depending on one resource or crop and they are trying to diversify their economies. To **diversify** is to add variety. When Latin American nations try to diversify their economies, it means that they are looking for other ways to make money. Many are building factories to make products that can be sold to bring more money into the economy. Factories also provide jobs for people.

Venezuela has been trying to set up more factories and farms rather than relying only on oil production. Brazil has been building up its various industries, exporting machinery, steel, and chemicals, and encouraging cotton farming. El Salvador used to depend too heavily on its coffee crop. Now, cotton, sugar, corn, and other crops play an important role in the nation's economy.

SECTION 3 ASSESSMENT

AFTER YOU READ

RECALL

1. Identify: (a) Jamaica, (b) Venezuela, (c) Brazil, (d) Colombia

2. Define: (a) hydroelectricity (b) diversify

COMPREHENSION

3. Describe the important natural resources of Latin America.

4. Why is it important for Latin American nations to diversify their economies?

CRITICAL THINKING AND WRITING

5. **Exploring the Main Idea** Review the Main Idea statement at the beginning of this section. Then, write a paragraph explaining how the economies of the nations of Latin America are tied to its resources.

6. **Recognizing Cause and Effect** Suppose a disease destroyed Colombia's coffee crop. How would this loss affect coffee-plantation workers and their families?

ACTIVITY

 Take It to the NET

7. **Writing a Position Paper** Write a paper discussing your views about the conservation of the rainforests. Visit the World Explorer: People, Places, and Cultures section of **phschool.com** for help in completing this activity.

Using Reliable Information

SEARCH ENGINE

Search | options

Yellow Pages - People Search - City Maps -- Today's News - Stock Quotes - Sports Scores

- **Arts and Humanities**
  Architecture, Photography, Literature ...
- **Business and Economy [Xtra!]**
  Companies, Investments, Classifieds ...
- **Computers and Internet [Xtra!]**
  Internet, WWW, Software, Multimedia ...
- **Education**
  Universities, K-12, College Entrance ...
- **Entertainment [Xtra!]**
  Cool Links, Movies, Music, Humor ...
- **Government**
  Military, Politics [Xtra!], Law ...
- **Health [Xtra!]**
  Medicine, Drugs, Diseases, Fitness ...
- **News and Media [Xtra!]**
  Current Events, Magazines, TV, Newspapers ...
- **Recreation and Sports [Xtra!]**
  Sports, Games, Travel, Autos, Outdoors ...
- **Reference**
  Libraries, Dictionaries, Phone Numbers ...
- **Regional**
  Countries, Regions, U.S. States ...
- **Science**
  CS, Biology, Astronomy, Engineering ...
- **Social Science**
  Anthropology, Sociology, Economics ...
- **Society and Culture**
  People, Environment, Religion ...

Learn the Skill

You know that you can find a great deal of information on the Internet, which provides contact with other computers around the world. People use the Internet to search for information on nearly every topic. However, you need to make sure that the information you find is reliable and accurate.

You can follow these steps to help you decide if the information you find is reliable.

A. Is the information true?

- Make sure any facts you find are supported. Remember that a fact can proven true, but opinions cannot. Be on the lookout for opinions presented as facts.
- Look for spelling or grammatical mistakes. These mistakes may show that the information was not checked or reviewed.

B. Who is responsible for the information?

- Check to see what person or organization put the information on the Internet. Is this person or organization qualified to provide information about this topic? How do you know? Is there a way to contact the author or organization by email or phone?

C. Is the information fair?

- Check to see if the information provides a balanced view on the topic.
- Identify the purpose of the information. Are you being persuaded to believe or do something? Is the information provided by a business that wants to sell you a product or service? If so, the information might not be as reliable as it seems.

D. Is the information up to date?

- Check to see when the Web page was first created. Also, make sure you can tell when the page was last updated. If there are no dates on the page, then the information might not be reliable.

E. How in-depth is the information?

- Decide if the Web page goes into enough detail on the topic. Also, check to see if there are links to other resources and Web sites. Are these links working?

You may not be able to find answers to all these questions for every Web page you visit. However, it's important for you to keep these questions in mind when you use the Internet.

Practice the Skill

Use the Internet to find out information about Latin America. First, write a question that you can answer, such as "What kinds of animals live in the Andes Mountains?" Then, use a search engine to find Web pages related to your topic. Choose three Web sites from your search and follow the steps you learned to decide if the information on each page is reliable. Record your observations.

Apply the Skill

See the Chapter Review and Assessment at the end of this chapter for more questions on using reliable information.

CHAPTER 9 Review and Assessment

Creating a Chapter Summary

On a separate piece of paper, draw a web like this one, and include the information that summarizes part of the information in Section 1. Then, add more ovals to summarize the remaining information you learned in this chapter.

Physical Geography

Physical Enviroment

Latin America

Geographic features divide Latin America into three smaller regions.

Natural Resources

Reviewing Key Terms

Complete each sentence with a word from the list below.

hydroelectricity   elevation

coral   plateau

isthmus

1. An _____ is a narrow strip of land that has water on both sides and joins two larger bodies of land.

2. _____ refers to the height of land above sea level.

3. A large, raised area of mostly level land is called a _____.

4. _____ generates power using moving water.

5. _____, a rock-like substance, is formed by the skeletons of tiny sea animals.

Reviewing the Main Ideas

1. List the three main regions of Latin America. Then choose two and describe their physical features. (Section 1)

2. In what ways do the physical features of Latin America affect the people and their way of life? (Section 1)

3. How does elevation affect climate? (Section 2)

4. Give an example of how climate in one region of Latin America affects the vegetation that grows there. How does this affect the way in which people live? (Section 2)

5. List two natural resources found in each of the three regions of Latin America. (Section 3)

6. What problems arise when a country depends too heavily on a single source of income? Support your answer with one or two examples. (Section 3)

Map Activity

For each place listed below, write the letter from the map that shows its location.

1. Colombia   **4.** Mexico

2. Brazil   **5.** Venezuela

3. Jamaica

 Take It to the NET

Enrichment For more map activities using geography skills, visit the social studies section of **phschool.com**.

Writing Activity

1. Writing a Letter Imagine that you are a visitor to Latin America. You are touring the whole region: Mexico, Central America, the Caribbean, and South America. Write a letter home describing your trip. Write about such items as these: the weather, interesting facts you've learned about Latin America's physical features, places that you liked or didn't like, and the economy in at least one of the regions.

2. Writing a Report Choose a country in Latin America for further study. Visit the library or the Internet and gather information on the physical geography and climate of that country. Write a short report explaining how the geography and climate affect the economy and way of life in that country.

Applying Your Skills

Turn to the Skills for Life activity on p. 179 to help you complete the following activity.

Use the Internet to search for information about the Amazon River. Find one web page that is a good example of reliable information and one that is a bad example. Support your choices using the information you learned on p.179.

Critical Thinking

1. Supporting a Point of View Write a paragraph using examples to support this point of view: "The weather in Latin America is a great friend to the people, but also an enemy."

2. Drawing Conclusions "How a country uses its natural resources affects the well-being of its people." Do you agree or disagree with this statement? Explain your answer.

3. Making Comparisons Compare the physical geography of the Caribbean to that of South America. Which region do you think has a more beneficial geography? Explain.

 Take It to the NET

Activity Draw or trace a map of Latin America. Label each country and capital. Then label at least five countries with a number indicating their current population. Visit the World Explorer: People, Places, and Cultures section of **phschool.com** for help in completing this activity.

Chapter 9 Self-Test As a final review activity, take the Chapter 9 Self-Test and get instant feedback on your answers. To take the test, visit the Social Studies section of **phschool.com**.

LATIN AMERICA:
Shaped by History

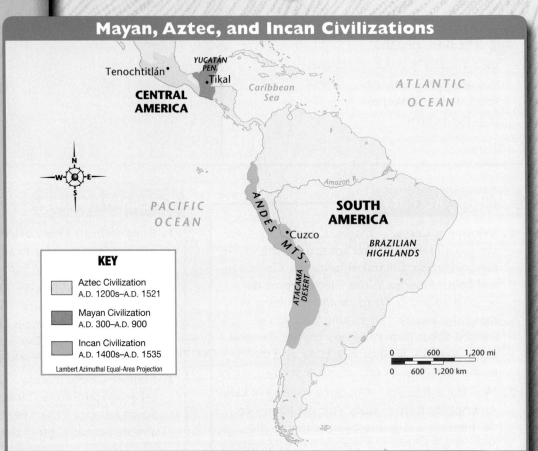

Mayan, Aztec, and Incan Civilizations

Tenochtitlán

YUCATÁN PEN.

Tikal

CENTRAL AMERICA

Caribbean Sea

ATLANTIC OCEAN

PACIFIC OCEAN

Amazon R.

ANDES MTS.

•Cuzco

SOUTH AMERICA

BRAZILIAN HIGHLANDS

ATACAMA DESERT

KEY

Aztec Civilization
A.D. 1200s–A.D. 1521

Mayan Civilization
A.D. 300–A.D. 900

Incan Civilization
A.D. 1400s–A.D. 1535

Lambert Azimuthal Equal-Area Projection

0   600   1,200 mi
0   600 1,200 km

USING A MAP

This map shows the location of three civilizations in Latin America that existed before Europeans arrived in the region.

Understanding Ancient Civilizations

Each of these civilizations was highly advanced. Visit your local library or the Internet to find out some of the major accomplishments of each of these civilizations. Make a list of your findings.

Evaluating the Geography

Look at the map and describe the location of each of the three civilizations. Which civilization do you think was the most difficult to defend from invaders? Explain your answer.

Early Civilizations

READING FOCUS

1. What were the chief cultural characteristics and accomplishments of the Mayan civilization?
2. What were the chief cultural characteristics and accomplishments of the Aztec civilization?
3. What were the chief cultural characteristics and accomplishments of the Incan civilization?

KEY TERMS

maize
hieroglyphics
aqueduct

KEY PLACES

Copán
Valley of Mexico
Tenochtitlán
Cuzco

NOTE TAKING

Copy the Venn diagram below. As you read the section, complete the diagram to show how the ancient Mayan, Aztec, and Incan civilizations were alike and how they were different.

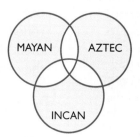

MAIN IDEA

The Mayas, Aztecs, and Incas had developed unique civilizations in Latin America before Europeans arrived.

Setting the Scene

Fans cheered as the players brought the ball down the court. Suddenly, the ball flew into the air and sailed through the hoop. Fans and players shouted and screamed. Although this may sound like a championship basketball game, it is actually a moment of a game played over 1,000 years ago. Pok-a-tok was a game played by ancient Mayas.

Mayan Civilization and Culture

Mayan civilization thrived in Central America and southern Mexico from about A.D. 300 to A.D. 900. By studying ruins, scientists have learned much about Mayan civilization.

The Mayas built great cities that were also religious centers. Two of these cities were **Copán** (ko PAHN) in present-day Honduras and Tikal (tee KAHL) in Guatemala. Large pyramid-shaped temples, where Mayas worshipped, stood in the center of the cities. Mayan farmers worked in the fields surrounding the cities.

Ancient Mayan Games

CULTURE This pok-a-tok court is in Copán, Honduras. **Critical Thinking** In what ways do you think sporting events or games played by the ancient Mayas were similar to those played today?

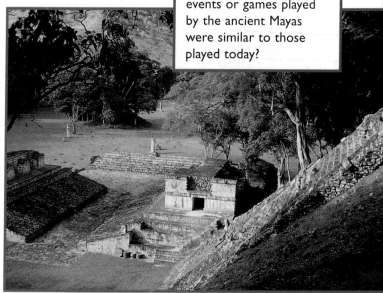

LINKS TO
Math

The Concept of Zero
The Mayas created a numbering system that included the idea of zero. Zero is important in math because it is a symbol that shows that there is none of something. For example, to write the number 308, you need a symbol to show that there are no tens. Mathematicians consider the idea of zero to be one of the world's greatest inventions.

Aztec Calendar

SCIENCE AND TECHNOLOGY

The Aztecs observed the stars and planets carefully and like the ancient Greeks, named them after their gods. The Aztecs used their knowledge of astronomy to make calendars like the one below. **Critical Thinking** Who do you think designed and used the calendar? Why?

Science, Technology, and Religion The most important Mayan crop was **maize,** or corn, which was the main food in the Mayan diet. Farmers also grew beans, squash, peppers, avocados, and papayas. Mayan priests studied the stars and planets and designed an accurate calendar, which they used to decide when to hold religious ceremonies. They also developed a system of writing using signs and symbols called **hieroglyphics** (hy ur oh GLIF iks) along with a number system similar to the present-day decimal system.

The Great Mystery of the Mayas About A.D. 900, the Mayas suddenly left their cities, but no one knows why. Crop failures, war, disease, drought, or famine may have killed many, or perhaps people rebelled against the control of the priests and nobles. The Mayas left their cities, but stayed in the region and millions of them still live in the countries of Mexico, Belize, Guatemala, Honduras, and El Salvador.

Aztec Civilization and Culture

Another ancient civilization is that of the Aztecs. They arrived in the **Valley of Mexico** in the 1100s. The Valley of Mexico is in Central Mexico.

The Aztecs found a permanent home in 1325 when they settled on an island in Lake Texcoco. They changed the swampy lake into a magnificent city, which they called **Tenochtitlán** (tay nawch tee TLAHN). Tenochtitlán stood on the site of present-day Mexico City.

The Aztecs Expand Their Empire In the 1400s, Aztec warriors conquered other people in the region. They forced the people they conquered to pay tribute, or taxes. Tribute was paid in food, cotton, gold, or slaves. The Aztecs grew rich from the tribute.

An emperor ruled over all Aztec lands and their society had several classes. Nobles and priests helped the emperor, warriors fought battles, and traders carried goods throughout the empire and beyond. Craftworkers created jewelry, garments, pottery, sculptures, and other goods. Most people, however, were farmers.

Aztec Science and Technology Tenochtitlán was a center of trade and learning. Aztec doctors made more than 1,000 medicines from plants. Aztec astronomers predicted eclipses and the movements of planets. Aztec priests kept records using hieroglyphics similar to those used by the Mayas.

Incan Civilizations and Culture

In about 1200, the Incas settled in **Cuzco** (KOOS koh), a village in the Andes that is now a city in the country of Peru. Most Incas were farmers who grew maize and other crops. Through wars and conquest, the Incas won control of the entire Cuzco Valley, one of many valleys that extend from the Andes to the Pacific Ocean.

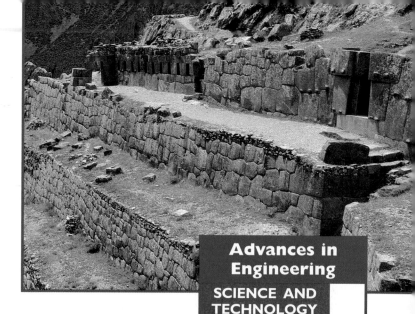

At one time, the Incan Empire stretched some 2,500 miles (4,023 km) from what is now Ecuador south along the Pacific coast through Peru, Bolivia, Chile, and Argentina. The 12 million people ruled by the Incas lived mostly in small villages and their descendants still live in present-day Peru, Ecuador, Bolivia, Chile, and Colombia. They speak Quechua (KECH wah), the Incan language.

Incan Accomplishments The Incan capital, Cuzco, was the center of government, trade, learning, and religion. The emperor and the nobles who helped him run the empire lived in the city near the central plaza. Most of the farmers and workers lived outside Cuzco in mud huts.

The Incas were excellent farmers, builders, and managers. They built more than 19,000 miles (30,577 km) of roads. The roads went over some of the most mountainous land in the world. This road system helped the Incas to govern their vast empire. They increased their farmland by building stone terraces into the sides of steep slopes and **aqueducts,** pipes or channels designed to carry water from a distant source. Aqueducts allowed the Incas to irrigate land to grow crops.

SECTION I ASSESSMENT

AFTER YOU READ

RECALL

1. Identify : (a) Copán, (b) Valley of Mexico, (c) Tenochtitlán, (d) Cuzco

2. Define: (a) maize, (b) hieroglyphics, (c) aqueduct

COMPREHENSION

3. What were the main accomplishments of the Mayan civilization?

4. What were the main accomplishments of the Aztec civilization?

5. What were the main accomplishments of the Incan civilization?

CRITICAL THINKING AND WRITING

6. **Exploring the Main Idea** Review the Main Idea statement at the beginning of this section. Then, describe some of the ways that the ancient civilizations of the Mayas, Aztecs, and Incas influenced Latin America's present-day cultures.

7. **Distinguishing Fact from Opinion** Tell if the following statements are facts or opinions. Explain why.

(a) Mayan calendars were very accurate. (b) Aztec civilization was more important than Mayan civilization.

ACTIVITY

 Take It to the NET

8. **Exploring Early Latin American Civilizations** Imagine you are an archeologist and examine some of the artifacts you see on the Web site. Interpret the object's use or purpose, and how it represents the culture. Visit the World Explorer: People, Places, and Cultures section of **phschool.com** for help in completing this activity.

European Exploration
Short and Long Term Effects

BEFORE YOU READ

READING FOCUS

1. Why did Europeans sail to the Americas?
2. What were some of the short-term effects of European exploration in Latin America?
3. What were some of the long-term effects of European rule over Native Americans in the region?

KEY TERMS

Treaty of Tordesillas
treaty
Line of Demarcation
conquistador
mestizo
hacienda

KEY PEOPLE

Hernán Cortés
Christopher Columbus
Moctezuma
Francisco Pizarro

NOTE TAKING

Copy the chart below. As you read the section, fill in the chart with information about the causes and effects of Spain's colonization of Latin America.

MAIN IDEA

As European explorers expanded their wealth and claimed land in Latin America for their countries, their exploration and conquests damaged many Native American civilizations.

Early Navigation

SCIENCE AND TECHNOLOGY

Sailors in the 1400s guided their ships using only the stars, a compass, and an astrolabe. Above is a drawing of an astrolabe. **Critical Thinking** Why did sailors use the stars? How could they do that?

Setting the Scene

Hernán Cortés was the Spanish soldier who conquered the Aztecs. He landed in Mexico in 1519 and soon met Malinche (mah LIHN chay), the daughter of a Mayan leader. Malinche quickly learned Spanish and became Cortés's main translator. She also kept an eye on Aztec spies. Without Malinche, Cortés could not have conquered the Aztecs.

Europeans Arrive in the Americas

In the 1400s, Spain and Portugal searched for new trade routes to Asia. They knew that in Asia they would find expensive goods such as spices and silks that could be traded for a profit.

Explorer **Christopher Columbus** thought he could reach Asia by sailing west across the Atlantic Ocean. Columbus knew the world was round, but he believed the distance around the world was shorter than it was.

Columbus asked Spain to sponsor a voyage, and he set sail in early August 1492. On October 12, he spotted land. Columbus thought he had reached the East Indies in Asia, so he described the people there as Indians. In fact, the land he saw was an island in the Caribbean Sea.

Spain and Portugal soon became fierce rivals. Each country tried to stop the other from claiming land in the Americas. In 1494, Spain and Portugal signed the **Treaty of Tordesillas** (tor day SEE yas). A **treaty** is an agreement in writing made between two or more countries. The treaty set an imaginary line from the North Pole to the South Pole at about 50° longitude, called the **Line of Demarcation.** It gave Spain the right to settle and trade west of the line. Portugal could do the same east of the line. The only part of South America that is east of the line is roughly the eastern half of present-day Brazil. Because of the Treaty of Tordesillas, the language and background of Brazil are Portuguese.

Spanish explorers heard stories of wealthy kingdoms in the Americas where they hoped to find gold and other treasures. Spanish rulers did not pay for the trips of the explorers. Instead, they gave the **conquistadors** (kon KEES ta dors), or conquerors, the right to hunt for treasure. In exchange, conquistadors agreed to give Spain one fifth of any treasures they found.

Cortés Conquers the Aztecs

In 1519, Hernán Cortés sailed to the coast of Mexico in search of treasure. He brought a small army of 500 men and 16 horses with him. The Aztec ruler **Moctezuma** (mahk tuh ZOOM uh) heard that a strange ship was offshore and sent spies to find out about it. The spies, who had never seen horses before, described the Spanish as "supernatural creatures riding on hornless deer, armed in iron, fearless as gods." Moctezuma thought Cortés might be a god.

When Cortés and his soldiers arrived in Tenochtitlán, Moctezuma welcomed them. But the peace did not last. Spanish soldiers killed some Aztecs and a bloody battle began. Moctezuma was killed, and with the help of native groups who were enemies of the Aztecs, Cortés surrounded and attacked Tenochtitlán. In 1521, the Aztecs surrendered after nearly 240,000 Aztecs and 30,000 of Cortés's allies had died. The Aztec Empire lay in ruins.

Pizarro Conquers the Incas **Francisco Pizarro** (fran SIS koh pih ZAR oh), like Cortés, was a Spanish conquistador. He heard stories about the rich Incan kingdom in South America, so in 1531, Pizarro set sail with a small force of 180 Spanish soldiers. Pizarro captured and killed the Incan emperor and other leaders. By 1535, Pizarro had conquered most of the Incan empire, including the capital, Cuzco.

Within 15 years, the conquistadors defeated the two most powerful empires in the Americas. They had guns, cannons, and horses that Native Americans had never seen. The Europeans also carried diseases, such as smallpox, that wiped out entire villages.

A Court Welcome

HISTORY This historical painting shows Moctezuma welcoming Cortés to his court. **Critical Thinking** Based on this painting, what conclusions can you draw about Aztec wealth?

Colonization

By the 1540s, Spain claimed land throughout much of the Americas. Spain's lands stretched from what today is Kansas all the way south to the tip of South America. Brazil was claimed by Portugal.

Spain Organizes Its Empire   Spain divided its territory into provinces and set up a strong government. The two most important provinces were New Spain and Peru. The capital of New Spain was Mexico City and Lima became the capital city of Peru.

The most powerful citizens lived in the center of Lima. They either came from Spain or had Spanish parents. **Mestizos,** people of mixed Spanish and Native American descent, lived on the outskirts of the city. Native Americans, the least powerful class, continued to live in the countryside. The Spanish forced them to work on haciendas. A **hacienda** (hah see EN duh) was a plantation owned by Spaniards or the Catholic Church.

The Effect of European Rule   Spain gave its settlers rights to demand taxes or labor from Native Americans. Many Native Americans died from overwork, malnutrition, and European diseases. In 1519, New Spain had a Native American population of 25 million. Only 3 million survived the first 50 years of Spanish rule.

A Family in the Americas

CULTURE   This painting shows a Native American man, his Mestizan wife, and their child.   **Critical Thinking** What do you think the family in this painting is doing?

SECTION 2 ASSESSMENT

AFTER YOU READ

RECALL

1. Identify : (a) Hernán Cortés, (b) Christopher Columbus, (c) Moctezuma, (d) Francisco Pizarro

2. Define: (a) Treaty of Tordesillas, (b) treaty, (c) Line of Demarcation, (d) conquistador, (e) mestizo, (f) hacienda

COMPREHENSION

3. What did European explorers originally hope to achieve by sailing west across the Atlantic Ocean?

4. What were the short-term effects of European exploration of Latin America?

5. How did Spanish colonization affect Native Americans?

CRITICAL THINKING AND WRITING

6. **Exploring the Main Idea** Review the Main Idea statement at the beginning of this section. Then, write a paragraph listing some of the factors that led to the decline of Native American cultures in the Americas.

7. **Recognizing Bias** Native Americans were not asked about the Treaty of Tordesillas, though it directly affected their lives. What do you think this says about European attitudes toward Native Americans?

ACTIVITY

8. **Writing to Learn** Write two paragraphs: one by a Native American who has just seen a European for the first time and another by a European who has just seen a Native American for the first time.

Independence and the Spread of Democracy

BEFORE YOU READ

READING FOCUS

1. How did Latin American nations win independence from their European rulers?
2. How did the American and French revolutions influence events in Latin America?
3. What are some of the challenges Latin America faced as a result of gaining independence?

KEY TERMS

revolution
criollo
caudillo
invest
economy

KEY PEOPLE

Toussaint L'Ouverture
Miguel Hidalgo
Agustín de Iturbide
Simón Bolívar
José de San Martín

NOTE TAKING

Copy the chart below. As you read the section, fill in the chart with information about how and when Latin American countries gained independence.

Late 1770s: British colonies in North America revolt for freedom from British rule

Late 1780s: French citizens revolt against royal rulers

Criollos in Latin America become interested in revolutions

| Haiti | Mexico | Western South America | Brazil |

MAIN IDEA

Inspired by revolutions in other countries, Latin American countries fought for and gained their independence from European rule.

Setting the Scene

The first colony in Latin America to start a revolution was Saint-Domingue (san duh MANG) in the Caribbean. Tired of French colonial rule and mistreatment by white masters, and led by a former slave, **Toussaint L'Ouverture** (too SAN loo vur TOOR), the slaves there fought for 10 years and finally gained independence in 1804. They called their new country Haiti.

The flame of liberty sparked in Haiti soon spread across Latin America. By 1825, most of the region was independent. Latin Americans would no longer be ruled by Europe.

Independence in Mexico

Haiti's leaders drew encouragement from two famous revolutions. One type of **revolution** is a political movement in which the people overthrow a government and set up another. During the 1770s and early 1780s, the 13 British colonies in North America fought a war to free themselves from Britain's rule. In 1789, the common people of France staged a violent uprising against their royal rulers. These actions inspired not only the people of Haiti, but also people across Latin America.

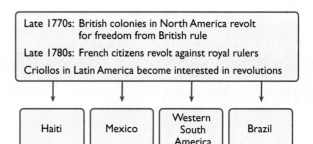

HISTORY Toussaint L'Ouverture was captured by the French, but his followers won Haiti's independence. **Critical Thinking** What qualities do you think make a hero? Why?

Haitian Independence

AS YOU READ

Draw Conclusions
What do you think the attitude of Mexican criollos was toward the revolution?

Criollos (kree OH yohz) paid particular attention to these events. A **criollo** had Spanish parents, but had been born in Latin America. Criollos often were the wealthiest and best-educated people in the Spanish colonies but few criollos had any political power because only people born in Spain could hold government office.

The "Cry of Dolores" Mexico began its struggle for self-government in 1810. **Miguel Hidalgo** (mee GEHL ee DAHL goh) led the way. He was a criollo priest in the town of Dolores. With other criollos in Dolores, he planned to begin a revolution.

In September 1810, the Spanish government discovered Hidalgo's plot. But before the authorities could arrest him, Hidalgo took action. He wildly rang the church bells. A huge crowd gathered. "Recover from the hated Spaniards the land stolen from your forefathers," he shouted.

Hidalgo's call for revolution became known as the "Cry of Dolores." It attracted some 80,000 fighters in a matter of weeks, mostly mestizos and Native Americans. They wanted revenge against the Spanish government. The rebels won some victories, but their luck changed and by the beginning of 1811, they were in full retreat. Hidalgo tried to flee the country but was captured. He was tried, convicted of treason, and executed in July 1811.

The Cry of Dolores

CULTURE Father Hidalgo made the "Cry of Dolores" on September 16. Mexico celebrates every year on that day. **Critical Thinking** Why do you think that the painter of this mural included so many people in the background behind Father Hidalgo? What can you tell about these people?

Independence Finally Comes Small rebel groups kept fighting. Then **Agustín de Iturbide** (ee toor BEE day) joined the rebels. He was a high-ranking officer in the Spanish army. Many people who had opposed the rebellion felt they could trust Iturbide to protect their interests. They decided to support the rebellion and in 1821, Iturbide defeated the Spanish and declared Mexico independent.

South American Independence

Simón Bolívar (see MOHN boh LEE vahr) almost certainly was the greatest Latin American revolutionary leader.

Bolívar joined the fight for Venezuelan independence in 1804. Six years later he became its leader. By 1822, Bolívar's troops had freed a large area from Spanish rule (the future countries of Colombia, Venezuela, Ecuador, and Panama). This newly liberated region formed Gran Colombia. Bolívar became its president.

José de San Martín (san mahr TEEN), an Argentine, had lived in Spain and served in the Spanish army. When Argentina began its fight for freedom, he quickly offered to help. In 1817, he led his soldiers through the high passes in the Andes into Chile. This bold action took the Spanish completely by surprise and in a matter of months, Spain was defeated. San Martín declared Chile's independence. Then he turned his attention to Peru.

Again, San Martín took an unexpected action. This time, he attacked from the sea. In July 1821, San Martín pushed inland and seized Lima, the capital of Peru.

A year later, San Martín met with Bolívar to discuss the fight for independence. Afterward, San Martín suddenly gave up his command and left Bolívar to continue the fight alone. Eventually, Bolívar drove the remaining Spanish forces out of South America altogether. By 1825, only Cuba and Puerto Rico were still ruled by Spain.

Brazil Takes a Different Route to Freedom   In the early 1800s, French armies invaded Spain and Portugal. Portugal's royal family fled to Brazil for safety. The king returned to Portugal in 1821, and left his son, Dom Pedro, to rule the colony. Dom Pedro declared Brazil independent in 1822. Three years later, Portugal quietly admitted that Brazil was independent.

Challenges of Independence

After winning independence from Europe in the mid-1800s, Latin American leaders faced hard challenges and had to decide how to govern their nations. Bolívar set the standard for Latin American leaders, most of whom were **caudillos** (kow DEE yohs), military officers who ruled very strictly with unlimited powers. Unlike Bolívar, though, most caudillos just wanted to stay in power and get rich. Following years of fighting and now under strict control, Latin American nations were very poor.

Agriculture and the Economy
ECONOMICS
Many large-scale farming operations in Latin America are still foreign-owned. **Critical Thinking** How would having many foreign-owned farming operations affect a country's economy?

Building Televisions on an Assembly Line

ECONOMICS In the last 50 years, Latin American countries have begun to produce many more products in factories like this one in Brazil. **Critical Thinking** What skills do you think these factory workers need?

Economic Issues

In the 1900s, many foreign companies **invested**—spent money to earn more money—in Latin America. As a result, foreign companies became powerful in Latin American **economies**—the ways that goods and services are produced and made available to people. Foreign companies made huge profits without helping Latin American economies.

In the 1970s, Latin American countries began to build their own factories and to grow different kinds of crops to develop their resources. But in the 1980s, the price of oil to run factories rose and prices for Latin American goods dropped. Latin American countries spent more money but were making less, forcing them to borrow money and causing huge foreign debt. In some Latin American countries, these economic problems became too much for the people to bear. In Argentina, for example, debt, unemployment, and other economic problems caused riots in the streets and forced the Argentinian president to resign in 2000.

Today, Latin American countries continue to expand their economies. Foreign countries still invest in Latin America, but most Latin American countries now limit how investments can be made. Recently, Latin American countries have also tried to improve their economies by cooperating with one another in trade organizations, such as the North American Free Trade Agreement (NAFTA) between Mexico, The United States, and Canada. Efforts to improve the economies and welfare of the people in Latin America continue.

SECTION 3 ASSESSMENT

AFTER YOU READ

RECALL

1. Identify: (a) Toussaint L'Ouverture, (b) Miguel Hidalgo, (c) Agustín de Iturbide, (d) Simón Bolíver, (e) José de San Martín

2. Define: (a) revolution, (b) criollo, (c) caudillo, (d) invest, (e) economy

COMPREHENSION

3. Describe how Latin American countries won their independence.

4. What world events influenced the independence movement in Latin America?

5. What steps did Latin American countries take to improve their economies after winning independence?

CRITICAL THINKING AND WRITING

6. **Exploring the Main Idea** Review the Main Idea statement at the beginning of this section. Then, list some of the political and economic challenges faced by the new, independent countries of Latin America.

7. **Making Predictions** Write a paragraph explaining what you think might have happened to Latin American economies if the countries had not gained independence and had stayed under colonial rule.

ACTIVITY

8. **Writing to Learn** Imagine you are a poet and have been asked to write a patriotic poem for a newly independent country in Latin America. Write a poem about the country's independence. Be sure to include the country's name and details about its struggle for independence.

Making Decisions

IDENTIFY THE SITUATION

GATHER INFORMATION

CONSIDER THE OPTIONS
Option 1
Option 2
Option 3

PREDICT THE CONSEQUENCES
1.
2.
3.

MAKE A DECISION

Learn the Skill

Making good decisions requires thought and effort. To make good decisions, follow these steps:

A. Identify the Situation. Make sure you have a clear picture of the issues involved. It is sometimes helpful to write out the situation, explaining reasons why it needs to be considered and what needs to be changed.

B. Gather Information. To clarify the issues further, it is helpful to collect specific information about the situation being considered. A situation develops over the course of time. Often this history—the history of the situation—can offer facts that will aid you in making your decision.

C. Consider the Options. Before jumping to conclusions and acting too quickly, take some time to write down several options, or different possible courses of action. When Christopher Columbus wanted to find a better trade route to the East, he probably considered several different routes. Brainstorming as many ideas as possible and writing them down will give you more information to work with.

D. Predict the Consequences. Think about each option and the possible consequences of each action. Write down the risks as well as the outcome not only for yourself, but for everyone involved. Some decisions affect not only you but your family, school, and community. Others, such as which candidate to vote for or which political issue to support, may affect your entire state or country. It's better to know these possible outcomes before your decision is made.

E. Make a Decision. Choose one of the options. Using what you have learned, decide what action to take that is best for everyone involved. The best decision is not always the easiest solution or the one that brings the quickest results. Choose the one that will best solve the problem in the long run.

Practice the Skill

Miguel Hidalgo began a revolution that led to Mexican independence. No doubt this priest struggled with his decision to rally the people to war. He may have pondered his decision over a period of months or even years. Think about the decision he made and examine it in light of the five decision-making steps. What was the situation? What were the options? Consider the consequences of each option. Tell why you think Hidalgo made the decision he did. Do you think he made the right decision? Tell why or why not.

Apply the Skill

See the Chapter Review and Assessment at the end of this chapter for more questions on making decisions.

Review and Assessment

Creating a Chapter Summary

On a separate piece of paper, draw a diagram like this one, and include the information that summarizes the first section of the chapter. Then, fill in the second and third boxes with summaries of Sections 2 and 3.

LATIN AMERICA: SHAPED BY HISTORY

Section 1
Three advanced civilizations—those of the Mayas, Aztecs, and Incas—existed in Latin America before the arrival of Europeans. Each had its own important cultural practices and institutions.

Section 2

Section 3

Reviewing Key Terms

Match the definitions in Column I with the key terms in Column II.

Column I

1. a pipe or channel designed to carry water from a distant source
2. conqueror
3. a kind of writing, using signs and symbols
4. a political movement in which people overthrow the government and set up another
5. people of mixed Spanish and Native American descent
6. the ways in which goods and services are produced and made available

Column II

a. revolution
b. conquistador
c. hieroglyphics
d. economy
e. aqueduct
f. mestizo

Reviewing the Main Ideas

1. Name one major accomplishment of each of the Mayan, Aztec, and Incan civilizations. (Section 1)
2. Give two examples of how the Mayan, Aztec, or Incan civilizations affect culture in Latin America today. (Section 1)
3. How were the Incas able to change their environment in order to grow more food? (Section 1)
4. List two ways in which the Mayan and Aztec civilizations were alike. (Section 1)
5. Why did Spain gain control over most of Latin America while Portugal gained control over only Brazil? (Section 2)
6. What role did the criollos play in the fight for Latin American independence? (Section 3)
7. How have many Latin American countries been trying to improve their economies in recent years? (Section 3)

Map Activity

For each civilization or place listed below, write the letter from the map that shows its location.

1. Andes

2. Incan civilization

3. Mayan civilization

4. Aztec civilization

 Take It to the NET

> **Enrichment** For more map activities using geography skills, visit the social studies section of **phschool.com**.

Writing Activity

1. Writing a Song The Mayas, Aztecs, and Incas had spoken histories. Information is passed from generation to generation in stories and songs. Imagine that you lived at the time of the Spanish conquest. Write a song that tells about the conquest from a Mayan, Aztec, or Incan point of view.

2. Writing a Journal You are supporter of Miguel Hidalgo who has just heard the "Cry of Dolores." Write a journal entry telling how you feel about Hidalgo's efforts toward making Mexico an independent nation, free of Spanish rule.

Critical Thinking

1. Recognizing Cause and Effect What were two causes of the fall of the Aztec and Incan civilizations? What were two long-term effects of European rule on the Native American people of the region?

2. Recognizing Point of View Hidalgo shouted to the people, "Recover from the hated Spaniards the land stolen from your forefathers!" Why would criollos, who had Spanish parents but who had been born in Latin America, be sympathetic to his cry for freedom from Spain?

 Take It to the NET

Activity Read about the conquistadors and early civilizations in Latin America. How have the conquistadors influenced life in present-day Latin America? Visit the World Explorer: People, Places, and Cultures section of **phschool.com** for help in completing this activity.

Chapter 10 Self-Test As a final review activity, take the Chapter 10 Self-Test and get instant feedback on your answers. To take the test, visit the Social Studies section of **phschool.com**.

Applying Your Skills

Turn to the Skills for Life page to answer the following questions.

1. During which step of the decision-making process would you ponder the consequences of your actions?

    a. Identify the Situation   **b.** Gather Information

    c. Consider the Options   **d.** Predict the Consequences

    e. Make a Decision

2. Identify an issue in your life for which you must make a decision, such as what topic to choose for a special report. Use the steps in the decision-making process to make your decision. Finally, write a list of action steps you would take to implement your decision.

LATIN AMERICA:
Rich in Culture

"Wind and Water and Stone" by Octavio Paz

*The water hollowed the stone,
the wind dispersed the water,
the stone stopped the wind.
Water and wind and stone.*

*The wind sculpted the stone,
the stone is a cup of water,
the water runs off and is wind,
Stone and wind and water.*

*The wind sings in its turnings,
the water murmurs as it goes,
the motionless stone is quiet.
Wind and water and stone.*

*One is the other, and is neither;
among their empty names
they pass and disappear,
water and stone and wind.*

UNDERSTANDING LITERATURE

Analyzing Poetry

A poet often attempts to give meaning to something through the words he or she uses. The poet, Octavio Paz, shows the relationship between wind, water, and stone in this poem. Reread the poem and then choose one of the poem's four stanzas and draw or paint a picture that you think captures the images used in this poem. You might recreate the scene as the poet describes it, or use symbolism or abstract art to illustrate the stanza.

Creating a Poem

Read the poem by Octavio Paz again. What do you think the poet is saying about the relationship between wind, water, and stone? How do these three elements relate to each other? Think of other elements in nature that have a close relationship, such as the ocean's tides and the beach, clouds and rain, or sun and light. Write a poem that illustrates such a relationship, using images from nature.

The Cultures of Mexico

BEFORE YOU READ

READING FOCUS

1. What are three of the cultures that influence Mexico?
2. What population trends affect Mexico today?
3. What economic factors have caused emigration from Mexico to the United States?

KEY TERMS

campesinos
rural
urban
maquiladora
emigrate

KEY PLACES

Mexico City

NOTE TAKING

Copy the concept web below. As you read the section, fill in the web with information about the culture of Mexico. Add more ovals as you need them.

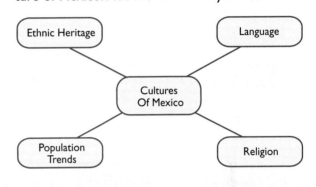

Ethnic Heritage — Language
Cultures Of Mexico
Population Trends — Religion

MAIN IDEA

Mexico's diverse peoples are affected by shifting population patterns and economic circumstances.

Setting the Scene

Modern Mexico is greatly influenced by its past. For centuries it was the home of advanced, ancient Native American civilizations. When the Spanish colonized the region in the 1500s, they brought their language, religion, architecture, and music with them. The combination of these two cultures gave rise to another culture, the mestizo. Mexico blends these cultures.

Mexico's Cultural Influences

Mestizos have both Spanish and indigenous ancestors. About 20 percent of the people of Mexico are indigenous people, but Spanish is the first language for most Mexicans. Some Mexicans also speak Native American languages.

Religion is important to the people of Mexico. In the 1500s and 1600s, Spanish Catholic missionaries converted many Native Americans to Christianity and the Roman Catholic Church has been important to this region ever since. Native Americans, however, have blended many elements of their religions with Christianity.

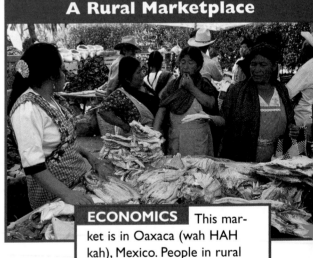

A Rural Marketplace

ECONOMICS This market is in Oaxaca (wah HAH kah), Mexico. People in rural Mexico buy many of their groceries and housewares from markets like these. **Critical Thinking** What details in this photograph show similarities between rural markets and urban supermarkets? What details show differences?

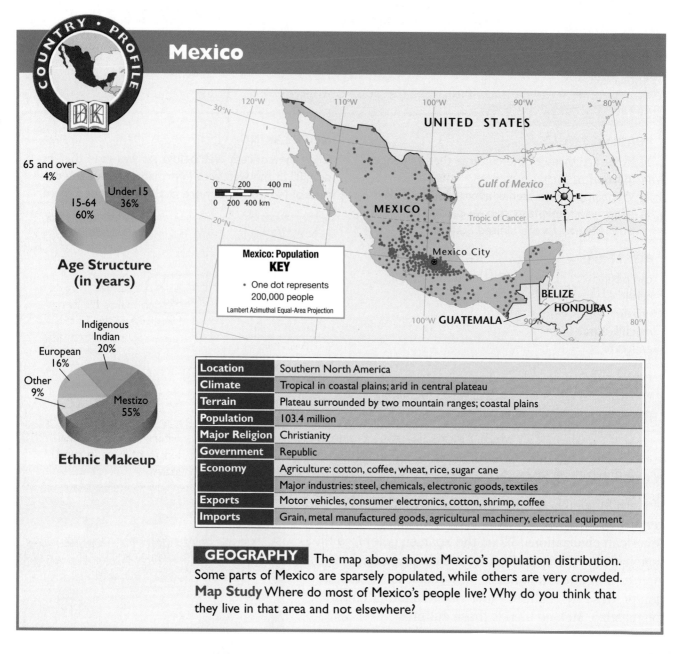

Age Structure (in years)

- 65 and over 4%
- Under 15 36%
- 15-64 60%

Ethnic Makeup

- Indigenous Indian 20%
- European 16%
- Other 9%
- Mestizo 55%

Mexico: Population KEY
- One dot represents 200,000 people

Lambert Azimuthal Equal-Area Projection

Location	Southern North America
Climate	Tropical in coastal plains; arid in central plateau
Terrain	Plateau surrounded by two mountain ranges; coastal plains
Population	103.4 million
Major Religion	Christianity
Government	Republic
Economy	Agriculture: cotton, coffee, wheat, rice, sugar cane
	Major industries: steel, chemicals, electronic goods, textiles
Exports	Motor vehicles, consumer electronics, cotton, shrimp, coffee
Imports	Grain, metal manufactured goods, agricultural machinery, electrical equipment

GEOGRAPHY The map above shows Mexico's population distribution. Some parts of Mexico are sparsely populated, while others are very crowded. **Map Study** Where do most of Mexico's people live? Why do you think that they live in that area and not elsewhere?

Changing Population Patterns

Most farm families in Mexico are poor. The poor farmers, who are known as **campesinos** (kahm peh SEE nohs), plow the land and harvest their crops by hand because they cannot afford expensive equipment.

Although some people of Mexico live in **rural,** or countryside, areas, about 74 percent live in cities and large towns. Mexico's population has risen dramatically over the last 20 years, growing at a rate of more than two percent each year—a rate that will cause the poulation to double in 20 to 30 years. Rapid population growth makes it hard for young people in rural areas to find jobs and many leave home to look for work in **urban,** or city, areas.

Many people have moved from rural areas to **Mexico City,** Mexico's largest city. If you count the people in all the outlying areas,

Mexico City has more than 23 million people. There are many contrasts between the lives of city dwellers in Mexico City. Wealthy people in Mexico City have a lifestyle similar to that of wealthy people in the United States. For the poor, however, life in the city can be very hard.

Economics and Emigration

Some people in Mexico move to towns along the border with the United States. There they can work in factories owned by American companies, but located in Mexico because wages are lower than in the United States. These border factories are called **maquiladoras** (ma kee la DOR as).

As people flood into Mexican cities and border towns, jobs become scarcer and some people have decided to emigrate. **Emigrate** means to move permanently from one country to another. Thousands of people have emigrated from Mexico to the United States. Some of these emigrants enter the United States illegally, a problem that the U.S. and Mexican governments are attempting to solve.

Fermin Carrillo (fair MEEN kah REE yoh) is one worker who did just that. Because there were no more jobs and his parents needed food and medical care, he left his hometown in Mexico and moved to Oregon. He found work in a fish processing plant and sends most of the money he earns home to his parents.

Rural and Urban Living

ECONOMICS

Above, a farmer in rural Mexico makes his living by raising alfalfa. To the left, people hurry to destinations in Mexico City. **Critical Thinking** How do you think the challenges of living in urban areas in Mexico might be different from the challenges of living in rural areas?

SECTION 1 ASSESSMENT

AFTER YOU READ

RECALL

1. Identify: (a) Mexico City

2. Define: (a) campesinos, (b) rural, (c) urban, (d) maquiladora, (d) emigrate

COMPREHENSION

3. What cultures influence Mexico today?

4. Why is the population in Mexico shifting from rural to urban areas?

5. Describe economic factors that have influenced emigration from Mexico to the United States.

CRITICAL THINKING AND WRITING

6. **Exploring the Main Idea** Review the Main Idea statement at the beginning of this section. Then write a paragraph telling how and why the population patterns in Mexico are changing.

7. **Supporting a Point of View** Write a journal entry from the point of view of a person moving from a rural to urban setting. Write about how the person's life has changed as a result of his or her move.

ACTIVITY

 Take It to the NET

8. **Mexican Culture and Cooking** Food and cooking are important aspects of Mexican culture. Cook some of the recipes you find on the Web site and sample some traditional Mexican food. Visit the World Explorer: People, Places, and Cultures section of **phschool.com** for help in completing this activity.

The Cultures of Central America

BEFORE YOU READ

1. What is the cultural heritage of the people of Central America?
2. How does religion affect the lives of Central Americans?
3. Why have many Central Americans moved to cities or to the United States?

KEY TERMS

diversity
injustice

KEY PLACES

Honduras

MAIN IDEA

There is great diversity and rich heritage among the cultures of Central America.

NOTE TAKING

Copy the Venn diagram below. As you read the section, fill in the diagram with information about rural and urban life in Central America.

Rural Life   Urban Life

Farming Methods

SCIENCE, TECHNOLOGY, AND SOCIETY

In El Salvador, many farmers do not have modern farming equipment. They use traditional wooden plows and oxen. **Critical Thinking** How might modern farming equipment change farming methods in El Salvador? How would this affect the economy?

Setting the Scene

Elvia Alvarado (el VEE ah ahl vah RAH doh) walks the back roads of rural **Honduras** to help poor campesinos make a living. Honduran campesinos, like rural people in all of Central America, have little land of their own. It is hard for them to make enough money to support their families.

Alvarado is a mother and grandmother and she works for an organization of campesinos. She helps people get loans to buy seeds and farm machinery and to get more land. She also works with community groups.

Alvarado's work is not easy. "The communities we work in are hard to get to," she says. "Sometimes I don't eat all day, and in the summertime the streams dry up and there's often no water to drink." Sometimes Alvarado does not get paid. "But I couldn't be happy if my belly was full while my neighbors didn't have a plate of beans and tortillas to put on the table," she says. "My struggle is for a better life for all Hondurans."

Cultural Heritage

Honduras, where Alvarado lives and works, is one of seven nations in Central America. Together these countries form a crooked, skinny isthmus. The isthmus links Mexico and South America.

One Region, Many Faces   There is much **diversity,** or variety, among the people of Central America. Hondurans, like Alvarado, are mostly mestizo with both Spanish and indigenous ancestors. About half of Guatemala's people are mestizo while the other half are indigenous. Many Costa Ricans are direct descendants of Spaniards, and more than half the people of Belize are of African or mixed African and European descent.

Spanish is the main language in six of the seven countries. However, these countries have many other languages. Guatemala is home to more than 20 languages. Spanish is the language of government and business, but the indigenous people in Guatemala speak their own languages, as do indigenous people in Panama, El Salvador, and Nicaragua. People in Belize speak English.

Religion and Citizenship

Religion is important to the people of Central America. Just as in Mexico, Spanish Catholic missionaries who came to Central America in the 1500s and 1600s converted many Native Americans to Christianity. Today, most Central Americans are Catholic but some Native American religions also blend elements of their traditional religions with Christianity.

The Roman Catholic Church fights injustice in Central America. **Injustice** is the unfair treatment of people and often happens in countries with undemocratic governments. Examples of injustice include people having their property taken away from them and people being imprisoned without first having a fair trial. Catholic clergy members work for the fair treatment of the people, and many citizens take their own steps to end poverty and injustice.

Art and Heritage

CULTURE   The people of El Salvador are mostly mestizo, and this mixed heritage often is reflected in their art. **Critical Thinking** Why would people choose to reflect their mixed heritage in the art they create?

Harvesting Crops

ECONOMICS

Many immigrants from Central America come to the United States to find jobs on farms, harvesting crops. The worker in the photograph is harvesting broccoli in Texas' Rio Grande Valley. **Critical Thinking** Why must people who make a living harvesting crops move around so often?

A Search for Economic Opportunity

Much like the population of Mexico, Central America's population is growing rapidly. The population has increased dramatically in both the rural and urban areas. As the population expands in rural areas, many campesinos have decided that making a living from the land is just too difficult. They have left the land and gone to the cities in the hopes of finding better economic opportunities. This move has resulted in the rapid growth in the populations of large cities, where populations have increased the most.

In the cities, the wealthy people live in big houses on wide streets. They send their children to good schools and can afford to pay for medical care. For the poor, however, city life is difficult since there is a housing shortage. Rising prices have made living even more expensive. It is not easy to find work, or to feed a family.

Most people in Central America move somewhere else within their own country if they cannot find work. Some have left their countries to find work in places such as the United States. They have become immigrants, people who have moved into one country from another. Some of these immigrants want to remain in the countries to which they have moved. Others want to return home after earning some money to help their families.

Although some Central Americans have left the region in search of a better life, many more have followed Elvia Alvarado's example. They have stayed and begun to build a better life for themselves at home.

SECTION 2 ASSESSMENT

AFTER YOU READ

RECALL

1. Identify: (a) Honduras

2. Define: (a) diversity, (b) injustice

COMPREHENSION

3. (a) What are the main language and religion of the people of Central America? (b) How do the languages and religions of the region reflect Central America's history?

4. What role does religion play in the lives of Central Americans?

5. What is one reason that Central Americans are immigrating to the United States?

CRITICAL THINKING AND WRITING

6. Exploring the Main Idea Review the Main Idea statement at the beginning of this section. Then write a paragraph describing the diversity of cultures found in Central America.

7. Identifying Cause and Effect Imagine that you are an immigrant from Central America who has come to the United States. Write a journal entry telling about the reasons that led to your immigration and about the effects your immigration has had on you and your family.

ACTIVITY

8. Making a Cultural Map Make a map showing the countries of Central America and labeling each with the cultures found in that country. Include labels for major cities.

SECTION 3
The Cultures of the Caribbean

BEFORE YOU READ

READING FOCUS

1. How did European, African, and Native American cultures come together to create unique Caribbean cultures?
2. Which cultures influence the ethnic groups, religions, and languages found in the Caribbean today?
3. What are the key cultural elements that make up the present-day cultures of the Caribbean?

KEY TERMS

ethnic group
Carnival

KEY PLACES

Jamaica
Cuba
Trinidad and Tobago

MAIN IDEA

Caribbean lifestyles, music, foods, art, and entertainment are influenced by a rich blend of cultures.

NOTE TAKING

Copy the outline below. As you read the section, fill in the outline with information about the cultures of the Caribbean islands.

I. **Cultural Links with the Past**
   A. Native American, indigenous people
   B.
   C.
   D.
II. **Ethnic Variety and Cultural Traits**
   A. Race
   B. Language
   C. Religion
III. **Cultural Blend of Past and Present**
   A. Sports/Entertainment
   B. Food
   C. Caribbean Music
   D. Carnival

Setting the Scene

Dorothy Samuels is a ten-year-old from **Jamaica,** a tropical island in the Caribbean Sea. She lives in a village near the ocean and goes to a village school. She hopes one day to go to college in Kingston, Jamaica's capital city. Jamaican laws require that women have as much opportunity for education as men have.

Dorothy's family are farmers. They plant vegetables, fruits, and cocoa beans. Every Saturday, Dorothy's mother and grandmother take their fruits and vegetables to the market to sell. All the traders at the market are women.

The People and Cultures of the Caribbean

Many Jamaicans, like most Caribbean people, are descendants of enslaved Africans. Africans were brought to the Caribbean to work on sugar plantations built by Europeans. Today, a variety of cultures are found in this region.

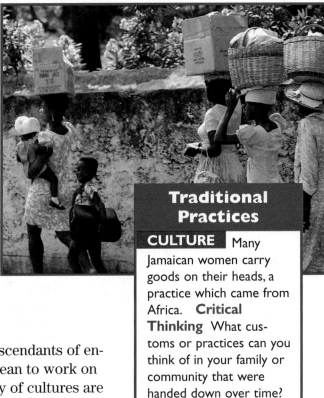

Traditional Practices

CULTURE Many Jamaican women carry goods on their heads, a practice which came from Africa. **Critical Thinking** What customs or practices can you think of in your family or community that were handed down over time?

AS YOU READ

Use Prior Knowledge
What ethnic groups do you think live in the Caribbean today?

The First People of the Caribbean

The island chain that makes up the Caribbean stretches some 2,000 miles (3,219 km) through the Caribbean Sea. Jamaica, like other Caribbean islands, has fertile soil and adequate rainfall that is especially good for sugar and cotton production. Small valleys produce fruits and vegetables.

Native Americans called the Ciboney (SEE boh nay) lived on the islands for thousands of years. In about 300 B.C., a South American group called Arawaks (AR ah wahks) joined them. In about A.D. 1000, another South American group called the Caribs (KA ribs) joined the population and gave the region its name. They lived there for more than 400 years before the first Europeans came to the area.

When Christopher Columbus landed on the Caribbean islands, he thought he had reached the Indies in Asia, so he called the native peoples there Indians. Columbus and other explorers, who sailed from Spain to the Caribbean islands, enslaved the Native Americans, and as a result, most of the Caribs, Arawaks, and other groups died of overwork and of diseases the Spanish brought with them. Today, just a few hundred Caribs still live on the island of Dominica.

Dutch, French, and English colonists followed the Spanish. They claimed territory in the 1600s and brought enslaved Africans to work on their plantations. The descendants of the Africans, Europeans, and of immigrants who came to the Caribbean from China, India, and the Middle East add to the rich blend of present-day Caribbean cultures.

Ethnic Variety and Cultural Traits   The Caribbean population has grown to about 37 million. Nearly one-third of these people live on the region's largest island, **Cuba.**

Because so many people came to the Caribbean as colonists, slaves, or immigrants, the area has great ethnic variety. An **ethnic group** is a group of people who share race, language, religion, or cultural traditions. The ethnic groups of the Caribbean are Native American, African, European, Asian, and Middle Eastern.

The people of the Caribbean islands speak one of several European languages or their language may be a mixture of European and African languages. Most West Indians are Christians, but there are also small groups of Hindus, Muslims, and Jews. Some people practice traditional African religions.

A Caribbean Family

CULTURE

Family life is very important to people in the Caribbean. This family, from Montserrat, British West Indies, is made up of parents and their children. Many people in the Caribbean live in family groups that also include grandparents, uncles, aunts, and cousins.

Critical Thinking

What members make up your family? How does your family compare to a Caribbean family?

A Cultural Blend of Past and Present

Caribbean culture is known for its liveliness. People play music, dance, and tell stories. People also play many sports. Baseball, soccer, and track and field are popular.

Food Caribbean food is a mixture from all the cultures of the islands. Caribbean people enjoy abundant seafood. Bammy—a bread made from the cassava plant—is still made the way the Arawaks made it. People also cook spicy curries from India, sausages from England, and Chinese dishes.

Music Caribbean music is famous around the world. Calypso, which originated in Trinidad and Tobago, is a form of song that often is played on steel drums. These instruments are made from recycled oil drums. A steel drum can be "tuned" so that different parts of it play different tones. Reggae is another popular form of music from the Caribbean, which originated in Jamaica.

Carnival Many islanders observe the Roman Catholic tradition of Lent, which is the period of 40 days before Easter Sunday. People consider Lent to be a very solemn time, so just before Lent they throw a huge party called **Carnival.**

Different countries celebrate Carnival in different ways. The biggest Carnival takes place in **Trinidad and Tobago.** People spend all year making costumes and floats. At 5 a.m. the Monday before Lent, people go into the streets in their costumes. Calypso bands play and thousands of fans follow the bands through the streets, dancing and celebrating. At the stroke of midnight Tuesday, the party stops. Lent has begun.

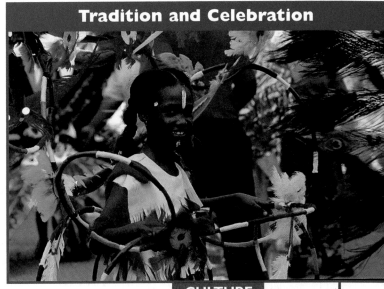

Tradition and Celebration

CULTURE Many people in Caribbean countries dress in lavish, colorful costumes to celebrate Carnival. **Critical Thinking** What similar celebrations take place in the United States?

SECTION 3 ASSESSMENT

AFTER YOU READ

RECALL

1. Identify: (a) Jamaica, (b) Cuba, (c) Trinidad and Tobago

2. Define: (a) ethnic group, (b) Carnival

COMPREHENSION

3. How did the Caribbean's unique cultures come together?

4. Which cultures have influenced the ethnic makeup, language, and religion of the Caribbean?

5. What are some of the customs that contribute to present-day Caribbean culture?

CRITICAL THINKING AND WRITING

6. **Exploring the Main Idea** Review the Main Idea statement at the beginning of this section. Then list at least four different cultures that influence the traditions, food, art, entertainment, and music found in the Caribbean.

7. **Making Comparisons** What common elements in their histories have shaped the cultures of the various Caribbean islands?

ACTIVITY

8. **Comparing Cultures** Select one aspect of Caribbean culture (food, music, religion, and so on) and take notes on what you have learned about it in this section. Then, write ways in which it is similar to and different from your own culture.

The Cultures of South America

BEFORE YOU READ

READING FOCUS

1. How has geography created diversity in South America?
2. How does farming shape the lives of South Americans?
3. How has rapid population growth affected the cities of South America?

KEY TERMS

subsistence farmer
import

KEY PLACES

Andes Mountains

MAIN IDEA

Within South America's four cultural regions, there is great diversity in lifestyles.

NOTE TAKING

Copy the chart below. As you read the section, fill in the chart with information about the different cultural regions of South America.

Cultural Regions of South America			
Colombia Venezuela Guyana Suriname French Guiana	Peru Ecuador Bolivia	Chile Argentina Uruguay Paraguay	Brazil

Setting the Scene

Between Peru and Bolivia is a deep lake called Lake Titicaca. It lies high in the **Andes Mountains.** This area is bitterly cold with few trees. Native Americans here make their living from totora reeds, a kind of thick, hollow grass that grows on the lakeshore. They use these reeds to make houses, boats, mats, hats, ropes, sails, toys, roofs, and floors. They eat the reeds, feed them to livestock, and brew them into tea. Totora reeds can even be made into medicine. Long ago, some Native American groups built floating islands with totora reeds. They used the islands to hide from the Incas. Today, some Native Americans live on floating islands.

Building Boats

CULTURE The Native Americans who live on Lake Titicaca use totora reeds to make boats. **Critical Thinking** What forms of transportation might the Native Americans use to travel through the Andes?

The People of South America

Most South Americans today are descended from Native Americans, Africans, or Europeans. In this way, they are like the people of Mexico and Central America. South America's history is also like that of its neighbors to the north. It was colonized mainly by Spain, so most South Americans speak Spanish and are Catholic. Each nation has its own unique culture, however.

Regions Within South America

There are four cultural regions in South America. The first region includes Colombia, Venezuela, Guyana, Suriname, and French Guiana, which are in the northern part of South America. They each border the Caribbean Sea. The cultures of these countries are like those of the Caribbean islands.

To the south and west, the culture is very different. Peru, Ecuador, and Bolivia are Andean countries. Many Native Americans live high in the Andes. In Bolivia, there are more indigenous people than mestizos. The Quechua and Aymara (eye MUH rah) people each speak their own languages.

The third cultural region consists of Chile, Argentina, and Uruguay. The long, thin country of Chile has mountains, beaches, deserts, forests, and polar regions. Most people in Chile are mestizos. The big cities of Argentina and Uruguay, however, are very diverse, and many different ethnic groups live there. Another culture exists on Argentina's Pampas, or plains. On the Pampas, gauchos (GOW chohz), or cowhands, herd cattle.

Brazil is South America's largest country and fourth region. Brazil was a colony of Portugal so its people speak Portuguese. However, Brazil is culturally diverse. Many Native Americans live in Brazil and so do people of African and mixed descent.

Rural and Urban Life

South America is made up of very large cities, along with numerous villages throughout the countryside. However, there are vast areas with hardly any people at all.

Farming in South America
Outside of Chile, Argentina, and Uruguay, most rural people with small plots of land are **subsistence farmers.** That means they grow only enough food for their families to eat. Farmers plant corn, beans, potatoes, and rice.

Raising Llamas in Peru

CULTURE Some of the indigenous people of the Andes raise llamas, a relative of the camel.
Critical Thinking How do you think the people of the Andes use llamas?

LINKS TO
Language Arts

Gabriela Mistral
Chilean poet Gabriela Mistral was awarded the Nobel Prize for Literature in 1945. But Mistral considered herself to be more a teacher than a writer. Mistral taught school in rural Chile in the early 1900s, but she was frustrated by the low quality of the textbooks that were available. In response, Mistral began to write poetry and prose for children.

Brasília: Brazilian Innovation

Brasília is a planned city. Some people think the layout of the city looks like a bow and arrow. Others think it looks like a jet plane. Government offices and shopping areas are located in the center of the city, where the two "wings" meet. The Plaza of the Three Powers is the center of government. The Presidential Palace is located at the tip of the city, on Lake Paranoa. The wings contain superblocks, or residential neighborhoods. Each includes 10 to 16 apartment buildings, a school, and shops.

Very large farms grow crops such as coffee, sugar, and cocoa, to export to other countries. Export farming uses so much land for cash crops that South America has to import food to eat. To **import** means to buy from another country.

The population of South America is booming. Latin America is the fastest-growing region in the world. Like Mexicans and Central Americans, South Americans cannot find enough jobs in rural areas. Every day, thousands of rural South Americans move to the cities looking for work.

Urban Issues The cities of South America illustrate the region's mix of cultures. Many major cities—Lima, Peru, and Buenos Aires, Argentina, for example—were built by Spanish colonists more than 400 years ago. Some of the buildings follow Native American designs. In contrast, modern office blocks and apartment buildings of concrete, steel, and glass tower above the downtown areas. Brasília, the Brazilian capital, was constructed in the 1950s. It was a completely planned city, designed to draw people to the country's interior.

By contrast, slums in many South American cities were unplanned. They are called favelas (FUH vez luz) in Brazil and barrios (BAR ee ohs) in Venezuela. As more and more people migrate into the cities they have ended up in these poor neighborhoods. City governments try to provide electricity and running water to everyone. But people move into cities so quickly that it is hard for city governments to keep up.

SECTION 4 ASSESSMENT

AFTER YOU READ

RECALL

1. Identify: Andes Mountains

2. Define: (a) subsistence farmer, (b) import

COMPREHENSION

3. Name two ways in which the geography of South America has shaped how people live.

4. How does farming contribute to the lives of the people and to the economies of South America?

5. What pressures does rapid population growth place on the cities of South America?

CRITICAL THINKING AND WRITING

6. **Exploring the Main Idea** Review the Main Idea statement at the beginning of this section. Then list the ways in which life differs in rural and urban areas of South America.

7. **Recognizing Cause and Effect** Write a paragraph explaining two causes and two effects of rapid population growth in the cities of South America.

ACTIVITY

8. **Creating a Travel Brochure** Design a travel brochure for a region in South America. Tell what countries a traveler might visit and what the people are like there. Include other facts that someone visiting might like to know. Illustrate your brochure with a drawing or a map.

Analyzing Images

Learn the Skill

Have you stopped to think about how the images around you communicate meaning? Understanding how images communicate meaning can help you analyze their messages. Follow these steps to help you analyze this image:

A. Identify the subject of the image. From looking at the painting, you can see that it depicts some kind of a celebration that is taking place in front of a church.

B. Look at the elements of design. Elements of design include line and color. Line refers to the overall shapes and patterns of elements in the image. Color is one of the most important elements in images. You can see that the painting above has very strong patterns of circles and lines. Also, by putting the church in the center of the painting, the artist draws the viewer's attention to it. In addition, the use of bright colors creates a very festive atmosphere.

C. Think about the purpose of the image. Why was the image created? Some images, such as advertisements, are created to persuade you to buy something or think a certain way. Other images, such as those in a magazine article, are meant to inform you about a topic. This painting was probably meant to entertain the viewer and capture the excitement of a celebration.

D. Respond to the image. Think about the feelings that the subject matter and design elements create in you. How does the image make you feel? Happy? Sad? Scared? In the painting above, the people dancing, the fireworks, and the bright colors work together to create a sense of joy and excitement in the viewer.

Practice the Skill

Turn to p. 190 in Chapter 10 of your book. Look at the mural of Father Hidalgo. Answer the following questions to help you analyze the image:

- What is the subject matter of this mural?
- What elements of design are in the mural? Pay careful attention to and describe the artist's use of line and color.
- Why do you think the artist created it?
- How does the mural make you feel? Why?

Apply the Skill

See the Chapter Review and Assessment at the end of this chapter for more questions on analyzing images.

CHAPTER 11 Review and Assessment

Creating a Chapter Summary

On a separate piece of paper, draw a chart like this one, and include the information that summarizes the first section of the chapter. Then, fill in the remaining boxes with information that summarizes what you learned about the cultures of Latin America.

Mexico	• The cultures of Mexico include Spanish, Native American, and mestizo influences. • Due to Mexico's increasing population, more people are searching for new places to live and make a living.
Central America	
Caribbean	
South America	

Reviewing Key Terms

Decide whether the definition for each term below is correct. If it is incorrect, rewrite the definition to correct it.

1. Campesinos are poor farmers who plant and harvest their crops by hand.

2. Maquiladoras are people who move permanently from Mexico to the United States.

3. Injustice is the unfair treatment of people.

4. A subsistence farmer grows only enough food to feed his or her family.

5. To import means to sell goods to another country.

Reviewing the Main Ideas

1. Name the predominant cultures of Mexico. (Section 1)

2. Name one way Mexico's population pattern is changing. (Section 1)

3. What are the main religion and language of Central America? (Section 2)

4. To which country are some Central Americans going to find jobs? (Section 2)

5. What blend of three cultures makes up a unique culture found in the Caribbean today? (Section 3)

6. Name some of the key elements of present-day Caribbean culture. (Section 3)

7. What are the three main cultural groups found in South America today? (Section 4)

8. Name one way the cities of South America have been affected by rapid population growth. (Section 4)

Map Activity

For each place listed below, write the letter from the map that shows its location.

1. Andes   5. Jamaica
2. Argentina   6. Mexico City
3. Brazil
4. Honduras

 Take It to the NET

Enrichment For more map activities using geography skills, visit the social studies section of **phschool.com**.

Writing Activity

1. **Writing a Magazine Article** In this chapter, you've taken a guided tour of the cultures of Latin America. Write an article for a travel magazine describing the "high points" of your tour. As you write, consider how historical events and geography influenced the region's culture.

2. **Writing a Dialogue** You are a young adult from a campesino family in Mexico who is planning to leave the farm to live in Mexico City. Write a dialogue between you and one of your parents as you explain why you think you need to go to the city.

Critical Thinking

1. **Making Comparisons** Consider these regions of Latin America: Mexico, Central America, the Caribbean, South America. What do the cultures of these regions have in common? How are they different?

2. **Recognizing Cause and Effect** What is the main reason that many Latin Americans move from rural to urban areas?

3. **Drawing Conclusions** In what ways are maquiladoras important to the economy of Mexico?

Applying Your Skills

Turn to the Skills for Life activity on p. 209 to help you complete the following activity.

With a partner, look through magazines and newspapers to find three or four images. Try to choose a variety of images—an advertisement, a photograph, and a drawing. Follow the steps you learned to analyze the images you chose.

 Take It to the NET

Activity Examine the paintings found on the Web site. Choose one and write a short description describing what is happening in the painting and what it tells you about the Mayan community. Visit the World Explorer: People, Places, and Cultures section of **phschool.com** for help in completing this activity.

Chapter 11 Self-Test As a final review activity, take the Chapter 11 Self-Test and get instant feedback on your answers. To take the test, visit the Social Studies section of **phschool.com**.

MEXICO AND CENTRAL AMERICA: Exploring the Region Today

Artistic Mexico

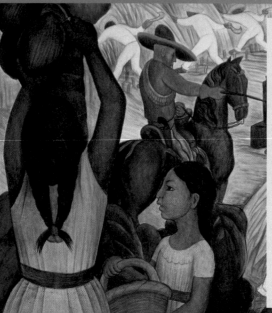

"The walls of the new Ministry of Education building were the great prize for any of the muralists, but it was Diego Rivera who seized his opportunity and through artistic skill, force of personality, and a ruthless will made himself the painter of Mexico. Here in the Ministry of Education, beginning on March 23, 1923, he created one of his undisputed masterpieces, and one of the enduring artistic triumphs of twentieth-century art..."

—Pete Hamill, *Diego Rivera*
(Harry N. Abrams, Inc. Publishers, 1999, p. 87)

Jose Diego Maria Rivera, "Sugar Cane," 1931. Fresco. 57 1/8 x 94 1/8 in. (145.1 x 239.1 cm). Philadelphia Museum of Art. Gift of Mr. and Mrs. Herbert Cameron Morris, 1943-46-2. (C)Banco de Mexico Diego Rivera Museum Trust.

USING BIOGRAPHY

If you visit any public buildings in Mexico, chances are you will see the work of Mexican artist Diego Rivera, best known for painting large wall murals. He chose as his themes his country's revolution and the social problems of the early 1900s.

Understanding Biographies

Read the excerpt from the biography of Diego Rivera. A biography is a book written about the life of a real person. What does this excerpt tell you about Diego Rivera?

Using Biographies

Choose a well-known person who is of interest to you, and find a biography written about that person. Make a list of questions that you would like to answer by reading the biography, such as, "Where did this person live?" "How was this person affected by where he or she lived?" "How did the influence of family and friends affect this person's life?" Read the biography and try to answer as many of the questions on your list as possible.

Mexico
Urban Migration

BEFORE YOU READ

READING FOCUS

1. Why have many Mexicans been moving from rural to urban areas?
2. What challenges do Mexicans from the country face when they build new lives in the city?
3. What environmental problems result when urban areas like Mexico City experience rapid population growth?

KEY TERMS

migrant farmworker
squatter

KEY PLACES

Mexico City

NOTE TAKING

Copy the table below. As you read the section, fill in the table with information about rural and urban life in Mexico.

Life in Rural Mexico: Benefits	Life in Rural Mexico: Drawbacks	Life in Urban Mexico: Benefits	Life in Urban Mexico: Drawbacks

MAIN IDEA

In recent times, many Mexicans have begun migrating to urban areas where they must meet the challenge of finding housing and jobs, and of living with pollution.

Setting the Scene

Ramiro Avila (rah MEE roh ah VEE lah) is one of seven children. He grew up in the state of Guanajuato (gwah nuh HWAH toh), in central Mexico. In his small village, Ramiro knew everyone and everyone knew him.

Ramiro's family were campesinos who owned no land. Even as a young child, Ramiro had to work to help support the family and he and his father had jobs as **migrant farmworkers.** Migrant farmworkers do not own land, but work on large farms owned by rich landowners and travel from one area to another, picking crops that are in season. Ramiro and his father made less than a dollar a day. There is not enough farm work for all the migrant workers, so many move to the cities because they cannot find work in the countryside.

Urban Migration to Mexico City

Ramiro's village is located in the southern part of the Mexican Plateau. This area has Mexico's best farmland, and is home to more than half of the country's people. Not surprisingly, it is the location of Mexico's largest city—**Mexico City.**

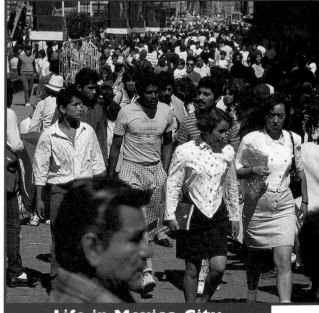

Life in Mexico City

CULTURE This photo shows people walking on a crowded street in Mexico City. **Critical Thinking** How do you think the challenges of living in a city might be different from the challenges of living in a rural area?

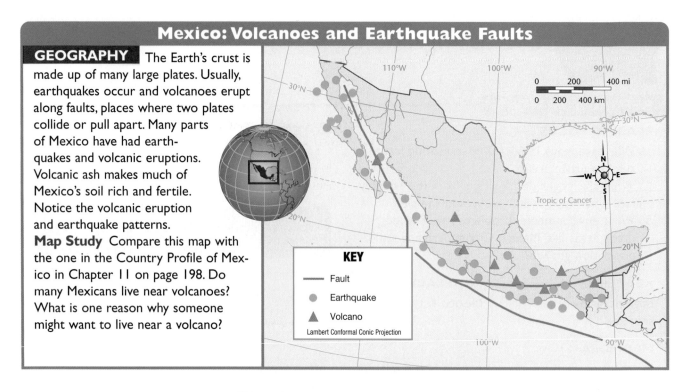

Mexico: Volcanoes and Earthquake Faults

GEOGRAPHY The Earth's crust is made up of many large plates. Usually, earthquakes occur and volcanoes erupt along faults, places where two plates collide or pull apart. Many parts of Mexico have had earthquakes and volcanic eruptions. Volcanic ash makes much of Mexico's soil rich and fertile. Notice the volcanic eruption and earthquake patterns.

Map Study Compare this map with the one in the Country Profile of Mexico in Chapter 11 on page 198. Do many Mexicans live near volcanoes? What is one reason why someone might want to live near a volcano?

KEY
— Fault
● Earthquake
▲ Volcano
Lambert Conformal Conic Projection

When Ramiro was 13, his parents decided to move the family to Mexico City where they hoped to find better work. The city was far away and their lives would be completely different, but moving offered them a chance to make a decent living.

Life in the City

Like thousands of other campesino families coming to the city, Ramiro's family did not have much money. When they arrived in Mexico City, they could not afford a house. They went to live in Colonia Zapata, which is one of many neighborhoods where poor people become **squatters.** That means they settle on someone else's land without permission. Many small houses of squatters cling to the sides of a steep hill in the Colonia. The older houses near the bottom of the hill are built of concrete. However, most people cannot afford to make sturdy houses when they first arrive. Therefore, many of the newer houses higher up the hill are constructed of scrap metal.

Ramiro's family made a rough, one-room house of rock. Ramiro felt that his new house was ugly. He and his family hoped that soon they would be able to buy land from the government. Then they could build a real house with a garden and a patio.

In Mexico City small neighborhoods of very wealthy people are tucked away from the rest of the city. But most of the residents are not wealthy. The poor live in all areas of the city, but many of the poorest, like Ramiro and his family, live on the outskirts. Some must travel hours each day to get to and from their jobs.

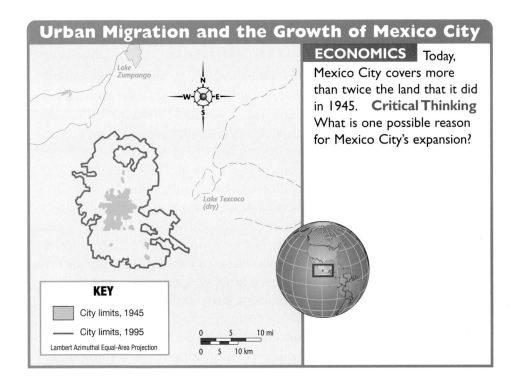

Urban Migration and the Growth of Mexico City

Lake Zumpango

Lake Texcoco (dry)

ECONOMICS Today, Mexico City covers more than twice the land that it did in 1945. **Critical Thinking** What is one possible reason for Mexico City's expansion?

KEY

City limits, 1945

City limits, 1995

Lambert Azimuthal Equal-Area Projection

0   5   10 mi

0   5   10 km

Mexico City is huge. Its population sprawls over a large area. It is a megacity, an urban center where many of Mexico's people live. Unlike most big cities, Mexico City does not have many skyscrapers and major streets. Two- and three-story buildings still form its downtown, and only a few streets are wide enough for the city's traffic. The subway, or underground railroad system, carries thousands of people each day.

Shortages and the Economy   Large cities offer many ways to make a living. Factories and offices employ millions of people. Ramiro works as a cook in a tiny restaurant from 7 A.M. to 2 P.M. For these seven hours of work he earns about $3. His mother and some of his brothers and sisters work, too. Ramiro's sister, Carmela, works as a street vendor. She sells juice at a stand in the bus station near their neighborhood. Every morning, she gets up at 5:30 to make juice from oranges and carrots. People on their way to work buy her juice for their long trip into the city.

Ramiro also goes to a school in Mexico City that holds night classes. After work, he attends classes until 9:30 at night.

Ramiro's father could not get a job in Mexico City. He decided to go to Texas in the United States. He found work as a migrant farmworker. He sends money home every month. It became Ramiro's job to look after his younger brothers and sisters while his father is gone. Ramiro's life is very different from how it had been in his village where life changed little over the years.

AS YOU READ

Monitor Your Reading What problems might occur as more people move into a city?

Pollution and the Environment

GEOGRAPHY Even on a sunny day, buildings a few blocks away appear dim and blurry in Mexico City because of heavy smog. **Critical Thinking** Why do you think Mexico City has so much smog? How can people living in Mexico City work to protect the environment from pollution?

Urban Growth and the Environment

The cities in Mexico have grown so large and so rapidly that they now face problems found in cities throughout the world. Mexico's capital and other large cities in the region are trying to deal with the problems of pollution and heavy traffic. Four million cars and trucks jam Mexico City's narrow streets and they compete with taxis, trolleys, and buses. Mexico City's geographic location causes pollution to be trapped close to the city. The city spreads across a bowl-shaped valley, and the mountains surrounding the valley stop winds from carrying away factory smoke, automobile exhaust fumes, and other pollution. The pollution creates smog that hangs over the city like a dark cloud.

Mexico City is not the only city that is growing. All of Mexico's major cities are becoming more crowded. This is especially true near Mexico's northern border, where the North American Free Trade Agreement (NAFTA) has greatly expanded trade between Mexico and the United States. People have moved to these cities for jobs in industries that export products across the border.

SECTION 1 ASSESSMENT

AFTER YOU READ

RECALL

1. Identify: (a) Mexico City

2. Define: (a) migrant farmworker, (b) squatter

COMPREHENSION

3. Why have many people from rural areas in Mexico been migrating to urban areas?

4. What are some of the problems that people from rural areas face when they move to Mexico City?

5. How has urban migration affected Mexico City's physical environment?

CRITICAL THINKING

6. **Exploring the Main Idea** Review the Main Idea statement at the beginning of this section. Then list two benefits and two drawbacks for people who leave Mexico's rural areas for its cities.

7. **Making Predictions** Write a paragraph about the future of Mexico City. Tell what you think will happen to the environment and to the city's residents as more and more people move there.

ACTIVITY

8. **Writing a Journal** Write an entry in your Explorer's Journal comparing and contrasting Ramiro's life with your own. How are your lives different? What similarities do you notice?

Guatemala and Nicaragua
Economic and Political Change

BEFORE YOU READ

READING FOCUS

1. What are the main issues that the indigenous people of Guatemala face?

2. What kinds of changes have been taking place in Guatemala recently?

3. What political events have led to Nicaragua's unstable economy?

KEY TERMS

ladino
political movement
strike
Creole
dictator
guerrilla

KEY PLACES

Guatemala
Nicaragua

MAIN IDEA

While the Maya people of Guatemala have struggled for hundreds of years to earn a voice in their government, in Nicaragua, the people struggle to keep the government and economy stable.

NOTE TAKING

Copy the outline below. As you read the section, complete the outline with information about Guatemala and Nicaragua.

> **I. Guatemala: Struggle for Land**
>   A. History
>   1.
>   2.
>   3.
>   4.
>   B. Mayas Struggle for Rights
>   1.
>   2.
>   3.
>   4.
> **II. Nicaragua: Changes in Government**
>   A. History
>   1.
>   2.
>   3.
>   B. Many Changes in Government
>   1.
>   2.

Setting the Scene

Many Latin American countries are working hard to keep their democratic republics alive. Struggles for land, conflicts among people, and changes in government are often part of everyday life. Two countries in Central America—**Guatemala** and **Nicaragua**—share similar histories. Both countries were conquered and colonized by the Spanish in the early 1500s. Yet their challenges are different.

The Struggle for Land in Guatemala

Guatemala has the largest population among Central American countries. The Native Americans are the majority of the population. They form 23 ethnic groups, each with its own language and customs. The largest group is the Quiche Maya.

In Guatemala, most Mayas live in the mountains because at one time it was the only land available to Native Americans. Most land in Guatemala belongs to a few rich landowners called **ladinos** (luh DEE nohs), mestizos who are descended from Native Americans and Spaniards.

Rural Challenges

ECONOMICS Most Mayas who live in the highlands of Guatemala have only small plots of land to farm. **Critical Thinking** What challenges face Mayas who have only small farms?

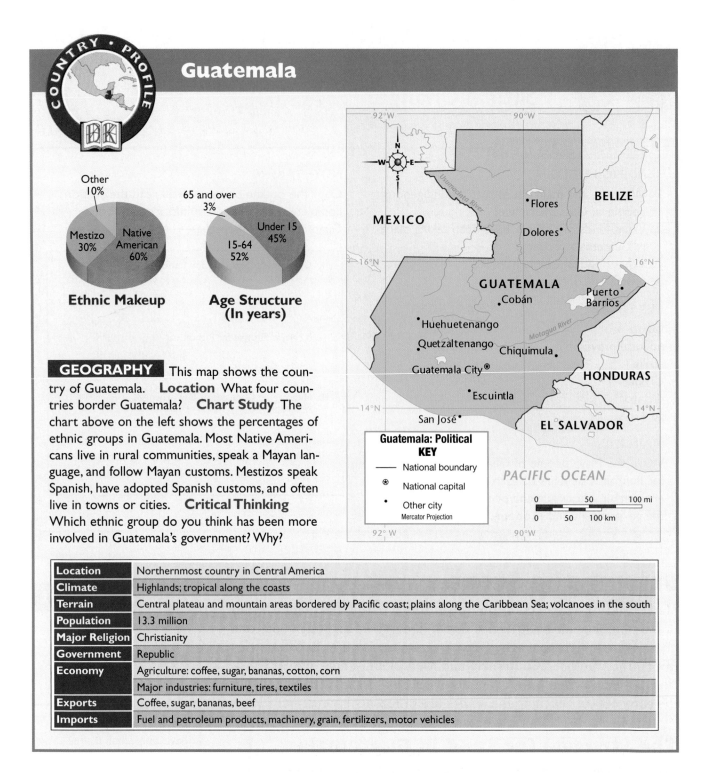

COUNTRY · PROFILE

Guatemala

Ethnic Makeup

Other 10%

Mestizo 30%

Native American 60%

Age Structure (In years)

65 and over 3%

Under 15 45%

15-64 52%

GEOGRAPHY This map shows the country of Guatemala. **Location** What four countries border Guatemala? **Chart Study** The chart above on the left shows the percentages of ethnic groups in Guatemala. Most Native Americans live in rural communities, speak a Mayan language, and follow Mayan customs. Mestizos speak Spanish, have adopted Spanish customs, and often live in towns or cities. **Critical Thinking** Which ethnic group do you think has been more involved in Guatemala's government? Why?

Guatemala: Political KEY

—— National boundary

⊛ National capital

• Other city

Mercator Projection

Location	Northernmost country in Central America
Climate	Highlands; tropical along the coasts
Terrain	Central plateau and mountain areas bordered by Pacific coast; plains along the Caribbean Sea; volcanoes in the south
Population	13.3 million
Major Religion	Christianity
Government	Republic
Economy	Agriculture: coffee, sugar, bananas, cotton, corn
	Major industries: furniture, tires, textiles
Exports	Coffee, sugar, bananas, beef
Imports	Fuel and petroleum products, machinery, grain, fertilizers, motor vehicles

Though Native American families work hard to make their land produce crops, they have many challenges to overcome since the soil is not very good, and soil erosion is a serious problem. Also, most Native Americans in Guatemala cannot read or write. Many have not filed papers with the government showing that they own land. As a result, they have no way to prove that their land belongs to them.

The Struggle for Change

When a civil war started in Guatemala in 1961, it caught many Mayas in the middle. In hundreds of villages, soldiers came to challenge the Mayas. Sometimes the soldiers were sent by landowners to claim the Mayas' land. Other times, they wanted to exert control over the Mayas by taking away their land and possessions. Most Mayan survivors lost all of their belongings and were forced out of their villages.

Some Mayas started **political movements,** large groups of people who work together to defend their rights or to change the leaders in power. They teach people the history of their land and how to read. They also help organize meetings, protests, and **strikes,** or work stoppages. Above all, they are determined to defend Native American land rights.

All of these efforts have brought about change in Guatemala. For the first time, Mayas have a voice in their own government. For example, Guatemala appointed 21 Mayan priests to advise officials about Mayan culture and the government has promised to rebuild indigenous communities damaged by civil war. Now, the people of Guatemala must make sure that justice is carried out.

Nicaragua: Political and Economic Divisions

Nicaragua is the largest country in Central America, yet it is the least populated. The majority of Nicaraguans are mestizos. Spanish is spoken throughout most of Nicaragua and most of the people are Roman Catholics.

Just as Guatemalans have struggled with injustice and civil war, so have their neighbors to the south in Nicaragua. Many of Nicaragua's struggles are a result of political revolts and changes in government.

Nicaragua shares a similar history with its neighbors in Middle America. Spanish colonists established two cities, Leon and Granada, where a history of political and economic conflicts emerged between conservatives, who favored traditional political ideals, and liberals, who favored non-traditional ideals. British colonists established a logging industry on Nicaragua's eastern coast on the Caribbean Sea.

Spanish is spoken by nearly everyone in the fertile Pacific lowlands and central highlands, where most of the country's population lives. English is spoken on the Caribbean side, which is sparsely populated by people of indigenous, African, and Creole descent. A **Creole** is a person born in the Caribbean of European, usually French, and African descent. Miskito, an indigenous language, is also spoken on the Caribbean side.

LINKS TO Language Arts

The Mosquito Coast (1986) *The Mosquito Coast* is a film about an American inventor, Allie Fox (played by Harrison Ford), who moves his family to a rain forest in Central America to create a simpler life alongside nature, while bringing progress to the indigenous population. While mosquitoes are part of the film's jungle setting, the word *mosquito* in the film's title actually refers to the region on the east coast of Nicaragua and Honduras. This region is named for the Miskito, the native people who inhabit the area.

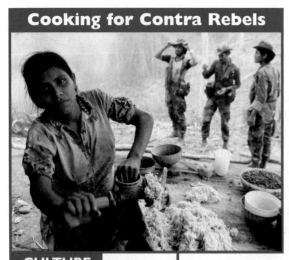

Cooking for Contra Rebels

CULTURE In the picture above, a Nicaraguan woman prepares food for Contra rebels. **Critical Thinking** How do you think women and children were affected by Nicaragua's civil war?

Independence and Political Changes For much of the twentieth century, civil war and political differences tore Nicaragua apart. In 1979, Sandinista **guerrillas**—people taking part in undeclared warfare as part of an independent group—took power and introduced land reform and other socialist policies. Civil war continued as the U.S.-backed Contra rebels fought the Sandinistas.

With the help of neighboring countries, the Sandinistas and Contras reached a compromise and stopped fighting in the early 1990s. Free elections were held in 1990, 1996, and again in 2001. Different factions continued to compete for power, but the government of Nicaragua continues pushing for peaceful democracy.

Economic and Social Changes Years of civil war had disastrous effects on the Nicaraguan economy. The government placed controls on the people and took land from citizens. Some of the leaders even took money from the country. At the same time, the government borrowed money from other countries and built up a huge debt.

Today, Nicaragua is one of the poorest nations in Latin America. Although the economy has grown as exports have risen, many people remain poor, and unemployment and foreign debt remain high. Nicaragua's main hope is its wealth of unused natural resources. Using these wisely, Nicaragua could experience economic growth in the 21st century.

SECTION 2 ASSESSMENT

AFTER YOU READ

RECALL

1. Identify: (a) Guatemala (b) Nicaragua

2. Define: (a) ladino, (b) political movement, (c) strike, (d) Creole, (e) dictator, (f) guerrilla

COMPREHENSION

3. What are some of the current economic and political difficulties that the indigenous people of Guatemala face?

4. How has the Mayan role in the Guatemalan government changed over time?

5. How have the changes in government affected the economy of Nicaragua?

CRITICAL THINKING AND WRITING

6. **Exploring the Main Idea** Review the Main Idea statement at the beginning of this section. Then list three steps the Mayas of Guatemala have taken to gain in voice in their government.

7. **Making a Prediction** What do you think the future holds for the economy of Nicaragua?

ACTIVITY

8. **Writing a Journal** Write a journal entry explaining what you would have done if you were a Mayan villager of Guatemala or a campesino whose land was taken away by the government in Nicaragua during a civil war. Then, explain what you would do if you were the president of either Guatemala or Nicaragua.

Panama
A Transportation Corridor

READING FOCUS

1. What geographic and political challenges did the builders of the Panama Canal face?

2. How did Panama eventually gain control of the Canal?

KEY TERMS

lock
transportation corridor

KEY PLACES

Panama
Panama Canal
Canal Zone

MAIN IDEA

The Panama Canal is an important transportation corridor providing a shortcut across the Western Hemisphere between the Atlantic and Pacific Oceans.

NOTE TAKING

Copy the flow chart below. As you read the section, fill in the chart with information about the Panama Canal. Add more boxes as needed.

> **1500s** - Sailors dream of transportation corridor through Central America
> ↓
> ↓
> ↓

Setting the Scene

Cruising through the Pacific Ocean, ships filled with cargo or passengers approach the country of **Panama** heading for the **Panama Canal.** When they reach the canal, they will get in line and perhaps wait for up to 20 hours. Ships pass through this 40-mile (64.4-km) canal 24 hours a day, 365 days a year. A trip through the canal takes at least eight hours and costs thousands of dollars.

It is a worthwhile shortcut, the only way in the Western Hemisphere to get from the Pacific to the Atlantic Ocean by ship without going around the tip of South America. The Panama Canal eliminates about 7,800 miles (12,553 km) in travel distance.

Ships enter the Panama Canal at sea level. But parts of the canal go through mountains. The ships need to be raised and lowered several times in locks as they travel through the canal. A **lock** is a section of waterway in which a ship is raised and lowered by adjusting the water level. Each ship passes through a set of gates into a lock chamber. The water in the chamber starts at sea level. Then, more water comes pouring into the chamber. When the water rises high enough, the ship passes through a second set of gates and enters a small lake. It proceeds to the next lock. Ships pass through two more sets of locks and zigzag through a passage cut through the mountains. After sailing through a huge lake, they exit at the city of Colón (kuh LOHN) into a bay in the Atlantic Ocean.

Panama's Tropical Rain Forest

GEOGRAPHY

Panama's Barro Colorado rain forest is near the Panama Canal. **Critical Thinking** This photograph shows a trail through the rain forest. Where is the trail? Based on this photograph, what difficulties might Panama Canal workers have faced?

Panama

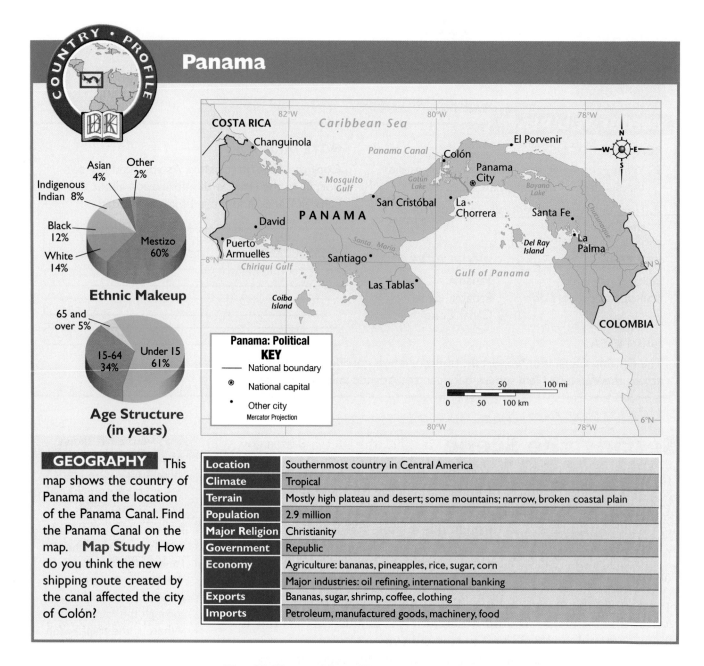

Ethnic Makeup

- Asian 4%
- Other 2%
- Indigenous Indian 8%
- Black 12%
- White 14%
- Mestizo 60%

Age Structure (in years)

- 65 and over 5%
- 15-64 34%
- Under 15 61%

Panama: Political
KEY
- ⎯ National boundary
- ⊛ National capital
- • Other city

Mercator Projection

0 50 100 mi
0 50 100 km

GEOGRAPHY This map shows the country of Panama and the location of the Panama Canal. Find the Panama Canal on the map. **Map Study** How do you think the new shipping route created by the canal affected the city of Colón?

Location	Southernmost country in Central America
Climate	Tropical
Terrain	Mostly high plateau and desert; some mountains; narrow, broken coastal plain
Population	2.9 million
Major Religion	Christianity
Government	Republic
Economy	Agriculture: bananas, pineapples, rice, sugar, corn
	Major industries: oil refining, international banking
Exports	Bananas, sugar, shrimp, coffee, clothing
Imports	Petroleum, manufactured goods, machinery, food

Building the Panama Canal: Geographic and Political Challenges

Since the 1500s, sailors dreamed of a transportation corridor through Central America to shorten the trip from the Atlantic to the Pacific. A **transportation corridor** is a passageway through which people can travel by foot, vehicle, rail, ship, or airplane. A canal would cut the cost of shipping goods.

In 1881, when Panama was part of Colombia, Colombia gave a French company the rights to build a canal. Digging through Panama posed several problems. The builders struggled with mudslides. A mountain range blocked the way. In addition, tropical diseases such as malaria and yellow fever killed 25,000 workers. After a few years, the French company went bankrupt and work on the canal stopped.

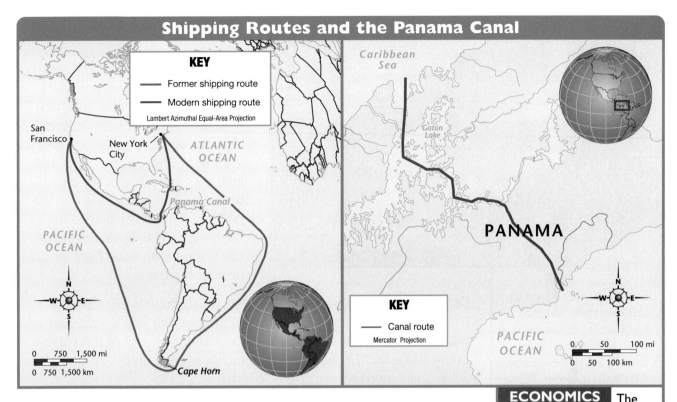

Shipping Routes and the Panama Canal

KEY
— Former shipping route
— Modern shipping route
Lambert Azimuthal Equal-Area Projection

San Francisco
New York City
ATLANTIC OCEAN
Panama Canal
PACIFIC OCEAN
Cape Horn

0   750   1,500 mi
0   750   1,500 km

Caribbean Sea
Gatún Lake
PANAMA
PACIFIC OCEAN

KEY
— Canal route
Mercator Projection

0   50   100 mi
0   50   100 km

The United States Takes a Role   In 1902, the United States government tried to get the rights to continue building the canal. Colombia refused and Panamanians who had hoped that the Canal would bring business to Panama were disappointed. Many Panamanians wanted freedom from Colombia's rule and they saw the canal as a chance to win independence.

In November 1903, the United States helped Panama revolt against Colombia. Two weeks after Panama declared independence, the United States received the rights to build the Canal.

Scientific Developments Make the Canal a Reality   Builders continued to face problems building the Canal. Whenever the diggers carved a hole in the soft earth, more dirt slid into its place. A dam needed to be built to form a lake. Locks needed to be designed and built. But, the biggest problems were malaria and yellow fever.

In the early 1900s, doctors discovered that mosquitoes carried malaria and yellow fever. The mosquitoes bred in swamps and in drinking water. In 1904, the Panama Canal Company hired a doctor and a large crew to deal with the mosquito problem. Workers burned sulfur in every house to kill mosquitoes and they covered drinking water sources with wire mesh and filled swamps with dirt.

Without modern medicine and the scientific innovations of the early 1900s, as well as good planning, the Panama Canal could not have been built. Still, it took eight years and 45,000 workers, mostly Caribbean islanders, to make the waterway. The Panama Canal remains one of the greatest engineering feats of modern times.

ECONOMICS   The map on the left shows shipping routes from New York to San Francisco before and after construction of the Panama Canal. The map on the right is a close up of the Panama Canal route. Before the Panama Canal was built, ships had to travel more than 13,000 miles (20,900 km) around South America. After the Canal was built, ships only had to travel 5,200 miles (8,370 km). **Map Study** What kind of savings would occur by shortening the trip 7,800 miles?

Building the Canal

Control of the Canal

When the United States gained the rights to build the canal, it signed a treaty with Panama that also gave the United States control over the Panama Canal forever. The United States also controlled the **Canal Zone,** which included land on either side of the canal, the ports, the port cities, and the railroad. The treaty placed the Zone under U.S. laws and gave the United States the right to protect the canal.

Conflict and Resolution   Many Panamanians felt this gave the United States too much power over Panama. For years, Panama talked with the United States about regaining control of the canal and in the 1960s and 1970s, many Panamanians grew angry about the situation and rioted to protest U.S. control.

In 1978, U.S. President Jimmy Carter signed two new treaties with Panama. These treaties gave Panama more control over the canal. In 1999, Panama finally gained full control of the Panama Canal.

SECTION 3 ASSESSMENT

AFTER YOU READ

RECALL

1. Identify: (a) Panama, (b) Panama Canal, (c) Canal Zone

2. Define: (a) lock, (b) transportation corridor

COMPREHENSION

3. What were some of the political and geographical difficulties that the builders of the canal faced?

4. What countries controlled the Panama Canal at one time or another? How did Panama eventually gain control of the canal?

CRITICAL THINKING AND WRITING

5. **Exploring the Main Idea** Review the Main Idea statement at the beginning of this section. Then list at least three reasons why the Panama Canal is an important transportation corridor.

6. **Recognizing Point of View** Write a paragraph explaining why it has been important both politically and economically to Panamanians to have control of the Panama Canal.

ACTIVITY

 Take It to the NET

7. **Creating a Timeline** The Panama Canal is an engineering marvel. Create a timeline of significant events pertaining to the construction of the Panama Canal. Visit the World Explorer: People, Places, and Cultures section of **phschool.com** for help in completing this activity.

Using Standard English

Learn the Skill

Even in places where the same language is spoken, variations occur in different regions. In the United States, English phrases and accents are different in the South than in the North or West. Different ethnic and cultural groups also develop their own ways of speaking.

Most national and state standardized tests require you to know what is called "standard English." Questions on these tests usually require you to read a passage and answer multiple-choice questions. (See the sample test on this page.)

Standard English is what you learn when you study grammar, spelling, capitalization, and punctuation rules. Use these strategies to help you answer questions about English when taking tests:

A. Recognize grammar errors. Remember the rules you've learned. Don't confuse common spoken language for Standard English, for example, "ain't" instead of "am not." Check to see if the subject and verb agree, for example, "land and resources affect an economy," instead of "land and resources affects an economy."

B. Recognize spelling errors. Check the spelling of the words in the passage you are being tested on. Pay special attention to homophones (to, too, two), double vowels ("squeak," not "squeek"), suffixes ("*-ness*," not "*-nes*"), and words containing *-ie* or *-ei*.

C. Check for capitalization errors. Make sure that the first word in a sentence is capitalized, that proper nouns are capitalized, and that no words are capitalized unnecessarily. All the words in a compound proper noun should be capitalized, for example, "National Preparatory School."

D. Recognize punctuation errors. Check end punctuation, make sure that all necessary commas and no unnecessary commas are there, notice if both pairs of quotation marks are present, and look for a question mark where needed.

Practice the Skill

Read the sample test and try to find the errors in Standard English.

(1) Have you ever visited the Panama Canal.

A Spelling error   B Punctuation error
C Grammar error   D No error

(2) It crosses through Panama in central America.

A Capitalization error   B Punctuation error
C Grammar error   D No error

(3) The Canal Zone use to be controlled by the United States.

A Spelling error   B Punctuation error
C Grammar error   D No error

(4) In 1999, Panama finally gained complete control of it.

A Spelling error   B Capitalization error
C Grammar error   D No error

Apply the Skill

See the Chapter Review and Assessment at the end of this chapter for more questions on Standard English.

Review and Assessment

Creating a Chapter Summary

On a separate piece of paper, draw a diagram like this one, and include the information that summarizes the first section of the chapter. Then fill in the second and third boxes with summaries of Sections 2 and 3.

MEXICO AND CENTRAL AMERICA: EXPLORING THE REGION TODAY

Section 1
In recent times, many Mexicans have begun moving to urban areas like Mexico City. This migration from rural to urban areas brings many new challenges for people.

Section 2

Section 3

Reviewing Key Terms

Match the definitions in Column I with the Key Terms in Column II.

Column I

1. ruler who has complete power
2. work stoppage
3. large group of people who work together to defend their rights
4. passageway through which foot, vehicle, rail, shipping, or airplane traffic can travel
5. a section of waterway in which a ship is raised and lowered by adjusting the water level
6. rich landowner of Guatemala or Nicaragua, or a Native American who follows European ways
7. landless farm worker who travels with the seasons and the crops
8. person who settles on someone else's land without permission

Column II

a. strike
b. transportation corridor
c. migrant farmworker
d. dictator
e. squatter
f. ladino
g. lock
h. political movement

Reviewing the Main Ideas

1. Describe Mexico's urban migration. Why are so many people making this move? (Section 1)
2. What housing and environmental problems has Mexico City experienced as a result of its rapid population growth? (Section 1)
3. What are the main challenges that indigenous Guatemalans face? (Section 2)
4. Name two steps Mayas in Guatemala are taking to ensure their rights. (Section 2)
5. How have political changes affected Nicaragua's economy? (Section 2)
6. Name one way civil war has played a role in Nicaragua's history. (Section 2)
7. Why was the Panama Canal so difficult to build? (Section 3)
8. Why is control of the Panama Canal important to Panama? (Section 3)

Map Activity

For each place listed below, write the letter from the map that shows its location.

1. Guatemala
2. Colón, Panama
3. Panama
4. Mexico City
5. Nicaragua
6. Panama City

 Take It to the NET

Enrichment For more map activities using geography skills, visit the social studies section of **phschool.com.**

Writing Activity

1. **Writing News Stories** Imagine you are a writer for a radio program. Write two brief news stories on urban migration in Mexico and the history of the Panama Canal.

2. **Writing a Dialogue** Imagine that you are a Maya from Guatemala. Write a dialogue between you and a person from Nicaragua. Discuss the political changes in your countries.

Critical Thinking

1. **Making Comparisons** What do people who move from rural Mexico to the city have to gain? What do they have to lose?

2. **Drawing Conclusions** Over the years, the United States has exercised economic and political influence in Central America. How does the history of the Panama Canal demonstrate U.S. influence in the region?

Applying Your Skills

Choose the letter answer below that correctly identifies the type of error in each sentence shown.

1. nicaragua is a country in Central America.

  A Spelling error   **B** Punctuation error

  C Capitalization error   **D** No error

2. Mayas in Guatemala now have a voice in their own goverment.

  A Capitalization error   **B** Spelling error

  C Grammar error   **D** No error

3. If you're planning too take a trip to South America, bring me along to!

  A Capitalization error   **B** Spelling error

  C Grammar error   **D** No error

 Take It to the NET

Activity Create a graph illustrating the population growth in Mexico City over the past 50 years. What are some negative effects of such a rapid increase in population? What are some possible solutions? Visit the World Explorer: People, Places, and Cultures section of **phschool.com** for help in completing this activity.

Chapter 12 Self-Test As a final review activity, take the Chapter 12 Self-Test and get instant feedback on your answers. To take the test, visit the Social Studies section of **phschool.com.**

THE CARIBBEAN AND SOUTH AMERICA:
Exploring the Region Today

U.S. Petroleum Imports From Venezuela, 1990–2000

UNDERSTANDING GRAPHS

Petroleum is one of the most valuable resources in the world. It comes from deep within the Earth in the form of crude oil, which is refined to use as fuel and to create thousands of other products. Venezuela has one of the largest reserves of petroleum in South America. The United States, which uses more petroleum than it can produce, imports petroleum from Venezuela.

Using the Graph

Study the graph, and then write a series of questions about the information in the graph. For example, about how many more millions of barrels were imported in 1998 than in 1992? Between what two years did petroleum imports increase the most? When you are finished, trade your questions with a partner and use the graph to answer them.

Researching Petroleum Products

Use your local library or the Internet to learn more about the uses of petroleum and the different kinds of products that are made from it. Write a brief report on your findings. Then, work with your classmates to create a bulletin board display showing the different kinds of products that are made from petroleum.

The Caribbean
Economic and Political Challenges

BEFORE YOU READ

READING FOCUS

1. What are the major industries in the Caribbean?
2. What are some of the political challenges facing countries in the Caribbean?

KEY TERMS

one-crop economy
dictator

KEY PEOPLE

Jean-Bertrand Aristide

MAIN IDEA

The island nations of the Caribbean, some of which are independent and some of which remain dependent on other countries, have struggled with poverty and political unrest.

NOTE TAKING

Copy the diagram below. As you read the section, complete the diagram with information from the text.

Caribbean Industries

When farmer Pierre Joseph stands at the top of his land on the island of Haiti, he can see the calm waters of the Caribbean. When he looks down, he sees the dry, cracked earth of his one acre of land.

About two thirds of the people in Haiti make their living by farming. However, much of the land has been overused. Most trees have been cut down to make way for farmland and rain often washes the topsoil into the sea. "The land just doesn't yield enough," says Joseph. He points to the few rows of corn and beans that he can grow on his one acre.

Economic Challenges

Agriculture The Caribbean islands have very fertile soil and are located in a tropical region with moderate temperatures and adequate rainfall. This makes the land suitable for farming. Agriculture, therefore, is the chief economic activity on the Caribbean islands, and over half of the working population works in this industry. Sugar cane is the leading crop grown on the islands. It is grown on large plantations and exported to other countries. Other crops grown on large plantations include bananas, coffee, and cotton.

Sugar Cane Plantation

ECONOMICS

A Caribbean farm worker harvests sugar cane on a plantation in Saint Kitts. Sugar cane plantations in the Caribbean, like this one, were first established by Spanish and Portuguese settlers. **Critical Thinking** Judging from the photo, do you think harvesting sugar cane is an easy or difficult task? Why?

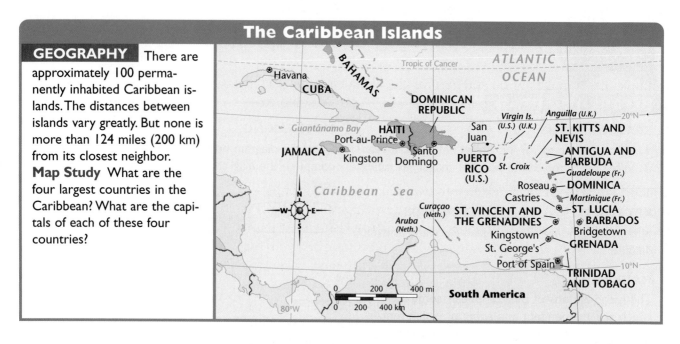

The Caribbean Islands

GEOGRAPHY There are approximately 100 permanently inhabited Caribbean islands. The distances between islands vary greatly. But none is more than 124 miles (200 km) from its closest neighbor. **Map Study** What are the four largest countries in the Caribbean? What are the capitals of each of these four countries?

Many people who live in rural areas on the islands work as small farmers, like Pierre Joseph. They raise yams, corn, sweet potatoes and tropical fruits such as guavas and mangoes. Most of these farmers are poor, working one or two acres of land with simple farming tools. In addition to these farms, ranches are found throughout the Caribbean, where cattle, pigs and other livestock are raised.

For years, many Caribbean countries have relied on one type of crop for a majority of their income. Sugar cane, for example, is one of Cuba's largest crops, accounting for three-quarters of the country's agricultural exports.

Many Caribbean nations have begun to vary the crops that they raise. They have learned that it can be very risky to rely on a **one-crop economy,** in which only one crop provides a majority of a country's income. A single crop can be destroyed by disease or ruined by natural disasters, such as a hurricane, which could seriously hurt a country's economy.

Tourism   Tourism is another important economic activity for these islands. Each year, millions of tourists travel to the islands to take advantage of the beautiful beaches and tropical weather. Shops, hotels, and restaurants employ about one third of the population. Because many Caribbean nations are so dependent on tourism, their economies can be badly hurt by natural disasters, such as hurricanes, or social problems. Jamaica, for example, has faced many social problems, including poverty and unemployment. In the 1960s and 1970s, Jamaicans became so upset that they began to riot and violent crimes began to increase, which adversely affected the tourism industry.

Manufacturing and Mining Many goods are also produced on the islands. Clothing and medicine are just some of the products that are produced. A few islands are rich in natural resources. Trinidad, for example, has supplies of oil and natural gas. Jamaica is rich in bauxite, a mineral that is used to make aluminum. It is mined and exported to the United States and Canada.

Political Challenges

Today, the Caribbean islands fall into two major political groups—those countries that are independent and those that are still dependent on other countries. Some countries, such as Cuba, Haiti, and the Dominican Republic, have been independent from colonial powers for many years. Others have gained their independence more recently. However, there are still many countries in the Caribbean, including Puerto Rico, that are dependent on other countries' governments in one form or another. These countries usually manage their own affairs, but receive economic and military aid from their ruling powers.

Haiti's Journey to Democracy Haiti became the first independent Caribbean nation in 1804. In the 1790s, enslaved Africans working on plantations began to revolt against their French masters. One former enslaved African, Toussaint L'Ouverture, took control of the government and offered Haitians a new way of life based on the idea that all people could live as equals. Unfortunately, he was captured by the French army and imprisoned in France. In the years that followed, Toussaint L'Ouverture's goal of freedom and equality was never fully realized. Most of Haiti's presidents became dictators when they got into power. A **dictator** is a person who rules with complete power and authority.

More recently, there have been attempts to bring democracy to Haiti. In 1990, **Jean-Bertrand Aristide** was elected president. He was the first person to be democratically elected in many years. Aristide, however, only served as president for seven months. Haiti's military took control and forced him to leave the country. However, with help from the United States, Aristide came back to Haiti in 1994, restoring democratic government. Successful elections in 1995 resulted in Rene Preval, an ally of Aristide, being elected president of Haiti.

In national elections held in 2000, it seemed that Aristide's party had won control of the legislature, and Aristide again assumed the presidency. But the election results were challenged. Because of the disputed election, international aid to Haiti stopped, and the weak Haitian economy got worse. Many Haitians called for Aristide to resign. In early 2004, rebels opposed to Aristide's government gained control of much of Haiti; Aristide was forced to flee the country. An interim government has called for democratic elections, but the future of democracy in Haiti remains uncertain.

> **Democracy in Haiti**
> **GOVERNMENT**
> Haitian President Jean-Bertrand Aristide returned to Haiti in 1994 amid cheers of support. **Critical Thinking** Why was Aristide's return to Haiti so important to Haitians?

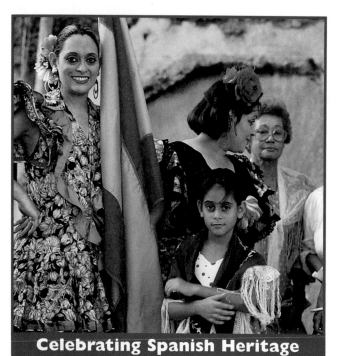

Celebrating Spanish Heritage

CULTURE These women are celebrating Puerto Rico's Spanish heritage. Puerto Ricans celebrate many holidays with traditional music and dancing.
Critical Thinking What similar celebrations take place in the United States?

Puerto Rico's Ties to the U.S. Puerto Rico is an island of old cities as well as beautiful countryside. Farming is still very important to the economy. However, about 70 percent of Puerto Ricans live in cities and many of them work in factories. The standard of living is high in Puerto Rico and its economy is the strongest of all the Caribbean islands.

After defeating Spain in the Spanish-American War in 1898, the United States took control of Puerto Rico, which had been a Spanish colony. In 1951, Puerto Ricans voted to adopt their own constitution. A constitution is a statement of a country's basic laws and values. This gave the country its own group of lawmakers, but it was still connected to the United States. Puerto Rico is a commonwealth of the United States. A commonwealth is a place that has its own government but also has strong ties to another country. Puerto Ricans are U.S. citizens, but they cannot vote in U.S. presidential elections. They do not pay U.S. taxes and they have only a non-voting representative in the U.S. Congress.

SECTION I ASSESSMENT

AFTER YOU READ

RECALL

1. Identify: (a) Jean-Bertrand Aristide

2. Define: (a) one-crop economy

COMPREHENSION

3. What are some of the main industries of the Caribbean islands?

4. How did Haiti win its independence?

5. What is the political relationship between the United States and Puerto Rico?

CRITICAL THINKING

6. **Exploring the Main Idea** Review the Main Idea statement at the beginning of this section. Then, write a short paragraph discussing some economic and political challenges faced by the countries of the Caribbean.

7. **Drawing Conclusions** Some people in Puerto Rico want the country to separate from the United States. Others feel that it should become a state so that they can enjoy all the privileges of U.S. citizens. Write a paragraph in support of either Puerto Rico's becoming a

state or separating completely from the United States.

ACTIVITY

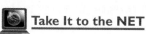 Take It to the NET

8. **Writing a Travel Journal** Cuba is one of our nearest neighbors, but life in Cuba is very different from life in the United States. Use the information on the web site to write a travel journal of a trip to Cuba, and include information about daily life in Cuba. Visit the World Explorer: People, Places, and Cultures section of **phschool.com** for help in completing this activity.

SECTION 2

Brazil
Natural Resources and Industry

BEFORE YOU READ

READING FOCUS

1. Why are Brazil's rain forests a global concern?
2. How do the rain forests in Brazil affect its economy?

KEY TERMS

campesinos
canopy
photosynthesis

KEY PEOPLE AND PLACES

Rio de Janeiro
Brasília

MAIN IDEA

Brazil looks for ways to develop new industries, aware that what happens to its rain forests is important not only to Brazil, but also to the rest of the world.

NOTE TAKING

Copy the outline below. As you read the section, fill in the outline with information about the natural resources of Brazil.

Brazil's Natural Resource: Rain Forests
I. Importance of rain forests to Brazil
  A.
  B.
II. Importance of Brazil's rain forests to the world
  A.
  B.

Setting the Scene

Land is a valuable natural resource in Brazil. It provides places for people to settle and live, and places to grow crops. It contains valuable resources that can be used, made into other goods, or traded to other countries. It provides places for factories and cities to develop. How land is used and what happens to the resources the land produces greatly affect the economy of Brazil.

Brazilian Rain Forests: A Global Concern

Brazil, the largest country in South America, is nearly as large as the United States. It is also one of the richest countries in the world in land and resources. Until recently, its immense rain forests remained undisturbed. Only the few Native American groups that had lived in them for centuries ever explored them.

Brazil's rain forests take up about one half of the country. The rain forests are important to Brazil's economy. People cut timber, mine for gold, and farm there. In the past, the government of Brazil gave land to landless peasants and poor farmers, known as **campesinos** (kahm peh SEE nohs). The government moved the campesinos to the Amazonian rain forests where the farmers burned down trees to clear the land for their farms. After a few years, however, the soil in the rain forest became unfit for farming.

People around the world expressed concern about the clearing of the rain forest. Many scientists think that when people come to the rain forest, they upset the delicate balance of nature. Other people worry that the traditional way of life of native people who live in the rain forest may be altered or damaged.

Farming in a Rain Forest

ECONOMICS

This pepper farmer has cleared land on an island in the Amazon River, in northern Brazil.
Critical Thinking How does pepper farming contribute to Brazil's economy?

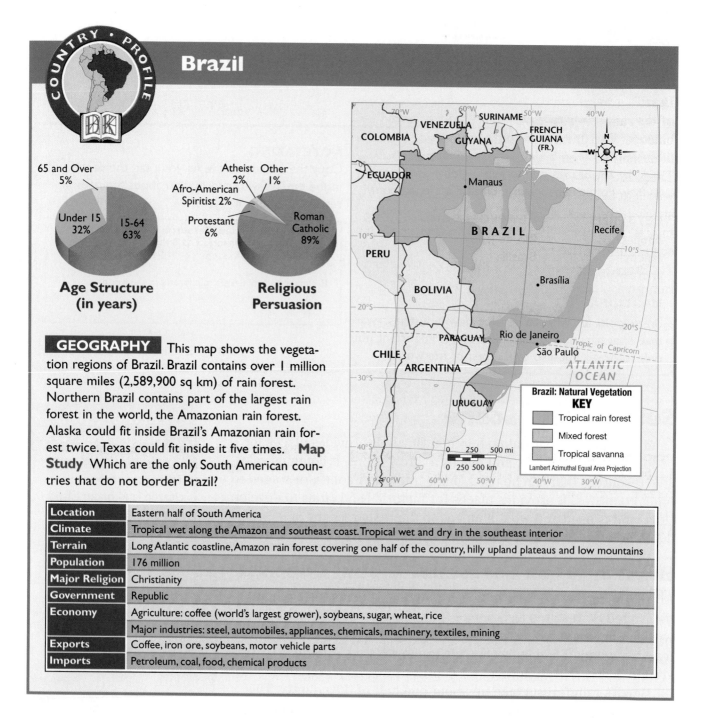

COUNTRY · PROFILE

Brazil

Age Structure (in years)

- 65 and Over 5%
- Under 15 32%
- 15-64 63%

Religious Persuasion

- Atheist 2%
- Other 1%
- Afro-American Spiritist 2%
- Protestant 6%
- Roman Catholic 89%

Brazil: Natural Vegetation KEY
- Tropical rain forest
- Mixed forest
- Tropical savanna

Lambert Azimuthal Equal Area Projection

GEOGRAPHY This map shows the vegetation regions of Brazil. Brazil contains over 1 million square miles (2,589,900 sq km) of rain forest. Northern Brazil contains part of the largest rain forest in the world, the Amazonian rain forest. Alaska could fit inside Brazil's Amazonian rain forest twice. Texas could fit inside it five times. **Map Study** Which are the only South American countries that do not border Brazil?

Location	Eastern half of South America
Climate	Tropical wet along the Amazon and southeast coast. Tropical wet and dry in the southeast interior
Terrain	Long Atlantic coastline, Amazon rain forest covering one half of the country, hilly upland plateaus and low mountains
Population	176 million
Major Religion	Christianity
Government	Republic
Economy	Agriculture: coffee (world's largest grower), soybeans, sugar, wheat, rice
	Major industries: steel, automobiles, appliances, chemicals, machinery, textiles, mining
Exports	Coffee, iron ore, soybeans, motor vehicle parts
Imports	Petroleum, coal, food, chemical products

A Valuable Natural Resource

Deep in the rain forest in Brazil, the light barely penetrates. At the top of the trees, the leaves form a dense, roof-like mass called a **canopy.** More species of plants and animals than any other place on Earth can be found living in and under the rain forest canopy. Scientists also estimate that rain forests produce about one third of the world's oxygen. In a process called **photosynthesis** (foht oh SIN thuh sis), green plants produce their own food using water and carbon dioxide, and oxygen is given off. The rain forests also hold about one fifth of the world's fresh water.

Using Technology to Protect the Rain Forest

Brazil's government is trying to use the resources of the rain forest without upsetting the natural balance. The government has begun using satellite technology to keep an eye on the rain forest. There are many threats for the government to watch out for. When part of the forest is destroyed, the animals and plants that live there may not survive. When plant life is destroyed, less oxygen is produced.

There is also a problem with smuggling in the rain forest. Each year, Brazil loses about 12 million animals to smugglers. Many of these animals are endangered. It is illegal to capture and kill these animals, but the smugglers often get away with it.

In the late 1980s, the discovery of gold attracted many miners to the rain forest. Gold mining caused pollution in streams in the rain forest, and made people in several villages sick. The government of Brazil passed strict laws about mining in the rain forest. As they work to protect the rain forests, Brazilian leaders must also look for ways to use the rain forest's resources to ensure Brazil's economic progress.

Brazil's African Heritage

CULTURE In Salvador, Brazil, people cook food similar to the food eaten in West Africa. Food in both places is seasoned with coconut milk, pepper, and palm oil, and cooked in earthenware pots. The women of Salvador wear lacy dresses and turbans, like many of the women of West Africa. **Critical Thinking** Why do you think these women dress in a West African fashion even though they live in Brazil?

Economic Challenges and Developing Industry

The Native Americans living in the rain forests were some of the first people to live in Brazil. Today, most Brazilians are a mix of Native American, African, and European heritages. Many parts of African culture still flourish in Brazil. Most of the people of African descent are ancestors of the millions of Africans brought to Brazil as slaves and forced to work the coffee plantations. Brazil used their labor to become the world's largest coffee grower. When the slaves were freed in the late 1800s, they became paid but cheap labor.

Coffee prices dropped in the first few years of the 1900s. Brazilians realized that they could not depend on one or two crops to survive. In the 1930s, the government discouraged coffee production and tried to diversify the economy by building more factories. Today, Brazil produces many goods, including iron and steel, cars, and electrical equipment. Since 1960, about 30 million people have left farms and plantations to get jobs in the large cities near the coast, such as **Rio de Janeiro** (REE oh day zhuh NER oh), far from the rain forests.

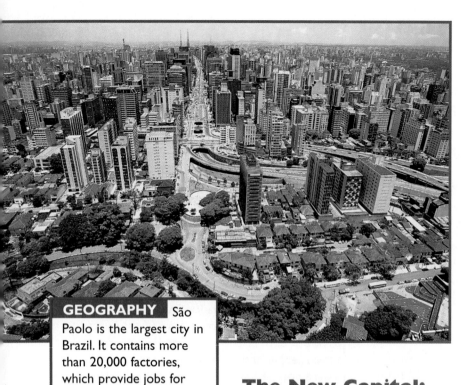

GEOGRAPHY São Paolo is the largest city in Brazil. It contains more than 20,000 factories, which provide jobs for about 600,000 workers. **Critical Thinking** In what ways does São Paolo look similar to large cities in the United States? In what ways does it look different?

Brazilian cities are home to the rich and the very poor. Rio de Janeiro is a good example of these contrasts. Expensive hotels and shops for tourists are located in the south part of the city. Old palaces and government buildings are found in the downtown area, and north of the city are clusters of small houses where factory workers live. Beyond the factory workers' homes is an even poorer area. It is crowded with homes that have no electricity or running water. About a quarter of Rio's 12 million people live in these neighborhoods known as *favelas* (fuh VEH lus).

The New Capital: A Move for the Economy

In the 1950s, the Brazilian government moved the capital to a new city, **Brasília,** away from the coast and closer to the rain forest. The government thought that moving the capital there would attract some people from the coastal areas and help develop industry using resources from the rain forest. Brazilian leaders continue to face challenges as they try to help the economy without destroying the rain forest.

SECTION 2 ASSESSMENT

AFTER YOU READ

RECALL

1. Identify: (a) Rio de Janeiro, (b) Brasília

2. Define: (a) campesinos, (b) canopy, (c) photosynthesis

COMPREHENSION

3. Why is the Brazilian rain forest an important environmental concern for the world?

4. In what ways does the Brazilian economy depend upon the rain forests?

CRITICAL THINKING AND WRITING

5. Exploring the Main Idea Review the Main Idea statement at the beginning of this section. Then, list one way the Brazilian government is working to protect its rain forests, and one way it is trying to use resources from the rain forest to improve its economy.

6. Supporting a Point of View Some people want Brazil to stop using rain forests completely. Is this reasonable? What do you think it would do to Brazil's economy?

ACTIVITY

7. Creating a Rain Forest Display Work with a partner to find images that show the vegetation and animal life found in Brazil's rain forests. Write captions for the images you select and then create a classroom display.

SECTION 3

Chile and Venezuela
Growing Economies

BEFORE YOU READ

READING FOCUS

1. How does Chile's government work to protect the environment?

2. Why is agriculture important to Chile's economy?

3. How did Venezuela's oil boom affect its people and its economy?

KEY TERMS
boom
privatization

KEY PEOPLE AND PLACES
Santiago
Caracas

NOTE TAKING

Copy the chart below. As you read the section, fill in the chart with information about the economies of Chile and Venezuela.

	Chile	Venezuela
Economy Before 1980s		
Economy After Mid-1980s		

MAIN IDEA

As Chile and Venezuela develop and expand new industries and resources, their governments must meet the challenges of keeping their economies strong while protecting the environment.

Setting the Scene

Both Chile and Venezuela have experienced the prosperity and problems associated with growing economies. Before the 1980s, Chile's economy depended mostly on its copper exports and the primary industry of mining. In the early 1980s, world copper prices began to drop and Chile could no longer depend on copper to survive. One way to improve Chile's economy was to focus on agriculture.

Agriculture and the Economy

By the late 1980s, agriculture was especially important for Chile. It had become a billion dollar industry, providing jobs for about 900,000 Chileans. Like Chile, Venezuela experienced an economic **boom,** or period of increased prosperity. Venezuela's boom was in the sale of oil products. During the 1970s the price of oil went up. Then, like copper prices in Chile, the oil prices started to fall. Now, Venezuela must find other ways to make money. As demand for products has risen and fallen, so too have standards of living.

Chile's Varied Landscape

GEOGRAPHY

The Atacama Desert in Chile is barren and empty, but other areas of Chile are fertile and green. **Critical Thinking** What factors do you think make it possible for one country to have such different climates?

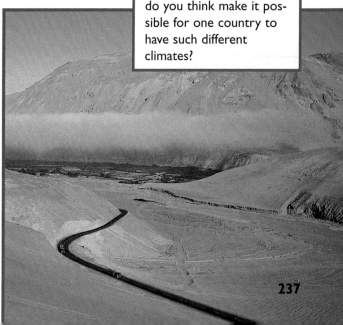

237

Chile's Physical Environment

Look at the physical map of Latin America in the Activity Atlas on page 164. Find the Andes Mountains. They extend down the whole length of the continent like a giant spine. Chile stretches 2,650 miles (4,265 km) down the Pacific Coast, and it reaches all the way to the tip of South America. It is the longest, narrowest country in the world.

Chile contains an amazing variety of lands and climates. In the north is the Atacama Desert. The long central valley near the coast has rolling hills, high grasses, and dense forests. This is the region where most of the people live.

Chile's Cultural Ties

Chile's early Spanish settlers married Native Americans already living there. Today, these mestizos make up about 75 percent of the population. Only 3 percent of Chileans are Native Americans.

The lifestyles of Chileans vary from region to region. In the far south, people raise sheep. Farther north in the central valley, farmers grow many vegetables and fruits. Few people live in the Atacama Desert of the far north. But the desert is rich in copper and dotted with copper mines. Chile exports more copper than any country in the world.

A visit to the city of **Santiago** is unforgettable. Old Spanish buildings stand near gleaming skyscrapers. The city is in the valley of the central plain, so the altitude is low enough to produce mild weather. The sea makes the air humid. Palm trees grow in the public parks with a backdrop of the snowcapped Andes in the east.

Protecting the Environment

The beautiful sights of Santiago, Chile's capital, are sometimes blocked by a thick layer of smog. How did pollution get to be so bad in Santiago? One cause is the city's location. It is surrounded by the Andes on three sides. The mountains trap the exhaust fumes from vehicles and smoke from factories in the valley.

Another cause is that in the early 1980s, the government relaxed the laws that protected the environment from pollution. Government leaders thought that if the laws were too strict, some private industries would not survive. Encouraging private industry was good for Chile's economy. The standard of living rose, but so did pollution levels. More people moved to the cities to get jobs in the new industries. More than 80 percent of Chile's people now live in cities.

During the 1990s, Chile's government took action to reduce the problems of pollution in the city. On days when the wind does not blow, industries are shut down, and only a limited number of cars may enter the city. The government may also require new cars to have special exhaust systems that do not produce much pollution.

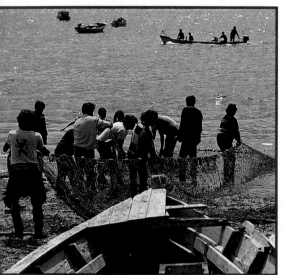

Net Fishing Off Chile's Coast

ECONOMICS

In northern Chile, the soil is not very good for farming. Many people here fish for a living. Chile's fishing industry is one of the largest in the world. **Critical Thinking** What difference do you see between people who fish for a living and those who fish for fun?

AS YOU READ

Use Prior Knowledge What cities in the United States have problems with pollution? Which of these cities, like Santiago, are surrounded by mountains?

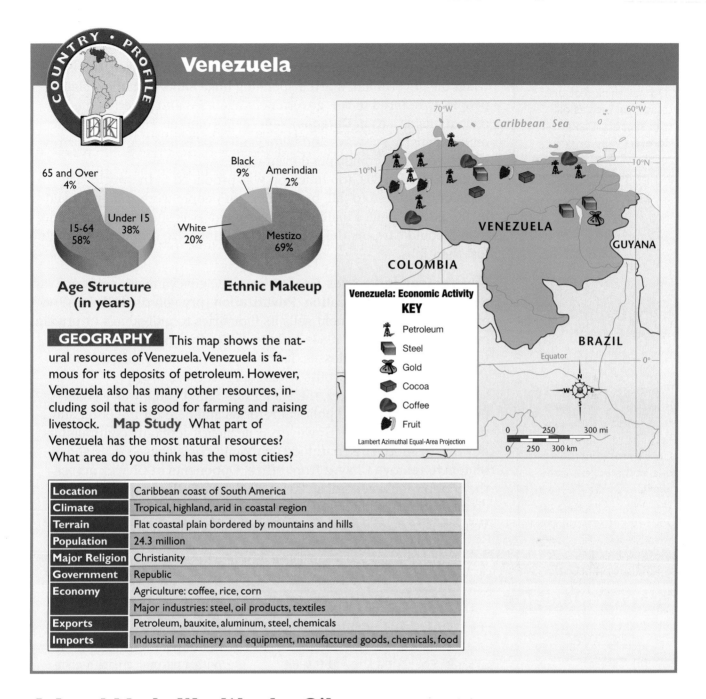

COUNTRY · PROFILE

Venezuela

Age Structure (in years)

65 and Over 4%

15-64 58%

Under 15 38%

Ethnic Makeup

Black 9%

Amerindian 2%

White 20%

Mestizo 69%

GEOGRAPHY This map shows the natural resources of Venezuela. Venezuela is famous for its deposits of petroleum. However, Venezuela also has many other resources, including soil that is good for farming and raising livestock. **Map Study** What part of Venezuela has the most natural resources? What area do you think has the most cities?

Venezuela: Economic Activity

KEY

Petroleum

Steel

Gold

Cocoa

Coffee

Fruit

Lambert Azimuthal Equal-Area Projection

Caribbean Sea

VENEZUELA

COLOMBIA

GUYANA

BRAZIL

Equator

0   250   300 mi

0   250   300 km

Location	Caribbean coast of South America
Climate	Tropical, highland, arid in coastal region
Terrain	Flat coastal plain bordered by mountains and hills
Population	24.3 million
Major Religion	Christianity
Government	Republic
Economy	Agriculture: coffee, rice, corn
	Major industries: steel, oil products, textiles
Exports	Petroleum, bauxite, aluminum, steel, chemicals
Imports	Industrial machinery and equipment, manufactured goods, chemicals, food

A Land Made Wealthy by Oil

Venezuela, located in the north of South America, has vast supplies of oil. The map above shows where this oil is located. Venezuela's oil has earned billions of dollars on the world market. Because of this, people have migrated from the countryside to work for the oil companies.

Venezuela's oil was discovered about 75 years ago. Since then, Venezuela has pumped about 67 billion barrels of oil. Except for the Persian Gulf region, Venezuela has the biggest oil reserves in the world.

AS YOU READ

Monitor Your Reading
Do you think that one resource, such as oil, can support a country forever? Why or why not?

During the 1970s, the price of oil went up and an oil boom began. The standard of living of many Venezuelans began to rise. That is when the government started spending huge sums of money. Many people were hired to run government agencies and government-owned businesses in **Caracas,** Venezuela's capital. The government built expensive subways and high-quality roads and began to borrow money so that it could spend even more.

In the mid-1980s, too much oil was produced in the world. The price of oil started to fall, but millions of people were still employed by the government. Finally, the government was spending much more than it could earn. As the price of oil continued to drop, many people lost their jobs.

Government Industries Go Public The government's solution was a new policy of privatization. **Privatization** (pry vuh tih ZAY shun) occurs when the government sells its industries to individuals or private companies. In the late 1980s and the 1990s, the government decided to privatize some businesses. It hoped that the corporations would make big profits. The profits would help workers.

In 1998, Hugo Chavez, the leader of a failed coup, was elected president. He promised political reforms and help for the poor, and won reelection in 2000. However, Venezuela's economy continued its downward slide. The continued economic crisis caused riots and attempts to remove Chavez from office. Opponents of Chavez across the country led a general strike in 2002, nearly shutting down the country and crippling oil production. Despite the wealth of oil that Venezuela possesses, the future for this country remains uncertain.

SECTION 3 ASSESSMENT

AFTER YOU READ

RECALL

1. Identify: (a) Santiago, (b) Caracas
2. Define: (a) boom, (b) privatization

COMPREHENSION

3. What steps has the government taken to prevent pollution in Chile's cities?
4. Why did Chile begin developing its agricultural industry?
5. How has Venezuela's oil boom affected the economy in the past and more recently?

CRITICAL THINKING AND WRITING

6. **Exploring the Main Idea** Review the Main Idea statement at the beginning of this section. Then, list ways that Chile and Venezuela have worked to keep their economies strong, and their people and environment in good health.
7. **Drawing Conclusions** Write a paragraph about what you think Venezuela should do to avoid economic problems in the future, without harming the environment.

ACTIVITY

8. **Writing an Advertisement** With a partner, create a commercial to advertise a new product that would help the economies of either Chile or Venezuela. Make a poster to use as a prop for your commercial. Write a script that takes no longer than 60 seconds to present and that explains why it is important to have new products to help the economy.

SECTION 4

Argentina
A Cultural Center

BEFORE YOU READ

READING FOCUS

1. How is Argentina's ethnic makeup different from other countries in South America?
2. What are two of Argentina's distinct cultural groups?
3. How is the gaucho of Argentina's Pampas region like the American cowboy of the Great Plains in the United States?

KEY TERMS

cosmopolitan
gauchos
porteños
bolas
estancias

KEY PEOPLE AND PLACES

Buenos Aires
Pampas

NOTE TAKING

Copy the diagram below. As you read the section, fill in the diagram with information about the cultures of Argentina.

People of
Buenos Aires

People of
the Pampas

MAIN IDEA

Argentina's cultural heritage is an unusual blend of European influences found in the capital city of Buenes Aires with a uniquely Argentinian culture from the plains.

Setting the Scene

Walking through the colorful streets of **Buenos Aires,** the capital of Argentina, a traveler is likely to hear the country's official language, Spanish, being spoken with an Italian accent. Buenos Aires is a **cosmopolitan** city, or a city whose population is composed of people from many parts of the world.

Not far from Buenos Aires lies an area called the **Pampas** [PAHM puhs], a vast, flat grassland similar to the Great Plains in the United States. It was here, in the mid-18th century, that nomadic cowboys called **gauchos** (GOW chohz), became legends portrayed in ballads and stories.

Geographical and Cultural Diversity

Argentina spreads across almost the entire southern half of South America and it is the eighth largest country in the world. Argentina's geographical diversity begins in the north with

The Pampas

GEOGRAPHY The grasslands known as the Pampas in Argentina are perfect for raising cattle. **Critical Thinking** How are these grasslands similar to the Great Plains in the United States?

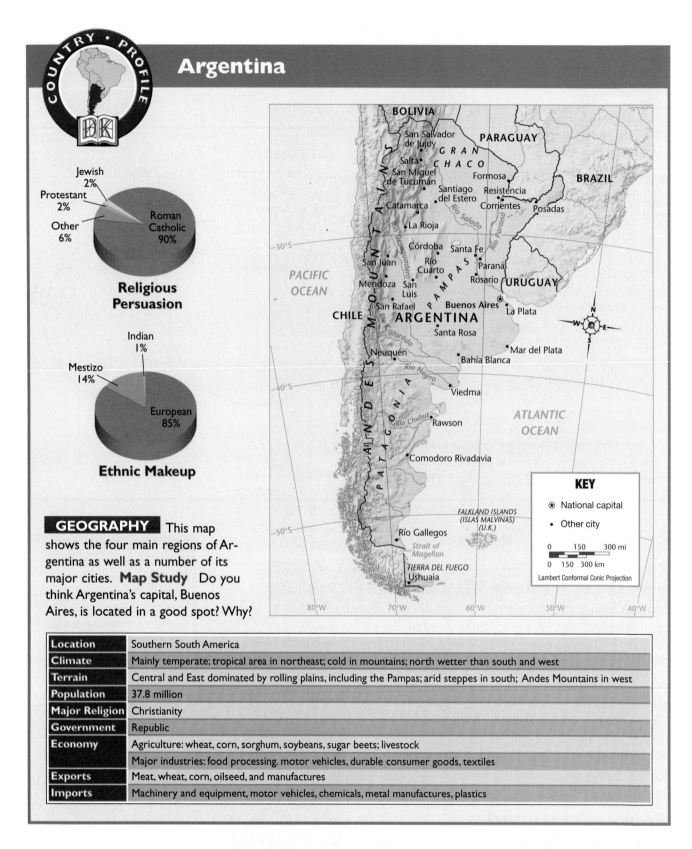

Argentina

Religious Persuasion

- Jewish 2%
- Protestant 2%
- Other 6%
- Roman Catholic 90%

Ethnic Makeup

- Indian 1%
- Mestizo 14%
- European 85%

GEOGRAPHY This map shows the four main regions of Argentina as well as a number of its major cities. **Map Study** Do you think Argentina's capital, Buenos Aires, is located in a good spot? Why?

Location	Southern South America
Climate	Mainly temperate; tropical area in northeast; cold in mountains; north wetter than south and west
Terrain	Central and East dominated by rolling plains, including the Pampas; arid steppes in south; Andes Mountains in west
Population	37.8 million
Major Religion	Christianity
Government	Republic
Economy	Agriculture: wheat, corn, sorghum, soybeans, sugar beets; livestock
	Major industries: food processing. motor vehicles, durable consumer goods, textiles
Exports	Meat, wheat, corn, oilseed, and manufactures
Imports	Machinery and equipment, motor vehicles, chemicals, metal manufactures, plastics

a heavily forested, low, wet, hot region called the Gran Chaco. The central plains, or Pampas, lie south of the Gran Chaco and encompass a stretch of land from the East Coast, where Buenos Aires is located, to increasingly dry land toward the west. The Pampas is mostly flat, fertile land with a temperate climate where nearly 98 percent of the population lives. To the south of the Pampas is an arid region called Patagonia. This windswept plateau also contains some grassy valleys. The Andes Mountains in the west make up Argentina's fourth geographic region.

Political and Economic History

Argentina became a Spanish colony in the 16th century. Under Spanish control, Argentina was forbidden to trade with foreign countries. This trade policy angered the colonists. In the early 1800s, Argentina finally gained its independence from Spain. By the 1900s European immigrants came to farm and invest in businesses in Argentina.

Following its independence, a long struggle took place between the *centralists*, those who wanted more central government control, and the *federalists*, who favored local control. In recent times, the government has become more stable, and industry and agriculture have developed. Today, Argentina has a free market economy and people there enjoy one of the highest standards of living in Latin America.

Two Distinct Cultures

Argentina's ethnic makeup is part Spanish but also a blend of European from other countries like Italy, England, France, and Germany, with nearly one half of the population of Italian descent. Also, unlike its neighbor Brazil and countries of the Caribbean, African slaves were not imported. Two distinct social groups of people settled in this vast land that we now call Argentina. One group crossed the Andes from Peru and established themselves in the fertile interior and central Pampas. Most of them were mestizos, or people of Spanish and Native American heritage. Others were of mixed European and African ancestry. The people of the interior learned to raise cattle and adopted rural lifestyles.

The people who settled in and around Buenos Aires were Europeans who came to the port city for trade. The **porteños** as they are sometimes called, wanted to make Buenos Aires a city much like those in Europe. These people of European heritage far outnumbered the small groups of mestizos who settled on the plains.

An Argentine Cultural Center

More than one third of Argentina's population lives in the capital city of Buenos Aires. Buenos Aires is located along the Rio de la Plata estuary and its location on the Atlantic coast in the sea lanes between the South Atlantic and South Pacific oceans places it in an important transportation corridor for trade.

GOVERNMENT

Working Together

From 1976 to 1983, Argentina had a military government. The government took thousands of people prisoner. Many were never seen again. The mothers and grandmothers of the "disappeared" marched in protest every day for six years in Buenos Aires. They wanted their marches to remind the government to keep investigating the disappearance of their relatives.

The Gauchos of Argentina

CULTURE This gaucho displays his horse on a ranch on the Pampas. **Critical Thinking** Today, many Argentinian cowboys still wear the costume of the early gauchos. Why do you think they still dress like gauchos?

Like a European city, Buenos Aires is composed of small neighborhoods, each with its own special characteristics. It also houses tall, cosmopolitan skyscrapers that tower over homes built in the 19th century. Spanish colonial design with Italian and French influences enriches the city's fine buildings. The city offers a great variety of cultural activities such as opera, ballet, concerts, plays, literary events, and film festivals.

The Culture of the Pampas

Beyond Buenos Aires, where the Pampas stretches into the rich, fertile grassland of the interior, is the birthplace of the gaucho. The nomadic gauchos established a unique culture found only in Argentina. They wandered the Pampas and hunted herds of wild horses and cattle using lassos, knives, and **bolas** (BOH lahs), a set of leather cords and three iron balls or stones that they threw at the legs of animals to capture them.

The gauchos were part of a profitable, although illegal, trade in hides and tallow in the frontier regions near Buenos Aires. Known for their expert horsemanship, the gauchos played a major role in Argentina's history. They helped bring civilization to the Pampas, and fought in the struggle for independence and stability.

By the late 1800s, most of the Pampas had been fenced in as part of the huge **estancias** (eh STAHN see yahs), or estates owned by private owners. The gauchos became hired farmhands rather than the free-spirited cowboys they had once been.

SECTION 4 ASSESSMENT

AFTER YOU READ

RECALL

1. Identify: (a) Buenos Aires, (b) Pampas

2. Define: (a) cosmopolitan, (b) gauchos, (c) porteños, (d) bolas, (e) estancias

COMPREHENSION

3. What is unique about the ethnic makeup of the people in Argentina?

4. Describe Argentina's two distinct cultural groups.

5. What are some similarities between the gauchos of the Pampas and the cowboys of the Great Plains?

CRITICAL THINKING AND WRITING

6. **Exploring the Main Idea** Review the Main Idea statement at the beginning of this section. Then, write a paragraph describing how two distinct cultures came to exist in Argentina.

7. **Drawing Conclusions** Why do you think nearly 98 per-

cent of the population lives in a small geographic area of Argentina called the Pampas?

ACTIVITY

8. **Learning About Gauchos** Find out more about gauchos by doing research on the Internet or in your school library. Write a short report about your findings and include any images that you find while doing your research.

Making Generalizations

Quality of Life

	Gross national product per capita (in U.S. dollars)	Life expectancy in years	People per doctor	Literacy rate	Infant mortality (per 1,000 live births)	Cars per 1,000 people
United States	$29,080	77	400	99%	7 deaths	489
Venezuela	$3,480	72	625	92%	21 deaths	68
Haiti	$380	54	10,000	46%	58 deaths	4
Brazil	$4,790	67	714	84%	34 deaths	128
Chile	$4,820	75	909	95%	11 deaths	71

Learn the Skill

A generalization is a broad statement that is based on data, or facts. It is a statement that links information or ideas together. To make a generalization based on data from a chart, follow these steps:

A. Study the information on the chart. Determine what information the chart provides by reading the title and the labels for each column and row. Also check out the data to determine ranges in numbers of percentages. Which numbers are highest? Which numbers are lowest? Are the numbers decimals? Are numbers provided in the millions?

B. Look for relationships in the information. On the chart on this page, for example, you can look for a relationship between life expectancy and the number of people per doctor. Look for other relationships that the chart reveals.

C. Make a general statement based on the facts. This statement might be a conclusion based on relationships that you've noted. You can make a general statement, or generalization, regarding a relationship between life expectancy and the number of people per doctor in the chart: As the number of people per doctor increases, life expectancy usually decreases.

Practice the Skill

Use the chart titled "Quality of Life" to practice making generalizations. To help you get started, answer these questions. Then, come up with your own generalizations by looking for relationships among data.

1. What are some characteristics of societies with high gross national products per capita?

2. What would you say are the characteristics of societies with low gross national products per capita?

3. What two suggestions would you make to improve the quality of life in societies that are less industrialized?

4. What relationship do you see between the number of people per doctor and infant mortality? What general statement about this relationship can you make?

Apply the Skill

See the Chapter Review and Assessment at the end of this chapter for more questions on making generalizations.

Creating a Chapter Summary

On a separate piece of paper, draw a diagram like this one, and include the information that summarizes the first section of the chapter. Then, fill in the remaining boxes with summaries of Sections 2, 3, and 4.

THE CARIBBEAN AND SOUTH AMERICA

Section 1
The nations of the Caribbean face many economic and political challenges. Often, they have been influenced by the United States.

Section 2

Section 3

Section 4

Reviewing Key Terms

Match the definitions in Column I with the key terms in Column II.

Column I

a. people who own only small tracts of land in Latin America

b. nomadic cowboys of Argentina

c. the process of a government selling its industries to individuals and private companies

d. one crop provides a majority of a country's income

e. estates owned by private owners

f. a period of increased prosperity

Column II

1. boom
2. campesinos
3. privatization
4. one-crop economy
5. gauchos
6. estancias

Reviewing the Main Ideas

1. Why is agriculture the leading industry of most Caribbean nations? (Section 1)

2. How have Haiti's political problems influenced its economic problems? (Section 1)

3. What political ties exist between Puerto Rico and the United States? (Section 1)

4. Why are Brazil's rain forests a global concern? (Section 2)

5. How has producing more crops and increasing agriculture helped Chile's economy? (Section 3)

6. How did its oil boom affect Venezuela's people and its economy? (Section 3)

7. What makes Argentina's culture so unique? (Section 4)

8. What are two of Argentina's distinct cultural groups? (Section 4)

Map Activity

The Caribbean and South America

For each place listed below, write the letter from the map that shows its location.

1. Cuba
2. Haiti
3. Puerto Rico
4. Brazil
5. Chile
6. Brasília
7. Venezuela
8. Argentina

 Take It to the NET

Enrichment For more map activities on the Caribbean and South America, visit the World Explorer section of **phschool.com.**

Writing Activity

1. **Using Primary Sources** Visit your school or local library or use the Internet to find newspaper and magazine articles and other primary sources with information about the current status of the Brazilian rain forests. Write a persuasive argument describing why it is important to protect the rain forests. Create a poster to illustrate your argument.

2. **Writing a Journal** You are a citizen of Puerto Rico. Tomorrow an election will be held to decide if Puerto Rico should remain a commonwealth, become the 51st state in the United States, or declare independence from the United States. Write how you feel about this decision in your journal. Include your feelings about how you will vote and why.

Applying Your Skills

Use the chart titled "Quality of Life" on p. 245. Look for a relationship by answering the questions, then write a generalization for each one based on data from the chart. Be sure to write in complete sentences.

1. Does the gross national product seem to have a bearing on the amount of cars owned?

2. Are the countries with the highest literacy rates the countries that are most industrialized or least industrialized?

Critical Thinking

1. **Making Comparisons** Compare the environmental concerns faced by the governments of Brazil and Chile. How are they similar? How are they different?

2. **Making Generalizations** What generalization can you make about the culture and people of Argentina?

 Take It to the NET

Activity Search your home and make a list of items you find that are made from resources found in the rainforest. How can resources from the rainforest be used in sustainable ways? Visit the World Explorer: People, Places, and Cultures section of **phschool.com** for help in completing this activity.

Chapter 13 Self-Test As a final review activity, take the Chapter 13 Self-Test and get instant feedback on your answers. To take the test, visit the Social Studies section of **phschool.com.**

ANCIENT CIVILIZATIONS

Deep in the tropical forests of Mexico, the Mayan people created a sophisticated and advanced civilization. It reached its height between A.D. 250 and 900. The Mayas were great scholars who developed systems of mathematics and astronomy. They also created their own writing system and used it to record their history on stone plaques.

In the 12th century, Native Americans founded the Incan civilization in the Andes Mountains. By the 15th century, the empire stretched down the South American coast to include 12 million people. The Incas had a powerful army. Inca engineers built a network of paved roads that linked far-reaching parts of the empire. Relays of imperial messengers carried information, news, and messages to and from the capital city of Cuzco.

In the 13th century, a wandering tribe of Native Americans founded the Aztec civilization in the Valley of Mexico. Borrowing ideas from the Toltec and Olmec peoples with established civilizations in the area, the Aztec empire grew to 12 million people over a two hundred-year span.

? How have ancient civilizations influenced contemporary society in Latin America?

GLYPHS
Mayan writing was made up of a series of signs that archaeologists call glyphs. Many of the glyphs were simplified pictures of the objects they stood for. The Maya used glyphs to record their calendar and to write inscriptions about their history.

Outer shell of stone concealed earth base and royal tomb.

Temple contains historic inscriptions.

Priests used the main staircase.

People taking part in ceremonies could stand on the main stepped levels.

PALENQUE

The Temple of Inscriptions at Palenque was a famous Mayan pyramid. Deep inside the base was a secret chamber. It contained the tomb of Pacal. Pacal was a local king who died in about A.D. 684. A temple was built on top of the pyramid. Inside were stone tablets carved with glyphs that recorded the history of the local kings up to Pacal's reign.

TENOCHTITLÁN

The Aztec capital was Tenochtitlán. It has been called a "floating city" because it was built on one natural island and a series of artificial islands in Lake Texcoco. Raised roads, or causeways, and canals linked the islands to the mainland. Today, Mexico City stands on the site of the ancient city.

Aztec pyramid with temple at top

Victim being sacrificed on top of temple

Preaching priest

The bodies of sacrificed victims were thrown to the ground

Causeway

Temple precinct at Tenochtitlán

TRIBUTES

The Aztecs became very rich by collecting tributes (payments) from conquered tribes. Porters brought cloth, corn, pottery, and luxury goods to Tenochtitlán from the conquered cities. Goods were exchanged in four huge markets. Officials used picture writing to make lists of all the tributes that were paid. The Aztecs declared war on any tribe that refused to pay tribute.

QUIPU

The Incas did not have a written language. Instead, they used lengths of knotted string to record every aspect of their daily life. The strings were called quipu. Information about historic events, laws, gold reserves, population statistics, and other news was accurately stored using these knotted strands.

Welcome to Europe and Russia

ECONOMICS

Shop with the new European currency ...

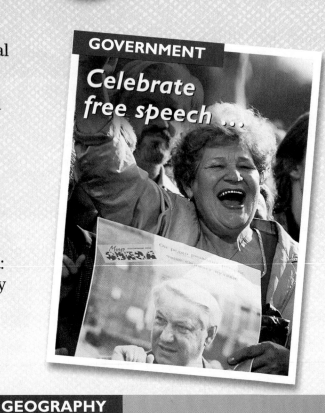

GOVERNMENT

Celebrate free speech ...

GEOGRAPHY

Explore important physical features ...

What do you want to learn?

CITIZENSHIP
Climb over the Berlin Wall ...

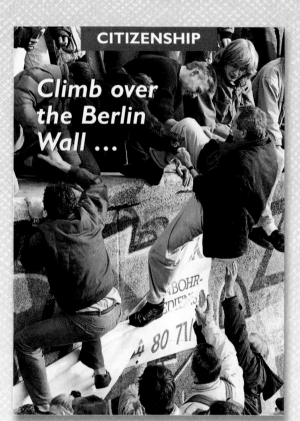

CULTURE
Listen to the music of Italy ...

HISTORY
Explore the ancient ruins of the Colosseum ...

SCIENCE, TECHNOLOGY, AND SOCIETY
Travel through France on a high-speed train ...

A journal can be your personal record of discovery. As you learn about Europe and Russia, you can create journal entries about what you read, write, think, and create. For your first entry, choose a region of Europe or Russia that you would like to visit. How might the history of this region be similar to the history of the region where you live? How might it be different?

EXPLORER'S JOURNAL

Guiding Questions

What questions do I need to ask to understand Europe and Russia?

Asking questions is a good way to learn. Think about what information you would want to know if you were visiting a new place, and what questions you might ask to find out. The questions on these pages can help guide your study of Europe and Russia. You might want to try adding a few of your own!

GEOGRAPHY

The continent of Europe is surrounded on three sides by water. Rivers wind through the land, leading to coastal harbors and inland seas. The steep slopes of ancient mountains separate regions of land and people. In the north, winters are long and cold, and in the south, summers are hot and dry. In the east, the Ural Mountains separate Europe from the vast, isolated region known as Siberia.

❶ How has the geography of Europe and Russia influenced economic, political, and cultural differences in the region?

HISTORY

Events of the past have shaped the modern European world. These events include ethnic conflicts, colonization of distant lands, shifting political borders, and changing economic systems. To understand how Europeans are living today, it is important to understand how history has shaped the course of their lives.

❷ How have the turbulent and triumphant events of the past influenced present-day Europe?

CULTURE

Some countries in Europe share a common language and religion, while others attempt to blend many different cultures successfully. Some regions have changed governments over centuries of war and peace. Different beliefs and customs have spread across the European continent for hundreds of years, but each nation manages to retain a cultural identity that is uniquely its own.

❸ What are some cultural traits that European nations share, and what are some traits that make each nation unique?

GOVERNMENT

For many years, Western Europe was separated from Eastern Europe and Russia by an invisible but strong boundary called the Iron Curtain. In Eastern Europe, behind the Iron Curtain, dictatorships maintained strict control over all aspects of the people's lives. In Western Europe, governments were democratic and the people were free to choose their leaders and make and enforce their own laws. Both of these regions have seen great political change in recent times, and look forward to more change in the future.

4 How are people's lives changing in the free–market economies of Eastern Europe?

ECONOMICS

The countries that share the continent of Europe also share limited natural resources. Economic stability and the ability to compete in worldwide markets depend on open transportation corridors and fair trade agreements. With these factors in mind, many countries of Europe have come together to form the European Union.

5 What are the economic advantages of participating in the European Union?

CITIZENSHIP

In democratic countries, citizens are allowed to be involved in government and are encouraged to participate in the political process. In countries where civil and human rights are violated, the freedom of all the people might depend on a group of citizens or even an individual leader speaking out for change, and inspiring reforms.

6 Why is it important for people in democratic societies to exercise their responsibilities as citizens?

SCIENCE, TECHNOLOGY, AND SOCIETY

People have moved from the cities to the countryside across the continent of Europe over the last century. Rapid technological advances in industry and telecommunications have made the world a smaller place. However, these advances have threatened traditional ways of life, especially in Europe's countryside.

7 How can people take advantage of new technologies and still maintain links to more traditional ways of life?

 Take It to the NET

For more information on Europe and Russia, visit the World Explorer: People, Places, and Cultures companion Web site at **phschool.com.**

ACTIVITY ATLAS

Europe and Russia

◆ ◆ ◆ ◆ ◆ ◆ ◆ ◆ ◆ ◆ ◆ ◆ ◆ ◆ ◆ ◆ ◆ ◆

Learning about Europe and Russia means being an explorer and a geographer. No explorer would start out without first checking some facts. Begin by exploring the maps of Europe and Russia on the following pages.

Relative Location

1. LOCATION

Locate Europe and Russia A geographer must know where a place is. Use the map at left to describe Europe and Russia's location relative to the United States. Which area is closer to the Equator, Europe and Russia or the United States? Which is closer to the Arctic Circle? Many people think the climates of Europe and the United States are similar. Look at the map. Then list three reasons why this might be so.

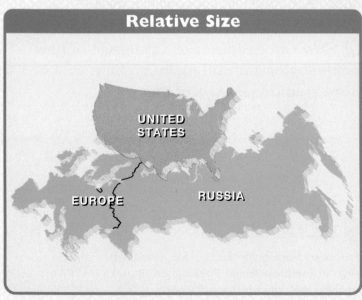

Relative Size

2. PLACE

Compare the Size of Europe, Russia, and the United States Are Europe and Russia together larger or smaller than the United States? How does the size of Russia alone compare to that of the continental United States?

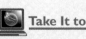 Take It to the NET

Items marked with this logo are periodically updated on the Internet. To get current information about the geography of Europe and Russia, go to **phschool.com.**

Europe and Russia: Climate Regions

KEY

- Semiarid
- Arid
- Mediterranean
- Humid subtropical
- Marine west coast
- Humid continental
- Subarctic
- Tundra
- Highlands

Mercator Projection

0   500   1000 mi
0   500   1000 km

3. REGIONS

Compare Climates in Europe and Russia Find Russia on the map. What are its three major climate regions? How does Russia's latitude, or distance from the Equator, affect its climate? Compare Russia's climate regions with those in Europe. Does Europe have a greater or lesser variety of climate regions than Russia? Find Moscow and Rome on the map. Which city do you think has a warmer climate? Why?

4. HUMAN-ENVIRONMENT INTERACTION

Predict the Effect of Climate on How People Live In warm countries such as Spain, many people live in houses with thick walls, which remain cool in the hot sun. In colder countries like Sweden, houses often have steep roofs to keep the snow from piling up on them. In what other ways do you think people have adapted to their climates?

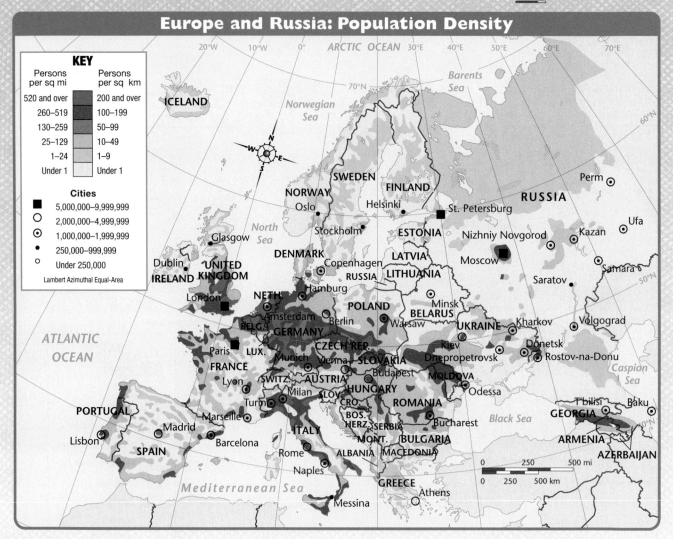

Europe and Russia: Population Density

KEY

Persons per sq mi	Persons per sq km
520 and over	200 and over
260–519	100–199
130–259	50–99
25–129	10–49
1–24	1–9
Under 1	Under 1

Cities

■ 5,000,000–9,999,999
○ 2,000,000–4,999,999
◉ 1,000,000–1,999,999
• 250,000–999,999
○ Under 250,000

Lambert Azimuthal Equal-Area

5. PLACE

Compare Population Densities Population density is the average number of people living within an area. Compare the parts of Europe that have many people to the parts that have only a few people. Do the same for Russia. How would you describe the pattern of population density of the two regions? Why is the population density different from place to place? Now compare the population densities of individual countries. How does Germany's population density compare to that of Norway? What might explain the difference?

6. MOVEMENT

Analyze Population and Transportation Notice the population density in the northernmost part of Europe and European Russia. Now look at the same region on the railroad map on the next page. How many railroads do you see in this region compared to regions in central and southern Europe and European Russia? Do regions with more people tend to have more or fewer rail routes? In what other ways might population and transportation affect each other?

7. MOVEMENT

Organize a Journey by Railway You've always wanted to visit Europe and Russia. Now you have the chance. Your family will be exploring Europe and Russia next summer by train. Together, you've set the following goals. Use the map below to plan which routes to take.

A. Your flight from the United States will land in Paris. From there, you want to travel to Warsaw. What's the shortest route? List the cities you'll pass through.

B. From Warsaw, you will go to Moscow. What other Russian city can you visit on the way?

C. After Moscow, you are going to Rome. You want to see as many major cities as you can on the way. What's your route?

D. From Rome, you must head straight back to Paris. Can you find the shortest route?

BONUS

Your trip is planned for March. What clothing should you pack for each part of your journey? Use the climate map on page 255 and information from the Map and Globe Handbook.

Europe: Major Railroad Lines

KEY
— Railroads
⊛ National capital
• Other city
Robinson Projection

ACTIVITY ATLAS

Former Republics of the Soviet Union

KEY
— National boundary
⊛ National capital
• Other city
Two-Point Equidistant Projection

8. REGIONS

Identify Countries of the Former Soviet Union From the 1920s until
1991, some of the countries in Eastern Europe were republics of the Soviet
Union. Today, all of these countries are independent nations. The map
above shows the former Soviet Union. The former republics are shown by
different colors. Look at Russia's western border. According to the map,
how many countries in Eastern Europe are former Soviet republics?

9. REGIONS

Describe the Size of Russia You can see from the map that, in terms of
size, Russia dominated the other Soviet republics. Use the scale of miles
on the map. About how far is it from the eastern border of Russia to the
western border of Russia? Moscow is the capital of Russia. It was also the
capital of the Soviet Union. How far is Moscow from Vladivostok? Do you
think your measurements are accurate? Are the actual distances greater or
less than your measurements? Why?

The Biggest Lakes and Rivers

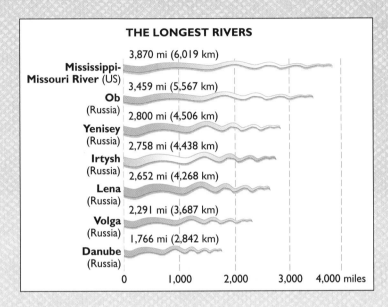

THE LONGEST RIVERS

Mississippi-Missouri River (US) — 3,870 mi (6,019 km)

Ob (Russia) — 3,459 mi (5,567 km)

Yenisey (Russia) — 2,800 mi (4,506 km)

Irtysh (Russia) — 2,758 mi (4,438 km)

Lena (Russia) — 2,652 mi (4,268 km)

Volga (Russia) — 2,291 mi (3,687 km)

Danube (Russia) — 1,766 mi (2,842 km)

0   1,000   2,000   3,000   4,000 miles

10. PLACE

Compare Physical Features Study these charts and diagrams. Using the maps in this Activity Atlas to locate the places listed in Russia and Europe. What lake has the largest volume of water? Some geographers say that the Caspian Sea is a lake. Others say it is a sea because its waters are salty. How does it compare to other lakes in size? What countries border it? What is the longest river in Russia and Europe?

LARGEST VOLUMES OF WATER

Lake Baikal — 22,995 cubic km — 18%

Lake Tanganyika (Africa) — 18,900 cubic km — 15%

All other freshwater lakes — 57%

Lake Superior (US–Canada) — 12,230 cubic km — 10%

LARGEST LAKES

Lake Balkhash — 7,115 sq mi — 18,482 sq km

Lake Ladoga — 7,000 sq mi — 18,130 sq km

Aral Sea — 13,000 sq mi — 33,800 sq km

Lake Baikal — 12,162 sq mi — 31,500 sq km

Caspian Sea — 152,239 sq mi — 394,299 sq km

Lake Superior (US–Canada) — 31,820 sq mi — 82,414 sq km

CHAPTER 14

EUROPE AND RUSSIA: Physical Geography

Trans-Siberian Railroad

KEY
— Trans-Siberian Railroad
— National boundary
⊛ National capital
• Other city
Two-Point Equidistant Projection

USING MAPS

This map shows the route of the Trans-Siberian Railroad, completed in 1916. The route is thousands of miles long, but it covers only a part of Siberia, which has many natural resources but few transportation routes. An addition to the rail line would make it easier to transport some of the region's many natural resources to other parts of Russia.

Planning a New Railroad Line

Look up Russia and Siberia in an encyclopedia. Make a list of Siberian mineral resources and where each can be found. Using this list, and other maps of Siberia, decide where you think a new rail line should run. Write down a list of cities and towns the route might pass through, and then draw a map showing both the old route and the new route.

Writing a Proposal

Write a proposal to persuade the Russian government to build a new rail line in Siberia. Start with a brief history of the Trans-Siberian Railroad. Then, tell where the new rail line will run, what purpose it will serve, and how the project will be paid for.

Physical Features

Setting the Scene

Eurasia is the world's largest landmass. It is made up of the continents of **Europe** and Asia and much of it lies in the northern latitudes. There the climate is colder and the growing season is shorter than in countries farther south.

Look at the map of Europe and Russia in the Activity Atlas on page 256. The continent of Europe is made up of 48 different countries and each country is about the size of an average state in the U.S. Included on the European continent is part of **Russia,** the largest country in the world. Beyond the **Ural** (YOOR uhl) **Mountains** that mark the boundary between Europe and Asia, the Russian region of **Siberia** (sy BIHR ee uh) extends for thousands of miles.

The Physical Features of Europe and Russia

Europe has four major land regions: The Northwestern Highlands, the North European Plain, the Central Uplands, and the Alpine Mountain System.

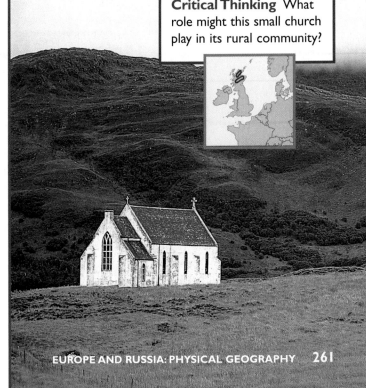

Far to the North

CULTURE This small church is located in the Scottish Highlands, which are in the Northwestern Highlands region.
Critical Thinking What role might this small church play in its rural community?

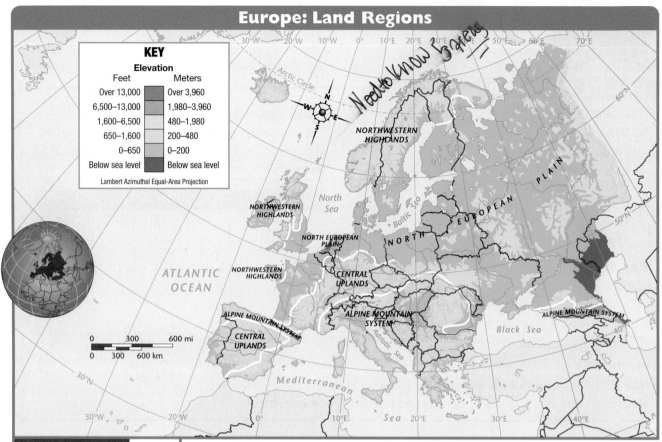

Europe: Land Regions

KEY

Elevation

Feet	Meters
Over 13,000	Over 3,960
6,500–13,000	1,980–3,960
1,600–6,500	480–1,980
650–1,600	200–480
0–650	0–200
Below sea level	Below sea level

Lambert Azimuthal Equal-Area Projection

0   300   600 mi
0   300   600 km

NORTHWESTERN HIGHLANDS

NORTHWESTERN HIGHLANDS

NORTH EUROPEAN PLAINS

NORTH EUROPEAN PLAIN

NORTHWESTERN HIGHLANDS

CENTRAL UPLANDS

ALPINE MOUNTAIN SYSTEM

CENTRAL UPLANDS

ALPINE MOUNTAIN SYSTEM

ALPINE MOUNTAIN SYSTEM

Arctic Circle

North Sea

Baltic Sea

ATLANTIC OCEAN

Adriatic Sea

Black Sea

Mediterranean Sea

GEOGRAPHY

This map shows the four major land regions of Europe. **Map Study** Which of the four land regions covers the greatest area? Where in Europe can you find land that is below sea level?

The Northwestern Highlands

The ancient mountains of the Northwestern Highlands are found in the northern parts of France, Great Britain, and Scandinavia. These have been eroded by centuries of wind and weather. Few people live here, where the climate is severe, the soil is thin, and the farming is poor.

Plains and Uplands

The North European Plain extends from Southern England and France to the foot of the Ural Mountains in Russia. This is a region of rich soil, productive farmland, and a high population density, which is the average number of people living in an area.

The Central Uplands stretch across the center of southern Europe. This region is made up of mountains and **plateaus** (pla TOHZ), which are large raised areas of level land. The soil in this region is too rocky for farming, but the land is rich in minerals and is good for grazing goats and sheep.

Alpine Mountain System

The Alpine Mountain System is a series of high mountain ranges that cross Europe from Spain to the Balkans and extend to Georgia east of the Black Sea. The Alps in Switzerland (SWIT sur lund) are a spectacular part of this region, and their majestic, snow-capped peaks are a favorite vacation spot for hikers and skiers. This region is home to families who work small farms in the valleys and meadows high in the mountains.

Siberia

Beyond the Ural Mountains lies a vast, low, marshy expanse called the West Siberian Plain. It covers more than a million square miles (2.58 million sq. km). It is known for its long, cold winters, harsh living conditions, and small, scattered population. At the eastern edge of the plain, the Central Siberian Plateau slopes upward. The land continues to rise, forming the East Siberian Uplands. This is a desolate region of rugged mountains, stark plateaus, and more than twenty active volcanoes.

River Resources and Transportation Corridors

The highlands of Europe and Russia are the source for many important rivers. High in the Swiss Alps, melting glaciers form two streams that combine to become the Rhine (RYN) River. The Rhine winds for 865 miles (1,391 km) through forests and plains and past castles, factories, and cities before it flows into the North Sea. The Rhine and its canals and **tributaries** (TRIB yoo tehr eez), which are the smaller rivers and streams that connect to the main channel, form a network of transportation corridors that reach every part of Western Europe.

The Volga (VAHL guh) River is the longest river on the continent of Europe. It flows for 2,291 miles (3,687 km) through western Russia and empties into the Caspian Sea. Its tributaries and canals link the Volga to the Arctic Ocean and the Baltic Sea. However, the river is frozen for three months of the year, so during the winter, the Volga and many other rivers of Russia are not **navigable** (NAV ih guh bul), which means ships cannot travel on them.

The Danube (DAN yoob) River begins in the mountains of Germany and flows through eight countries before it empties into the Black Sea. It is the second longest river in Europe, and it is navigable year round. These factors make it an important transportation corridor for trade and travel. Ships from the Mediterranean Sea can travel up the Danube to ports in Romania. From there, the cargo can be transferred to smaller boats that can continue up the river.

ECONOMICS

These farm workers in Siberia are havesting strawberries. The best farming country in Siberia lies in the region's southwestern section. Here, in addition to strawberries, farm workers harvest wheat, oats, and rye. **Critical Thinking** Based on this photograph, what do you think a job harvesting strawberries would be like?

Ocean Patterns and Processes

The continent of Europe forms a **peninsula** (puh NIN suh luh), a body of land nearly surrounded by water. It juts into the Atlantic Ocean and is bordered by the Mediterranean Sea, the North Sea, and the Norwegian Sea. The entire continent is affected by all of this water. The warm ocean current called the Gulf Stream begins in the Gulf of Mexico and flows northeast to join the North Atlantic Current that flows into the Arctic Ocean. The warm water keeps the northern coastlines of Great Britain and Norway from freezing in the winter, even if the land is covered in ice and snow.

Moist, warm air blows inland from the coast, sweeping across the North European Plain. West of the mountains, rainfall is heavy. When the moist air rises over the mountains, it cools and falls as snow along the ridges of the Alpine Mountain System. Not much moisture makes it over to the east side of the mountains, so this area is hotter and dryer.

The waves that have battered the coastline for millions of years, have formed bays, inlets, coves, and harbors. Look at the maps in the Activity Atlas on pages 255–256 to see how these natural features affect the climate and influence where people live.

SECTION 1 ASSESSMENT

AFTER YOU READ

RECALL

1. Identify: (a) Eurasia, (b) Europe, (c) Russia, (d) Ural Mountains, (e) Siberia

2. Define: (a) plateau, (b) tributary, (c) navigable, (d) peninsula

COMPREHENSION

3. Why does the North European Plain have the highest population density of all the major land regions?

4. What makes the Danube River a major transportation corridor?

5. What keeps the harbors of Northern England and Norway from freezing in the winter?

CRITICAL THINKING AND WRITING

6. **Exploring the Main Idea** Review the Main Idea statement at the beginning of this section. Write a paragraph to describe how your life would change if you moved from a farm in the North European Plain to a farm in the Alpine Mountain System.

7. **Comparing and Contrasting** Write a paragraph comparing life at a port city on the Rhine to life in a remote village in the Scottish highlands. In which place would you rather live? Give reasons for your answer.

ACTIVITY

 Take It to the NET

8. **Creating a Map of Siberia** The physical geography of Siberia is varied and beautiful. Imagine that you are walking along the routes described on the Web site. Write a detailed account of your experience, including geographical features, climate, and vegetation. Visit the World Explorer: People, Places, and Cultures section of **phschool.com** for help in completing this activity.

Humans and the Physical Environment

BEFORE YOU READ

READING FOCUS

1. How do people adapt to climate conditions in different parts of Europe and Russia?
2. How have people learned to modify and use the physical environment and natural vegetation of Europe and Russia?

KEY TERMS

deciduous
coniferous
taiga
prairies
steppe
tundra
permafrost

KEY PLACES

Barcelona
Irkutsk
Norway
Iceland

NOTE TAKING

Copy the concept web below. As you read the section fill in the concept web with information about the natural vegetation of Europe and Russia.

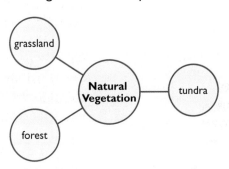

MAIN IDEA

People find ways to adapt to the climate and to modify the natural vegetation where they live.

Setting the Scene

It is February in **Barcelona** (bar suh LOH nuh), Spain. Twelve-year-old Isabella wakes up to a warm, sunny Saturday morning. It is 65°F (18°C)—the perfect day for a bike ride.

At that same moment, it is late afternoon in **Irkutsk** (ihr KOOTSK), a city in Southern Siberia. It is a clear, cold, sunny day. The temperature is –15°F (–26°C). Alexy is skiing home after a visit with his grandmother.

In Barcelona, which is located on the Mediterranean Sea, the winters are mild and rainy, while the summers are hot and dry. In Siberia, snow covers the ground for six months of the year. Winters are severe, with temperatures falling to –50°F (–46°C). Summers are cool and short. The temperature on a pleasant summer day in Irkutsk is the same as the temperature on a chilly winter day in Barcelona.

Humans Adapt to the Physical Environment

In Section 1, you read about how the ocean affects climate. Much of northwestern Europe, including the coast of **Nor-**

Skiing in Siberia

GEOGRAPHY In areas such as Siberia, where winters are long and snow covers the ground for six months of the year, cross-country skiing is an efficient way to get from place to place. **Critical Thinking** What other forms of transportation have people developed in response to their climate or physical environment?

265

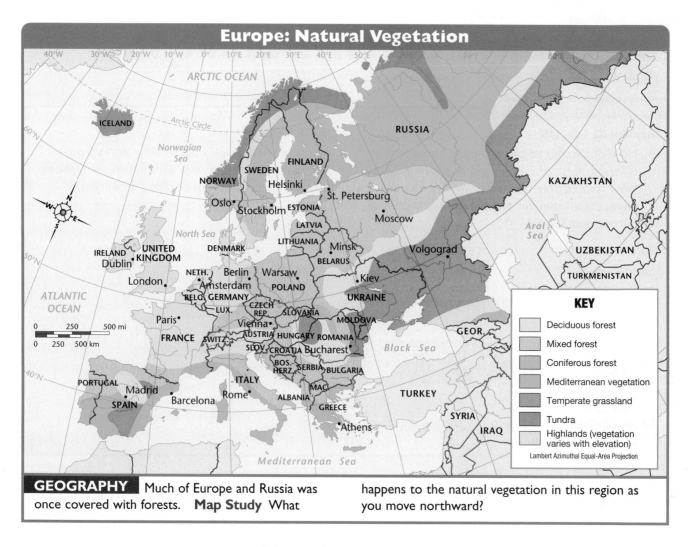

Europe: Natural Vegetation

KEY
- Deciduous forest
- Mixed forest
- Coniferous forest
- Mediterranean vegetation
- Temperate grassland
- Tundra
- Highlands (vegetation varies with elevation)

Lambert Azimuthal Equal-Area Projection

GEOGRAPHY Much of Europe and Russia was once covered with forests. **Map Study** What happens to the natural vegetation in this region as you move northward?

way and the southern tip of **Iceland,** has a marine west coast climate and is rainy year round.

The countries that ring the Mediterranean have a climate similar to that of Barcelona. Much of this region is in the rain shadow of the mountains of the Alpine Mountain System. A rain shadow is an area on the dry, sheltered side of a mountain that receives little rainfall.

Most of Eastern Europe is in the humid continental region. As you travel inland, you move out of the range of the warm, moist air blowing in from the Atlantic. People living here are prepared for longer, colder winters and very hot summers.

Few people live in the climate regions of the subarctic and tundra areas of Europe and Asia because during the long, dark winters, temperatures stay well below zero. In the summer, temperatures do not get much above freezing.

Modifying the Physical Environment

Temperature, rainfall, altitude, and latitude are factors that determine the natural vegetation, or plant life, of an area. Compare the vegetation map to the climate and landform maps you have seen.

Forests and Grasslands

Deciduous (duh SID joo us) forests, made up of trees that lose their leaves, once covered most of Europe. Over many years, people cleared the trees to create farmland and build cities. In Northern Europe and in Russia, there are large **coniferous** (koh NIF ur us) forests, which have trees with cones that carry and protect the seeds. In Russia, the **taiga** (TY guh), as this forested region is called, covers more than 4 million square miles (6.4 million sq km). The soil is not so good for farming, and the growing season is short.

The central and southern parts of the North European Plain were once covered with grasslands called **prairies.** People created farmland in this region. In Russia, the grasslands are called **steppes.** The fertile, black soil is good for farming.

Tundra

The **tundra** is a treeless plain where only grasses and mosses grow. Here, the ground is **permafrost,** or permanently frozen soil, and there is only a very short growing season. In Iceland, Norway, and northern Russia, the people have had to find ways to raise food and construct shelters without the natural resources that forests provide.

The Frozen Tundra

GEOGRAPHY The tundra stretches from northern Europe into northern Russia. The shapes visible on the ground here are caused by upheavals in permafrost. **Critical Thinking** What are some ways that people living here might raise food and construct shelters in the absence of natural resources?

SECTION 2 ASSESSMENT

AFTER YOU READ

RECALL

1. Identify: (a) Barcelona, (b) Irkutsk, (c) Norway, (d) Iceland

2. Define: (a) deciduous, (b) coniferous, (c) taiga, (d) prairie, (e) steppe, (f) tundra, (g) permafrost

COMPREHENSION

3. What are the advantages of living in the rain shadow of the Alps?

4. What makes the taiga an important resource for people living in Siberia?

CRITICAL THINKING AND WRITING

5. Exploring the Main Idea Review the Main Idea statement at the beginning of this section. Then, imagine that you are either Isabella or Alexy and write a letter describing your day. Explain how you stayed comfortable and what you saw when you were out.

6. Drawing Conclusions Considering the difficulties posed by the physical environment of the tundra, why do you think people choose to live there?

ACTIVITY

7. Design a House Design a house for life in the French countryside and for the tundra of Norway. Use materials found in each region. How will this house protect you from the climate? Include illustrations that detail your design ideas and construction methods.

Geographic Factors and Natural Resources

READING FOCUS

1. Where do fossil fuels come from and how do they benefit Europe and Russia?
2. How are water resources used in Europe and Russia?
3. What geographic features contribute to the fertile soil of Europe and Ukraine?

KEY TERMS

fossil fuels
nonrenewable resources
turbine
hydroelectric power
loess

KEY PLACES

North Sea
Ruhr Valley
Silesia
Ukraine

MAIN IDEA

Europe and Russia are rich in both renewable and nonrenewable natural resources.

NOTE TAKING

Copy the Venn diagram below. As you read the section fill in the diagram with information about the natural resources of Europe and Russia.

Europe — Both — Russia

Off-Shore Oil Rigs

ECONOMICS Great Britain, Norway, and other nations around the North Sea depend on the oil and natural gas drilled from underwater petroleum deposits. **Critical Thinking** Do you think it is expensive to drill for oil in the North Sea? Why?

Setting the Scene

Europe is a wealthy region and a world leader in economic development. Part of this wealth and success comes from Europe's rich supply of natural resources, such as fertile soil, water, and fuels. Russia has a wide variety of resources, but its harsh climate, frozen rivers, and huge transportation distances have made it difficult to turn these resources into wealth.

Physical Processes that Produce Fossil Fuels

Fossil fuels in the form of oil, natural gas, and coal provide energy for industries. They are called fossil fuels because they are formed over millions of years from the remains of ancient animals and plants. Fossil fuels are **nonrenewable resources;** once they are used up, they are gone.

Millions of years ago, marine plants and animals called plankton died and settled on the ocean floor. Over the years, the plankton was

Europe and Russia: Natural Resources

KEY

- Hydroelectric power
- Iron
- Copper
- Bauxite
- Phosphates
- Gold
- Nickel
- Uranium
- Coal
- Petroleum
- Lead
- Natural gas
- Tungsten
- Diamonds

Lambert Azimuthal Equal-Area Projection

covered with mud and sand. The weight of this material gradually changed the plankton into oil trapped inside of porous rock. Oil drilling equipment cuts through the rock and removes the oil, which is called crude oil. Crude oil is then cleaned to make refined oil products that are used to run cars and heat homes.

There are oil and gas deposits under the ocean floor in the **North Sea** and Siberia. However, these resources in remote parts of Russia are thousands of miles from the country's industrial centers. They must be transported by pipeline.

Coal is made from ancient plant and animal materials that decay to form peat. Over millions of years, the pressure of materials heaped on top of peat deposits gradually changed the peat into brown coal. Increased pressure changed the brown coal into what is called soft coal that is used in industries worldwide.

Coal is mined in Great Britain; the **Ruhr Valley** of Germany; the industrial center called **Silesia** (sy LEE shuh), where Poland, the Czech (chek) Republic, and Germany come together; **Ukraine** (yoo KRAYN); and Russia, which has one-third of the world's coal reserves.

Russia also has great reserves of iron ore, which is used to make steel. Most of these mineral deposits are west of the Ural Mountains, which is where Russia's industrial centers are located.

GEOGRAPHY

Europe and Russia are rich in natural resources that are important for the development and strength of the economy of the region. **Map Study** How does the distribution of natural resources match the major population centers of Europe?

AS YOU READ

Monitor Your Reading What kinds of natural resources have you used so far today?

Geographic Processes

In Western Europe, water is an important resource. People use the water supply for personal use, irrigating crops, and transporting goods. People also use water as an energy source. The force of water flowing from a waterfall or from a dam on a river can spin machines called **turbines** (TUR bynz). Spinning turbines generate, or create, electricity. This is called **hydroelectric** (hy dro ee LEK trik) **power**; *hydro* is the Greek word for water.

Many countries use their water resources for power. Norway gets almost all of its electric power from water, and factories in Sweden, Switzerland, Austria, Spain, and Portugal all run on power generated by dams on rivers that flow out of the mountains.

Except in the southern and western part of the country, the frozen rivers in Russia and Siberia cannot be used to generate hydroelectric power. In addition, they are polluted by industrial waste. These polluted rivers will need to be restored before they can be developed as a natural resource.

Over thousands of years, winds have deposited fertile, dust-like soil called **loess** (LOH ess) across the North European Plain. This soil, combined with the plentiful rainfall and a long growing season, enables European farmers to produce abundant crops. In Ukraine, a black soil called *chernozem* (CHEHR nuh zem) is very fertile. It is extremely important for food production in this region.

SECTION 3 ASSESSMENT

AFTER YOU READ

RECALL

1. Identify: (a) North Sea, (b) Ruhr Valley, (c) Silesia, (d) Ukraine

2. Define: (a) fossil fuels, (b) nonrenewable resources, (c) turbine, (d) hydroelectric power, (e) loess

COMPREHENSION

3. Why are fossil fuels more beneficial to the economy of Europe than to the economy of Russia?

4. What prevents hydroelectric power from being developed in Russia compared to Europe?

5. Explain the physical processes that produce renewable soil resources across the North European Plain.

CRITICAL THINKING AND WRITING

6. **Exploring the Main Idea** Review the Main Idea statement at the beginning of this section. Then, write a paragraph identifying the most important natural resource for Europe and for Russia. Give reasons for your ideas.

7. **Making Predictions** What will Russia's major natural resource be in twenty years? Write a paragraph describing the development of the resource and tell how it will affect the country's economy.

ACTIVITY

8. **Writing a Journal** Imagine that you are on an oil rig in the North Sea. Write a journal entry describing your important, dangerous work on the high seas.

Interpreting Graphs

Learn the Skill

Graphs are helpful because they organize information in a simple, easy-to-read way. One of the most common types of graph is the line graph. A line graph shows how data values change over time.

Bar graphs use bars to show amounts. The length of the bar tells you the number value it represents.

Circle graphs use slices of the circle (like a pie) to show proportion, or the parts of a whole. The value of the entire circle is 100 percent.

To read a graph:

A. Read the title to find out what information the graph shows.

B. Figure out what kind of graph it is. Study the three graphs on this page. Which one is a line graph? Which is a circle graph? Which is a bar graph?

C. Read the information on the graph. Read the line graph to tell which month has the hottest weather in Irkutsk, Russia. Read the bar graph to tell which country produces the most oil. Read the circle graph to tell which method is used to generate the most electricity in Russia.

Practice the Skill

Compare the three graphs on this page. How does each type of graph show the value of the data? Do you think a circle graph could be used to show yearly temperature changes? Could a line graph show oil production in different countries?

Apply the Skill

See the Chapter Review and Assessment at the end of this chapter for more questions on comparing graphs.

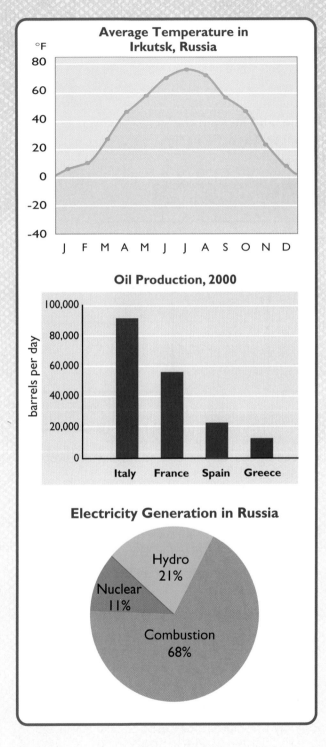

Average Temperature in Irkutsk, Russia

Oil Production, 2000

Electricity Generation in Russia

Review and Assessment

Creating a Chapter Summary

On a separate piece of paper, draw a diagram like this one, and include the information that summarizes the first section of the chapter. Then, fill in the remaining boxes with summaries of Sections 2 and 3.

EUROPE AND RUSSIA: PHYSICAL GEOGRAPHY

Section 1
Europe and Russia have four major land regions. The population density in each of these regions depends on the climate, the quality of the soil, and the access to navigable rivers.

Section 2

Section 3

Reviewing Key Terms

Match the definitions in Column I with the key terms in Column II.

Column I

1. Russian grassland
2. electricity generated by water
3. rich, dust-like soil
4. rivers or streams that connect to a larger river
5. able to be used by ships
6. treeless plain where the ground is permafrost
7. fuels—coal, oil, and natural gas—that come from remains of ancient plants and animals

Column II

a. navigable
b. tundra
c. fossil fuels
d. steppe
e. hydroelectric power
f. loess
g. tributaries

Reviewing the Main Ideas

1. Identify the four major land regions of Europe. (Section 1)
2. Identify the part of Russia that is in Asia. (Section 1)
3. Name the mountain range that separates Europe and Asia. (Section 1)
4. What is the longest river on the continent of Europe? (Section 1)
5. What is a marine west coast climate? (Section 2)
6. What kind of vegetation covered most of Europe long ago? (Section 2)
7. What parts of Europe have large reserves of coal? (Section 3)
8. Why is it difficult for Russia to take advantage of its natural resources? (Section 3)

Map Activity

Europe and Russia

For each place listed below, write the letter from the map that shows its location.

1. Europe
2. Ural Mountains
3. Alps
4. Siberia
5. Volga River
6. North Sea

 Take It to the NET

Enrichment For more map activities using geography skills, visit the social studies section of **phschool.com.**

Writing Activity

1. **Using Primary Sources** Find out more about one of the land regions of Europe or the expanse of Siberia. Visit your school or local library and use primary sources such as newspaper and magazine articles to find out more information about the towns in the region, details of daily life, how people make a living, and so on. Use the information to create a profile of a typical family in the region.

2. **Write Catalogue** You work for a coat manufacturer. You have just received a shipment of two new coats. One is perfect for the drizzle of London. The other is designed to keep off the Siberian chill. Write a paragraph describing the features of the two coats for your company catalogue, including details from the climate in these places.

Applying Your Skills

Turn to the Skills for Life Activity on page 271 to answer the following questions.

1. Which graph would you NOT use to show population increases in Great Britain during the past 10 years?

   A line graph

   C bar graph

   B circle graph

   D none of the above

2. Which kind of graph would best show the percent of days with rain in Southern France?

   A line graph

   C bar graph

   B circle graph

   D both a and c

Critical Thinking

1. **Identifying Main Ideas** How does the Gulf Stream affect the climate of the North European Plain? How does it affect the coastline of Norway?

2. **Recognizing Cause and Effect** Russia has had to build an extensive rail system and pipelines to transport resources out of Siberia. What are the reasons for needing to build these transportation corridors?

 Take It to the NET

Activity Read about Europe's diverse physical geography. How are some of the geographic features of Europe similar to and different from the region where you live? Visit the World Explorer: People, Places, and Cultures section of **phschool.com** for help in completing this activity.

Chapter 14 Self-Test As a final review activity, take the Chapter 14 Self-Test and get instant feedback on your answers. To take the test, visit the Social Studies section of **phschool.com.**

EUROPE AND RUSSIA:
Shaped by History

Inventions in Industry

Michael Faraday's first electric generator

1733 John Kay, flying shuttle *England*

1765 James Watt, improved steam engine *Scotland*

1779 Samuel Crompton, spinning mule *England*

1803 Richard Trevethick, first successful steam locamotive *Wales*

| 1725 | 1750 | 1775 | 1800 | 1825 | 1850 | 1875 |

1764 James Hargreaves, spinning jenny *England*

1800 Alessandro Volta, electric battery *Italy*

1831 Michael Faraday, electric generator *England*

1859 Jean-Joseph-Etienne Lenoir, first successful internal combustion engine *France*

James Watt's steam engine changed heat into energy, which could be used to power machinery.

USING TIME LINES

This time line shows European inventions in industry from the 1700s and 1800s.

Exploring Early Inventions

Many of the inventions shown on the time line helped pave the way for more advanced technology. Visit the library or use the Internet to gather information on three of the inventions shown on the time line. Include the inventor's role in the discovery and how the invention crossed the boundaries of societies and helped shape the world. Prepare a brief oral report on your findings and be prepared to share it with the rest of the class.

Making a Time line of Modern Inventions

People continue to invent technologies that change the world. Make a list of eight modern-day inventions that you would like to know more about. Use the library or the Internet to gather information about these inventions, including the year they were invented, who invented them, and what their purpose is. Create a time line showing the information you gather.

From Ancient Greece to Feudal Europe

BEFORE YOU READ

1. What were the main accomplishments of the ancient Greeks and Romans?
2. What impact did Christianity and feudalism have on life during the Middle Ages?

KEY TERMS

policy
empire
Pax Romana
feudalism
Middle Ages
serf

KEY PEOPLE AND PLACES

Greece
Athens
Alexander the Great
Rome
Jesus
Palestine

MAIN IDEA

Many achievements of the empires of the ancient world have had a lasting impact throughout history, and continue to this day.

NOTE TAKING

Copy the outline below. As you read the section, fill in the outline with information about ancient times and the Middle Ages.

I. **Ancient Greeks and Romans**
  A. Greeks
    1.
    2.
    3.
    4.
  B. Romans
    1.
    2.
    3.
    4.
II. **Middle Ages**
  A. Feudalism
    1.
    2.
    3.
    4.

Setting the Scene

Athletes compete in the Olympics. Buildings are designed in a classical style. Judges make rulings based on written law. Citizens pay taxes to the state. All of these activities can be traced to ancient times.

Achievements of the Ancient Greeks and Romans

The ancient Greeks were Europe's first great philosophers, historians, poets, and writers. They borrowed ideas from older civilizations of Mesopotamia and Egypt and used them to develop new ways of thinking. Their observations led to scientific ways of gathering knowledge. Their method of rule led to democracy.

Origins of Democracy In ancient times, **Greece** was divided into over 100 city-states. Each city-state acted as an independent nation. The most famous was **Athens.** In Athens, free men were allowed to vote on their leaders, laws, and **policies.** Policies are the methods and plans a government uses to do work. Women, slaves, and non-Greeks could not vote. Even so, the idea that people should have a voice in how they are ruled had a strong impact on history.

Aristotle

HISTORY The Greeks and Romans made sculptures of their political and cultural figures. This is a sculpture of Aristotle, Alexander the Great's teacher. Aristotle is known for his observations about the natural world and creating rules for drama that are still used for plays, TV, and movies today.

Critical Thinking
Why do you think the Greeks and Romans made sculptures of their political and cultural figures?

The Roman Empire

GEOGRAPHY This map shows the regions conquered by the Romans. These regions became part of the Roman Empire, which lasted for hundreds of years. **Map Study** Using what you know about the resources, climate, and natural barriers of Europe, describe the geography of the Roman Empire.

Map: The Roman Empire, A.D. 150

North Sea · Britannia · London · Germania · Paris · Gallia · Rhine R. · ATLANTIC OCEAN · Milan · Marseille · Florence · Italy · Rome · Hispania · Corduba · Dalmatia · Adriatic Sea · Dacia · Danube River · Black Sea · Byzantium · Istanbul · Cappadocia · Pergamum · Athens · Syracuse · Carthage · Mediterranean Sea · North Africa · Libya · Egypt · Nile River · Red Sea · Arabia · Petra · Jerusalem · Syria · Mesopotamia · Euphrates River · Tigris River · Armeni · Parthia · Caspian Sea

LINKS TO Science

The Volcano and the City of Pompeii The city of Pompeii stood at the foot of a volcano called Mt. Vesuvius. In A.D. 79, the volcano erupted. Smoke, ash, and cinders rained on the city. In two days, the eruption covered the city with about 20 feet (6.6 m) of ash. It sealed the city like a volcanic "time capsule." Archaeologists have uncovered Pompeii's buildings, almost perfectly intact. They have even found loaves of bread in ovens!

Spread of Greek Culture   Greek language, ideas, and culture were spread throughout the Mediterranean by **Alexander the Great,** a king of Macedonia. Between 334 B.C. and 323 B.C., Alexander conquered an **empire** that spread eastward to the Indus River. An empire is a collection of lands ruled by a single government. When the Romans took over Alexander's lands they borrowed many Greek ideas.

The Roman Empire   The Romans began to build their empire after Alexander died. Augustus, the first emperor of **Rome,** came to power in 27 B.C. His rule began 200 years of Roman peace, or **Pax Romana** (pahks ro MAH nah). During this time, Rome was the most powerful state in Europe. Magnificent cities were built, new technologies were developed, and the economy prospered.

Judges in the Roman Empire followed written laws to make decisions. These written laws protected all citizens in the empire, not only the rich and powerful. Modern ideas about law and citizenship used by democratic governments are based on Roman law.

The Pax Romana was followed by hundreds of years of war. More and more soldiers were needed to defend the empire's boundaries. The taxes raised to maintain the army hurt the economy. The emperor could no longer govern such a huge area, and the empire was divided into two parts. The western half of the empire began to crumble.

The Fall of Rome   The Christian religion was based on the teachings of **Jesus,** who lived in the eastern Mediterranean region of **Palestine.** When the Roman emperor Constantine became a follower of Christianity, the religion quickly spread throughout the empire. Later, the empire collapsed. Government, law and order, and trade broke down, but Christianity survived. Without the empire, people were living in difficult, dangerous times. Christianity gave them hope.

Europe in the Middle Ages

Along with Christianity, **feudalism** (FYOOD ul iz um) was an important part of society in the **Middle Ages,** the time period that falls between ancient and modern times. Feudalism was a way to organize society when there was no central government. Peasants made up about 90% of the population. They worked as **serfs,** farming the land on manors owned by lords. The lords collected taxes for the king. The serfs were not slaves, but they had to follow the lord's rules. In return, they were given work and protection.

Over the centuries, life in Europe changed. Trade increased. Many serfs bought their freedom from the lords and moved into towns, where they could practice trades and take advantage of opportunities. Towns grew into cities. By the 1400s, a new way of life had begun to develop in Europe.

Notre Dame

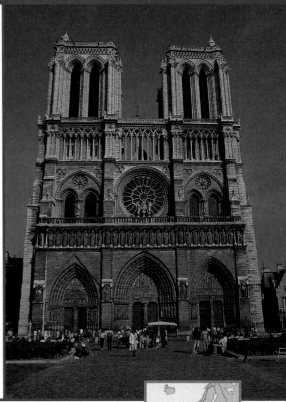

CULTURE Picture a building like a hollow mountain of stones. Graceful arches sweep to the sky. This building is a cathedral, a great church. Many cathedrals were built in Europe during the Middle Ages. It took 150 years to build the cathedral of Notre Dame. Workers devoted their lives to the work, believing it was God's wish. This strong religious faith was a key part of life in Europe during the Middle Ages. **Critical Thinking** How do you think this long-term building project based on faith in God affected the society?

SECTION 1 ASSESSMENT

AFTER YOU READ

RECALL

1. Identify: (a) Greece, (b) Athens, (c) Alexander the Great, (d) Rome, (e) Jesus, (f) Palestine

2. Define: (a) policy, (b) empire, (c) Pax Romana (d) feudalism, (e) Middle Ages, (f) serf

COMPREHENSION

3. How did the ancient leaders of Greece and Rome unite their empires?

4. What were the positive effects of feudalism on Europe in the Middle Ages?

CRITICAL THINKING AND WRITING

5. **Exploring the Main Idea** Review the Main Idea statement at the beginning of this section. Write a paragraph describing how you have been influenced by the culture and ideas of the ancient world.

6. **Compare and Contrast** Describe some ways in which Europe under the Pax Romana was different from Europe in the Middle Ages.

ACTIVITY

7. **Writing a Journal** You are a Roman governor in Britain, far from your home and family in Rome. Write a journal entry describing the things you miss about Rome. Be as specific as you can.

Renaissance and Revolution

Fine Art

CULTURE Painters were still creating works to celebrate Marco Polo's adventures more than 100 years after his journey. **Critical Thinking** Why were Europeans excited by the idea of Marco Polo's travels?

Setting the Scene

At the end of the thirteenth century, **Marco Polo** traveled from Venice to the east and brought back marvelous tales of the voyage. He visited the Spice Islands, sources of cinnamon, nutmeg, and cloves—spices that Europeans loved. He earned great riches, only to be robbed on his way home to Italy. For centuries after, explorers searched the globe for routes that would lead to more riches.

The Age of Discovery

Two hundred years later, Christopher Columbus was inspired by Marco Polo's travels to set sail on a voyage of his own. Columbus believed that sailing west would lead to a new route to China, Japan, the Spice Islands, and India. Instead, Columbus came ashore in the New World and claimed it for Spain.

While Columbus was sailing across the Atlantic, the Portuguese were making their way down the western coast of Africa. They set up a very profitable trade in gold, ivory, and slaves. When they finally traveled around the Cape of Good Hope and reached the Indian Ocean, they were able to open trade corridors to the Spice Islands. To people in Europe, spices were more precious than any other resource.

Other European nations were quick to send explorers to faraway lands, seeking new trade routes and sources for exotic items. The rulers of Spain, France, England, and the Netherlands all wanted a share in the riches that the Portuguese enjoyed. As a result, wonderful goods poured into Europe. In additions to spices, there were precious minerals, gold and silver, and fur and tobacco.

The Renaissance   The Age of Exploration made the European monarchs very rich. **Monarchs** were the king and queen in control of a nation. The traders and merchants got rich, too, and formed the new **middle class,** a group between the very poor and the very rich. The middle class paid taxes to the monarchs and soon, the monarchs did not need the support of the feudal lords. Feudalism began to disappear.

Members of the middle class used their money to support artists and scholars. They now had time to enjoy art and learning. This rebirth of interest in learning and art is called the **Renaissance** (REN uh sahns). It began in Italy in the 1300s and spread over the rest of the continent. It reached its peak in the 1500s.

Renaissance scholars and artists rediscovered the ideas of ancient Greece and Rome, and what they learned changed the culture. They began writing fresh, powerful poetry. They built glorious buildings and filled them with breathtaking paintings and sculpture. People focused on improving this world rather than hoping for a better life after death. This new approach to knowledge was called **humanism.**

The Age of Revolution

Revolution in Government   Over time, the monarchs of Europe unified their countries and made them stronger. The kings were absolute monarchs who exercised complete power. **Louis XIV**, a powerful king of France from 1643 to 1715, said, "I am the state." His wishes were the law, and no one dared to disagree with him. He believed that his power to rule came from God. The French monarchs taxed citizens heavily to pay for their luxurious lifestyle.

By the end of the Age of Revolution, Europe was a continent of powerful nations. They were bustling with trade and bursting with new scientific ideas. Europe was about to begin a new kind of revolution. This time it would be an economic one—the rise of industry.

Europeans began to question their governments and think about

Leonardo da Vinci

CULTURE   Leonardo da Vinci (above), one of the best-known artists of the Renaissance, is famous for his paintings and drawings. But he also excelled as a scientist, an engineer, and an inventor.

AS YOU READ

Use Prior Knowledge How might humanism have influenced the Scientific Revolution?

The Seeds of Change

The idea of a limited government spread from Great Britain to the thirteen colonies in North America. A colony is a territory ruled by another nation, usually one that is far away. In 1776, the colonies rebelled against the British king, and in 1789, the French Revolution overthrew King Louis XVI.

change—even the far-reaching change in government called **revolution.** In the 1600s, when England's king refused to share his power with **Parliament** (PAHR luh munt), the elected legislature, he was overthrown. For a time, there was no monarch in England. The monarchy was later restored, but not before the people realized the kind of limited government they wanted. The modern age of science and democracy had begun.

The Scientific Revolution At the time of the revolutions in America and in France, there was also a revolution going on in the world of science. For centuries European scientists had studied nature to explain how the world fit with their religious beliefs. During the Age of Revolution, that approach changed. Scientists started to base theories on facts by watching carefully to see what really happened in the world. This change is called the **Scientific Revolution.** The Scientific Revolution required new procedures, called the scientific method, in which ideas are tested with experiments and observation.

The scientific method led to dramatic advances. For example, in the Middle Ages, Europeans believed that the Earth was at the center of the universe. Renaissance scientists challenged this belief, but they could not prove their ideas. Then, during the Scientific Revolution, scientists used a new form of mathematics called calculus (KAL kyoo lus) to study the movement of the moon and planets.

SECTION 2 ASSESSMENT

AFTER YOU READ

RECALL

1. Identify: (a) Marco Polo, (b) Louis XIV

2. Recall: (a) monarch, (b) middle class, (c) Renaissance, (d) humanism, (e) revolution, (f) Parliament, (g) Scientific Revolution

COMPREHENSION

3. What factors led to Europe's voyages of exploration?

4. What groups formed the new middle class in Europe during the Age of Revolution?

5. How did government and science in Europe change during the Age of Revolution?

CRITICAL THINKING AND WRITING

6. **Exploring the Main Idea** Review the Main Idea statement at the beginning of this section. Imagine you are a merchant at a European port. Write a letter to a friend describing the changes in your life as trade ships arrive from all over the world.

7. **Making Valid Generalizations** The French Revolution took place thirteen years after the American Revolution. With a partner, write a dialogue between an American traveling in Europe in 1780

and a French worker who is thinking about the benefits of limited power in a ruler.

ACTIVITY

8. **Research the Scientific Revolution** Do research to learn more about scientific discoveries made during the Scientific Revolution by such scientists as Galileo, René Descartes, Isaac Newton, and Louis Pasteur. Choose two scientists, describe their discoveries, and explain how the influence of these discoveries crossed the boundaries of societies and helped shape the world.

Industrial Revolution and Nationalism

BEFORE YOU READ

READING FOCUS

1. How are the Industrial Revolution and the Age of Imperialism connected?
2. How did the Industrial Revolution influence nationalism?

KEY TERMS

Industrial Revolution
textiles
imperialism
nationalism
alliance

NOTE TAKING

Copy the flow chart below. As you read the section, fill in a flow chart with information about the Industrial Revolution, imperialism, and nationalism.

Invention of Spinning Mule → ☐ → ☐ → ☐ → Workers Gain Power

Countries Build Factories → ☐ → ☐ → ☐ → Export Goods to Colonies

Destructive Nationalism → ☐ → ☐ → ☐ → Creative Nationalism

MAIN IDEA

The 1800s represent a century of change for the nations of Europe, change that left its mark on history and continues to influence contemporary life worldwide.

Setting the Scene

Until the late 1700s, everything that people needed was handmade. Goods were either produced at home or bought from small local shops. Then, inventors began to create machines that could make goods quickly and cheaply. Huge factories housed the machines. People left their homes to work in the factories and keep the machines running. This change in the way goods were made was called the **Industrial Revolution.** It was also a revolution in the ways people lived and worked.

Factories in England

GEOGRAPHY This picture from the 1800s shows factory smokestacks along the Don River in Sheffield, an industrial city in northern England. **Critical Thinking** Why are factory towns often located on or near rivers?

Technological Innovation Shapes the World

The Industrial Revolution began in Great Britain. The first machines were invented to speed up the spinning of thread and the weaving of **textiles,** or cloth products. Spinning mules were huge machines that could spin fiber such as cotton or linen into thread. A person using a spinning wheel would have to spin full time for nearly four years to produce the amount of thread that the spinning mule could produce in a single day.

European Imperialism, 1900

KEY
- Russia
- Portugal
- France
- The Netherlands
- Germany
- Britain
- Spain

Robinson Projection

ARCTIC OCEAN

CANADA

PACIFIC OCEAN

GREAT BRITAIN

RUSSIAN EMPIRE

PACIFIC OCEAN

FRENCH WEST AFRICA

EGYPT

ANGLO-EGYPTIAN SUDAN

INDIA

Arabian Sea

ATLANTIC OCEAN

BRITISH EAST AFRICA

INDIAN OCEAN

DUTCH EAST INDIES

AUSTRALIA

UNION OF SOUTH AFRICA

0   2,000   4,000 mi

0   2,000   4,000 km

GEOGRAPHY This map shows the colonies held by the various countries of Europe in 1900. **Map Study** Which three countries had the most colonies? Why do you think the Americas were mostly free of colonies? What geographic features prevented Russia from colonizing far-away lands?

AS YOU READ

Find Main Ideas How did the Industrial Revolution promote democracy?

The new factories made their owners very wealthy, and the revolution spread to other countries. By 1900, factories produced almost all goods made in the United States and most of Western Europe.

The Industrial Revolution changed life across Europe. For centuries, farmers had worked the land. Now they moved to cramped, dirty quarters in rapidly growing cities to find factory work.

The changes that people made in their lives were difficult. For many years, factory owners took advantage of workers. Factory conditions were not safe, and wages were low. Conditions gradually improved as workers formed unions that spoke up for their rights and laws were passed to protect them.

Governments had to respond to workers' complaints. Making and selling goods became a big part of each country's economy, and the work force was an important resource. Nations became more democratic as working people were given a stronger voice in passing laws and setting policies.

At the same time, European governments were becoming more aggressive abroad. During the 1800s, many nations took over other countries and turned them into colonies. This is called **imperialism.** Factories needed raw materials, such as cotton, wood, and metals, which colonies could provide. With plenty of raw materials, the factories were able to produce more goods than people could buy. Colonies also became a source for new customers.

The late 1800s are called the Age of Imperialism, but European nations had a long tradition of colonizing other parts of the world. They began colonizing the Americas in the 1500s. By 1900, most of the colonies in America had gained their independence. Belgium,

France, Italy, Spain, Portugal, and Great Britain concentrated their efforts on managing colonies in Africa, Southeast Asia, and the South Pacific. In time, struggles between these colonial powers would bring disaster to Europe.

Nationalism and Historic Events

At the start of the 1900s, the people of Europe were filled with **nationalism,** or pride in their country. Nationalism can be either destructive or creative, depending on how people express it.

Destructive Nationalism   Destructive nationalism can make anger and hatred erupt between nations as they compete with each other for the world's resources, wealth, and power. In the early 1900s, this sense of competition made the nations of Europe team up. They made **alliances** (uh LY un sez), or agreements, to help each other in case of attack. Soon, Europe was divided into two alliances, with Germany, Austria-Hungary, and Italy on one side and Great Britain, France, and Russia on the other. When fighting broke out between these alliances, World War I began, and millions of people were killed.

In 1939, World War II broke out between the Axis powers and the Allies. The Axis powers included Germany, Italy, and Japan; the Allies were Great Britain and the Soviet Union, joined by the United States. More than fifty nations were involved in this war, the most destructive ever fought. When it ended in 1945, the Allies had won.

Creative Nationalism   This period of war was followed by an era of creative nationalism. The United States and the Soviet Union took over as the world's leading nations while the Europeans rebuilt and repaired their societies. They began working together to establish a new type of European nationalism.

A Tunnel Connecting Britain to France

GEOGRAPHY   In 1987, French and English workers began digging a tunnel underneath the English Channel separating Great Britain and France. In 1994, the men in this picture broke through to link the two nations. Today, trains use this tunnel known as "the Chunnel." **Critical Thinking** Do you think nationalism could have kept Great Britain and France from building the Chunnel before 1987?

SECTION 3 ASSESSMENT

AFTER YOU READ

RECALL

1. Define: (a) Industrial Revolution, (b) textiles, (c) imperialism, (d) nationalism, (e) alliance

COMPREHENSION

2. How did European nations' colonies help to boost the economy and increase wealth?

3. What happened in Europe as countries competed for wealth and power?

CRITICAL THINKING AND WRITING

4. **Exploring the Main Idea** Review the Main Idea statement at the beginning of this section. Write a paragraph describing the most important change that took place in Europe during the 1800s.

5. **Identifying Cause and Effect** Write an editorial that speaks out against the destructive nationalism that led

Europe into the first world war.

ACTIVITY

6. **Writing a First-Person Account** During the Industrial Revolution, many people your age worked in factories 12 hours a day, 6 days a week. Imagine that you work in a spinning factory. Write a first-person account describing your very long, hard day.

The Russian Monarchy and Soviet Communism

BEFORE YOU READ

READING FOCUS

1. What events led to the overthrow of the Russian czars?
2. Why did Communism fail in the Soviet Union?

KEY TERMS

westernization
czar
Duma
Communism
dictator
Cold War

KEY PEOPLE

Golden Horde
Ivan the Terrible
Catherine the Great
Vladimir Lenin
Mikhail Gorbachev

NOTE TAKING

Copy the concept web below. As you read the section, fill in the concept web with information about the history of Russia under the czars and under Communism.

MAIN IDEA

Russia has changed from a small, occupied state into an empire stretching across Asia, into a communist dictatorship and now into an independent nation.

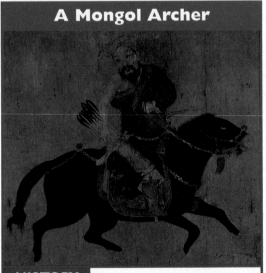

A Mongol Archer

HISTORY Mongol warriors like this archer plundered and burned Kiev and other Russian towns. They killed so many Russians that a historian claimed "no eye remained to weep for the dead."
Critical Thinking Do you think life for the Russian people was better under Mongol rule, or Czarist rule? Why?

Setting the Scene

While Western Europe was exploring the world and establishing colonies, Russia was building a vast empire. The history of Russia is a story with three themes: expansion, the harsh treatment of the common people, and slow westernization. **Westernization** is the process of becoming more like Western Europe and North America.

The Rise and Fall of the Russian Czars

Muscovy (MUHS kuh vee), or Moscow, was once a collection of lands ruled by weak princes who did not get along. Kiev (KEE ev), the most important city in the region, was ruled by the grand prince. In 1238, Mongol conquerors called the **Golden Horde** swept into the region from Asia and quickly defeated the weak princes. By 1240, the Mongols had conquered Kiev. The whole territory became part of the Mongol empire that lasted for 250 years.

The Mongols kept the people cut off from the culture of Western Europe. They demanded service in the army and high taxes, which were collected by princes they appointed. Little by little, the princes gained land and power until they were able to overthrow the Mongolian rule.

The Rise of the Czars   As Muscovy spread its control throughout Russia, its grand prince became known as a **czar** (ZAR), or emperor. The first czar, Ivan IV, was crowned in 1547. He conquered western Siberia and the Mongol lands to the southeast. He was known as **Ivan the Terrible** because of his cruelty.

After Ivan IV's death, Russians suffered through 30 years of war until 1613, when the Romanov (ROH muh nawf) family came to power. The Romanovs continued to expand Russian territory. Over time, seaports on the Baltic (BAWL tik) and Black seas were added to the empire, along with territories in Poland, Turkey, China, and Sweden.

In 1689, Peter the Great came to power, and in 1762, **Catherine the Great** took the throne. Both of them opened their court to the teachers, thinkers, and scientists of Western Europe and encouraged their people to adopt western customs.

However, the serfs of Russia wanted freedom, and the czars would not give it to them. The Russian people became divided between the very rich and the very poor, and the poor were starving. Finally, in 1905, violence erupted. Serfs and workers demonstrated, demanding reforms. Hundreds were killed and Czar Nicholas II was forced to establish the **Duma** (DOO mah), a congress whose members were elected by the people. Establishing the Duma was not enough, however, to save the monarchy.

The Rise and Fall of Soviet Communism

Russian involvement in World War I caused severe food and fuel shortages at home. The people listened to leaders speaking out to overthrow the government. In November 1917, **Vladimir Lenin** and his supporters took over the government and set up a new communist regime. **Communism** (KAHM yoo nizum) is a form of unlimited government in which the state owns the farms and factories and decides what will be grown and produced. Lenin turned the Russian Empire into the Union of Soviet Socialist Republics (U.S.S.R.) called the Soviet Union.

Catherine the Great

GOVERNMENT

Catherine the Great was a German princess who came to Russia as a young bride of 16. Her husband became czar, but he was a weak ruler. With the support of the people, the military, and the church, Catherine seized control of the throne. **Critical Thinking** What qualities might Catherine the Great have had that appealed to the people?

Vladimir Lenin

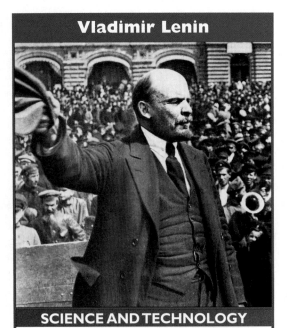

SCIENCE AND TECHNOLOGY

In this picture, Lenin is seen giving a fiery speech to the workers of Moscow. **Critical Thinking** How might today's technology have affected the way Lenin called people to action? How would today's technology have made it difficult to cut the Soviet people off from the west?

Iron Curtain   The Communists jailed or killed anyone who was an enemy of the revolution. When Lenin died in 1924, Josef Stalin took his place as **dictator** (DIK tayt ur). A dictator is a leader with unlimited power. All of the Soviet Union lived in terror of Stalin's harsh policies.

When World War II ended, the Communists established governments across Eastern Europe. The imaginary barrier called the Iron Curtain was created, again cutting the people off from the west.

The Cold War   In the decades following World War II, Communism was seen by the United States as a corrupt system of government. Both countries developed enough weapons to destroy the planet while they engaged in a **Cold War,** a period of tension without actual warfare. At the same time, the people were losing faith in unlimited control by the communist system. Their labor supported state projects instead of their families.

Government Reform   In 1985, **Mikhail Gorbachev** (mee khah EEL GOR buh chawf) came into power. He granted the people more personal freedom and fewer economic controls. By 1991, the Soviet Union had broken apart into independent nations struggling for democracy. After years of harsh rule, the Eastern European and Russian people now control their own fate.

SECTION 4 ASSESSMENT

AFTER YOU READ

RECALL

1. Identify: (a) Golden Horde, (b) Ivan the Terrible, (c) Catherine the Great, (d) Vladimir Lenin, (e) Mikhail Gorbachev

2. Define: (a) westernization, (b) czar, (c) Duma, (d) Communism, (e) dictator, (f) Cold War

COMPREHENSION

3. How did the living conditions of serfs lead to opposition to the czars?

4. What happened in the Soviet Union under the leadership of Lenin and Stalin?

CRITICAL THINKING AND WRITING

5. **Exploring the Main Idea** Review the Main Idea statement at the beginning of this section. Imagine you are a serf. Write a journal entry explaining how frustrated you are by your way of life but how strongly you are connected to Russia's land and people.

6. **Comparing and Contrasting** Some people in Russia want to go back to the old communist way of life. Write a paragraph comparing life before and after communism, and arguing against a return to communism.

ACTIVITY

 Take It to the NET

7. **Creating a Timeline of the Russian Revolution** The Russian Revolution began an era of communist dictatorship in Russia that lasted until the end of the twentieth century. Create a timeline showing significant events leading up to and following the Russian Revolution of 1917. Visit the World Explorer: People, Places, and Cultures section of **phschool.com** for help in completing this activity.

Supporting a Position

Learn the Skill

> Ivan IV was one of Russia's cruelest and most violent czars.

When you write a paper, give a speech, or debate a point, it's very important to support your position or argument. By providing support for your ideas, your position becomes more persuasive, or believable. For example, in the statement above, the writer says that Ivan IV was a cruel and violent leader. However, the statement would be much more persuasive if the writer supported her idea with details and examples. Follow these steps to learn how to support a position or argument:

A. Use facts and statistics to reinforce your position. Remember that your position or argument is an opinion that needs to be supported by facts.

B. Use explanations and definitions to make your ideas more clear. Don't assume that your readers will understand all the terms and words that you use. Your argument will be clearer if you take the time to explain and define your ideas.

C. Use examples to strengthen your argument. Examples can help illustrate your ideas and make your argument more convincing to readers.

D. Use quotations to offer support for your position. By using the words of other writers and experts, you can make your own argument more persuasive.

Practice the Skill

Read this passage about Ivan IV. Then, answer the questions that follow.

> **The Reign of Terror**
> Ivan IV was one of Russia's cruelest and most violent czars. As legend states, a terrible thunderstorm shook Moscow on the day that he was born. A Russian priest warned Ivan's father that a wicked son would succeed him.
>
> As a child, Ivan began to distrust everyone around him. He believed that the Russian nobles and ministers around him wanted him dead so that they could control the country. When he became czar in 1547, his suspicions only grew. Ivan ordered many arrests and executions to protect himself. He also passed a new code of laws that only he could change. Once, in a fit of rage, he even killed his own son. Ivan died in 1584, ending his reign of terror.

A. What is the writer's position or argument?

B. Identify the ways in which the writer supports her position.

C. Do you think the writer's position is well-supported and convincing? Why?

D. What other ways could the writer support her position to make it more convincing?

Apply the Skill

See the Chapter Review and Assessment at the end of this chapter for more questions on supporting a position.

Creating a Chapter Summary

On a separate piece of paper, draw a chart like this one, and include the information that summarizes the first section of the chapter. Then, fill in the chart with summaries of Sections 2, 3, and 4.

Section 1	• The ancient Greek and Roman empires spread cultural ideas and practices throughout Europe. • The influence of these ancient empires is still felt today.
Section 2	
Section 3	
Section 4	

Reviewing Key Terms

Complete each sentence with a term from the list below.

czar	communism	dictator
Industrial Revolution		Renaissance

1. A _____ is a leader who rules with unlimited power.

2. The _____ was a period of artistic and intellectual rebirth.

3. During the _____, there were many changes in the ways that goods and products were made.

4. A ruling emperor or empress in Russia was called a _____.

5. _____ is a system of government in which the state decides what is best for its citizens.

Reviewing the Main Ideas

1. Identify how the accomplishments of the Greeks and Romans influence our lives today. (Section 1)

2. Identify how Christianity and feudalism affected the lives of people in the Middle Ages. (Section 1)

3. Describe life under the rule of Europe's absolute monarchs. (Section 2)

4. What factors led to the French Revolution? (Section 2)

5. How did the Industrial Revolution change life for people in Europe? (Section 3)

6. How did nationalism in Europe lead to world war? (Section 3)

7. Describe the ways in which the rule of the Russian czars was different from the rule of the Soviet dictators. (Section 4)

8. What factors led to the fall of Soviet communism? (Section 4)

Map Activity

Europe and Russia

For each place listed below, write the letter from the map that shows its location. Use the maps in the Activity Atlas to help you.

1. Athens
2. Rome
3. Italy
4. France

5. Great Britain
6. Russia
7. Greece
8. Spain

 Take It to the NET

Enrichment For more map activities using geography skills, visit the social studies section of **phschool.com**.

Writing Activity

1. Using Primary Sources Find out more about what is going on in the former Soviet Union today. Visit your school or local library and use primary sources such as newspaper and magazine articles to find out more information about the people, current leaders, the economy, and the culture. Use the information to write a brief report on life in Russia today.

2. Writing an Interview Choose a historical figure from this chapter. Think of questions that you would like to ask that person. Find out more about the person so that you can get a better idea of how he or she might have answered you. Then write the "interview" as if you were asking that person the questions and he or she was answering them.

Applying Your Skills

Turn to the Skills for Life activity on p. 287 to help you complete the following activity.

Write a one-page report supporting the argument that the Renaissance was one of the most creative periods in European history. You may want to find more information about the Renaissance in the library or on the Internet to help you support this position.

Critical Thinking

1. Identifying Main Ideas Describe some of the advantages of feudalism.

2. Drawing Conclusions How did the growth of towns lead to strong monarchies and increased nationalism?

3. Recognizing Cause and Effect Why did the Communist dictators consider exposure to western ideas and culture such a danger?

 Take It to the NET

Activity The Industrial Revolution was a time of great change that shaped the way we live and work today. How would your life be different if the Industrial Revolution had never happened? Visit the World Explorer: People, Places and Cultures section of **phschool.com** for help in completing this activity.

Chapter 15 Self-Test As a final review activity, take the Chapter 15 Self-Test and get instant feedback on your answers. To take the test, visit the Social Studies section of **phschool.com.**

EUROPE AND RUSSIA: Rich in Culture

Pearl in the Egg

Sir Geoffrey was lord of the manor, which included his great stone house and all the land surrounding it. He owned this tiny village. He even owned most of the people in it. A few, like the baker, the miller, and the soapmaker, were freemen and free women. They worked for themselves and paid the lord taxes....

But the serfs were not free. They could never leave the manor, or marry without the lord's permission. They could not fish in the streams or hunt in the forest....The serfs also paid taxes. Each year they gave Sir Geoffrey a portion of their crops. He took a share of their eggs; if a flock of sheep or geese increased, he took a share; and if a cow had a calf, he took that also. On certain days of the week each family had to send a man—and an ox if they had one—to help plow the lord's fields, harvest his crops, and do their work. Each woman had to weave one garment a year for the lord and his family.

—from *Pearl in the Egg* by Dorothy Van Woerkom

USING LITERATURE

This description of life in the Middle Ages is from a novel based on the life of a girl who lived in the 1200s. Because it is set during a certain historical period, it reveals a great deal about life in that particular place and time.

Connecting to Today

Do you think the society that the author describes sounds like a fair one? Write a paragraph comparing life in the medieval village the author describes, to life in a town or city today. What are the similarities? What are the differences?

Writing a Descriptive Paragraph

If the author were writing about your community, how might she describe it? Reread her description of the village in the novel. Then, make a list of important points to include in a description of the place where you live. Use your notes to write a paragraph describing it to someone who might live 500 years from now.

The Cultures of Western Europe

BEFORE YOU READ

READING FOCUS

1. How has industry shaped the cities of Western Europe?

2. How do immigrants enrich Europe's cultural centers?

3. How has the development of the European Union influenced Western Europe?

KEY TERMS

urbanization
multicultural
tariff

KEY PLACES

Paris
London
Madrid
Berlin
Stockholm

NOTE TAKING

Copy the flow chart below. As you read the section, fill in the chart with information about Western Europe.

Farm machinery is developed. → ☐ → ☐ → ☐ → ☐

MAIN IDEA

Western Europe has prospered because of the change from an agricultural to an industrial economy, from a closed to a multicultural society, and from several competing nations to a single union.

Setting the Scene

The capital cities of Western Europe have distinctive characters. **Paris,** France attracts scholars, writers, and artists. **London,** England is known for its grand historic buildings, theaters, and parks. **Madrid** (muh DRID), Spain is friendly and relaxing. **Berlin,** Germany is full of activity. **Stockholm,** Sweden combines Viking history with modern design.

Most Western European cities are a mix of the old and the new. Buildings from the Middle Ages stand beside modern apartments and office complexes. Cars and buses travel over cobblestone streets built by the Romans. People travel to these cities to enjoy the cultural attractions, past and present.

Growth in Industry

The prosperity, or wealth, of Western Europe is based on industry. Factories in Western Europe make consumer goods that are in great demand around the world, as well as steel, cars, machines, and many other important products.

British Theater

CULTURE "The Mousetrap," a play by mystery writer Agatha Christie, has been playing continuously in London since its opening in November 1952. **Critical Thinking** What cultural activities and events help to define the city or town where you live?

The Labor Force in Selected Western European Countries

Netherlands

- Services 71%
- Industry 25%
- Agriculture 4%

Norway

- Services 75%
- Industry 19%
- Agriculture 6%

Spain

- Services 51%
- Industry 37%
- Agriculture 12%

Austria

- Services 58%
- Industry 34%
- Agriculture 8%

Services
Industry
Agriculture

ECONOMICS Today, most people in the Netherlands, Norway, Spain, and Austria make their living in services, performing tasks for other people. Workers in industry make products. Workers in agriculture grow crops and raise livestock. **Chart Study** Of the countries shown, which two have the largest proportions of service workers? Which two have the largest proportions of industrial workers? Would you expect to find service and industrial workers in cities or in rural areas? Why?

The Louvre

CULTURE Construction of the Louvre, which is the national museum of France, began in 1546 on the site of a 12th century fortress. The glass pyramid entrance was added in the mid-1980s. **Critical Thinking** How do the two parts of the Louvre shown here represent Western European culture?

Technological Innovation

Two hundred years ago, most Europeans worked in agriculture. As machinery was developed and farming techniques were improved, fewer workers were needed on the land.

The need for farmworkers decreased just as the Industrial Revolution began. Farmworkers moved to the cities to fill factory jobs. This growth of cities, or **urbanization** (ur bun ih ZAY shun), increased after World War II. Money from the United States to help Western Europe recover from the destruction of the war helped make the region's industrial centers stronger than ever.

Today, most Western Europeans work in factories or in service industries such as banking, education, and health care. And most Western European workers earn good wages and have comfortable lives. For example, a visitor to Germany would see a fast-paced society that is run without a lot of waste or extra effort by hardworking people. City streets, buses, parks, and playgrounds are clean. Hotels are efficient. German cars are well designed and long-lasting. Travel from place to place is swift, either on the excellent highway system or on high-speed trains.

However, life is not all hard work. Many people are given up to six weeks of vacation each year. The mountains and rivers are popular spots for all forms of outdoor recreation. Cities offer many cultural festivals and celebrations, as well as museums, plays, and concerts that are enjoyed by citizens and tourists alike.

Immigration and Culture

Life in Western Europe was not always so good. In the 1800s and early 1900s, millions of people left Europe to find a better life in the United States, Canada, and South America. However, since World War II, the direction of human movement has changed. As industry developed in the postwar years, more workers were needed. Western Europeans did not leave their homeland, and people began moving in from other parts of the world, including Eastern Europe, North Africa, Asia, and the Middle East. Today, these immigrants make up about 6 percent of the workforce in Western Europe.

When immigrants leave their homelands, they bring their languages, religious beliefs, values, and customs. But most immigrants make changes in their way of life. They may change the way they dress, or discover new ways of cooking. Most of them learn the language of their new country.

Immigration has changed the cultures of Western Europe. In countries such as Britain and France, people from many different backgrounds live and work together. They learn about each other's way of life, and in the process, they begin to blend their backgrounds. As a result, many Western European countries are multicultural. **Multicultural** (mul ti KUHL chur ul) means a country's way of life is influenced by many different cultures.

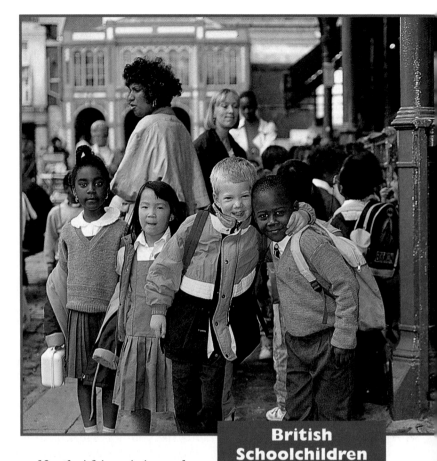

British Schoolchildren

CULTURE The children in this picture are on a school outing in London. **Critical Thinking** How do you think the culture these children experience is different from that of their parents? Their grandparents?

The Influence of the European Union

If you look at a map of Europe, you can see that most of the countries are small and close together. High-speed trains can take travelers from one country to another in a matter of hours. Ideas, goods, and raw materials can travel very quickly as well. The open exchange of ideas and items has helped make Western Europe prosperous and strong.

Europe's New Money—The Euro

ECONOMICS

To make it easier for member nations to trade among themselves, the European Union adopted a single currency called the European Currency Unit, or ECU. Later, the ECU was renamed the Euro. In 1999, consumers began using the Euro, but only through checks, credit cards, or bank transfers. Actual bank notes and coins appeared in 2002, replacing the national currencies of participating EU members. **Critical Thinking** How might the Euro make travel and trade among the European countries easier?

It was not always so easy for people, goods, and ideas to move throughout Western Europe. Until World War II, many countries kept their borders closed. Changes began in 1950, when France and Germany agreed to work together to rebuild after World War II. Other nations soon joined them to create an organization called the European Union (EU). By 2004, the EU had 25 member nations with plans for adding more. The EU works to expand trade in Europe. One way to do this is to end **tariffs,** or fees that a government charges for goods entering the country. Between 1958 and 1970, when these tariffs were ended, there was six times more trade between EU member nations and three times more trade with the rest of the world. The EU hopes to maintain an alliance that continues to enable people, money, goods, and services to move freely among member countries.

SECTION 1 ASSESSMENT

AFTER YOU READ

RECALL
1. Identify: (a) Paris, (b) London, (c) Madrid, (d) Berlin, (e) Stockholm
2. Define: (a) urbanization, (b) multicultural, (c) tariff

COMPREHENSION
3. What caused the shift in Western Europe from an agricultural to an industrial economy?
4. What are the strengths of a multicultural society?

5. What has the European Union accomplished over the past 50 years?

CRITICAL THINKING AND WRITING
6. **Exploring the Main Idea** Review the Main Idea statement at the beginning of this section. Write a paragraph describing how change has benefited Western Europe and helped it to prosper.

ACTIVITY

Take It to the NET

7. **Exploring Baroque Architecture** Architecture can teach you about the history and culture of past societies. View the images on the web site. What does the Baroque architecture tell you about the time period, the people, and the culture? Visit the World Explorer: People, Places and Cultures section of **phschool.com** for help in completing this activity.

SECTION 2

The Cultures of Eastern Europe

BEFORE YOU READ

READING FOCUS

1. How have Slavic cultures shaped life in Eastern Europe?
2. What are the causes of ethnic conflict in Eastern Europe?

KEY TERMS

migration
ethnic group
NATO

KEY PLACES

Czech Republic
Slovakia

MAIN IDEA

The people of Eastern Europe share many cultural traits, but it is their cultural differences that give them a national identity.

NOTE TAKING

Copy the concept web below. As you read the section, complete the web with information about the cultural traits of Eastern Europeans. Add additional ovals as needed.

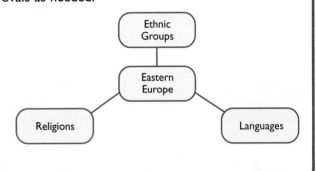

Setting the Scene

Look at a map of Europe in 1900 and you may notice something odd. Poland is missing. From 1795 to 1918, this nation disappeared from the maps of Europe.

A geographer could quickly solve this mystery of the missing country. Poland lies on the North European Plain. There are few mountains or other natural barriers to keep invaders out. In 1795, Russia, Prussia, and Austria moved into Poland and divided it among themselves. Poland did not become independent again until the end of World War I.

Movement throughout much of Eastern Europe is easy. For thousands of years, groups have entered or crossed this region. This movement from place to place, called **migration** (my GRAY shun), is still happening today.

There are many reasons for migration in Eastern Europe. Long ago, people moved to find places with a good supply of natural resources. Sometimes people moved to escape enemies. In more recent times, people have fled places where their religious or political beliefs put them in danger. And they have often moved to find a better life.

Europe in 1871

GEOGRAPHY

From 1795 to 1918, the nation of Poland disappeared from maps such as the one shown here. **Critical Thinking** How did the geography of Eastern Europe affect the takeover of Poland?

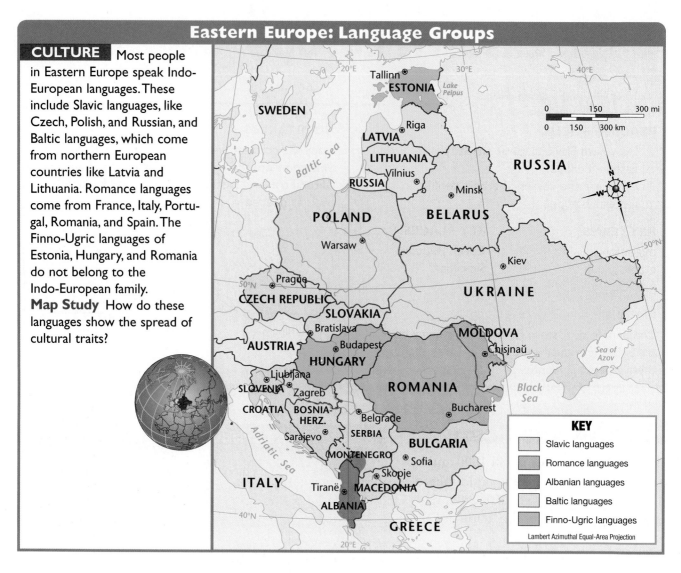

Eastern Europe: Language Groups

CULTURE Most people in Eastern Europe speak Indo-European languages. These include Slavic languages, like Czech, Polish, and Russian, and Baltic languages, which come from northern European countries like Latvia and Lithuania. Romance languages come from France, Italy, Portugal, Romania, and Spain. The Finno-Ugric languages of Estonia, Hungary, and Romania do not belong to the Indo-European family.

Map Study How do these languages show the spread of cultural traits?

KEY
- Slavic languages
- Romance languages
- Albanian languages
- Baltic languages
- Finno-Ugric languages

Lambert Azimuthal Equal-Area Projection

Ethnic Groups in Eastern Europe

Among the groups that long ago migrated to Eastern Europe were the Slavs (slahvz). These people first lived in the mountains of modern Slovakia (sloh VAH kee uh) and Ukraine. By the 700s, they had spread south to Greece, west to the Alps, and north to the coast of the Baltic Sea.

Slavic Cultures   Today, the Slavs are one of the major ethnic groups in Eastern Europe. People of the same **ethnic group** share things, such as a culture, a language, and a religion, that set them apart from their neighbors. Two thousand years ago, there was a single Slavic language. But as the Slavs separated, different Slavic languages were born. Today, some 10 Slavic languages are spoken in Eastern Europe. These include Czech, Polish, and Russian.

Though the Slavs now have different languages and live in different nations, they still have many of the same customs. Large numbers of Eastern Europeans still work as farmers, and live in rural areas where customs change more slowly than in cities.

Other Ethnic Groups Such countries as Poland, Croatia (kroh AY shuh), Slovenia (sloh VEE nee uh), and the **Czech Republic** are almost entirely Slavic. But many other ethnic groups live in Eastern Europe. About 95 percent of the people of Hungary belong to an ethnic group called the Magyars (MAG yarz). In the country of Romania, most people belong to yet another ethnic group, the Romanians. Similarly, the Bulgars of Bulgaria and the Albanians of Albania are separate ethnic groups. And people belonging to the German ethnic group live in several of the countries of Eastern Europe.

Ethnic Conflict

In some Eastern European countries, people of different ethnic groups live together in harmony. But in other places, there have been ethnic conflicts.

Czechs and Slovaks: A Peaceful Division For most of the 1900s, Czechoslovakia (CHECK uh sloh VAH kee uh) was a single country. The two main ethnic groups were the Czechs and the Slovaks.

Czechoslovakia was a parliamentary democracy from 1918 to 1935, but after World War II, the Soviet Union controlled Czechoslovakia. Almost overnight, the Communist Party took over the country. Many people were not happy with the communist government. From the 1960s to the 1980s, students and writers formed groups promoting a return to democracy. Vaclav Havel, a playwright, was a major voice of protest. He spoke out against the government for more than 20 years and was repeatedly put in jail. The government urged him to move out of the country, but he always refused.

Mass protests forced the communist government to consider changes. In 1989, the Communist Party gave up its power and worked in cooperation with the democratic groups. This generally nonviolent change is called the Velvet Revolution. Havel later was elected president of Czechoslovakia.

The Czechs and the Slovaks disagreed about how to carry out the goals of the newly democratic country. In 1993, they agreed to separate, and the countries of the Czech Republic and **Slovakia** were born. Perhaps because most Czechs and Slovaks already lived in separate parts of the country, the split was peaceful.

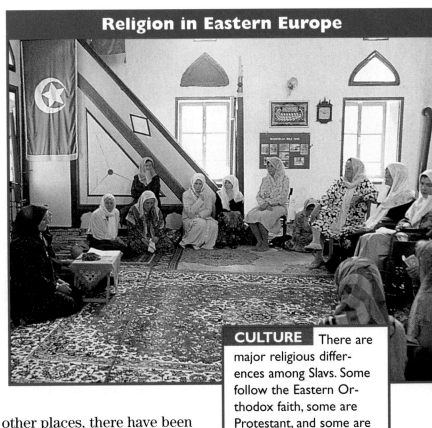

Religion in Eastern Europe

CULTURE There are major religious differences among Slavs. Some follow the Eastern Orthodox faith, some are Protestant, and some are Roman Catholic. The women in this photograph are Muslims. **Critical Thinking** How can religious differences in a region lead to cultural conflicts?

A Fragile Peace

HISTORY In the war-torn country of Bosnia-Herzegovina, United Nations troops struggle to keep a fragile peace among the warring parties. **Critical Thinking** How would it feel to live in a city with armed troops patrolling the streets?

Yugoslavia: Violent Division

Most of the people of Yugoslavia were part of the same ethnic group—the Slavs. However, various groups within the country had distinct religions and cultures, which led to the breakup of Yugoslavia in 1991. The new countries of Bosnia-Herzegovina (BAHZ nee uh herts uh goh VEE nuh), Croatia, Slovenia, Serbia and Montenegro, and Macedonia were formed. War broke out, and thousands of people, mainly Bosnians, were killed. In 1995, **NATO** forces helped bring peace to the region. NATO (North Atlantic Treaty Organization) is an alliance among the United States, Canada, and other western nations.

NATO forces were once again needed to stop violence in Yugoslavia in 1999, this time between Serbians and ethnic Albanians who live in Kosovo, a province of Serbia. Although NATO troops ended the violence and enforced a fragile peace in the region, unrest continued. Because of UN sanctions, the government of Yugoslavia was overthrown in 2000. In 2003, the country was divided into Serbia and Montenegro. Peace was restored to the area, but tensions continue and the region remains unstable.

SECTION 2 ASSESSMENT

AFTER YOU READ

RECALL

1. Identify: (a) Czech Republic, (b) Slovakia

2. Define: (a) migration, (b) ethnic group, (c) NATO

COMPREHENSION

3. What influence have Slavic cultures had in Eastern Europe?

4. What factors have contributed to ethnic conflict in Eastern Europe?

CRITICAL THINKING AND WRITING

5. **Exploring the Main Idea** Review the Main Idea statement at the beginning of this section. Write a paragraph describing the cultural differences between the Serbs and Albanians.

6. **Recognizing Cause and Effect** Why do you think cultural traits change more slowly in rural areas than in urban areas?

ACTIVITY

7. **Writing a Journal** Write a paragraph in your Explorer's Journal about why you think Eastern Europe has been called "the powder keg of Europe."

SECTION 3 — The Cultures of Russia

BEFORE YOU READ

READING FOCUS

1. How have ethnic groups in and around Russia affected Russian history?
2. How are the people of Russia reconnecting with their cultural traditions?

KEY TERMS

heritage
repress
propaganda

KEY PEOPLE AND PLACES

Leo Tolstoy
Peter Tchaikovsky
St. Petersburg

MAIN IDEA

Although the Soviet government of the 20th century tried to control the Russian people's religious beliefs and creative expression, many of their cultural traditions have survived.

NOTE TAKING

Copy the table below. As you read the section, fill in the table with information about cultural expression in Soviet Russia and in present-day Russia.

Cultural Expression in Soviet Union	Cultural Expression in Federation of Russia
forbid practice of religious beliefs	renewed practice of religious beliefs

Setting the Scene

For many years, Russians passing the Church of Saints Cosmas and Damian in Moscow never heard a choir or religious services. The communist government of the Soviet Union owned the church and used it as a printing shop. In the Soviet Union, people were restricted from practicing religion.

In 1991, the Soviet Union collapsed. Two years later, Russians who had never given up their faith took back their church. Now Saints Cosmas and Damian is filled with people singing songs of worship. In recent years, hundreds of other churches in Moscow and across all of Russia have reopened their doors. It is one way the Russian people are reclaiming their culture.

Russia's Ethnic Mix

The Russian Orthodox religion, a branch of Christianity, has been a powerful bond among Russians for hundreds of years. It is part of the Russian **heritage** (HEHR ut ij), the customs and practices that are passed from one generation to the next. Another part of the Russian heritage is ethnic identity.

Reclaiming Cultural Traditions

CULTURE Under communism, worship in Soviet churches was restricted. Now, the doors of churches all over the former Soviet Union are open again for worshippers. **Critical Thinking** How would you feel if your government did not allow you to freely practice your religion? What could you do about it?

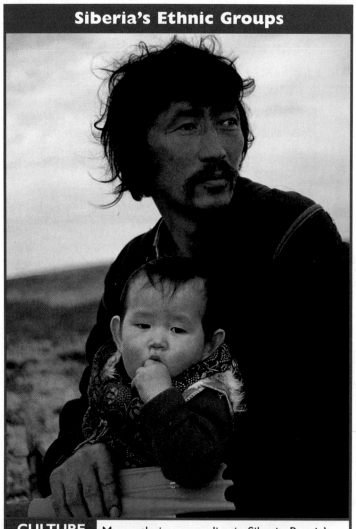

Siberia's Ethnic Groups

CULTURE Many ethnic groups live in Siberia, Russia's largest region. This father and child are Nentsy, an ethnic group that lives in northwest Siberia. **Critical Thinking** Would the isolation of Siberia from the rest of Russia affect the cultural traits of its different ethnic groups? In what ways?

More than 80 percent of the Russian people belong to the ethnic group of Russian Slavs. These people generally speak the Russian language and live in western parts of the country.

Other Ethnic Groups   Besides the Slavs, more than 75 different ethnic groups live in Russia. The Finns and Turks live in regions of the Ural and Caucasus (KAW kuh sus) mountains. Armenians and Mongolians live along Russia's southern edges. The Yakuts (yah KOOTS) live in small areas of Siberia. These groups speak languages other than Russian and they also follow different religions. Muslims make up Russia's second-largest religious group, after Russian Orthodox.

United or Divided?   When the Soviet Union came apart, some non-Russian ethnic groups broke away from Russia and formed their own countries. Since that time, other ethnic groups have tried to break ties with Russia. Recently, the Russian army has been locked in battle with rebels in Chechnya who are fighting for independence.

The new Russian government has tried to keep the country unified by giving ethnic groups the right to rule themselves. At times, however, groups have called for complete independence from Russia. In response, the Russian government has sent the army to **repress,** or put down, the independence movements.

Russian Culture Past and Present and Education

Russia has produced many great artists, thinkers, and writers. Russia's artistic heritage includes outstanding architecture, fine religious paintings, great plays, and intricate art objects. Novelist **Leo Tolstoy** (TOHL stoy) wrote powerful stories of life in Russia in the 1800s. **Peter Tchaikovsky** (chy KAWF skee) composed moving classical music. Russian painters, such as Vasily Kandinsky (kan DIN skee), were leaders in the modern art movement in the early 1900s. In a way, creating works of art is a tradition among Russians.

Under communism, the creation of great new works of art nearly came to a halt. The Soviet government believed that the purpose of art was to glorify communism. The government banned any art it did not like and jailed countless artists. The only art that the government did like was **propaganda**—the spread of ideas designed to support some cause, such as communism. With the collapse of communism, the Russian people eagerly returned to creating new works of art.

Elegant St. Petersburg   An important center of Russian culture is the city of **St. Petersburg.** Visitors to the city can clearly see the Russian mixture of European and Slavic cultures. Peter the Great founded it in 1703. His goal was to create a Russian city as beautiful as any Western European city.

Elegant is the best word for St. Petersburg. The Neva (NYEH vuh) River winds gracefully through the city. Along the river's banks are palaces and public buildings hundreds of years old. St. Petersburg's grandest sight, the Winter Palace, is on the Neva. This 1,000-room palace was the winter home of Russia's czars. Part of the palace is the Hermitage (HUR mih tij) Museum. This museum houses one of the world's finest art collections.

Education in Russia   One of the few strengths of the old Soviet Union was its free public education. Under this system, the number of Russians who could read and write rose from about 40 percent to nearly 100 percent.

The new Russia has continued free public schooling for children between ages 6 and 17. Schools are updating their old courses of study, which told only the communist point of view. New courses, such as business management, are preparing students for the new, non-communist Russia. Some private schools run by the Orthodox Church offer similar courses, as well as religious instruction.

A Monument to Heroic Workers

CULTURE   Socialist realism was the only style of art permitted in the Soviet Union. Socialist realist paintings and sculptures showed idealized views of heroic workers and farmers, often struggling against great odds. The only purpose of socialist realist art was to further the aims of the Soviet government. This sculpture in Moscow is a monument to Soviet workers. The two workers are holding aloft a hammer and sickle, the symbols of the Soviet Union.

Critical Thinking What aspects of socialist realist art does this sculpture illustrate?

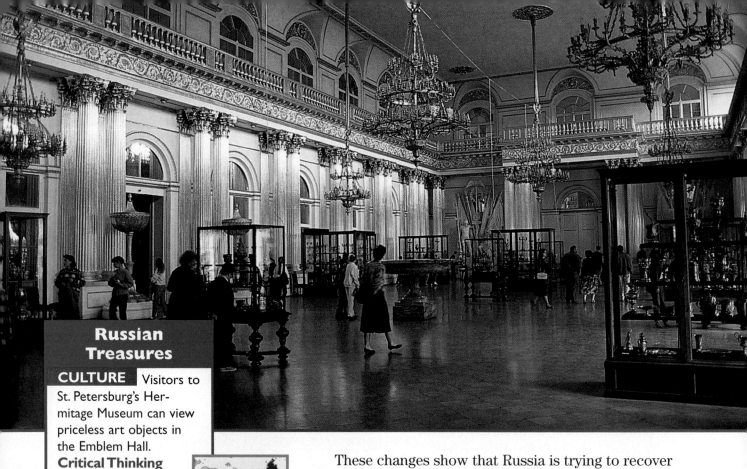

Russian Treasures

CULTURE Visitors to St. Petersburg's Hermitage Museum can view priceless art objects in the Emblem Hall.

Critical Thinking Why do you think it is important to Russians to preserve the homes of the czars even though Russia is no longer ruled by a czar?

These changes show that Russia is trying to recover the riches of its past even as it prepares for a new future. Religion and art, two important parts of Russia's cultural heritage, can now be freely expressed. And Russia's young people, unlike their parents, can grow up making more decisions for themselves.

SECTION 3 ASSESSMENT

AFTER YOU READ

RECALL

1. Identify: (a) Leo Tolstoy, (b) Peter Tchaikovsky, (c) St. Petersburg

2. Define: (a) heritage, (b) repress, (c) propaganda

COMPREHENSION

3. (a) What is Russia's major ethnic group? (b) How has the government treated Russia's smaller ethnic groups?

4. What role has art played in connecting the Russian people with their cultural heritage?

CRITICAL THINKING AND WRITING

5. **Exploring the Main Idea** Review the Main Idea statement at the beginning of this section. Write a paragraph describing the role that language may have played in preserving the cultural traditions and traits of ethnic peoples across Russia.

6. **Identifying Point of View** Some of Russia's ethnic groups have demanded their independence. Write a speech in favor of independence for a group you belong to.

ACTIVITY

7. **Writing a Letter** Imagine that you are on a visit to St. Petersburg. Write a letter to your family, describing the works of art and other expressions of the Russian culture that you are experiencing.

Synthesizing Information

SKILLS FOR LIFE ✓

The diamond at the top of the egg covers a portrait of the czarina.

The colors of the egg match the colors of the gown Czarina Alexandra wore when she and Czar Nicholas II were crowned in 1896.

The windows of the coach are made of a clear type of rock crystal quartz.

The egg holds a model of the coach used for the czar and czarina's crowning. The coach has working doors and folding steps.

This handcrafted egg was given by Czar Nicholas II to his wife, Czarina Alexandra. It was made by the jewelry company Fabergé. The egg is 5 inches (12.6 cm) tall. The miniture coach, encrusted with diamonds, rubies, and rock crystal, is about 3 3/4 inches (9.3 cm) long. Fabergé made 56 Imperial eggs for the czars. Master goldsmiths, jewelers, enamelers, and miniature painters worked on each egg. The eggs never failed to hold a surprise. Inside, something either moved or played a song. Some eggs even contained other objects like this one.

Learn the Skill

When you combine details from different sources to make decisions or draw conclusions, you are synthesizing information. You've already had practice with this skill by looking at images and reading captions in your text and then answering questions about the information. Synthesizing helps you to better understand the information you see, hear, and read. To learn how to synthesize information, follow these steps:

A. Identify the common topic of the different sources of information.

B. Identify the main idea and details of each source of information. The purpose of this skill is to get information on a particular topic from different sources. Before you can compare these sources, you need to focus on each one separately.

C. Identify the similarities and differences between or among the sources. Paying attention to these similarities and differences will help you better understand the topic.

D. Draw conclusions based on the information.

Practice the Skill

Study the two pieces of information above about Fabergé eggs. Then, answer the questions below to help you practice the skill.

- What is the topic of these two sources of information?
- What information about the egg does the photograph contain? The text?
- Based on the information, how special do you think a Fabergé egg was? Do you think a single egg was expensive to produce? Why?

Apply the Skill

See the Chapter Review and Assessment at the end of this chapter for more questions on synthesizing information.

Creating a Chapter Summary

On a separate piece of paper, draw a web like this one, and include the information about the cultures of Western Europe. Then, add more ovals and summarize the information you learned about the culture of Eastern Europe and Russia.

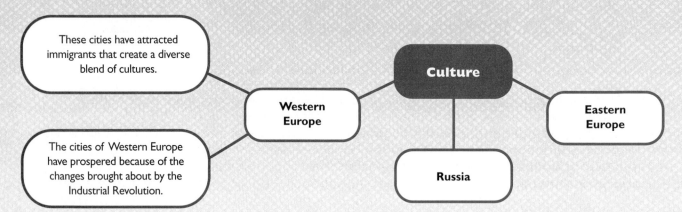

These cities have attracted immigrants that create a diverse blend of cultures.

The cities of Western Europe have prospered because of the changes brought about by the Industrial Revolution.

Western Europe

Culture

Russia

Eastern Europe

Reviewing Key Terms

Complete each sentence with a term from the list below.

propaganda	ethnic group	heritage
tariff	migration	

1. An _____ is made up of people who share language, culture, and religion.

2. The fee a government charges for goods entering a country is called a _____.

3. _____ is the movement of people from place to place.

4. The spread of ideas designed to support a cause is called _____.

5. A person's _____ is made up of customs passed down from older generations.

Reviewing the Main Ideas

1. What features make the cities in Western Europe great centers for culture? (Section 1)

2. How do open borders and free trade affect the way Western Europeans live? (Section 1)

3. Who are the Slavs and why are they an important part of the population of Eastern Europe? (Section 2)

4. How was the breakup of Czechoslovakia different from the breakup of Yugoslavia? (Section 2)

5. How have non-Russian ethnic groups reacted to recent events in Russia? (Section 3)

6. What traditions are Russians reviving following the collapse of the Soviet Union? (Section 3)

Map Activity

Europe and Russia

For each place listed below, write the letter from the map that shows its location.

1. France

4. Germany

2. Poland

5. Slovakia

3. Russia

6. St. Petersburg

 Take It to the NET

Enrichment For more map activities using geography skills, visit the social studies section of **phschool.com.**

Writing Activity

1. Using Primary Sources Visit your school or local library and use primary sources such as newspaper and magazine articles to gather information on the lives of non-Russian ethnic groups since the collapse of the Soviet Union. Use the information to describe a day in the life of a non-Russian person.

2. Create a Travel Guide Choose six cultural centers from Western Europe, Eastern Europe, and Russia. Create a travel guide that describes a cultural tour that visits each of these six places. Describe the highlights of the trip for each place. Provide as much interesting background information as possible, in order to convince travelers to take the tour.

Applying Your Skills

Turn to the Skills for Life Activity on p. 303 to help you complete the following activity.

Choose a current movie in theaters that you have not yet seen. Look through a newspaper for an ad for the movie. Locate a few reviews for the film in a newspaper or on the Internet. Use these sources to write a paragraph that analyzes and synthesizes the information you found.

Critical Thinking

1. Drawing Conclusions Why do Western Europeans generally have a higher standard of living than Eastern Europeans?

2. Identifying Central Issues How has life changed for the Russian people since the collapse of the Soviet Union?

 Take It to the NET

Activity Examine the paintings found at the Web site. What can you learn about Russia and Russian culture from looking at these paintings? Visit the World Explorer: People, Places and Cultures section of **phschool.com** for help in completing this activity.

Chapter 16 Self-Test As a final review activity, take the Chapter 16 Self-Test and get instant feedback on your answers. To take the test, visit the Social Studies section of **phschool.com.**

WESTERN EUROPE: Exploring the Region Today

A Masterpiece of the Renaissance

USING ART

This painting is the *Mona Lisa* by Italian Renaissance painter Leonardo da Vinci. The *Mona Lisa* is one of the world's most famous paintings. The subject is the wife of an Italian merchant named Giocondo. The artist managed to capture a slight smile and eyes that seem to follow the viewer. Images of the *Mona Lisa* appear in modern art and her name is mentioned in literature and music throughout the world.

Comparing Portraits

Da Vinci painted the *Mona Lisa* with oil paints in a style that was popular in his time. Visit the library and find examples of more modern portrait paintings. Choose one and compare and contrast it with the painting of the *Mona Lisa*. How is the style different? What does each painting reveal about its subject?

Creating a Self-Portrait

In da Vinci's time, portraits were often used to capture and preserve an image of a person for history. Think about the ways that painters may reveal things about their subjects' lives. They may paint the subject with a certain facial expression, certain clothing, or certain way of sitting and show other objects or symbols in the painting. Draw or paint a self-portrait that says something about who you are.

SECTION 1

Great Britain and Ireland
Historic Roots of Modern Conflict

BEFORE YOU READ

READING FOCUS

1. How did democracy develop in Britain?
2. What key issues and events have contributed to the conflict in Northern Ireland?

KEY TERMS

Parliament
representative
constitutional
  monarchy
persecution

KEY PEOPLE AND PLACES

Northern Ireland
King John
Queen Elizabeth II
King Henry VIII

MAIN IDEA

Ireland has fought for unity and independence from Great Britain for centuries, though Great Britain has a long history of colonial and democratic rule.

NOTE TAKING

Copy the cause and effect chart below. As you read the section, fill in the chart with information about conflicts throughout Ireland's history.

Cause
1.
2.
3.

Event: Conflict in Ireland

Effects
1.
2.
3.

Setting the Scene

The United Kingdom is made up of England, Scotland, Wales, and **Northern Ireland.** The four countries have their own histories and cultures but are ruled by a single government. Though *United Kingdom of Great Britain and Northern Ireland* is the country's official name, people often call this region *Britain* or *Great Britain* instead. This is because most of the people live on the island of Great Britain. The government of the United Kingdom is a constitutional monarchy that is headed by a king or queen—a symbol of Britain's past and its customs.

A Democratic History

The roots of British democracy go back many hundreds of years. During the Middle Ages, British kings could not take major actions without the approval of a group of rich nobles. Over time, the power of this group grew. In 1215, the group forced one English monarch, **King John,** to sign a document called the Magna Carta, or "Great Charter." The Magna Carta strengthened the power of the nobles and limited the power of the king.

St. Edward's Crown

HISTORY St. Edward's crown, one of several crowns kept at the Tower of London, is a copy of a crown worn by Edward the Confessor. He ruled England from 1042 to 1066. **Critical Thinking** What kind of influence do you think Britain's history has on its people today?

Britain's Parliament

Britain's Parliament is divided into two houses, the House of Commons and the House of Lords. Members of the House of Commons are elected by the country's citizens and they pass Britain's laws. Members of the House of Lords can delay, but not block, a House of Commons bill. The House of Lords also serves as the final court of appeal in the British legal system. Britain's Parliament has served as a model for legislative bodies throughout the world.

In time, the group of nobles became known as the **Parliament.** This word comes from the French word *parler* (PAHR lay), which means "to talk." The Parliament later gained more power. It helped to decide the kinds of taxes paid by citizens and elected people from areas of the country to serve as **representatives.** A representative represents, or stands for, a group of people. In time, the people themselves elected these representatives.

Limited Power   Britain's **Queen Elizabeth II** was crowned in 1953. The Queen may approve or reject laws passed by Parliament, but no British monarch has rejected a law since the 1700s. The royal family may participate in national ceremonies and may represent Britain on trips to other countries.

However, Britain's monarchs today do not have the power to make laws or collect taxes because Great Britain is now a **constitutional monarchy.** A constitution is a set of laws that describes how a government works. In a constitutional monarchy, the power of kings and queens is limited. British laws are made by Parliament, not by the king or queen.

British Parliament, Present and Past

GOVERNMENT

The modern Parliament consists of the House of Commons, whose members actually make the nation's laws, and the House of Lords. The Prime Minister is the chief executive.   **Critical Thinking** How do the houses of Parliament compare to the U.S. Congress?

Ireland: One Island, Two Nations

Ireland's struggle for independence goes back centuries. Originally the island was divided into small settlements controlled at different times by Irish chiefs, Catholic bishops, Viking invaders, Norman conquerors, and British planters. There was no unified central govern-

United Kingdom

COUNTRY · PROFILE

Age Structure (in years)

- Under 15: 19%
- 65 and over: 16%
- 15-64: 65%

Ethnic Makeup

- West Indian, Asian and Other: 4%
- Northern Irish: 4%
- Welsh: 2%
- Scottish: 10%
- English: 80%

United Kingdom: Political

KEY

— National boundary
⊛ National capital
• Other city

Lambert Azimuthal Equal-Area Projection

0   50   100 mi
0   50 100 km

Shetland Islands

Orkney Islands

Wick

SCOTLAND

Loch Ness

Aberdeen

Dundee

Loch Lomond

Edinburgh

Glasgow

Tweed River

North Sea

GREAT BRITAIN

Londonderry

NORTHERN IRELAND

Belfast

North Channel

Newcastle

Carlisle

Middlesbrough

ATLANTIC OCEAN

Isle of Man

Irish Sea

Leeds

Liverpool

Manchester

Sheffield

IRELAND

WALES

Nottingham

Cardigan Bay

Severn River

Birmingham

Aberystwyth

ENGLAND

Ipswich

Saint George's Channel

Swansea

Cardiff

Thames River

London

Dover

Strait of Dover

BELGIUM

Bristol Channel

Bristol

Portsmouth

Plymouth

Isle of Wight

English Channel

FRANCE

Location	An island in the north Atlantic Ocean
Climate	Marine west coast
Terrain	Mountainous highlands in the north, plains and rolling hills in the south
Population	59.8 million
Major Religions	Protestantism, Roman Catholicism
Government	Constitutional monarchy
Economy	Agriculture: wheat, barley, potatoes, sugar beets, dairy, livestock
	Major industries: steel, metals, vehicles, shipbuilding, textiles, chemicals, electronics
Exports	Manufactured goods, machinery, fuels, chemicals, transport goods and equipment
Imports	Manufactured goods, machinery, semifinished goods, foodstuffs, consumer goods

HISTORY

For centuries, Ireland struggled for independence. This map shows how the island was divided. Great Britain still controls the northern counties of the island. **Map Study** What are the advantages and disadvantages of being part of the United Kingdom?

ment so these individual settlements were easy prey. At the same time, the scattered settlements made it difficult for an outside force to take complete control of the island. In 1541, England's **King Henry VIII** declared himself King of Ireland and head of the Church. The colonization of Ireland by the English began.

The Irish Famine

By 1841, the population of Ireland had grown to more than 8 million. Only small plots of land were available, and rents were high. Farm families lived on a diet of potatoes because they were easy to grow and did not take a lot of time to tend. Then, between 1845 and 1849, a blight rotted the potato crop creating a famine, or food shortage.

As a result of the Great Famine, it is estimated that one million people died from hunger and disease, and one million people emigrated to North America.

Religious Conflict Over the centuries, Ireland's religious heritage and ties to the Roman Catholic Church have been the cause of bitter disputes. Catholics were often **persecuted,** or mistreated, because of their beliefs, by both the government and by settlers sent over from England to establish plantations. Time and again the Irish were driven from their lands. They fought back, demanding equal rights, political independence, and religious freedom.

For a while, the British government had to lift trade restrictions on Irish goods and grant political power to the Irish parliament. Ireland's freedom, however, was short lived. In 1801, England passed the Act of Union, joining Ireland to England.

Political Conflict Efforts to set up an Irish parliament that would govern Irish affairs, or "Home Rule," were opposed by Protestant landowners who held the majority there and did not want political independence from Great Britain. Cutting ties to the British Parliament was not in their best interests because, in a unified Irish nation, they would be outnumbered and voted out of power. The Irish movement for Home Rule took many forms, including peaceful opposition, political force, and war.

A treaty signed in 1922 said that Northern Ireland, where the Protestants of Ulster held power, would remain part of Great Britain. It granted independence to most of the rest of Ireland, which became the Irish Republic in 1949.

In 1998, the Good Friday Agreement was approved by voters in Northern Ireland and in the Irish Republic. This agreement gives the Catholics in Northern Ireland a stronger voice in their government but does not cut ties to Britain.

SECTION I ASSESSMENT

AFTER YOU READ

RECALL

1. Identify: (a) Northern Ireland, (b) King John, (c) Queen Elizabeth II, (d) King Henry VIII

2. Define: (a) Parliament, (b) representative, (c) constitutional monarchy, (d) persecution.

COMPREHENSION

3. What two houses comprise Britain's Parliament?

4. What happened after Ireland was partitioned?

CRITICAL THINKING AND WRITING

5. **Exploring the Main Idea** Review the Main Idea statement at the beginning of this section. Then, write a paragraph about the importance of fair political representation in Parliament.

6. **Making Predictions** Imagine that it is the year 2025. Write a newspaper article describing life in Northern Ireland. Has the first quarter of the 21st century been peaceful? Why or why not?

ACTIVITY

7. **Researching the Great Famine** Visit the library or the Internet to learn more about Ireland's Great Famine. Write a short report that provides important details about the famine and how it affected life in Ireland.

SECTION 2

Belgium and the Netherlands
Changing Economies

BEFORE YOU READ

READING FOCUS

1. What are the main products and industries of Belgium and the Netherlands?
2. How might the European Union affect the relationship between Belgium and the Netherlands?

KEY TERMS

polders
Flemish

KEY PLACES

Flanders
Wallonia
Walloons
Brussels
Amsterdam
Rotterdam

NOTE TAKING

Copy the concept web below. As you read the section, fill in the web with information about Belgium and the Netherlands.

MAIN IDEA

Belgium and the Netherlands share borders and ties with neighboring countries, but they have unique economies and cultures.

Setting the Scene

Much of the region that makes up Belgium and the Netherlands is below sea level. To reclaim the land that would normally be under water, long walls called dikes were built to hold it back. Excess water is pumped into canals that empty into the North Sea. The reclaimed patches of land are called **polders** (POHL durz), and they are home to farmland and large cities.

Resources and Industry

For hundreds of years, control of the region that is now Belgium and the Netherlands was passed down from one European ruler to the next. In 1648, the Dutch occupying the Northern Netherlands, known as Holland, were granted independence from Spain. They rapidly built a strong economy through shipping, the spice trade, and colonization. In 1794, the Southern Netherlands, known as Belgium, was annexed to France. Industries developed and manufacturing centers flourished. In 1814, the provinces of the Northern and Southern Netherlands were combined to form one kingdom. But by 1830, differences in religion and language caused Belgium to break away from the Netherlands, and two separate nations were formed.

Reclaimed Land
GEOGRAPHY

Polders like the one beside this canal add 3,000 square miles (7,770 sq km) of land to the Netherlands. In the crowded conditions of the Netherlands, this land that was once underwater is home to 3.5 million people. **Critical Thinking** How has the need for polders, and their uses, changed over the centuries?

311

Belgium and the Netherlands

Ethnic Makeup (Belgium)

Italian 2%
Moroccan 1%
Other 6%
Walloon 33%
Fleming 58%

Ethnic Makeup (Netherlands)

Turkish 2%
Moroccan 1%
Other 2%
Dutch 96%

GEOGRAPHY The ports at Antwerp and at Rotterdam are two of the busiest in the world. **Map Study** What geographical advantages does the Netherlands have?

National boundary
⊛ National capital
• Other city

0   200   400 mi
0   200   400 km
Lambert Conformal Conic Projection

Location	Belgium: Western Europe
Climate	Temperate; humid and mild at coast; cold winters, hot summers in southeast, with heavy rains, fog, and drizzle
Terrain	Low-lying coastal plain in northwest; central plateau with waterways and valleys; wooded highlands southeast
Population	10.3 million
Major Ethnic Groups	Fleming, Walloon
Government	Parliamentary democracy under constitutional monarchy
Economy	Agriculture: grains, vegetables; livestock, dairy; Major Industries: machinery, chemicals, textiles, shipbuilding
Exports	Machinery and equipment, chemicals, diamonds, metals and metal products
Imports	Machinery and equipment, chemicals, metals and metal products

Location	Netherlands: Western Europe
Climate	Temperate; cool summers and mild winters common
Terrain	Lowlands: much of west below sea level; some land reclaimed from sea; east flat to gently rolling
Population	16.1 million
Major Ethnic Groups	Dutch
Government	Constitutional monarchy
Economy	Agriculture: Grains, fruits, vegetables; livestock
	Major Industries: metal products, machinery, chemicals, machinery, chemicals, petroleum, fishing, construction
Exports	Machinery and equipment, chemicals, fuels, foodstuffs
Imports	Machinery and transport equipment, chemicals, fuels, foodstuffs, clothing

Belgium's Industries in the South Belgium is made up of three distinct regions. In the north, the people of **Flanders** speak Dutch, or **Flemish.** In the south, the people of **Wallonia,** called **Walloons,** speak French. The region around the capital, **Brussels,** at the center of the country and at the heart of Europe, is bilingual.

For hundreds of years, the region of Wallonia supported the primary industry of coal mining. Coal was used to power factories throughout the country. However, the reserves of coal, a nonrenewable resource, eventually ran out. Most coal mines closed down in the 1960s, and all coal mining had stopped by 1992. Coal now must be imported to keep the factories going and to provide heating.

The steel and textile industries that were located in the coal mining region went into a decline as mining ceased. The government has stepped in with reforms designed to help strengthen these industries, but regaining a healthy balance of trade has been slow.

Belgium's Industries in the North Industry in the more heavily populated region of Flanders has continued to grow. A strong transportation network supports the export of products. Over time, manufacturing has steadily replaced agriculture as a major industry, but agricultural production has become more efficient. Better use is made of the land and the crops that are grown have higher yields. These crops include cereals, potatoes, sugar beets, fruits, and vegetables.

Industry in the Netherlands Like Belgium, the Netherlands is not rich in natural resources. Exceptions include coal mining, and natural gas and petroleum exploration. The Netherlands has a successful dairy and cheese industry, and flower bulbs generate an important source of agricultural income.

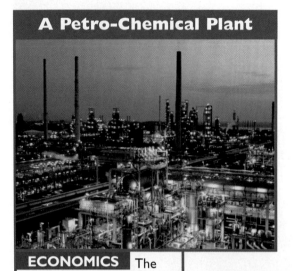

A Petro-Chemical Plant

Raw materials are imported to the Netherlands to support industries that concentrate on manufacturing products. These include the production of textiles, metals, processed foods, plastics, and chemicals.

The city of **Amsterdam** is a major financial center for international banking. The busy port of **Rotterdam** supports the merchant marine and foreign trade with worldwide destinations for Amsterdam's many exports including machinery, textiles, petroleum products, fruits and vegetables, and meat.

Tourism is also an important part of the economy, and the careers of many people in Amsterdam are devoted to sharing Dutch history and culture with visitors.

ECONOMICS The Netherlands is not a country rich in natural resources. However, petroleum exploration and Holland's international ports support industries like the petro-chemical plant above. **Critical Thinking** How might a petro-chemical plant benefit and burden the communities nearby?

The European Union

During the 1950s, six European countries, including the Netherlands, agreed to form a common market. Now, the number of countries involved in this union, called the European Union, has risen to twenty-five. Both Belgium and the Netherlands have been leaders in the European Union. The growth of the union paves the way for more international activities that will cross the national and economic borders of the countries of Europe. A single currency, called the euro, is shared by all of the countries in the union. The European Union may help Belgium and the Netherlands to overcome cultural and historical disputes that have kept them apart in years past.

SECTION 2 ASSESSMENT

AFTER YOU READ

RECALL

1. Identify: (a) Flanders, (b) Wallonia, (c) Walloons, (d) Brussels, (e) Amsterdam, (f) Rotterdam

2. Define: (a) polders, (b) Flemish

COMPREHENSION

3. Name three industries that are important to Belgium, and three industries that are important to the Netherlands.

4. How might the European Union bring Belgium and the Netherlands closer together?

CRITICAL THINKING AND WRITING

5. **Exploring the Main Idea** Review the Main Idea statement at the beginning of this section. Then write a paragraph describing some of the similarities and differences between Belgium and the Netherlands.

6. **Draw Conclusions** Reclaimed patches of land in Belgium and the Netherlands would normally be under the North Sea, if not for polders. Without the polders, how might life be different in this region?

ACTIVITY

7. **Writing a Report** Find out more details about the unification, conflict, and separation that mark the history of Belgium and the Netherlands. What role did cultural identity play in the differences and disagreements between the Dutch, the Belgians, the Flemish, and the Walloons? Organize the information you collect into a brief report.

Germany
Political and Economic Reunion

BEFORE YOU READ

READING FOCUS

1. Why was Germany divided and how did it become reunited?

2. How are Germans dealing with the issues of a reunited nation?

KEY TERMS
Holocaust
genocide
reunification

KEY PEOPLE
Adolf Hitler

NOTE TAKING
Copy the table below. As you read the section, fill in the table with comparisons about Germany before and after reunification.

Germany before Reunification	Germany after Reunification

MAIN IDEA
The United States, Great Britain, France, and the Soviet Union divided Germany and its capital city, Berlin, into two parts at the end of World War II, and West Germany prospered, the East German economy collapsed, paving the way for political reunification in 1990.

Setting the Scene

In 1961, a policeman named Conrad Schumann stood guard at a barbed wire fence separating East Berlin from West Berlin. At that time, East Berlin was part of the communist government of East Germany and the fence was built to prevent people from escaping to West Berlin. Schumann had orders to shoot anyone who tried. Schumann thought about the colorful culture of West Berlin. He thought about political freedom and economic opportunities in the democracy of West Germany. So he jumped over the barbed wire fence separating East and West Berlin. Soon after Schumann's escape, the Berlin Wall was built to replace the fence, dividing the city in half.

Germany's Dark History

To understand the importance of the Berlin Wall, you need to understand part of Germany's past. After losing World War I in 1918, the German government had to pay billions of dollars as punishment for attacking other countries. To make things even worse, the German economy collapsed. Prices soared. Germans everywhere felt desperate.

A Leap to Freedom

CITIZENSHIP
Conrad Schumann's responsibility was to prevent his fellow citizens from escaping into West Berlin. From West Berlin, people could reach democratic West Germany. **Critical Thinking** What might you have done if you were in Schumann's position?

Germany

Age Structure (in years)

- 65 and over 16%
- Under 15 16%
- 15-64 68%

Ethnic Makeup

- Other 3%
- Turkish 2%
- Other European 3%
- German 92%

Location	Central European country to the east of France
Climate	Marine west coast
Terrain	Flat in the north, hilly in the central and western portions, mountainous in Bavaria
Population	83 million
Major Religions	Protestantism, Roman Catholicism
Goverment	Federal republic
Economy	Agriculture: grains, potatoes, sugar beets, fruit
	Major industries: steel, ships, vehicles, machinery, electronics, coal, chemicals, iron
Exports	Precision tools, chemicals, motor vehicles, steel, agricultural products, raw materials, fuels
Imports	Manufactured products, agricultural products, fuels, raw materials

Germany: Political KEY

- ——— National boundary
- ⊛ National capital
- • Other city

Albers Equal-Area Projection

0   50   100 mi
0   50   100 km

GEOGRAPHY This map shows Germany's borders and major cities. It also shows the network of rivers that flow through the country. **Map Study** How are the locations of Bonn, Bremen, Hamburg, and Dresden similar?

Hitler and World War II **Adolf Hitler** (AY dahlf HIT lur), a young German soldier, had wept bitterly in 1918 when he learned that Germany had lost the war. He promised himself that his country would never suffer such a defeat again. Hitler became deeply involved in politics. In speech after speech, he promised to make Germany great again. By 1933, this once unknown soldier was dictator of Germany.

Hitler blamed Germany's economic problems on the Jews. He spread hateful theories about Jews, gypsies, and other ethnic groups in Germany. He claimed they were inferior to, or not as good as, other Germans. He claimed that true Germans were a superior ethnic group—and believed that this superior group deserved a larger country.

Many people did not believe Hitler's threats. But Hitler was deadly serious. He ordered attacks on neighboring countries and forced them under German rule. His actions led to the start of World War II in 1939. Great Britain, the Soviet Union, and the United States joined other nations to stop Hitler and the Germans. By the end of the war, Europe was in ruins. People around the world learned that the Germans had forced countless Jews, Gypsies, Slavs, and others into death prison camps. Millions of people were systematically murdered in these camps. Most of those killed in the camps were Jews. This horrible mass murder of six million Jews is called the **Holocaust** (HAHL uh kawst). The deliberate murder of a racial, political, or ethnic group is called **genocide.**

The Cold War   At the end of the war, the Americans, the British, the French, and the Soviets divided Germany. The American, British, and French sections were joined into a democratic country called West Germany. The Soviet Union created communist East Germany.

Berlin was in the Soviet part of Germany. But the western half of it, called West Berlin, became part of democratic West Germany. This turned the western half of Berlin into an island of democracy in the middle of communism. The Berlin Wall separated the two halves of the city. But it divided more than Berlin. It was a symbol of a divided world. Little wonder that some people called it the "Wall of Shame."

East Germans led far different lives than West Germans. The communist government required people to obey without asking questions. It even encouraged people to spy on family members and neighbors. Children were taught to respect only those things that helped communism. Things from the West—including movies, music, books, and magazines—were seen as harmful to communism.

The Communists Weaken   In time, communist rule started to change. One reason was that the East German economy was falling further behind the West German economy. The average West German had a much better life than the average East German. To keep East Germans happy, the government softened its rules and let some East Germans visit West Germany. Conrad Schumann's mother, who was then in her late seventies, was allowed to see him. But he still was not allowed to go to East Berlin to see her. If he crossed the border, he would be arrested and put in prison.

In the late 1980s, changes in the Soviet Union helped to cause the collapse of East Germany. Soviet leader Mikhail Gorbachev made it clear that he would not use force to protect communism in Eastern Europe. Fear of the Soviets had helped keep the East German government in power. Now this fear was gone and East Germany's government collapsed.

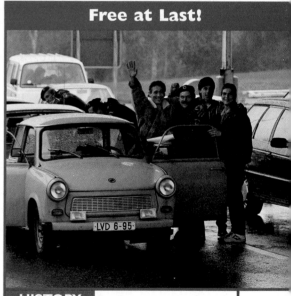

Free at Last!

HISTORY   In the summer of 1989, many East Germans crossed into West Germany to begin new lives.   **Critical Thinking** Why do you think that no efforts were made to prevent East Germans from fleeing to the West?

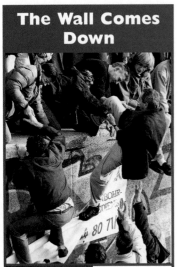

The Wall Comes Down

HISTORY Crowds began to destroy the Berlin Wall on November 9, 1989. They held a huge party on and around the wall, while people from both sides helped each other up and over. **Critical Thinking** Judging from the behavior of the crowds, how do you think Germans felt about the Berlin Wall?

The Berlin Wall collapsed as well. On November 9, 1989, crowds of Germans began scrambling over the wall. Some people raced to see friends and relatives. Others just wanted to enjoy a different life. People helped each other over the top of the wall to the other side. Crowds tore at the wall and took it apart block by block. Less than a year later, the governments of East and West Germany united. Germany had become a single country again.

Germany Reunited

Most Germans were thrilled about the fall of the Berlin Wall. The cultures of East and West Germany had remained similar in many ways. People in both Germanys spoke the same language and ate the same foods. They knew the same German composers, writers, and painters. Still, the process of becoming unified again, called **reunification** (ree yoo nuh fih KAY shun), would not be easy.

Germans spent millions of dollars to rebuild the economy of what was East Germany. For the first time since World War II, East Germans are enjoying modern televisions, cars, and washing machines. They have new shopping malls and better roads.

Easterners may have more televisions and cars since the reunification, but they have fewer jobs. In communist East Germany, people were guaranteed a job and food to eat. There are no such guarantees under the Western democratic system. This is one of the prices of freedom, and most former East Germans are willing to pay it.

When Germany was reunited in 1990, so was Berlin. The next year, the German legislature restored this city to its traditional role as the nation's capital. By 1999, most government offices had moved back to Berlin from the West German capital of Bonn.

SECTION 3 ASSESSMENT

AFTER YOU READ

RECALL

1. Identify: (a) Adolf Hitler

2. Define: (a) Holocaust, (b) genocide, (c) reunification

COMPREHENSION

3. Describe the events that led to the division of Germany and the events that led to its reunification.

4. How has the reunification of Germany affected life in the former East Germany?

CRITICAL THINKING AND WRITING

5. **Exploring the Main Idea** Review the Main Idea statement at the beginning of this section. Then, imagine that you are living in East Berlin. Write a letter to a relative in Bonn, describing how your life has changed since reunification.

6. **Making Comparisons** Compare personal freedom in East and West Germany during the Cold War.

ACTIVITY

 Take It to the NET

7. **Reporting on the Berlin Wall** Choose a significant event related to the rise of the Berlin Wall. Imagine you are a newspaper reporter and write an article reporting on the event. Visit the World Explorer: People, Places, and Cultures section of **phschool.com** for help in completing this activity.

France and Italy
Cultural Influence on the World

BEFORE YOU READ

READING FOCUS

1. How is contemporary French culture connected to the past?
2. What cultural traits help to define the people of France?
3. What role does religion play in Italy?
4. What are the cultural characteristics of Italy?

KEY TERMS
manufacturing
emigrate

KEY PLACES
Aix-en-Provence
Paris
Vatican
Rome
Milan
Locorotondo

NOTE TAKING

Copy the Venn diagram below. As you read the section, fill in the diagram with comparisons about the cultures of France and Italy.

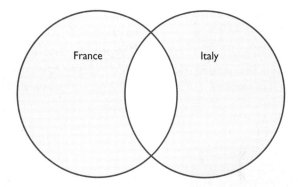

France   Italy

MAIN IDEA

Cultural traditions and institutions in France and Italy can be traced back through the centuries.

Setting the Scene

Catherine and Victoire are sisters. Both are in their 20s—just one year apart in age. The two look so much alike that some people think they are twins. They grew up in the south of France, in a city called **Aix-en-Provence** (EKS ahn praw VAHNS). It is a quiet, pretty town, a trading center for olives, almonds, and wine.

Catherine and Victoire are very different. Catherine still lives in Aix. She is married and has two children. Her husband works as a pastry chef, making cakes and other desserts. He follows French recipes that were created 150 years ago.

Victoire is single and lives in **Paris,** the capital of France. She works for a publisher. Her job is to get American books translated into French.

French Influence

CULTURE These girls are carrying baguettes, which are long, crusty loaves of bread. This type of bread is known throughout the world as "French bread." **Critical Thinking** What other familiar things are described using the adjective "French?"

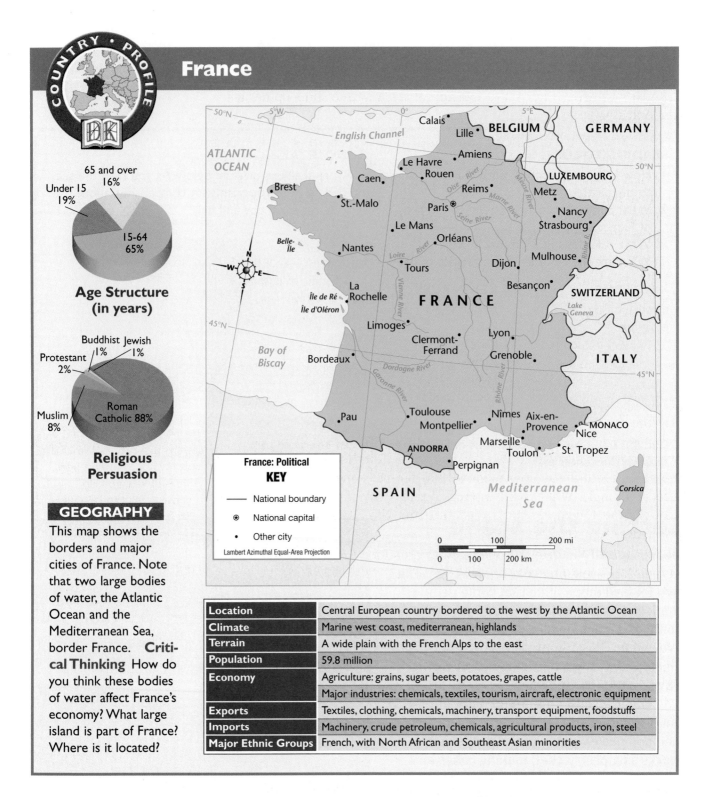

France

Age Structure (in years)

Under 15 19%

65 and over 16%

15-64 65%

Religious Persuasion

Buddhist 1%

Jewish 1%

Protestant 2%

Muslim 8%

Roman Catholic 88%

GEOGRAPHY

This map shows the borders and major cities of France. Note that two large bodies of water, the Atlantic Ocean and the Mediterranean Sea, border France. **Critical Thinking** How do you think these bodies of water affect France's economy? What large island is part of France? Where is it located?

France: Political
KEY

—— National boundary

⊛ National capital

• Other city

Lambert Azimuthal Equal-Area Projection

Location	Central European country bordered to the west by the Atlantic Ocean
Climate	Marine west coast, mediterranean, highlands
Terrain	A wide plain with the French Alps to the east
Population	59.8 million
Economy	Agriculture: grains, sugar beets, potatoes, grapes, cattle
	Major industries: chemicals, textiles, tourism, aircraft, electronic equipment
Exports	Textiles, clothing, chemicals, machinery, transport equipment, foodstuffs
Imports	Machinery, crude petroleum, chemicals, agricultural products, iron, steel
Major Ethnic Groups	French, with North African and Southeast Asian minorities

Contemporary Culture in France

The cultural traditions of France can be traced back for centuries. Despite rapid change in industrial centers and large cities, particularly over the last century, long-standing traditions and customs are still practiced in the more rural provinces and towns throughout the countryside. These traditions provide a cultural foundation that the French are proud to share with the rest of the world.

Traits that Define

Catherine and Victoire show us two sides of the French character. Each side values French culture differently. Catherine sums up her attitude this way:

> "We French are as modern as anyone else. But there is something very special about our culture. Take our language. It's very exact. In the seventeenth century [we] invented a standard for speaking correct French. Since then, an organization called the French Academy has tried to keep our language as correct as possible. We French love our traditions."

Catherine is right about the Academy. Since 1635, it has published dictionaries that give all the words accepted in the French language. The Academy makes rules about how these words should be used. This is an example of how the French work to preserve their culture.

Highlights of French Culture French culture has always had a lasting influence on the rest of the world. France has produced world-famous poets, philosophers, visual artists, and politicians, and the great city of Paris has been at the center of many of the major artistic and literary movements of the twentieth century.

In the 1920s, soon after the end of World War I, artists from all over the world flocked to Paris because they felt the city offered them the freedom to experiment with different forms of art, literature, and music. While living in Paris, writers such as Ernest Hemingway, F. Scott Fitzgerald, T. S. Eliot, Gertrude Stein, and James Joyce produced many of their most famous literary works. The Spanish painter, Pablo Picasso, the American photographer Man Ray, and France's own Jean Cocteau and André Breton were major figures in the visual arts.

France is also known for its cooking. In 1805, a French pastry chef named Marie-Antoine Carême (MUH ree ahn twahn kuh REM) began making desserts for rich and powerful people in France.

In 1833, Carême wrote a book on the art of French cooking. It set strict standards of excellence. Ever since Carême's book was published, French cooking has been one of the most respected kinds of cooking in the world.

Religion in Italy

The vast majority of French and Italian citizens are Roman Catholic and the world headquarters of the Roman Catholic Church are in the tiny nation called the **Vatican** (VAT ih kun). It is an independent city-state located within **Rome,** and its leader is the pope. Roman Catholicism unites about one billion people around the world, and it especially unites Italians. Not every Italian is Catholic, but Italy's history is closely tied to the history of Catholicism. Until recently, Catholicism was the official religion of the country.

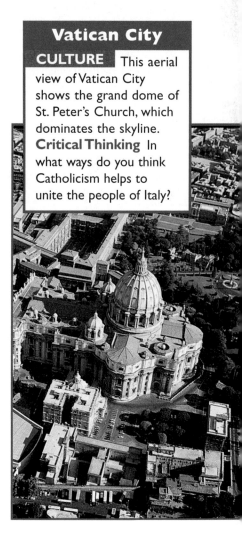

Vatican City

CULTURE This aerial view of Vatican City shows the grand dome of St. Peter's Church, which dominates the skyline. **Critical Thinking** In what ways do you think Catholicism helps to unite the people of Italy?

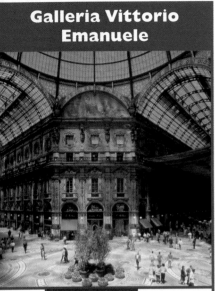

Galleria Vittorio Emanuele

CULTURE This building was designed by Giuseppe Mengoni in 1861. It consists of a domed area, creating a covered shopping mall. **Critical Thinking** In what ways does this photograph show how Milan is a mix of the old and the new?

Cultural Differences in Northern and Southern Italy

Life in the North   Milan (mih LAN) is typical of northern Italy. It is one part of a triangle of cities—with the cities of Turin and Genoa—that are home to most of Italy's manufacturing industries. **Manufacturing** is the process of turning raw materials into finished products. It also caters to international business.

Milan has a flashier side, too. Every season, people interested in fashions crowd into Milan to see collections from clothing designers. Italian fashion has become so important that Milan is second only to Paris as a fashion capital. Milan's factories also produce cars, planes, leather goods, and plastics.

Rural Culture in Southern Italy   Southern Italy is very different from Milan. **Locorotondo** (loh koh roh TAWN doh) is a typical town located on the "heel" of the Italian "boot." Farming is the way most people here make a living, and wheat, olives, and fruits are grown here. Fishing is also an important industry. Southern Italian traditions and the family still rule everyday life.

Changing Cultures   The cultures of both France and Italy will keep changing. As more and more people **emigrate,** or move in from other parts of the world, the cultures will become more diverse. At the same time, institutions and traditions that make each nation unique will be preserved and will continue to influence people all over the world for generations to come.

SECTION 4 ASSESSMENT

AFTER YOU READ

RECALL

1. Identify: (a) Aix-en-Provence, (b) Paris, (c) Vatican, (d) Rome, (e) Milan, (f) Locorotondo

2. Define: (a) emigrate, (b) manufacturing

COMPREHENSION

3. What are some cultural traditions of France that have influenced people around the world?

4. How has the Catholic religion influenced life in Italy?

5. What are three differences between life in Milan and life in a southern Italian village?

CRITICAL THINKING AND WRITING

6. **Exploring the Main Idea** Review the Main Idea statement at the beginning of this section. Work with a partner to make a list of ways in which cultural traditions in France and Italy can be traced back to these countries' pasts.

ACTIVITY

7. **Holding a Debate** It is important to the French to maintain certain standards in the French language. Hold a class debate about why preserving language is important and how it provides a link to cultural traditions.

Solving Problems

Swedish automobile makers can't compete with firms from other countries because they cannot make cars as quickly and cheaply as other countries

Possible Solutions

1. Look for economic growth in other areas, such as natural resources.
2. Make cars of less quality to increase production.
3. Partner with an American company and use their methods to increase production.
4. Hire more workers and allow less time for vacations.

Learn the Skill

Many countries today face problems. The problems are often economic—how to increase growth or reduce taxes so people have more money to spend and save. You probably face problems as well—how to earn spending money, get good grades, or make new friends.

One way to solve problems is to study how other people have solved the same problem. For example, governments can study successful solutions that other governments have come up with.

Another way to solve problems is to make a list of possible solutions and choose the best alternative. To solve problems, you can use a Problem-Solution Chart such as the one shown on this page. To complete the chart, follow these steps:

A. Identify the problem. Write it in the first box in the chart. In the sample chart, the problem is one faced by automobile makers in Sweden. They aren't able to sell many cars, because they cannot make them fast enough or cheap enough. How can the automobile makers and the government work together to increase sales and thereby boost Sweden's economy?

B. List possible solutions. Brainstorm and write down as many ideas as you can, even

if you think the solution is not a good one, as it might lead to a better idea. Talk to others and get their ideas as well. Many governments have found solutions by studying what was done to correct a similar problem in another country. This is a time to call on experts and get as many ideas to choose from as possible.

C. Choose the best solution. Study each possible solution carefully. Think about the long-term effects of each. If you are with others, talk with them to find out if they are willing to help, and come up with a plan for working together. Then, choose the best solution and circle it. The solution that Sweden chose was to work with an American firm and learn how to increase production. Sweden was able to solve its problem.

D. Put the solution you chose into action.

E. Evaluate the results. If you aren't satisfied, build on your experiences and try another solution. Keep working with the problem until you are successful.

Practice the Skill

Working in a small group, make a list of problems facing your community or city. Choose one of the problems and create a Problem-Solution Chart like the one shown. First, define the problem. Then, work with your group to brainstorm several solutions. Discuss each solution thoroughly to determine if it will yield the results you want. Choose the solution that you think will work the best, and circle it. Explain your process and your chart to another small group.

Apply the Skill

See the Chapter Review and Assessment at the end of this chapter for more questions on solving problems.

Review and Assessment

Creating a Chapter Summary

On a separate piece of paper, draw a diagram like this one, and include the information that summarizes the first section of the chapter. Then fill in the remaining boxes with summaries of Sections 2, 3, and 4.

WESTERN EUROPE

Section 1

Great Britain is a constitutional monarchy whose laws are set by Parliament. As part of the United Kingdom, Northern Ireland is also governed by the British parliament. The Republic of Ireland is an independent nation.

Section 2

Section 3

Section 4

Reviewing Key Terms

Match the definitions in Column I with the key terms in Column II.

Column I

1. polders
2. persecution
3. reunification
4. Parliament
5. constitutional monarchy
6. Flemish
7. Holocaust

Column II

a. oppression
b. government in which the power of kings and queens is limited by law
c. Dutch-speaking Belgian
d. mass murder of millions of Jews and others by Germans during World War II
e. land reclaimed from the sea
f. representative body that makes the law in Great Britain
g. process of Germany's becoming unified again

Reviewing the Main Ideas

1. How does the monarchy help to unify Great Britain? (Section 1)
2. Why do the Protestants of Northern Ireland oppose Home Rule? (Section 1)
3. How does the Netherlands get raw materials for manufacturing? (Section 2)
4. What are some of the differences between northern and southern Belgium? (Section 2)
5. How was Germany divided and why was it reunified? (Section 3)
6. What kept Germans unified in their thinking even when their country was divided? (Section 3)
7. How do the French keep their cultural traditions? (Section 4)
8. Why is religion an important part of Italian culture? (Section 4)

Map Activity

Western Europe

For each place listed below, write the letter from the map that shows its location.

1. Aix-en-Provence   **4.** Italy

2. London   **5.** Berlin

3. The Netherlands   **6.** Brussels

 Take It to the NET

Enrichment For more map activities using geography skills, visit the social studies section of **phschool.com.**

Writing Activity

1. Using Primary Sources News about the current events described throughout this chapter can be researched at your school or local library. Use primary sources such as journal accounts, autobiographies, letters, and first-hand accounts to write a press release that gives an update on a current event in Great Britain, Ireland, Belgium, the Netherlands, Germany, France, or Italy.

2. Writing a Travel Journal Imagine that you have traveled to each country mentioned in this chapter. Write a journal entry describing some of the cultural or historical sites you visited, traditions you learned about, or experiences you enjoyed. Visit the library or Internet to help you complete the activity.

Applying Your Skills

Turn to the Skills Activity on p. 323 to complete the following activity.

Think of a problem that you are having in your own life, and then create a Problem-Solution Chart to find the best solution.

Critical Thinking

1. Making Comparisons Compare the partitioning of Germany with the partitioning of Ireland and the separation of the Netherlands from Belgium. What factors are similar? What factors are different?

2. Drawing Conclusions How do you think Germany will change in the future? How might Germans react to these changes?

 Take It to the NET

Activity Take a virtual tour of Paris using the interactive map. Create a travel guide for your own town or city. Include photos or illustrations of sights, a map, and information about each point of interest. Visit the World Explorer: People, Places, and Cultures section of **phschool.com** for help in completing this activity.

Chapter 17 Self-Test As a final review activity, take the Chapter 17 Self-Test and get instant feedback on your answers. To take the test, visit the Social Studies section of **phschool.com.**

EASTERN EUROPE AND RUSSIA:
Exploring the Region Today

Peace, Not War

Thursday, December 3, 1992
Dear Mimmy,

Today is my birthday. My first wartime birthday. Twelve years old. Congratulations. Happy birthday to me!

As usual there was no electricity. Auntie Melica came with her family (Kenan, Naida, Nihad) and gave me a book.... The whole neighborhood got together in the evening. I got chocolate, vitamins, a heart shaped soap, a key chain, a pendant made of a stone from Cyprus, a ring (silver) and earrings.

The table was nicely laid, with little rolls, fish and rice salad, cream cheese (with Feta), canned corned beef, a pie, and of course—a birthday cake. Not how it used to be, but there's a war on. Luckily, there was no shooting, so we could celebrate.

It was nice, but something was missing. It's called peace!
Your Zlata

USING LITERATURE

This letter was written by Zlata Filipovic, a young girl who lived through the civil war in the country of Bosnia. She wrote the letter in her diary, which she called "Mimmy." During the war in Bosnia, Zlata and her family spent their days in the basement to avoid gunfire. Schools closed. Food and water became scarce.

Using a Diary or Journal
Many people write in a diary or journal what they would tell no other person. Diaries can give people hope and courage, especially during hard times. What does this diary entry tell you about war? How do you think the experience of living through a war affected Zlata?

Keeping a Diary
Keep a diary for a week, writing one entry each day. Write about what makes you happy as well as things that bother or upset you. At the end of the week, write an entry telling what you think about keeping a diary.

Poland
The Growth of Free Enterprise

BEFORE YOU READ

READING FOCUS

1. How is Poland's economy changing?

2. What are some of the challenges faced by all Polish citizens?

KEY TERMS

free enterprise

KEY PEOPLE

Pope John Paul II

MAIN IDEA

In Poland, communism once controlled people's lives and livelihood. Now, Poles are learning about freedom's rewards and responsibilities.

NOTE TAKING

Copy the table below. As you read the section, fill in the table with information about Poland's changing economy.

Changes in the Cities	Changes in the Countryside

Setting the Scene

After World War II, Poland was dominated by the Soviet Union. The Polish people were made to follow strict rules governing the economy, education, and free speech, but they would not give up their language or their strong connection to the Roman Catholic Church. **Pope John Paul II,** a Polish citizen, was made head of the Church in 1978. His leadership helped to reinforce traditional beliefs and to gain support for the Polish bid for freedom. In 1989, the communist government in Poland came to an end. The Polish people were committed to democracy and were ready to meet the challenges of freedom.

Changes in the Towns and Economy

Ever since the fall of communism, Poland has undergone rapid change in its economy. Under communism, the government owned and ran all of the businesses. Now the Poles have adopted a **free enterprise** system like that of the United States. In a free enterprise system, businesses can compete with each other for profit, with little government control.

Small businesses soon blossomed all over Poland's capital, Warsaw. Traders set up booths on the streets where they sold everything from American blue jeans to old Soviet army uniforms. Some traders earned enough money to take over stores that the government had once owned. Poland's economy

Cultural Traditions

CULTURE Christians across the world make decorated eggs at Easter. These brightly colored eggs are similar to those that Polish people exchange at Easter. **Critical Thinking** Why was it so important to many Polish people to maintain their religious customs during communist rule?

Poland

COUNTRY · PROFILE

Other and non-religious 5%

Eastern Orthodox 2%

Roman Catholic 93%

Religious Persuasion

Under 15 23%

65 and over 11%

15-64 66%

Age Structure (in years)

ECONOMICS This map shows the ways people make a living in different parts of Poland. **Map Study** How do you think most people make a living in the cities that are shown on this map?

Poland: Economic Activity
KEY
- Forestry
- Commercial farming
- Manufacturing and trade

Lambert Conformal Conic Projection

0   50   100 mi
0   50   100 km

Location	Baltic Sea in eastern Central Europe
Climate	Humid continental and marine west coast
Terrain	Mostly lowlands forming part of the Northern European Plain; mountains along the southern border
Major Ethnic Groups	Polish, with German and Ukrainian minorities
Population	38.6 million
Government	Democratic state
Economy	Agriculture: potatoes, fruits, vegetables, wheat; major industries: shipbuilding, chemicals, metals, machinery
Exports	Machinery, transport equipment, foodstuffs
Imports	Machinery, transport equipment, intermediate goods, chemicals, fuels

began growing faster than any other in Eastern Europe. Today, the standard of living of its people is growing stronger every day.

Challenges for the Future

Merchants and industrial workers are benefiting from their hard work. But people in rural areas are working harder and are not benefiting. Farmers, with no government support, find it hard to compete

Standard of Living in Eastern European Countries

Country	Percent of Population with Televisions	Percent of Population with Telephones
Albania	10%	2%
Czech Republic	33%	33%
Hungary	50%	20%
Poland	25%	14%
Serbia	17%	20%
United States	83%	77%

ECONOMICS One way to study a country's economic health is to take a look at its basic services, such as communications. This chart shows the percentage of people that have TVs and telephones in several European countries, as well as in the United States. **Chart Study** Based on this information, which country probably has the weakest economy?

in the European market. Many young people in rural areas feel that they have little chance to make a decent living. Some have moved to the city in the hope of finding jobs.

Migration to the cities, however, can cause overcrowding. Today, 60 percent of all Poles live in towns or cities, a huge increase from just 50 years ago. In response, the government is building apartment buildings and expanding suburban areas.

The new life is good in some ways and hard in others. Many Poles have things they never had before. For these people, the new way of life is good.

However, you can also see people with nothing to do. This, too, is a change. There are more people without jobs than there were under communism. The Poles will have to find ways to deal with such challenges. The Polish people are ready to do whatever is needed because, for the first time in many years, their future is in their own hands.

SECTION 1 ASSESSMENT

AFTER YOU READ

RECALL

1. Identify: (a) Pope John Paul II
2. Define: (a) free enterprise

COMPREHENSION

3. What economic changes have taken place in Poland since the end of communist rule?
4. What challenges have people in Poland's rural areas had to face in recent times?

CRITICAL THINKING AND WRITING

5. **Exploring the Main Idea** Review the Main Idea statement at the beginning of this section. Then, write a paragraph describing the changes in Poland after communist rule.
6. **Comparing and Contrasting** Many Polish people left farms to move to cities like Warsaw in order to earn a better living. How was life in the city different from life in rural areas?

ACTIVITY

7. **Creating an Advertisement** Imagine that you are a business owner in Warsaw. Decide what your business is and then think of a way to promote it. Create a magazine advertisement for your business.

SECTION 2

The Balkans
Cultural and Political Power Struggles

Mostar, Bosnia-Herzegovina

CULTURE This bridge in Mostar, Bosnia-Herzegovina, stood for more than 400 years. It was destroyed in 1993 during a war between ethnic groups. **Critical Thinking** In what ways might war damage the culture of a particular region?

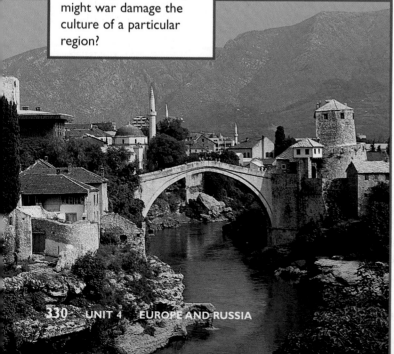

Setting the Scene

The **Balkans** is a region made up of several countries, including Yugoslavia. The region is located south of the Danube River and gets its name from the Turkish word for "mountain." The land here features rugged mountains, which form natural barriers around fertile valleys and isolated alpine villages. To the west of the Balkan Peninsula is the Adriatic Sea, to the southwest is the Ionian Sea, and to the east is the Black Sea.

A centuries-old clash of cultures divides the states that once were part of Yugoslavia. The area has been devastated by years of war and, for many people in the Balkans, the future is uncertain.

Geographic Barriers Lead to Cultural Differences

For centuries, the Ottoman Empire controlled the Balkans region. The people living there were cut off from the west until after World War I, when the countries of the Balkans region were finally established. These new countries were poor and unstable, and could not stand up to their more powerful neighbors. One of those neighbors, the Soviet Union, dominated the region after World War II.

Under a Soviet-influenced communist government, people gave up freedom in an effort to develop stronger industries and a more stable economy.

Distinct Cultural Groups

The mountains of the Balkan region form natural barriers. Cultural groups developed without interference from each other, forming strong traditions and beliefs. Bringing these different groups together has had tragic results.

Many of the people in the Balkans share a Slavic background even though they belong to different ethnic groups. The largest groups in Yugoslavia are the Serbs, Croats (KROH atz), and Muslims, also called Bosniaks. Smaller groups are the Slovenes, Macedonians (mas uh DOH nee unz), and Montenegrins (mahn tuh NEH grins). Although these groups were unified under the communist government, they each have distinct languages and cultural identities.

Cultural Profile of the Balkan Countries

Country	Major Ethnic Groups	Major Religions	Languages
Albania	Albanian 95% Greek 3% Other 2%	Muslim 70% Albanian Orthodox 20% Roman Catholic 10%	Albanian Greek
Bosnia-Herzegovina	Serb 31% Bosniak 44% Croat 17% Other 8%	Muslim 40% Orthodox 31% Roman Catholic 15% Other 14%	Croatian Serbian Bosnian
Bulgaria	Bulgarian 83% Other 17%	Bulgarian Orthodox 84% Muslim 13% Other 3%	Bulgarian
Croatia	Croat 78% Serb 12% Other 10%	Roman Catholic 76% Orthodox 11% Muslim 1% Other 12%	Croatian Other
Former Yugoslav Republic of Macedonia	Macedonian 67% Albanian 23% Other 10%	Macedonian Orthodox 67% Muslim 30% Other 3%	Macedonian Albanian Turkish Serbo-Croatian
Romania	Romanian 89% Other 11%	Romanian Orthodox 87% Roman Catholic 5% Protestant 4% Other 4%	Romanian Hungarian German
Yugoslavia (Serbia and Montenegro)	Serb 62% Albanian 17% Montenegrin 5% Bosniak 3% Hungarian 3% Other 10%	Orthodox 65% Muslim 19% Roman Catholic 4% Protestant 1% Other 11%	Serbian Albanian
Slovenia	Slovene 88% Croat 3% Serb 2% Bosniak 1% Other 6%	Roman Catholic 71% Lutheran 1% Muslim 1% Atheist 4% Other 23%	Slovenian Serbo-Croatian

CULTURE This chart shows the ethnic, religious, and language groups of the people in the Balkan countries. **Chart Study** Which countries would you expect to be the most stable? Which countries would you expect to be the least stable? Give reasons for your answers.

Differences in Language

Serbs and Croats both speak the Serbo-Croatian language, but they do not use the same alphabet to write. Slovenian, Macedonian, and Bulgarian languages are related to Serbo-Croatian, but they are not identical to it. Albanians and Romanians speak languages that are not closely related to those of their Slavic neighbors. Differences in language set the people in each group apart from each other.

Differences in Religion

In the Balkans, the majority of the people are Christian Orthodox, Roman Catholic, or Muslim. People who want to live, work, and socialize only with people who share their religious beliefs have tried to rid their communities, often through the use of violence, of those people who do not share the same beliefs.

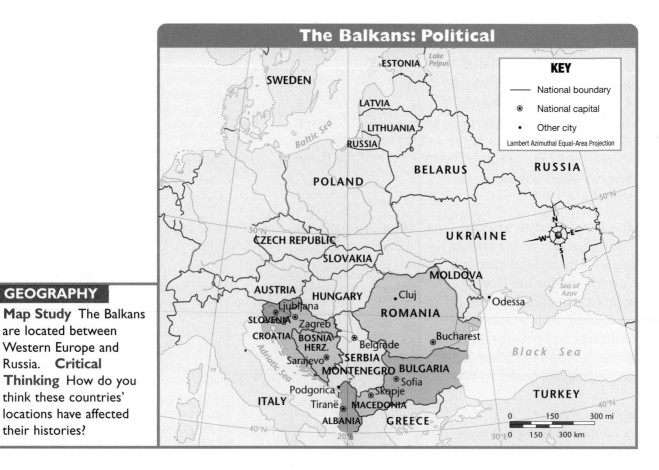

The Balkans: Political

KEY

— National boundary

⊛ National capital

• Other city

Lambert Azimuthal Equal-Area Projection

SWEDEN
ESTONIA
Lake Peipus
LATVIA
LITHUANIA
RUSSIA
Baltic Sea
BELARUS
RUSSIA
POLAND
50°N
CZECH REPUBLIC
UKRAINE
SLOVAKIA
MOLDOVA
AUSTRIA
HUNGARY
•Cluj
•Odessa
Sea of Azov
Ljubljana
SLOVENIA ⊛ Zagreb
ROMANIA
CROATIA BOSNIA-HERZ.
⊛Bucharest
Black Sea
Adriatic Sea
⊛Belgrade
Sarajevo⊛ SERBIA
MONTENEGRO BULGARIA
Podgorica⊛ ⊛Sofia
⊛Skopje
TURKEY
ITALY Tiranë⊛ MACEDONIA
40°N
ALBANIA GREECE
40°N
0   150   300 mi
20°E
30°E 0   150   300 km

Map Study The Balkans are located between Western Europe and Russia. **Critical Thinking** How do you think these countries' locations have affected their histories?

Cultural Division and Destruction

In 1991, tensions among the Serbs, the Croats, and other groups in Yugoslavia came to a breaking point. The Serbs controlled the government of Yugoslavia, and some provinces did not want to live under Serbian rule.

Slovenia, Croatia, the Former Yugoslavian Republic of Macedonia, and Bosnia-Herzegovina all declared their independence and drew up borders to form their own countries.

Under communism, industries were concentrated in large factories near the natural resources needed for raw materials. The formation of independent countries divided the natural resources, industries, and transportation corridors in the region. The newly independent countries faced great challenges as they tried to build their new economies.

Adding to these challenges were cultural differences. Serbs maintained control of what remained of Yugoslavia, the country later renamed Serbia and Montenegro, as shown on the map above. Serbs living in Croatia and Bosnia-Herzegovina worried about living under non-Serb governments. Likewise, Croatians living outside of Croatia worried about living under non-Croatian governments.

Eventually, these cultural conflicts resulted in bitter warfare. In Bosnia-Herzegovina, fighting broke out among three main ethnic groups—Serbs, Croats, and Bosnian Muslims. Tens of thousands of lives were lost, and the capital city of Sarajevo was destroyed. Troops were sent in by the **United Nations,** a group of 189 countries that work together to bring about peace and cooperation among the nations of the world. They brought food and medicine to people cut off from supplies by Serbian forces. A peace treaty was finally signed in 1995 to divide Bosnia and Herzegovina into the Federation of Bosnia and Herzegovina and the Bosnian Serb Republika Srpska.

In 1999, fighting broke out again when Serbs fought against Albanians seeking independence in **Kosovo.** The international community was quick to respond, first with bombing attacks against Serbia and then by sending peace-keeping troops. The Yugoslavian government was overthrown in 2000, and in 2003 the country was divided into Serbia and Montenegro.

These ongoing conflicts have prevented economic development in the Balkans region. Refugees fleeing from one part of the region to another have put huge financial burdens on poor countries. Bombing raids have destroyed bridges, communication lines, railways, and roads. Some countries, however, that have been able to avoid conflict and concentrate their efforts on establishing industries, building the economy, and lowering unemployment, are beginning to get results. Slovenia, Bulgaria, and Romania are all working toward becoming members of the European Union.

The Long War in Bosnia

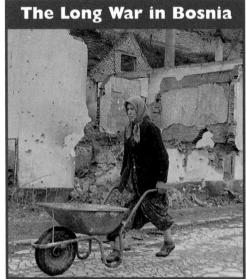

HISTORY The war in Bosnia claimed thousands of lives and reduced cities to rubble. One relief worker there said, "Everyone in this city has memories of . . . when they had no water or electricity and they couldn't go out on the streets without fear of being shot." **Critical Thinking** What do you think would be some of the challenges of living in a country destroyed by war?

SECTION 2 ASSESSMENT

AFTER YOU READ

RECALL

1. Identify: (a) Balkans, (b) Kosovo

2. Define: (a) United Nations

COMPREHENSION

3. How has physical geography contributed to the separation of cultural groups in the Balkans?

4. What are the main cultural differences that have led to the conflicts in countries of the former Yugoslavia?

CRITICAL THINKING AND WRITING

5. Exploring the Main Idea Review the Main Idea statement at the beginning of this section. Then, write a paragraph describing the causes leading to the conflict in the Balkans, and how these conflicts might have been avoided.

6. Making Predictions What do you think will happen in the Balkan countries that were once part of Yugoslavia? Write an update for the year 2015.

ACTIVITY

 Take It to the NET

7. Writing to a Pen Pal Establish a pen pal relationship with a student in Bosnia and ask questions that will help you to understand what life is like there. Share with your pen pal what life is like for you in the United States. Visit the World Explorer: People, Places, and Cultures section of **phschool.com** for help in completing this activity.

The Czech Republic

An Economic Success Story

BEFORE YOU READ

READING FOCUS

1. How did the history of the Czech Republic prepare it for independence?
2. What economic challenges does the Czech Republic face?

KEY TERMS

privatization

KEY PLACES

Slovakia

MAIN IDEA

Before World War II, Czechoslovakia was a democratic nation with a strong economy, and now the Czech Republic is using its experience to rebuild the economy and compete in worldwide markets.

NOTE TAKING

Copy the outline below. As you read the section, fill in the outline with information about the Czech Republic.

I. **Czechoslovakia to 1989**
  A. World War I
    1.
    2.
  B. World War II
    1.
    2.
    3.
    4.
  C. Communist Takeover
    1.
    2.

II. **Czechoslovakia since 1989**
  A. Communist Collapse
    1.
    2.
  B. Czech Republic
    1.
    2.

The Struggle for Independence

HISTORY After decades of Soviet domination, Czechs demanded freedom and independence in 1989. **Critical Thinking** What would it be like to live in a country where you were punished for protesting and speaking your mind?

Setting the Scene

In 1918 the Czechs and Slovaks joined together to form a single independent nation that enjoyed rapid growth and prosperity.

By 1939, when the German army began its occupation of the country during World War II, Czechoslovakia was one of the ten most developed nations in the world.

The Road Back to Independence

After World War II, the Czechoslovakian Republic and its democratic government were re-established, until a communist takeover in 1948. All private property was seized for the state. Political freedom and human rights were taken away from the Czech people.

Over the years, Czechoslovakians tried to keep their commitment to freedom alive even in a totalitarian state. The Soviet Union sent troops

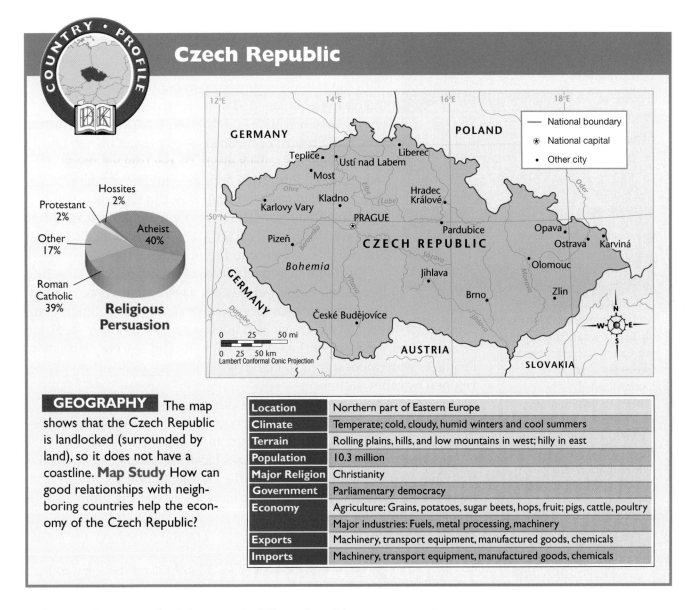

Czech Republic

COUNTRY · PROFILE

Religious Persuasion

- Atheist 40%
- Roman Catholic 39%
- Other 17%
- Protestant 2%
- Hossites 2%

GEOGRAPHY The map shows that the Czech Republic is landlocked (surrounded by land), so it does not have a coastline. **Map Study** How can good relationships with neighboring countries help the economy of the Czech Republic?

Location	Northern part of Eastern Europe
Climate	Temperate; cold, cloudy, humid winters and cool summers
Terrain	Rolling plains, hills, and low mountains in west; hilly in east
Population	10.3 million
Major Religion	Christianity
Government	Parliamentary democracy
Economy	Agriculture: Grains, potatoes, sugar beets, hops, fruit; pigs, cattle, poultry
	Major industries: Fuels, metal processing, machinery
Exports	Machinery, transport equipment, manufactured goods, chemicals
Imports	Machinery, transport equipment, manufactured goods, chemicals

to keep strict control of the people. When the citizens rose up to protest, they were suppressed with harsh punishments.

Restoring a Free Enterprise System When the Soviet Union collapsed in 1989, Czechoslovakia regained its freedom. Within a few years, the Czech Republic peacefully separated from **Slovakia** to form its own nation.

Under communism, almost all goods manufactured in Czechoslovakia were sold only to the Soviet Union or other countries under Soviet control. Most manufacturers did not compete in world markets, and products did not have to meet the demands of the international marketplace. Even so, companies whose goods were exported built up strong reputations. The quality of the glassware, vehicles, planes, motorcycles, and textile machinery earned loyal customers and worldwide respect.

Better Factories, Better Products

ECONOMICS These workers are on an assembly line at a car factory in the Czech Republic. Many Czech factories were modernized and improved to help improve the country's economy. **Critical Thinking** How would this car factory's modernization help improve the Czech Republic's economy?

Meeting New Economic Challenges

With the fall of communism, manufacturing in the Czech Republic needed to be restructured. The first step was to privatize state-owned businesses. **Privatization** is the return of businesses to private ownership and management. To help do this, citizens bought coupon booklets. The coupons could be exchanged for shares in companies. In this way, the citizens bought the companies from the state. Only the largest industries are still owned by the state, and little by little they are being transferred to the private sector.

During the split with Slovakia, some of the Czech Republic's industrial centers were lost. To make up for this loss, manufacturing plants needed to be upgraded. Productivity needed to increase and quality needed to improve. Some product lines were discontinued, and some factories were shut down. Products were modernized to compete with state-of-the-art goods developed by other nations.

In order to strengthen trade with other countries, imports were decreased, sales of exports were increased, and marketing strategies were developed in order to win contracts.

Meeting these economic challenges has been an enormous task. But each step in the process makes the Czech economy stronger and more stable. Today, Czech-made products are becoming more visible in the international marketplace.

SECTION 3 ASSESSMENT

AFTER YOU READ

RECALL

1. Identify: Slovakia

2. Define: privatization

COMPREHENSION

3. How has past experience helped the Czech Republic build an independent nation?

4. What are some of the economic challenges the Czech Republic has faced since the return of free enterprise?

CRITICAL THINKING AND WRITING

5. **Exploring the Main Idea** Review the Main Idea statement at the beginning of this section. Then make a list of the strategies the Czech Republic is using to strengthen its economy.

6. **Draw Inferences** Imagine that you are a worker in the Czech Republic. How has the free enterprise system changed your ideas about what you do? How do you feel about improving the quality of the prod-

ucts you help to manufacture? How can you benefit from the free enterprise system?

ACTIVITY

7. **Creating a Business Directory** Use library and Internet sources to find out about businesses and products that are being developed in the Czech Republic. Use the information you gather to create business profile cards that describe goods being developed and marketed around the world.

Russia

New Democracy, Unstable Economy

BEFORE YOU READ

READING FOCUS

1. How has life in Siberia changed since the fall of communism?

2. How has life in Moscow changed since the fall of communism?

KEY TERMS

investor

KEY PLACES

Kemerovo
Moscow

MAIN IDEA

The change to a free enterprise system after years of communist rule has been difficult for Russians, but the new system allows them to pursue economic opportunities that were once impossible.

NOTE TAKING

Copy the table below. As you read the section, fill in the table with comparisons about life in Russia during and after communism.

	During Communism	After Communism
Life in Siberia		
Life in Moscow		

Setting the Scene

Inessa Krichevskaya (in es UH kree chev SKY uh) has surprising feelings about change in Russia. "You know," she says, "it's a very difficult period in our country right now, but we will just have to live through it, because this is the right direction.... We can never go back to what was before."

Why are Inessa's feelings so surprising? For more than 30 years, she was a loyal communist. She lived and worked in the city of Moscow as an engineer. Like all other Russians, she always expected that the government would send her monthly checks when she grew too old to work. That was part of the communist system. But then Russia switched to the free enterprise system. Now Inessa is in her 60s and is retired. The amount she receives from the government is much less than she expected. Inessa gets about 1,300 rubles a month—only about $8.

The change from communism to democracy and a free enterprise system has not been easy. From Moscow to Siberia, Russian people have suffered many hardships to gain freedom.

Life in Siberia

During the Soviet years, the government tried to change Siberia, the huge region of eastern Russia. It built factories to take advantage of the region's rich reserves of

The Voice of Democracy

GOVERNMENT In countries like the United States, it is easy to take freedom for granted. Only after the collapse of communism were Russians able to speak freely about politics.

Critical Thinking How do you think the Russian people feel about being able freely to voice their ideas and beliefs?

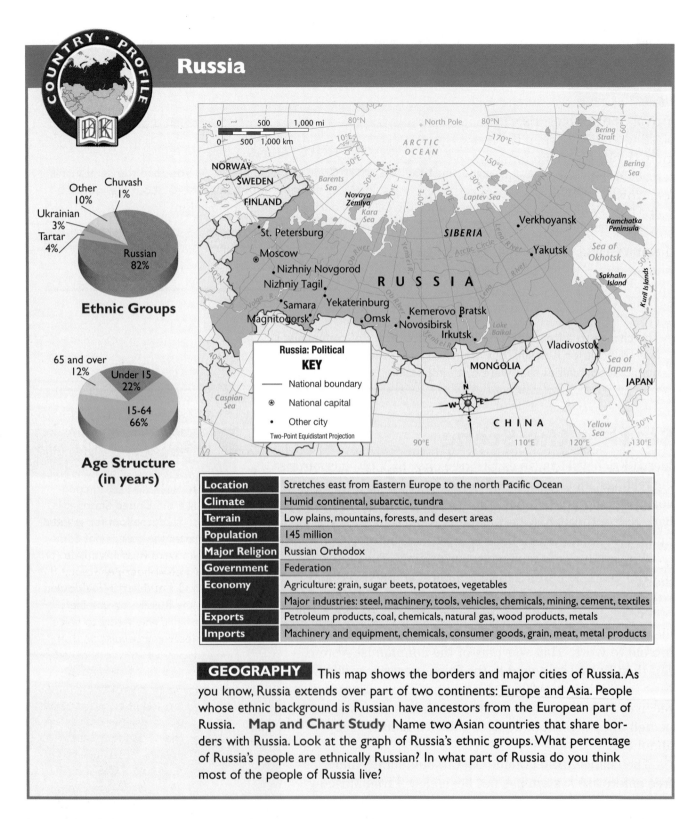

Russia

COUNTRY · PROFILE

DK

Ethnic Groups

Other 10%
Chuvash 1%
Ukrainian 3%
Tartar 4%
Russian 82%

Age Structure (in years)

65 and over 12%
Under 15 22%
15-64 66%

Location	Stretches east from Eastern Europe to the north Pacific Ocean
Climate	Humid continental, subarctic, tundra
Terrain	Low plains, mountains, forests, and desert areas
Population	145 million
Major Religion	Russian Orthodox
Government	Federation
Economy	Agriculture: grain, sugar beets, potatoes, vegetables
	Major industries: steel, machinery, tools, vehicles, chemicals, mining, cement, textiles
Exports	Petroleum products, coal, chemicals, natural gas, wood products, metals
Imports	Machinery and equipment, chemicals, consumer goods, grain, meat, metal products

GEOGRAPHY This map shows the borders and major cities of Russia. As you know, Russia extends over part of two continents: Europe and Asia. People whose ethnic background is Russian have ancestors from the European part of Russia. **Map and Chart Study** Name two Asian countries that share borders with Russia. Look at the graph of Russia's ethnic groups. What percentage of Russia's people are ethnically Russian? In what part of Russia do you think most of the people of Russia live?

coal, gold, iron, oil, and natural gas. The government took advantage of the Trans-Siberian Railroad to transport materials to and from Siberia. But today, many of the factories are outdated. In the Siberian city of **Kemerovo** (KEM uh roh voh), factories still release black smoke into the air. Other buildings in the town are crumbling. Rusty cars move slowly down the muddy streets.

Traditional ways still continue in Siberia. Change is slow, especially in rural villages. But the fall of communism and the arrival of free enterprise are starting to affect life in the region. Under the communist system, everyone was guaranteed a job. Now Siberians who work in factories and coal mines must worry about losing their jobs. On the other hand, for the first time in more than 70 years, Siberians are able to buy their own homes. Before, they had to live in houses that belonged to the state. People can also now buy stock in the companies where they work.

Life in Moscow

In **Moscow,** where Inessa lives, buying shares in businesses is a big business in itself. Investors from everywhere, including the United States, have come to Moscow to make money. An **investor** is someone who spends money on improving a business in the hope of getting more money when the business succeeds. Some investors have become very wealthy. When the first American fast-food chain in Russia opened in Moscow, people lined up in the streets to try it out. The restaurant served 30,000 people on the first day.

A New Middle Class In big cities like Moscow, investors have brought big changes. Just outside the city, a new skyscraper reaches the sky. At its top is a fine restaurant, enclosed in stone and glass. The building is the world headquarters of Gazprom (GAHS prahm), Russia's only natural gas company. Started by a former communist official, it makes a huge amount of money.

The head of Gazprom is one of Russia's richest people. Many other former government leaders have become wealthy in the new Russian democracy. Another group of newly rich Russians leads criminal gangs. Both of these groups worry ordinary Russians—neither rich nor poor—who are members of the new middle class.

New investment and the creation of businesses, restaurants, and services have contributed to the rise of a middle class in Russia. Members of this middle class have been working hard since the collapse of communism in Russia. They dream of starting their own new business or opening a small factory. They have been studying Western ways of doing business and gaining knowledge from the Internet, which has

Siberian Industry: A Mixed Blessing

SCIENCE AND TECHNOLOGY

Black smoke belches into the cool air in the Siberian town of Ulan Ude (oo LAHN oo DAY) along the Trans-Siberian Railroad. The railroad, completed in 1916, helped to link Siberia's rich natural resources to more densely populated areas of Europe. When towns along the tracks of this railroad became industrial centers, the number of available jobs increased, but so did pollution. **Critical Thinking** What are some ways that these industrial centers can deal with the problem of pollution?

Building Anew in Moscow

ECONOMICS Since the fall of communism, people in Moscow, Russia's capital, have started over. They have constructed new buildings and started many new businesses. The number of cars in Russia has tripled, and the streets of the capital, once empty, are always busy. **Critical Thinking** How does starting a new business create jobs?

become popular in Russia. More than during Soviet times, ordinary Russians can own appliances and can sometimes afford to travel.

Like middle classes in other countries in the world, ordinary Russians are at a disadvantage when the economy does not thrive. Though Russians work hard to make capitalism succeed, they have had a lot of challenges to overcome. In 1998, the value of the ruble fell, causing prices of goods to skyrocket and bringing heavy inflation. In addition, Russia faced a severe food shortage. Vladimir Putin, the Russian president elected in 2000, made some progress reforming Russia's economy, but great differences still separate the rich from the poor in Russia.

Tradition and Change Free enterprise is changing Moscow, but old Russian ways survive alongside the new. After all, Russia is a huge country with many different ways of life. Russia faces many challenges in the future. Can a country with many different ethnic groups and an area of more than 6 million square miles (9 million sq km) hold itself together? Will the old ways and new ways become one common way for everyone? The answers to these questions are not yet clear. But Russians are united in the hope for a better future for all.

SECTION 4 ASSESSMENT

AFTER YOU READ

RECALL

1. Identify: (a) Kemerovo, (b) Moscow

2. Define: (a) investor

COMPREHENSION

3. How has the fall of communism affected life in Siberia?

4. How have the fall of communism and the growth of free enterprise affected life in Moscow?

CRITICAL THINKING AND WRITING

5. **Exploring the Main Idea** Review the Main Idea statement at the beginning of this section. Then, write an account of some of the biggest hardships you might face as a new business owner in Moscow.

6. **Comparing and Contrasting** Create a chart that shows the similarities and differences between life in Siberia, and life in Moscow.

ACTIVITY

7. **Writing a Business Report** Write a business report for a store that you have opened in Moscow. Explain what the business is, where you get your products, who your customers are, how many employees have, and why you think the business will succeed.

Drawing Inferences

Facts	Inferences
During communism the people in Yugoslavia got along. After communism, civil war erupted.	Communist rule kept the people from expressing ethnic tensions.
Ukraine means "border-land." Ukraine is surrounded by many countries. Ukraine has vast natural resources. The Ukraine has been invaded many times.	Other countries invade the Ukraine to gain its natural resources.
Six months after a nuclear accident at Chernobyl, people returned to work at the nuclear plant. But no one lived in the area.	
When the first American fast-food chain in Russia opened in Moscow, people lined up in the streets to try it out. The restaurant served 30,000 people on the first day.	

Learn the Skill

Writers do not always state everything directly. Sometimes when you read, you have to "read between the lines" in order to figure out what is not directly stated. When you read between the lines, you are drawing inferences. To help you draw inferences when you read, follow these steps:

A. Study what is stated, and look for facts. Knowing the facts when you read is an essential first step to drawing inferences. For example, you know from reading the first fact in the chart that the people in Yugoslavia got along during communism. After communism, civil war erupted. These are facts.

B. Draw inferences from the facts by using what you already know. Ask yourself, "What does this information suggest?" "What conclusions can I draw from these facts?" Use prior knowledge and common sense. Think about what is an obvious conclusion that is not stated in the material. Regarding what you know about Yugoslavia, you can conclude that below the surface during communism, serious differences existed between the people. Communist rule must have kept the people from expressing their tensions.

C. Read the facts in the second row of the chart about Ukraine. The facts are that Ukraine has lots of natural resources and has been taken over many times by other countries. To draw an inference, think about why the country is invaded. It's because the other countries want the natural resources. When you come to this conclusion as you read, you are drawing an inference.

Practice the Skill

The chart shown is incomplete. Make your own two-column chart. Label the first column "Facts." Label the second column "Inferences." Copy the information into your chart. Then, draw inferences to complete the last two rows of the chart. To do so, use your common sense and prior knowledge about people to figure out why no one lived near the Chernobyl plant and why so many Russians were interested in trying American fast food.

Apply the Skill

See the Chapter Review and Assessment at the end of this chapter for more questions on drawing inferences.

Creating a Chapter Summary

On a separate piece of paper, draw a diagram like this one, and include the information that summarizes the first section of the chapter. Then fill in the remaining boxes with summaries of Sections 2, 3, and 4.

EASTERN EUROPE AND RUSSIA

Section 1
Since the fall of communism, the people of Poland are adjusting to a new way of life, while retaining their long-standing cultural traditions.

Section 2

Section 3

Section 4

Reviewing Key Terms

Match the definitions in Column I with the key terms in Column II.

Column I

1. person who spends money to help improve business in the hope of getting more money in return

2. a system that allows private businesses to compete with one another for profit, and with little government control

3. the return of businesses to private ownership and management

4. an international organization of countries that work together to bring about peace and cooperation worldwide

Column II

a. free enterprise
b. United Nations
c. privatization
d. investor

Reviewing the Main Ideas

1. What parts of Polish life have not changed? (Section 1)

2. What forces are changing some basic parts of Polish town life and country life? (Section 1)

3. What conflicts led to the breakup of Yugoslavia? (Section 2)

4. Name some things that Bosnians, Croats, and Serbs in the Balkans region have in common. Name some differences. (Section 2)

5. What challenges have the citizens of the Czech Republic faced in the change to a free enterprise system? (Section 3)

6. What are some differences between life in Siberia and life in Moscow? (Section 4)

7. How have recent events affected the people of Russia in different ways? (Section 4)

Map Activity

Eastern Europe

For each place listed below, write the letter from the map that shows its location.

1. Czech Republic
2. Poland
3. Sarajevo
4. Bosnia-Herzegovina
5. Serbia and Montenegro
6. Warsaw

 Take It to the NET

Enrichment For more map activities using geography skills, visit the social studies section of **phschool.com.**

Writing Activity

1. **Using Primary Sources** Nations are trying to work together to help resolve the conflicts between people in the Balkans. Visit your school or local library and use primary sources such as newspaper and magazine articles to find additional information on the events. Diaries, letters, and autobiographies of people who are involved in these conflicts may also be available. Write a character sketch to describe what life is like for a student, an athlete, a political leader, or some other citizen living in the region. Use your character sketch to introduce the person to your classmates.

2. **Writing an Advertisement** Write an advertisement for a hat shop in Warsaw. In the advertisement, explain why people should buy from new shops instead of from older stores that used to be run by the government.

Applying Your Skills

Turn to the Skills Activity on p. 341 to help you draw inferences from the following facts.

1. For centuries, the Ottoman Empire controlled the Balkans region. After World War I, the countries of the Balkans region were established.

2. Under communism, industries in Yugoslavia were concentrated in large factories near the natural resources needed for raw materials. After the fall of communism, Yugoslavia broke apart into independent countries.

Critical Thinking

1. **Making Comparisons** Compare Poland's change to a free enterprise system after the fall of communism to that in Russia. What similarities and differences are there in the way that their rural populations have been affected?

2. **Identifying a Problem** What do you think would help bring lasting peace to the Balkans? Explain your answer.

 Take It to the NET

Activity Read about the dissolution of the USSR and life in Russia today. Choose one of the interactive activities found under "A Nation in Transition" or "Russia Today." Visit the World Explorer: People, Places, and Cultures section of **phschool.com** for help in completing this activity.

Chapter 18 Self-Test As a final review activity, take the Chapter 18 Self-Test and get instant feedback on your answers. To take the test, visit the Social Studies section of **phschool.com.**

PAINTERS

Artists use paint to express ideas. Painters can capture the likeness of a face or a flower, but they do more than just paint realistic images. They also work with color, texture, and shape to create eye-catching images of the world as they see it. Cultures throughout history have produced their own great painters. There have been many different groups, or movements, in painting, such as classicism, cubism, and pop art. Painters change the way we see the world. They use different kinds of techniques and media (materials) to achieve a certain effect. Whatever the medium or the style, the work of any painter reflects his or her cultural traits.

? How is art used to express ideas and beliefs in a culture?

EARLY PAINTERS
The artists of ancient Egypt decorated the walls of tombs with scenes of gods and goddesses and of hunting and feasting. The Minoan people of early Greece painted their houses and palaces with pictures of dancers, birds, and flowers. Roman artists painted gods and goddesses and scenes from classical mythology.

RENAISSANCE

One of the greatest periods of European painting was the Renaissance, which reached its height in Italy in the early part of the 16th century. During the Renaissance, painters studied perspective to develop a more realistic style of painting landscapes and portraits.

MICHELANGELO
Italian Michelangelo Buonarroti (1475–1564) is one of the best known painters of the Renaissance. He painted the ceiling of the Sistine Chapel at the Vatican in Rome between 1508 and 1512.

MEDIEVAL PAINTERS
In medieval times, most artists in Europe and Russia painted only subjects from Christianity. Painters used rich colors and thin layers of gold on wood panels for altarpieces or directly onto church walls. This style may look somewhat flat to us, but the images are powerful and reflect the deep religious feelings in western culture at that time.

REMBRANDT
Like Michelangelo, the Dutch artist Rembrandt van Rijn (1606–1669) is widely known by only his first name. Rembrandt's famous portraits, such as the self-portrait shown here, are powerful and full of expression.

ROMANTIC MOVEMENT

During the late 18th and early 19th centuries, a new style of painting became known as the romantic movement. The romantics flooded their paintings with light and color. This is a detail from a painting called *The Swing* by a French romantic artist Fragonard (1732–1806).

IMPRESSIONISM

The artists of the impressionist movement painted dabs of color to create the effect of light and shade that defines objects. Artists of the impressionist movement include Claude Monet, Camille Pissarro, Pierre Auguste Renoir, Edgar Degas, Mary Cassatt, and Alfred Sisley.

MONET
Claude Monet (1840–1926) was the leader of the impressionist movement. He painted many pictures of his garden and of the French countryside, including The Poppy Field *shown here. Up close, the painting consists of many brushstrokes of different colors. From a distance, the dabs of color come together to form a field of red flowers.*

PICASSO
Spanish painter Pablo Picasso (1881–1973) was one of the most creative and influential artists of the 20th century. His restless personality led him to paint in many different styles at different times of his life. His pictures of people painted using distorted shapes and sharp angles led to a movement called cubism.

MARY CASSATT
Mary Cassatt (1845–1926) was born in the United States but spent much of her life in France. Like many artists of the day, she painted in the style of the French impressionists. Many of Mary Cassatt's paintings show the daily lives of women, often with their children. This painting is called Mother About to Wash her Sleepy Child, *1880.*

Welcome to Africa

GOVERNMENT

Witness the election of a new president ...

CULTURE

Listen to tales from the past ...

CITIZENSHIP

Work towards equal rights in South Africa ...

What do you want to learn?

ECONOMICS

Tend crops on a farm in Tanzania ...

HISTORY

Explore the ruins of Great Zimbabwe ...

SCIENCE, TECHNOLOGY, AND SOCIETY

Explore modern farming methods ...

GEOGRAPHY

Watch the sun set on the African plains ...

A journal can be your personal record of discovery. As you learn about Africa, you can create journal entries about what you read, write, think, and create. For your first entry, think about the history of Africa. What are some of the ways that history is passed down from one generation to the next in Africa? Compare how history is passed down in your culture.

EXPLORER'S JOURNAL

Guiding Questions

What questions do I need to ask to understand Africa?

Asking questions is a good way to learn. Think about what information you would want to know if you were visiting a new place, and what questions you might ask to find out. The questions on these pages can help guide your study of Africa. You might want to try adding a few of your own!

GEOGRAPHY

African cultures have been shaped by the need to survive in nearly every type of land on the Earth. The giant continent has people-packed cities, mountaintop coffee farms, and grasslands where zebras gallop. The geography of Africa presents huge barriers to movement, such as giant deserts and thick rain forests. Yet, from early times, Africans discovered ways to overcome these barriers.

❶ How has geography affected the way African societies have developed?

HISTORY

Africa gave birth to some of the world's oldest civilizations. Early Africans traded widely beyond their borders, but much of the continent, especially beyond the coasts, was little known to the outside world until modern times. In myths, poetry, and stories, Africans passed down their history, telling of great kingdoms, family customs, and human wisdom. These histories shape Africans' sense of identity today.

❷ How have Africans been affected by their history?

CULTURE

A culture is the set of beliefs and customs shared by a group of people. There is no single African "culture" because Africa has hundreds of cultures. Some are the unique traditions of people who lived in isolation. Yet more often ideas, customs, and inventions spread across Africa, varying as they passed from region to region.

❸ How do Africa's many cultures differ from place to place?

GOVERNMENT

Africa's history includes powerful kingdoms, empires, and nations. Until recent times, though, Africans usually ruled themselves in smaller clans, villages, or towns. Today, many African national governments give their citizens American-style freedoms, such as the right to vote, to worship freely, and to choose where they live and work.

4 **How do African governments compare with the United States government?**

CITIZENSHIP

The nature of citizenship varies among the different regions of Africa. Citizens have different roles and responsibilities, and they participate in the political process in different ways. In some countries, citizens have fought hard to participate in their government's political process, and in other countries, they have brought about change using different methods.

6 **How have Africans struggled to participate in their government's political processes?**

ECONOMICS

As they have for generations, many Africans raise crops and livestock, both to consume and to sell. Yet Africa's economy is becoming more industrialized. People work in everything from factories to restaurants to road construction. World demand for African products—oil, gold, coffee, and cocoa—provides jobs to millions of workers.

5 **What are some of the ways that Africans make a living?**

SCIENCE, TECHNOLOGY, AND SOCIETY

Africa has an economy largely based on agriculture and the raising of livestock. Scientific innovations in farming are beginning to improve the economy in many African countries, and advances in technology and science are making Africa's economy increasingly industrialized.

7 **How has Africa's relative isolation from the rest of the world affected the use of science and technology?**

 Take It to the NET

For more information on Africa, visit the World Explorer: People, Places, and Cultures companion Web site at **phschool.com.**

ACTIVITY ATLAS

Africa

Learning about Africa means being an explorer and a geographer. No explorer would start out without first checking some facts. Begin by exploring the maps of Africa on the following pages.

Relative Location

UNITED STATES

ATLANTIC OCEAN

Tropic of Cancer

AFRICA

Equator

Tropic of Capricorn

Relative Size

UNITED STATES

AFRICA

1. LOCATION

Explore Africa's Location One of the first questions a geographer asks about a place is "Where is it?" Use the map to describe Africa's location relative to the United States. What ocean lies between Africa and the United States? Note that the Equator extends through Africa. What role might their location on the Equator play in the climates of nearby countries? How do you think climates of the United States might differ from the climates of Africa?

2. REGIONS

Explore Africa's Size How big is Africa compared to the United States? On a separate sheet of paper, trace the map of the United States and cut it out. How many times can you fit it inside the map of Africa?

 Take It to the NET

Items marked with this logo are periodically updated on the Internet. To get current information about the geography of Africa, go to **phschool.com**.

Africa: Political

30°W 20°W 10°W 0° 10°E 20°E 30°E 40°E 50°E 60°E

Strait of Gibraltar

Algiers
⊛Tunis
TUNISIA
Rabat
Casablanca⊛ Tripoli

MOROCCO

Mediterranean Sea

Alexandria ⊛Cairo
Giza• Suez Canal

30°N

WESTERN SAHARA (MOROCCO)

ALGERIA

LIBYA

EGYPT

Lake Nasser

Red Sea

30°N

Tropic of Cancer

20°N

CAPE VERDE
⊛Nouakchott
MAURITANIA
MALI

NIGER

CHAD

Khartoum⊛

ERITREA
⊛Asmara
DJIBOUTI

Gulf of Aden

20°N

•Praia SENEGAL
Dakar⊛ THE GAMBIA
Banjul• Bamako⊛ Ouagadougou⊛
Niamey⊛

•Kano

SUDAN

L. Chad

N'Djamena⊛

Djibouti•

L. Tana

10°N

GUINEA-BISSAU
Conakry⊛
Freetown⊛
SIERRA LEONE
Monrovia⊛
LIBERIA

•Bissau
GUINEA
CÔTE D'IVOIRE
Yamoussoukro⊛
Abidjan

BURKINA FASO
GHANA
TOGO
BENIN
Lomé⊛
Accra⊛
Malabo⊛

NIGERIA
⊛Abuja
Lagos•
Porto-Novo⊛

CAMEROON
⊛Yaoundé

Benue R.

CENTRAL AFRICAN REPUBLIC
Bangui⊛

Addis Ababa⊛

ETHIOPIA

SOMALIA

⊛Mogadishu

10°N

EQUATORIAL GUINEA
SÃO TOMÉ AND PRÍNCIPE ⊛
São Tomé•

⊛Libreville
GABON

Congo R.

Kisangani•

Congo R.

UGANDA
Kampala⊛
Kigali⊛
RWANDA

Kampala•
Lake Victoria

L. Turkana

KENYA
Nairobi⊛

Mombasa•

INDIAN OCEAN

Victoria•
SEYCHELLES

0°

Equator

Prime Meridian

DEM. REP. OF THE CONGO
Brazzaville⊛
CABINDA (ANGOLA)
⊛Kinshasa

BURUNDI
Bujumbura⊛
Dodoma⊛
Dar es Salaam•

0°

ATLANTIC OCEAN

Luanda⊛

L. Tanganyika

TANZANIA

10°S

400 800 mi
400 800 km

ANGOLA

Lubumbashi•

ZAMBIA
Lusaka⊛

MALAWI
L. Nyasa
Lilongwe⊛

COMOROS
•Moroni

10°S

Harare⊛

MOZAMBIQUE

Antananarivo•

MAURITIUS
Port Louis⊛

20°S

Tropic of Capricorn

NAMIBIA
Windhoek⊛

ZIMBABWE
BOTSWANA

Zambezi R.

Limpopo R.

MADAGASCAR

RÉUNION (FR.)

20°S

Gaborone⊛
Johannesburg•
Orange R.

⊛Pretoria
SWAZILAND
Maseru⊛
LESOTHO
SOUTH AFRICA
Cape Town•

Maputo⊛
⊛Mbabane
Durban•

Mozambique Channel

30°S

KEY

—— National boundary
⊛ National capital
• Other city

Lambert Azimuthal Equal Area Projection

0° 10°E 20°E 30°E 40°E 50°E 60°E

3. MOVEMENT

Explore the Influence of Geography on the Economy Fifteen African nations are landlocked. That is, they do not border any ocean. Point to them on the map. Make a list of them. Landlocked nations are often poor. How do you think being landlocked might affect a nation's economy?

ACTIVITY ATLAS

Africa: Physical

KEY

Elevation

Feet	Meters
Over 13,000	Over 3,960
6,500–13,000	1,980–3,960
1,600–6,500	480–1,980
650–1,600	200–480
0–650	0–200
Below sea level	Below sea level

Lambert Azimuthal Equal Area Projection

4. PLACE

Describe Africa's Physical Features Find Southern Africa on the map
above. It extends south of 10°S. Steep cliffs rise up from the narrow
coastal plains, where the dark green areas meet the lighter green. Trace
these cliffs north with your finger. Inside this line of cliffs, how would you
describe the physical features of the interior of Southern Africa?

5. REGIONS

Identify Africa's Physical Features An adventurous friend has flown off to Africa, but she hasn't told anyone where she is going. She sends you clues. Use the maps on pages 351, 352, and 353 to find her location.

A. I've landed in a city in Ethiopia. It's in a region of tall grasses and few trees. The city is near 10°N and 40°E. What city am I in?

B. The area around me has Mediterranean vegetation. But I'm not anywhere near the Mediterranean Sea! I am flying over a city on a very narrow coastal plain. Nearby are steep cliffs. What city is below me?

C. Today, I flew above tropical rain forests along the Equator. Going north, the forests changed into savanna. I'm in a city north of where the Benue River meets the Niger River. Where am I?

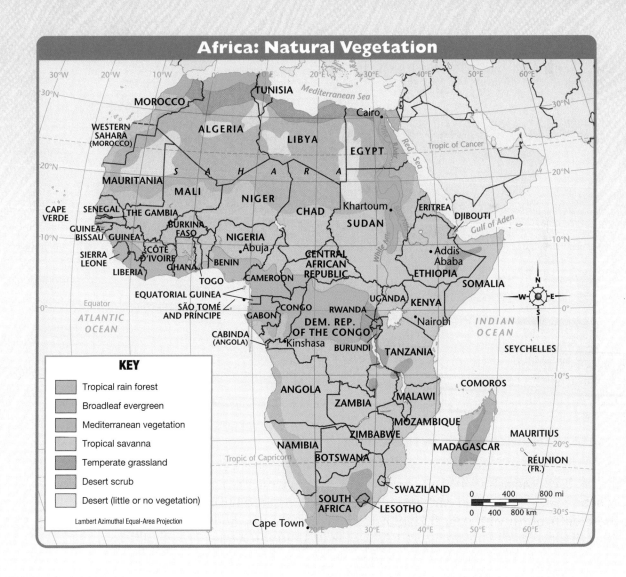

Africa: Natural Vegetation

KEY

- Tropical rain forest
- Broadleaf evergreen
- Mediterranean vegetation
- Tropical savanna
- Temperate grassland
- Desert scrub
- Desert (little or no vegetation)

Lambert Azimuthal Equal-Area Projection

ACTIVITY ATLAS

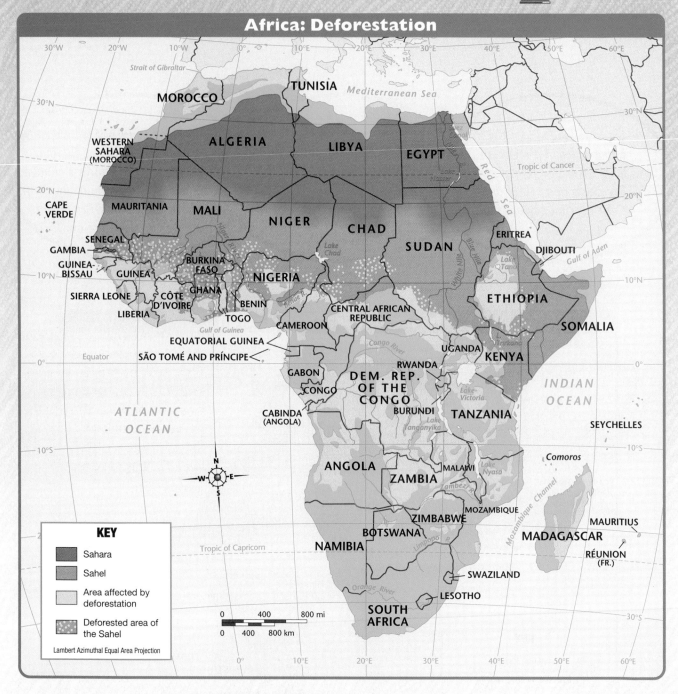

Africa: Deforestation

KEY

- Sahara
- Sahel
- Area affected by deforestation
- Deforested area of the Sahel

Lambert Azimuthal Equal Area Projection

0   400   800 mi
0   400   800 km

6. HUMAN-ENVIRONMENT INTERACTION

Explore the Effects of Physical Processes A loss of trees and forest is called deforestation. It causes droughts, raises temperatures, reduces animal life, and helps create deserts. Deforestation comes mainly from farmers and herders who clear trees to make farming and grazing land. On the map above, which regions are affected by deforestation? How can you tell?

Africa's Deepest, Largest, Tallest, and Longest . . .

DEEPEST LAKES

Lake Victoria
area 26,828 sq mi
depth 270 ft

Lake Chad (wet season)
area 10,000 sq mi
depth 25 ft

Lake Turkana
area 2,471 sq mi
depth 240 ft

Lake Michigan
(U.S.)
area 22,300 sq mi
depth 923 ft

Lake Chad (dry season)
area 4,000 sq mi
depth 25 ft

Lake Nyasa
area 11,430 sq mi
depth 2,310 ft

Lake Tanganyika
area 12,750 sq mi
depth 3,465 ft

LARGEST DESERTS

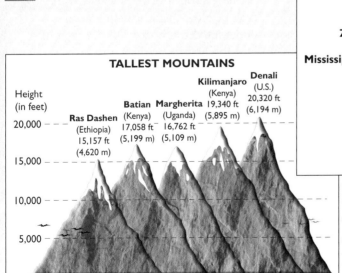

Namib
800 sq mi
(1,200 sq km)

Mojave (U.S.)
25,0000 sq mi
(65,000 sq km)

Nubian
100,000 sq mi
(259,000 sq km)

Kalahari
275,000 sq mi
(712,250 sq km)

Libyan
450,000 sq mi
(1,165,500 sq km)

Sahara
3,500,000 sq mi
(9,065,500 sq km)

Take It to the NET

7. PLACE

Compare Physical Features
Study the diagrams on this page. Using the maps in this Activity Atlas, locate each of the African features shown. What part of Africa—northern, southern, eastern, western, or central—has the (a) tallest mountain; (b) longest river; (c) deepest lake; (d) largest desert?

LONGEST RIVERS

Orange 1,350 mi (2,173 km)

Zambezi 2,200 mi (3,540 km)

Mississippi (U.S.) 2,350 mi (3,780 km)

Niger 2,600 mi (4,180 km)

Congo 2,720 mi (4,375 km)

Nile 4,000 mi (6,437 km)

0   1,000   2,000   3,000   4,000 miles

TALLEST MOUNTAINS

Height
(in feet)

Ras Dashen
(Ethiopia)
15,157 ft
(4,620 m)

Batian
(Kenya)
17,058 ft
(5,199 m)

Margherita
(Uganda)
16,762 ft
(5,109 m)

Kilimanjaro
(Kenya)
19,340 ft
(5,895 m)

Denali
(U.S.)
20,320 ft
(6,194 m)

20,000 —

15,000 —

10,000 —

5,000 —

AFRICA: Physical Geography

Nile River Valley

USING MAPS

Because they cover such a large area, world maps lack the detail to show much about a specific part of the world. That is why people use regional maps. Regional maps focus on one part of the world, showing it in greater detail. This map shows the region in Africa known as the Nile River valley.

KEY

Elevation

Feet	Meters
6,500–13,000	1,980–3,960
1,600–6,500	480–1,980
650–1,600	200–480
0–650	0–200
Below sea level	Below sea level

⊛   National capital

•   Other city

Lambert Conformal Conic Projection

Understanding Regional Maps

A region is an area of the Earth that shares some common characteristics. What region is shown on this map? What defines the region? What landforms can be found on either side of the Nile River valley? Where are most of the cities in the Nile River valley located? Why might the Nile River be important to people in Egypt?

Exploring the Nile River Valley

Why would this map be useful in learning about the ways of life in this region? How might it help you to understand the history of the region? Use the library or the Internet to gather more information about the Nile River valley. Write a brief report describing the ways that the Nile River has shaped people's lives in this region.

Africa
Physical Features

READING FOCUS

1. What are the four regions of Africa and how do they differ geographically?
2. What are Africa's three major landforms?
3. What effects do Africa's rivers have on the land and people?

KEY TERMS

plateau
elevation
escarpment
rift
cataract
transportation barrier
silt
fertile
tributary

KEY PLACES

Sahara
Great Rift Valley
Nile River
Congo River
Niger River
Zambezi River

NOTE TAKING

Copy the chart below. As you read the section, fill in the chart by noting the regions in which each physical feature is located.

Physical Features	North	West	East	Central/South
Sahara				
Plateaus				
Great Rift Valley				
Nile River				
Congo River				
Niger River				
Zambezi River				

MAIN IDEA

Africa is a huge continent with a variety of regions and physical features that affect how people live and work in different regions.

Setting the Scene

Africa is a giant. More than three times bigger than the United States, it covers close to 11,700,000 square miles (more than 30,000,000 sq km). That is about one fifth of all of the land in the world. If you drove across Africa at its widest point going 65 miles (105 km) per hour, without stopping for gas or sleep, it would take you about 72 hours. Traveling north-to-south, the trip would take about 77 hours.

Africa's Contrasting Geography

Africa can be divided into four regions: 1) North, 2) West, 3) East, and 4) Central and Southern. Each region contains many different climates and physical features.

North Africa is marked by rocky mountains and the world's largest desert, the **Sahara.** The Sahara is almost the size of the United States.

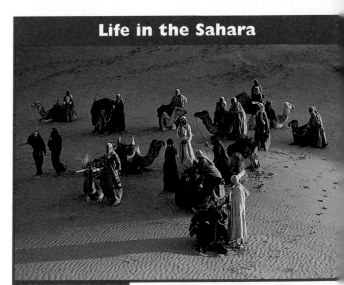

Life in the Sahara

GEOGRAPHY The Sahara covers about 3 1/2 million square miles (9 million square km). It has a poulation of less than 2 million people. **Critical Thinking** What are some of the difficulties that people might face living in the Sahara?

West Africa, the continent's most populated region, consists mostly of grasslands. The soil in the grasslands is good for farming.

East Africa contains many mountains, and **plateaus**, which are large raised areas of mostly flat land. The East also has areas of grasslands and hills.

Much of Central and Southern Africa is flat or rolling grassland. The region also contains thick rain forests, mountains, and swamps. The Namib (NAHM eeb) Desert of the country of Namibia and the Kalahari (kal uh HAHR ee) Desert of Botswana are in this region.

Africa's Major Landforms

Africa can be described as an upside-down pie. If you were to slice Africa in half from east to west, you would see that much of the continent is a plateau that drops off sharply near the sea.

Plateaus   Africa is often called the "plateau continent," because the elevation of much of the land area is high. **Elevation** is the height of land above sea level.

Each of Africa's four regions has mountains, but the highest are in East Africa. Mount Kilimanjaro is Africa's tallest mountain, rising to a height of 19,341 feet (5,895 m).

Coastal Plains   Along much of Africa's coast is a strip of coastal plain. This strip of land is dry and sandy at some points, and marshy and moist at other places. In the city of Accra, in the West African

Africa's Coastal Plains

ECONOMICS

Narrow coastal plains line much of Africa's coast, like this one at Cape Coast, Ghana. **Critical Thinking** Based on this photograph, how do you think people living on Africa's coastal plains might make a living?

country of Ghana (GAHN uh), the coastal strip is only 16 miles (25 km) wide. It ends at a long **escarpment**, or steep cliff, that is about as high as a 100-story skyscraper.

The Great Rift Valley Mount Kilimanjaro is located on the edge of the **Great Rift Valley** in East Africa. The Great Rift Valley was formed millions of years ago, when the continents pulled apart. A **rift** is a deep trench. The rift that cuts through East Africa is 4,000 miles (6,400 km) long. Most of Africa's major lakes are located in or near the Great Rift Valley.

The Rivers of Africa

Four large rivers carry water from the mountains of Africa's plateaus to the sea. They are the **Nile,** the **Congo,** the **Niger** (NI jur) and the **Zambezi.** The rivers are useful for traveling but they are broken in places by **cataracts,** or rock-filled rapids. These cataracts act as transportation barriers because they make it impossible for ships to sail from Africa's interior to the sea. **Transportation barriers** are physical features that make it difficult to travel or transport goods from one region to another.

The Nile River The Nile is the longest river in the world. Its length, more than 4,000 miles (6,400 km), is more than the width of the United States. The sources of the Nile are the White Nile in the country of Uganda and the Blue Nile in the highlands of Ethiopia. From these two sources, the river flows north and spills into the Mediterranean Sea.

People have farmed the land surrounding the Nile for thousands of years. At one time, the Nile flooded its banks regularly. Farmers planted their crops to match the flood cycle of the river. The floods provided water for the crops and left behind a layer of **silt**, which is the tiny bits of rock and dirt that build up on the bottoms of rivers and lakes. Silt helps make soil **fertile**, containing substances that plants need in order to grow well.

In 1960, Egypt's government began building the Aswan High Dam to control the flooding of the Nile. As the water backed up behind the dam, it created Lake Nasser. Lake waters are channeled to water crops that grow in the desert, while water rushing through the dam makes electricity.

The Great Rift Valley

KEY

Great Rift Valley

Lambert Azimuthal Equal-Area Projection

GEOGRAPHY The Great Rift Valley is so large that more than 30 Grand Canyons could fit inside it. Some of Africa's most spectacular mountains, volcanoes, and waterfalls can be found here. **Map Study** What sea is part of the Great Rift Valley? What bodies of water in the Great Rift Valley form natural borders between countries?

A River Without a Delta The Congo River's current is so strong that the river does not empty into the ocean at ground level (known as a *delta*). Instead, the river has cut a deep, wide canyon beneath the sea for a distance of about 125 miles (200 km).

The Congo River The Congo River flows through the rain forest of the country of Congo (KAHNG oh) in Central Africa. At 2,720 miles (4,375 km), the Congo is Africa's second-longest river. It is fed by hundreds of **tributaries**, or small rivers and streams that flow into a larger river. People in this region grow grains and cassava, a starchy plant similar to a potato. They also catch fish in the Congo with basket traps.

The Niger River Africa's third-longest river, the Niger, begins its journey in the West African country of Guinea (GIN ee). The river flows north and then bends south for 2,600 miles (4,180 km). The Niger provides water for farms in the river valley. People make a living catching fish in the river.

The Zambezi River The fourth-longest of Africa's rivers, the Zambezi, is in Southern Africa. It runs through or forms the borders of six countries: Angola, Zambia, Namibia, Botswana, Zimbabwe (zim BAHB way), and Mozambique (moh zam BEEK). The Zambezi is 2,200 miles (3,540 km) long. People have used the Zambezi's strong current to make electricity. About halfway to its outlet in the Indian Ocean, the Zambezi plunges into a canyon, creating Victoria Falls. The African name for Victoria Falls is "the smoke that thunders." People can see the mist and spray from 40 miles away.

SECTION 1 ASSESSMENT

AFTER YOU READ

RECALL

1. Identify: (a) Sahara, (b) Great Rift Valley, (c) Nile River, (d) Congo River, (e) Niger River, (f) Zambezi River

2. Define: (a) plateau, (b) elevation, (c) escarpment, (d) rift, (e) cataract, (f) transportation barrier, (g) silt, (h) fertile, (i) tributary

COMPREHENSION

3. Describe a major geographic feature from each of Africa's four regions.

4. Why is Africa called "the plateau continent?"

5. How do people use the rivers of Africa? What makes the rivers difficult to use?

CRITICAL THINKING AND WRITING

6. **Exploring the Main Idea** Review the Main Idea statement at the beginning of this section. Then, select 3 landforms in Africa that you would like to visit. Explain why you would like to go there and what you would do during your visit.

7. **Drawing Conclusions** Most of North Africa's population lives north of the Sahara near the Mediterranean Sea. If the Sahara were a grassland region with rivers and forests, would this change where people in North African countries live? Why?

ACTIVITY

8. **Writing a Journal** Imagine that you are traveling across each of Africa's four regions, and keeping a journal of your adventure. Write an entry for each region describing where you are and what sights you are seeing.

Humans and the Physical Environment

READING FOCUS

1. What physical features affect Africa's climate?
2. How have people in Africa learned to adapt to their environment?

KEY TERMS:

irrigate
oasis
savanna
nomad

MAIN IDEA

Different climate regions in Africa have different weather patterns and physical features, affecting the way people live.

NOTE TAKING

Copy the chart below. As you read the section, fill in the chart with information about the physical features of Africa and the ways that people in those regions have adapted to the environment.

	Rain Forest	Savanna	Desert
Physical Features			
Ways people adapt			

Setting the Scene

Visualize the continent of Africa with all of its different physical features: mountains, plateaus, rivers, forests, grasslands, and deserts. Now visualize people living and working in all of those different places. They must adapt the ways that they live and work in order to make the best use of their physical environment.

Physical Features and Climate

Look at the climate map on the following page. Find the Tropic of Cancer and the Tropic of Capricorn. Much of Africa lies between these two lines of latitude, which means that most of Africa is in a tropical climate region. The Equator runs through this midsection of the continent. These regions are usually hot.

Location near the Equator is not the only influence on climate. The climate of a place may depend on how close it is to large bodies of water. Major landforms and elevation also affect climate.

Living near the Equator A place's location in relation to the Equator influences the seasons. North of the Equator, winter and summer occur at the same time as in the

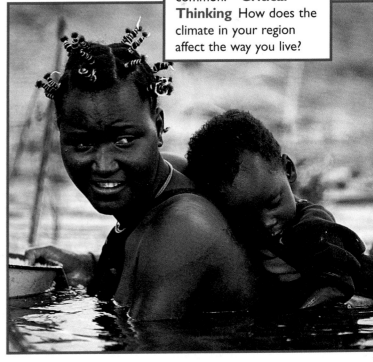

Ways People Adapt

GEOGRAPHY

In Botswana during the rainy season, floods like this one, on the Okavango River Delta, are common. **Critical Thinking** How does the climate in your region affect the way you live?

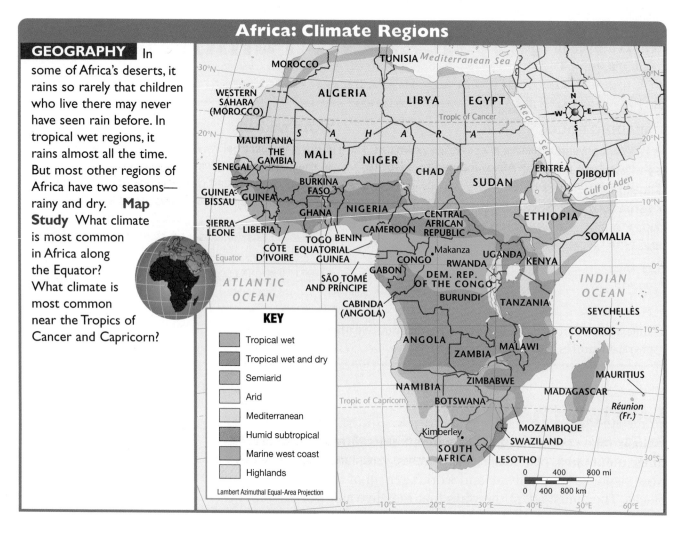

Africa: Climate Regions

GEOGRAPHY In some of Africa's deserts, it rains so rarely that children who live there may never have seen rain before. In tropical wet regions, it rains almost all the time. But most other regions of Africa have two seasons—rainy and dry. **Map Study** What climate is most common in Africa along the Equator? What climate is most common near the Tropics of Cancer and Capricorn?

KEY

- Tropical wet
- Tropical wet and dry
- Semiarid
- Arid
- Mediterranean
- Humid subtropical
- Marine west coast
- Highlands

Lambert Azimuthal Equal-Area Projection

United States. South of the Equator, the seasons are reversed, with winter beginning in June.

Climate and Farming Elevation, or height above sea level, also affects climate. The higher the elevation, the cooler a place tends to be. The countries of Ethiopia and Somalia are about the same distance from the Equator, yet they have different climates. Ethiopia is on a very high plateau and has mild temperatures and much rain. Farmers can grow a wide range of crops—including bananas, coffee, dates, and oats. Because Ethiopia usually gets plenty of rain, many farmers there do not **irrigate**, or artificially water their crops.

Somalia, at a lower elevation than Ethiopia, is hot and dry. Farming is possible only near rivers. Far from the rivers, farmers rely on oases to water their herds. An oasis is a place where springs and fresh underground water make it possible to support life in a dry region.

Adapting to the Land

The land in Africa's different regions is varied. People in these different regions understand how to adapt to the seasons and to the land in order to make a living.

Tropical Rain Forests Tropical rain forests are regions where it rains nearly all the time. The moisture supports a rich environment of trees, plants, and animals. This region used to be much larger. It covered much of Central Africa. Through the years, people cut trees from the forest for wood or to clear land for farming. Once the trees were cut, heavy rains washed away the nutrients that make soil fertile.

Tropical Savannas Much of Africa north and south of the rain forest is tropical **savanna**. The savanna is a region of tall grasses. The climate of the savanna is tropical wet and dry. The savanna has two seasons: dry and wet. During the dry season, farming is impossible. People trade, build houses, and visit friends. In the wet season, the land turns green and farmers plant their crops.

Deserts in Africa Beyond the savanna lie the deserts. In the south lie the Kalahari and the Namib. The immense Sahara extends across most of North Africa. **Nomads** make their living in the Sahara. Nomads move to various places to make a living. Some nomads are traders, and others hunt game and gather food. Most nomads are herders. They travel to where they can get water and food for their goats, camels, or sheep.

The southern edge of the Sahara meets the savanna in a region called the Sahel (SAH hel), which is the Arab word for shore or border. The Sahel is very hot and dry. It receives only 4 to 8 inches (10 to 20 cm) of rain per year. Small shrubs, grass, and some trees grow there.

AS YOU READ

Monitor Your Reading Picture the rain forest. What might it look like and sound like? Feel like? Smell like?

SECTION 2 ASSESSMENT

AFTER YOU READ

RECALL

1. Define: (a) irrigate, (b) oasis, (c) savanna, (d) nomad

COMPREHENSION

2. How do physical features affect the climate in Africa?

3. What are some of the ways that people have adapted to the climate in different regions of Africa?

CRITICAL THINKING AND WRITING

4. **Exploring the Main Idea** Review the Main Idea statement at the beginning of this section. Then, imagine that you are taking a trip to Africa where you will be visiting several different climate regions. Make a packing list for your trip and explain why you are bringing each item.

5. **Summarizing** Africans face many environmental challenges because of their varied climate. Write a paragraph in which you summarize the major climate-related problems and solutions discussed in this section.

ACTIVITY

 Take It to the NET

6. **Life in the Desert** Use the information on the web site to write a brief report about how humans and animals have adapted to life in the Sahara. Visit the World Explorer: People, Places, and Cultures section of **phschool.com** for help in completing this activity.

Geographic Factors and Natural Resources

READING FOCUS

1. What are Africa's agricultural resources?

2. What are Africa's mineral and energy resources?

3. How is Africa preparing for the economic future?

KEY TERMS

subsistence farming

cash crop

NOTE TAKING

Copy the chart below. As you read the section, fill in the chart with information about Africa's crops and mineral resources.

Crops	Minerals
• cacao beans	• copper
• yams	• diamonds
•	•
•	•

MAIN IDEA

Geographic factors influence how Africa's natural resources are used and who benefits from them.

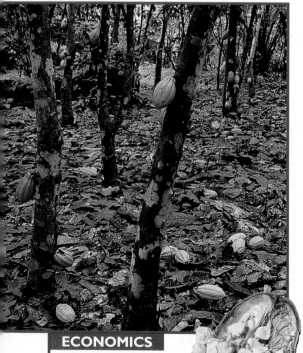

ECONOMICS

The cacao bean, now a natural resource of Ghana, is exported as chocolate. **Critical Thinking** Do you think that cacao beans are a valuable crop? Why?

Setting the Scene

Geographic factors, such as climate, limit the ability of some regions in Africa to develop adequate natural resources, while other regions are rich in resources, such as minerals.

Agricultural Resources

Some Africans are farmers living in areas with fertile soil and much rain. But many Africans have land that is difficult or impossible to farm because of poor soil or too little rain.

Subsistence Farming Most of Africa's land is used for **subsistence farming**. Subsistence farmers raise crops to support their families. Generally, they have little or nothing left over to sell or trade. In northern African countries such as Morocco, farmers raise barley and wheat. Farms at Saharan oases in Egypt produce dates and small crops of barley and wheat. In the dry, tropical savannas of Burkina Faso (bur KEE nuh FAH soh) and Niger, subsistence farmers grow grains. In regions with more rainfall, farmers also grow vegetables, fruits and roots such as yams and cassava. In West Africa, corn and rice are important crops.

Africa: Mineral and Energy Resources

ECONOMICS Most of Africa's people work in agriculture, yet most of Africa's exports are produced by miners. **Map Study** Southern Africa is famous for its diamond industry. What other regions of Africa produce diamonds? Which resource is most prevalent in Northern Africa?

KEY

- Bauxite
- Coal
- Cobalt
- Copper
- Diamonds
- Gold
- Iron
- Petroleum
- Hydroelectric power

Lambert Azimuthal Equal-Area Projection

Cash Crops

In all regions of Africa, farmers raise crops to sell. These are called **cash crops**. Farmers in Côte d'Ivoire (koht deev WAR), Ghana, and Cameroon grow cash crops of coffee and cacao. Farmers in Kenya, Tanzania, Malawi, Zimbabwe, and Mozambique grow tea as a cash crop.

In recent years, more and more farmers have planted cash crops. As more land is used for cash crops, less land is planted with crops to feed families. In some regions, this has led to food shortages when cash crops have failed.

Mineral and Energy Resources

An economy is a system for producing, distributing, consuming, and owning goods, services, and wealth. Farming is the major part of Africa's economy. Mining is also important to Africa's economy.

Parts of Africa are rich in mineral resources. In North Africa, nations such as Libya and Algeria have large amounts of petroleum, which is used to make oil and gasoline. In West Africa, the country of Nigeria is a major oil producer. Ghana was once called the Gold

AS YOU READ

Summarize What are some examples of cash crops in Africa?

Mining a Natural Resource

South Africa is the world's leading supplier of gold, providing about 500 metric tons a year, more than half of the world's supply. A gold miner in South Africa works more than two miles underground in a huge mine, which operates both night and day. The gold from these mines is used to make jewelry, coins and even teeth for people around the world.

A modern underground mine uses vehicles, railroad cars, elevators that hold dozens of workers at a time, a power supply, and a ventilation shaft which pumps clean air into the mine. Safety is an important issue in the mining process, and most mines try hard to protect the workers and their equipment.

Critical Thinking Compare working in a gold mine to working on a cash crop farm in Africa. Which would you prefer and why?

Coast because it was a leading exporter of African gold. Other mineral resources from Africa include copper, silver, uranium, and diamonds.

Africa's Future Economic Development

Most of Africa's workers are farmers. When a nation's economy is dependent on one kind of industry, such as farming, it is called a specialized economy. In Africa, specializing in just farming makes the economy sensitive to rainfall and the price of crops. For this reason, African countries are now trying to diversify their economies. To diversify means to add variety. These countries are working to produce a variety of crops, raw materials, and manufactured goods. A country with a diverse economy will not be hurt as much if a major cash crop fails or if world prices for one of its major mineral exports suddenly drop.

Mining requires many workers and costly equipment. Throughout much of Africa, foreign companies mine African resources and take the profits. This system does little to help African economies. In addition, Africa has few factories to make products from its own raw materials. Therefore, many African countries want to diversify their economies to include manufacturing.

SECTION 3 ASSESSMENT

AFTER YOU READ

RECALL

1. Define: (a) subsistence farming, (b) cash crop

COMPREHENSION

2. What are Africa's agricultural resources?

3. What are Africa's mineral and energy resources?

4. How are Africans preparing for their economic future?

CRITICAL THINKING

5. Exploring the Main Idea Review the Main Idea statement at the beginning of this section. Then, write a paragraph describing and comparing subsistence farming and farming for cash crops.

6. Identifying Central Issues Why is it important for countries in Africa to diversify their economies?

ACTIVITY

7. Writing to Learn List some of Africa's natural resources that you and your family use. Then, write a paragraph that explains which you would miss most if you did not have it—and why you would miss it.

Comparing and Contrasting

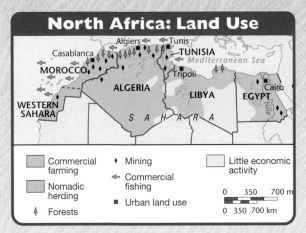

North Africa: Land Use

Casablanca — MOROCCO — Algiers — Tunis — TUNISIA — *Mediterranean Sea* — Tripoli — ALGERIA — LIBYA — Cairo — EGYPT — WESTERN SAHARA — S A H A R A — *Nile*

- Commercial farming
- Nomadic herding
- Forests
- Mining
- Commercial fishing
- Urban land use
- Little economic activity

0   350   700 m
0   350 700 km

Learn the Skill

When you compare and contrast, you look for similarities and differences between or among objects and ideas. Finding these similarities and differences can help you organize, understand, and draw conclusions from the information you read.

The map above shows land use in North Africa. Using the map, you can compare and contrast land use in Algeria and Libya. To compare and contrast, follow these steps:

A. Determine the purpose for comparing and contrasting. What are you being asked to compare and contrast? In this case, you are being asked to compare and contrast land use in Algeria with land use in Libya.

B. Examine the information carefully. First, locate each country on the map. Then, read the information in the map key. Using the key, identify each type of land use in each country. From the map, you can see that land is used in Algeria primarily for nomadic herding, with areas in the north

of the country used for commercial farming and mining. There are a few areas where there is little economic activity. In Libya, most of the land is used for nomadic herding, with some areas used for commercial farming. Almost half of the country has little economic activity.

C. Identify the similarities between or among the objects or ideas. Both countries use a majority of the land for nomadic herding, with smaller areas of commercial farming. In addition, both countries have areas with little economic activity.

D. Identify the differences. Algeria uses a larger percentage of the land for both nomadic herding and commercial farming than Libya. Algeria also uses land for mining, which Libya does not. Libya has a larger amount of land with little economic activity than Algeria.

E. Summarize these similarities and differences in order to draw conclusions. From the map, you can conclude that Algeria uses more of its land for a wider variety of economic activities than Libya does.

Practice the Skill

Continue to study the map to learn more about land use in North Africa. Follow the steps you learned to compare and contrast land use in Morocco and Egypt.

Apply the Skill

See the Chapter Review and Assessment at the end of this chapter for more questions on comparing and contrasting.

CHAPTER 19 Review and Assessment

Creating a Chapter Summary

On a separate piece of paper, draw a web like this one, and include the information that summarizes the information in each of the sections of the chapter. Add more ovals to the web as necessary.

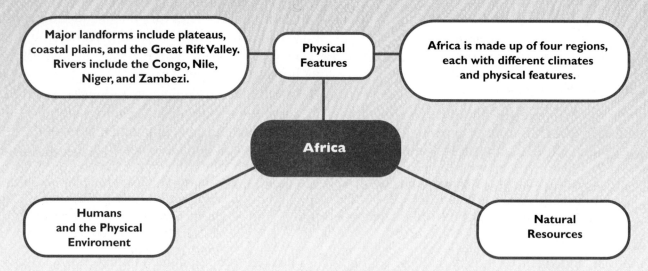

Major landforms include plateaus, coastal plains, and the Great Rift Valley. Rivers include the Congo, Nile, Niger, and Zambezi.

Physical Features

Africa is made up of four regions, each with different climates and physical features.

Africa

Humans and the Physical Enviroment

Natural Resources

Reviewing Key Terms

Use the following key terms to complete the sentences below.

cash crop   nomads   savanna   rift
irrigate

1. A _____ is a deep trench.

2. Because Ethiopia receives adequate rainfall, most farmers do not _____ their crops.

3. _____ are people who move from place to place to earn a living.

4. A crop sold for a profit is known as a _____.

5. A _____ is a region of tall grasses.

Reviewing the Main Ideas

1. List four major physical features of Africa. (Section 1)

2. Why might some parts of Africa have a cool climate even though they are near the Equator? (Section 2)

3. Explain why there is little or no farming in much of North Africa and parts of Southern Africa. (Section 2)

4. How is subsistence farming in Africa different from farming to raise cash crops? (Section 3)

5. List three cash crops grown in Africa, and where they are grown. Name one mineral resource found in Africa, and where it is found. (Section 3)

6. Explain why many African nations are trying to diversify their economies. (Section 3)

Map Activity

Africa

For each place listed, write the letter from the map that shows its location.

1. Nile River
2. Congo River
3. Sahara
4. Zambezi River
5. Niger River
6. Great Rift Valley

 Take It to the NET

> **Enrichment** For more map activities using geography skills, visit the social studies section of **phschool.com**.

Writing Activity

1. **Writing a Report** Describe some challenges Africans face that are caused by Africa's landforms or climate. Give examples of how Africans overcome, or are working to overcome, these challenges.

2. **Writing a Letter** Imagine that you have just returned from a trip to Africa. Write a letter to a friend describing some of the physical features and climates that you encountered in several different regions of Africa. Describe how the landscape and climate were similar to or different from the landscape and climate where you live.

Applying Your Skills

Study the map of Africa's mineral and energy resources on page 365. Refer to the Skills for Life activity on page 367 to help you complete the following activity.

Compare and contrast the resources of North Africa with those of Southern Africa.

Critical Thinking

1. **Identifying Central Issues** Explain the meaning of this statement. Give an example to support it. "People in Africa tend to live in grassland regions."

2. **Recognizing Cause and Effect** How did the yearly flooding of the Nile affect farmers in the Nile Valley? How did the building of the Aswan Dam affect the farmers?

 Take It to the NET

Activity Create a map of Africa and include major geographical features, climate, and natural resources. Visit the World Explorer: People, Places, and Cultures section of **phschool.com** for help in completing this activity.

Chapter 19 Self-Test As a final review activity, take the Chapter 19 Self-Test and get instant feedback on your answers. To take the test, visit the Social Studies section of **phschool.com**.

AFRICA: Shaped by History

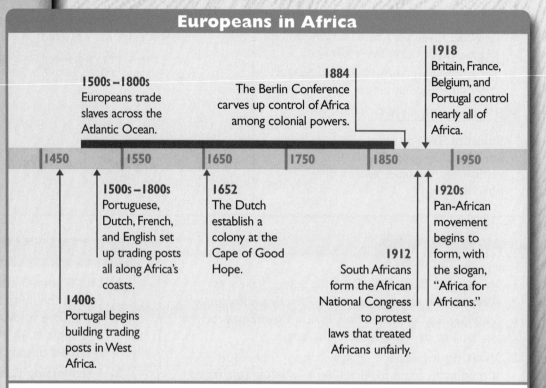

Europeans in Africa

1500s–1800s
Europeans trade slaves across the Atlantic Ocean.

1884
The Berlin Conference carves up control of Africa among colonial powers.

1918
Britain, France, Belgium, and Portugal control nearly all of Africa.

1450　　1550　　1650　　1750　　1850　　1950

1500s–1800s
Portuguese, Dutch, French, and English set up trading posts all along Africa's coasts.

1652
The Dutch establish a colony at the Cape of Good Hope.

1912
South Africans form the African National Congress to protest laws that treated Africans unfairly.

1920s
Pan-African movement begins to form, with the slogan, "Africa for Africans."

1400s
Portugal begins building trading posts in West Africa.

USING TIME LINES

Africans resisted European colonization, but as this time line shows, Europe slowly took control of more and more of Africa.

Exploring Europeans in Africa

Study the time line of Europeans in Africa. Which European country was the first to become involved with Africa? What does the time line reveal about why the first Europeans came to Africa? What European countries controlled most of Africa by 1918? Why do you think it was possible for Europeans to colonize Africa?

Making a Time Line

The last entry on the time line is for the 1920s. What happened next in African history? Use the library and the Internet to research major events in Africa's history from the 1920s to the present. Choose eight significant events from this period and create a time line showing the dates and events that you chose.

Africa's First People

BEFORE YOU READ

READING FOCUS

1. How did early Africans adapt to their environment?
2. How did the emergence of farming and herding change life for early Africans?
3. What are the features of a civilization?
4. How did important ideas and discoveries spread throughout Africa?

KEY TERMS

hunter-gatherer
domesticate
fertile
surplus
civilization
migrate
ethnic group

KEY PEOPLE AND PLACES

Louis Leakey
Egypt
Nubia
Bantu-speakers

NOTE TAKING

Copy this chart. As you read the section, complete the chart to show important facts or new ideas and discoveries of early Africans.

Stone Age	Farmers	Nile Civilizations

MAIN IDEA

Africa's first peoples survived by developing tools and techniques for farming and herding, and they later spread out and settled into societies.

Setting the Scene

Today the dry sands of the Sahara cover most of North Africa. Until about 4,000 years ago, however, this large area held enough water to support many people and animals. Scientists think that Africa's first farmers lived there. Paintings on cliffs and cave walls tell their story.

But the continent's first people lived in East Africa. We know this because of the stones and bones they left behind.

Hunter-Gatherers

The earliest humans probably survived by gathering wild fruits, nuts, and roots. These **hunter-gatherers** also hunted animals for meat and clothing. They made tools out of wood, animal bones, and then stone. The first use of stone tools marks the beginning of a period scientists call the Stone Age.

These stone tools worked very well. The scientist **Louis Leakey** found some of the first evidence of early people in East Africa. He also taught himself to make and use tools he had discovered.

CULTURE This painting was originally found in Algeria. **Critical Thinking** Do you think the horns on this woman's helmet suggest that the Sahara may once have supported animal life? Why?

Farming and Herding

When hunter-gatherers began to farm and to herd animals, they probably planted wild grains such as wheat, barley, sorghum, and millet. At first, gatherers just protected the areas where these grains grew best. Then, they began to save some seed to plant for the next year's crop.

Later, people began to **domesticate** plants, or adapt them for their own use. People also domesticated animals by taming them and developing ways to use them.

Domesticating plants and animals meant people could plant their own crops. They did not have to travel to places where grains were already growing. As a result, they could settle in a certain place, usually where the land was **fertile,** or productive. Some communities produced a food **surplus,** or more than they needed. Surpluses allowed some people in the community to do work other than farming.

Civilizations on the Nile

A **civilization** is a society with cities, a government, and social classes. Social classes form when people do a variety of jobs. Civilizations also have architecture, writing, and art. One civilization arose on the Nile River about 5,000 years ago.

Egypt   Each summer, the Nile River flooded its banks. It left a layer of fertile silt that was ideal for farming. People began farming along the banks of the Nile by around 4000 B.C. They settled in scattered villages. Over the centuries, these villages grew into the civilization of ancient **Egypt.**

Ancient Egypt was ruled by kings and queens called pharaohs (FAY rohz). The people believed the pharaohs were gods as well as kings. When some pharaohs died, they were buried in pyramids. People painted murals and picture-writings called hieroglyphics (hy ur oh GLIF iks) on the walls in these pyramids.

Egyptian civilization included more than just the pyramids. The Egyptians were advanced in paper-making, architecture, medicine, and mathematics.

Nubia   Starting in about 6000 B.C., several civilizations arose south of Egypt. This area was called **Nubia.** The final and greatest Nubian kingdom arose in the city of Meroë (MER oh ee) during the 500s B.C. It thrived until about the middle of the A.D. 300s. Meroë was probably the first place in Africa where iron was made.

Ancient Art

CULTURE

This Egytian wall painting shows Nubian princes arriving in Egypt. At first, Egypt ruled Nubia, but later, Nubia conquered much of Egypt.

Critical Thinking

What objects are the figures walking behind the princes carrying? Why do you think they are carrying these items?

The Bantu Migrations

By about 500 B.C., West Africans had learned to heat and shape iron. They used it to form parts of tools such as arrowheads, ax heads, and hoe blades. The strong iron tools made farming easier and created food surpluses. As a result, West Africa's population increased.

Around 4,000 years ago, a group of people who spoke Bantu (BAN too) languages began to **migrate,** or move, out of West Africa, perhaps looking for new land to farm. Over hundreds of years, these **Bantu-speakers** settled in Central and Southern Africa. They introduced farming, herding, and iron tools to these regions. Today, people in this part of Africa belong to hundreds of **ethnic groups,** or groups that share languages, religions, family ties, and customs. But almost all of these ethnic groups speak Bantu languages.

SECTION I ASSESSMENT

AFTER YOU READ

RECALL

1. Identify: (a) Louis Leakey, (b) Egypt, (c) Nubia, (d) Bantu-speakers

2. Define: (a) hunter-gatherer, (b) domesticate, (c) fertile, (d) surplus, (e) civilization, (f) migrate, (g) ethnic group

COMPREHENSION

3. What techniques did the earliest Africans use to work and feed themselves?

4. What caused early Africans to begin settling in permanent communities?

5. What were two important early civilizations in Africa?

6. How did the Bantu-speakers contribute to the development of Africa?

CRITICAL THINKING AND WRITING

7. **Exploring the Main Idea** Review the Main Idea statement at the beginning of this section. Then, create a time line showing dates and the sequence of some important developments from the earliest people in East Africa lead-

ing up to the civilizations along the Nile.

8. **Identifying Central Issues** Write a paragraph describing some of the important contributions of early Africans.

ACTIVITY

9. **Writing to Learn** Imagine you are in ancient Egypt. Write a message that might be found in hieroglyphics on a pyramid wall about an important event that you want to record for history.

Kingdoms and Empires

BEFORE YOU READ

READING FOCUS

1. Why was trade so significant to East Africa's kingdoms?
2. How did the Islamic religion spread from East Africa to other parts of Africa?
3. What were the important trade routes within and outside of East Africa?

KEY TERMS
Quran
pilgrimage
Swahili
city-state

KEY PEOPLE AND PLACES
Aksum
Ghana
Mali

Songhai
Mansa Musa
Tombouctou
Kilwa

NOTE TAKING

Copy these webs. As you read the section add information in the empty ovals about the important features of East Africa and West Africa.

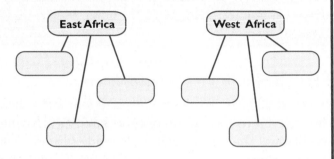

East Africa

West Africa

MAIN IDEA

African societies were influenced by traders from other cultures who brought not only goods, but also new religions and languages.

Trade in East Africa

ECONOMICS As early as A.D. 1100, traders in East Africa bought and sold goods from many parts of the world. Traders bought animal skins, gold, and ivory, or elephant tusks (shown) from Africa and sold them in India and China. **Critical Thinking** How did trade help people in East Africa to learn about other cultures?

Setting the Scene

Adulis was the most important city in Aksum, a bustling trade center along the Red Sea. In the year A.D. 1, a Greek writer made a list of things you could buy there:

"Cloth made in Egypt…and brass, which is used for ornament and cut pieces instead of coin; sheets of soft copper, used for cooking utensils and cut up for bracelets and anklets for the women; iron, which is made into spears…."

An East African Kingdom

Aksum was located in East Africa, in what is now Ethiopia and Eritrea. Around 1000 B.C., African and Arab traders began settling along the west coast of the Red Sea. These were the ancestors of the people of Aksum. Over time, Aksum came to control trade in the Red Sea. In time, Aksum would control a trade network that stretched from the Mediterranean Sea to India.

Ideas, as well as goods, traveled along these trade routes. The Christian religion traveled to Aksum along these routes. In fact, Aksum became a center of the early Ethiopian Christian Church. But Aksum began to decline in the 600s. Then, Arabs took control of much of the region's trade.

West African Kingdoms

As Aksum declined, great kingdoms arose on the other side of the continent, in West Africa. The power of these kingdoms was based on the trade of salt and gold. People need salt to survive, especially in hot areas like West Africa, but the people there had no local sources of salt. However, they had plenty of gold. For the people of North Africa, the opposite was true; they had salt, but no gold.

A brisk trade between North Africa and West Africa quickly grew. Control of this trade brought power and riches to three West African kingdoms—**Ghana** (GAH nuh), **Mali** (MAH lee), and **Songhai** (SAWNG hy).

Ghana   The kingdom of Ghana was located between the Senegal and Niger rivers. From this location Ghana controlled trade across West Africa. Ghana's kings grew rich from the taxes they charged on the salt, gold, and other goods that flowed through their land. The flow of gold was so great that Arab writers called Ghana "land of gold." But in time, Ghana lost control of the trade routes. It gave way to a new power, the kingdom of Mali.

Mali and the Spread of Islam   The kingdom of Mali arose in the mid-1200s in the Upper Niger Valley. Mali's powerful kings controlled both the gold mines of the south and the salt supplies of the north. In Mali, the king was called Mansa, which means "emperor."

Mali's most famous king, **Mansa Musa,** brought peace and order to the kingdom during his 25-year reign. He based his laws on the **Quran** (koo RAHN), the holy book of the religion of Islam. Over the centuries, Muslim traders had spread their religion into many parts of Africa.

In 1324, Mansa Musa made a **pilgrimage**—a religious journey—to the Arabian city of Mecca, a Muslim holy place where Muhammad, the prophet who first preached Islam, was born. Mansa Musa brought 60,000 people and eighty camels with him. Each camel carried 300 pounds (136 kg) of gold, which Mansa Musa gave to people along the way.

Mansa Musa's pilgrimage brought about new trading ties with other Muslim states. It also displayed Mali's wealth. Hearing the reports, Europe's rulers grew interested in African gold.

Songhai   In time, Songhai became West Africa's most powerful kingdom. Its rulers controlled important trade routes and wealthy trading cities, such as **Tombouctou** (tohm book TOO), also a great Muslim learning center.

Songhai people still live near the Niger River, and Islam remains important in the region.

The Kingdom of Mali

CULTURE   This image, showing Mansa Musa on his throne, is a detail from an old map of trading routes in Europe, Africa, and Asia. After Mansa Musa's pilgrimage to Mecca, Mali began to appear on maps throughout Asia and Europe. **Critical Thinking** Why do you think other countries in Asia and Europe became so interested in Mali?

East African Trade Routes

KEY

→ Trade routes

Lambert Azimuthal Equal-Area Projection

To Mediterranean

Cairo

Mecca

To India

Mogadishu

Malindi

Mombasa

Kilwa

INDIAN OCEAN

To East Asia

Great Zimbabwe   Sofala

0   500   1,000 mi

0   500   1,000 km

GEOGRAPHY Traders visiting East African city-states could buy gold from Africa, cotton from India, and porcelain from China. **Map Study** How were the East African city-states ideally located to become centers of trade?

East African City-States

As in West Africa, trade helped East African cities to develop. Around the time that Aksum declined, trading cities arose along East Africa's coast. Traders from these cities carried animal skins, ivory, and gold and other metals to India and China. The traders brought back many different goods.

Some of the traders who visited the area were Arab Muslims. In time, a new language called **Swahili** (swah HEE lee), developed in the area. It was a Bantu language with some Arab words mixed in. Today, many East Africans speak Swahili.

Some East African cities grew into powerful **city-states.** A city-state has its own government and controls much of the surrounding land. Among the greatest of these city-states were Malindi (muh LIN dee), Mombasa (mahm BAH suh), and **Kilwa** (KIL wah). These city-states grew rich from trade and huge taxes traders paid on goods they brought into the city.

Kilwa Ibn Batuta (ihb UHN ba TOO tah), a Muslim traveler from North Africa, visited Kilwa in 1331. He had seen great cities in China, India, and West Africa, but he wrote that Kilwa was "one of the most beautiful and best-constructed towns in the world." There, people lived in three-and four-story houses made of stone and sea coral.

SECTION 2 ASSESSMENT

AFTER YOU READ

RECALL

1. Identify: (a) Aksum, (b) Ghana, (c) Mali, (d) Songhai, (e) Mansa Musa, (f) Tombouctou, (g) Kilwa

2. Define: (a) Quran, (b) pilgrimage, (c) Swahili, (d) city-state

COMPREHENSION

3. What were the wealth and power of East African kingdoms based on?

4. In addition to goods, what else spread over West African trade routes?

5. What were the main trade routes of East Africa?

CRITICAL THINKING AND WRITING

6. **Exploring the Main Idea** Review the Main Idea statement at the beginning of this section. Then, make a list of the things introduced into African culture, past and present, by traders from other cultures.

ACTIVITY

 Take It to the NET

7. **Exploring Daily Life in Ancient Egypt** Using the information on the Web site, write several journal entries from the perspective of a young child, including what you eat, how you live, and what you wear. Visit the World Explorer: People, Places, and Cultures section of **phschool.com** for help in completing this activity.

European Influence and African Independence

BEFORE YOU READ

READING FOCUS

1. What were the effects of European rule in Africa?
2. How did African nations win independence from European rule?
3. What challenges did African leaders face after independence?

KEY TERMS

colonize
nationalism
Pan-Africanism
boycott

KEY PEOPLE

Leopold Sedar Senghor
Kwame Nkrumah

MAIN IDEA

For many centuries, Africans suffered the loss of their freedom, their land, and many of their traditions; many African countries have fought and succeeded in regaining their independence, and have faced the challenges of self-government.

NOTE TAKING

Copy this chart. As you read the section, complete the chart to show the events leading from the 1400s to Africa's independence.

1400s	
1500s	
1600s	
1700s	
1800s	
1900s	
1920	
1950s–1990s	

Setting the Scene

On the island of Gorée (gaw RAY), off the coast of the West African country of Senegal, stands a museum called the House of Slaves. It honors over 20 million Africans who were enslaved and shipped across the Atlantic Ocean. Many Africans passed through this building. Their last view of Africa was an opening called "The Door of No Return." Beyond it lay the ocean and the slave ships bound for the Americas.

Trade with Europeans

Contact between Europeans and Africans began in North Africa with Europeans trading for gold and salt by bringing copper, clothing, and crops such as corn from the Americas.

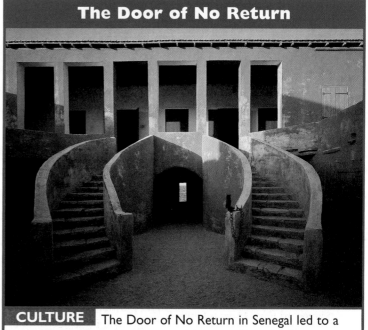

The Door of No Return

CULTURE The Door of No Return in Senegal led to a pier, where slave ships were waiting to sail to the Americas. **Critical Thinking** Why is it important to have monuments like this one? What do they represent?

Protecting Trade

HISTORY In 1482, the Portuguese built this fort, Elmina Castle, in Ghana to protect and supply their trade with West Africa. **Critical Thinking** Why do you think the Portuguese would need a fort to protect their trade in this region?

The Slave Trade

Even before the arrival of the Europeans, slavery was common in Africa. Beginning around 1450 Europeans began transporting Africans across the Atlantic to work on the plantations and mines in North and South America. At the same time, Swahili traders in East Africa relied heavily on slaves for labor and exported African slaves to Arabia, the Mediterranean, and to lands bordering the Indian Ocean. While the British put an end to the Atlantic slave trade by about 1850, the slave trade in East Africa continued until about 1900. The effects of slavery for Africans were disastrous.

The Effects of Colonization

Many Europeans wanted to **colonize** Africa, or settle it and take over its governments. When the slave trade ended, some Europeans saw Africa's natural resources as a new way to build wealth and empires. In 1884 fourteen countries, including Germany, France, Great Britain, and Belgium, met at the Berlin Conference to divide up Africa among themselves. By 1900, most parts of Africa were colonized. Though not all were ruled in the same way, in most cases Africans had little power in the governments that ruled them.

Europeans had gained power in part by encouraging Africans to fight each other. They also took the best land to farm and, in some areas, forced Africans to work under terrible conditions. The new political boundaries drawn up by the Europeans divided some ethnic groups and forced others together. This caused much conflict, some of which continues in Africa today.

The Growth of African Independence

Many Africans dreamed of independence in the late 1800s. Mankayi Sontanga (mun KY ee suhn THAN guh) put this dream to music. His song, called "Bless, O Lord, Our Land of Africa," expressed the growing nationalism of Africans. **Nationalism** is a feeling of pride in one's homeland. African leaders saw that to end colonial rule, they would have to build a spirit of togetherness among many ethnic groups.

In 1912, a political party was formed in South Africa and its members protested laws that limited the rights of black South Africans. Today this party is the African National Congress (ANC). In British West Africa, African lawyers formed the West African National Congress, a group that worked to gain Africans the right to vote.

The Pan-African Movement

A movement called **Pan-Africanism** was formed in the 1920s. Unity and cooperation among all Africans, whether they live in Africa or not, was stressed and their motto was "Africa for Africans." One of the greatest leaders of Pan-Africanism was **Leopold Sedar Senghor** (SAN gawr) of Senegal. Senghor, a poet and political leader, encouraged Africans to study their traditions and to be proud of their culture. Senghor became the first president when Senegal became independent in 1960.

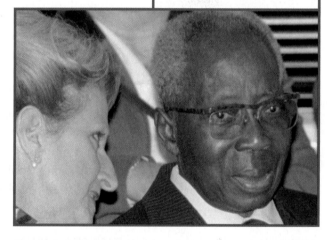

The First President of Senegal

HISTORY Leopold Sedar Senghor, shown here with his wife at a celebration marking his 90th birthday, served as president of Senegal for 20 years. **Critical Thinking** What kind of challenges do you think Senghor faced when he became president of the newly-independent Senegal?

Paths to Independence

A major boost to African independence came in the 1930s and 1940s when some African countries joined with Great Britain, France, and the United States to fight the armies of Germany, Italy, and Japan. African soldiers, drivers, and transportation workers took part in the war effort. When World War II was over, Africans wanted their own freedom. Some European countries let go peacefully, as when Ghana won its independence from Britain. But Algeria had to fight for its freedom against France.

Ghana: From Past to Present In the British West African colony of the Gold Coast, **Kwame Nkrumah** organized protests against British rule in the early 1950s. These protests took the peaceful form of strikes and **boycotts.** In a boycott, people refuse to buy or use certain products or services. The British put Nkrumah in jail for his actions, but the protests continued without him. In 1957, he achieved his goal: independence for the Gold Coast. The country took the new name of Ghana, after the great trading kingdom that lasted until the 1200s. It was a name that recalled Africa's earlier greatness. Nkrumah became Ghana's first president in 1960.

Gambians Celebrate Independence

HISTORY Gambia won its independence from Great Britain through peaceful elections in 1965. School-children celebrate Gambian independence every year. **Critical Thinking** How is this celebration similar to Fourth of July celebrations in the United States?

The Challenges of Independence

Africa's new leaders had spent many years working for independence. But they had little experience actually governing a country. As a result, some new governments in Africa were not very stable.

In some African countries, military leaders took control of the government by force. Military governments are not always fair since the people often have few rights, and citizens may be jailed if they protest. But this form of government has held together some African countries that otherwise would have been torn apart by war.

Other African countries have a long history of democracy. In a democracy, citizens help to make governmental decisions. Some countries have made traditional ways a part of democratic governing. For example, in Botswana, lively political debates take place in "freedom squares." These outdoor meetings are like the traditional kgotla (KUHT luh), in which people talk with their leaders.

Most African countries are less than 40 years old. In contrast, the stable, democratic country of the United States is over 200 years old. Many Africans feel that building stable countries will take time. One leader commented, "Let Africa be given the time to develop its own system of democracy."

SECTION 3 ASSESSMENT

AFTER YOU READ

RECALL

1. Identify: (a) Leopold Sedar Senghor, (b) Kwame Nkrumah

2. Define: (a) colonize, (b) nationalism, (c) Pan-Africanism, (d) boycott

COMPREHENSION

3. How did relations between Africa and Europe change between the 1400s and the 1900s?

4. Describe Ghana's road to independence.

5. In what ways did colonial rule cause problems for African countries after independence?

CRITICAL THINKING AND WRITING

6. Exploring the Main Idea Review the Main Idea statement at the beginning of this section. Then, describe some of the challenges that African countries have faced after gaining their independence.

7. Supporting a Point of View Write a brief speech that a leader in the Pan-Africanism movement might give to persuade others to join the movement.

ACTIVITY

8. Writing to Learn Choose one African country that won its independence after 1950. Write a headline and a brief article for a newspaper that might have appeared on the day that country became independent.

Organizing by Sequence and Category

Learn the Skill

Being able to follow a sequence of events and being able to categorize are skills that will help you when you read. Sequence is simply another name for the order of events. Categorizing is sorting items into groups.

Organizing by Sequence. You may have noticed in reading your textbook that some historical events are told in the order in which the events occurred. For example, war against the colonizers usually occurred before independence. You will probably read first about the steps that led to war, the war itself, and, finally, the new government. To find the sequence of events when reading, follow these steps:

A. Look for dates. They are usually included when you need to be able to follow a sequence of events. If you find a date that is missing the year, read the information that comes before it. Writers may refer to several dates in the same year without repeating the year.

B. Find clue words that refer to time, such as day, week, month, or year. These clues will help you keep the sequence of events clear.

Organizing by Category. When you read about economic issues, note how the topics are categorized. For example, you will probably read a section about farming, then a section on mining. This kind of text is organized by category. In this case, the categories are economic categories. Each topic might be further categorized. The section on mining might first address copper mining, then silver mining. You can also categorize information as you read. To do this, follow these steps:

A. Read the information and decide what topics are covered. Think about what the text is about and how the information could be sorted into categories.

B. Decide what categories you will use. For example, if reading about trade in ancient Africa, you might think of each type of good as a separate category. You could develop separate categories for food, clothing, jewelry, and tableware.

C. Once you have decided on the categories, you can sort information into them. Under food, for example, you might list: salt, oil, sugar, grain.

Practice the Skill

The chart below lists several countries in Africa and tells where they are found and the year in which they gained independence. Use the information in the chart to create two more charts. First, list the countries in a particular sequence. You decide what the sequence should be. Then, organize the countries into several categories. You decide what the categories should be. When finished, compare your two charts with the chart in your book. Which one(s) are the easiest to read and understand? How are sequencing and categorizing useful?

Country	Location	Year of Independence
Egypt	North Africa	1922
Kenya	East Africa	1963
Ghana	West Africa	1957
Somalia	East Africa	1960
South Africa	South Africa	1910
Algeria	North Africa	1962
Congo	Central Africa	1960
Tanzania	East Africa	1961
Nigeria	West Africa	1960
Ethiopia	East Africa	1941

Apply the Skill

See the Chapter Review and Assessment at the end of this chapter for more questions on organizing by sequence and category.

Creating a Chapter Summary

On a separate piece of paper, draw a diagram like this one, and include the information that summarizes the first section of the chapter. Then, fill in the remaining boxes with a summary of sections 2 and 3.

AFRICA

Section 1
The continent's first people lived in East Africa. They survived by developing tools of stone and iron, and by becoming farmers and hunter-gatherers.

Section 2

Section 3

Reviewing Key Terms

Match the definitions in Column I with the key terms in Column II.

Column I

1. a society with cities

2. a movement that stressed unity among all Africans

3. a city that controls much of the land around it and has its own government

4. person who gathers wild food and hunts animals to survive

5. to settle in an area and take over or create a government

6. the holy book of the religion Islam.

7. a feeling of pride in one's home-land

8. a government in which citizens have power through their elected representatives

Column II

a. hunter-gatherer

b. nationalism

c. Quran

d. civilization

e. Pan-Africanism

f. colonize

g. democracy

h. city-state

Reviewing the Main Ideas

1. List some of the ways in which early Africans made a living. (Section 1)

2. What were Africa's earliest civiliza-tions like? (Section 1)

3. How did Africa's kingdoms and city-states become wealthy? (Section 2)

4. How did trade help the spread of ideas among different cultures and regions? (Section 2)

5. How did relationship between Africans and Europeans change over time? (Section 3)

6. What were some of the effects of the Atlantic slave trade on Africa? (Section 3)

7. What factors helped lead to inde-pendence for many African coun-tries? (Section 3)

Map Activity

Africa

For each place listed below, write the letter from the map that shows its location.

1. Senegal

2. Tombouctou

3. Kilwa

4. Kingdom of Mali

5. Nubia

6. Aksum

 Take It to the NET

Enrichment For more map activities using geography skills, visit the social studies section of **phschool.com.**

Writing Activity

1. Writing a Speech In the 1800s, many people in the United States spoke out against slavery. They were called abolitionists because they wanted to abolish, or put an end to, slavery. Pretend that you are an abolitionist living in the 1800s. Use what you have learned about the slave trade to write a speech that will help persuade people that slavery is wrong.

2. Writing a Letter Today is Independence Day in your country. It is a day to remember those who fought for the freedom to govern themselves. Write a letter to your ancestors and tell them how you feel today.

Applying Your Skills

Turn to the Skills for Life activity on p. 381 to answer the following questions.

1. Reread pp. 374–376. How is the information about African kingdoms organized—by sequence or by category?

2. Reread pp. 378–380. How is most of this information organized? How can you tell?

Critical Thinking

1. Recognizing Cause and Effect Many of Africa's cities and countries are located along trade routes. How has trade affected Africa's history?

2. Expressing Problems Clearly The Atlantic slave trade lasted from the 1500s to the 1800s. How did the slave trade and the colonization of Africa affect traditional African cultures?

3. Drawing Conclusions How do you think most Africans feel about their hard-won independence? Explain your answer.

 Take It to the NET

Activity Read about Africa's history. Choose a specific area to focus on and prepare a presentation of what you learned. Visit the World Explorer: People, Places, and Cultures section of **phschool.com** for help in completing this activity.

Chapter 20 Self-Test As a final review activity, take the Chapter 20 Self-Test and get instant feedback on your answers. To take the test, visit the Social Studies section of **phschool.com.**

CHAPTER 2

AFRICA:
Rich in Culture

Drums Go Drumming

USING MUSIC

Music has many roles in the cultures of African countries—to send messages, tell a story, organize work, or celebrate a special occasion. People in African countries rarely play music by itself. Most often, they combine music with dance, theater, words, games, or visual art.

Exploring Musical Instruments

In many African cultures, drums play an important role in traditional and modern music. Use the library and the Internet to find out more about traditional African drums and how they differ. When you do research, look under subject headings such as African Arts, African Music, and Musical Instruments.

Making an African Drum

As you gather information about African drums, choose one as a model for making your own. Learn as much as you can about this kind of drum. Build your own drum using this information. If possible, use materials that are similar to the materials the traditional drums are made from. Experiment with different methods to see which sounds best.

The Cultures of North Africa

BEFORE YOU READ

FOCUS QUESTIONS

1. What is culture?
2. What are the major influences on the culture of North Africa?
3. How has their Mediterranean location affected the cultures of North Africa?

KEY TERMS

culture
cultural diffusion

MAIN IDEA

The culture, or way of life, in a society is influenced by different ethnic groups that may share common bonds, such as religion, language, and the influence of neighboring societies.

NOTE TAKING

Copy this web diagram. As you read the section, complete the web by adding the institutions and characteristics that are basic to all societies and which help to define culture.

Culture

Setting the Scene

Thirteen-year-old Meena lives in the city of Marrakech (muh rah kehsh) in Morocco, a country in North Africa. Every morning she works in a factory, weaving carpets. She learned to weave carpets from her mother, who learned the skill from her mother. Carpets play an important role in Moroccan life. In some Moroccan homes, they serve as more than just floor coverings, and are used as chairs, beds, and prayer mats. They are also important exports for the country. In the afternoon, Meena leaves the factory to attend school. Her day ends at sunset, when she hears the crier who calls out from the nearby mosque, a Muslim house of worship. Muslims are followers of the religion of Islam. When she hears the call, Meena recites this prayer in Arabic: "There is no God but Allah, and Muhammad is His prophet."

What Is Culture?

When a group of people share similar beliefs and customs they are said to share a **culture.** Culture has many elements, including food, clothing, homes, jobs, and language. It can also be shared ideas, such as how people view the world and practice a religion. In some cultures, for example, people take time to pray every day. Culture shapes the way people behave.

Moroccan Carpets

CULTURE Moroccan weavers decorate their carpets with intricate designs. **Critical Thinking** Why are carpets an important part of Moroccan culture? What similar traditions do we have in the United States?

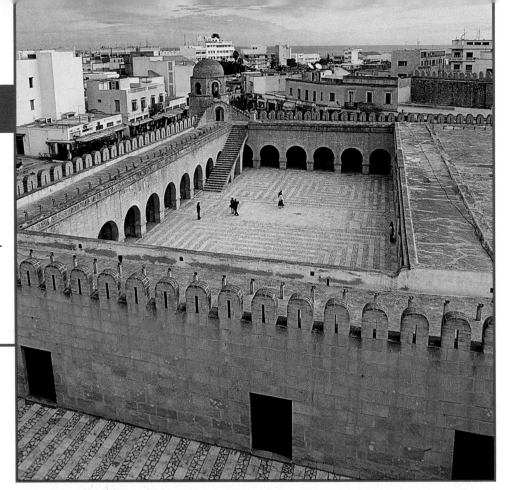

Community Centers

CULTURE Muslims often build a large, empty space into the middle of their mosques. Why? The empty space can be used for many different kinds of activities, including education. **Critical Thinking** How are religious buildings in your town or city used? Do they look like this one?

How Culture is Influenced

Religion is an important part of North African culture. More than 95 percent of North Africans practice Islam and are Muslims. Like Jews and Christians, Muslims believe in one God. Allah is the Arabic word for God.

The Influence of Islam In North Africa, many aspects of daily life are affected by the sacred book of Islam, the Quran. Like the Hebrew Torah and the Christian Bible, the Quran provides a guide to life and forbids lying, stealing, and murder. The Quran also prohibits gambling, eating pork, and drinking alcohol. North African countries use some Islamic laws to govern family life, business practices, banking, and government.

Religion and Language Unify The People In North Africa, the religion of Islam and the Arabic language unify people of many different ethnic backgrounds and ways of life. These people live in a large region that includes the countries of Egypt, Libya, Tunisia, Algeria, and Morocco. People here have many different backgrounds and ways of life.

An ethnic group is a group of people who share language, religion, and cultural traditions. Most North Africans are Arabs but the region has other ethnic groups, too. The largest of these is the Berbers, who live mainly in Algeria and Morocco. Most Berbers speak Arabic as well as Berber. Some live in cities, but most live in small villages in rugged mountain areas and make their living by herding and farming.

The Tuareg (TWAH reg) are a group of Berbers who live in the Sahara and make their living by herding camels and goats.

In large cities like Cairo (KY roh), Egypt and Tunis, Tunisia, people live with a mix of the traditional and modern ways of life. Some weave carpets or sell baskets. Others are scientists or sell computers in modern stores. The peoples of North Africa live vastly different lives, yet almost all consider themselves to be Muslims.

How Culture Spreads

Cultures are constantly changing as people and ideas move from one place to another. This movement of customs and ideas is called **cultural diffusion.** The word *diffuse* means "to spread out."

North Africa has been part of the diffusion process because of its Mediterranean location. Throughout history, it has been a hub of trade with Europe, Asia, and other parts of Africa. Wars, too, affected culture as one empire would conquer another. Thus, North Africans have influenced, and been influenced by, the cultures of many different places.

Contemporary North African Culture   Like other parts of the world, North Africa has felt the influence of Western culture in recent decades. Some North Africans are concerned that their countries are becoming too Western. More people are wearing Western clothes, buying Western products, seeing Western films, and adapting Western ideas. All over Africa, people face the challenge of how to preserve the traditions they value as their countries modernize.

AS YOU READ

Monitor Your Reading
What sights might you see if you were walking through a city in North Africa? How would these sights be different from what you might see walking through a city in the United States?

SECTION 1 ASSESSMENT

AFTER YOU READ

RECALL

1. Define: (a) culture, (b) cultural diffusion

COMPREHENSION

2. How does a common culture bind people together?

3. How does Islam affect everyday life in North Africa?

4. How has North Africa's location contributed to cultural diffusion?

CRITICAL THINKING AND WRITING

5. **Exploring the Main Idea** Review the Main Idea statement at the beginning of this section. Then, make a list of the common bonds that North Africans share. Which ones are common bonds in your culture?

6. **Comparing and Contrasting** Visualize a map of the United States. Which regions do you think have been culturally influenced by neighboring countries and in what ways? How is this similar to the influences on North Africa by other cultures? Write a paragraph to explain your thinking.

ACTIVITY

7. **Writing an Essay** What traditions in your culture do you think are worth preserving? Write an essay describing the customs you value most.

The Cultures of West Africa

BEFORE YOU READ

READING FOCUS

1. Why does West Africa have such a variety of cultures?

2. What effects do family ties have on West African culture?

3. How has urbanization affected the cultures of West Africa?

KEY TERMS

cultural diversity
kinship
nuclear family
extended family
lineage
clan
griot

MAIN IDEA

Since West Africa has a wide variety of cultures and ethnic groups, West Africans are not united by a single religion or a common language.

NOTE TAKING

Copy this chart. As you read the section, complete the chart by filling in information you read that helps to define kinship.

Kinship

Setting the Scene

Like North Africans, West Africans see themselves as members of a number of groups. Just as you belong to a family, an ethnic group, and a country, so do West Africans. The culture of West Africa is created both by the similarities and by the differences of its people and their ways of life. There are 17 countries in this region with hundreds of ethnic groups. West Africa is famous for its **cultural diversity**—it has a wide variety of cultures.

Cultural Differences

With so many ethnic groups in West Africa, most West Africans learn to speak more than one lan-

A Market in Dakar, Senegal

ECONOMICS At this open-air market in Dakar, Senegal, customers can buy many kinds of groceries, including fresh fish. Senegal has built up its fishing industry so much that fish are its most important export. **Critical Thinking** Besides the people who catch the fish, who benefits from Dakar's fishing industry?

guage. Many can communicate in four or five languages and use these languages to conduct business or when traveling. This ability is an important way that a culturally diverse country can be unified in spite of its differences.

AS YOU READ

Draw Inferences How do you think the cultural diversity of West Africa affects the lives of its people?

Different Ways of Making a Living

The working life of West Africans can be as different as herding camels across the Sahara or working in a hotel in a large city. Most West Africans live in a village surrounded by farmland and grow cash crops. But, in some countries, such as Cote d'Ivoire, almost half of the people live and work in cities.

Cultural Ties

One of the strongest bonds West Africans have is the bond of **kinship,** which refers to a family relationship. The first level of kinship is the **nuclear family,** which consists of parents and their children. The next level is the **extended family,** which includes all other relatives. West Africans often live as an extended family, all working together and taking care of each other. This custom is reflected in the well-known African proverb, "It takes a village to raise a child."

In many rural areas, a group of families may trace their descent back to a common ancestor. Such a group forms a **lineage.** Several lineages form a **clan,** all with roots back to an even earlier ancestor.

Preserving Culture

Family ties remain strong in West Africa, but with more people moving from rural villages to urban areas, or cities, family life is changing. This trend, called urbanization, is occurring in Africa and in the world. Often the young men go to the cities to find jobs, while the women stay to raise the children and farm the land. The men return to visit and share what they have earned.

One way for West Africans to adapt, change, and keep their family ties strong, is to pass on their history, values, and traditions to their children. They do this through storytelling, usually spoken rather than written. A storyteller called a **griot** (GREE oh) passes this oral tradition from one generation to the next.

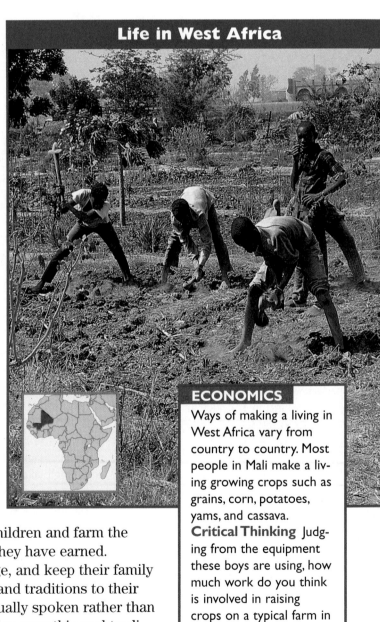

Life in West Africa

ECONOMICS

Ways of making a living in West Africa vary from country to country. Most people in Mali make a living growing crops such as grains, corn, potatoes, yams, and cassava.
Critical Thinking Judging from the equipment these boys are using, how much work do you think is involved in raising crops on a typical farm in West Africa?

The Influence of West African Culture

West African traditions have greatly influenced other cultures, especially American culture. Enslaved West Africans brought their ideas, stories, dances, music, and customs to the United States. The stories of Brer Rabbit as well as blues and jazz music have their roots in West Africa. In recent years, three Nobel Prize winners for literature have been African. One of them, Wole Soyinka (WHO lay shaw YING kah) is from the West African country of Nigeria.

SECTION 2 ASSESSMENT

AFTER YOU READ

RECALL

1. Define: (a) cultural diversity, (b) kinship, (c) nuclear family, (d) extended family, (e) lineage, (f) clan, (g) griot

COMPREHENSION

2. In what ways is West Africa culturally diverse?

3. Describe the importance of family ties to West Africans.

4. How has urbanization changed the lives of West Africans?

CRITICAL THINKING AND WRITING

5. **Exploring the Main Idea** Review the Main Idea statement at the beginning of this section. Imagine that you live in a small village in an extended family in West Africa. Make a list of what you might have in common with someone in the next village, and what differences you might have.

6. **Drawing Conclusions** How has the extended family helped to develop a sense of community among West Africans? Write a paragraph explaining your answer.

ACTIVITY

 Take It to the NET

7. **Writing a Myth or Fable** Read the myths and fables on the Web site. Using these stories as a guide, write your own myth or fable. Visit the World Explorer: People, Places, and Culture section of **phschool.com** for help in completing this activity.

The Cultures of East Africa

BEFORE YOU READ

1. How has location affected the development of East African cultures?
2. What role does the Swahili language play in East African cultures?
3. How and why are ideas about land ownership changing in East Africa?

KEY TERMS

plantation

MAIN IDEA

East Africa is a region of great cultural diversity where the migration of people from other continents has influenced cultural development and the current society.

NOTE TAKING

Copy the diagram below. As you read the section, complete the diagram by filling in the information that shows the common characteristics shared by the cultures of East and West Africa.

East Africa — Bantu Language — West Africa

Setting the Scene

Alemeseged Taddesse Mekonnen (ah lem uh SEH ged TAH day say meh KOH nen) is an Ethiopian who works in a bakery in St. Louis, Missouri.

Mekonnen misses life with his close-knit family in Ethiopia. "At home we ate every meal together. If anyone was missing, we waited until they came home," he says. Mekonnen hopes to return home someday. He lives in the United States, but his heart is in Ethiopia.

Location Leads to Cultural Borrowing

Like West Africa, East Africa has many ethnic groups who speak different languages. In Ethiopia, alone, more than 70 languages are spoken. East Africa's diversity is the result of its location and people have been migrating to it for at least 2,000 years, when the Bantu-speaking people of West Africa arrived. From across the Indian Ocean, explorers from Arab countries, from India, and from China arrived and settled along East Africa's long coastline.

A Kenyan Family

CULTURE Shown below is a family from Kenya. Families in East Africa traditionally eat their meals together, using one bowl or plate. **Critical Thinking** What foods do people in the United States share from one plate or bowl? Why?

391

A Family Farm in Rwanda

CULTURE On his family farm in Rwanda, this farmer grows potatoes, corn, beans, and cabbage. East Africans sometimes move away from their farms, but they almost always hope to return to them one day. **Critical Thinking** What ties people to the places that they call home? Put your answer in the form of a chart with three headings: People, Ideas, Things.

Blended Cultures

Along the east coast of Africa from Somalia to Mozambique live Africans who have mixed African and Arab ancestry. They are the Swahili. The Swahili language, with its mixture of Bantu and Arabic words, is widely used for business and communication throughout the region. It is the official language of Kenya and Tanzania, although children here are also educated in English. By promoting the continuation of this language, these nations of blended cultures are trying to preserve their African heritage.

Like languages, religious beliefs in East Africa reflect its diversity. Islam was introduced into the region by Arab traders. Christianity spread to the region from North Africa and, later, through European influence. Traditional religions and practices also remain alive in East Africa and throughout the continent.

Changing Ideas About Land

The ways in which East Africans view and work the land form an important part of their culture. Traditionally, Africans did not own their own land. The idea of buying or selling the land did not exist. Extended families farmed plots of land near the village and produced crops for the whole group. Men cleared the land, women planted and harvested, and, meanwhile, men herded livestock or traded goods.

European settlers brought with them the idea of privately owned land. The British set up **plantations,** large farms where cash crops were grown. With independence, many countries broke up the old colonial plantations and the land was sold to individual Africans.

Increasing Urbanization

Like the rest of Africa, East Africa is becoming increasingly urban. Yet even people who spend most of their time in a city do not call it home. If asked where home is, an East African will name the village of his or her family or clan. Most people consider their life in the city to be temporary. They expect to return to their villages some day.

Some land in East Africa is still available to buy. But much of it is poor farmland in areas where few people live. In fertile areas like the Ethiopian Highlands and the Rift Valley, land for farming is scarce. Many people live in these areas where the farmland is fertile. In densely populated countries, such as Rwanda and Burundi, conflicts have developed over land.

CULTURE Kampala is Uganda's largest city and leading trade center. It is a religious center as well. You can find Muslim mosques, Hindu temples, and Christian churches here. **Critical Thinking** What does the presence of these religious buildings tell you about the religious make-up of Uganda?

SECTION 3 ASSESSMENT

AFTER YOU READ

RECALL

1. Define: (a) plantation

COMPREHENSION

2. Describe some ways in which East Africa's location along the Indian Ocean has affected its cultures.

3. Why is Swahili spoken by so many people in East Africa?

4. Explain the changes in ideas about land ownership in East Africa.

CRITICAL THINKING AND WRITING

5. Exploring the Main Idea Review the Main Idea statement at the beginning of this section. Think about the many people who migrated to East Africa and choose the group that you think had the most lasting influence. Use examples to support your choice.

6. Making Comparisons How did traditional East African ideas about land differ from the ideas of Europeans who took over parts of Africa?

ACTIVITY

7. Writing a Descriptive Paragraph Write a paragraph describing one of the cultural institutions in your society, such as your school or church. Explain why this institution is important to you and your family.

The Cultures of South Africa

BEFORE YOU READ

READING FOCUS

1. How has the country of South Africa influenced the entire region of Southern Africa?
2. How did migrant labor give rise to a new group identity among the peoples of Southern Africa?

KEY TERMS
migrant worker

KEY PLACES AND PEOPLE
Republic of South Africa
Nelson Mandela

MAIN IDEA
The culture of South Africa has developed around two issues, the conflict over basic rights between black South Africans and white South Africans, and the influence of the organized mine workers who also seek equal rights.

NOTE TAKING
Copy the outline below. As you read the section, complete the outline to show important events in the recent history of South Africa.

> I. **Modern History of the Nation of South Africa**
>   A. European minority rule
>   1. separation of people into categories
>   2.
>   B.
>   1.
>   2.
>   C.
>   1.
>   2.

The Fight for Equal Rights

GOVERNMENT South African blacks organized the African National Congress (ANC) to fight for equality. The ANC used boycotts, rallies, and work strikes to protest the government. **Critical Thinking** Do similarities exist between the fight for equal rights in South Africa, and the fight for equal rights in the United States? If so, why?

Setting the Scene

The African National Congress (ANC), a political party in the **Republic of South Africa,** played a key role in gaining political and civil rights for all South Africans. Until 1991, white South Africans had denied equal rights to blacks, who make up a majority of the population. Three countries—Tanzania, Zambia, and Zimbabwe—adopted the ANC anthem for their national anthem. Here are the words to the ANC anthem:

> "Bless, O Lord, our land of Africa
> Lift its name and make its people free.
> Take the gifts we offer unto Thee
> Hear us, faithful sons.
> Hear us, faithful sons."

The Influence of South Africa

South Africa is just one country in Southern Africa, but it has had, by far, the greatest impact on the region. Its influence has touched the lives of millions of people.

Political Influence

Until the 1990s, a minority group of white people ruled South Africa, and everything in the country was separated into categories by skin color. People of African descent were classified as black, people of European descent as white, people of mixed ancestry as colored, with Asians forming a fourth category. Only people considered to be white were allowed to vote and have other basic rights of citizenship.

Growing Sense of Nationalism

White settlers, not blacks, had established the nation of South Africa. But as black South Africans struggled to gain political rights they began to think of themselves as full members of the nation. Soon there was a sense of nationalism that led eventually to black South Africans winning the rights of equal citizenship and, as the majority, the right to rule the nation.

In 1912, South African blacks organized the African National Congress (ANC) to fight for equality. Many ANC members, including **Nelson Mandela,** were jailed for their actions. Mandela spent almost 30 years in jail. The struggle finally paid off. In the 1990s, South Africa ended its discriminatory laws and gave nonwhite South Africans the right to vote for the first time. Mandela became South Africa's president. The struggle for majority rule inspired similar movements elsewhere in the region.

Economic Influence

South Africa is the richest and most industrialized country on the continent of Africa. Its economic power has affected all of

GOVERNMENT

A New South Africa

South Africa's first one-person one-vote election took place April 26–29, 1994. Millions of people waited patiently in mile-long lines to vote for the first time in their lives. The election was won by the African National Congress (ANC) with nearly two-thirds of the vote. Under a new South African flag, ANC president Nelson Mandela, freed after 27 years as a political prisoner, was inaugurated as president of the republic and head of a government of national unity. He invited the former president, F.W. de Klerk, to become a deputy president as a way to bring all South Africans together under a new government.

A South African Gold Miner

ECONOMICS

This miner crawls through cramped tunnels until he reaches this "room," where he does not have space to stand up. **Critical Thinking** What do you think a work day for this gold miner would be like? Why do you think a worker would choose to leave his country to work in the mines?

Southern Africa because of its demand for labor, especially for mining workers. A huge work force of hundreds of thousands of **migrant workers,** people who move from place to place to find work, was soon created.

Migrant Workers Form a New Group Identity

Mine workers in South Africa were from many countries. They lived together in compounds, or fenced-in groups of homes. They were far from their families, clans, and ethnic groups. They worked long hours in dangerous conditions for low wages.

They began to think of themselves as a group—as workers. This kind of group identity was new for southern Africans. It was not based on family or ethnic group. Group identity is very important in Africa. This is reflected in the African proverb "A person is a person because of people." It means that a person is who he or she is because of his or her relationships with other people. The migrant workers formed a new identity based on how they related to each other as workers.

Mine Workers Form a Union   In the 1980s, the mine workers in South Africa formed a union—the National Union of Mineworkers. This union was illegal at the time, but it played a leading role in the drive for equal rights. The union workers sometimes went on strike in support of their causes. Thus, the new identity of the mine workers led them to take group action.

AS YOU READ

Summarize How did South Africa's mines affect its culture?

SECTION 4 ASSESSMENT

AFTER YOU READ

RECALL

1. Identify: (a) Republic of South Africa, (b) Nelson Mandela

2. Define: (a) migrant worker

COMPREHENSION

3. Describe the political and economic effects South Africa has had on the entire region of Southern Africa.

4. What was unusual about migrant workers in South Africa forming a group identity as workers?

CRITICAL THINKING AND WRITING

5. **Exploring the Main Idea** Review the Main Idea statement at the beginning of this section. Then, write a paragraph summarizing the information in this section that supports this main idea.

6. **Recognizing Cause and Effect** What positive and/or negative effects might South Africa's labor needs have had on the economies of nearby countries?

ACTIVITY

7. **Writing a Song** Consider the life of a mine worker in a South African gold mine in the 1970s. Write the first verse of a song about miners' living and working conditions and wages.

Finding the Main Idea

supporting details

Music in Africa may be used to send messages or to a story. Horns, bells, and drums may be used to organize work. Xylophones, lutes, harps, flutes, and clarinets may be used to celebrate a special occasion. Music has many roles in the cultures of African countries.

main idea

Main Idea
Music has many roles in the cultures of African countries.
Supporting Details
Music can be used to send messages, tell a story, organize work, or celebrate a special occasion.
Supporting Details
Instruments include horns, bells, drums, xylophones, lutes, harps, flutes, and clarinets.

Learn the Skill

Each paragraph in a textbook contains a main idea and supporting details. The main idea is the most important idea about the paragraph's topic. Locating the main idea will help you figure out what the paragraph is about. To locate the main idea and supporting details in a paragraph, follow these steps:

A. Read the paragraph carefully.

B. Search the paragraph for the main idea. The main idea is often stated in the paragraph's first or last sentence. Reread the first and last sentences to see if they contain the main idea. Note that the last sentence contains the main idea in the sample paragraph above. If neither the first or last sentence states the main idea, look for a main idea sentence in the middle of the paragraph. A main idea can also be unstated. When the main idea is not stated, readers must figure it out on their own, and state it in their own words.

C. After you have found the main idea, look for details that support the main idea. Supporting details are small pieces of information that tell more about the main idea. Some details may be more interesting than others, but all details tell about the topic. You should be able to find several supporting details in each paragraph.

Practice the Skill

Using what you have learned, find the main idea and supporting details of the paragraph on the Dogon people of Mali. Then, make a Main Idea-Supporting Details chart like the one shown on this page.

The Dogon people of Mali use granaries to store grain. The granaries are made of twigs and mud but have stylized wooden doors. The Dogon believe the tree from which the wooden door was made contains a spirit that protects the stored grain. Although the rain and sun often wear down the granaries, the Dogon transfer the symbolic door from one granary to another.

Apply the Skill

See the Chapter Review and Assessment at the end of this chapter for more questions on finding the main idea.

Creating a Chapter Summary

On a separate piece of paper, draw a diagram like this one, and include the information that summarizes the first section of the chapter. Then, fill in the remaining boxes with summaries of Sections 2, 3, and 4.

THE CULTURES OF AFRICA

Section 1
North Africa's location on the Mediterranean, and its history as a trading center have greatly influenced its culture, which is a blend of African, European, and Southwest Asian elements. The religion of Islam plays an important role in North African life.

Section 2

Section 3

Section 4

Reviewing Key Terms

Match the definitions in Column I with the key terms in Column II.

Column I

1. parents and their children
2. people who move in order to find work
3. shared beliefs and customs
4. large farms of cash crops
5. a family relationship
6. a spreading of culture
7. several lineages with a common ancestor
8. a wide variety of cultures

Column II

a. cultural diffusion
b. culture
c. kinship
d. cultural diversity
e. clan
f. migrant worker
g. plantation
h. nuclear family

Reviewing the Main Ideas

1. Describe how Islam has influenced the culture of North Africa. (Section 1)
2. What factor has greatly aided cultural diffusion in North Africa? (Section 1)
3. In what ways is West Africa culturally diverse? (Section 2)
4. What role do family ties play in West African culture? (Section 2)
5. Explain how location has affected East African cultures. (Section 3)
6. How does the language of Swahili help unite the people of East Africa? (Section 3)
7. How has South Africa affected the cultures of the entire region of Southern Africa? (Section 4)
8. What major effect did migrant labor have on the people of Southern Africa? (Section 4)

Map Activity

Africa

For each place listed below, write the letter from the map that shows its location.

1. Mediterranean Sea
2. North Africa
3. West Africa
4. East Africa
5. Southern and Central Africa

 Take It to the NET

Enrichment For more map activities using geography skills, visit the social studies section of **phschool.com.**

Writing Activity

1. Writing a Dialogue An exchange student from an African country has come to stay at your home for six weeks. You and your family are sharing your first dinner with the visitor. Write a dialogue in which you ask your visitor about African culture. Use what you have learned in this chapter to write your visitor's answers.

2. Writing a Newspaper Article You are a news reporter in South Africa and you have the opportunity to interview Nelson Mandela. Prepare a list of the questions you would most want to ask him, and then visit your school or local library to try to find the answers to your questions. When you are finished with your research, write a newspaper article based on the information you have gathered.

Applying Your Skills

Read the first paragraph under the heading "Cultural Ties" on p. 389. Create a chart like you did on p. 397 to identify the main idea of the paragraph and the details used to support this main idea.

Critical Thinking

1. Identifying Central Issues Explain why the proverb "A person is a person because of people" is particularly suited to African culture.

2. Making a Valid Generalization What benefits and problems have come with modernization in Africa?

3. Drawing Conclusions Which organization founded in the 20th century do you think has had the greatest effect on the events of modern Africa? Explain your answer.

 Take It to the NET

View art and personal objects from Africa. Think about art and personal objects you've seen from your region of the world. What do these things reflect about your region's culture and history? Visit the **phschool.com** for help in completing this activity.

Chapter 21 Self-Test As a final review activity, take the Chapter 21 Self-Test and get instant feedback on your answers. To take the test, visit the Social Studies section of **phschool.com.**

NORTH AND WEST AFRICA:
Exploring the Region Today

Heavenly Bodies

USING ART

Education is a priority in the religion of Islam, one of the major religions practiced in Africa. From the 600s on, Muslims have studied art, literature, philosophy, math, astronomy, and medicine. Muslim mathematicians invented algebra, and Muslim astronomers accurately mapped the locations of the stars. A Muslim astronomer drew this comet in the 1500s.

Drawing Conclusions
It wasn't until the 1500s that Galileo, an Italian, discovered that the planets revolve around the sun. Study the illustration carefully. Think about what the Muslim astronomer might have known about the heavens. Make a list of what you think he knew, and why.

Exploring Science through Art
Make a list of the facts you can recall about astronomy and outer space. Then use the facts to create an illustration that reveals what you know. Compare your drawing to the Muslim illustration. How are they alike? How are they different?

SECTION 1

Egypt
A Nation Shaped by Islam

BEFORE YOU READ

READING FOCUS

1. How does religion affect Egypt's culture?
2. How does life differ for Egyptians living in rural and urban areas?

KEY TERMS

bazaar
fellaheen

KEY PLACES

Cairo

NOTE TAKING

Copy this chart. As you read the section, complete the chart to show the aspects of daily Egyptian life that help define Muslim culture.

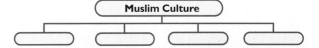

MAIN IDEA

Even though some Egyptians live in modern cities and others live in rural areas, most are unified by their faith in Islam.

Setting the Scene

At noon, the restaurants in Cairo stand empty. It's the Muslim holiday of Ramadan (RAM uh dahn) and for a month followers of Islam will fast, or go without food, from dawn to dusk. Muslim culture is one of the strongest elements that unify Egyptian society.

Egypt's Religious Culture

Egypt is across the Red Sea from Saudi Arabia, where the messenger of Islam, Muhammad, was born. Like most countries in North Africa, Islam is now the major religion in Egypt. In fact, it is the country's official religion.

Cairo's Busy Streets

GEOGRAPHY

More people live in Cairo than in any other city in Africa. Most of the people who live here are Muslim Arabs. **Critical Thinking** What similarities and differences do you see between this busy street in Cairo, and cities in the United States? Make a list.

Egypt

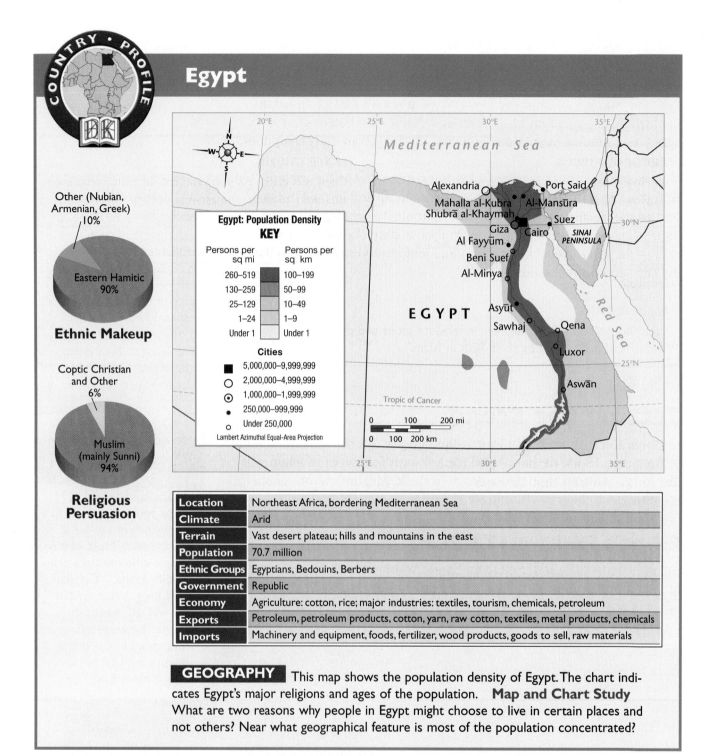

Other (Nubian, Armenian, Greek) 10%

Eastern Hamitic 90%

Ethnic Makeup

Coptic Christian and Other 6%

Muslim (mainly Sunni) 94%

Religious Persuasion

Egypt: Population Density
KEY

Persons per sq mi	Persons per sq km
260–519	100–199
130–259	50–99
25–129	10–49
1–24	1–9
Under 1	Under 1

Cities

■	5,000,000–9,999,999
○	2,000,000–4,999,999
◉	1,000,000–1,999,999
●	250,000–999,999
○	Under 250,000

Lambert Azimuthal Equal-Area Projection

Location	Northeast Africa, bordering Mediterranean Sea
Climate	Arid
Terrain	Vast desert plateau; hills and mountains in the east
Population	70.7 million
Ethnic Groups	Egyptians, Bedouins, Berbers
Government	Republic
Economy	Agriculture: cotton, rice; major industries: textiles, tourism, chemicals, petroleum
Exports	Petroleum, petroleum products, cotton, yarn, raw cotton, textiles, metal products, chemicals
Imports	Machinery and equipment, foods, fertilizer, wood products, goods to sell, raw materials

GEOGRAPHY This map shows the population density of Egypt. The chart indicates Egypt's major religions and ages of the population. **Map and Chart Study** What are two reasons why people in Egypt might choose to live in certain places and not others? Near what geographical feature is most of the population concentrated?

Muslim Beliefs

Muslims believe that the Quran, their holy book, contains the words of God and that they were revealed to Muhammad during the month of Ramadan. Muslims believe in many of the teachings presented in the Jewish Torah and the Christian Bible.

Muslims pray five times a day, often in a mosque, a building used for worship. They face in the direction of Mecca, the city in Saudi Arabia, where Islam's holiest shrine is located.

An Islamic Renewal

Praying and fasting are two ways that Egyptian Muslims have brought their religion into their daily lives. While most Muslims believe that the laws of Egypt should be based on Islamic law, there is some disagreement among Egyptians. One area of disagreement is the public behavior of women.

Muhammad taught that men and women are equal in the eyes of God. Both are required by Islamic law to dress modestly in public. One part of the debate is whether women should be required to cover their faces with a veil. Some people feel women should be covered except for their eyes. Other Egyptians feel that women should have the right to choose in this case.

Diversity of Life in Egypt

While the people of Egypt share the common bond of their religious practice, their lives differ greatly depending on whether they live in a city or a rural village.

Urban Life About half of all Egyptians live in cities. **Cairo,** the nation's capital and largest city has more than 9.5 million people, more people than live in Los Angeles and Chicago combined.

It is Africa's largest city. Some parts of the city are more than 1,000 years old, while other parts look like a modern western city. Apartment buildings with air-conditioning are common. Shopping takes place in open-air markets called **bazaars.**

Many people move to the cities from rural areas. They hope to find jobs and better education. As a result, Cairo is very crowded. There are traffic jams and housing shortages. Some people live in tents that they have set up on rowboats on the Nile. Others live in homes they have built in the huge graveyards on the outskirts of Cairo. So many people live in the graveyards that they are considered suburbs of the city, and the government has provided the graveyards with electricity.

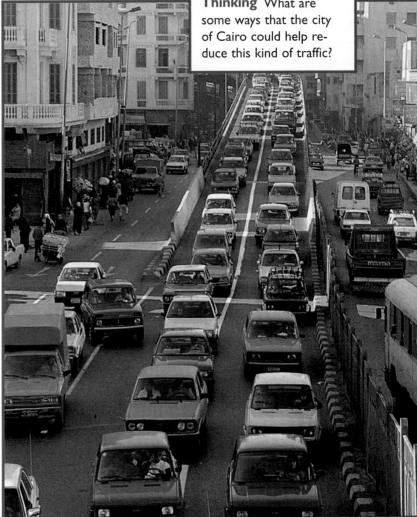

A Traffic Jam in Cairo

CULTURE Some people think that Cairo is the loudest city in the world because of its honking horns and roar of car engines. More than 9.5 million people live in the city, but millions more drive or take buses and trains in from the suburbs each day. **Critical Thinking** What are some ways that the city of Cairo could help reduce this kind of traffic?

A Farm in Egypt

ECONOMICS With power from a water buffalo, a fellaheen woman runs a traditional machine that separates the seeds of grain from the plants. **Critical Thinking** What conclusions about farming as a way of life in Egypt can you draw based on this photograph?

Rural Life In the rural areas of Egypt, most people live in villages along the Nile or the Suez Canal. Most villagers make their living by farming. These farmers are called **fellaheen** (fel uh HEEN) and, because land is scarce along the river banks, most have small, rented plots of land. Others work in the fields of rich landowners. Fellaheen live in homes built of mud bricks or stones, with one to three rooms and a courtyard that is shared with the animals.

Whether living in a city or in a rural area, most Egyptians hope that renewing their Muslim faith every day will help them to maintain traditional values and customs in a modern age.

SECTION 1 ASSESSMENT

AFTER YOU READ

RECALL

1. Identify: (a) Cairo
2. Define: (a) bazaar, (b) fellaheen

COMPREHENSION

3. Give two examples of how Islam affects everyday life in Egypt.
4. Compare the lives of city and village dwellers in Egypt.

CRITICAL THINKING AND WRITING

5. **Exploring the Main Idea** Review the Main Idea statement at the beginning of this section. Then, write a paragraph about the ways that Egyptians are united by their Islamic faith.

ACTIVITY

6. **Writing to Learn** In a journal entry, describe how the clothes people wear and the music they listen to may reflect their beliefs. Use examples from your own experience as well as from this section.

SECTION 2

Algeria
Urban and Rural Ways of Life

BEFORE YOU READ

READING FOCUS

1. What are some differences and similarities between the Berbers and the Arabs of Algeria?
2. How is life in Algerian cities different from life in the villages?

KEY TERMS

terrace
souq
casbah

KEY PEOPLE AND PLACES

Berber
Arab

NOTE TAKING

Copy this chart. As you read the section, complete the chart by filling in information on Algeria and its people. Add more circles to the web as you go.

MAIN IDEA

While Algeria's two main ethnic groups, the Berbers and the Arabs, have similar cultural traditions, important aspects of their cultures set them apart.

Setting the Scene

Like many people in many parts of the world, Algerians adapt to their climate by resting during the hottest hours of the day. If you were visiting Adrar, an oasis city in the Algerian Sahara, during midday, the temperature outside would be about 124 degrees F (51 degrees C). To survive in that heat, people must drink enough water to produce 2 to 4 gallons (7.6 to 15.2l) of perspiration a day.

Algeria's Ethnic Groups

The Sahara covers all of Algeria south of the Atlas Mountains and water is in short supply in this area. For this reason, fewer than three percent of Algeria's people live here. But because of their resourcefulness, **Berber** and **Arab** nomads have survived in the Sahara for hundreds of years.

The Berbers and Arabs The Berbers and the Arabs are Algeria's two main ethnic groups. The Berbers have lived in North Africa since at least 3000 B.C. Many historians think they migrated from Southwest Asia. They settled in the Atlas Mountains and on plains near Algeria's coast. Most Berbers live in villages in rural areas and continue to follow traditional ways of life. Their households form an extended family, but each married couple in a family has its own home opening onto the family courtyard. In this way, grandparents, parents, sons, daughters, and cousins can all live close together.

A Desert Lifestyle

CULTURE These men live in the Sahara's Ahaggar Mountains. Even in the mountains, the sun is so hot that people must wear clothes that cover most of their skin. **Critical Thinking** How do the clothes these men are wearing help them adapt to living in the desert?

405

Algeria

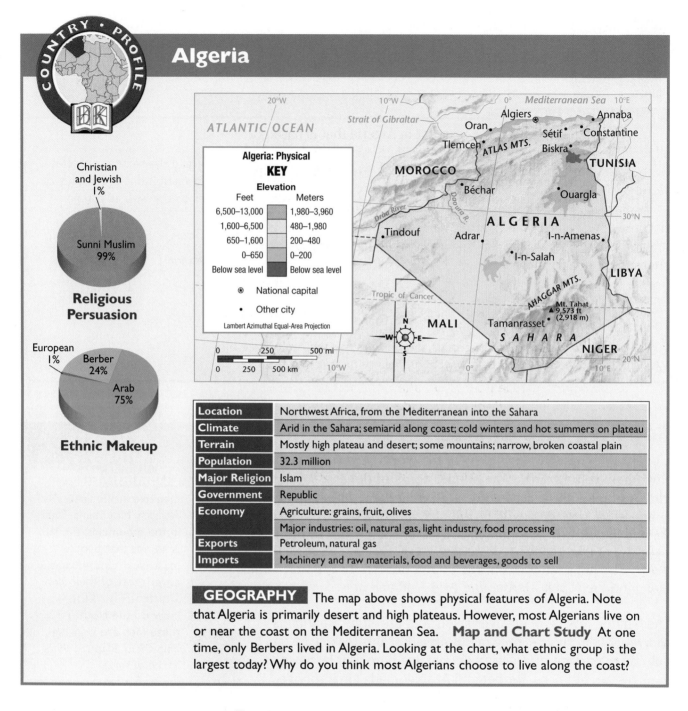

Religious Persuasion

Christian and Jewish 1%

Sunni Muslim 99%

Ethnic Makeup

European 1%

Berber 24%

Arab 75%

Algeria: Physical
KEY

Elevation

Feet		Meters
6,500–13,000		1,980–3,960
1,600–6,500		480–1,980
650–1,600		200–480
0–650		0–200
Below sea level		Below sea level

⊛ National capital

• Other city

Lambert Azimuthal Equal-Area Projection

0   250   500 mi
0   250   500 km

Location	Northwest Africa, from the Mediterranean into the Sahara
Climate	Arid in the Sahara; semiarid along coast; cold winters and hot summers on plateau
Terrain	Mostly high plateau and desert; some mountains; narrow, broken coastal plain
Population	32.3 million
Major Religion	Islam
Government	Republic
Economy	Agriculture: grains, fruit, olives
	Major industries: oil, natural gas, light industry, food processing
Exports	Petroleum, natural gas
Imports	Machinery and raw materials, food and beverages, goods to sell

GEOGRAPHY The map above shows physical features of Algeria. Note that Algeria is primarily desert and high plateaus. However, most Algerians live on or near the coast on the Mediterranean Sea. **Map and Chart Study** At one time, only Berbers lived in Algeria. Looking at the chart, what ethnic group is the largest today? Why do you think most Algerians choose to live along the coast?

Family is so important to the Berbers that their village governments are based on it. The head of each family is a member of the village assembly, which makes laws for the village.

Most rural Berbers make a living by farming and herding. They get up as soon as it is light and work until the sun is hottest. Then, people rest for several hours before going back to work until dark. In the mountains, the Berbers build **terraces,** or platforms cut into the mountainside, for their crops. The terraces increase farmland and keep the soil in place when it rains.

Arabs in Algeria The Berber way of life changed in the A.D. 600s, when Arabs spread across North Africa. The Arabs conquered North

Africa gradually, over hundreds of years. Peace in the region came about when most Berbers accepted the religion of Islam.

Arab traditions are like Berber traditions in many ways. For example, both Arabs and Berbers often live with extended families. However, Arabs and Berbers do differ.

Arabs created a central government in Algeria that is based on Islam. The Berber tradition is for each village to govern itself. But Berbers adapted to Arab rule by keeping their own governments along with the new one.

Most Arabs were nomads. They usually camped near a well or stream in the summer and herded animals across the desert during the rest of the year. As a result of Arab influence, many Berbers changed from a farming to a nomadic lifestyle. However, most Berbers today are farmers, while some Berber nomads still migrate.

Life in the Cities   About half of Algeria's people live in cities where mosques and open-air marketplaces called **souqs** (sooks) are common. Older parts of the cities are called **casbahs** (KAHZ bahz). The houses and stores here are close to each other on narrow, winding streets. Newer parts of the cities look like cities in Europe and the United States, with tall buildings and wide streets.

Berbers and Arabs Today

Berbers and Arabs have mixed over the centuries. Both groups are Muslim, and most Berbers speak Berber and Arabic. Because France ruled Algeria for part of its history, many Berbers and Arabs also speak French. The Berbers and the Arabs of Algeria have had many conflicts in the past. However, there have also been long periods during which they learned from each other peacefully. Algeria's future will continue to mix Berber and Arab, old and new.

SECTION 2 ASSESSMENT

AFTER YOU READ

RECALL

1. Identify: (a) Berber, (b) Arab

2. Define: (a) terrace, (b) souq, (c) casbah

COMPREHENSION

3. How did Arabs change the Berber way of life?

4. How are Arabs and Berbers similar today?

CRITICAL THINKING AND WRITING

5. Exploring the Main Idea Review the Main Idea statement at the beginning of this section. Then, write a paragraph about differences between Berbers and Arabs.

6. Recognizing Cause and Effect Why do you think that the Berbers maintained their language and traditions after Arabs came to Algeria?

ACTIVITY

 Take It to the NET

7. Creating a Guidebook Create a guidebook for your region. Include the same categories of information that you found on the Web site. Visit the World Explorer: People, Places, and Cultures section of **phschool.com** for help in completing this activity.

BEFORE YOU READ

READING FOCUS

1. How have events in history led to a multiethnic Nigeria?
2. How are Nigeria's main ethnic groups similar to and different from each other?

KEY TERMS
multiethnic
census

KEY PLACES
Lagos
Abuja
Kano

NOTE TAKING

Copy this chart. As you read the section, complete the chart with information about each of Nigeria's three main ethnic groups.

Hausa-Fulani	Yoruba	Ibo

MAIN IDEA

Nigeria is Africa's most populated country, with many ethnic groups that have learned to cooperate and unify as one independent nation.

Calabash Carver in Kurmi Market

CULTURE A carver decorates a calabash, or empty gourd, at his stall in Kano's Kurmi Market. At this market, people can buy goods from many African countries. **Critical Thinking** How might Nigeria's culture be influenced by the presence of so many different ethnic groups?

Setting the Scene

The language of Nigeria is not Nigerian because there is no such language. Nigerians speak more than 250 languages!

The languages of Nigeria match its ethnic groups. Nigeria's three most widely spoken languages are Hausa, Yoruba, and Ibo and there are places called Hausaland, Yorubaland, and Iboland. But these places are not countries. In fact, Hausaland and Yorubaland both lie partly in Nigeria and partly in other countries. Look at the map in the Country Profile on the next page. You can see that Nigeria's borders do not match the borders of any one ethnic group. Nigeria is **multiethnic,** which means that many ethnic groups live within its borders.

Nigeria's History

Why are there so many ethnic groups and languages within one country? Before Europeans arrived, what is now Nigeria was ruled by many ethnic groups, including the Hausa, the Yoruba, and the Ibo. But when Europeans drew Nigeria's borders, they did not think about ethnic groups.

By 1914, Great Britain had taken over the government of Nigeria. The borders of the British colony of Nigeria included part of Hausaland, part of Yorubaland, and Iboland. When Nigeria became independent in 1960, ethnic groups that had always lived separately became part of one nation. To help unify the country, in 1991 the government moved the nation's capital from **Lagos,** in the south, to **Abuja** (ah BOO jah) in the central portion of the country.

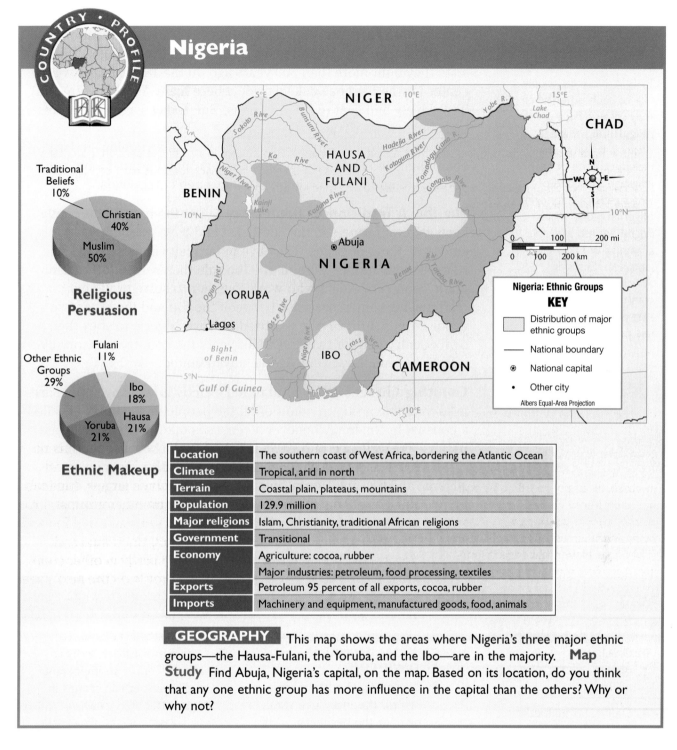

Country Profile

Nigeria

Religious Persuasion

- Traditional Beliefs 10%
- Christian 40%
- Muslim 50%

Ethnic Makeup

- Other Ethnic Groups 29%
- Fulani 11%
- Ibo 18%
- Hausa 21%
- Yoruba 21%

Location	The southern coast of West Africa, bordering the Atlantic Ocean
Climate	Tropical, arid in north
Terrain	Coastal plain, plateaus, mountains
Population	129.9 million
Major religions	Islam, Christianity, traditional African religions
Government	Transitional
Economy	Agriculture: cocoa, rubber
	Major industries: petroleum, food processing, textiles
Exports	Petroleum 95 percent of all exports, cocoa, rubber
Imports	Machinery and equipment, manufactured goods, food, animals

GEOGRAPHY This map shows the areas where Nigeria's three major ethnic groups—the Hausa-Fulani, the Yoruba, and the Ibo—are in the majority. **Map Study** Find Abuja, Nigeria's capital, on the map. Based on its location, do you think that any one ethnic group has more influence in the capital than the others? Why or why not?

Three Different Cultures

The Hausa and the Fulani make up about 33 percent of Nigeria's people and most are Muslims. For hundreds of years, the Hausa-Fulani have made an important part of their living by trading goods from as far away as Spain, Italy, and Egypt. The Hausa-Fulani built cities at the crossroads of trade routes. Each of these cities had its own ruler, was enclosed by walls, and had a central market. **Kano,** the oldest city in West Africa, is a Hausa city and has been a center of trade for over 1,000 years.

Pidgin How do people talk to each other when they speak different languages? One way is to create a language that includes a little of each language. This kind of language is called pidgin. Nigerian pidgin mixes English words with the grammar of Nigerian languages. Enslaved Africans and their captors may have been the first people in Africa to use pidgin.

The Yoruba: Farmers Near the Coast   About 20 percent of Nigeria's people are Yoruba and many of them still live in Lagos, the city-state they built more than 500 years ago. In the 1800s, Lagos was a center for the European slave trade where many Yoruba were sold into slavery and sent to the Americas. But, today, Lagos is a more peaceful center of trade.

Most Yoruba are farmers. They live with their families in large compounds which have several houses grouped around a big yard. A Yoruba community is made up of many such compounds.

The Ibo: A Tradition of Democracy   The Ibo have traditionally lived as rural farmers in the southeast and have not built any large cities like Kano or Lagos. They live in farming villages. Unlike the Hausa-Fulani and the Yoruba, the Ibo rule themselves with a democratic council of elders who work together to solve problems.

Tensions sometimes arise between the Ibo and the other two major groups. In 1967, the Ibo tried to leave Nigeria to start their own country and for two and a half years the country was torn by war. In the end, however, Nigeria stayed united.

Counting Citizens   It is hard to tell exactly how many people are in each ethnic group. A count of all the people in a country is called a **census.** In Nigeria, whenever a census is taken, it causes debate because the largest group will have the most power in government.

In 1991, the census showed that over 88 million people live in Nigeria, and that the Hausa-Fulani are the country's largest ethnic group. This gives them more political power than other groups.

SECTION 3 ASSESSMENT

AFTER YOU READ

RECALL

1. Identify: (a) Lagos, (b) Abuja, (c) Kano

2. Define: (a) multiethnic, (b) census

COMPREHENSION

3. How did the arrival of Europeans in the region affect the ethnic groups that live in the region?

4. What are the three largest ethnic groups in Nigeria, and where does each group live?

CRITICAL THINKING AND WRITING

5. **Exploring the Main Idea** Review the Main Idea statement at the beginning of this section. Then, write a paragraph summarizing some of the reasons why Nigeria was able to bring together many ethnic groups to work together in self-government. Think about past influences and contributions of modern leaders.

6. **Cause and Effect** Why is taking a census so important to different ethnic groups in Nigeria?

ACTIVITY

7. **Writing to Learn** Currently, Nigeria does not have one national language. Based on what you have learned, do you think a national language might be useful for Nigeria? Why or why not? Write a paragraph explaining your opinion.

Ghana
Origins of a Democratic Government

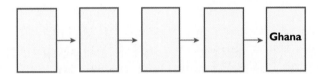
Setting the Scene

In 1935, **Kwame Nkrumah,** a 26-year-old student, sailed from Ghana to the United States. At that time, Ghana was called the Gold Coast and it had been ruled by Great Britain for over 60 years. Nkrumah was well aware that the people of his country did not have true freedom or equality, and when he saw the Statue of Liberty for the first time, it made him determined to bring freedom not only to his country, but to the whole continent.

Moving Toward Independence

In 1947, Nkrumah returned to the Gold Coast. The Gold Coast was named for its gold, which is one of the country's most important natural resources. The Country Profile on the next page shows the country's other important resources.

While the Gold Coast had many resources, most of its people were poor. Nkrumah believed that the people should benefit from the wealth of their own country, so he began traveling all over the country to convince the people to demand independence from Great Britain.

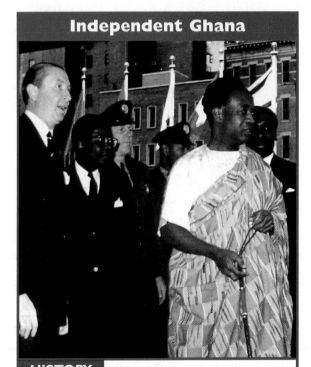

Independent Ghana

HISTORY Kwame Nkrumah, the first leader of independent Ghana, showed his respect for African traditions by wearing traditional clothing. **Critical Thinking** What African traditions do you think Kwame Nkrumah might have felt were most important to maintain in Ghana? Why?

Ghana

Religious Persuasion

Other 8%
Traditional Beliefs 38%
Muslim 11%
Christian 43%

Ethnic Group

Indigenous African Groups 99%
Other 1%

Ghana: Political
KEY

— National boundary
⊛ National capital
• Other city

Albers Equal-Area Projection

ECONOMICS

This political map shows Ghana's major cities and waterways. Locate the capital city, Accra.
Map and Chart Study What advantage does Accra's location offer?

Location	Southern coast of West Africa, bordering the Atlantic Ocean
Climate	Tropical wet and dry
Terrain	Low fertile plains and plateaus
Population	20.2 million
Major religions	Traditional African religions, Islam, Christianity
Government	Constitutional democracy
Economy	Agriculture: cocoa, coffee, rice
	Major industries: aluminum, light industry mining
Exports	Cocoa beans and products, gold, timber, bauxite and aluminum
Imports	Petroleum, goods to sell, foods, equipment

Traditional Government in Ghana

The Akan are the largest ethnic group in Ghana. When the Akan give power to a new leader, they also give a warning: If the leader does not rule fairly, the people can give power to a new ruler. In this way, the Akan are democratic since the people have control over who rules them.

While the Europeans were trading in gold and slaves on the coast, some Akan groups formed the Asante kingdom. This kingdom became very rich from trade and controlled parts of the northern savanna and the coastal south. The Asante used all their power to try to stop the Europeans from taking over west Africa.

The Influence of Colonialism   In 1874, Great Britain made the Gold Coast a colony and tried to control the economy. It encouraged farmers to grow cocoa for British chocolate factories and exported timber and gold. As these raw materials left the country, goods from other countries were shipped in. People grew fewer food crops because growing cash crops like cocoa brought in more money and food had to be imported. People also spent more time on farming and less on traditional crafts. The British sold food and factory-made goods to the people of the Gold Coast. Soon, the Gold Coast began to depend on these imports.

The British also built schools in the Gold Coast. Foreign missionaries ran the schools and Christianity began to replace traditional religions. By the time Ghana became independent in 1957, many new ideas and lifestyles had come to traditional communities. Kwame Nkrumah, for example, was a Christian. But he also believed in parts of the traditional African religion. Nkrumah's respect for old and new ways helped him govern when Ghana became independent.

Independence

In 1957, Nkrumah gave a moving speech to his people. Great Britain, he said, had finally agreed to grant them **sovereignty** (SAHV run tee), or political independence. Cheering, the people carried Nkrumah through the streets. Crowds sang victory songs to celebrate a dream come true.

Nkrumah became the leader of the new country and later, the president. The government changed the country's name to Ghana, after an African kingdom that had ruled the region hundreds of years ago. Ghana was the first African colony south of the Sahara to become independent.

Since independence, Ghana has worked to balance new technology with traditional culture. Modern health care, electricity, transportation, and education are things that most Ghanaians want.

AS YOU READ

Draw Inferences How does your community blend traditional ways of life with modern ways?

ECONOMICS   Since colonization, many Ghanaian women purchase machine-made cotton fabrics, instead of traditional Kente cloth, for everyday dresses and head scarves.   **Critical Thinking** Do you think this effect of colonization is positive or negative? Why?

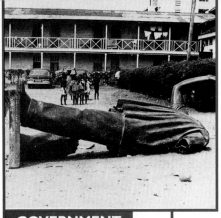

Pulled down by angry citizens, the headless statue of Kwame Nkrumah lies on the grounds of the central police station in Accra. Nkrumah was out of the country when the government was overthrown, in February 1966. He never returned to Ghana, but lived in exile in the nearby country of Guinea.

Nkrumah's Government Is Overthrown   Nine years after being carried through the streets as a hero, Nkrumah was thrown out of office by a military **coup** (koo), or takeover. Most Ghanaian citizens did not protest. In fact, many celebrated. People pulled down statues of Nkrumah.

How did this hero become an enemy? Nkrumah had big plans for Ghana. He borrowed huge amounts of money to make those plans happen fast. But when world prices fell for cocoa, the country's chief export, Ghana could not pay back its loans. Many people blamed Nkrumah for the country's economic problems.

Nkrumah's downfall did not end Ghana's problems. The country alternated between military and democratically elected governments. Few were successful. In the meantime, people began to think better of Nkrumah. Many felt that he had done his best to help the country. When he died in 1972, he was hailed as a national hero.

Ghana's Economy and Culture Today   In the 1980s, Ghana's president, **Jerry Rawlings,** tried to reform Ghana's politics and economy. Rawlings was a military officer who had taken part in some of the earlier coups. Rawlings stressed the traditional African values of hard work and sacrifice. Ghanaians supported Rawlings, and as a result, Ghana's economy began to grow.

Ghana is still dependent on the sale of cocoa. Even so, the economy has grown so much that Ghana has been able to build better roads and irrigation systems. The government plans to improve education and health care. People have formed groups so they can voice concerns about issues that affect their lives.

Ghana's culture, as well as its economy, has benefited from Rawlings's renewal of traditional values. Ghana has special centers that have been set up to keep the country's traditional culture alive.

SECTION 4 ASSESSMENT

AFTER YOU READ

RECALL
1. Identify: (a) Kwame Nkrumah, (b) Jerry Rawlings

2. Define: (a) sovereignty, (b) coup

COMPREHENSION
3. How did colonization affect Ghana's economy and its push for independence?

4. What challenges have leaders of independent Ghana faced?

CRITICAL THINKING AND WRITING
5. **Exploring the Main Idea** Review the Main Idea statement at the beginning of this section. Then, write a paragraph describing the beliefs and traditions Ghanaians drew on to successfully form an independent democracy.

6. **Recognizing Cause and Effect** Kwame Nkrumah went from being a Ghanaian hero to an unpopular figure to a hero again. What caused this change in people's attitudes?

ACTIVITY
7. **Writing an Essay** Write an essay about one or two changes you would like to see in your country or community. Describe the obstacles that might stand in the way of this change, and how these obstacles could be overcome.

Using Models

What You Need

To make a model showing the desertification process, you will need:

▶ a three-sided box
▶ blow-dryer
▶ piece of sod as wide as the box
▶ sand
▶ goggles

Learn the Skill

A model is a small copy of something, used to represent an object or a process. For example, a globe is a model of the Earth. Models are useful because they make it easier to see and understand the object or process being represented.

In this activity, you will make a model that will help you explore and understand one cause of desertification. Desertification occurs when land that was once fertile becomes a desert. The land becomes dry and salty, underground water dries up, erosion occurs, and plant life dies.

The Sahara is expanding into the edge of the savanna, or the Sahel. The desertification of the Sahel affects not only the environment, but also the people living there.

A. Set up your model. Place the box so that the open end is in front of you. Put on your goggles. Lay the sod in the box, with some space between the sod and the back of the box. Pour the sand in a pile across the open end of the box, directly in front of the sod. Hold the blow-dryer at the open end of the box so that it will blow across the sand toward the sod.

B. Create a windstorm by using the blow-dryer to create wind. Lift handfuls of sand and let it sift through your fingers in front of the blow-dryer, so that the sand is blown across the grass. This represents the sandy winds that blow across the desert and over grassy lands. Do this for about one minute,

holding the blow-dryer no higher than the top of the sod. Note how much sand gets caught in the grass.

C. Begin the desertification process. Thin the vegetation by removing about half of the grass in the sod. This is similar to what happens when vegetation is grazed or dies from climate change. Use the blow-dryer and handfuls of sand to create another windstorm, again for one minute. How much sand is in the sod this time? How does the grass look?

D. Continue the desertification process. This time remove almost all of the grass in the sod. This represents more overgrazing and the death of vegetation. Make a final one-minute windstorm. How much sand is in the sod now? How does the sand affect the soil?

Practice the Skill

Record your observations from the activity. What happened to the sand as it blew across the grass? What happened to the remaining grass and topsoil as the sand blew across the "overgrazed" sod? Imagine you are a cattle herder who needs to feed your cattle. You know that if you let your animals graze, you might contribute to desertification. But if your animals do not eat, they will die. What would you do?

Apply the Skill

See the Chapter Review and Assessment at the end of this chapter for more questions on using models.

Creating a Chapter Summary

On a separate piece of paper, draw a chart like this one, and include the information that summarizes what you learned about Eygpt. Then, fill in the remaining boxes by summarizing the information you learned about the other three countries.

Egypt	Egyptians are a diverse people, but they are unified by their Islamic beliefs. The religion of Islam affects all aspects of Egyptian life.
Algeria	
Nigeria	
Ghana	

Reviewing Key Terms

Use each of the following words in a sentence that explains its meaning.

1. fellaheen (p. 404)
2. souq (p. 407)
3. census (p. 410)
4. bazaar (p. 403)
5. multiethnic (p. 408)
6. casbah (p. 407)
7. coup (p. 414)
8. sovereignty (p. 413)

Reviewing the Main Ideas

1. How do Egyptians show their faith in Islam in their daily lives? (Section 1)
2. How does life in Egypt's cities differ from life in Egypt's rural areas? (Section 1)
3. What do Berbers and Arabs have in common and what sets them apart? (Section 2)
4. How does Algeria's geography affect the people who live there? (Section 2)
5. What are Nigeria's three largest ethnic groups? (Section 3)
6. How are politics in Nigeria affected by its census? (Section 3)
7. What role did Kwame Nkrumah play in Ghana's move to independence? (Section 4)
8. How has Ghana changed since it became independent? (Section 4)

Map Activity

North Africa

For each place listed below, write the letter from the map that shows its location.

1. Cairo
2. Algeria
3. Mediterranean Sea
4. Egypt
5. Sahara
6. Nigeria
7. Ghana
8. Lagos
9. Abuja
10. Algiers

 Take It to the NET

Enrichment For more map activities using geography skills, visit the social studies section of **phschool.com**.

Writing Activity

1. **Writing a News Report** Choose one of the recent events described in this chapter and write a news report about it. Remember to describe these five things for your readers: who, what, when, where, and why.

2. **Writing a Poem** The Berber languages are rarely written down. Most Berber history is preserved by professional poets. Pretend that you are a professional poet living in the 600s, when Arabs first came to North Africa. Write a poem explaining some of the differences and similarities between Arabs and Berbers.

Critical Thinking

1. **Making Comparisons** Compare Egypt's geography to that of Ghana. How do you think each country's geography affected its history?

2. **Making Valid Generalizations** Choose one feature or aspect of culture that best portrays the country and its people for each of the four countries studied in this chapter.

 Take It to the NET

Activity Read about the people, history, and culture of Ghana. How is life in Ghana different from life in the United States? Visit the World Explorer: People, Places, and Cultures section of **phschool.com** for help in completing this activity.

Chapter 22 Self-Test As a final review activity, take the Chapter 22 Self-Test and get instant feedback on your answers. To take the test, visit the Social Studies section of **phschool.com**.

Applying Your Skills

Turn to the Skills for Life activity on p. 415 to answer the following questions.

1. Explain how using models helps you to learn about an object or process.

2. How did using the desertification model help you understand the process of desertification? Do you think you would have understood the process as well if you had only read about it and not used the model? Why?

EAST, CENTRAL, AND SOUTH AFRICA:
Exploring the Region Today

A Lifetime of Struggle

"I cannot pinpoint a moment when I became politicized, when I knew that I would spend my life in the liberation struggle. I had no epiphany, no singular revelation, no moment of truth, but a steady accumulation of a thousand slights, and a thousand indignities produced in me an anger, a desire to fight the system that imprisoned my people."

—Nelson Mandela from
Mandela: An Illustrated Autobiography

USING AUTOBIOGRAPHIES

This excerpt is from an autobiography written by Nelson Mandela. An autobiography is a book written about a person's life, by that person. Nelson Mandela was elected president of South Africa in 1994, after spending 28 years in prison for fighting apartheid.

Understanding the Author

Use a dictionary to find the meaning of the words, *politicized, epiphany, revelation, slight,* and *indignity.* What does Nelson Mandela say was the cause of his efforts to fight apartheid? What does this excerpt reveal about Nelson Mandela? What does it reveal about his struggle to fight apartheid?

Learning More about the Author

This is only a brief excerpt from Nelson Mandela's autobiography. What else would you like to know about his life? Make a list of six questions about Mandela's life that you would like to have answered. Use the library and the Internet to find the answers, and then write a brief report on Mandela that you can share with the rest of the class.

Rwanda and Burundi
Torn By Ethnic Conflict

BEFORE YOU READ

READING FOCUS

1. What are the three main ethnic groups in Rwanda and Burundi and how did they arrive in the region?
2. What has been the history of conflict between two of the major ethnic groups in these countries?

KEY TERMS

aristocratic
mwami
ganwa
vassal
refugee

KEY PEOPLE

Hutu
Tutsi
Twa

NOTE TAKING

Copy this chart. As you read the section, complete the chart with information on the Hutu and Tutsi people of Rwanda and Burundi.

	Hutu	Tutsi
• Orgin		
• Place in Society		
• Religion		
• Occupation		

MAIN IDEA

Since independence in the 1960s, both Rwanda and its neighboring country, Burundi, have experienced civil war between two major ethnic groups, the Hutu and the Tutsi.

Setting the Scene

The kingdoms of Rwanda and Burundi date back to the 15th and 16th centuries.

Both countries have rich and varied wildlife including elephants, antelopes, zebras, and buffalo. Rare mountain gorillas live in one of the last remaining sanctuaries in Rwanda's Volcanoes National Park. The people of this region, primarily **Hutu** and **Tutsi,** share common social structures and religious beliefs. Rwanda and Burundi are neighbors but they have a long and unhappy history of conflict that has not yet been resolved.

Cultural Origins

The first inhabitants of both Rwanda and Burundi were the **Twa,** a Pygmy people, who were hunters and pottery makers. Today, the Pygmies live in areas near the Equator.

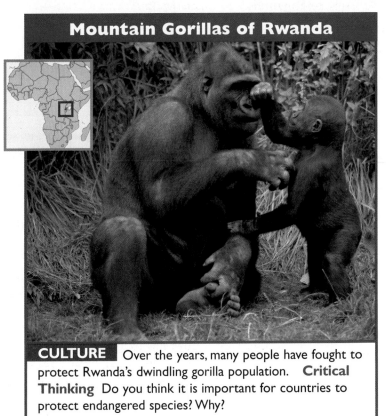

Mountain Gorillas of Rwanda

CULTURE   Over the years, many people have fought to protect Rwanda's dwindling gorilla population.   **Critical Thinking** Do you think it is important for countries to protect endangered species? Why?

Rwanda and Burundi

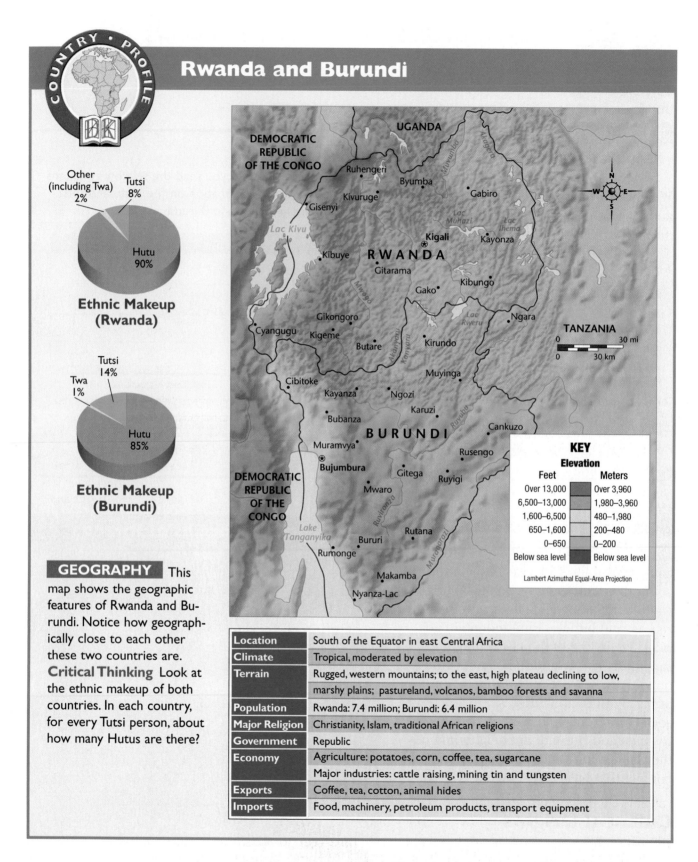

Ethnic Makeup (Rwanda)

Other (including Twa) 2%
Tutsi 8%
Hutu 90%

Ethnic Makeup (Burundi)

Tutsi 14%
Twa 1%
Hutu 85%

GEOGRAPHY This map shows the geographic features of Rwanda and Burundi. Notice how geographically close to each other these two countries are. **Critical Thinking** Look at the ethnic makeup of both countries. In each country, for every Tutsi person, about how many Hutus are there?

KEY		
Elevation		
Feet		Meters
Over 13,000		Over 3,960
6,500–13,000		1,980–3,960
1,600–6,500		480–1,980
650–1,600		200–480
0–650		0–200
Below sea level		Below sea level

Lambert Azimuthal Equal-Area Projection

Location	South of the Equator in east Central Africa
Climate	Tropical, moderated by elevation
Terrain	Rugged, western mountains; to the east, high plateau declining to low, marshy plains; pastureland, volcanos, bamboo forests and savanna
Population	Rwanda: 7.4 million; Burundi: 6.4 million
Major Religion	Christianity, Islam, traditional African religions
Government	Republic
Economy	Agriculture: potatoes, corn, coffee, tea, sugarcane
	Major industries: cattle raising, mining tin and tungsten
Exports	Coffee, tea, cotton, animal hides
Imports	Food, machinery, petroleum products, transport equipment

The Hutu arrived next. They were Bantu-speakers who migrated to the region from West Africa. Finally, the Tutsi settled here, and are believed to have come from either the Nile River Valley or from Ethiopia.

The ethnic makeup of both Rwanda and Burundi is similar. The Hutu account for 85–90% of the population. The Tutsi form the other significant portion of the population, while the Twa comprise just a tiny fraction. Despite this, it is the Tutsi who have always held a dominant place in both societies.

The Aristocratic Minority

When the Tutsi arrived in this region, the Hutu were well established and made their living as subsistence farmers. But the Hutu were soon under the control of the Tutsi, who had superior military skills. The Tutsi, who were herdsmen, gained control of the land. They became **aristocratic** rulers, those who are in the minority but are considered a privileged, upper class. A political system developed headed by a **mwami** (king) who divided the land among his **ganwa** (princes or lords). This Tutsi form of government continued until both countries gained independence from Belgium in 1962.

Life for the Hutu Majority

The Hutus in these societies were considered to be **vassals,** or servants, of the Tutsi landowners.

The Hutus' task was to safeguard the cattle herds, but they also raised crops of plantains, corn, and yams. The Tutsi lords, who in modern times were called chiefs and military captains, required the Hutu to support them through their labor. The Hutu accepted this role until civil war erupted in 1959 and, then again, after independence in 1962.

Cultures at War

Belgium had occupied both Rwanda and Burundi after World War I but its influence was declining in the late 1950s. It was then that the Hutu majority began to demand a more equal role in society. In Rwanda, the Hutu succeeded in overthrowing the ruling Tutsi king, and thousands of Tutsis were killed, while others were driven into exile in neighboring countries. By 1994, the Tutsi were again in power. This time, as many as 2 million Hutu fled the region and became **refugees,** people who seek safety in another country.

In Burundi, rebellions by the Hutu were brutally put down by the Tutsi, who controlled the country until the l993 elections gave power to the Hutu.

AS YOU READ

Summarize How did the role of the Hutu in society differ from that of the Tutsi?

Refugees Return Home

CULTURE Thousands of Hutu refugees returned to Rwanda after fleeing the country for their safety.
Critical Thinking Why do you think these refugees wanted to return to Rwanda after facing so much danger and violence?

421

World Leaders Intervene

Both Rwanda and Burundi have experienced continual military coups, assassinations, and outbreaks of ethnic violence. In 1994, the rest of the world began to recognize the desperate situation in these countries. In April of that year, the presidents of both Rwanda and Burundi died when their airplane was shot down. In Rwanda, extreme Hutu soldiers soon killed hundreds of thousands of civilians, most of them Tutsi. Since 1999, world leaders have organized peace talks in hopes of ending the violence in neighboring Burundi.

GOVERNMENT In 2000, President Bill Clinton traveled to Tanzania to take part in the Burundi Peace Talks. **Critical Thinking** Why do you think international leaders intervened in the conflict in Burundi?

Contemporary Issues

Both Rwanda and Burundi continue to struggle for peace and prosperity. In Rwanda, battles between the Hutu and Tutsi began to end after 1994, but many challenges remain. Fighting continues on a smaller scale between the two groups despite much international assistance and free elections in 1999. Burundi faces similar problems. A temporary government was established in 2001 to end the fighting, but violence continues. The effects of war will cause suffering in these countries even after the struggles end.

SECTION 1 ASSESSMENT

AFTER YOU READ

RECALL

1. Identify: (a) Tutsi, (b) Hutu, (c) Twa

2. Define: (a) aristocratic, (b) mwami, (c) ganwa, (d) vassal, (e) refugee

COMPREHENSION

3. Who were the first inhabitants of both Rwanda and Burundi? Where do they live now?

4. How did the minority Tutsi people first gain and keep control over the majority Hutu?

CRITICAL THINKING AND WRITING

5. Exploring the Main Idea Review the Main Idea statement at the beginning of this section. Then, write a paragraph comparing and contrasting the Hutu and Tutsi peoples, and discussing each group's historic role in the region.

6. Making Predictions How will the years of war affect life in Rwanda and Burundi even after the fighting stops? What problems would you predict for education, culture, families, the environment, and the economies?

ACTIVITY

7. Creating a Timeline Using the information you learned in this section, create a timeline that shows the major events in the history of Rwanda and Burundi.

Kenya
Diverse Cultures, Shared Goals

BEFORE YOU READ

READING FOCUS:

1. How have Kenyans worked together to preserve the things they value most?
2. How do Kenyans who move to Nairobi from rural areas maintain ties to their homes and families?

KEY TERMS

harambee

KEY PEOPLE AND PLACES

Mount Kenya
Jomo Kenyatta
Nairobi

NOTE TAKING

Copy this chart. As you read the section, complete the chart with information about the values, traditions, and natural resources that contribute to Kenya's economy.

Values and Traditions	Natural Resources

MAIN IDEA

Kenya's diverse people belong to more than 40 different ethnic groups, but they are all loyal to their homeland and work together to preserve their values and families.

Setting the Scene

"Where is your shamba?" This is a question that two Kenyans usually ask each other when they first meet. A shamba is a small farm owned and run by a Kenyan family. Even Kenyans who live in the city think of the piece of land where they were born as home and return to it throughout their lives. Land is very important to Kenyans.

Kenya's Geography and People

Kenya is a country in central East Africa. **Mount Kenya,** Kenya's highest mountain, lies just south of the Equator, but its twin peaks are covered with snow all year. Southwest of Mount Kenya is a region of highlands. Its average temperature is 67°F (19°C). The area also gets plenty of rain, so the land is good for farming. Most of Kenya's people are farmers, who live in shambas dotting the countryside in the highlands.

The land near the coast is warmer but also has good farmland. Farther inland, plains stretch across Kenya, and here there is little rainfall so the plains can support only bushes, small trees, and grasses. North of the plains lie deserts, where the temperature can sometimes climb as high as 135°F (57°C).

A Kenyan Shamba

CULTURE This series of buildings is part of a shamba. It was built by a family that is part of Kenya's Kikuyu ethnic group. The whole shamba is considered the family home. **Critical Thinking** What do you think "home" means to the Kenyan people?

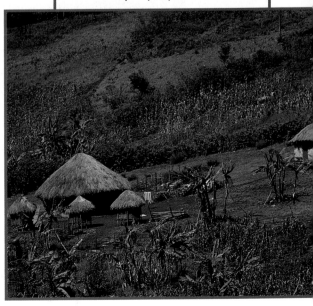

Kenya

Population Age Breakdown

Female

Age					
81–100	0.4%				
61–80	2%				
41–60	5%				
21–40	13.5%				
0–20	29.5%				

Male

Age					
81–100	0.4%				
61–80	1.9%				
41–60	5%				
21–40	12.7%				
0–20	29.6%				

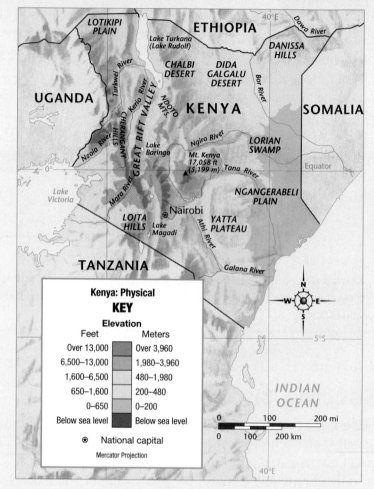

Kenya: Physical
KEY

Elevation

Feet	Meters
Over 13,000	Over 3,960
6,500–13,000	1,980–3,960
1,600–6,500	480–1,980
650–1,600	200–480
0–650	0–200
Below sea level	Below sea level

⊛ National capital

Mercator Projection

GEOGRAPHY This map shows land elevation in Kenya. **Map and Chart Study** Look at the map showing land elevation in Kenya. What areas have the highest elevation? The lowest elevation?

Location	East Africa, bordering Indian Ocean
Climate	Semiarid, highland
Terrain	Low coastal plain and plateau to the south; the Great Rift Valley enters country north-south flanked by high mountains
Population	31.3 million
Major Religion	Christianity, Islam, traditional African religions
Government	Republic
Economy	Agriculture: coffee, corn, tea; major industries: tourism, light manufacturing, petroleum products
Exports	Tea, coffee, petroleum products
Imports	Machinery and equipment, petroleum and petroleum products, iron and steel, raw materials, food, goods to sell

The Diversity of Kenya's People   Nearly all of Kenya's people are indigenous Africans who belong to more than 40 different ethnic groups, each with its own culture and language. Most Kenyans are Christian or Muslim.

Despite the differences among Kenya's people, they have many things in common. As they value the land, Kenyans also value their families, which often have six or more children. People consider their cousins to be almost like brothers and sisters.

Harambee—Working Together After Kenya gained independence in 1963, the new president, **Jomo Kenyatta** (JOH moh ken YAH tuh), began a campaign he called **harambee** (hah RAHM bay). The word is Swahili for "let's pull together." One example is Kenyatta's approach to education in which the government pays for some of a child's education, but the people work together to build and support schools.

AS YOU READ

Summarize What is the concept behind harambee? What is an example of this campaign?

Kenya's Labor Moves to the Cities

The people who live in the rural areas of Kenya are farmers. Like farmers all over Africa, most are women, who grow fruits and vegetables to eat and herd livestock. Men also farm, but they usually raise cash crops, such as coffee and tea.

Farming in the Highlands The Kikuyu (ki KOO yoo) are Kenya's largest ethnic group. Many Kikuyu live on the highlands near Mount Kenya. The Kikuyu grow food and cash crops such as coffee and sisal, which is used to make rope.

Children in a farming village have more responsibilities than most children in the United States. To see what a typical day is like for a Kenyan child, look at the schedule below.

City Life The way of life of many Kenyans is changing. As the population increases, people are moving to the city to find work. Most women and children, however, stay in the rural areas. It is expensive for them to move to the city and easier to support their families by farming.

Nairobi: Kenya's Capital City Every day, new residents arrive in **Nairobi** (ny ROH bee) by train, bus, or matatu (muh TAH too)—a minibus. Nairobi's population grew from one million in 1985 to three

A Typical Day for Some Young Kenyans

Time	Activity	Time	Activity	Time	Activity
5:45 A.M.	Get up, wash, and dress.	10:20 A.M.	Break	5:30 P.M.	Reach home. Wash uniforms. Lock up goats and sheep. Help prepare supper.
6:15 A.M.	Eat breakfast.	11:00 A.M.	Lessons		
6:30 A.M.	Start walking to school.	12:45 A.M.	Lunch break. Children bring their own lunch.		
7:00 A.M.	Arrive at school. Help clean the school.	1:00 P.M.	Play.	7:00 P.M.	Eat supper.
		2:00 P.M.	Lessons start.	7:30 P.M.	Wash up.
7:30 A.M.	Prepare for lessons.	4:00 P.M.	Lessons end. Help clean the school or work on the school shamba.	8:00 P.M.	Do homework every night.
7:45 A.M.	Assembly. Sing national anthem.			8:30 P.M.	Wash and prepare for bed.
8:00 A.M.	Lessons start.	5:00 P.M.	Start walking home.	9:00 P.M.	Go to bed.

CULTURE Like you, many Kenyan children spend most of each day in school. **Chart Study** Compare your schedule with this one. How might your day be different if you lived in Kenya? How might it be similar?

million in 1995, making it bigger than the city of Chicago in the United States. By the year 2000, the city had more than four million residents.

Many men move to Nairobi in order to earn money to support their families. When men move to the city without their families, they often feel homesick for their loved ones in rural villages. Meanwhile, the women who are left behind must do twice as much work. Many people have responded to this situation in the spirit of harambee—working together.

Women's Self-Help Groups   One of the best examples of harambee in rural Kenya are women's self-help groups, which women in rural areas all over Kenya have formed to solve problems in their communities. In addition to the crops they grow for their families to eat, the women grow cash crops, sell them, and save the money as a group. The women then meet to decide what to do with the money they have saved.

In Mitero, a village in the mountains north of Nairobi, Kikuyu women's groups have built a nursery school and installed water pipes for the community. They also loan money to women who want to start small businesses. Sometimes, they give money to women who need to buy such things as a cow or a water tank.

Men in the City   Moses Mpoke (MOH zuz uhm POHK ay) is from a Maasai village and he traditionally made a living farming and herding. Mpoke finished high school and now works in Nairobi. He has land in his home village, but the land is too dry for farming and he could not find good grazing for his livestock. He left the village to find work.

Men who move to the city work hard. Men in Nairobi who are from the same ethnic group often welcome each other, share rooms, and help each other.

SECTION 2 ASSESSMENT

AFTER YOU READ

RECALL

1. Identify: (a) Mount Kenya, (b) Jomo Kenyatta, (c) Nairobi

2. Define: (a) harambee

COMPREHENSION

3. Describe a typical day in the life of a young Kenyan.

4. Why do so many Kenyan men move to Nairobi?

CRITICAL THINKING AND WRITING

5. **Exploring the Main Idea** Review the Main Idea statement at the beginning of this section. Then, write a paragraph that discusses how Kenyans work together to preserve their values and families.

6. **Expressing Problems Clearly** How are women in rural villages affected when men move to the city?

ACTIVITY

7. **Journal Writing** Write a journal entry from the point of view of a Kenyan man who has just left his home and moved to the city. What new opportunities have brought him there and what problems must he overcome?

The Democratic Republic of the Congo

A Government in Turmoil

Setting the Scene

Since the 1930s, the Democratic Republic of the Congo (often called the Congo) has become one of the world's main sources of copper. The Congo also has supplies of many other resources, including gold, diamonds, forests, water, and wildlife which have played an important role in the nation's history. Even so, a small part of the country's natural resources have been developed.

Mining and Other Natural Resources

The Democratic Republic of the Congo is located in west Central Africa and is equal in size to the United States east of the Mississippi River. It is Africa's third largest country.

Although about two-thirds of the Congo's people work as farmers, mining produces most of the country's wealth. The Congo has huge copper deposits in the southern province of **Shaba** (SHAB uh), the Swahili word for copper. The country also has reserves of gold and other minerals and produces more diamonds than any other country, except Australia.

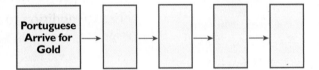

Copper Mining in the Congo

ECONOMICS In the Congo, miners take copper out of the ground in layers, leaving an open pit behind. **Critical Thinking** How might a country's natural resources affect its history?

The Democratic Republic of the Congo

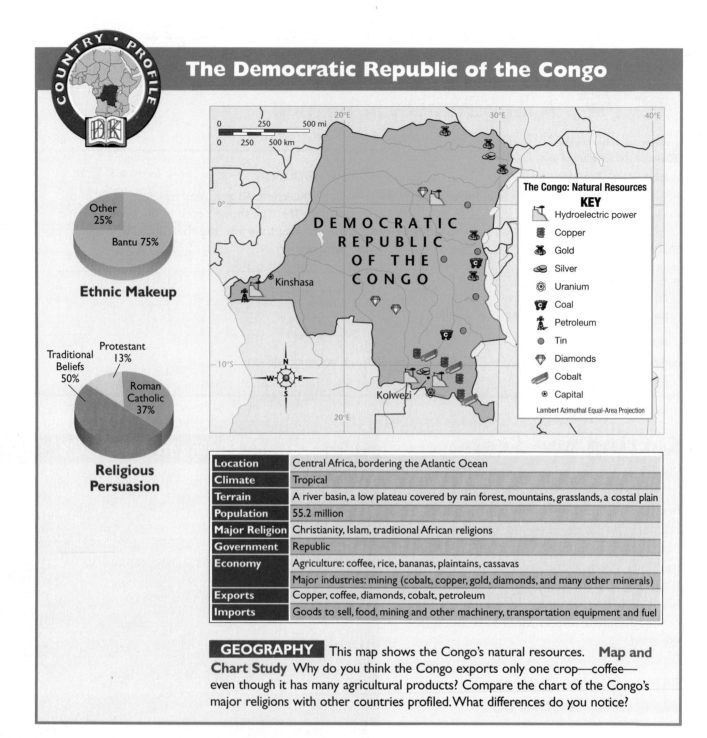

Ethnic Makeup

- Other 25%
- Bantu 75%

Religious Persuasion

- Traditional Beliefs 50%
- Protestant 13%
- Roman Catholic 37%

The Congo: Natural Resources

KEY

- Hydroelectric power
- Copper
- Gold
- Silver
- Uranium
- Coal
- Petroleum
- Tin
- Diamonds
- Cobalt
- Capital

Lambert Azimuthal Equal-Area Projection

Location	Central Africa, bordering the Atlantic Ocean
Climate	Tropical
Terrain	A river basin, a low plateau covered by rain forest, mountains, grasslands, a costal plain
Population	55.2 million
Major Religion	Christianity, Islam, traditional African religions
Government	Republic
Economy	Agriculture: coffee, rice, bananas, plaintains, cassavas
	Major industries: mining (cobalt, copper, gold, diamonds, and many other minerals)
Exports	Copper, coffee, diamonds, cobalt, petroleum
Imports	Goods to sell, food, mining and other machinery, transportation equipment and fuel

GEOGRAPHY This map shows the Congo's natural resources. **Map and Chart Study** Why do you think the Congo exports only one crop—coffee—even though it has many agricultural products? Compare the chart of the Congo's major religions with other countries profiled. What differences do you notice?

Natural Resources in the Congo's History

Events relating to natural resources dominate the history of the Congo. The power of the ancient kingdoms of Kongo, Luba, and Lunda was based on their knowledge of ironworking. In the 1480s, the Portuguese came to the Congo in search of gold. When Belgium colonized the area 400 years later, it forced Africans to harvest wild rubber, but later was interested only in the Congo's other resources, especially its copper and diamonds.

The Challenges of Independence

In the Congo's first years of independence, various groups fought each other for power. The foreign companies that controlled many of the country's industries feared this unrest would hurt their businesses. In 1965, they helped a military leader, **Mobutu Sese Seko** (muh BOO too SAY say SAY koh) take power.

Mobutu tried to restore order through an **authoritarian** government. An authoritarian government is one in which a single leader or small group of leaders has all the power. This type of government is not democratic. First, Mobutu renamed the country Zaire. Then, he **nationalized,** or put under government control, the foreign-owned companies. But this economic decision failed when government officials ran the companies poorly. When the world price of copper fell sharply in the 1970s, Zaire's export income fell and the nation could not pay back its debts.

Agriculture in Eastern Congo
GEOGRAPHY

Although the Congo is rich in natural resources, not all Congolese make a living as miners. Many Congolese work as farmers. They grow bananas, plantains, cassavas, corn, peanuts, and rice for their families. Others make a living growing cash crops such as cocoa, coffee, cotton, and tea. **Critical Thinking** The fields shown in this photograph are in a hilly area of the Congo. How do you think the shape of the land here creates challenges for farmers?

Economic Collapse Leads to Conflict

When Zaire's economy collapsed, Mobutu cut government spending. This hit the poor people of Zaire especially hard. Unemployment rose and political groups began forming to challenge Mobutu's policies.

Throughout the 1980s, Mobutu continued to rule harshly, and Zaire's economy continued to decline. Calls for reform came from inside and outside Zaire. In the early 1990s, Mobutu's grip on the country weakened. He began to promise major changes, but failed to carry through on any of them. In 1996, a minor uprising began in a region of eastern Zaire. A small ethnic group, with the help and support of neighboring countries, grew into a rebel army. Within months, they took control of eastern Zaire and, in 1997, took over the capital city of Kinshasa. Mobutu was expelled from the country and later died in Morocco.

A New Government and Continued Conflict

The rebels renamed the country the Democratic Republic of the Congo and promised to establish a new constitution and hold national elections. However, rebel groups with differing ideas continued sporadic fighting until 2002. The new president, Joseph Kabila, negotiated the withdrawal of the troops from neighboring countries. Soon after, an agreement was signed that ended fighting between the rival groups and set up a new, unified national government.

GOVERNMENT While Mobutu was successful in encouraging a sense of nationhood, he accumulated a large personal fortune through exploitation and corruption. **Critical Thinking** Considering the changes that Mobutu made when he took power, do you think he had the well being of his country in mind? Why?

SECTION 3 ASSESSMENT

AFTER YOU READ

RECALL

1. Identify: (a) Shaba, (b) Mobutu Sese Seko

2. Define: (a) authoritarian, (b) nationalize

COMPREHENSION

3. What are some of the Congo's mineral resources? What role have they played in the Congo's development as a nation?

4. What economic changes did Mobutu Sese Seko make when he took power? How successful were these changes?

CRITICAL THINKING AND WRITING

5. **Exploring the Main Idea** Review the Main Idea statement at the beginning of this section. Then, write a paragraph about the relationship that might exist between the Congo's political turmoil and the fact that the country has not fully developed its natural resources.

6. **Drawing Conclusions** Why do you think Congolese people's wages and living conditions have declined since independence?

ACTIVITY

7. **Writing a Description** Write a title and a short description for a book about the history of the Congo. Design a cover by deciding what images best represent the Congo's history.

South Africa
The End of Apartheid

BEFORE YOU READ

READING FOCUS

1. How did apartheid develop into the law of the land in the Republic of South Africa? How did the people of South Africa finally change the apartheid system?

2. How has life changed for the people of South Africa in the years since the end of apartheid?

KEY TERMS

apartheid
discriminate
homeland

KEY PEOPLE AND PLACES

Cape Town
F. W. de Klerk
Nelson Mandela

NOTE TAKING

Copy this chart. As you read the section, complete the chart with information about some of the effects of apartheid on black South Africans.

MAIN IDEA

The history of the Republic of South Africa is marked by racial division and social inequality, which only recently ended when black South Africans gained full citizenship rights and majority control of the government.

Setting the Scene

The Republic of South Africa lies at the southern tip of Africa and is larger than the states of Texas and California combined. Like the United States, South Africa has seacoasts on two oceans—the Atlantic Ocean and the Indian Ocean. South Africa is one of the wealthiest African countries. Yet, until recently, white people controlled almost all its riches because society was divided by law along racial and ethnic lines. How did such a system come to be?

Rule by Few

The ancestors of most black South Africans arrived some 1,500 years ago during the Bantu migrations. White Europeans first arrived about 400 years ago when Dutch settlers set up a colony at Cape Town. In time, they thought of themselves as Africans. They called themselves Afrikaners (af rih KAHN erz) and spoke their own language, Afrikaans. British, French, and German settlers arrived later and, by the late 1800s, these white settlers had forced black South Africans off of the best farmlands.

Divided Society
GOVERNMENT

Under apartheid, blacks and whites were even forced to sit separately at sports events. **Critical Thinking** Does any historical situation in the United States parallel South African apartheid?

South Africa

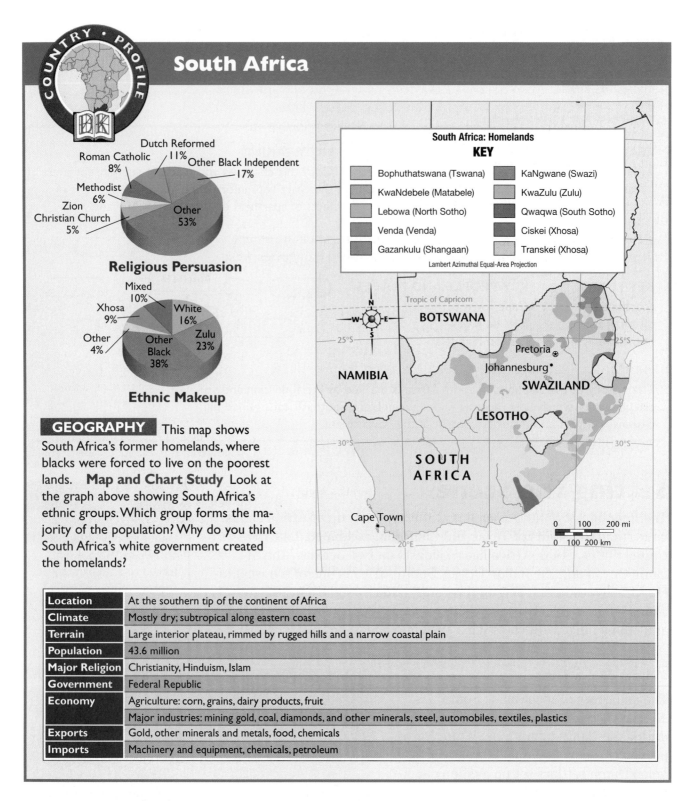

Religious Persuasion

Dutch Reformed 11%
Roman Catholic 8%
Other Black Independent 17%
Methodist 6%
Zion Christian Church 5%
Other 53%

Ethnic Makeup

Mixed 10%
Xhosa 9%
White 16%
Other 4%
Zulu 23%
Other Black 38%

South Africa: Homelands
KEY

- Bophuthatswana (Tswana)
- KwaNdebele (Matabele)
- Lebowa (North Sotho)
- Venda (Venda)
- Gazankulu (Shangaan)
- KaNgwane (Swazi)
- KwaZulu (Zulu)
- Qwaqwa (South Sotho)
- Ciskei (Xhosa)
- Transkei (Xhosa)

Lambert Azimuthal Equal-Area Projection

Tropic of Capricorn
BOTSWANA
NAMIBIA
Pretoria
Johannesburg
SWAZILAND
LESOTHO
SOUTH AFRICA
Cape Town

0   100   200 mi
0   100 200 km

GEOGRAPHY This map shows South Africa's former homelands, where blacks were forced to live on the poorest lands. **Map and Chart Study** Look at the graph above showing South Africa's ethnic groups. Which group forms the majority of the population? Why do you think South Africa's white government created the homelands?

Location	At the southern tip of the continent of Africa
Climate	Mostly dry; subtropical along eastern coast
Terrain	Large interior plateau, rimmed by rugged hills and a narrow coastal plain
Population	43.6 million
Major Religion	Christianity, Hinduism, Islam
Government	Federal Republic
Economy	Agriculture: corn, grains, dairy products, fruit
	Major industries: mining gold, coal, diamonds, and other minerals, steel, automobiles, textiles, plastics
Exports	Gold, other minerals and metals, food, chemicals
Imports	Machinery and equipment, chemicals, petroleum

The British and Afrikaners eventually fought each other for control of South Africa. To get away from the British, the Afrikaners founded their own states, Transvaal (tranz VAHL) and Orange Free State. Soon, however, diamonds and gold were discovered in the Transvaal. British prospectors pushed Afrikaners off their farms. The British and the Afrikaners fought for three years over the territory. Britain finally won, and declared South Africa an independent country in 1910.

Minority White Rule in South Africa The government of the new country passed laws to keep land and wealth under control of the white population. Blacks could not own land. They could work in white areas, but the best jobs and the highest pay were reserved for whites.

In 1948, the Afrikaners' political party, the National Party, was elected to run the country. New laws were added to the system of white power. The system was called **apartheid** (uh PAHR tayt), Afrikaans for "separateness." Apartheid laws placed every South African into one of four categories based on race and made it legal to discriminate in this way.

To **discriminate** means to treat people differently, and often unfairly, based on race, religion, or sex. The four racial categories were black, white, colored, and Asian.

Coloreds, or people of mixed race, and Asians, usually people from India, had a few rights but blacks were denied citizenship rights, including the right to vote. The system kept them in low-paying jobs, poor schools, and kept them out of white restaurants and hospitals. In addition they were forced to move to 10 poor rural areas called **homelands.** These homelands had the driest and least fertile land.

A Country Unites Against Apartheid

Many South Africans, black and white, fought apartheid through peaceful and organized protests. The well-armed South African government responded with deadly force, resulting in many deaths and jailings. But the demonstrations kept growing.

Countries around the world joined the movement against apartheid. Many nations stopped trading with South Africa. Its athletes were banned from the Olympic games and other international sporting events.

In 1990, faced with a weakening economy and continuing protests, South Africa's president, **F. W. de Klerk,** helped pass laws to end apartheid. South Africans of all colors peacefully elected a president, for the first time, in April of 1994 when they chose **Nelson Mandela,** a black leader who had spent many years in prison for fighting apartheid.

First Multiracial Elections, 1994

CITIZENSHIP Women in Johannesburg joyously displayed the identification papers that allowed them to vote in the historic election on April 26, 1994. Blacks had to wait in line for as long as eight hours to cast ballots for the first time in their lives. **Critical Thinking** How do you think black people felt voting for the first time in this historic election? Is this different from or similar to the way people think about voting in the United States?

AS YOU READ

Draw Inferences What do you think South Africans could learn from people who remember integration efforts in the United States?

Building a New Nation

Despite the end of apartheid under Mandela's government and new opportunities for millions of blacks, South Africa remained a divided society. The white population still held a lot of power and many did not like the changes in South Africa. Mandela's government had to find ways to reassure whites while making certain that blacks had an equal chance for a good life.

To help heal South Africa, Nelson Mandela's government set up a Truth and Reconciliation Commission which was to examine the crimes of the apartheid era. In 1998, the commission issued its final report. It condemned human rights abuses by both white and black South Africans. It also granted amnesty, or forgiveness, to some people who had committed crimes.

In June 1999, South Africa held its second election open to all races. Mandela's party stayed in power, but Nelson Mandela ended his political career. Thanks to his work, democracy continues in South Africa. In April 2004, South Africa held its third free and fair elections without problems or violence. The South African people continue to work together to build a peaceful and prosperous nation.

SECTION 4 ASSESSMENT

AFTER YOU READ

RECALL

1. Identify: (a) Cape Town, (b) F.W. de Klerk, (c) Nelson Mandela

2. Define: (a) apartheid, (b) discriminate, (c) homeland

COMPREHENSION

3. How did apartheid affect South Africans? How did the system of apartheid ultimately end?

4. What changes have taken place in South Africa since the collapse of apartheid?

CRITICAL THINKING AND WRITING

5. **Exploring the Main Idea** Review the Main Idea statement at the beginning of this section. Then, write a paragraph from the point of view of a black South African fighting apartheid laws. Explain how discrimination affects that person and what equality will mean for them.

6. **Expressing Problems Clearly** What challenges must the South African government meet in order to build a new nation based on equality for all?

ACTIVITY

 Take It to the NET

7. **Understanding Apartheid** Gather information on apartheid from the web site, and then write a position paper in which you discuss your views and thoughts about the subject. Visit the World Explorer: People, Places, and Cultures section of **phschool.com** for help in completing this activity.

Drawing Conclusions

Clues from your reading
+
What you already know
↓
Conclusion

Learn the Skill

You probably draw conclusions several times a day in your daily activities. Drawing conclusions is a skill that will help you get the most out of what you read. Drawing conclusions means making sensible decisions or forming reasonable opinions after thinking about the facts and details in what you are reading. To draw conclusions, follow these steps:

A. When you read look for clues, or evidence, that can lead to more understanding. For example, you might see a picture of Somali women wearing hajeebs—long, plain gowns with veils that completely cover their hair and neck. This clothing can serve as a clue to Somali culture.

B. Use what you already know. From reading about life in Egypt in an earlier chapter, for example, you might already know that Muslim women wear this type of clothing.

C. Add the clues that you found and what you already know, and then draw a conclusion. When you add the appearance of the Somali women to your knowledge of the way Muslim women dress, you can conclude that the Somali women are Muslims.

D. Stop to evaluate the decision you made. Ask yourself if the conclusion make sense. Is it the only reasonable alternative? Is it based on inaccurate facts or false assumptions? If you think the conclusion is faulty, try again to draw a conclusion that makes sense.

Practice the Skill

Read each of the following short pieces of information. Use clues from them and what you already know to write at least one conclusion. Then evaluate your conclusion by giving reasons why it makes sense. The first one is done for you.

I. Lake Victoria in East Africa is named after Queen Victoria of England.
Conclusion: This area was previously colonized by the British.
Evaluation: It makes sense, because East Africans or colonizers from another country would not have named their lake after Queen Victoria of England.

2. As a tourist, you find both Muslim mosques and Christian churches in Addis Ababa, the capital of Ethiopia.

3. Swahili is a language that contains a mix of African and Arab words. Swahili has become the language of East African trade.

Apply the Skill

See the Chapter Review and Assessment at the end of this chapter for more questions on drawing conclusions.

Creating a Chapter Summary

On a separate piece of paper, draw a diagram like this one and include the information that summarizes the first section of the chapter. Then, fill in the remaining boxes with summaries of Sections 2, 3, and 4.

EAST, CENTRAL, AND SOUTH AFRICA

Section 1
The Central African countries of Rwanda and Burundi have been devastated by the war between both countries' two major ethnic groups, the Hutu and the Tutsi. Hundreds of thousands of people have died in fighting.

Section 2

Section 3

Section 4

Reviewing Key Terms

Match the definitions in Column I with the key terms in Column II.

Column I

1. under government control
2. system of laws legalizing racial discrimination
3. Swahili word for "let's pull together"
4. person seeking safety outside their country
5. when a single leader or group has all the power
6. rural areas where black South Africans were forced to live
7. to treat people in a different way based on race, religion, or sex

Column II

a. refugee
b. harambee
c. discriminate
d. homelands
e. nationalize
f. apartheid
g. authoritarian

Reviewing the Main Ideas

1. Identify the three ethnic groups populating Rwanda and Burundi. (Section 1)
2. What is the source of conflict between the two largest ethnic groups in Rwanda and Burundi? (Section 1)
3. Why has the concept of harambee been important to individual Kenyans and to Kenya as a country? (Section 2)
4. What are Congo's greatest natural resources? (Section 3)
5. How has mining played a role in Congo's past and present? (Section 3)
6. What were the beginnings of the apartheid system in South Africa? (Section 4)
7. What people and events finally brought an end to the apartheid system? (Section 4)

Map Activity

Location

For each place listed below, write the letter from the map that shows its location.

1. Nairobi
2. Kenya
3. Cape Town
4. Johannesburg
5. Kinshasa
6. Democratic Republic of the Congo
7. South Africa

 Take It to the NET

Enrichment For more map activities using geography skills, visit the social studies section of **phschool.com.**

Writing Activity

1. **Writing Interview Questions** Choose either South Africa or the Congo. Write a list of five interview questions you would ask someone who has been elected president of the country. Consider the challenges the new president faces. Then exchange questions with a partner. Pretend that you are the president. Write answers to your partner's questions.

2. **Writing a Journal Entry** The countries currently experiencing civil wars—the Congo, Rwanda, and Burundi—share similar histories and consequences of war. Write a journal entry that explores some of these similarities.

Applying Your Skills

Turn to the Skills for Life activity on p. 435 to answer the following questions.

1. Explain why drawing conclusions is an important skill to use when reading.

2. Read the following excerpt from p. 433. What conclusion about the demonstrators can you draw from this information?

Many South Africans, black and white, fought apartheid through peaceful and organized protests. The well-armed South African government responded with deadly force, resulting in many deaths and jailings. But the demonstrations kept growing.

Critical Thinking

1. **Drawing Conclusions** South Africa's new government is trying to persuade skilled white workers to remain in the country. Based on what you know about apartheid, why do you think the country faces a shortage of skilled workers?

2. **Recognizing Cause and Effect** The people of Kenya believe in large, extended families working together. How did this attitude benefit the country in its struggle for independence and solving problems after independence?

 Take It to the NET

Activity Compare and contrast city life in Kenya to city life in America, as well as rural life in both countries. Visit the World Explorer: People, Places, and Cultures section of **phschool.com** for help in completing this activity.

Chapter 23 Self-Test As a final review activity, take the Chapter 23 Self-Test and get instant feedback on your answers. To take the test, visit the Social Studies section of **phschool.com.**

ORGANIZING TO GOVERN

Governments make decisions and pass laws that determine how a country will be run. The government decides how money will be raised and how it will be spent. Services that the government provides might include health, education, welfare, and the armed forces. The government may also see to public safety through the police force and civil defense; public transportation through roads, bridges, railways, and airports; and public enrichment through libraries, museums, and universities. Because of historical, cultural, and economic differences, governments vary from country to country. There are, however, three main ways in which governments are organized: republic, monarchy, and dictatorship. In a republic, the people limit the power of the head of state. They vote in an election to choose their government and chief executive. In a monarchy, the head of the royal family is the head of state, though a parliament may be elected to set policy and pass laws. In a dictatorship, a single ruler has unlimited power, and the people do not have any say in the affairs of state.

? How have conflicts between different forms of government influenced world history?

MONARCHY

In a monarchy, a king or queen rules the country. For centuries, the monarchs of Europe made laws and collected taxes. Today only a few monarchs, such as the king of Swaziland, have political power.

PLATO
More than 2,000 years ago, the Greek philosopher Plato wrote the first book about governments and how they rule people—what today we call politics. His book, The Republic, *set out a plan for an ideal government ruled by a philosopher king who always seeks to achieve good.*

PRESIDENCY

In a republic, the people vote to choose the head of state. In South Africa, for example, the president holds real political power and is responsible for the administration of the country and for its foreign policy. To the left, Thabo Mvuyelwa Mbeki is sworn in as president of the Republic of South Africa in 1998.

In the United States, the seat of government is Washington, D.C. In the Capitol Building, members of Congress (made up of the Senate and the House of Representatives) meet to discuss policies and pass laws.

SEATS OF POWER

Every government has a meeting place that is the seat of power. In the seat of power, federal laws are passed to provide a structure for the entire country. State or provincial governments and local governments carry out the federal laws and set policies according to federal guidelines outlined in the constitution.

INDEPENDENCE

The coming of independence to much of Africa after 1956 did not always bring peace or prosperity to the new nations. Many were weakened by famines and droughts or torn apart by civil wars. Few have managed to maintain civilian governments without periods of military dictatorships.

BENIN
The west African Kingdom of Benin reached the height of its power between the 14th and 17th centuries. Above is a Benin bronze mask.

NELSON MANDELA
In 1994, Nelson Mandela, a leader of the ANC, became the president of South Africa.

APARTHEID

In 1948, the National Party came to power in South Africa. Years of segregation, known as apartheid, followed. The policy gave white people power but denied black people many rights, including the vote. In 1990 the African National Congress (ANC), a banned black nationalist movement led by Nelson Mandela, was legalized, and the apartheid laws began to be dismantled. In 1994, the first-ever free elections were held.

Welcome to

Asia

GEOGRAPHY

Climb the steep sides of Mount Fuji ...

SCIENCE, TECHNOLOGY, AND SOCIETY

Explore innovations in computer technology ...

HISTORY

Visit the ancient Taj Mahal ...

What do you want to learn?

GOVERNMENT

Witness a handshake for peace ...

ECONOMICS

Increase productivity at a Japanese seafood plant ...

CULTURE

Act out China's traditional myths and legends ...

CITIZENSHIP

Demonstrate for better wages in South Korea ...

A journal can be your personal record of discovery. As you learn about Asia, you can create journal entries about what you read, write, think, and create. For your first entry, think about the geography of Asia. What are some of Asia's most distinctive geographic features? Compare and contrast them to geographic features in the place where you live.

EXPLORER'S JOURNAL

Guiding Questions

What questions do I need to ask to understand Asia?

Asking questions is a good way to learn. Think about what information you would want to know if you were visiting a new place, and what questions you might ask to find out. The questions on these pages can help guide your study of Asia. You might want to try adding a few of your own!

GEOGRAPHY

Asia is a region of extremes, with some of the driest deserts, longest rivers, and highest mountains in the world. The giant continent has cities crowded with people, small villages where people struggle to adapt to their physical environment, busy shipping ports, and a region of volcanic islands. Bodies of water such as the Pacific Ocean and the Indus River shape the lives of people who live near their shores.

❶ How has geography affected the way Asian societies have developed?

HISTORY

Some of the world's first great civilizations arose in Asia. Traders, explorers, and travelers passed through the region bringing new ideas that Asians borrowed and adapted. Architectural treasures, traditional art forms, and a diversity of languages reflect the region's rich history. This history continues to shape Asians' sense of identity today.

❷ How have history and the achievements of historic figures influenced life in Asia today?

CULTURE

Many of the world's religions began in Asia. Today, religious beliefs and practices help to define the many cultures of this vast region. In Southwest Asia, religious law and civil law are often the same. In South Asia and East Asia, religious observances and celebrations play a major part in daily life.

❸ How has religion affected the way Asian societies have developed?

GOVERNMENT

Asian governments in the past have included powerful dynasties and empires, as well as periods of foreign rule. Today the governments of Asia vary widely. They include the communist governments of China and North Korea, and the more democratic governments of Japan and South Korea. In the Southwest Asian country of Israel, democracy prevails, but old conflicts still threaten the stability of the region.

4 How do Asian governments compare with each other and with the government of the United States?

CITIZENSHIP

The nature of citizenship in the different regions of Asia is largely defined by the history of those regions. Some Asian countries have only recently gained independence from colonial rule. Their governments face great challenges in building a political process that is acceptable to all, and in which citizens can participate in the decision-making process.

6 How does participation in the political process differ in Asia and in the United States?

ECONOMICS

As they have for generations, many Asians raise crops both to support their families, and to sell or export for profit. Many Asian nations are industrialized, while others are becoming more so. The industries that support the people of Asia range from small-scale production of traditional crafts, to large-scale factory production of auto parts. World demand for oil has brought great wealth to some countries in Southwest Asia.

5 How do physical geography and natural resources affect the ways that Asians earn a living?

SCIENCE, TECHNOLOGY, AND SOCIETY

Asia has long been a region defined by excellence in scientific and technological innovation, and it maintains that distinction today. Israelis have devised irrigation methods to help develop important agricultural areas in desert land. Farmers in Saudi Arabia have used technology to adapt to a climate of hot summers and cold winters. Japan has become a world leader in computer technology.

7 How have geographic factors affected the development of science and technology in Asia?

 Take It to the NET

For more information on Asia, visit the World Explorer: People, Places, and Cultures companion Web site at **phschool.com.**

ACTIVITY ATLAS

Asia

◆ ◆

Learning about Asia means being an explorer and a geographer.
No explorer would start out without first checking some facts.
Begin by exploring the maps of Asia on the following pages.

Relative Location

Relative Size

1. LOCATION

Locate Asia and the United States Look at the map at left. The land that is colored green is Asia. What ocean lies between Asia and the United States? If you lived on the west coast of the United States, in which direction would you travel to reach Asia?

2. REGIONS

Estimate Asia's Size The Relative Size map on the left shows the United States superimposed over the southern part of the Asian continent. How large is this part of Asia compared to the continental United States? Use a ruler to measure the greatest distance across this portion of Asia from east to west. Now make the same measurement for the United States. About how many times wider is this portion of Asia from east to west than the United States?

 Take It to the NET

Items marked with this logo are periodically updated on the Internet. To get current information about the geography of Asia, go to **phschool.com**.

Asia: Political

KEY

— National boundary

⊛ National capital

• Other city

Two-Point Equidistant Projection

3. PLACE

Identify Countries in Asia Asia is the largest continent on the Earth. The map above shows countries in Asia. Which Asian country on the map do you think is the biggest? Asia also includes many countries that are located on islands. Find three island countries on the map. What are their names? Asia extends far to the west and east. One country in the western part of Asia is Saudi Arabia. Name three countries that are near Saudi Arabia.

The continent of Asia also includes part of the country of Russia. Russia is such a big country that it is a part of two continents—Europe and Asia. Notice the location of Russia on the map. Most of Russia lies in Asia. Most Russians, however, live in the European part of Russia. For this reason, geographers often include Russia in discussions of Europe, rather than in discussions of Asia.

ACTIVITY ATLAS

Asia: Physical

KEY

Elevation

Feet		Meters
Over 13,000		Over 3,960
6,500–13,000		1,980–3,960
1,600–6,500		480–1,980
650–1,600		200–480
0–650		0–200
Below sea level		Below sea level

Two-Point Equidistant Projection

4. MOVEMENT

Analyze the Influence of Geography on the Economy The Himalaya Mountains are the highest mountains in the world. Asia has other high mountain ranges as well, and large, barren deserts. Find these physical features on the map. What effect do you think these barriers to transportation have on the economies of countries in Asia?

5. LOCATION

Identify Bodies of Water and Peninsulas in Asia Asia is surrounded by water on most sides. Use the map above to locate and name the bodies of water from the eastern side of Asia to the western side. Asia also has four major peninsulas. A peninsula is an area of land that is connected to a larger land and is surrounded by water on most sides. Asia's four major peninsulas are labeled on the map. What are their names?

6. HUMAN-ENVIRONMENT INTERACTION

Examine the Effect of Physical Processes Monsoons are great winds that blow across Southeast Asia and India every winter and summer. Winter monsoons blow dry air across the land and push clouds away from land toward the oceans. Summer monsoons blow clouds and moist air across the land, creating great rains. The map below shows the land use and monsoons in Asia. Read the following descriptions. Then use the map to answer the questions.

A. This country is on a peninsula that juts out into the Indian Ocean. The Bay of Bengal borders its east coast. What's the name of this country? What is most of the land used for in this country?

B. This is a large country with a long eastern coast. Nomadic herding takes place in the western half of the country. Wet monsoons blow from the south, affecting the southeastern coast. What is the name of the country?

C. Find Southeast Asia on the map. Much of this area has a tropical wet climate. What kind of monsoon affects this area the most? What two types of farming take place in this region?

Asia: Land Use and Monsoons

KEY
- Nomadic herding
- Hunting and gathering
- Forestry
- Livestock raising
- Commercial farming
- Subsistence farming
- Manufacturing and trade
- Little or no activity
- → Wet monsoon
- ← Dry monsoon

Two-Point Equidistant Projection

ACTIVITY ATLAS

Take It to the NET

Rainforests in Asia

KEY

- Present extent of rain forest
- Ancient extent of rain forest

Two-Point Equidistant Projection

7. HUMAN-ENVIRONMENT INTERACTION

Examine the Impact of People on the Environment Southeast Asia has high rainfall and is located near the Equator. As a result, much of the region was once covered with rain forest. In recent decades, many of these forests have disappeared. They are cut down by farmers who need land. Other forests are cleared by timber companies seeking wood for sale to other countries. Look at the map. Which nations have lost all of their rain forests? Where would you go to find the largest remaining rain forest?

Asia's Biggest

SIZE OF CONTINENTS

Australia
2,989,000 sq mi
(7,741,000 sq km)

Antarctica
5,400,000 sq mi
(14,000,000 sq km)

Europe
4,015,000 sq mi
(10,3398,000 sq km)

Africa
11,657,000 sq mi
(30,190,000 sq km)

South America
6,889,000 sq mi
(17,868,000 sq km)

North America
9,347,000 sq mi
(24,208,000 sq km)

Asia
16,992,000 sq mi
(44,008,000 sq km)

8. PLACE
Compare Physical Features

Study these charts and diagrams. They compare features of Asia with those of the rest of the world. How many of the world's seven longest rivers are in Asia? What is Asia's longest river? What percentage of the world's population lives in Asia? How many of the world's five highest mountains are in Asia? Where is Mount Everest located? List the three largest continents from largest to smallest.

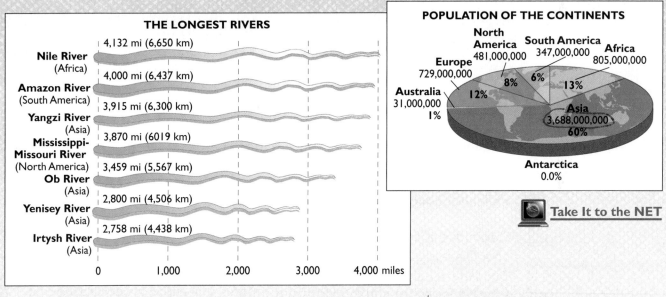

THE LONGEST RIVERS

River	Length
Nile River (Africa)	4,132 mi (6,650 km)
Amazon River (South America)	4,000 mi (6,437 km)
Yangzi River (Asia)	3,915 mi (6,300 km)
Mississippi-Missouri River (North America)	3,870 mi (6019 km)
Ob River (Asia)	3,459 mi (5,567 km)
Yenisey River (Asia)	2,800 mi (4,506 km)
Irtysh River (Asia)	2,758 mi (4,438 km)

0   1,000   2,000   3,000   4,000 miles

POPULATION OF THE CONTINENTS

North America 481,000,000 — 8%
South America 347,000,000 — 6%
Africa 805,000,000 — 13%
Europe 729,000,000 — 12%
Australia 31,000,000 — 1%
Asia 3,688,000,000 — 60%
Antarctica 0.0%

Take It to the NET

WORLD'S HIGHEST MOUNTAINS

feet: 30,000 / 25,000 / 20,000 / 15,000 / 10,000 / 5,000 / 0

Mt. Everest
29,035 ft./8,850 m
Nepal/Tibet, Asia

K2
28,250 ft./8,611 m
Pakistan, Asia

Kangchenjunga
28,169 ft./8,586 m
Nepal, Asia

Lhotse
27,920 ft./8,501 m
Nepal, Asia

Makalu I
26,758 ft./8,156 m
Nepal, Asia

ASIA:
Physical
Geography

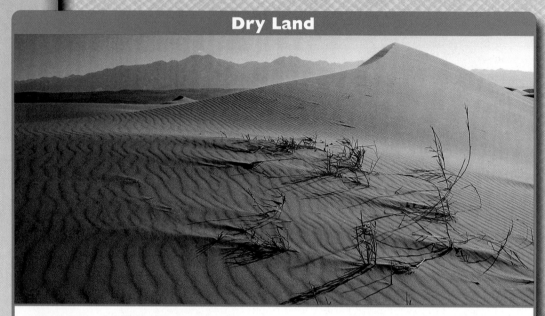

Dry Land

USING PICTURES

The Gobi is Asia's largest desert. Barren lands stretch for approximately 500,000 square miles across China and Mongolia. Very little rain falls here. The word "Gobi" is a Mongolian word meaning "place without water." Yet even with harsh weather and little water, people, plants, and animals manage to survive in this desert.

Charting a Trip across the Desert

Find and trace a map of the Gobi. Draw a dotted line on the map to chart the path of a trip you might take by truck through it. Use the map scale to determine how many miles you are planning to travel. To decide how many miles to travel each day, first answer these questions:

• How many miles an hour do you think your truck can travel across the desert sand?

• What might slow you down? How much time will you plan for emergencies and rest?

Keeping a Travel Journal

People who live in desert climates have devised ways of preserving water and staying cool during the day and warm at night. Research the Gobi's animals, plants, people, land, and weather. Then, use the information you find to write a journal about your desert travel. Describe what you think it feels like to spend nights and days in the desert. What discoveries, setbacks, or dangers might you encounter? Give details using all of your senses—sight, sound, smell, taste, and touch.

SECTION 1

Physical Features

BEFORE YOU READ

READING FOCUS

1. How have physical processes shaped the landscape of Asia?
2. Why are rivers important natural resources in Asia?
3. How do geographic factors affect where people live in Asia?

KEY TERMS

subcontinent

KEY PLACES

Himalaya Mountains
Yangzi
Huang He
Ganges River
Indus River
Tigris River
Euphrates River

NOTE TAKING

Copy the chart below. As you read the section, fill in the chart with information about Asia's physical features and population distribution.

	Major Landforms or Vegetation Regions	Major Bodies of Water	Major Areas of Population
Indian Subcontinent			
Southeast Asia			
Southwest and Central Asia			

MAIN IDEA

Asia's natural resources include rivers that provide water and transportation, and fertile valleys where it is easiest for people to live and grow food.

Setting the Scene

Two hundred million years ago, the land now called the Indian **subcontinent,** in the region of South Asia, was attached to the east coast of Africa. A subcontinent is a large landmass that is a major part of a continent. Scientists believe that at one time, all of the Earth's continents were joined.

About 200 million years ago, the land shifted and cracked and the continents began to break apart. The Indian subcontinent split off from Africa and crept slowly toward Asia. The landmass moved so slowly that it took about four years to travel the length of an average pencil.

About 40 million years ago, the Indian subcontinent collided with Asia. Just as the front ends of cars crumple in a traffic accident, northern India and southern Asia crumpled where they met. This area is the huge **Himalayan Mountain** range, which contains the tallest peaks in the world.

The Himalaya Mountains

GEOGRAPHY A stream fed by melting snow zigzags down through the rugged Himalaya Mountains in the Lahaul Valley of northern India. **Critical Thinking** Using the map on page 452, name two rivers whose sources are in the Himalaya Mountains.

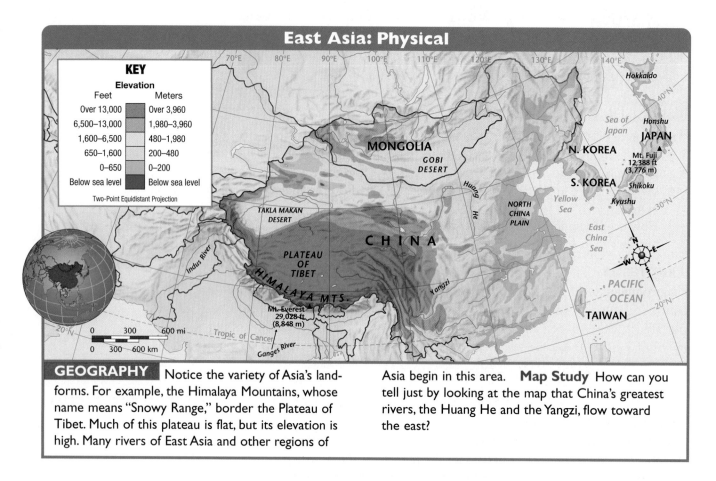

East Asia: Physical

KEY

Elevation

Feet	Meters
Over 13,000	Over 3,960
6,500–13,000	1,980–3,960
1,600–6,500	480–1,980
650–1,600	200–480
0–650	0–200
Below sea level	Below sea level

Two-Point Equidistant Projection

GEOGRAPHY Notice the variety of Asia's landforms. For example, the Himalaya Mountains, whose name means "Snowy Range," border the Plateau of Tibet. Much of this plateau is flat, but its elevation is high. Many rivers of East Asia and other regions of Asia begin in this area. **Map Study** How can you tell just by looking at the map that China's greatest rivers, the Huang He and the Yangzi, flow toward the east?

Powerful Physical Processes

Mountain ranges in China, northeast of India, also were formed by the collision of these two landmasses. This ancient mountain-building process continues today. Scientists estimate that Mount Everest is "growing" about 2 inches (5 cm) each year. Everest, the world's tallest mountain, rises 29,035 feet (8,850 m), or about five and a half miles high!

Farther east of China, natural forces also shaped the islands of Japan as earthquakes forced some parts of the earth to rise and others to sink. Erupting volcanoes piled up mountains of lava and ash, forming new mountains. Today, in many parts of Asia, earthquakes and volcanoes are still changing the landscape. Most of the islands here are mountainous because they are the peaks of underwater volcanoes.

Life Giving Rivers

Asia has many rivers which are natural resources providing not only water, but also means of transportation. One is China's **Yangzi** (yang ZEE), which flows 3,915 miles (6,300 km) to the East China Sea and is the only river in East Asia that is deep enough for cargo ships to sail on. More than 400 million people live along the banks of another river, the **Huang He** (hwahng hay), which runs through a fertile region called the North China Plain.

Mountain Beginnings   The two most important rivers in the region of South Asia—the **Ganges** and the **Indus**—begin high in the Himalaya Mountains.

The Ganges River flows in a wide sweeping arc across northern India while the Indus flows westward from the Himalaya Mountains into the country of Pakistan.

Rivers carry from the mountains the water and minerals necessary for good farming. The plains around the rivers, therefore, are quite fertile and, as a result, heavily populated.

Rivers in the Dry World   The regions of Southwest and Central Asia are nicknamed "the Dry World" because they contain some of the largest deserts on Earth. The Rub al-Khali is almost as big as the state of Texas. The Kara Kum covers 70 percent of Turkmenistan (turk men ih STAHN). While few plants grow in Southwest and Central Asian deserts, some of the most fertile soil in the world lies along the **Tigris, Euphrates** (yoo FRAYT eez), and Ural rivers. When these rivers flood, they deposit rich soil along their banks, soil that is good for growing crops. So, more people live in river valleys than anywhere else in the region.

Rivers are not only important as sources of water. They also provide means of transportation. The Tigris and Euphrates rivers, for example, both begin in Turkey and make their way south. They combine to form the Shatt-al-Arab Channel, in Iraq. This channel empties into the Persian Gulf, and gives Iraq its only outlet to the sea.

East Asia: Population Density

KEY

Persons per sq mi	Persons per sq km
520 and over	200 and over
260–519	100–199
130–259	50–99
25–129	10–49
1–24	1–9
Under 1	Under 1

Cities

☐ 10,000,000 and over
■ 5,000,000–9,999,999
○ 2,000,000–4,999,999

Two-Point Equidistant Projection

GEOGRAPHY   As you can see, the largest number of China's people is found in the east central part of the country.   **Map Study** Why do you think the population density is the way it is?

Geography and Population

As you can see on the map on the previous page, the population of East Asia is not spread evenly across the land because few people live in the deserts, highlands, and mountains. Yet, almost 1.5 billion people make their homes in China, North Korea, South Korea, and Japan. This means that people crowd into the lowland and coastal areas and these parts of East Asia have a very high population density, or average number of people living in a square mile (or square km).

In East Asia, level ground is scarce and must be shared by cities, farms, and industries. For example, almost half the population of Japan is crowded on less than 3 percent of the country's total land. Most of the population of China is located in the east.

Although East Asia is largely a rural region, and about 75 percent of China's people live in rural areas, East Asia also has some of the largest cities in the world. In Japan, 80 percent of the people live in cities, and in South Korea, Seoul, the capital city, has a population of more than 10 million.

Mainland Southeast Asia   The nations of mainland Southeast Asia are Vietnam, Cambodia, Laos (LAH ohs), Myanmar (MY AHN mar), and Thailand (TY land). Southeast Asia is about one-fifth the size of the United States. Much of this area is covered by forested mountains but most people live in the narrow river valleys between mountain ranges. Just as on the Indian subcontinent, rivers flow from the north and provide river valleys with the water and minerals necessary to grow crops.

GEOGRAPHY

Seoul, seen here at dusk, is one of East Asia's most densely populated cities. **Critical Thinking** Judging from this photograph, how do you think geographic factors affect population density in Seoul?

SECTION I ASSESSMENT

AFTER YOU READ

RECALL

1. Identify: (a) Himalaya Mountains, (b) Yangzi, (c) Huang He, (d) Ganges River, (e) Indus River, (f) Tigris River, (g) Euphrates River

2. Define: (a) subcontinent

COMPREHENSION

3. How did the collision of two landmasses shape the landforms of northern India and southern Asia?

4. In what two ways are the Tigris and Euphrates rivers important natural resources for people in Southwest Asia?

CRITICAL THINKING AND WRITING

5. **Exploring the Main Idea** Review the Main Idea statement at the beginning of this section. Then, write a paragraph describing the physical features of Asia.

6. **Supporting a Point of View** You are a travel agent with a client who wants to visit East Asia. Which landforms would you suggest that your client visit?

ACTIVITY

 Take It to the NET

7. **Journeying through the Himalayas** Imagine that you are a traveler who has come to explore the Himalayas. Use the information on the web site to write a journal account of your journey through the Himalayas. Visit the World Explorer: People, Places, and Cultures section of **phschool.com** for help in completing this activity.

Humans and the Physical Environment

READING FOCUS

1. How does the physical environment affect people's lives in Southwest Asia?
2. How does the physical environment affect people's lives in East Asia?
3. How does the physical environment affect people's lives in South and Southeast Asia?

KEY TERMS

arable land
monsoon

scarce

MAIN IDEA

Throughout Asia, humans must adapt to difficult, and sometimes dangerous, physical environments.

NOTE TAKING

Copy the outline below. As you read the section, fill in the outline with information about how the physical environment affects people's lives in Asia.

I. **Aspects and effects of the physical environment**
   A.
      1. Dry climate - People must adapt farming methods
      2. Limited arable land —
   B. East, South, and Southeast Asia
      1.
      2. Tropical climate (Southeast Asia) —

Setting the Scene

Muhammad bin Abdallah Al Shaykh (MOO ham ud BIN ub dul LAH AL SHAYK) and his family raise crops on what was once a huge, sandy plain in Saudi Arabia. Only thornscrub, a kind of short, stubby shrub, grows here. Before Muhammad and his family could grow any crops on their land, they had to drill a well more than 600 feet (183 m) deep.

Muhammad's family also dug irrigation canals throughout their 20 acres (8 hectares) of farmland. After they planted trees to help pro-tect the farm from the fierce desert winds, they planted date palms. Dates are an important crop in Southwest Asia because the palms survive well in desert conditions.

Dates are not the only crop grown by Muhammad's family. They also grow cucumbers, toma-toes, corn, and large crops of al-falfa. The extremely long roots of alfalfa plants can find moisture deeper in the ground. Growing plants with long roots is one way that farmers adapt to a climate of hot summers and cool winters.

The Date Palm
ECONOMICS

Muhammad bin Abdallah Al Shaykh inspects one of the date palms on his farm. These trees produce a sweet, nourishing fruit. In addition, the trunk pro-vides timber, and leaves provide fuel and the mak-ings of baskets and rope. **Critical Thinking** Why is the date palm a good plant to raise for sale?

Use Prior Knowledge
What parts of the
United States have
plenty of arable land?

Adapting to Harsh Conditions

Southwest Asia is a region of huge climate extremes. It has scorching summers and bitterly cold winters. In some places, temperatures change drastically every day. Southwest Asia is among the largest dry regions on the Earth. Water is a **scarce** resource there. A scarce resource is one that does not exist in sufficient quantities to satisfy all desires to use it.

Most workers in Southwest Asia work on farms. In Turkey and Syria, agriculture is the most important economic activity. But the amount of **arable land,** or land that can produce crops, is limited. In some places, the soil is not fertile or mountains make it hard to farm. Under such conditions, people have a hard time making a living.

A River in Flood

GEOGRAPHY

Like the Huang He, the Yangzi, China's other great river, sometimes floods. A 1998 flood was the worst in 44 years, killing 4,100 people and causing about $30 billion in damage. Here, three workers in Wuhan visit their store by rowboat. **Critical Thinking** How might a river like the Yangzi be both a blessing and a curse for the people living along its banks?

The Influence of Climate

Climate greatly affects life in East Asia. In China, the region around the Huang He, or Yellow River, is a good example. The river gets its name from the brownish yellow dirt that is blown by the desert winds. The river picks up the dirt and deposits it to the east on the North China Plain. The plain is a huge 125,000 square mile (32,375,000 hectare) area around the river and one of the best farming areas in China.

The river, nicknamed "China's Sorrow," is both a blessing and a curse for Chinese farmers who live along its banks because the Huang He can overflow its banks during the monsoons. **Monsoons** are winds that blow across the region at certain times of the year. In summer, Pacific Ocean winds blow west toward the Asian continent. They cause hot, humid weather and heavy rain.

In winter, the winds blow toward the east and bring cooler, drier air to the continent. In parts of China, the winter monsoons produce dust storms that last for days. Where they cross warm ocean waters, such as those of the South China Sea, these monsoons pick up moisture that later drops as rain or snow.

Stormy Asia

The monsoon rains in Asia provide water for half the world's population. But they affect life in South Asia in other ways as well. In India, students start school in June, after the first rains have fallen. Their long vacation comes during the spring, when hot, stifling temperatures make it hard to concentrate at school.

In Nepal, fierce monsoon rains can bring mudslides that destroy entire villages. The mud comes from hills that have been stripped of their trees. In Bangladesh, swollen rivers can overflow and flood two-thirds of the land.

Much of Southeast Asia has a tropical wet climate and is covered with rain forests. Vietnam owes its lush coastal rain forests to the winter monsoons. As these winter winds blow south from China toward Vietnam, they cross the South China Sea. The air picks up moisture, which falls as rain when the air reaches the coast.

The rain forests of Southeast Asia are lush and thick. However, there are disadvantages to living in the tropical climate of Southeast Asia—typhoons. When typhoons hit land, the high winds and heavy rain often lead to widespread property damage and loss of life.

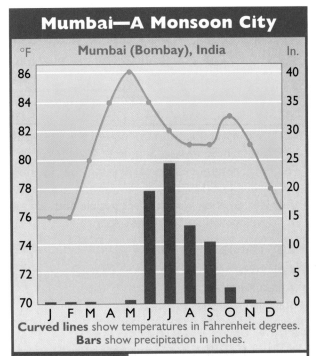

Mumbai—A Monsoon City

Mumbai (Bombay), India

Curved lines show temperatures in Fahrenheit degrees. **Bars** show precipitation in inches.

GEOGRAPHY This climate graph shows the average monthly temperature and precipitation for Mumbai (Bombay), India. As you can see on the graph, heavy rainfall starts in June. This marks the beginning of the summer monsoons. **Chart Study** What effect do the summer monsoon winds have on the temperature in Mumbai?

SECTION 2 ASSESSMENT

AFTER YOU READ

RECALL

1. Define: (a) arable land, (b) monsoon

COMPREHENSION

2. Analyze how farmers in Southwest Asia adapt to their physical environment, including extreme climates.

3. How do monsoons affect people's lives in South Asia?

4. What is one disadvantage to living in the tropical climate of Southeast Asia?

CRITICAL THINKING AND WRITING

5. **Exploring the Main Idea** Review the Main Idea statement at the beginning of this section. Then, make a list of different features of the physical environment in Asia, and how these features affect people's lives.

6. **Recognizing Cause and Effect** The climate of South Asia, and the lives of the people who live there, are greatly affected by the presence of the Himalaya Mountains. How

might the climate and lives of the people of South Asia be different if the Himalaya Mountains were not there? Write a paragraph to answer.

ACTIVITY

7. **Writing a Letter** You are traveling through Asia with a tour group. Write a letter to a friend or family member at home describing the different climates and vegetation where you have visited, and how they compare to the climate and vegetation where you live.

Geographic Factors and Natural Resources

BEFORE YOU READ

READING FOCUS

1. What natural resources do people use to make a living in South and Southeast Asia?
2. What natural resources do people use to make a living in East Asia?
3. How does oil wealth affect people and economic development in Southwest Asia?

KEY TERMS

cash crop
aquaculture
standard of living

MAIN IDEA

Land and water resources, along with oil, contribute to the way most people in South and Southeast Asia make their living.

NOTE TAKING

Copy this diagram. As you read the section, complete the diagram to show key resources in Asia and the problems involved in using these resources.

	Key Resources		Problems in Using Resources
South & Southeast Asia	cash crops such as tea and rubber	⇨	
East Asia	Precious metals & mineral resources	⇨	
Southwest Asia		⇨	

Harvesting Tea

ECONOMICS Tea is an important cash crop in the island nation of Sri Lanka. These workers can pick about 40 pounds (18 kg) of tea a day. **Critical Thinking** What might happen to the people of Sri Lanka if tea prices fell very low?

Setting the Scene

If you had been born in a small village in Thailand, you would probably live in a bamboo house built on stilts near a river. During the monsoon rains, the river might flood, and you would paddle home after school in a small boat. During the dry season, your family's prized possession, a water buffalo, would live between the stilts under your house. There it would be safe from wild animals.

Most of your time would be spent growing rice. Soon after planting seeds in boxes, you would transplant the sprouts to the fields just before the rains. Throughout the growing season, you would keep the fields flooded. You would carefully weed between the rice plants, using a knife or a sickle. All this is hard but necessary work. In Thailand, as in much of Asia, rice is the most important part of all meals.

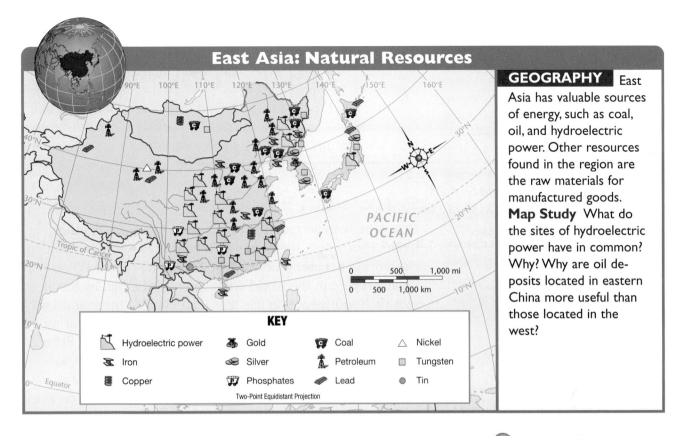

East Asia: Natural Resources

GEOGRAPHY East Asia has valuable sources of energy, such as coal, oil, and hydroelectric power. Other resources found in the region are the raw materials for manufactured goods. **Map Study** What do the sites of hydroelectric power have in common? Why? Why are oil deposits located in eastern China more useful than those located in the west?

KEY

Hydroelectric power	Gold	Coal	△ Nickel
Iron	Silver	Petroleum	▢ Tungsten
Copper	Phosphates	Lead	● Tin

Two-Point Equidistant Projection

PACIFIC OCEAN

Land and Water: Precious Resources

Most of the people of South and Southeast Asia make their living from the land. They live in small villages clustered along the fertile valleys of the region's mighty rivers where they build their own homes, often from bamboo, and grow their own food. Some use the same building and farming methods that their ancestors relied upon thousands of years ago.

Some countries of South and Southeast Asia produce cash crops such as tea, cotton, and rubber. A **cash crop** is one that is raised to be sold for money on the world market.

Cash crops often bring in a great deal of money, but they may also cause problems by making the economies of a region dependent on world prices for the crops. When prices are high, the people who produce the crops are able to buy food. But when world prices fall, the cash crops do not bring in enough money. Because they cannot eat tea or rubber, the people who produce these crops sometimes go hungry.

Using East Asia's Resources

The Pacific Ocean is an important resource for food in East Asia. Some people in East Asia catch fish using poles, nets, and even trained birds, called cormorants. But fishing is also a big business. Huge boats owned by corporations catch large numbers of fish and shellfish.

East Asians also practice **aquaculture,** or sea farming. In shallow bays throughout the area, people raise fish in huge cages and artificial reefs provide beds for shrimp and oysters. The lakes and rivers of

LINKS TO
Science

India's Salt Lake
During the hot months, the 90-square-mile (230-sq-km) Sambhar Lake in northwestern India is dry. Oddly, during this time the lake bed looks as though it is covered in snow. The white blanket is not snow but a sheet of salt. This salt supply was harvested as far back as the 1500s. It is an important resource for the region even today.

Working Together

During the Persian Gulf War of 1991, after the Iraqi Army set fire to Kuwait's oil wells, a group of brave oil-firefighters from Texas, led by a man named Red Adair, saved the day. Working with Kuwaitis, they smothered the fires with nitrogen. The work was dangerous; firefighters breathed smoke; the heat melted desert sands into glass. It took eight months to put out the fires.

China are also important sources of food. In fact, almost twice as many freshwater fish are caught in China as in any other country in the world.

Although East Asia's lands and waters are filled with natural resources, some are too difficult or too expensive to obtain. The resource map on page 459 will help you understand the distribution of this region's natural resources.

Petroleum: Black Gold

Petroleum can be found in only a few places around the globe. As a result, petroleum-rich countries play a key role in the world's economy. Southwest Asia is the largest oil-producing region in the world and is greatly affected by its oil wealth. Southwest Asia has more than half of the world's oil reserves, but some countries in the region have little or no oil. These countries tend to have a lower **standard of living,** or quality of life, than their oil-rich neighbors because they do not have the income that petroleum brings. However, these countries benefit from oil wealth income another way. When their citizens work in oil-rich nations, they bring money home.

Kazakstan is one of three Central Asian countries that contain large oil reserves. Uzbekistan (ooz BEK ih stan) and Turkmenistan are the others. They have developed less of their petroleum reserves than other nations in Southwest Asia. Many countries want to help Kazakstan and its neighbors develop a larger oil industry. They offer equipment, training, and loans, in return for a share in the wealth.

SECTION 3 ASSESSMENT

AFTER YOU READ

RECALL
1. Define (a) cash crop, (b) aquaculture, (c) standard of living

COMPREHENSION
2. How do people in South and Southeast Asia use land and water resources?
3. How do people in East Asia use the Pacific Ocean as a resource for food?
4. How might Southwest Asian countries work together to best use the oil reserves of the region?

CRITICAL THINKING AND WRITING
5. **Exploring the Main Idea** Review the Main Idea statement at the beginning of this section. Then, write a paragraph explaining how natural resources affect the standard of living in different regions.
6. **Writing to Learn** The economy of Southwest Asia depends on oil and on water. (There are few permanent water sources in the region.) Write a 1-page report explaining ways in which water and oil can be conserved.

ACTIVITY
7. **Learning about Gems** The mineral wealth of South and Southeast Asia includes valuable gems. Myanmar, Thailand, Sri Lanka, and India are the source of fine rubies and sapphires. Do research in the library or on the Internet to find out more about the kinds of gems found in Asia and how the resources contribute to the various countries' economies. Share your findings in a class presentation.

Analyzing Images

Learn the Skill

You encounter images every day in your life—on television, in newspapers and magazines, and on the Internet. These images convey information, communicate ideas, and influence attitudes. It is important to know how to read these images, just as it is to know how to read the words on this page. Follow these steps to learn how to analyze images:

A. Identify the content of the image. Pay careful attention to all of the elements that make up the image. Which elements are the most important?

B. Identify the emotional elements in the image. Artists and photographers often use color and form to communicate their ideas and emotions. What feelings are conveyed by the elements of the image?

C. Identify and read any text that appears with the image. Often, an image will have a title, caption, or other text that can help you to analyze it. What does the text tell you about the image?

D. Identify the purpose of the image. Images are created for many different reasons. Some provide information, some try to persuade, and others are meant to entertain. Thinking about why an image was created can help you better understand it.

E. Respond to the image. Identify the emotions the image causes you to feel. Think about how these emotions relate to the purpose of the image. How effective is the image in its intended purpose?

Practice the Skill

Practice analyzing the image "Mount Haruna" by reviewing the steps you learned and answering the questions that follow.

View of Mount Haruna Under the Snow, Japanese print, early 1800's

- What are some of the important elements in this print? Which element is the most important? Why?
- How does the artist use color to convey emotion in this print?
- What information about the print does the caption provide?
- Why do you think this print was created? What is its purpose?
- What emotions and feelings does this print convey?

Apply the Skill

See the Chapter Review and Assessment at the end of this chapter for more questions on analyzing images.

Creating a Chapter Summary

On a separate piece of paper, draw a diagram like this one, and include the information that summarizes the first section of the chapter. Then, fill in the remaining boxes with summaries of Sections 2 and 3.

ASIA: PHYSICAL GEOGRAPHY

Section 1
Natural forces have shaped Asia's physical landscape and continue to do so today. The world's tallest mountains and some of the world's largest deserts are found in Asia. There are also many important rivers.

Section 2

Section 3

Reviewing Key Terms

Read each statement below. Decide whether it is true or false. If it is false, rewrite the underlined portion to make the statement true.

1. A country's standard of living refers to <u>the size of its population</u>.

2. A <u>subcontinent</u> is a large landmass that is a major part of a continent.

3. If land is <u>arable</u>, it can produce crops.

4. East Asians practice aquaculture, which <u>raises crops to be sold for money</u>.

5. <u>Monsoons</u> are winds that blow across East Asia at certain times of the year.

Reviewing the Main Ideas

1. Name two natural forces that shaped Asia's landscape. (Section 1)

2. What do rivers provide for people in Asia? (Section 1)

3. Why is population density high in areas such as coastal lowlands and river valleys? (Section 1)

4. How does limited arable land affect the lives of people in Southwest Asia? (Section 2)

5. How do monsoons affect the lives of people in East and South Asia? (Section 2)

6. What benefits has Southwest Asia gained from its oil reserves? (Section 2)

7. What are two natural resources that people in South, Southeast, and East Asia use to make their living? (Section 3)

Map Activity

Asia

For each place listed below, write the letter from the map that shows its location.

1. Ganges River
2. Indus River
3. Thailand
4. Himalaya Mountains
5. Yangzi
6. Huang He
7. Sri Lanka

 Take It to the NET

Enrichment For more map activities using geography skills, visit the social studies section of **phschool.com**.

Writing Activity

1. **Writing a Report** China's Huang He has created rich soil for the surrounding lands. This makes these lands the best agricultural areas in China. However, China's monsoon season causes the river to overflow frequently. Do some research to find out how people protect fields from flood damage. Write a report that contains suggestions for the farmers who live along the banks of the Huang He to protect their crops.

2. **Writing a Pamphlet** In order to have enough water to meet the needs of the population, irrigation systems must be used throughout Southwest Asia. Sometimes these irrigation systems can cause environmental problems or deprive other countries of water. Select a country in Southwest Asia. Write a pamphlet that describes the advantages a dam might bring to this country. Also, mention possible problems the dam might bring and offer solutions to those problems.

Applying Your Skills

Turn to the Skills for Life activity on p. 461 to help you complete the following activity.

Choose an image from a newspaper or magazine and analyze it. Record your analysis on a sheet of paper.

Critical Thinking

1. **Drawing Conclusions** The Yangzi is the only river in East Asia that is deep enough for cargo ships to sail on. How might this affect the population density of the lands surrounding the river? Of East Asia?

2. **Recognizing Cause and Effect** Most of Southwest Asia has an arid or semi-arid climate. What are two effects of this lack of water?

 Take It to the NET

Activity Explore Asia's vast and diverse physical features. Create a map of Asia that includes major geographical features such as mountain ranges, rivers, lakes, and forest areas. Visit the World Explorer: People, Places, and Cultures section of **phschool.com** for help in completing this activity.

Chapter 24 Self-Test As a final review activity, take the Chapter 24 Self-Test and get instant feedback on your answers. To take the test, visit the Social Studies section of **phschool.com**.

ASIA: Shaped by History

Mohandas K. Gandhi

"He was perhaps the greatest symbol of the India of the past, and of the future…. We stand on this perilous edge of the present, between the past and the future, and we face all manner of perils. And the greatest peril is sometimes the lack of faith which comes to us, the sense of frustration that comes to us, the sinking of the heart and of the spirit that comes to us when we see ideals go overboard, when we see the great things that we talked about somehow pass into empty words, and life taking a different course. Yet, I do believe that perhaps this period will pass soon enough."

—*Jawaharlal Nehru*

USING SPEECHES

Mohandas K. Gandhi (1869–1948) was a greatly beloved spiritual and political leader in India who played an important role in India gaining its freedom from Great Britain in 1947. Jawaharlal Nehru, India's first Prime Minister, delivered this speech in 1948 after Gandhi's death.

Understanding the Speech

In his speech, Nehru speaks of the perils, or dangers, that face the new nation of India, and "the sinking of the heart and spirit" that comes when ideals are lost. Do research to find out what some of the perils faced by India were, and what happened after Gandhi's death. Why do you think people felt discouraged at Gandhi's death?

Writing a Speech

Great speechmakers often use repetition of phrases to create a sense of rhythm when they talk. Examine Nehru's speech for words or phrases that are repeated. Read the speech aloud, listening for the repetition. Then, prepare a short speech on a topic that you feel strongly about, using repetition to emphasize key points in your speech. Present your speech to the class.

SECTION 1

East Asia

BEFORE YOU READ

READING FOCUS

1. What are some of ancient East Asia's major achievements?
2. How did culture traits spread within East Asia and from East Asia to the West?
3. How did Western trade pressure contribute to the rise of communist nations in East Asia after World War II?

KEY TERMS

civilization
emperor
dynasty
migration

clan
cultural diffusion

MAIN IDEA

Discoveries and advances in science, technology, and the arts spread within East Asia and to Western nations before conflicts within and beyond East Asia erupted during World War II.

NOTE TAKING

Copy the diagram below. As you read the section, fill in the diagram to show causes and effects in East Asian history.

Cause	Effects
• Chinese wanted to keep rest of the world out	• Built Great Wall of China

Setting the Scene

Over two thousand years ago, Confucius (kun FYOO shus), one of the most important thinkers of ancient times, advised his pupils:

"Let the ruler be a ruler and the subject be a subject."

"A youth, when at home, should act with respect to his parents, and, abroad, be respectful to his elders."

Confucius taught that everyone has duties and responsibilities. If a person acts correctly, the result will be peace and harmony. Confucius' ideas helped both China's government run smoothly for years and Chinese culture to last for centuries.

East Asia's Achievements

A **civilization** has cities, a central government, workers who do specialized jobs, and social classes. Of the world's early civilizations, only China's has survived. This makes it the oldest continuous civilization in the world.

The Glory That Was China   For much of its history, China had little to do with the rest of the world. The Great Wall of China—started before 206 B.C.—is a symbol of China's desire to keep the

Statue of Confucius

CULTURE   This statue of Confucius stands in the Chinatown section of New York City.   **Critical Thinking** Why do you think that Chinese people all over the world still admire Confucius?

AS YOU READ

Monitor Your Reading
Think of two questions
you might ask about
the achievements of
China.

world at a distance. Chinese leaders named their country the Middle Kingdom because to them, it was the center of the universe.

The Chinese had reason to be proud. They invented paper, gunpowder, silk weaving, the magnetic compass, the printing press, clockwork, the spinning wheel, and the water wheel. Chinese engineers were experts at digging canals, building dams and bridges, and setting up irrigation systems.

Ancient China was governed by an **emperor**—a ruler of widespread lands and groups of people. A series of rulers from the same family was a **dynasty.** Chinese history is described by dynasties.

Migration Influences Korea Around 1200 B.C., during a time of troubles in China, some Chinese migrated to the Korean Peninsula. A **migration** is a movement of people from one country or region to another to make a new home. Later, other Chinese settled in the southern part of the peninsula. These migrations led to a transfer of Chinese knowledge and customs to the Koreans.

Years of Japanese Isolation For much of Japan's history, **clans,** or groups of families who claimed a common ancestor, fought each other for land and power. Around A.D. 500, one clan, the Yamato (yah mah toh), became powerful. Claiming descent from the sun goddess, Yamato leaders took the title of "emperor." Many emperors sat on Japan's throne. For a long time they had little power. Instead, shoguns (SHOH gunz), or "emperor's generals," made the laws. Warrior nobles, the samurai (SAM uh rye), enforced these laws. Together, the shoguns and samurai ruled Japan for more than 700 years.

Japanese leaders came to believe that isolation, or separation, was the best way to keep the country united. Thus, Japan was isolated from the outside world from 1640 to 1853.

HISTORY The time line highlights some important events and cultural contributions of several dynasties.
Chart Study Under which dynasty do you think China made the most important achievements? Why?

Major Dynasties of China

1500 B.C.	1000 B.C.	500 B.C.	A.D. 1	A.D. 500	A.D. 1000	A.D. 1500

Shang
1700 B.C.–1100 B.C.
• Writing
• Wheeled chariots

Zhou
1100 B.C.–256 B.C.
• Confucius lived
• First canals built

Qin
221 B.C.–206 B.C.
• China took its name from this dynasty
• Great Wall built
• Standard weights and measures

Han
206 B.C.—A.D. 220
• Chinese trace their ancestry to this dynasty
• Paper, compass, seismograph invented
• Buddhism comes to China from India

Tang
A.D. 618—A.D. 907
• Art and poetry flourish
• Chinese goods flow to Southwest Asia and Europe
• First book printed

Song
A.D. 960—A.D. 1279
• Block printing and paper money

Ming
A.D. 1368—A.D. 1644
• Artists and philosophers make China a highly civilized country

Qing
A.D. 1644—A.D. 1911
• Last dynasty ends with Emperor Pu Yi

Events in Japanese History

c. 300 B.C.
Japanese learn irrigated rice cultivation and metalworking from Asian continent.

Swords were the weapons of the samurai.

A.D. *c.* 538
Buddhism is introduced.

A.D. 1000
A woman writes the world's first novel, *The Tale of Genji.*

A.D. 1853
Commodore Perry and American warships arrive in Japan. Japanese then agree to trade with the United States and other nations.

A.D. 1543
Portuguese traders introduce guns and Christianity.

| 400 B.C. | A.D. I | A.D. 400 | A.D. 800 | A.D. 1200 | A.D. 1600 |

A.D. 405
Japan accepts Chinese characters to write Japanese.

A.D. 712
Japan's first history and poetry collections are put together.

A.D. 1640
Japan closes its borders to the rest of the world.

Culture Traits Spread

In ancient times, China led the world in inventions and discoveries. Many Chinese discoveries then spread to Korea and Japan. This **cultural diffusion,** or spreading of ideas, happened early and the teachings of Confucius were among the first ideas to be passed along. The religion of Buddhism (BOOD izm), which China had adopted from India, later spread to Korea and Japan.

Cultural diffusion was not always friendly. For example, Korean potters so impressed the Japanese that they were captured and taken back to Japan in 1598. East Asian culture owes much to early exchanges among China, Japan, and Korea. The countries changed what they borrowed until the tradition became their own.

HISTORY Japan has interacted with outside nations except for one period in it history. **Chart Study** Name three examples of cultural diffusion shown in the time line.

Trade Pressure and Communism

Although at times East Asia was not interested in the rest of the world, the world was interested in East Asia. In the 1800s, Europeans and Americans began to produce great amounts of manufactured goods. East Asia seemed like a good place to sell these products, so Western trading ships sailed to Asian ports.

In 1853, U.S. Commodore Matthew Perry sailed with four warships to Japan to force it to grant trading rights to the United States. The Japanese adapted Western ways and inventions that were useful to them, helping Japan to become the strongest nation in Asia.

The opening up of China was different. Foreign countries wanted to control parts of China and its wealth and it became clear that the country was not strong enough to protect itself as the British, French, Dutch, Russians, and Japanese gained control over parts of China. The United States feared losing the opportunity to share in China's riches and, in 1899, announced a policy opening China for trade with all nations equally. For a while, this halted efforts to divide up China.

Conflict and Communism   Many Chinese blamed the emperor for the growing foreign influence. In 1911, revolution broke out in China, the rule of emperors ended, and a republic was set up.

Meanwhile, Japan's leaders sought to control other Asian countries. They wanted to make sure that Japan would have resources to fuel its growing industries. Japanese attacks on other Asian and Pacific lands led to World War II in East Asia. Ultimately, the United States and its allies defeated Japan. The United States then helped Japan recover and create an elected government.

After World War II, civil war broke out in China. Some people, the Nationalists, wanted to strengthen China so it could manage its own affairs without other nations. Others, the Communists, wanted to break the power of the landlords and other wealthy people and drive out all foreign influences. The Communists won the civil war in 1949 and made China a communist nation.

After World War II, Korea was split in two. Communists ruled North Korea and South Korea turned to Western nations for support. In 1950, the two Koreas exploded into a bloody civil war when North Korea invaded South Korea. The United States and other United Nations countries sent 480,000 troops to help South Korea, while China sent troops to help North Korea. The war dragged on for three years, killing about 54,000 U.S. soldiers and as many as 1.8 million Korean soldiers and civilians. Neither side won. The battle line at the end of the war, in 1953, remains the border between the two Koreas today.

SECTION I ASSESSMENT

AFTER YOU READ

RECALL

1. Define: (a) civilization, (b) emperor, (c) dynasty, (d) migration, (e) clan, (f) cultural diffusion

COMPREHENSION

2. What are some major achievements of ancient East Asian civilizations?

3. How did China and North Korea change in the years after Western trade opened up with East Asia?

CRITICAL THINKING AND WRITING

4. Exploring the Main Idea Review the Main Idea statement at the beginning of this section. Then, choose an invention of the Chinese. Write a paragraph explaining why the invention is important or the difference that the invention might make in people's lives.

5. Making Inferences and Drawing Conclusions Write one or two sentences explaining why isolating a country from its neighbors might help keep it united.

ACTIVITY

 Take It to the NET

6. Mapping the Silk Road The ancient trade route known as the Silk Road was actually several routes connecting the cities and cultures of the east and west. Create a map outlining the Silk Road. Visit the World Explorer: People, Places, and Cultures section of **phschool.com** for help in completing this activity.

Southeast Asia

BEFORE YOU READ

READING FOCUS

1. How did culture traits spread from China, India, Southwest Asia, and Europe to Southeast Asia?
2. How did colonial rule influence Southeast Asia?

KEY PLACES

Angkor Wat

MAIN IDEA

Culture traits spread from other countries to Southeast Asia through conquest, trade, missions, and colonization.

NOTE TAKING

Copy the word web below. As you read the section, fill in the word web with information about how culture traits spread from other countries to Southeast Asia.

Setting the Scene

Deep in the rain forests of Cambodia lies the Hindu temple **Angkor Wat**—the largest temple in the world. It was built in the A.D. 1100s by the Khmer (kuh MEHR), whose empire included Cambodia and much of Laos, Thailand, and Vietnam. The empire enjoyed great wealth and it is said that the king, wearing gold and pearls, rode on an elephant whose tusks were wrapped in gold. The remains of Angkor Wat stand today as proof of the great civilization.

Culture and Conquest

From time to time, Chinese armies swept into Southeast Asia. In 111 B.C., the Chinese took over Vietnam and they ruled the country for more than 1,000 years. During that time, the Vietnamese began using Chinese ways of farming. They also began using the ideas of Confucius to run their government.

Angkor Wat

CULTURE Angkor Wat is almost one square mile (2.6 sq km) in area. Its inner walls are covered with carvings of figures from Hindu myths.
Critical Thinking Why do you think the Khmer built such a grand structure?

Religion   The Indians were another influence on Southeast Asia. For example, around A.D. 100, Indians introduced Hinduism to the region and, today, there are Hindus in Bali and parts of Malaysia. Buddhists eventually outnumbered Hindus in the region and today there are many Buddhists in Myanmar, Thailand, Laos, and Cambodia.

During the 800s and 900s, Arab traders introduced Islam to Southeast Asia. Today, Islam is the religion of millions in Malaysia, Indonesia, the southern Philippines, and other Asian countries.

European missionaries brought Christianity to the area in the 1500s. Today, most Filipinos are Christian and there are groups of Christians in other Southeast Asian countries, too.

From Colonial Rule to Independence

Europeans brought more than Christianity to Southeast Asia. Traders from Europe first arrived in the region in the 1500s. To gain control of the rich trade in silks, iron, silver, pearls, and spices, they built trading posts in the region. By the 1800s, European nations had gained control of most of Southeast Asia.

Colonial Rule in Southeast Asia, 1914

KEY

- Britain
- France
- Portugal
- The Netherlands
- United States

Names of present-day countries are shown in parentheses.

Two-Point Equidistant Projection

HISTORY   The United States was not the first Western power to rule the Philippines. The Spanish ruled these islands for 333 years. In 1898, the United States defeated Spain in the Spanish-American War and took control of the colony.   **Map Study**   Which country colonized the most land in Southeast Asia?

Effects of Colonial Rule Outside nations gained control of the Southeast Asian economy and forced their colonies to grow cash crops. On the island of Java, the Dutch forced farmers to grow and sell coffee. This caused rice production to fall, which meant that there was not enough food for people to eat.

Colonial rulers built a network of roads, bridges, and railroads in Southeast Asia making it easier to move people and goods across the region. The colonial powers also built schools and universities, which helped to produce skilled workers for colonial industries. These educated Southeast Asians would eventually lead the struggle for freedom.

Fighting for Freedom By the early 1900s, nationalists were organizing independence movements throughout Southeast Asia. During World War II, invading Japanese drove out European colonial powers and many Southeast Asians hoped that a Japanese victory would end colonialism in the region. However, Japanese rule proved to be as harsh as, or harsher than that of the former colonial powers.

After the Japanese were defeated in World War II, Western nations hoped to regain power in Southeast Asia. But Southeast Asians had other hopes; they wanted independence. In fact, most Southeast Asian countries did gain independence, though some, like Malaysia and Indonesia, had to fight for it.

After independence, the nations of Southeast Asia worked to create new governments. Some were democratic but others were controlled by dictators, leaders who have absolute power.

CITIZENSHIP

Working Together For Freedom

East Timor takes up half of a small island several hundred miles from the capital of Indonesia, Jakarta. A former Portuguese colony, East Timor was invaded by Indonesia in 1975 and ruled harshly. Some people, however, fought back. Carlos Filipe Ximenes Belo, a Roman Catholic bishop, and José Ramos-Horta, a politician, worked peacefully on behalf of the Timorese people. They were awarded the 1996 Nobel Peace Prize for their efforts. In 1999, East Timor voted to become an independent nation, and in 2002 it was internationally recognized as the world's newest independent democracy.

SECTION 2 ASSESSMENT

AFTER YOU READ

RECALL
1. Identify: (a) Angkor Wat

COMPREHENSION
2. Name four ways that culture spread from other countries to Southeast Asia.
3. How did colonial rule affect the economies of Southeast Asia?

CRITICAL THINKING AND WRITING
4. **Exploring the Main Idea** Review the Main Idea statement at the beginning of this section. Then, write a paragraph describing cultural diffusion in Southeast Asia.
5. **Hypothesizing** Imagine that the Southeast Asian countries did not gain independence from the colonial powers. How would life in these countries be different today?

ACTIVITY
6. **Delivering a Speech** Write a speech urging Southeast Asians to support independence from European rule. Make sure your speech has a persuasive argument. When you are finished, deliver your speech to your class.

South Asia

Mohenjo-Daro

GEOGRAPHY The people of Mohenjo-Daro built their city on mounds of earth to protect it from the floods of the Indus River. **Critical Thinking** Why was the Indus River valley a likely place for scientists to come across the ruins of an ancient civilization?

Setting the Scene

In 1922, scientists digging near the Indus River came upon the ruins of an ancient city they called Mohenjo-Daro (moh HEN joh DAH roh). The city had wide, straight streets and large buildings. It had a sewer system and a large walled fortress. Mohenjo-Daro was part of a civilization that developed about 4,500 years ago.

The people who lived there were part of one of the world's oldest civilizations. Over the centuries, many other people moved into the region. Some came peacefully. Others marched in with swords in their hands.

The Birth of Hinduism

Between 2000 B.C. and 1500 B.C., invaders known as Aryans (AIR ee unz) swept down on the people of the Indus Valley. The Indus Valley farmers were no match for the Aryan soldiers in horse-drawn chariots, and the Aryans took control of the area. In time, they moved eastward to the Ganges River, laying claim to much of northern India.

The Aryans ruled northern India for more than 1,000 years. They introduced new ways of living. For instance, they divided people into three classes—priests, warriors, and ordinary working people. This division grew out of Aryan religious writings called the Vedas (VAY duz). In time, the Aryans drew the

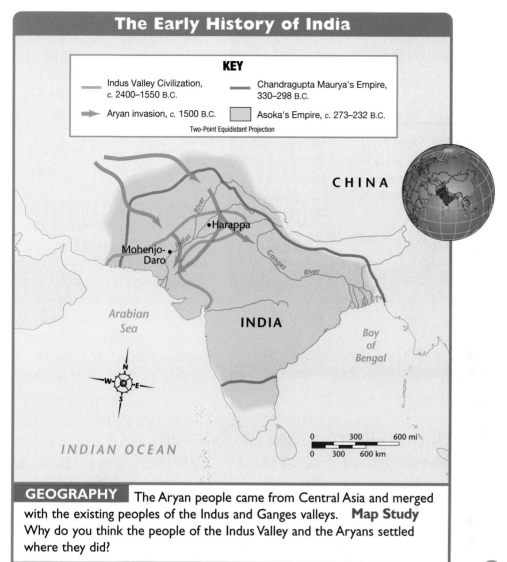

The Early History of India

KEY

― Indus Valley Civilization, c. 2400–1550 B.C.

➤ Aryan invasion, c. 1500 B.C.

― Chandragupta Maurya's Empire, 330–298 B.C.

▢ Asoka's Empire, c. 273–232 B.C.

Two-Point Equidistant Projection

CHINA

•Harappa

Mohenjo-Daro •

Indus River

Ganges River

Arabian Sea

INDIA

Bay of Bengal

INDIAN OCEAN

0   300   600 mi

0   300   600 km

GEOGRAPHY The Aryan people came from Central Asia and merged with the existing peoples of the Indus and Ganges valleys. **Map Study** Why do you think the people of the Indus Valley and the Aryans settled where they did?

conquered people into their class system. By 500 B.C., there was a strict division of classes. Europeans later called it the **caste** system. Each caste, or class, had special duties and work.

The caste system became a central part of a new system of belief that also emerged from Aryan religious ideas and practices. This system of beliefs, Hinduism, is the world's oldest living religion.

Important Groups and People

For hundreds of years, India was divided into many small kingdoms. No one ruler emerged to unite them.

The Maurya Empire Around 330 B.C., a fierce leader named Chandragupta Maurya (CHUN druh gup tuh MAH ur yuh) conquered many kingdoms. By the time of his death in 298 B.C., he ruled an empire that covered much of the subcontinent.

Maurya's grandson, **Asoka** (uh SOH kuh), continued the conquests,

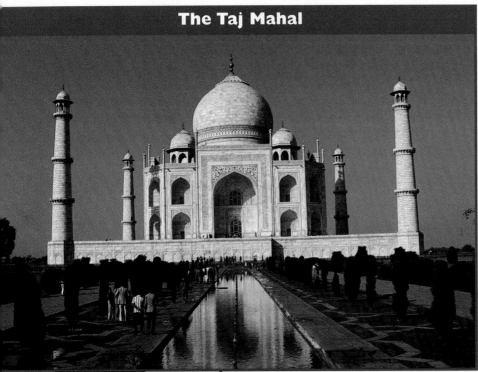

The Taj Mahal

but this soon changed. After one bloody battle, Asoka gave up war and violence and freed his prisoners. Later he changed his beliefs to Buddhism and vowed to rule peacefully.

Asoka kept his word and he showed concern for his people's welfare and he made laws requiring people to treat each other with respect, spreading the peaceful message of Buddhism throughout his empire.

The Maurya empire collapsed not long after Asoka's death. More than 1,500 years would pass before another empire as great ruled India.

CULTURE It took 20,000 workers 22 years to finish the Taj Mahal, the stunning monument Shah Jahan built to his wife. **Critical Thinking** How does the architecture of the Taj Mahal reflect its builder's Islamic religion?

The Mughal Empire In the A.D. 700s, people from the north began moving into northern India. They introduced Islam to the area. Islam is the set of beliefs revealed to the prophet Muhammad and he began teaching these beliefs around A.D. 610 in Southwest Asia. Islam spread westward into North Africa and eastward into South Asia.

The Mughals (MOO gulz) were among these Muslims, or followers of Islam, who settled in India. They arrived in the 1500s and established an empire ruled by Akbar (AK bar), from 1556 to 1605 who allowed all people to worship freely, regardless of their religion. He also supported the arts and literature.

Akbar's grandson, Shah Jahan (SHAH juh HAHN), built many grand buildings. Perhaps the greatest is the Taj Mahal (TAHZH muh HAHL), built as a magnificent tomb for Mumtaz (mum TAHZ) Mahal, his wife. But the cost of this and other of Jahan's building projects was enormous. It drained the empire of money and, eventually, helped to cause the empire's collapse in the 1700s.

AS YOU READ

Monitor Your Reading What questions do you have about how India won its freedom from Britain?

Colonization and Resistance During the 1700s, 1800s, and 1900s, European nations established many colonies in Asia, Africa, and the Americas. A **colony** is a territory ruled by another nation, usually one very far away. Through trade and war, the nations of Europe made colonies of most of South Asia. Britain took over most of the region, including India, and because of the riches it produced, the British called India the "jewel in the crown" of their empire.

While Britain treasured its empire, many Indians treasured their freedom and a strong independence movement grew up. Its greatest leader was **Mohandas K. Gandhi** (GAHN dee) who called for people to resist British rule. However, Gandhi stressed that they should do this through nonviolent means. For example, he urged a boycott of British goods. A boycott means a refusal to buy or use goods and services. Gandhi was jailed many times for opposing British rule, but this only made him a greater hero to his people. Gandhi's efforts played a major part in forcing Britain to grant India its freedom in 1947.

Past Conflicts Shape Current Conditions During the struggle for freedom in India, Hindus and Muslims had worked together. However, many Muslims feared that their rights would not be protected in a land with a Hindu majority. In 1947, Hindus and Muslims agreed on the **partition,** or division, of the subcontinent into two nations, India and Pakistan. This did not stop the fighting, and more than 500,000 people were killed. Ghandi himself was murdered, and conflict between the two nations continued. In recent years, both nations have tested missiles capable of carrying nuclear weapons, and a terrorist attack in India in 2001 nearly led to war between the two nations.

However, the early 21st century saw some hopeful improvements in relations between these two neighbors. The leaders of both India and Pakistan have offered concessions and begun negotiations to improve their relations. Although the situation remains tense, there is now hope that India and Pakistan can achieve a lasting peace.

Strength without Violence

HISTORY Mohandas K. Gandhi urged Indians to resist the British by following Hindu traditions. He preached the Hindu idea of *ahimsa,* or nonviolence and respect for all life. Because of his nonviolent approach, Indians call him *Mahatma,* or "Great Soul." **Critical Thinking** Why do you think Gandhi's nonviolent methods proved so successful?

SECTION 3 ASSESSMENT

AFTER YOU READ

RECALL

1. Identify: (a) Asoka, (b) Mohandas K. Gandhi

2. Define: (a) caste, (b) colony, (c) partition

COMPREHENSION

3. What social system did the Aryans introduce in South Asia?

4. Name two important people in South Asian history and tell one contribution of each.

CRITICAL THINKING AND WRITING

5. Exploring the Main Idea Review the Main Idea statement at the beginning of this section. Then, write a paragraph that describes some of the important influences that the Aryan invasion brought to South Asia.

6. Comparing and Contrasting Consider how the horse-drawn chariot enabled the Aryans to take control of the area where the

Indus Valley farmers lived. What technological innovations have given particular regions, countries, or groups power over others in recent times?

ACTIVITY

7. Writing to Learn Write a journal entry in which you discuss why you think Gandhi's being jailed made him more of a hero to the people of India.

SECTION 4

Southwest Asia

BEFORE YOU READ

READING FOCUS

1. What achievements did individuals and groups make in ancient Southwest Asia?
2. How have political boundaries intensified conflicts between different groups in Southwest Asia?

KEY PLACES

Mesopotamia
Palestine

MAIN IDEA

In modern times, political boundaries and ethnic differences have intensified regional conflicts between groups and countries in Southwest Asia.

NOTE TAKING

Copy the diagram below. As you read the section, complete the diagram with information about two ongoing conflicts in Southwest Asia.

Kurds vs. 3 Governments
a.
b.
c.

Land

Israelis vs. _____

Ancient Writing System

CULTURE The people of Mesopotamia used a writing system made up of wedge-shaped marks. This tablet shows the calculations for the area of a piece of land. **Critical Thinking** What other uses would this early civilization have had for a system of writing?

Setting the Scene

Hammurabi's Code was written about 3,800 years ago in Southwest Asia. People have described its laws as demanding "an eye for an eye." But there was more to the code than that:

"If the robber is not caught, the man who has been robbed shall formally declare whatever he has lost...and the city and the mayor...shall replace whatever he has lost for him."

The code punished people for wrong doings, but also offered justice to those hurt through no fault of their own.

Mesopotamia

Hammurabi ruled the city of Babylon from about 1800 B.C. to 1750 B.C. and he united the region along the Tigris and Euphrates rivers. This region is called **Mesopotamia,** which means "between the rivers."

People have lived in Mesopotamia for thousands of years, long before Hammurabi united it, and by 3500 B.C., the people made the area a center of farming and trade. The Tigris and Euphrates rivers flooded every year, leaving fertile soil along their banks. People dug irrigation ditches to bring water to fields that lay far from the river. Irrigation helped them to produce a crop surplus, or more than they needed.

Political Boundaries Intensify Conflicts and Challenges

After World War I, a conflict broke out between Arabs and Jews in Southwest Asia. Judaism has its roots in Southwest Asia. Over the centuries, a few Jews continued to live in their homeland, but many had settled in other parts of the world. In the late 1800s, Jews from around the world began to dream of returning to Palestine, an area along the eastern shore of the Mediterranean Sea. This alarmed the Arabs who lived there. **Palestine** was their homeland, too. When some Jews began moving to Palestine at the end of World War I, tensions rose.

Jews continued to migrate to Palestine during the 1930s. During World War II, millions of Jews in Europe were killed solely because they were Jewish. After the war, many of those who had survived decided to migrate to Palestine. On May 14, 1948, Jews declared the formation of their own state, Israel. Their state was recognized by the United Nations.

Arab-Israeli Conflict   The day after the state of Israel was declared, the Arab nations of Egypt, Iraq, Jordan, Lebanon, and Syria invaded Israel. These nations supported the Palestinians. Israel drove away the Arab forces. Hundreds of thousands of Palestinians fled from Jewish territory. Even larger numbers of Jews were forced to leave Arab countries, and most resettled in Israel. Since 1948, Israel and the Arab nations that border it have fought a number of bloody wars.

Efforts Toward Peace   In 1993, Israel and the Palestinian government—known as the Palestinian Liberation Organization (PLO)—formally recognized each other. In 2000, fighting broke out between Israel and the Palestinians once again. In 2003, the United States, Israeli leaders, and the PLO agreed on a new peace plan. The plan called for Israel to agree to the creation of a Palestinian State and for the PLO to agree to Israel's right to exist in peace. However, continuing violence has made it difficult for any progress to be made in bringing peace to this region.

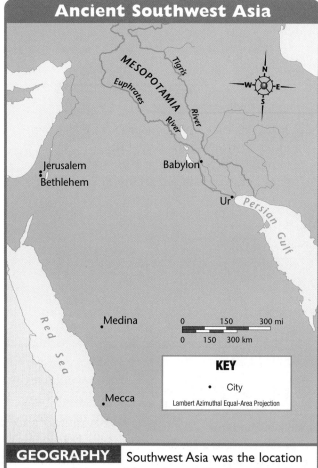

Ancient Southwest Asia

GEOGRAPHY   Southwest Asia was the location of some of the world's earliest civilizations. It is also the birthplace of Judaism, Christianity, and Islam. Jerusalem, Bethlehem, Mecca, and Medina all have religious connections.   **Map Study** Between which two rivers is Mesopotamia located?

Wars with Iraq In 1990, Iraqi armies, commanded by dictator Saddam Hussein, invaded the neighboring country of Kuwait. Although reluctant to get involved, the George H.W. Bush administration grew increasingly alarmed over the danger to its oil-rich ally Saudi Arabia and Saddam's investment in weapons of mass destruction. In January 1991, the United States and a coalition of 28 countries launched the Persian Gulf War. In just six weeks of fighting, Kuwait was liberated and Iraqi forces were driven out.

After Iraq's defeat in the 1991 Persian Gulf War, Saddam Hussein refused to cooperate with United Nations inspectors sent to ensure that Iraq destroyed its most dangerous weapons. In March 2003, U.S. forces attacked Iraq in an invasion supported by Great Britain and several other nations. Three weeks after the start of the war, Saddam fell from power and went into hiding. American officials began working with Iraqi leaders to set up a democratic system of government. In December 2003, U.S. troops captured Saddam.

HISTORY After successfully defeating Iraqi forces, American soldiers help topple a statue of Saddam Hussein.

SECTION 4 ASSESSMENT

AFTER YOU READ

RECALL

1. Identify: (a) Mesopotamia, (b) Palestine

COMPREHENSION

2. Name two achievements of Hammurabi and one achievement of more ancient people in Mesopotamia.
3. How has the drawing of political boundaries caused conflicts for Kurds, Arabs, and Jews in Southwest Asia?

CRITICAL THINKING AND WRITING

4. **Exploring the Main Idea** Review the Main Idea statement at the beginning of this section. Write a paragraph explaining the ongoing conflicts in Southwest Asia and describing the parties involved.
5. **Drawing Conclusions** Write a paragraph explaining how writing may have helped Mesopotamia leave its mark on the world.

ACTIVITY

6. **Writing to Learn** Review the information on page 477. Then, write a paragraph explaining why national security is so important to Israel.

Identifying Cause and Effect

CAUSE		EVENT		EFFECTS
Persecution in Europe	→	Jews left Europe to move to Palestine after WWII	→	Discord between Arabs and Jews
Palestine was homeland	→		→	Establishment of Israel

Learn the Skill

A cause is something that makes something else happen. The effect is what happens. Cause and effect can explain the relationship between events. History is full of causes and effects. A single event can have more than one cause or more than one effect. Also, an effect can in turn become the cause of more effects. Learning to correctly recognize causes and effects will help you to understand history.

To understand how cause-effect relationships work, make a cause-effect diagram of the information about Jewish people in Europe moving to Palestine after World War II. To make your cause-effect diagram, complete the following steps:

A. Identify the event. Jews left different European countries to move to Palestine after World War II. Write the event in the middle of a sheet of paper and circle it.

B. Identify the causes. What caused them to move to Palestine? You should be able to identify at least two causes. Not only did they move because they were being persecuted in Europe, but also because Palestine was their ancient homeland and Jerusalem their holy city. Write these causes to the left of the event, and draw a circle around each one. Then, draw an arrow from each cause to the event in the center.

C. Identify the effects. One effect was discord between Arabs and Jews. Another was the establishment of Israel as a nation. Write the effects to the right of the event, and circle each one. Then, draw an arrow from the event to each effect.

Now look your diagram over to see how it works. By following the arrows, you can trace the causes and effects of events.

Practice the Skill

Read the paragraph below. Look for cause-and-effect relationships between the events. Words and phrases such as "as a result" will give you clues that a cause-and-effect relationship exists. Make a list of the cause-effect relationships you find.

Sui Wendi

Sui Wendi ruled China as emperor from A.D. 581 to 604. As a young worker for the northern Chou dynasty, he helped the emperor gain control of most of northern China. As a result, he became a valued official.

As emperor, Sui Wendi invaded southern China. It had been divided from the rest of China for about 300 years. In 589, Sui Wendi became ruler of all of China. Long after his death, China remained united and powerful.

Sui Wendi also began reconstruction of the Grand Canal, which connects China's two greatest rivers. This improved transportation of goods in China. And he reformed the ways in which government officials were chosen by requiring civil service tests. The result is that he created a talented and skilled group of officials.

Apply the Skill

See the Chapter Review and Assessment at the end of this chapter for more questions on cause and effect.

Creating a Chapter Summary

On a separate piece of paper, draw a diagram like this one, and include the information that summarizes the first section of the chapter. Then, fill in the remaining boxes with summaries of Sections 2, 3, and 4.

ASIA: SHAPED BY HISTORY

Section 1	Section 2	Section 3	Section 4
The many achievements of East Asian civilizations spread to other regions via migration, invasion, and trade. Conflicts within the region helped spark World War II, after which China and North Korea became communist nations.			

Reviewing Key Terms

Match the key terms in Column I with the definitions in Column II.

Column I

1. dynasty
2. colony
3. boycott
4. caste
5. migration
6. dictator
7. cultural diffusion

Column II

a. class of people that performs special work

b. series of rulers from the same family

c. leader who has absolute power

d. territory ruled by another nation

e. spreading of ideas and culture through the movement of people

f. movement of people from one region to another

g. refusal to buy or use goods and services

Reviewing the Main Ideas

1. Name several discoveries made by early East Asian civilizations. (Section 1)

2. What was the effect of migration, invasion, and trade within East Asia and, ultimately, on Western nations? (Section 1)

3. How did culture traits spread from other countries to Southeast Asia? (Section 2)

4. By the early 1900s, what was Southeast Asians' growing response to colonization? (Section 2)

5. What new way of life did the Aryans establish in South Asia? (Section 3)

6. Identify two important leaders in the history of South Asia. (Section 3)

7. Identify one achievement of early Southwest Asia. (Section 4)

8. How do political boundaries in Southwest Asia affect Palestinians? (Section 4)

Map Activity

Asia

For each place listed below, write the letter on the map that shows the location. Use the Atlas at the back of the book to complete the exercise.

1. India
2. Vietnam
3. Pacific Ocean
4. China
5. Japan

Writing Activity

1. **Writing a Newspaper Editorial** Choose one conflict that you read about in this chapter. Write a newspaper editorial that gives your point of view on the conflict.

2. **Writing a Progress Report** Choose one of the countries discussed in this chapter and write a progress report about it. Do additional research, using primary or secondary sources, to find more information.
   Remember to address the problems the nation faces and the solutions being put forward to address those problems.

Applying Your Skills

Turn to the Skills for Life activity on page 479 to answer the following questions.

1. What is a cause?
2. What is an effect?
3. How are causes and effects related?
4. What were the causes of so many Jewish people moving to Palestine after World War II?
5. What were the effects of this move?

Critical Thinking

1. **Drawing Conclusions** Both ancient China and Japan attempted to isolate themselves from foreign influences. How did this affect both countries?

2. **Drawing Inferences** What sorts of conflicts might erupt in a very young country such as Israel?

 Take It to the NET

Activity Read about the Qin, Han, and Ming dynasties and the contributions they made to the world. Where do you see these contributions in society today? Visit the World Explorer: People, Places, and Cultures section of **phschool.com** for help in completing this activity.

Chapter 25 Self-Test As a final review activity, take the Chapter 25 Self-Test and get instant feedback on your answers. To take the test, visit the Social Studies section of **phschool.com**.

CHAPTER 26

ASIA: Rich in Culture

Sadako and the Thousand Paper Cranes

"What is it?" Sadako asked, staring at the paper.

Chizuko was pleased with herself. "I've figured out a way for you to get well," she said proudly. "Watch!" She cut a piece of gold paper into a large square. In a short time she had folded it over and over into a beautiful crane.

Sadako was puzzled. "But how can that paper bird make me well?"

"Don't you remember that old story about the crane?" Chizuko asked. "It's supposed to live for a thousand years. If a sick person folds one thousand paper cranes, the gods will grant her wish and make her healthy again." She handed the crane to Sadako. "Here's your first one."

USING LITERATURE

Sadako was a girl who lived in Hiroshima when the United States dropped an atom bomb there at the end of World War II. Sadako died at age 12 as a result of radiation from the bomb. Her story is told in the book *Sadako and the Thousand Paper Cranes* by Eleanor Coerr.

Exploring Japanese Legends

The story that Chizuko relates to Sadako about the paper cranes is an old Japanese legend. Use the library to research other Japanese legends. Choose one and write an updated version of the story using modern-day characters and plot. Create a display that shows copies of both the original version of the story, and your updated version. Display them both in the classroom.

Using Origami

Sadako decided to fold one thousand paper cranes to get well, but she was only able to fold 644 before she died. Her classmates folded 356 cranes so that one thousand were buried with Sadako. The art of paper folding in Japan is called origami. Find a book from the library on origami. Using colored paper, try making an origami crane or another origami figure.

SECTION 1

East Asia

BEFORE YOU READ

READING FOCUS

1. How does East Asia's past affect modern-day culture?

2. What similarities and differences in population exist within East Asia?

KEY TERMS

commune
dialect
nomad
homogeneous

MAIN IDEA

In East Asia, the past influences modern-day expressions of culture, whether in Communist China or technology-based Japan, and similarities and differences among nations are shown in the ethnic make-up of their populations.

NOTE TAKING

Copy the chart below. As you read the section, fill in the chart with details of how each nation blends tradition with modern practice.

Country	Mix of Old and New
China	
Korea	
Japan	

Setting the Scene

The Chinese game *weiqi* (way chee) has ancient cultural roots. One player has 180 black stones standing for night. The other has 180 white stones standing for day. The goal is to surround and capture the opponent's stones. But to the Chinese, weiqi is more than a game. For centuries, Buddhists have used it to discipline the mind and study behavior. Masters can look at a game record to see exactly when players became too greedy and doomed themselves to defeat. Today, you can see people playing this ancient game in any park in China.

Tradition Amid Change

In East Asia, tradition mixes with change. Businesspeople in Western suits greet each other with a bow. Ancient palaces stand among skyscrapers. In Japan, China, and the Koreas, reminders of the past mingle with activities of the present.

The Ideal Family

CULTURE The Chinese government uses billboard advertising to encourage people to limit the size of their families. **Critical Thinking** Why do you think the Chinese government wants people to have small families?

YOU SHENG YOU YU ZHEN XING ZHONG HUA

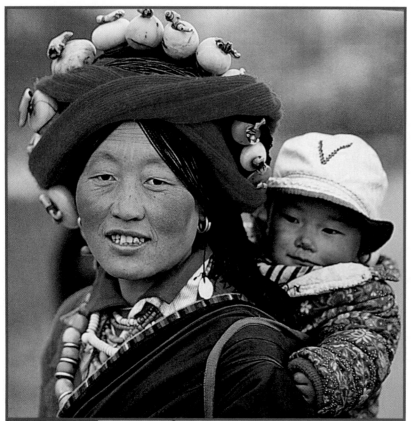

CULTURE This woman from Tibet, in the western part of China, reflects the tradition of her ethnic group in her headdress, jewelry, and the way she carries her baby. **Critical Thinking** In what ways do the clothes you wear reflect the traditions of your culture or ethnic group?

Communism Brings Change to China When the Communists came into power in 1949, they made major changes in the Chinese way of life. To begin with, the government created **communes,** communities in which land is held in common and where members live and work together. Chinese farmers were accustomed to living in family groups that worked together in small fields, so they resisted the communes. Food production fell, and China suffered terrible food shortages. Only when the government allowed some private ownership did food production grow.

The Communists also tried to slow China's population growth by attacking the idea of large families. Here, they had more success. Chinese couples are supposed to wait until their late twenties to marry. They are not supposed to have more than one child per family. Chinese families with only one child receive special privileges.

The mixture of old and new affects the lives of all Chinese. Even the cities retain aspects of the old China, as the streets are filled with three-wheeled cabs pedaled like tricycles. Tiny shops sell traditional cures made from herbs and exist alongside modern hospitals.

Changing Korea In Korea, daily life is affected by long-standing traditions. A family looks after the welfare of all its members. In rural areas, grandparents, parents, aunts, and uncles may live in one household. In the cities, a family is usually just parents and children.

As in China, modern ways are more popular in urban areas. Most Koreans wear modern clothes and save their traditional dress of trousers or a long skirt with a long jacket for holidays. Earlier, Korean women had few opportunities. Today, they can work and vote.

Japan's Blend of Old and New Japanese work at computers in skyscrapers and ride home on speedy trains. Once they reach home, however, they may follow traditional customs and change into kimonos, or robes and sit on mats at a low table to have dinner. Japanese students dress like students in the United States, though some wear the headbands of samurai warriors to show that they are getting ready for a challenge.

The Japanese try hard to preserve the past. For example, some years ago, the Japanese saw that traditional arts and crafts were dying out, so the government began offering lifetime salaries to some artists. Their main task is to teach young people who will keep the ancient arts alive.

Similarities and Differences in Population

One culture dominates within each East Asian country. Distinct sub-cultures persist in different regions of China because of its tremendous ethnic diversity.

China: The Han and Others   About 19 of every 20 Chinese people trace their ancestry to the Han, the people of China's second dynasty. As you can see on the map below, the Han live mostly in eastern and central China. Although they have a common language, they speak different **dialects,** or forms of a single language, from region to region. The other Chinese come from 55 different minority groups who live mainly in the western parts of China.

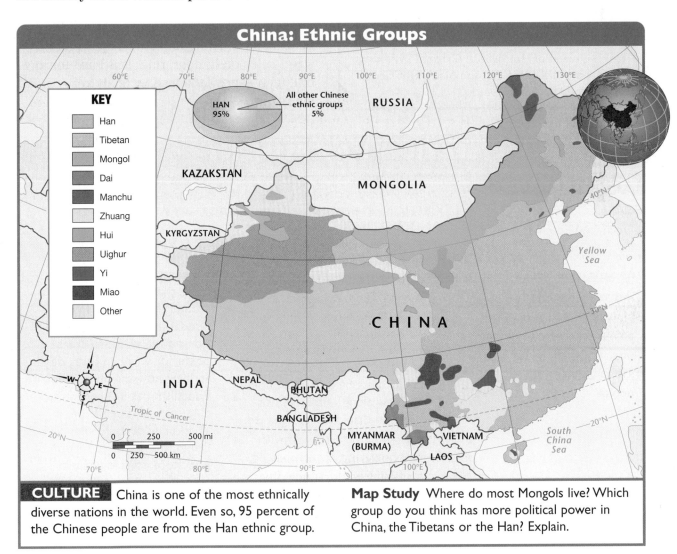

China: Ethnic Groups

KEY
- Han
- Tibetan
- Mongol
- Dai
- Manchu
- Zhuang
- Hui
- Uighur
- Yi
- Miao
- Other

HAN 95%

All other Chinese ethnic groups 5%

CULTURE   China is one of the most ethnically diverse nations in the world. Even so, 95 percent of the Chinese people are from the Han ethnic group.

Map Study Where do most Mongols live? Which group do you think has more political power in China, the Tibetans or the Han? Explain.

AS YOU READ

Draw Inferences What do you think it would be like to live in a country with a homogeneous population?

Korea and Japan: Few Minorities Historians believe that the ancient Koreans were descended from many different groups of **nomads** from Mongolia. Nomads are people who have no settled home.

They move from place to place in search of water and grazing for their herds. Over centuries, these groups lost their separate traditions. They formed one **homogeneous** (hoh muh JEE nee us) group. That is, the group's members were very similar. Today, even with the division of Korea into two countries, the population is homogeneous. There are few minority groups.

Because it was an island nation and it isolated itself from the world for part of its history, Japan has one of the most homogenous populations on the Earth. Nearly all of the people belong to the same ethnic group, a group that shares language, religion, and cultural traditions. Minority groups are few. One notable minority group is the Ainu (EYE noo), who may have been Japan's first inhabitants. Small numbers of Koreans and Chinese also live in Japan. However, Japan has strict rules on immigration. It is hard for anyone who is not Japanese by birth to become a citizen.

CULTURE These Ainu women are performing together in traditional dress. They have painted their lips in a traditional style as well. The Ainu live in parts of the Japanese island of Hokkaido. **Critical Thinking** What are some challenges that the Ainu might face as a minority group in Japan?

SECTION I ASSESSMENT

AFTER YOU READ

RECALL

1. Define: (a) commune, (b) dialect, (c) nomad, (d) homogeneous

COMPREHENSION

2. How does East Asia reflect past and present traditions?

3. Why are the populations of Korea and Japan homogeneous?

CRITICAL THINKING AND WRITING

4. **Exploring the Main Idea** Review the Main Idea statement at the beginning of this section. Then, write an outline for a three-day tour of East Asia. Include one day for each of these nations: China, Japan, and the Koreas. Identify and briefly describe elements of old and new along with ethnic distribution that visitors might see.

5. **Identifying Cause and Effect** Write a paragraph explaining why you think the Communists wanted to slow China's population growth.

ACTIVITY

 Take It to the NET

6. **Understanding Buddhism** More than 300 million people around the world practice Buddhism. Using the information on the web site, create a poster or write an essay describing how the philosophy of Buddhism has influenced the cultures of Asia. Visit the World Explorer: People, Places, and Cultures section of **phschool.com** for help in completing this activity.

Southeast Asia

BEFORE YOU READ

READING FOCUS

1. How is Southeast Asia's cultural heritage reflected in religion and the arts?
2. How is mineral wealth used to support an Islamic heritage in Southeast Asia?

KEY TERMS
The Ramayana

KEY PLACES
Brunei

MAIN IDEA

Religion, architecture, and the arts reflect a mix of tradition and change in Southeast Asia.

NOTE TAKING

Copy the chart below. As you read the section, fill in the chart to give examples of how the cultural heritage of Southeast Asia is reflected in modern-day life.

	Seen in
Cultural Heritage	
Religious Heritage	

Setting the Scene

Water puppet shows started in Vietnam centuries ago. With the pond for a stage, a puppeteer guides wooden figures so that they appear to wade through the water. The puppets are attached to rods and strings hidden under water. Audiences sit at the water's edge and stage settings of trees and clouds are placed on the pond.

At the same time, people in Southeast Asia enjoy the thrill of modern conveniences, like motorbikes, while retaining the beauty of traditional arts, like water puppet shows. Religion and architecture, like the arts, reflect a mix of tradition and change in Southeast Asia.

Arts and Religion in Cambodia

Most Cambodians are Buddhists, yet the cultural heritage of Hinduism is reflected in Cambodian arts. In the capital city of Phnom Pen, Cambodia's Royal Ballet has performed **The Ramayana,** a Hindu epic poem, since the 1700s. In Cambodian villages, this poem often is read aloud or acted out by shadow puppets.

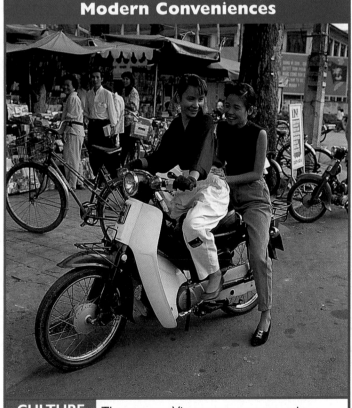

Modern Conveniences

CULTURE These young Vietnamese women enjoy traveling by motorbike. These vehicles are cheaper than cars and speedier than bicycles. **Critical Thinking** Use the description of water puppet shows and the photograph to identify one contrast that a visitor to Vietnam might observe. Can you think of others?

Displaced by War

HISTORY In the mid-1970s, civil war forced thousands of Cambodians to leave their homes and move to refugee camps near the border of Thailand and Cambodia. These children are in a refugee camp in Thailand.
Critical Thinking How can nations such as the United States help refugees like these children who were displaced by war?

Hindus believe that *The Ramayana*, completed in about 4 A.D., was revealed to its author by Brahma, the god of creation. The epic tells of a prince named Rama, who is ousted from his throne, and his beloved wife Sita, who is kidnapped by a demon king. *The Ramayana* is told and retold, in many different versions, throughout India and Southeast Asia. A tale of intrigue, betrayal, love, and loss, it goes beyond the boundaries of societies and conveys universal themes.

Today many Cambodians—about 90 percent—practice Buddhism, although at one time the Cambodian government discouraged the practice of religion. Two key ideas of Buddhism are that life includes suffering and that people live, die, and are reborn. These ideas may have helped Cambodians make sense of their recent history, during which many innocent people suffered and died.

A Heritage Maintained

The nations of Southeast Asia are rich in minerals. Indonesia, Myanmar, and the small kingdom of **Brunei** contain large deposits of oil. Brunei, on the northwestern coast of the island of Borneo, is only about the size of the state of Delaware. Yet this tiny nation boasts the world's biggest palace, the home of the Sultan of Brunei. This building covers 50 acres (20 hectares)—about the area of 36 football fields—and has 1,788 rooms.

Although not all of its people are Muslims, Brunei is an Islamic nation. It has used its oil wealth to sustain its people and to support Islamic traditions. The people of Brunei receive free health care, free education, and high wages on which they do not pay taxes. In return, they are expected to obey the government ruled by decree of Sultan Sir Hassanal Bolkiah.

Brunei's religious heritage is reflected in the sultan's government, which strictly enforces Islamic customs and traditions, and in its architecture, which reflects the nation's adherence to Islam.

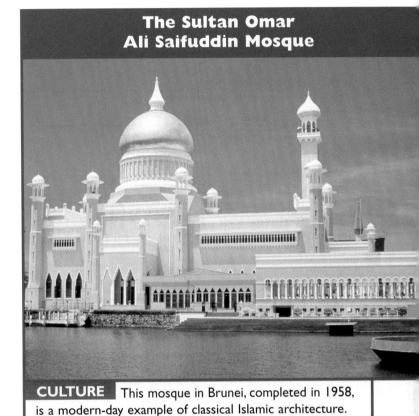

The Sultan Omar Ali Saifuddin Mosque

CULTURE This mosque in Brunei, completed in 1958, is a modern-day example of classical Islamic architecture. With its distinctive gold dome, the mosque dominates the city skyline. **Critical Thinking** Give an example of a building in your state or community that reflects an aspect of Americans' cultural heritage.

SECTION 2 ASSESSMENT

AFTER YOU READ

RECALL

1. Identify: Brunei

2. Define: *The Ramayana*

COMPREHENSION

3. How have key ideas of Buddhism helped Cambodians make sense of their recent history?

4. Give an example of how Brunei uses its mineral wealth to support its Islamic heritage.

CRITICAL THINKING AND WRITING

5. **Exploring the Main Idea** Review the Main Idea statement at the beginning of this section. Then, imagine that you are visiting a country in Southeast Asia. Write a journal entry describing sights that reflect a cultural mix of past and present.

6. **Making Inferences and Drawing Conclusions** Why do you think the Hindu epic *The Ramayana* is so popular in Cambodia, an overwhelmingly Buddhist country?

ACTIVITY

7. **Writing a Poem** Imagine that you have been displaced from your home by war. Write a poem describing your feelings about your present life and your hopes for the future.

South Asia

BEFORE YOU READ

READING FOCUS

1. What two religions have roots in South Asia?
2. What challenges does religious diversity present in South Asia?
3. How are many languages in South Asia related?

KEY PEOPLE

Siddhartha Gautama

MAIN IDEA

Many religions, including Islam and Sikhism, and languages are important in the politics and culture of South Asia.

NOTE TAKING

Copy this chart. As you read the section, complete the chart to show details about language and religion in South Asia. Add more ovals to the web as you go.

A Religious Festival

CULTURE The picture shows a religious festival in India.
Critical Thinking What does the picture tell you about the role of religion in everyday life in South Asia?

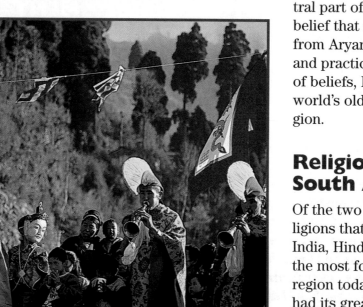

Setting the Scene

When the Aryans invaded the Indus Valley between 2000 B.C. and 1500 B.C., they brought with them new ways of living. One of these divided people into three classes—priests, warriors, and ordinary working people. This system, known as the caste system, was based on Aryan religious writings called the Vedas (VAY duz). It became a central part of a new system of belief that also emerged from Aryan religious ideas and practices. This system of beliefs, Hinduism, is the world's oldest living religion.

Religions of South Asia

Of the two major world religions that developed in India, Hinduism by far has the most followers in the region today. Buddhism had its greatest following in India in the 200s B.C.

Buddhism in India

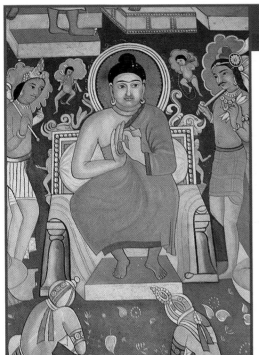

HISTORY The religion founded by the Buddha (left) had its greatest following during the time of the Indian ruler Asoka. The stone lions (right) topped one of the pillars that Asoka set up all over India. Asoka had Buddhist writings carved on these pillars. After Asoka's death, Buddhism nearly died out in India, but missionaries carried the religion to Japan, Korea, China, and Vietnam.

Critical Thinking How is the spread of Buddhism a good example of cultural diffusion?

Hinduism Hinduism is unlike other major world religions. It does not have one single founder. However, it has many great religious thinkers. Also, Hindus worship many gods and goddesses, but they believe in a single spirit. To Hindus, the various gods and goddesses represent different parts of this spirit. As an old Hindu saying states: "God is one, but wise people know it by many names." Today, Hinduism is the national religion of India and has 700 million followers there.

Buddhism Buddhism, like Hinduism, developed in India. According to Buddhist tradition, its founder was a prince named **Siddhartha Gautama** (shid DAHR tuh goh TUH MUH). He was born in about 560 B.C., in present-day Nepal. Gautama was a Hindu of high caste who lived a privileged life, safe from hunger and disease.

When he was 29 years old, Gautama left home to learn about his kingdom. For the first time, he saw people who were hungry, sick, and poor. He became so unhappy that he gave up his wealth and pledged his life to finding the causes for people's suffering.

Eventually, Gautama found what he believed was the solution. He taught that people can be free of suffering if they give up selfish desires for power, wealth, and pleasure. He then became known as the Buddha, or "Enlightened One." People of all backgrounds, princes and ordinary people alike, flocked to hear his sermons.

For a while after the Buddha's death, Buddhism had a huge following in India. Over time, however, it almost completely died out there.

AS YOU READ

Monitor Your Reading Think of three questions you might ask about the teaching of the Buddha.

India Welcomes Exiles

In 1950, Communist China invaded Tibet. Up until that time, Tibet had been an independent country ruled by the 14th Dalai Lama. Tibetan Buddhists consider the Dalai Lama to be the reincarnation of the first Dalai Lama and therefore the true spiritual and temporal ruler of Tibet. In 1959, the Dalai Lama and 100,000 followers fled Tibet and established a government-in-exile in India in an effort to preserve Tibet's religion and culture. In 1989, the Dalai Lama received the Nobel Prize for Peace for his nonviolent campaign to end Chinese occupation of Tibet.

The Challenge of Diversity

Today, about 80 percent of Indians are Hindus. Yet other religions remain important in Indian politics and culture. For example, Muslim traders brought Islam to India during the 700s A.D. and today about 14 percent of Indians are Muslim. Christianity and Sikhism are small but significant religious minorities in present-day India.

Armed conflict between religious groups endangers many people in India and presents a constant challenge to its government. Muslims and Hindus fight to control Kashmir, on the border between Pakistan and India. Sikhs have expressed their desire for more control of the Punjab area with terrorist attacks that are met by severe, sometimes brutal, reprisals by the Hindu-dominated government.

One Root, Many Languages

Just as two religions of South Asia—Buddhism and Hinduism—have common roots, so do many South Asian languages. They belong to a very large group of related

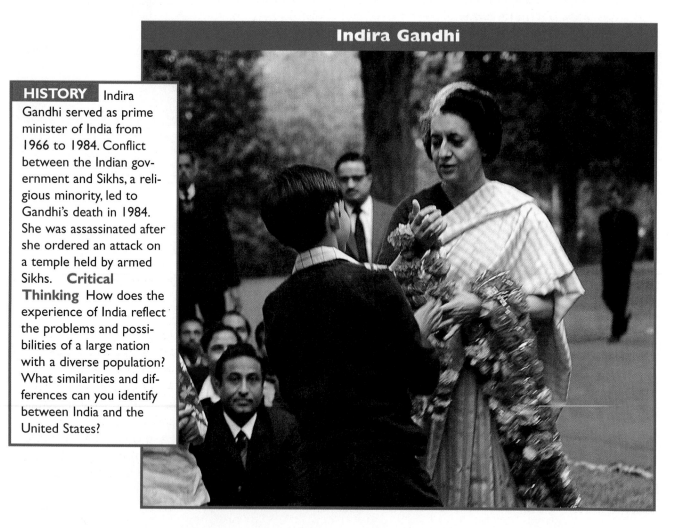

Indira Gandhi

HISTORY Indira Gandhi served as prime minister of India from 1966 to 1984. Conflict between the Indian government and Sikhs, a religious minority, led to Gandhi's death in 1984. She was assassinated after she ordered an attack on a temple held by armed Sikhs. **Critical Thinking** How does the experience of India reflect the problems and possibilities of a large nation with a diverse population? What similarities and differences can you identify between India and the United States?

Languages of South Asia	
Country	Major Languages
Afghanistan	Pashtu, Dari Persian, Turkic
Bangladesh	Bengali (official), English
Bhutan	Dzongkha (official), Gurung, Assamese
India	Hindi (official), Bengali, English, and 13 other languages
Nepal	Nepali (official) and many others
Pakistan	Urdu (official), English (official), Punjabi, Sindhi
Sri Lanka	Sinhalese (official), Tamil

CULTURE This chart shows the major languages spoken in South Asia. In India, for example, over 1,000 different languages and dialects are spoken. An official language is one chosen by a nation and used for government business. **Critical Thinking** Why do you think English is a major language in several South Asian countries?

languages which make up the Indo–Iranian branch of the Indo–European language group. Study the chart above to learn more about the languages spoken in South Asia.

Hindi, which is spoken mainly by South Asian Hindus, and Urdu, spoken mainly by South Asian Muslims, are dialects of this group.

More South Asian literature has been written in Bengali than in any other modern Indian language. Bengali is spoken in West Bengal, India, and throughout Bangladesh.

SECTION 3 ASSESSMENT

AFTER YOU READ

RECALL
1. Identify: Siddhartha Gautama

COMPREHENSION
2. Name two religions that have roots in South Asia.

3. Describe how religious diversity presents challenges to people who live in South Asia.

4. Explain how many languages spoken in South Asia are related.

CRITICAL THINKING AND WRITING
5. **Exploring the Main Idea** Review the Main Idea statement at the beginning of this section. Then, write a statement describing cultural heritage and diversity in South Asia, including specific examples.

6. **Making Predictions** Do you think the conflicts between different religious groups in South Asia will intensify or be resolved over time? Explain your thinking in a brief written prediction.

7. **Identifying Cause and Effect** Why do you think so many languages in South Asia have common roots? Write a paragraph to answer.

ACTIVITY
8. **Time Traveling** Locate your town on a map of the world showing time zones. Then, locate a city in South Asia such as Kathmandu, Nepal, or Kabul, Afghanistan. List that city's name and what time it is there when it is a) midnight, b) noon, and c) 5:00 p.m. in your town.

Southwest Asia

BEFORE YOU READ

1. Why are there so many cultures in Southwest Asia?

2. What three religions have roots in Southwest Asia?

KEY TERMS

muezzin
minaret

KEY PEOPLE AND PLACES

Abraham
Jerusalem
Jesus of Nazareth
Bethlehem
Muhammad
Mecca

MAIN IDEA

Three world religions—Christianity, Judaism, and Islam—and many different cultures have their roots in Southwest Asia, an area of great cultural diversity.

NOTE TAKING

Copy the diagram below. As you read the section, fill in the diagram to show some similarities and differences in three religions that have roots in Southwest Asia.

	Judaism	Islam	Christianity
birthplace			
holy city			
founder			
country of origin			
sacred text			

The Blue Mosque

CULTURE The mosque in the background is known as the Blue Mosque because of the blue tile decorating its interior. It is located in Istanbul, Turkey. The tall towers visible are the minarets, from which the muezzin calls Muslims to prayer. **Critical Thinking** What do you think it would be like to live in a place where everything stopped for prayer five times a day?

Setting the Scene

The sights and sounds of Islam are present everywhere in Southwest Asia. One sound is the call of the **muezzin** (moo EZ in), a person whose job it is to summon Muslims to pray from high atop the mosque in a **minaret.** Five times a day, wherever they are, Muslims stop what they are doing and pray.

Cultural Diversity

Southwest Asia's location has always made it an important link between Asia, Africa, and Europe. As a result, this region became a crossroad and hub of civilization. Throughout history, many empires have successively dominated the region. Most of these empires, such as the Hittite and Persian empires, originated in Southwest and Central Asia and they made lasting cultural contributions to the area. In addition, many of the people in this region were traders and traveled extensively throughout Asia, Africa, and Europe, which further promoted the cultural diffusion of ideas and traditions.

Birthplace of Three Religions

Christianity, Judaism, and Islam all developed in Southwest Asia. Judaism is believed to have started with **Abraham** over 3,000 years ago. Abraham and his family lived in Mesopotamia. According to the Torah, the collection of writings sacred to the Jews, God told Abraham to take his family west to another land called Canaan (present-day Israel). God promised Abraham that he would make him the father of a great nation. In return, Abraham promised that he and his descendants would worship only God. Today, **Jerusalem,** the capital of Israel, is a holy city for Jews.

The Rise of Christianity   Christianity began as a movement within Judaism. Around 30 A.D., a young man called **Jesus of Nazareth** began preaching to his fellow Jews, encouraging people to turn to God and lead moral lives.

Christian teachings tell that Jesus was born in **Bethlehem,** a town just outside of Jerusalem considered to be holy for Christians. Some people believed that he was the messiah, and they followed him until he was arrested, tried, and executed in Jerusalem. Accounts of Jesus's life were later written down by his followers and now form an important part of the New Testament in the Christian Bible.

After the death of Jesus, his followers began to form small communities, living and praying together. They began referring to Jesus

Jerusalem

CULTURE   Southwest Asia is the birthplace of Christianity, Judaism, and Islam. Jerusalem, capital of the country of Israel, is an ancient city. People have been living there since 1800 B.C. Jerusalem is holy to Christians, Jews, and Muslims because events important to their religions took place there. To the left is the silver dome of a Christian church. The golden-domed building is called the Dome of the Rock. It stands over the rock from which Muslims believe the prophet Muhammad rose into heaven to speak with God.

Critical Thinking Do you think it is easy for three religions to share a holy city? Why or why not?

West Bank Neighbors

CULTURE Israel has occupied the West Bank area since the late 1960s. In this picture, Israeli soldiers in the West Bank town of Hebron watch as two mothers, one Israeli (on the left), one Palestinian, walk with their children. **Critical Thinking** Why might cultural differences lead to conflict?

as Christ, which means "messiah." These followers were known as Christians. Gradually, these Christians began traveling along the ancient trade routes and preached the teachings of Jesus along the way. Soon, these small communities spread throughout the Roman Empire. Despite the persecution of its followers, Christianity would come to be the major religion of the Roman Empire, which helped the religion to flourish around the Mediterranean.

Muhammad and Islam **Muhammad,** the prophet of Islam, was born in the Arabian city of **Mecca** in approximately 570 A.D. Mecca, which is now a holy city for Muslims, is located in what is now Saudia Arabia. In the early 600s, Muhammad had a vision in which the angel Gabriel appeared to him and told him that he was to be the messenger of God, known as Allah in Arabic. Muhammad began teaching what he had learned. He taught the people of Mecca that Allah alone was God and that people would be judged by their actions and deeds, not by their wealth or power. These teachings form the basis of Islam's holy book, the Quran.

The Region Today

Southwest Asia is still a region of great cultural diversity. Dozens of different ethnic groups call this area home, and together they speak more than 30 languages, including Arabic, Turkish, Persian, Hebrew, and Armenian. However, with this cultural diversity has come conflict and violence—both within many of the countries and between many countries in this area.

SECTION 4 ASSESSMENT

AFTER YOU READ

RECALL

1. Define: (a) muezzin, (b) minaret

2. Identify: (a) Abraham, (b) Jerusalem, (c) Jesus of Nazareth, (d) Bethlehem, (e) Muhammad, (f) Mecca

COMPREHENSION

3. Describe the factors that account for the great cultural diversity of Southwest Asia.

4. Name the three religions that have their roots in Southwest Asia.

CRITICAL THINKING AND WRITING

5. Exploring the Main Idea Review the Main Idea statement at the beginning of this section. Then, write a paragraph describing some of the factors that link the three major religions in Southwest Asia.

ACTIVITY

6. Creating a Country Profile Create a country profile for one of the following Southwest Asian countries: Turkey, Iran, or Lebanon. Visit the library or the Internet to find out about the ethnic groups and religions in the country, and create a suitable chart that shows this information. Draw a map of the country, indicating the capital as well as important land forms to display along with the charts you create.

Explaining Points of View

Learn the Skill

A point of view is the position from which a person looks at something. Throughout history, various individuals and groups have held varying points of view. To recognize and explain varying points of view as you read, you must look closely at a person's argument to understand the reasons behind that belief. Understanding the viewpoints of groups of people and historical leaders will help you better understand what you read. To explain points of view, follow these steps:

A. Be on the lookout as you read for information on a person or group's point of view. This may be in the form of a statement within the text in which a viewpoint is given. Or a point of view may be revealed through the actions of people. The following sentences give the opposing religious viewpoints of the Soviet Union and ethnic Kazaks:

> When the Soviet Union took control of Kazakstan in the 1920s, they banned the practice of Islam and tried to stamp out Muslim culture. After the Cold War, ethnic Kazaks rebuilt the mosques and began celebrating their culture and religion once again.

B. Look for reasons why each side has a certain position, and analyze those reasons. The following sentences explain why the Soviets restricted the practice of religion in the Soviet Union:

> Wherever they went, the Soviets restricted the practice of religion, believing it was an "opium" of the people. The Soviets wanted people to celebrate communism, not religion. They believed the absence of religion would make their rule stronger.

C. Be able to explain both sides of the argument by giving reasons why different people take various positions on the same issue. To explain the practice of religion in Kazakstan, for example, you might write:

> The Kazaks were proud of their heritage and wanted the freedom to worship as they pleased and follow the religions of their ancestors.

Practice the Skill

Read the following information. Then follow the steps to write a summary to explain the two points of view.

The Soviet Union in Kazakstan

Ethnic Kazaks lived a nomadic lifestyle, taking their livestock to places where they could find food and water. But the Soviets believed it would be better for the Kazaks to become farmers and give up their nomadic lifestyle. They forced the Kazaks to work on collective farms. The Kazaks bitterly opposed plowing under their grazing land for crops. Then, the Soviets diverted so much water for irrigation from the Aral Sea, which the Kazaks live close to, that the sea shrunk in size, grounding many ships on what used to be the bottom of the sea. The irrigation has ended, but the Kazaks believe it will take 30 years for the Aral Sea to return to its normal size.

Apply the Skill

Turn to the Applying Your Skills section of the Chapter Review and Assessment for more questions on explaining points of view.

Review and Assessment

Creating a Chapter Summary

On a separate piece of paper, draw a diagram like this one, and include the information that summarizes the first section of the chapter. Then, fill in the remaining boxes with summaries of Sections 2, 3, and 4.

ASIA: RICH IN CULTURE

Section 1
History influences modern-day culture in East Asia. Countries in this region differ in the make-up of their populations. Japan and the Koreas have homogeneous populations, whereas China is one of the most ethnically diverse nations in the world.

Section 2

Section 3

Section 4

Reviewing Key Terms

Match the key terms in Column I with the definitions in Column II.

Column I	Column II
1. Jesus	**a.** very similar
2. dialects	**b.** founder of Buddhism
3. nomad	**c.** forms of a single language
4. deity	
5. homogeneous	**d.** founder of Judaism
6. Siddhartha Gautauma	**e.** a god
	f. founder of Islam
7. Abraham	**g.** person who has no settled home
8. Muhammad	**h.** founder of Christianity

Reviewing the Main Ideas

1. How do past and present blend in East Asia? (Section 1)

2. Which East Asian nations have homogeneous populations? Which is ethnically diverse? (Section 1)

3. What do religious practices, architectural style, and arts reveal about the relationship between past and present in Southeast Asia? (Section 2)

4. How is oil wealth used in Brunei? (Section 2)

5. What religions have roots in South Asia, and what other religions are important in the region today? (Section 3)

6. In what group of related languages are many languages of South Asia? (Section 3)

7. What three religions have their roots in Southwest Asia? (Section 4)

Map Activity

For each place below, write the letter from the map that shows its location. Use the maps in the Activity Atlas at the front of the book to help you.

1. China
2. Brunei
3. Japan
4. Vietnam
5. Israel
6. India
7. Nepal
8. North Korea
9. South Korea
10. Cambodia

 Take It to the NET

Enrichment For more map activities using geography skills, visit the Social Studies section of **phschool.com**.

Writing Activity

1. **Writing Sentences** Based on what you have read in this chapter, write five sentences describing how tradition and change exist together in Asia. Then, write five sentences describing how tradition and change exist together in the United States.

2. **Writing a Letter** You are visiting Asia to observe how the past and present intermingle in everyday life. Write a letter to a teacher describing your observations.

Applying Your Skills

Turn to the Skills for Life activity on p. 497 to answer the following questions.

1. Write a definition for point of view.

2. What did the ethnic Kazaks do after the Cold War that lets the reader know that they value their Islamic religion?

Critical Thinking

1. **Comparing and Contrasting** How do cultures in Southwest Asia compare to other Asian cultures you have studied?

2. **Generalizing** Each country in Asia is unique. However, many Asian countries have certain similarities in relation to their cultural heritage. What relationship to their heritages do many Asian countries share?

 Take It to the NET

Activity Examine some of the ceramic pieces in this exhibit. What do you learn about ancient Asian culture from looking at these objects? Visit the World Explorer: People, Places, and Cultures section of **phschool.com** for help in completing this activity.

Chapter 26 Self-Test As a final review activity, take the Chapter 26 Self-Test and get instant feedback on your answers. To take the test, visit the Social Studies section of **phschool.com**.

EAST AND SOUTHEAST ASIA:
Exploring the Region Today

City Life

USING PICTURES

Shanghai, located near the mouth of the Yangzi River, is China's leading port. With a population of 8 million people, it is the largest city in China.

Exploring Shanghai

Shanghai is a modern city. What are some of the details in the picture that show this? What effect do you think trade has had on the growth of the city of Shanghai? What effect do you think trade has had on culture in the city of Shanghai?

Making Predictions

China exports many goods to other countries around the world. Use an encyclopedia to gather information on China's natural resources. Make a list of the resources, and then brainstorm a list of products you think China might export to other countries, based on your list of resources. Use library and Internet sources to gather information and make a list of China's major exports. Check to see if your predictions about China's exports were accurate.

China
Political and Economic Changes

BEFORE YOU READ

READING FOCUS

1. How has communism changed the lives of many Chinese?
2. What steps has China recently taken to improve its economy?

KEY TERMS

radical
free enterprise

KEY PEOPLE AND PLACES

Mao Zedong
Red Guard
Taiwan

NOTE TAKING

Copy the diagram below. As you read the section, fill in the diagram to show similarities and differences—from 1949 to the present—between China and Taiwan.

China   Taiwan

MAIN IDEA

China has undergone tremendous political and economic change since 1949.

Setting the Scene

During the early 1980s, the streets of large Chinese cities were fairly quiet. Most people traveled by bicycle—200 million of them. At this time, the total number of vehicles in all of China was 100,000. In 1996, 670,000 cars, buses, and trucks crowded the streets of major cities. In the early 1980s, most houses were cramped, single-story dwellings made of clay and brick. Few had running water or flush toilets. Today, China's major cities have high-rise apartment and office buildings. New roads connect rural areas to the cities. Change is speeding up as China works to become an industrial nation.

Unlimited Government

When Chinese Communists took power from the Nationalists in 1949, they had few friends among the major nations of the world. The United States had backed the Nationalists, and the Soviet Union had been on the Communists' side, but later withdrew its support because it disagreed with China about how a communist society should be run.

The Communists faced enormous problems when they took control. China had not had peace for almost a century. Most Chinese were extremely poor. Their methods of farming and manufacturing were out of date.

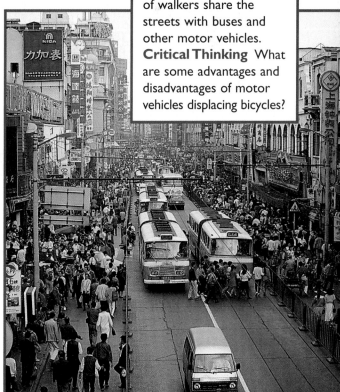

Busy Modern Streets

CULTURE China's streets are no longer packed with bicycles. In modern Shanghai, throngs of walkers share the streets with buses and other motor vehicles. **Critical Thinking** What are some advantages and disadvantages of motor vehicles displacing bicycles?

China

Religious Persuasion

- Buddhist 6%
- Muslim 2%
- Other 13%
- Traditional beliefs 20%
- Non-religious 59%

Labor Force

- Industry and commerce 25%
- Agriculture and forestry 60%
- Other 15%

China: Political
KEY

— National boundary

⊛ National capital

• Other city

Two-Point Equidistant Projection

Location	Eastern Asia
Climate	Very diverse; tropical in the south to subarctic in the north
Terrain	Mountains, high plateaus, and deserts in the west; plains, deltas, and hills in the east
Population	1.29 billion
Major Religion	Officially, atheism, but Buddhism, Daoism, and Confucianism are still practiced.
Ethnic Groups	Han Chinese and 55 East Asian minority groups
Government	Communist
Economy	Agriculture: rice, potatoes, sorghum, peanuts, tea, millet, barley, pork, cotton
	Major industries: iron and steel, coal, armaments, textiles and clothing, petroleum
Exports	Textiles, clothing, footwear, toys, machinery, weapons systems
Imports	Steel, motor vehicles, textile machinery, petroleum products, aircraft

GEOGRAPHY The map shows the country of China and its most important cities. **Map and Chart Study** In what part of China are the most cities located? Look at the graph of China's labor force. Based on the information in the graph, where do you think most Chinese workers live—in cities or rural areas? Why?

Under the leadership of **Mao Zedong** (MOW zuh DUNG), China made huge changes. The government seized land from large landowners, as well as taking over all factories and businesses. But Mao was not satisfied. Economic growth was too slow.

In the 1950s, Mao began a policy of **radical,** or extreme change. This policy, called the "Great Leap Forward," turned out to be a giant step backward. The Communists rushed to increase production on farms and in factories. But they ignored the need for experience and planning. For example, they ordered a huge increase in steel production. Thousands of untrained workers built furnaces for steel-making that never worked.

In 1966, Mao introduced another radical policy called the Cultural Revolution. His aim was to create a society with no ties to the past. Mao urged students to rebel against teachers and families. Students formed bands of radicals called the **Red Guard.** These bands destroyed some of China's most beautiful ancient buildings and beat up and imprisoned many Chinese artists and professionals such as lawyers and doctors.

Then, the Red Guard began to threaten Mao's government, and they were imprisoned, too. Mao ended the Cultural Revolution in 1969. The ill-conceived policy had left China in a shambles, with hundreds of thousands of citizens dead.

Improvement through Entrepreneurship

During the late 1970s, the Communists realized that their policies had hurt China. After Mao's death in 1976, more moderate Communists gained power. Over the next 20 years, they gradually introduced a limited form of **free enterprise.** Under this economic system, people are allowed to choose their own jobs, start private businesses, and make a profit. The new system also includes farming. Farmers can grow extra crops on private plots of land and can sell the crops for a profit.

Today, both the government and private citizens act as entrepreneurs. They form and manage small businesses, such as jade carving, porcelain making, and silk weaving. In addition, privately owned Chinese factories make cars, elevators, electronic equipment, watches, cameras, and bicycles.

The Growth of Taiwan

After their defeat by the Communists in 1949, the Nationalists

Taiwan: Physical

TAIWAN
Taiwan Strait
Tan shui
⊛ Taipei
Quemoy
South China Sea
Pescadores
Pescadores Channel
Tropic of Cancer
Tachia River
CHUNGYANG RANGE
Choshui River
Yu Shan 13,113 ft (3,997 m)
24°N
Tsengwen River
Chishan River
Lu I.
Philippine Sea
Lan I.
22°N
Oluan Point
Luzon Strait

KEY
Elevation

Feet	Meters
Over 13,000	Over 3,960
6,500–13,000	1,980–3,960
1,600–6,500	480–1,980
650–1,600	200–480
0–650	0–200
Below sea level	Below sea level

⊛ National capital

Lambert Conformal Conic Projection

0   50   100 mi
0   50   100 km

GEOGRAPHY

The island of Taiwan has an area of 13,900 square miles (35,980 sq km). This makes it almost twice the size of the state of New Jersey. Like much of East Asia, Taiwan is mountainous. Its farmers often build terraces for growing crops. **Map Study** Find Taiwan on the Country Profile map of China on page 502. How does Taiwan compare with mainland China in size? Now study this map. In what areas of Taiwan do you think most of the island's people live? Why?

The Three Gorges Dam

ECONOMICS

The construction of the Three Gorges Dam on China's Yangzi River is the largest hydroelectric project in the world. Begun in 1994, the project will generate up to one-ninth of China's power when completed around 2009. **Critical Thinking** How might the dam benefit the farmers who live and work along the banks of the Yangzi River? How might it harm them?

fled to **Taiwan,** an island 100 miles (161 km) off China's southeast coast. Here they set up a government they called the Republic of China.

Even in the 1950s, Taiwan's free enterprise economy was one of Asia's strongest. The Chinese on Taiwan started a program that allowed farmers to buy land at low prices. This increased farm output and brought in more money to the government. This money helped Taiwan build new ports and modern railroads, and with aid from the United States, Taiwan also built roads and helped industries. The Taiwanese then increased their trade with foreign nations. They sell computer chips, computers, and other electronic products to the rest of the world.

Challenges in China

Today, China is becoming a world economic force. Money to develop industry and business is pouring into the country, and China's middle class is growing. Yet progress has created some challenges. Rural areas of China have not prospered as much as urban areas. Farmers sometimes have trouble getting their crops to markets.

China is working on these problems. The government has built new communities in rural areas. Like tiny towns, they have schools, parks, and libraries. The government is encouraging the growth of business and industry in these communities and throughout rural China.

Another challenge China faces is its poor human rights record. With foreign investment and trade on the rise, China is under increasing pressure from the global community to foster civil rights among its citizenry.

SECTION 1 ASSESSMENT

AFTER YOU READ

RECALL

1. Identify: (a) Mao Zedong, (b) Red Guard, (c) Taiwan

2. Define: (a) radical, (b) free enterprise

COMPREHENSION

3. How did early communist policies affect the people of China?

4. In what ways has China's economy changed in recent years?

CRITICAL THINKING AND WRITING

5. **Exploring the Main Idea** Review the Main Idea statement at the beginning of this section. List some of the changes that China underwent after Mao Zedong came to power.

6. **Comparing and Contrasting** The governments of Communist China and Taiwan made very different political decisions when they were first formed. How did some of those decisions affect those countries' use of technology?

ACTIVITY

7. **Writing to Learn** Write a letter giving economic advice to a developing nation. Use what you have learned about China to suggest ways for the country to build a strong economy.

SECTION 2

Japan
An Economic Powerhouse

BEFORE YOU READ

READING FOCUS

1. How did Japan become one of the most successful developed nations in the world?
2. How do traditions inhibit change in Japan?

KEY TERMS

robot
subsidize
incentive
discrimination

MAIN IDEA

After World War II, Japan regained its status as an important manufacturing country and became a prosperous industrial nation.

NOTE TAKING

Copy the diagram below. As you read the section, fill in the diagram to show what caused Japan to develop a thriving market economy and to identify some of the current threats to this economy.

Japan becomes one of the most successful developed nations in the world.

Challenges

Setting the Scene

A Japanese company that makes **robots,** computer-driven machines that do tasks once done by humans, holds an Idea Olympics each year. Employees compete in thinking up ideas to improve the company. Nearly half of the employees work on these ideas on their own time.

Reorganizing Economic Systems

Some of Japan's ideas have come from outside the nation. Once Japan opened its ports to other countries in the 1800s, it welcomed new inventions from the West. For years, the Japanese worked to build major industries. By the 1920s, Japan had become an important manufacturing country. Its economy depended on importing natural resources and exporting manufactured goods.

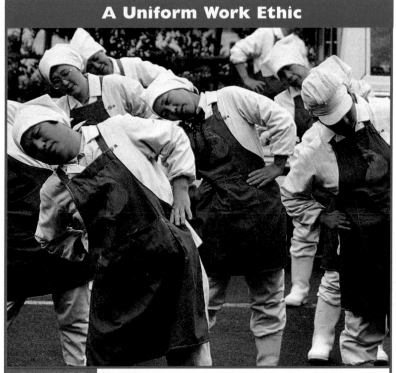

A Uniform Work Ethic

CULTURE Workers in neat uniforms exercise in unison at a seafood plant. The Japanese believe that such group activities make workers more productive. **Critical Thinking** Why do you think group activities would make these workers more productive? Explain your answer.

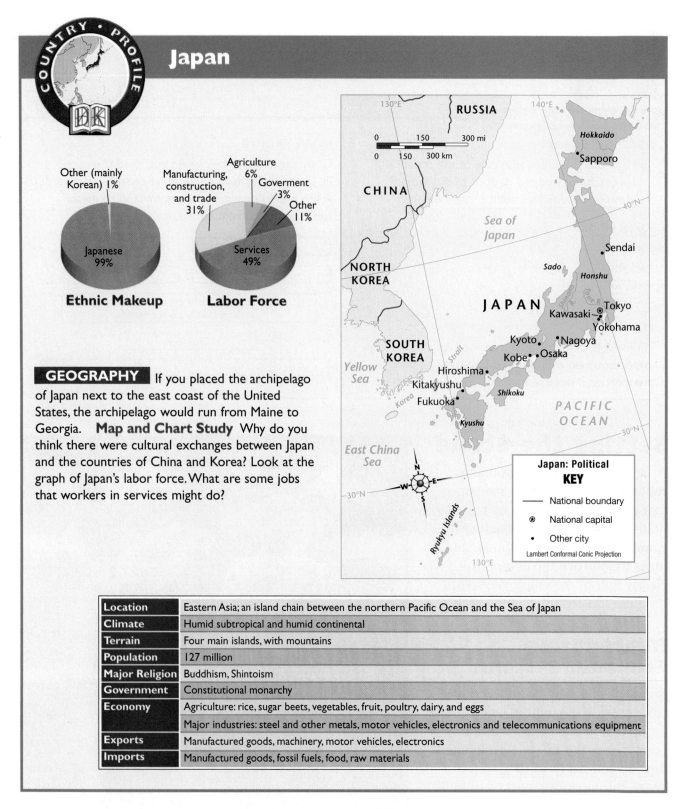

Japan

COUNTRY · PROFILE

Ethnic Makeup

Other (mainly Korean) 1%

Japanese 99%

Labor Force

Manufacturing, construction, and trade 31%

Agriculture 6%

Goverment 3%

Other 11%

Services 49%

GEOGRAPHY If you placed the archipelago of Japan next to the east coast of the United States, the archipelago would run from Maine to Georgia. **Map and Chart Study** Why do you think there were cultural exchanges between Japan and the countries of China and Korea? Look at the graph of Japan's labor force. What are some jobs that workers in services might do?

Japan: Political
KEY

——— National boundary

⊛ National capital

• Other city

Lambert Conformal Conic Projection

Location	Eastern Asia; an island chain between the northern Pacific Ocean and the Sea of Japan
Climate	Humid subtropical and humid continental
Terrain	Four main islands, with mountains
Population	127 million
Major Religion	Buddhism, Shintoism
Government	Constitutional monarchy
Economy	Agriculture: rice, sugar beets, vegetables, fruit, poultry, dairy, and eggs
	Major industries: steel and other metals, motor vehicles, electronics and telecommunications equipment
Exports	Manufactured goods, machinery, motor vehicles, electronics
Imports	Manufactured goods, fossil fuels, food, raw materials

World War II and Beyond After World War II, Japan was in ruins. Only a few factories were still running. They made shoes from scraps of wood, and kitchen pots and pans from soldiers' steel helmets. The idea that the Japanese might soon be able to compete with the industrial giants of the West seemed impossible.

Financial aid from the United States helped rebuild industry. Another reason Japan became a prosperous industrial nation was its ability to change and grow. The Japanese government helped industries by **subsidizing,** or financially supporting, them. This allowed companies to build large factories and buy modern machines. With more goods to sell, manufacturers could earn more money. Workers also earned more money, so they were able to spend more. This raised the demand for Japanese goods within Japan itself.

Since the 1960s, Japan has produced some of the world's most modern industrial robots. By the 1970s, the Japanese were making more watches and cameras than the Swiss and the Germans, and by the 1980s, Japan made and sold a large share of the world's cars, electronic goods, skiing gear, and bicycles. Japan also produced huge amounts of steel and many ships. You are probably familiar with personal stereos and small, hand-held electronic games. These were invented by the Japanese.

Japan's Workers

For many years, Japan has been known for its economic success. Japanese workers view themselves as members of a group, all working toward one goal. This dedication results in a Japanese economy comparable to developed nations of much greater size and population.

Although Japan still has one of the largest economies in the world, problems have surfaced in recent years. Poor trade relations combined with an economic recession in the early 1990s greatly hurt Japan's economy. Companies who in the past had always been loyal to their employees were forced to lay off workers, and unemployment in Japan rose. Japanese businesses were forced to re-think many traditional practices.

Limiting Government's Role   In Japan, there has always been a close cooperation between business and government. In the past, this has helped businesses to thrive. In recent years, however, it has hurt Japan's economy.

The Japanese government has always supported its citizens, no matter what the cost. Workers are rarely laid off, even when the companies they work for make no profits and cannot pay their salaries. The government has always stepped in to make companies and people happy. One way that it has been able to do this is by taking a strong role in Japan's banks and stock markets. The government controls bank loans, encourages consumers to save their money in banks, and regulates the stock market to expand and strengthen Japan's economy and create a high standard of living. In recent years, however, the economy has suffered. The government has not provided a banking system to regulate loans, and its control of the stock market has discouraged healthy competition.

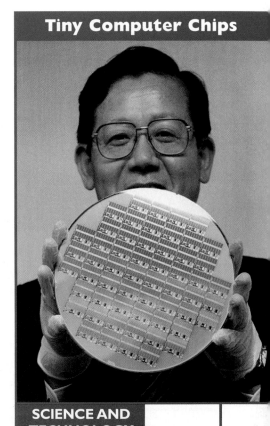

Tiny Computer Chips

SCIENCE AND TECHNOLOGY   In recent years, Japan has become a leader in computer technology. Here, a manager of a Japanese computer company displays dynamic random access memory, or DRAM, chips. These tiny chips, which measure about 0.5 inches (1 cm) by 0.75 inches (2 cm), are the "brains" of a computer.
Critical Thinking How did the Japanese government help computer technology and other industries to grow?

Women in the Labor Force

ECONOMICS

Employees of an American computer firm discuss a technical problem at the company's Japan headquarters. **Critical Thinking** What do you predict will happen to the role of Japanese women in economic life?

Tradition Inhibits Change

As elsewhere in East Asia, traditions are important in Japan. Times are changing, but change comes slowly. The role of women is one example. As in the past, being married is the most acceptable position for a Japanese woman. Large companies often have marriage bureaus to introduce their single employees.

Japan's hard-working wives and mothers support the economy and are in charge of their households. They make schooling decisions, handle the family finances, and take care of major purchases.

Japanese women often work before marriage. In the past, many worked in rice fields, fisheries, and factories, or as nurses or teachers. Today, though, some married women are venturing outside the home in a new direction—as part-time workers.

In the 1980s, the largest group of working women in Japan was the army of "office ladies." They served tea, did light cleaning, held doors, and answered the phone. Today, office ladies are rare. Instead, women are crowding the workplace, often working long hours beside male workers—who get higher salaries and good benefits.

At present, few women become managers in Japanese businesses and even when they do, they may meet with job **discrimination,** or unequal treatment. For this reason, many young women are not willing to join Japanese firms. Instead, they look for jobs with foreign businesses in Japan. They are also finding jobs in newer fields where there is less discrimination.

SECTION 2 ASSESSMENT

AFTER YOU READ

RECALL

1. Define: (a) robot, (b) subsidize, (c) incentive, (d) discrimination

COMPREHENSION

2. What are some reasons for Japan's economic success and for its recent downturn?
3. Do the roles played by women illustrate how tradition and change affect Japan today?

CRITICAL THINKING AND WRITING

4. **Exploring the Main Idea** Review the Main Idea statement at the beginning of this section. Then, imagine you are a Japanese grandparent. Write a descriptive paragraph for your grandchildren describing the economic changes you have seen since World War II.
5. **Making Inferences and Drawing Conclusions** Why does their view of work and incentives help Japanese employees produce more?
6. **Writing an Essay** Question several friends or people about their attitudes toward their jobs. Do they feel part of a team? Do they take pride in their work? What incentives do their employers offer? Write a short essay comparing American views with Japanese views.

ACTIVITY

Take It to the NET

7. **Graphing Japan's Economy** Find information on economic activities in Japan. Create a thematic graph to display information such as imports and exports. Visit the World Explorer: People, Places, and Cultures section of **phschool.com** for help in completing this activity.

North Korea: A Command Economy

North Korea is a communist country that has kept itself closed to much of the rest of the world. This has kept out new technology and fresh ideas. Yet North Korea is rich in mineral resources. Until the end of World War II, it was the industrial center of the Korean Peninsula.

Today, however, North Korea cannot compete with South Korea. It still manufactures goods in government-owned factories and these factories produce poor-quality goods. Little has been done to **diversify,** or add variety to, the economy.

Farming methods, too, are outdated in the north. Many farmers burn hillsides to prepare for planting crops. After a few years of destroying vegetation, the good soil can be washed away by rain. Then, the fields can no longer be farmed. In 1996, North Koreans faced **famine,** or a huge food shortage, and starvation. For the first time, they asked noncommunist countries for aid.

Why don't the two sides get together? They share a common heritage and language. Many families have members living on both sides of the DMZ. North Korea has great need of the food raised in the south. Its industries would also benefit from the technology of the south. South Korea's needs are fewer. It could make good use of the mineral resources of the north. But South Korea can easily buy what it needs with the money from exports. It is mainly political differences that keep the two countries from joining peacefully. Probably only the end of communism in the north will allow Korea to be unified again.

Student Demonstration in Seoul

CITIZENSHIP

In South Korea, groups often take to the streets to demand higher wages, better working conditions, new government programs, or friendlier relations with North Korea. Here, a group of college students march in such a parade, or demonstration, in Seoul. Sometimes, marchers clash with police. **Critical Thinking** What kinds of slogans do you think might be written on the colorful banners carried by the students?

SECTION 3 ASSESSMENT

AFTER YOU READ

RECALL

1. Define (a) demilitarized zone, (b) diversify, (c) famine

COMPREHENSION

2. Discuss the reasons for South Korea's economic success and recent downturn.

3. Why has North Korea's economy lagged behind South Korea's?

CRITICAL THINKING AND WRITING

4. Exploring the Main Idea Review the Main Idea statement at the beginning of this section. Then, list the industries and resources in South Korea and North Korea.

5. Comparing and Contrasting How do the governments of North and South Korea affect their economies?

ACTIVITY

6. Writing to Learn The division between North and South Korea has cut you off from family members. It has also influenced the way you live. Write a journal entry describing what it is like to live in either North or South Korea.

Vietnam
Rebuilding the Economy

READING FOCUS

1. What conflicts have divided Vietnam?

2. How are the Vietnamese rebuilding their economy?

KEY TERMS
refugee

KEY PEOPLE AND PLACES
Ho Chi Minh
Ho Chi Minh City

MAIN IDEA

After decades of conflict and war devastated Vietnam, a reunited country has struggled to rebuild its economy.

NOTE TAKING

Copy the diagram below. As you read the section, fill in the diagram to show what caused a long and devastating war in Vietnam, and to identify some of the problems war left behind.

War in Vietnam

War's Aftermath

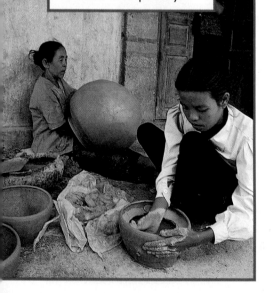

Setting the Scene

It is summer in northern Vietnam. Villagers cut, harvest, and plow rice fields just as their parents and grandparents did. Unlike their parents and grandparents, however, these villagers are making money. Rice farmers in the village of Phu Do return from the fields to a second job: noodle-making. Farmers in Son Dong carve religious statues from wood in their free time. Potters in Bat Trang, goldsmiths in Dong Sam, embroiderers in Thuong Tin—all are earning money from age-old crafts. Their success helps to rebuild the economy of Vietnam.

Decades of Conflict and War

In the mid-1800s, France took over Vietnam as a colony. The Vietnamese people resented French rule. They wanted to have their own government on their own soil. In 1946, many Vietnamese heeded the call to arms of independence leader **Ho Chi Minh** (hoh chee min).

Under Ho Chi Minh, the Vietnamese Communists defeated the French. The United States did not want Vietnam to become a communist country. After the French defeat, a treaty divided Vietnam into two nations. The northern nation was controlled by Communists. Under Ho Chi Minh, they tried to take over the south by force. In 1959, Ho Chi Minh's forces, the Viet Cong, launched a war to achieve this goal. As they threatened South Vietnam, the United States took an active role in the war.

COUNTRY · PROFILE

Vietnam

65 and over
5%

Under 15
36%

15-64
59%

**Age Structure
(in years)**

Chinese
4%

Thai
2%

Other
6%

Vietnamese
88%

Ethnic Makeup

GEOGRAPHY This map shows the locations of some cities in Vietnam. **Map and Chart Study** Look at the information about the exports of Vietnam. What generalization can you make about the country's exports?

CHINA

Dien Bien Phu

Hanoi ⊛

Haiphong

LAOS

Gulf of Tonkin

THAILAND

17th Parallel
Demarcation Line of 1954

Hue

Da Nang
(Tourane)

Chu Lai

Vietnam: Political
KEY

— National boundary

⊛ National capital

• Other city

Miller Cylindrical Projection

Plei Ku

CAMBODIA

VIETNAM

Ho Chi
Minh City
(Saigon)

Gulf of
Thailand

South China
Sea

| 0 | 100 | 200 mi |
| 0 | 100 | 200 km |

Location	Southeastern Asia
Climate	Tropical in the south; monsoons in the north with a hot, rainy season and a warm, dry season
Terrain	Low, flat in south and north, central highlands; mountainous in far north, northwest
Population	81.1 million
Major Religion	Buddhism, Hoa Hao, Cao Dai, Christianity, indigenous beliefs, Islam
Ethnic Groups	Mostly Vietnamese; also Chinese, Hmong, Thai, Khmer, Cham, and mountain groups
Government	Communist
Economy	Agriculture: paddy rice, corn, potatoes, rubber, soybeans, coffee, tea, bananas, sugar
	Major industries: food processing, garments, shoes, machine building, mining, cement
Exports	Crude oil, marine products, rice, coffee, rubber, tea, garments, shoes
Imports	Machinery and equipment, petroleum products, fertilizer, steel products, raw cotton

By the 1970s, Vietnam had been at war for more than 30 years. The United States government realized it was fighting a war it would never win. In addition, thousands of people in the United States were calling for an end to the war. By 1973, the United States finally ended its part in the war.

The Vietnamese Rebuild

After the United States pulled out, North Vietnam conquered the south and in 1976, the country was reunited under a communist government. Vietnam had been devastated by the war. Millions of Vietnamese had been killed or wounded, homes, farms, factories, and forests had been destroyed, bombs had torn cities apart, and fields were covered with land mines, or hidden explosives. The Vietnamese people were worn out. Still ahead was the huge effort of rebuilding.

In the years after the war, the communist government in Vietnam strictly controlled the lives of its citizens. Although it is still a communist country, Vietnam now allows some free enterprise. Still, most Vietnamese live in rural areas where whole families live on a few hundred dollars a year.

Vietnam's greatest economic successes have been in rebuilding its cities. Hanoi in the north is the capital. Saigon (sy GAHN), now called **Ho Chi Minh City,** is the most prosperous city in Vietnam and is the center of trade. Well-off Vietnamese buy designer clothing and watches, stereo systems, and jewelry. Many of these people run restaurants or hotels, buy and sell land or buildings, or own factories.

Although northern Vietnam has been much slower to modernize than the south, the desire for economic success has taken hold in that part of the country, too.

Thousands of former **refugees,** people who flee their country because of war, have returned to Ho Chi Minh City. Some ex-refugees attended business and law schools in the United States, and today they use their knowledge of Vietnam and the West to help wealthy foreigners do business in Vietnam.

SECTION 4 ASSESSMENT

AFTER YOU READ

RECALL

1. Identify: (a) Ho Chi Minh, (b) Ho Chi Minh City

2. Define: (a) refugee

COMPREHENSION

3. What conflicts have divided Vietnam?

4. What successes has Vietnam had in rebuilding its economy?

CRITICAL THINKING AND WRITING

5. **Exploring the Main Idea** Review the Main Idea statement at the beginning of this section. Then, list two challenges that Vietnam faced after the war and two ways that Vietnam is rebuilding its economy.

6. **Identifying Frame of Reference and Point of View** Why do you think Saigon was renamed Ho Chi Minh City after the war?

ACTIVITY

7. **Writing a Letter to the Editor** Imagine that you are a Vietnamese living in Saigon in 1954. Write a letter to a newspaper expressing your attitude towards Ho Chi Minh.

Recognizing Bias

Learn the Skill

Being biased means leaning toward a particular point of view. Sometimes, people who write about something only know one side of the story. Other people leave out information on purpose to give their own viewpoint. Biased writing takes a side, even if at first it seems not to. You need to be able to recognize bias in writing in order to know whether you're getting a fair picture of a situation. When you read, you can look for certain clues that will point out a writer's bias. To determine whether a writer is biased, do the following:

A. Look for opinions. Opinions are beliefs that cannot be proven. They are the opposite of facts, which can be proven. Biased writing often contains opinions disguised as facts. For example, the statement, "Life in South Vietnam was better than life in North Vietnam," may sound like a fact, but it is an opinion. It doesn't matter whether you agree with the opinion or think that it makes sense.

B. Look for loaded words and phrases that carry a hidden meaning. These words may give a positive or a negative impression. Read this sentence: "Vietnam's low flat deltas create picture perfect shorelines." The words "picture perfect" are loaded. They give a very positive impression. However, this hidden meaning cannot be proved. It is not fact.

C. Look for what isn't there. Biased writers often leave out information that does not support their bias. For example, the writer might tell you that "South Vietnam's president Ngo Dinh Diem distributed land among more farmers and built new factories during the 1950s," but leave out any negative actions of Diem's or any positive actions of North Vietnam's leader.

D. Think about the tone. Tone is the overall feeling of a piece of writing. It shows the writer's attitude toward the subject: "Water puppets became a crude form of entertainment." This sentence gives you the clear impression that the writer has negative feelings about Vietnamese forms of entertainment. Unbiased writing provides the facts and lets the reader form his or her own conclusions.

Practice the Skill

The selection in the box is a biased description of Vietnam today. To identify the bias, follow steps A through D. Consider these questions: Are there any opinions disguised as facts in the selection? What words give a positive or negative impression of Vietnam? What important facts about Vietnam does the writer fail to include? How would you describe the tone of the writing? Is it positive or negative? After you have finished, describe Vietnam today in one paragraph without bias.

Vietnam Today

It is unfortunate that Vietnam became a communist country. Today it is one of the poorest nations in Asia. Most houses have no indoor toilets or running water. The government of Vietnam would do well to model itself after the United States.

Apply the Skill

See the Chapter Review and Assessment at the end of this chapter for more questions on recognizing bias.

Review and Assessment

Creating a Chapter Summary

On a separate piece of paper, draw a diagram like this one, and include the information that summarizes the first section of the chapter. Then, fill in the remaining boxes with summaries of Sections 2, 3, and 4.

EAST AND SOUTHEAST ASIA TODAY

Section 1
In recent years, China has begun to repair its economy, which was devastated during the long rule of Mao Zedong. Taiwan has a free enterprise economy that, since the nation's founding, has been one of the strongest in Asia.

Section 2

Section 3

Section 4

Reviewing Key Terms

Match the key terms in Column I with the definitions in Column II.

Column I
1. subsidize
2. diversify
3. incentive
4. refugee
5. free enterprise
6. radical
7. discrimination

Column II
a. extreme
b. add variety
c. support financially
d. economic system that allows people to choose jobs, start private businesses, make a profit
e. person who flees his or her country because of war
f. benefit that inspires people to work hard
g. unequal treatment

Reviewing the Main Ideas

1. How did the policies of Mao Zedong affect China's economy? (Section 1)
2. What change has strengthened China's economy in recent years? (Section 1)
3. What has helped Taiwan to become and remain economically strong? (Section 1)
4. How did Japan regain economic strength after World War II? (Section 2)
5. What issues must Japan address to maintain a strong economy? (Section 2)
6. What political and economic differences divide North and South Korea? (Section 3)
7. How was Vietnam divided after it gained independence from France? (Section 4)
8. What change in economic policy is helping some Vietnamese attain a higher standard of living? (Section 4)

Map Activity

East and Southeast Asia

For each place listed below, write the letter from the map that shows its location. Use the Atlas in the back of your book to help you.

1. Japan
2. China
3. Taiwan
4. South Korea
5. North Korea
6. Hong Kong

 Take It to the NET

Enrichment For more map activities using geography skills, visit the social studies section of **phschool.com.**

Writing Activity

1. **Writing a Newspaper Editorial** Choose one conflict that you read about in this chapter. Write a newspaper editorial that gives your point of view on the conflict.

2. **Using Primary Sources** Choose one of the places discussed in the chapter to research. Visit your school library and use primary sources such as interviews found in newspaper or magazine articles and memoirs to find additional information on the place. Write a travel article that provides information and suggestions for what to see and how to act in the place.

Applying Your Skills

Look through a current newspaper or magazine to find a short article that interests you. Review the steps you learned to recognize bias. Read your chosen article and determine whether the writer is biased. Record your thoughts on a separate sheet of paper, making sure to support your decision with details from the article.

Critical Thinking

1. **Comparing and Contrasting** Compare the policies of the communist government of China before and after the late 1970s.

2. **Identifying the Main Ideas and Supporting Details** Why are Japan's people sometimes called its only natural resources?

 Take It to the NET

Activity Read the news article about the current state of Vietnam's economy and government. Who controls the economy in Vietnam? How is it different from the economy in the United States? Visit the World Explorer: People, Places, and Cultures section of **phschool.com** for help in completing this activity.

Chapter 27 Self-Test As a final review activity, take the Chapter 27 Self-Test and get instant feedback on your answers. To take the test, visit the Social Studies section of **phschool.com.**

SOUTH AND SOUTHWEST ASIA
Exploring the Region Today

A Tribute to Beauty

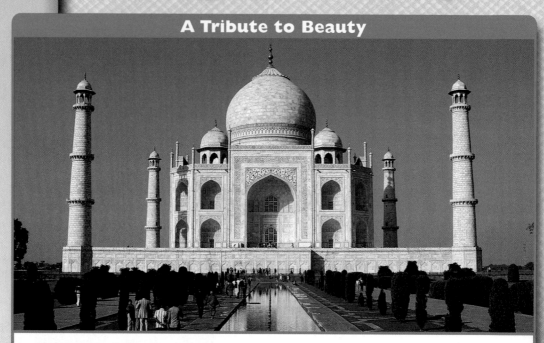

USING PICTURES

The Taj Mahal was built by Shah Jahan, a Muslim ruler from northern India. It represents the throne of God in paradise, but also served as a mausoleum (tomb) for the Shah and his wife when they died.

Taj Mahal Math
Construction of the Taj Mahal began in 1632. It took 20,000 workers eleven years to complete the mausoleum, and another eleven years to finish the entire complex. In what year was the mausoleum finished? How many years did it take to finish the entire complex?

Making a Model of the Taj Mahal
The Taj Mahal is made of white marble. The mausoleum rises about 120 feet into the air and covers an area of about 300 square feet. The minarets are 133 feet high. Notice the large dome in the center as well as other smaller domes. The large dome is 70 feet in diameter. Work with a partner. Use clay, a piece of cardboard for a base, and the photo on this page to create a model of the Taj Mahal.

Pakistan
Making Economic Progress

BEFORE YOU READ

READING FOCUS

1. How does the Indus River influence the relationship between Pakistan and India?
2. What has Pakistan done to help its farmers?
3. What economic growth has taken place in Pakistan?

KEY TERMS

drought

KEY PLACE

Kashmir

NOTE TAKING

Copy the outline below. As you read the section, add to the outline to show how Pakistan is making economic progress.

> I. **Geographical Issues**
>   A. Indus River is vital to Pakistan's economy
>   B.
> II. **Agriculture**
> III. **Industrial Growth**

MAIN IDEA

Most Pakistanis are farmers, but economic growth is taking place through the development of agricultural and other industries.

Setting the Scene

Many of us take water for granted. We turn on the tap, and water pours out. But many countries in the world lack water resources. **Drought,** or a long period without rain, is a major problem in Pakistan. It is one cause of the conflict over the region of **Kashmir** (KAZH mihr).

Geography Influences Politics

Kashmir is a land of high mountains and beautiful lakes. The Indus River flows from the high mountains of Kashmir. Therefore, whoever controls Kashmir, controls the water flow of the Indus River. Farmers need this water to irrigate crops because without the Indus River, Pakistan would be a dry, hot desert.

Kashmir is bordered by Pakistan, India, China, and Afghanistan. Both Pakistan and India claim Kashmir and want to control the waters of the Indus. The conflict over Kashmir has led to battles between India and Pakistan. This is how important water is to the region.

Terraced Farming

GEOGRAPHY Only about 6 percent of Kashmir's land is good for growing crops. Here, farmers have built terraces so they can grow crops on sloping land. **Critical Thinking** How does the snow on the mountain tops affect the river?

Pakistan

Age Structure (in years)

- 65 and over 4%
- Under 15 44%
- 15-64 52%

Religious Persuasion

- Christian 1%
- Hindu 2%
- Shi'a Muslim 20%
- Sunni Muslim 77%

GEOGRAPHY

This map shows the disputed territory of Kashmir. The line between the Indian and Pakistani sections of Kashmir is the truce line set in 1972. This dispute between Pakistan and India is still not settled. **Map and Chart Study** How can you tell from the map that the Indus River is important to Pakistan?

Pakistan: Economic Activity
KEY

- Area claimed and controlled by India; status disputed by Pakistan
- Area controlled by Pakistan and claimed by India
- – · – Line of control
- ······ Kashmir border
- ——— National boundary
- ⊛ National capital
- · City
- Wheat
- Cotton
- Sugar cane
- Rice
- Fruits and vegetables
- Hydroelectric power
- C Coal
- Petroleum
- Natural gas

Two-Point Equidistant Projection

Location	Southern Asia; bordering the Arabian Sea
Climate	Mostly hot, dry desert, with highlands climate in the mountains of the north
Terrain	Indus River Plain in the east; mountains in the north and west; plateau in the west
Population	147.7 million
Ethnic Groups	Punjabi, Sindhi, Pashtun, Baloch, others
Government	Republic
Economy	Agriculture: cotton, wheat, rice, sugar cane, fruits, vegetables, livestock
	Industries: textiles, food processing, construction materials, clothing, paper products
Exports	Cotton, textiles, clothing, rice, leather, carpets
Imports	Petroleum products, machinery, transportation equipment, vegetable oils, chemicals

An Agricultural Nation

Through hard work and clever farming methods, Pakistani farmers grow large amounts of wheat, cotton, and sugar cane. They also grow so much rice that they can export it to other countries. The great advances the country has made in agriculture could easily be lost without the much-needed water.

Irrigation Produces Larger Crops Pakistanis on the Indus Plain have built thousands of canals and ditches to move water to their fields. In this way, farmers maintain a steady flow of water, even during droughts. As more land is irrigated, more acres are farmed. This has increased the amount of crops.

At harvest time, the bright yellow flowers of Pakistan's five kinds of mustard blanket the fields. Improved farming methods allow Pakistani farmers to grow lentils, beans used in a spicy dish called dhal (dahl). Farmers also grow fruits, such as apricots and mangoes, and vegetables, such as chilis and peas.

Problems and Solutions Irrigation solves many farming problems, but it creates others. For example, river water contains small amounts of salts which, over time, build up in the soil and slow plant growth. Pakistani scientists are trying to find a way to treat the salt-damaged soil.

Pakistanis have another water problem. During the monsoon season, damaging floods occur. One solution is the large dams built by the government. The dams catch and hold monsoon rains. The waters are then released as needed, into irrigation canals.

Economic Development

In addition to helping farmers, dams speed industrial growth. Dams can release rushing water to create hydroelectric energy. In Pakistan, hydroelectric power plants produce energy to run mills and factories. Most industry is located near the sources of hydroelectric power, on the Indus Plain.

Wheat Harvest in Pakistan

ECONOMICS These Pakistani farmers are removing the husks from wheat grains by tossing the wheat into the air. In addition to such age-old practices, they also use modern farming methods. For example, they plant seeds developed by scientists that produce bigger crops. Since farmers started doing this in the 1960s, wheat production has doubled. Pakistan now grows more wheat than Kansas and Nebraska combined. **Critical Thinking** Why do you think some Pakistani farmers still rely on age-old agricultural practices even today?

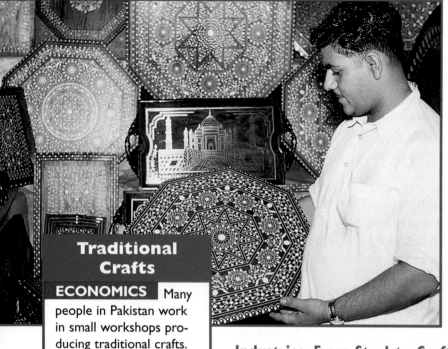

Traditional Crafts

ECONOMICS Many people in Pakistan work in small workshops producing traditional crafts. This worker from Karachi makes wooden trays and boxes that are inlaid with metal designs. Other traditional craft items produced in Pakistan include lace, carpets, pottery, and leather goods. **Critical Thinking** How might the development of traditional crafts help Pakistan's economy?

Industries Based on Agriculture At independence, Pakistan had few factories. Pakistan has worked hard to build its economy through agriculture and industry. Today, Pakistan is one of the more prosperous countries in Asia. Even so, only a few Pakistanis can afford such things as refrigerators, telephones, and cars.

Pakistan began its industrial growth by building on what its people knew best: farming. More than half of Pakistan's industrial output comes from turning crops such as cotton into manufactured goods such as socks.

Industries: From Steel to Crafts The nation also has other industries. The chemical industry produces paint, soap, and dye. Several steel mills allow Pakistan to make almost all the steel it needs, helping the country to save money.

Millions of Pakistanis work in small workshops, instead of in large factories. Workshops produce field hockey sticks, furniture, knives, saddles, and carpets. Pakistan is famous for its beautiful carpets. Some sell for as much as $25,000 in Pakistan—and $50,000 in New York or London.

Pakistanis are working hard to improve their future. By building industries and modernizing agriculture, they hope to raise their quality of life.

SECTION I ASSESSMENT

AFTER YOU READ

AFTER YOU READ
1. Identify: Kashmir
2. Define: drought

COMPREHENSION
3. Why is the Indus River crucial to Pakistani farmers?
4. What steps has Pakistan taken to improve its agriculture?
5. What industries have emerged since Pakistan became a nation?

CRITICAL THINKING AND WRITING
6. **Exploring the Main Idea** Review the Main Idea statement at the beginning of this section. Then, write a short paragraph discussing the impact you think Pakistan's industrial growth will have on its economy.
7. **Identifying a Problem** Write a paragraph explaining why Kashmir is important to both India and Pakistan.

ACTIVITY
8. **Make a List** Reread the descriptions of Pakistan's domestic policies, such as dam building, pursuing scientific advances in irrigation technology, and building hydroelectric plants. For each policy, identify and list geographic factors that helped shape it.

SECTION 2

India

A Democracy Rooted in Tradition

Setting the Scene

The whole village had turned up for the Hindu religious service—everyone from members of the highest caste to those of no caste, the Untouchables. After the service, the people sat down to a meal. No one seemed to mind who was sitting next to them. At the end of the meal, lower caste members and Untouchables began to clean up the dining room. Some higher caste members told them to stop, then did the work themselves. Stunned, an Untouchable said, "This is the first time in my life to see such a sight."

Opportunity for All Citizens

Why did the Untouchable express surprise? Because of the ancient traditions, such as the caste system, in which Indian culture is rooted.

The Caste System Traditional Hindu society divides its followers into four **castes,** or social groups. The castes put people in order from the bottom of society to the top. Below the lowest caste are the Untouchables. They are a "casteless" or outcast Hindu group.

Busy Streets

CULTURE An Indian barber shaves a customer. Many barbers in India work in the open air.
Critical Thinking What are economic reasons why a barber would want to work outside?

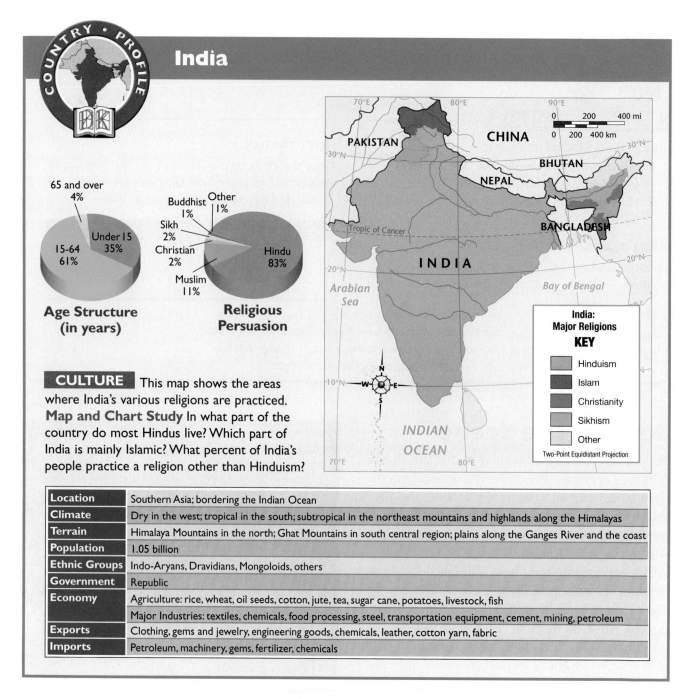

Country · Profile

India

Age Structure (in years)

65 and over 4%
Under 15 35%
15-64 61%

Religious Persuasion

Buddhist 1%
Other 1%
Sikh 2%
Christian 2%
Muslim 11%
Hindu 83%

India: Major Religions KEY
- Hinduism
- Islam
- Christianity
- Sikhism
- Other

Two-Point Equidistant Projection

CULTURE This map shows the areas where India's various religions are practiced. **Map and Chart Study** In what part of the country do most Hindus live? Which part of India is mainly Islamic? What percent of India's people practice a religion other than Hinduism?

Location	Southern Asia; bordering the Indian Ocean
Climate	Dry in the west; tropical in the south; subtropical in the northeast mountains and highlands along the Himalayas
Terrain	Himalaya Mountains in the north; Ghat Mountains in south central region; plains along the Ganges River and the coast
Population	1.05 billion
Ethnic Groups	Indo-Aryans, Dravidians, Mongoloids, others
Government	Republic
Economy	Agriculture: rice, wheat, oil seeds, cotton, jute, tea, sugar cane, potatoes, livestock, fish
	Major Industries: textiles, chemicals, food processing, steel, transportation equipment, cement, mining, petroleum
Exports	Clothing, gems and jewelry, engineering goods, chemicals, leather, cotton yarn, fabric
Imports	Petroleum, machinery, gems, fertilizer, chemicals

Over thousands of years, the caste system grew complex. The main castes divided into hundreds of groups, or subcastes. The people in each subcaste had the same job. Shopkeepers, barbers, and weavers, for example, each had their own subcaste. The caste system gave Hindus a sense of order. But for the Untouchables, life was hard. Untouchables could do only the dirtiest work. They were not allowed to mix with people of higher castes.

The System Weakens Today, however, the caste system is weakening. During India's struggle for independence, Mohandas Gandhi began to fight for the rights of Untouchables. He took Untouchables as his pupils. He called them *Harijans*, or children of God.

After independence from Britain in 1947, India became the world's largest democracy. In the spirit of democracy, India passed laws to protect the rights of Untouchables and to help them improve their lives. The government uses quotas to guarantee jobs to Untouchables. A **quota** is a certain portion of something, such as jobs, that is set aside for a group. Universities must also accept a quota of Untouchables as students.

The caste system is slower to change in rural areas. Here, it is hard to enforce laws to protect Untouchables. In a small village, everyone knows everyone else's caste. In some villages, Untouchables are still forbidden to draw water from the public well. Also, they may be allowed only certain jobs. However, some villages have loosened the rules. For example, Untouchables now are able to worship at village temples and, through India's public school system, the children of Untouchables are able to go to school.

In crowded cities, however, it is easier for Untouchables to blend into society. People there tend to be more tolerant.

Urban and Rural Life

GEOGRAPHY This street scene in Jaipur (JY poor), northern India (inset), illustrates well the hustle and bustle of Indian city life. In the countryside outside Jaipur (above), however, life is much quieter. **Critical Thinking** What other differences do you think exist between rural and urban life in India?

Change in India

Like the belief about castes, beliefs about men and women are changing in modern India. Healthcare and education have also seen major improvements in recent years.

Women Gain Rights   Gandhi urged women to play an active part in India's fight against Britain. Women took part in boycotts and prepared leaflets. Since independence, Indian women have gained many rights. They can now vote and engage in business. They are now free to take part in public life, participate in politics, and practice careers such as doctor and lawyer. For example, in 1966, a woman, Indira Ghandi, became prime minister.

Health Care   Disease and malnutrition are still problems for millions of Indian people. Yet progress has been made. The country has not suffered from major famine since the 1940s. The government has taken steps to improve health care. More government-paid doctors work in rural areas. The government has also launched programs that protect people from certain diseases.

Education   Another way that shows how well a country is taking care of its people is the literacy rate. A country's literacy rate shows the percentage of the population age 15 and over that can read and write. India's literacy rate is far lower than the literacy rate in the United States, but it is rapidly rising. In 1991, just over 50 percent of India's population was literate. In 2001, the literacy rate had risen to about 65 percent. Thanks to ongoing efforts to improve education, India's literacy rate is continuing to rise.

SECTION 2 ASSESSMENT

AFTER YOU READ

RECALL

1. (a) caste, (b) quota, (c) purdah, (d) parliament

COMPREHENSION

2. How is the caste system different in cities and rural villages?

3. How have women's roles in the political process changed since independence?

CRITICAL THINKING AND WRITING

4. **Exploring the Main Idea** Review the Main Idea statement at the beginning of this section. Then, write a paragraph explaining how the spirit of democracy can be seen in changes that have occurred in India.

5. **Making Inferences** List some reasons why you think the Indian government has taken the lead in helping Untouchables.

ACTIVITY

6. **Writing a Letter** Write a letter to Roda Mistry. Include some questions about the roles of women in India.

Saudi Arabia
Islam and the Oil Industry

BEFORE YOU READ

READING FOCUS

1. How has oil wealth changed Saudi Arabia?
2. How do Islamic beliefs affect women in Saudi Arabia?

KEY TERMS
hajj

KEY PLACES
Mecca
Riyadh

MAIN IDEA

Oil wealth has allowed Saudi Arabia to modernize its cities, build networks of transportation and communication, and educate its people, though at the same time maintaining tradition.

NOTE TAKING

Copy the diagram below. As you read the section, complete the diagram to show some outgrowths of Saudi Arabia's oil wealth and its traditional Islamic values. Add more circles to the web as you go.

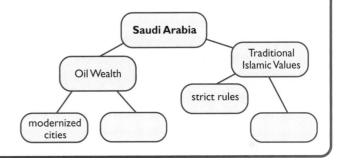

Setting the Scene

For more than a thousand years, Muslims from all over the world have been making pilgrimages to **Mecca,** Saudi Arabia. By going to Mecca, they honor the memory of Abraham, who is said to have built the first house of worship here. The pilgrimage is called the **hajj** (hahj). Muslims must make the hajj once in their lifetime if they can.

Oil and the Economy

In 1900, Mecca was a small and very poor town and the area known as Saudi Arabia was one of the poorest countries in the world. Many of its people made a living by herding livestock through the desert.

But in the 1930s, everything changed. People discovered oil on the Arabian Peninsula. Oil reserves changed the fortunes of Saudi Arabia and several other countries in the region. It made them rich.

Holy Pilgrimage

CULTURE Each year, over two million Muslims make the hajj to Mecca. Here, huge crowds worship at the Kabah, the holiest site in all of Islam. The Kabah is the cube-shaped structure to the left in the picture.

Critical Thinking How do you think making the hajj in the past compares to making this pilgrimage today? Use the photograph to help you.

Saudi Arabia

COUNTRY · PROFILE

65 and over
2%

Under 15
43%

15-64
55%

**Age Structure
(in years)**

**Afro-Asian
10%**

Arab
90%

Ethnic Groups

**Saudi Arabia: Economic Activity
KEY**

- Nomadic herding
- Commercial farming
- Little or no activity
- Petroleum

Lambert Conformal Conic Projection

ECONOMICS Only 1 percent of Saudi Arabia's land is good for farming, so it is not surprising that commercial farming is not a widespread activity. **Map and Chart Study** Where are most of Saudi Arabia's oil wells located? Look at the graph showing the age structure of the Saudi population. Why might the population be so young?

Location	Southwest Asia; bordering the Persian Gulf and the Red Sea
Climate	Dry, with great extremes of temperature
Terrain	Mostly desert, with highlands to the west
Population	23.5 million
Major Religion	Islam
Government	Monarchy
Economy	Agriculture: wheat, barley, tomatoes, melons, dates, citrus fruit, poultry, dairy products
	Major industries: petroleum production and refining, petro-chemicals, cement, construction, fertilizer, plastics
Exports	Petroleum and petroleum products
Imports	Machinery and equipment, chemicals, food, motor vehicles, textiles

Boom and Bust When night falls in **Riyadh** (ree AHD), Saudi Arabia's capital, the skyline begins to glow. The lights of the many apartment and office buildings flicker on. Large buildings line the city streets. When oil prices are high, buildings go up at a rapid pace. Money pours in, allowing communities like Riyadh to modernize. But when oil prices are down, the economy of the entire country is shaken. Many large building projects grind to a stop.

Saudi Arabia has the most important oil economy in the world. Under its deserts lie more than 250 billion barrels of oil, about one fourth of the world's supply. No other country on the Earth exports more petroleum.

Many Saudi leaders think that Saudi Arabia depends too much on oil, so the Saudis are trying to diversify their economy. They want to create many different ways for the country to earn money. But today, oil exports are still Saudi Arabia's main source of income.

Meanwhile, projects paid for with oil money have changed the lives of all Saudi Arabians. Before the oil boom, there were few roads in Saudi Arabia. Now roads link all parts of the country. In the past, people often lived without electricity and telephones. Now these luxuries are common in Saudi Arabia.

The nation's wealth has also made it possible to develop a good school system by building thousands of schools. In 1900, many Saudi Arabians could not read or write. But today, Saudi students are becoming doctors, scientists, and teachers.

Traditional Values   In Saudi Arabia, Islam regulates most people's lives. For example, cities like Riyadh contain department stores, hotels, and universities, but they have no movie theaters or nightclubs. The Sunni branch of Islam, which most Saudi Arabians follow, forbids this kind of entertainment. Also, alcohol and pork are illegal in Saudi Arabia and all shops must close during the five times a day when Muslims pray.

Saudi Arabians use many Western inventions to improve their lives. But they make sure these inventions do not interfere with their traditions.

The Role of Women in Saudi Arabia

Many laws in Saudi Arabia deal with the role of women, protecting them in certain ways, but also forbidding them to do some things. The role of women is changing, but traditional values remain strong.

Dual Lives

Old Ways and New Professions
In Riyadh, women who go out in public cover themselves with a full-length black cloak. Even their faces are usually covered. This is one of the rules of the country. Another rule is that women may not drive cars. At home, women stay in the part of the house designated for them if guests are visiting.

Samira Al Tuwaijri (suh MIH ruh al tuh WAY zhree), a young woman who lives in Riyadh, follows these rules. Tuwaijri is also a doctor in the King Fahd Hospital. She is studying to become a surgeon.

CULTURE   This doctor in Riyadh (above) wears Western-style clothes in her office. In the street, she wears a traditional full-length black cloak similar to the ones worn by these women in the Saudi city of Jidda (left).
Critical Thinking What can you tell about the women in each of these photographs?

"Traditionally, women have always…stayed at home to cook and look after the family. Working for a living was just not done," says Tuwaijri.

But when Saudi Arabia built new schools, women became better educated. "Women are no longer content to just stay at home….We are able to compete in a man's world," Tuwaijri says.

Despite the changes, women and men usually still remain separate. Boys and girls go to different schools and do not socialize with one another. Women choose careers where they will not have to work closely with men. Tuwaijri's patients are all women. "I could have entered general medicine, but I have been brought up strictly and it was difficult to adjust to examining male patients," she says.

Religion Shapes Culture   Most of the rules governing women's behavior in Saudi Arabia come from the Quran, the holy book of Islam. It requires fair treatment of women. Muslim women could own property long before Western women had that right. However, not all Muslims agree on how to apply the Quran to modern life.

"I suppose it is difficult for those who live in the West to understand why I am not allowed to be photographed," Tuwaijri says. "In Islam, the family is very important and a family decision is accepted by all members without question….Even if I disagreed with it, I would still abide by it."

Like many Saudi women, Tuwaijri is content with her role in a Muslim society. She does not want to live as Western women live. "There are many things in our culture which limit our freedom, but I would not want change overnight," she says. "It is important that we move into the future slowly and with care."

SECTION 3 ASSESSMENT

AFTER YOU READ

RECALL
1. Identify: (a) Mecca, (b) Riyadh
2. Define: hajj

COMPREHENSION
3. Name three changes that occurred in Saudi Arabia as the country grew wealthy from oil.
4. How do Saudi Arabian women keep a traditional Muslim way of life even with the changes brought by their oil wealth?

CRITICAL THINKING AND WRITING
5. **Exploring the Main Idea** Review the Main Idea statement at the beginning of this section. Then, pretend you are an older man or woman in Saudi Arabia. Write a journal entry describing what has changed in your life and what has stayed the same since the discovery of oil in the 1930s.
6. **Identifying Frame of Reference and Point of View** What is Samira Al Tuwaijri's point of view about the place of women in her culture?

ACTIVITY
7. **Making Observations** Using the map on page 528, make a list of observations about Saudi Arabia's geographic setting and the influence of this setting on the country. Include in your list observations about Saudi Arabia's neighbors, relative size, and access to water.

Israel
Building Its Economy

BEFORE YOU READ

READING FOCUS

1. How does geography affect Israel's economy?
2. How do people in Israel work together?
3. Why has Israel had to cooperate with neighboring countries?

KEY TERMS

moshavim
kibbutz

KEY PLACE

Negev Desert

NOTE TAKING

Copy the chart below. As you read the section, fill in the chart to show how the people of Israel have made it possible to farm in the desert.

```
                    ┌──────────────────┐
                    │ The Desert Blooms │
                    └──────────────────┘
              ↗              ↑              ↖
   ┌────────────┐   ┌──────────────┐   ┌──────────────┐
   │ Cooperation │   │              │   │              │
   └────────────┘   └──────────────┘   └──────────────┘
```

MAIN IDEA

By means of agricultural technology, the people of Israel have transformed a desert region to grow fruits and vegetables sold around the world.

Setting the Scene

Picture a land of rock and sand that is the lowest point on the Earth—1,310 feet (399 m) below sea level. Barely an inch of rain falls each year. Daytime temperatures can exceed 120°F (49°C). This is the **Negev Desert,** which makes up the southern two thirds of the country of Israel.

Technology Alters Geography

Israel's geography is similar to the rest of Southwest Asia and two thirds of the country is covered by desert. Throughout history, people in desert regions have made a living by herding animals across the desert, not by farming. In Israel, that has changed.

The people of Israel have used technology, new ideas, and hard work to make desert farming possible. Today, fruits and vegetables grown here are sold around the world as agriculture has become an important part of Israel's economy.

Kalman Eisenmann grows fruits and vegetables on Negev land that was once barren and dry. He uses an irrigation system that is controlled by a computer. It moves water underground through plastic tubes straight to the roots of the plants. This way of irrigating crops was invented in Israel. When it was developed, few people lived in this desert, but now half a million people live here.

Desert Farming

ECONOMICS With the sands of Israel's Negev Desert rising behind them, workers harvest strawberries.
Critical Thinking Why do you suppose this crop is grown under protective plastic sheeting?

Israel

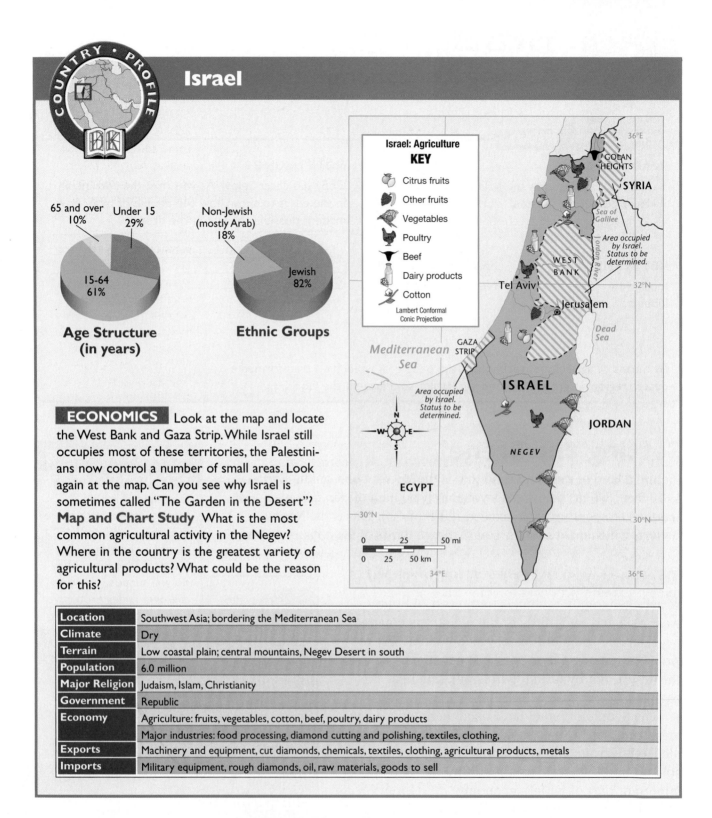

65 and over
10%

Under 15
29%

15-64
61%

**Age Structure
(in years)**

Non-Jewish
(mostly Arab)
18%

Jewish
82%

Ethnic Groups

**Israel: Agriculture
KEY**

🍊 Citrus fruits

🍇 Other fruits

🥦 Vegetables

🐓 Poultry

🐂 Beef

🥛 Dairy products

🌿 Cotton

Lambert Conformal
Conic Projection

GOLAN HEIGHTS

SYRIA

Sea of Galilee

Area occupied by Israel. Status to be determined.

WEST BANK

Tel Aviv

Jerusalem

Dead Sea

GAZA STRIP

Mediterranean Sea

Area occupied by Israel. Status to be determined.

ISRAEL

JORDAN

NEGEV

EGYPT

0   25   50 mi
0   25   50 km

ECONOMICS Look at the map and locate the West Bank and Gaza Strip. While Israel still occupies most of these territories, the Palestinians now control a number of small areas. Look again at the map. Can you see why Israel is sometimes called "The Garden in the Desert"? **Map and Chart Study** What is the most common agricultural activity in the Negev? Where in the country is the greatest variety of agricultural products? What could be the reason for this?

Location	Southwest Asia; bordering the Mediterranean Sea
Climate	Dry
Terrain	Low coastal plain; central mountains, Negev Desert in south
Population	6.0 million
Major Religion	Judaism, Islam, Christianity
Government	Republic
Economy	Agriculture: fruits, vegetables, cotton, beef, poultry, dairy products
	Major industries: food processing, diamond cutting and polishing, textiles, clothing,
Exports	Machinery and equipment, cut diamonds, chemicals, textiles, clothing, agricultural products, metals
Imports	Military equipment, rough diamonds, oil, raw materials, goods to sell

Working Together

Israel became a nation in 1948. Since then, it has almost doubled the amount of farmland within its borders. One reason for this success has been cooperation among farmworkers. In Israel, most people who do not live in cities live in **moshavim** (moh shah VEEM), small farming villages. The workers here cooperate. They combine their money to buy

Life on a Kibbutz

ECONOMICS On an Israeli kibbutz, all able-bodied adults work. While some adults tend crops such as oranges, others are busy cooking, doing the laundry, or teaching school. Children on a kibbutz may live with their parents, or they may stay in a Children's House, where they eat, sleep, and attend school. This kibbutz kindergarten class (right) is learning how to bake bread. **Critical Thinking** How is life for children on a kibbutz similar to your life? How is it different?

equipment and they tell each other about new methods of farming. They also pool their crops to get a better price.

The **kibbutz** (kih BOOTS) is another kind of cooperative settlement found in Israel. People who live on a kibbutz cooperate in all parts of life. They eat together, work together, and share profits equally. The people on a kibbutz do not earn any money while they work there, but the kibbutz provides their housing, meals, education, and health care.

On a kibbutz, people do more than farm. They may also work in factories, some of which make products such as electronic equipment and clothing. Manufacturing is an important part of Israel's economy since it exports products to many nations.

Israel and Its Neighbors

Israel has succeeded in making its dry lands come to life. However, like all countries in Southwest Asia, it must continue to manage its water carefully. To do this, Israel must cooperate with its neighbors.

Sharing the Jordan River   Galilee, in northern Israel, is a land of rolling green hills and valleys covered with wildflowers. Farmers pick bananas for market. Picnickers sit near the Sea of Galilee and toss scraps of bread to seagulls. Tourists who come to this fertile region may forget that Israel is a dry land. They may also find it hard to believe that Galilee has been the site of conflict between Israel and its Arab neighbors. The Jordan River, which runs through Galilee, is important both to Israel and to its Arab neighbors.

The Jordan River runs along Israel's borders with Syria and Jordan. It flows into the Dead Sea. In many places, this river is small and muddy. However, in Southwest Asia, the Jordan River is a vital resource. Israel, Syria, and Jordan each irrigate their crops with water

The Jordan River is the lowest river in the world. It begins in the springs of Mount Hermon in Syria and empties into the Dead Sea, approximately 1,310 feet (399m) below sea level. **Critical Thinking** How does the Jordan River's location affect the conflict between Israel and its Arab neighbors?

from the Jordan. For example, Israel uses water from this river to irrigate part of the Negev Desert.

Each country's use of Jordan River water affects its neighbors. The long conflict between Israel and the Arab states makes it hard for these neighbors to trust each other. Therefore, they watch each other's use of the Jordan River closely. When Israel began building a national irrigation system in the 1950s, Syria tried to stop the project. In the 1960s, Israel tried to stop Syria from channeling some of the river's waters. Today, the country of Jordan worries that it does not have enough water to meet its needs. It plans to build a dam near the Sea of Galilee. No building has begun, because if Jordan starts without Israel's approval, war could result.

SECTION 4 ASSESSMENT

AFTER YOU READ

RECALL
1. Identify: Negev Desert
2. Define: (a) moshavim, (b) kibbutz

COMPREHENSION
3. What geographical problems has Israel overcome to build a healthy economy?
4. How have Israelis worked together to overcome obstacles?
5. Why must Israel cooperate with its neighbors to manage its water resources?

CRITICAL THINKING AND WRITING
6. **Exploring the Main Idea** Review the Main Idea statement at the beginning of this section. Then, imagine you are a visitor in Israel. Write a postcard describing how the people of Israel grow crops on land that once was barren and dry.
7. **Comparing and Contrasting** What do you think would be some advantages and disadvantages of life on a kibbutz?

ACTIVITY
8. **Writing a Description** Using the information in the Country Profile on page 532, write a brief description of Israel's population.

Making Predictions

A. What I already know: Trees are sometimes planted to stop erosion.

B. Patterns: When other farmers have planted trees, the erosion has stopped.

C. List Possible Outcomes:

1) Farmland is more attractive.

2) Trees bear fruit.

3) Trees stop the wind from producing erosion.

D. Make a Prediction: The trees will stop the erosion.

E. Evaluation: The trees did not stop the erosion, but they did slow it down. Perhaps Dad planted the wrong kinds of trees, or not enough trees.

Learn the Skill

Imagine that you live in the Negev Desert in Israel where rainfall often erodes the desert soil. One day, your father plants trees where the erosion usually takes place. Can you predict what might happen as a result? When you make a prediction, you determine what the logical consequences of certain actions or decisions will be. Follow these steps to make predictions:

A. Think about what you already know, and write it down on paper. You might recall, for example, that trees are sometimes planted to stop erosion. This prior information will help you make a prediction.

B. Look for patterns. Maybe you have seen other farmers plant trees in eroded areas. Perhaps you noted that the erosion stopped or slowed. Think about what these patterns reveal. Write down any patterns that you've noted.

C. Make a list of possible outcomes. Brainstorm as many ideas as you can without

thinking about how valid they are. Write all of your ideas down. When you see trees planted in the desert, your list might look like the one shown on this page.

D. Use what you have learned from doing steps A, B, and C to make a prediction. First, analyze each outcome to determine which one is the most likely outcome. You will probably choose the most likely outcome.

E. Evaluate the results. Even though your prediction might be likely, things may not turn out as you had expected. You don't know yet whether the trees your father planted will actually stop the erosion. Only time will tell if your prediction was accurate.

Practice the Skill

Read each of the events listed below. Then, follow the steps to make a prediction.

1. Israel, Syria, and Jordan all need water from the Jordan River, which borders all three countries, to irrigate their crops. Predict the result.

2. Saudi Arabia improves transportation and lodging to make it easier for Muslim pilgrims to come to Mecca. Predict the result.

3. Saudi Arabian leaders think that Saudi Arabia depends too much on oil. Predict the result.

4. More and more women in Saudi Arabia are receiving a higher education. Predict the result.

Apply the Skill

See the Chapter Review and Assessment at the end of this chapter for more questions on making predictions.

Creating a Chapter Summary

On a separate piece of paper, draw a diagram like this one, and include the information that summarizes the first section of the chapter. Then, fill in the remaining boxes with summaries of Sections 2, 3, and 4.

SOUTH AND SOUTHWEST ASIA TODAY

Section 1
The conflict between India and Pakistan has been influenced by control of the Indus River, but Pakistan, a nation of farmers, is achieving economic growth through industrial development.

Section 2

Section 3

Section 4

Reviewing Key Terms

Match the key terms in Column I with the definitions in Column II.

Column I
1. moshavim
2. caste
3. drought
4. hajj
5. kibbutz
6. parliament

Column II
a. social group
b. small cooperative farming villages in Israel
c. long period without rain
d. Islamic pilgrimage to Mecca
e. law-making body
f. cooperative settlement

Reviewing the Main Ideas

1. What geographical factor influences the conflict between Pakistan and India? (Section 1)
2. How is Pakistan achieving economic growth? (Section 1)
3. What two groups have attained greater rights and access to the political process since Indian independence? (Section 2)
4. Where has social change occurred faster, in India's cities or its countryside? (Section 2)
5. How are Islamic values and traditions reflected in Saudi Arabia? (Section 3)
6. What challenge has the desert posed to Israel's economy? (Section 4)
7. How do farmers in Israel work together? (Section 4)

Map Activity

South and Southwest Asia

For each place or geographical feature listed below, write the letter from the map that shows its location.

1. Pakistan
2. Riyadh
3. Negev Desert
4. Mecca
5. Indus River
6. India

 Take It to the NET

Enrichment For more map activities using geography skills, visit the social studies section of **phschool.com**.

Writing Activity

1. **Writing a Briefing Paper** Find out about the political issues that have connected one of the following countries—Saudi Arabia or Israel—to the United States. Write a briefing paper for an incoming U.S. Senator or Representative summarizing your findings about involvement of the United States with this country.

2. **Writing a Speech** Choose one current issue discussed in the chapter to research. (Possibilities include the conflict over Kashmir or women's roles in Muslim society.) Visit your school or local library and use primary sources such as newspaper and magazine articles to find additional information about the issue. Write a speech that provides information about the issue and gives your opinion on how to address it.

Applying Your Skills

Turn to the Skills for Life activity on page 535 to answer the following questions.

1. Jordan builds a dam on the Jordan River. Predict the reaction of Syria and Israel.

2. India gains control over all of Kashmir. Predict the reaction of Pakistan.

Critical Thinking

1. **Making Comparisons** Compare the lives of women in India with those of women in Saudi Arabia.

2. **Recognizing Cause and Effect** What are some ways that low levels of rainfall might affect life in Southwest Asia?

3. **Drawing Conclusions** Explain why oil is such a valuable resource to Saudi Arabia.

 Take It to the NET

Activity Read about the histories, governments, and cultures of South Asia. How is democracy in India similar to and different from democracy in the United States? Visit the World Explorer: People, Places, and Cultures section of **phschool.com** for help in completing this activity.

Chapter 28 Self-Test As a final review activity, take the Chapter 28 Self-Test and get instant feedback on your answers. To take the test, visit the Social Studies section of **phschool.com**.

TECHNOLOGY

More than two million years ago, stone tools were invented, marking the beginning of technology. Technology is the way in which people use ideas and scientific principles to build machines that make tasks easier. Technology began in prehistoric times, but it advanced rapidly during the Industrial Revolution in the 18th century. Since that time, technology has continued to develop and to dramatically change our world. Technological advances in transportation, electronics, and communications have made the world a smaller place. Even the most isolated cultures of the world are accessible. Cooperation between cultures means that shared knowledge and ideas can benefit people worldwide.

Threshing machines help farmers separate the heads from the stalks of rice plants. Previously this job had to be done by hand.

? How have science and technology helped to shape the world?

COMPUTERS

The development of computers has been one of the most important recent advances in technology. The invention of the microchip changed the emphasis of producing goods from mechanical to electronic. Many tasks that were once done manually are now automated.

Microchips lie at the heart of a computer. These tiny devices store and process huge amounts of information at high speed.

Disabled members of the community can participate in more activities because of advanced technology and specially designed equipment.

COMMUNICATIONS

Today, people around the globe can communicate instantly with each other no matter where they are. Speech, pictures, and text are turned into signals and are transmitted to telephones, fax machines, computers, radios, and televisions. The signals travel via wires, cables, fiber optics, radio waves, and satellites.

Rockets and missiles have complex navigation systems.

Military satellite for spying and communication.

Videoconferencing enables people from all over the world to see each other during a meeting.

Satellite dish

Television

Mobile phone

Remote navigation and weapons system.

The Internet began as a military application.

Telephone

Radar

Personal computer

Harvesting machinery

Supermarkets and trucks use refrigeration to keep food fresh.

Space shuttle

Tank

Fax machine

Laptop

Submarine uses sonar to locate other vessels.

Greenhouses provide controlled growing conditions.

Irrigation waters crops

Pylons carry electricity

Efficient road network

Flying ambulance service

Concorde

Air-traffic control tower

Housing under construction

Wind turbines

Power station

Solar-power station

Bridge

Hovercraft ferry

Fishing trawler uses electronic sonar

Oil tanker

Underground transport tunnel

Factory uses automated assembly line

Business and commerce utilize latest technology.

Hydroelectric dam

Oil rigs drill deep beneath the land and sea.

Welcome to
The Pacific Realm

GOVERNMENT

Learn about parliamentary democracies ...

HISTORY *Study the giant statues of Easter Island ...*

SCIENCE, TECHNOLOGY, AND SOCIETY

Herd cattle in the Outback ...

What do you want to learn?

GEOGRAPHY
Explore the volcanic islands of Polynesia ...

ECONOMICS
Visit a busy city in New Zealand ...

CULTURE
Create a traditional painting ...

CITIZENSHIP
Meet Australia's young citizens ...

A journal can be your personal record of discovery. As you learn about the Pacific Realm, you can create journal entries about what you read, write, think, and create. For your first entry, think about the different cultures of the Pacific Realm. How have these cultures helped to define life in this region?

EXPLORER'S JOURNAL

Guiding Questions

What questions do I need to ask to understand the Pacific Realm?

Asking questions is a good way to learn. Think about what information you would want to know if you were visiting a new place, and what questions you might ask to find out. The questions on these pages can help guide your study of the Pacific Realm. You might want to try adding a few of your own!

GEOGRAPHY

Chains of islands lie in the Pacific Ocean, east of the Asian continent. Geography greatly affects the lives of people who live on these islands. The high islands have rich volcanic soil that is good for growing crops. Low islands have poor soil and a scarcity of natural resources, which makes earning a living difficult.

❶ **How has physical geography affected economic development in the Pacific Realm?**

HISTORY

Colonization and settlement have greatly affected the history of the Pacific Realm. Australia entered the world of nations as a penal colony. New Zealand attracted British settlers with its fine harbors and fertile soil. The Pacific islands appealed to Europeans as a site for trading posts and naval bases. Most nations in the Pacific Realm have attained freedom from colonial rule only within the last 125 years.

❷ **What characteristics of life in the Pacific Realm resulted from colonization?**

CULTURE

The diverse culture of the Pacific Realm is the result of its vibrant history, and a blending of the customs and heritages of its many peoples. The cultural traditions of indigenous peoples, early explorers and colonists, and more recent immigrants influence the arts, religion, language, and customs of the region.

❸ **How does the past influence contemporary expressions of culture in the Pacific Realm?**

GOVERNMENT

The governments of Australia and New Zealand are greatly influenced by the early colonization and settlement of these regions by the British. European governmental traditions continue to shape the governing institutions and laws, but increasingly, the indigenous peoples of the region are demanding and gaining a voice in government.

4 How do the governments of Australia and New Zealand compare with the government of Great Britain?

ECONOMICS

As they have for generations, many people in the Pacific Realm raise crops to sell. Australia and New Zealand are world leaders in wool production. A lack of natural resources poses economic challenges on many of the Pacific islands, where people are increasingly turning to the tourist industry to strengthen their economies.

5 What are some of the ways that people in the Pacific Realm earn a living?

CITIZENSHIP

The rights of citizenship vary among cultural groups in the Pacific Realm. In recent years, indigenous peoples have been fighting for, and gaining more rights. They are working hard to improve the quality of their lives, while still preserving the important traditions of their cultures.

6 How does the nature of citizenship vary among the different cultures of the Pacific Realm?

SCIENCE, TECHNOLOGY, AND SOCIETY

Scientific innovations in farming and ranching practices have contributed to the strong economies in Australia and New Zealand. New research into the potential health and medical benefits of coconut oil may bring increased prosperity to the Pacific islands.

7 How have geographical factors affected the use of science and technology in the Pacific Realm?

 Take It to the NET

For more information on the Pacific Realm, visit World Explorer: People, Places, and Cultures companion Web site at **phschool.com**.

ACTIVITY ATLAS

The Pacific Realm

◆ ◆

Learning about the Pacific Realm means being an explorer and a
geographer. No explorer would start out without first checking some facts.
Begin by exploring the maps of the Pacific Realm on the following pages.

Relative Location

1. LOCATION

Locate Australia and the Pacific Islands Use the map at the left to describe the location of Australia and the Pacific islands relative to the United States. What ocean would you cross to reach Australia from the west coast of the United States? In what direction would you travel? On which side of the Equator is Australia located? Where are the Pacific islands located relative to the Equator?

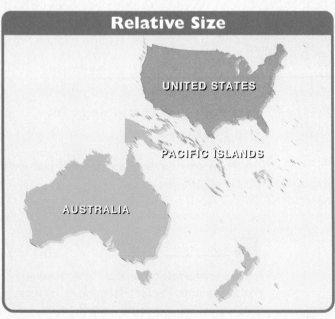

Relative Size

2. PLACE

Compare the Size of Australia, the Pacific Islands, and the United States Look at the map to the left. How large is Australia compared to the continental United States? Now compare the United States to the area covered by the Pacific islands. How do they compare east-to-west? North-to-south?

 Take It to the NET

Items marked with this logo are periodically updated on the Internet. To get current information about the geography of the Pacific Realm, go to **phschool.com.**

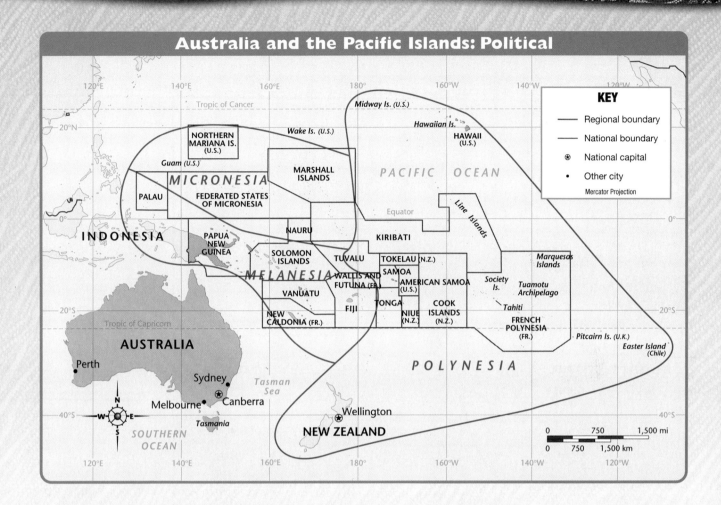

Australia and the Pacific Islands: Political

KEY
— Regional boundary
— National boundary
⊛ National capital
• Other city
Mercator Projection

120°E · 140°E · 160°E · 180° · 160°W · 140°W · 120°W

Tropic of Cancer

Midway Is. (U.S.)

Hawaiian Is.

Wake Is. (U.S.)

HAWAII (U.S.)

20°N

PACIFIC OCEAN

NORTHERN MARIANA IS. (U.S.)

Guam (U.S.)

MICRONESIA

MARSHALL ISLANDS

PALAU

FEDERATED STATES OF MICRONESIA

0°

Equator

Line Islands

INDONESIA

NAURU

PAPUA NEW GUINEA

KIRIBATI

Marquesas Islands

SOLOMON ISLANDS

TUVALU

TOKELAU (N.Z.)

MELANESIA

WALLIS AND FUTUNA (FR.)

SAMOA

AMERICAN SAMOA (U.S.)

Society Is.

Tuamotu Archipelago

VANUATU

FIJI

TONGA

COOK ISLANDS (N.Z.)

Tahiti

20°S

NEW CALDONIA (FR.)

NIUE (N.Z.)

FRENCH POLYNESIA (FR.)

Pitcairn Is. (U.K.)

Easter Island (Chile)

Tropic of Capricorn

AUSTRALIA

POLYNESIA

Perth

Sydney

Tasman Sea

Melbourne • Canberra

Tasmania

40°S

Wellington

NEW ZEALAND

SOUTHERN OCEAN

N W E S

0   750   1,500 mi
0   750   1,500 km

120°E · 140°E · 160°E · 180° · 160°W · 140°W · 120°W

---

3. PLACE

Explore the Pacific Realm Australia is both a continent and a country. Find it on the map. What is Australia's national capital? Most of the Pacific islands are tiny. Two of the larger islands make up the country of New Zealand. Where is New Zealand relative to Australia? The Pacific islands are divided into three groups. They are Micronesia, Melanesia, and Polynesia. These are regions, not countries. Each region is shown on the map above. In which region is Hawaii? Hawaii is also one of the fifty United States.

4. MOVEMENT

Analyze the Movement of Historical Societies The first people to live on the Pacific islands settled in New Guinea about 30,000 years ago. From there, they traveled across the Pacific Ocean by canoe. They reached Micronesia first. In what general direction did they travel? Then they traveled on to Polynesia. About how far did they travel from New Guinea to reach the Hawaiian Islands? How far to Easter Island?

ACTIVITY ATLAS

 Take It to the NET

Ring of Fire

RUSSIA

ALASKA (U.S.)

CANADA

UNITED STATES

CHINA

JAPAN

TAIWAN

PHILIPPINES

MEXICO

COLOMBIA

PACIFIC OCEAN

Tropic of Cancer

Equator

INDONESIA

PAPUA NEW GUINEA

ECUADOR

PERU

AUSTRALIA

Tropic of Capricorn

BOLIVIA

CHILE

NEW ZEALAND

ARGENTINA

KEY

— Major fault line

▲ Active volcano

Mercator Projection

0   1,000   2,000 mi

0   1,000   2,000 km

60°N   30°N   0°   30°S

120°E   150°E   180°   150°W   120°W   90°W   60°W

5. REGIONS

Explore Physical Processes in the Pacific Active volcanoes surround the Pacific Ocean. Many occur on the Pacific islands. Others are found in parts of North and South America. Use the map to name countries with several volcanoes. Now trace these strings of volcanoes with your finger. Why do you think this region is called the Ring of Fire?

6. REGIONS

Analyze Physical Processes Fault lines are breaks in the Earth's crust, where beneath lies hot, liquid rock. Find the fault lines on the map and trace them with your finger. Where do you find volcanoes in relation to fault lines? During earthquakes, the Earth's crust briefly opens, and sometimes liquid rock, or lava, escapes. What might this have to do with volcanoes?

7. PLACE

Locate Physical Features of Australia and New Zealand A favorite uncle has invited you to join him on a visit to Australia and New Zealand. You will be traveling widely and exploring the physical features of the region. Use the map below to plan your visit.

A. Your first stop will be New Zealand. You want to see the Southern Alps. Which island will you visit?

B. From New Zealand, you will be flying to Australia by the shortest route. Then the plane heads north, following the coast to the Great Barrier Reef. What mountain range is to your west?

C. You end up in the Kimberley Plateau, and then fly south to the Nullarbor Plain. What deserts will you pass over?

BONUS

Your trip is planned for July. What clothing should you pack for your visit to the Southern Alps? For the area around the Great Barrier Reef?

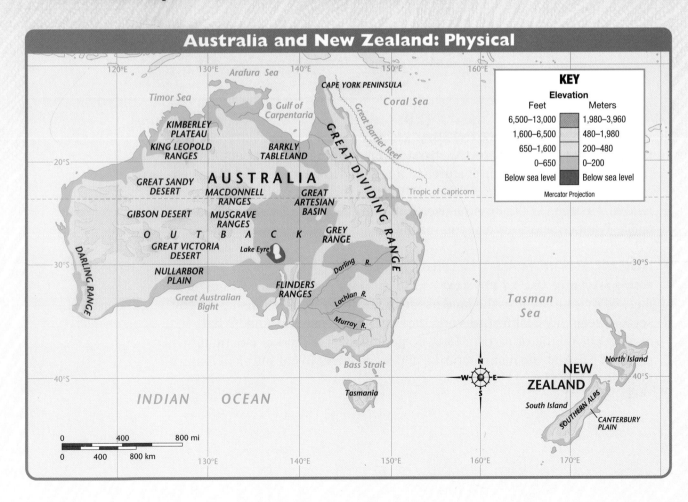

Australia and New Zealand: Physical

Take It to the NET

Land Use of Australia

Timor Sea
Darwin
Gulf of Carpentaria
PACIFIC OCEAN
Coral Sea
-20°S
AUSTRALIA
Tropic of Capricorn
Brisbane
-30°S
Perth
Great Australian Bight
Adelaide
Sydney
Melbourne
Tasman Sea
INDIAN OCEAN
-40°S
TASMANIA

Australia: Economic Activity
KEY
- Hunting and gathering
- Forest products
- Livestock raising
- Commercial farming
- Subsistence farming
- Manufacturing and trade
- Commercial fishing
- Little or no activity

Mercator Projection

0   400   800 mi
0   400   800 km

8. HUMAN-ENVIRONMENT INTERACTION

Examine Ways People Use the Physical Environment How people use the land is one of the main features of a region. How many different types of land use are identified on the map? What is the most widespread use of land in Australia? Compare the use of land in eastern and western Australia. What conclusions can you reach?

9. HUMAN-ENVIRONMENT INTERACTION

Compare Land Use to Physical Features Look at the physical map on page 547. Compare it to the land use map above. What relationship do you see between physical features and the way people use the land? What areas receive little or no use? How do people use the land in mountainous regions? Look at the manufacturing and trade areas. What physical feature is close to them?

Comparing the Pacific Realm's Longest, Highest, and Biggest

10. PLACE

Compare Physical Features What is the highest mountain in New Zealand? How much higher is the highest mountain in the world? About how many times larger is Australia's largest desert than the Mojave Desert? What is the longest river in Australia?

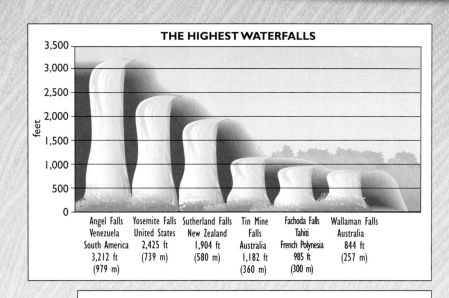

THE HIGHEST WATERFALLS

Angel Falls	Venezuela	South America	3,212 ft (979 m)
Yosemite Falls	United States	2,425 ft (739 m)
Sutherland Falls	New Zealand	1,904 ft (580 m)
Tin Mine Falls	Australia	1,182 ft (360 m)
Fachoda Falls	Tahiti	French Polynesia	985 ft (300 m)
Wallaman Falls	Australia	844 ft (257 m)

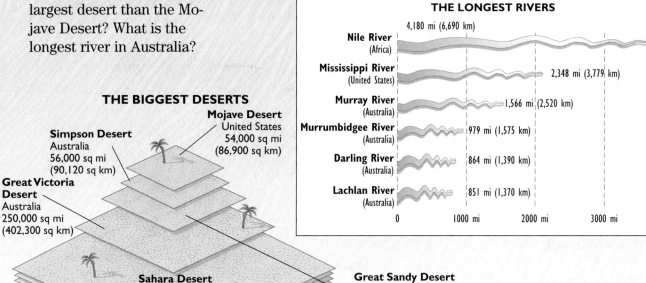

THE LONGEST RIVERS

Nile River (Africa) — 4,180 mi (6,690 km)

Mississippi River (United States) — 2,348 mi (3,779 km)

Murray River (Australia) — 1,566 mi (2,520 km)

Murrumbidgee River (Australia) — 979 mi (1,575 km)

Darling River (Australia) — 864 mi (1,390 km)

Lachlan River (Australia) — 851 mi (1,370 km)

0   1000 mi   2000 mi   3000 mi

THE BIGGEST DESERTS

Mojave Desert
United States
54,000 sq mi
(86,900 sq km)

Simpson Desert
Australia
56,000 sq mi
(90,120 sq km)

Great Victoria Desert
Australia
250,000 sq mi
(402,300 sq km)

Sahara Desert
Africa
3,5 million sq mi
(5.6 million sq km)

Great Sandy Desert
Australia
150,000 sq mi
(241,400 sq km)

THE HIGHEST MOUNTAINS

Mt. Everest	Mount McKinley	Mount Cook	Mount Tasman	Mount Dampier	Mount Silberhorn	Mount Kosciuszko
29,035 ft./ 8,850 m	20,320 ft./ 6,194 m	12,349 ft./ 3,764 m	11,483 ft./ 3,500 m	11,286 ft./ 3,440 m	10,757 ft./ 3,279 m	7,309 ft./ 2,228 m
Nepal/ Tibet	United States	New Zealand	New Zealand	New Zealand	New Zealand	Australia

AUSTRALIA, NEW ZEALAND, AND THE PACIFIC ISLANDS: Physical Geography

The Pacific Region

KEY
— Regional boundary
⊛ National capital
• Other city
Mercator Projection

USING MAPS

The Pacific region includes the continent of Australia and many islands. The largest islands are those that make up New Guinea and New Zealand, but there are thousands of others.

Understanding the Pacific Islands Region

Look at the map scale. What important fact does the map scale tell you about the Pacific region? Name the three large groups of Pacific islands. Why isn't Australia included in one of the regional boundaries? Locate the Pacific region on another map or globe.

Making Connections

The Pacific region is one of the largest in the world. But only about 29 million people live there. That is less than 1 percent of the world's population. Why do you think so few people live in this region? Write a short description, telling what you think life on a small island in the Pacific might be like.

Physical Features

READING FOCUS

1. How has plate movement affected the environments of Australia and New Zealand?

2. What are the major physical features of New Zealand?

3. What is the difference between high islands and low islands?

KEY TERMS

marsupial
tectonic plate
geyser
fiord
atoll

coral

MAIN IDEA

Earth movement and location have caused unique and diverse plant and animal life in both Australia and New Zealand.

NOTE TAKING

Copy the table below. As you read the section, mark the correct box or boxes beside each area in the Pacific realm to show some features of its physical geography.

Physical Geography				
	Reefs and Atolls	Unique Animal Life	Geysers and Fiords	Volcanoes
Australia				
New Zealand				
Pacific islands				

Setting the Scene

What strange-looking bird has a long bill, does not fly, and only comes out at night to hunt? If you said a kiwi, you are right. The people of New Zealand are so proud of this unusual bird that they have made it their national symbol. They even call themselves "Kiwis." The bird is just one of many unique animals found in New Zealand and its neighbor to the west, Australia.

Unique Environments

Australia and New Zealand lie between the Pacific Ocean and the Indian Ocean. Both are in the Southern Hemisphere, south of the Equator. This means that their seasons are the opposite of those in the United States. They are far from other landmasses, which has made them unique.

New Zealand and Australia are so far from other large landmasses that many of their plants and animals are found nowhere else on the Earth. Only in New Zealand can you find kiwis

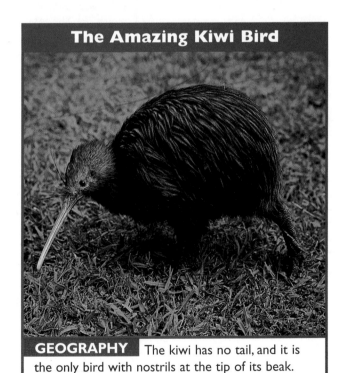

The Amazing Kiwi Bird

GEOGRAPHY The kiwi has no tail, and it is the only bird with nostrils at the tip of its beak. These help it sniff out insects and berries.
Critical Thinking Why do you think the people of New Zealand would call themselves "Kiwis"?

Australia and New Zealand: Physical

KEY

Elevation

Feet	Meters
6,500–13,000	1,980–3,960
1,600–6,500	480–1,980
650–1,600	200–480
0–650	0–200
Below sea level	Below sea level

Mercator Projection

GEOGRAPHY Apart from the Great Dividing Range, most of Australia is quite flat. The huge area to the west of the Great Dividing Range is made up of plains or low plateaus. In contrast, New Zealand is mountainous or hilly. **Map Study** Where are most of Australia's deserts located? Which of New Zealand's two islands is more mountainous?

and yellow-eyed penguins. Eighty-four percent of the vegetation in New Zealand's forests grows nowhere else. Australia has many unique creatures, such as the kangaroo and the koala. These animals are biologically unique, too. They are **marsupials** (mar SOO pea ulz), or animals that carry their young in a body pouch. Marsupials are found elsewhere in the world. The opossum of North America, for instance, is a marsupial. But in Australia, almost all mammals are marsupials. This is not true anywhere else on the Earth.

The uniqueness of New Zealand and Australia results from forces beneath the Earth's surface. The outer "skin" of the Earth, or the crust, is broken into huge pieces called **tectonic plates.** Australia, New Zealand, and the Pacific islands are all part of the Indo-Australian plate. Once that plate was part of a landmass that included Asia. Then, several hundred million years ago, the plate broke away. Slowly—only an inch or two each year—it moved southeast in the Pacific Ocean.

As the plate moved, the distance between the islands and Asia increased. Over the centuries, small changes occurred naturally in the islands' animals and plants. For instance, many birds have lost the ability to fly, even though they still have small wings. Because of the islands' isolation, these living things did not spread to other regions.

Physical Features

Australia is the Earth's largest island and smallest continent. It is about as large as the continental United States. That means the part of the United States located between Canada and Mexico.

Look at the map on page 552 and find New Zealand, which lies about 1,200 miles (1,900 km) southeast of Australia. Made up of two islands, North Island and South Island, New Zealand is much smaller than Australia. Yet it is one of the largest countries in the Pacific region—about the size of the state of Colorado.

Here, the land forms have been shaped by volcanoes. They, in turn, were caused by the movement of tectonic plates. Like other island groups, New Zealand's North and South Islands were formed by volcanoes when these plates collided.

Both North and South Island have highlands, forests, lakes, and rugged, snowcapped mountains. In the middle of North Island lies a volcanic plateau. Three of the volcanoes are active. North of the volcanoes, **geysers** (GY zurz), or hot springs, shoot scalding water over 100 feet (30.5 m) into the air.

South Island has a high mountain range called the Southern Alps. Mount Cook, the highest peak in the range, rises to 12,349 feet (3,764 m). Glaciers cover the mountainsides. Below, crystal-clear lakes dot the landscape. **Fiords** (fyordz), or narrow inlets, slice the southwest coastline. Here, the mountains reach the sea. To the southeast lies a flat fertile land called the Canterbury Plain.

LINKS TO
Science

Steam Heat Geysers are found in three places in the world: the northwestern United States, Iceland, and New Zealand. In these places, movements of tectonic plates have created deep cracks in the Earth's crust. Water seeps down into the cracks until it reaches very hot rocks. The heat raises the temperature of the water until it is so hot that it bursts upward in a shower of water and steam.

Changing the Earth

Continent
Volcano
Ocean
Magma

GEOGRAPHY New Zealand and its volcanoes were formed when the Pacific and Indo-Australian plates crashed together. The Pacific plate slid downwards into the Earth, forcing the edge of the Indo-Australian plate upwards. Friction and heat from inside the Earth melted the rock at the edges of the two plates. This molten rock, or magma, rose to the surface, causing volcanic eruptions. **Chart Study** Which is the Pacific plate, the one on the left of the diagram or the one on the right? What do the two arrows indicate?

A Coral Atoll

1　**2**　**3**

GEOGRAPHY The diagrams above show how a coral atoll is formed. It begins as a "fringe" of coral around a volcanic island. This coral reef continues to build as the island is worn away. Eventually, only the coral reef is left. **Chart Study** Why do you think coral islands cannot support much agriculture?

The Pacific Islands: High and Low

Geographers divide the Pacific islands into high islands and low islands. Volcanoes form high islands. They usually have mountains and the soil, which consists of volcanic ash, is very fertile.

Low islands are reefs or atolls. An **atoll** (a TAWL) is a small coral island in the shape of a ring which encloses a shallow pool of ocean water called a lagoon. Often the lagoon has at least one opening to the sea. An atoll often rises only a few feet above the Pacific. Low islands have this shape and low elevation because they are built on coral reefs. **Coral** is a rocklike material made up of the skeletons of tiny sea creatures. A reef expands until it nears the surface. Then sand and other debris accumulate on the reef's surface, raising the island above the level of the water.

SECTION I ASSESSMENT

AFTER YOU READ

1. Define (a) marsupial, (b) tectonic plate, (c) geyser, (d) fiord, (e) atoll, (f) coral

COMPREHENSION

2. How has plate movement affected the environments of Australia and New Zealand?

3. What are some physical features of New Zealand?

4. What is the difference between high islands and low islands?

CRITICAL THINKING AND WRITING

5. **Exploring the Main Idea** Review the Main Idea statement at the beginning of this section. Then, imagine you are visiting Australia, New Zealand, or the Pacific islands. Write a postcard to a friend describing some of the physical features that you see.

6. **Drawing Conclusions** What might be one advantage and one disadvantage of living in a region where there are volcanic mountains?

ACTIVITY

7. **Writing a Report** Find out more about the unique plants and animals of Australia and New Zealand. Choose one that interests you. Write and illustrate a report about it.

Take It to the NET

8. **Creating a Model Volcano** Using the information on the web site, create a model of a volcano and label its major parts. Write a short report describing how a volcano is formed and what causes an eruption. Visit the World Explorer: People, Places, and Cultures section of **phschool.com** for help in completing this activity.

Humans and the Physical Environment

BEFORE YOU READ

READING FOCUS

1. What geographic factors help explain where most people in Australia live?
2. What is one energy resource found on North Island and how is it used?
3. How are Australia and New Zealand similar and different?

KEY PLACES

Great Dividing Range
Outback

MAIN IDEA

There are many similarities and differences in the topography and climates of New Zealand and Australia.

NOTE TAKING

Copy the diagram below. As you read the section, complete the diagram to show ways in which people in Australia and New Zealand have responded to their physical environment.

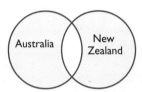

Setting the Scene

Although Australia is about as large as the continental United States, Australia has a much smaller population. Most Australians live on narrow plains along Australia's eastern and southeastern coasts. Australia's physical geography reveals why.

Australia: Climate and Population

Find the region along Australia's east coast on the map on page 552. This plain has Australia's most fertile farmland and receives ample rain. Winds flowing westward across the Pacific Ocean pick up moisture. As the winds rise to cross the **Great Dividing Range**—mountains just to the west of the coastal plain—the moisture falls as rain. These winds also help make the climate mild and pleasant. Australia's most important rivers, the Murray and the Darling,

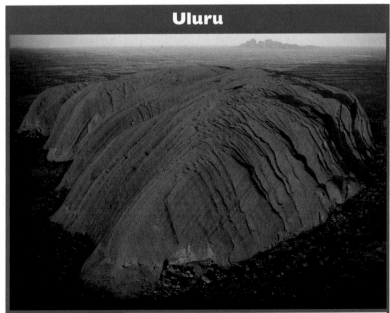

Uluru

GEOGRAPHY Uluru, once known as Ayers Rock, is 1.5 miles (2.4 km) long and 1,000 feet (305 m) high. This huge red monolith, or rock mass, is a major landmark in Australia's Outback. Rock paintings, made thousands of years ago, cover the walls of many caves in Uluru. In 1985 the Australian government returned the land where the monolith stands to native people who live in the region. **Critical Thinking** Why do you think Uluru is so important to the native people who live there? What could have been the purpose of the rock paintings?

New Zealand's Population

GEOGRAPHY The picture above shows towering Mount Cook on New Zealand's South Island. Sheep, like these grazing in the hills below Mount Cook, far outnumber New Zealand's human inhabitants. **Critical Thinking** Why do you think that most of the country's people live in harbor cities, like Auckland on New Zealand's North Island? (Shown on the left)

flow through the region. Most Australians live here, in cities.

The rest of Australia is very different. Just west of the Great Dividing Range is a rain shadow. This is a region that gets little precipitation because of the mountain range and is made up of semiarid plateaus and desert lands. Since rain seldom falls here, and there are few rivers, people depend on wells for fresh water. Farther west, the huge central plain called the **Outback** is desert and dry grassland.

New Zealand: Climate and Energy

Although New Zealand is more than 1,000 miles (1,600 km) long, no place is more than 80 miles (129 km) from the sea. The country's mild climate and abundance of rainfall help support farming and ranching. Farmers produce most of New Zealand's crops in the fertile

Canterbury Plain. Ranchers also raise sheep and cattle there. New Zealand's climate is not as hot as Australia's because New Zealand is farther from the Equator.

Recall from Section 1 that hot springs called geysers are found on North Island in New Zealand. New Zealanders use steam from these geysers as a source of electricity. To harness energy from geysers, workers drill into them and insert pipes. The pipes transport the steam in geysers to generators that use steam power to produce electricity.

Comparing Australia and New Zealand

Although Australia and New Zealand are often spoken of together, they are completely different countries separated by some 1,200 miles (1,900 km) of ocean. They do have some similarities: both are located in the South Pacific, both have important natural resources, and both raise sheep and cattle and grow similar crops. In both countries, most of the population lives in cities along the coast.

Australia, however, is mostly flat, while most of New Zealand is mountainous with some active volcanoes. Part of Australia has a tropical climate while about half of it has an arid climate. New Zealand's temperature is mild with plenty of rainfall.

SECTION 2 ASSESSMENT

AFTER YOU READ

RECALL

1. Identify: (a) Great Dividing Range, (b) Outback

COMPREHENSION

2. Why do most people in Australia live along the coast?

3. How do New Zealanders use the geysers on North Island?

4. What are some differences and similarities between Australia and New Zealand?

CRITICAL THINKING AND WRITING

5. **Exploring the Main Idea** Review the Main Idea statement at the beginning of this section. Then, draw a thematic map that shows the population distribution in Australia and New Zealand. You can use the information in this section and in a reference source, such as an atlas, to help you.

6. **Identifying Cause and Effect** How has Australia's physical geography affected where people live?

7. **Making Inferences** Since they can use geysers to generate electricity, can people on North Island use all the energy that they want, without thinking about conservation?

ACTIVITY

8. **Writing to Learn** Find out more about the natural resources of Australia and New Zealand. Write a brief report about these resources.

Geographic Factors and Natural Resources

BEFORE YOU READ

READING FOCUS

1. What is the physical geography of the Pacific islands?
2. What are some natural resources of the Pacific islands?

KEY PLACES

Melanesia
Micronesia
Polynesia
Papua New Guinea

NOTE TAKING

Copy the chart below. As you read the section, fill in the chart with important facts about the Pacific islands.

The Pacific Islands		
Melanesia	Micronesia	Polynesia
• mostly high islands		

MAIN IDEA

Geographic factors such as location and physical features help determine the climate and vegetation of the Pacific islands.

Nauru's Natural Resources

ECONOMICS

This picture shows a phosphate mine on Nauru. Phosphate is Nauru's only natural resource. **Critical Thinking** What kinds of industry might the people of Nauru develop instead of mining?

Setting the Scene

Luana Bogdan lives in Nauru (nah OO roo), the smallest country in the world. Tomorrow, she will be 12 years old. She is very excited, but she is also sad. Luana knows her family may soon have to leave Nauru.

Nauru's economy depended on its phosphate mines. But now the phosphate, used to make fertilizer, is almost gone. Even worse, mining has stripped the tiny island of its trees and vegetation. Nauru's leaders are trying to restore the island's ruined environment. If they fail, the Nauruans will have to find a new homeland.

The Pacific Islands: Physical Geography

The islands of the Pacific are geographically diverse. If you visited a high island, you might see three types of forests: mangrove forests ringing the coast, palm forests further inland, and monsoon forests in the center. If you visited a typical coral atoll, you would see much less plant life—only shrubs, small trees, grasses, and coconut palm trees.

Three Regions   The region known as the Pacific islands is divided into three areas. **Melanesia** (mel uh NEE zhuh) means "black islands." **Micronesia** (my kruh NEE zhuh) means "small islands." **Polynesia** (pahl uh NEE zhuh) means "many islands." Any island that falls inside the boundaries of a particular region belongs to that group.

The island region with the most people is Melanesia, which is north and east of Australia. Most of Melanesia's large islands are high islands. New Guinea, for example, has two ranges of high mountains and is divided into two countries. The western half of the island is called Irian Jaya (IHR ee ahn JAH yuh). It is part of the country of Indonesia. The eastern half is **Papua New Guinea** (PAP yuh wuh noo GIN ee), the largest and most populated Melanesian country. Some smaller Melanesian islands are Fiji, the Solomon Islands, and New Caledonia.

Most of the islands of Micronesia lie north of the Equator. Made up largely of low islands, Micronesia covers an area of the Pacific as large as the continental United States. Some of Micronesia's 2,000 islands are less than 1 square mile (2.6 sq km) in area. The largest is Guam, which is just 210 square miles (544 sq km). Most of Micronesia's islands are divided into groups. The largest are the Caroline, Gilbert, Marshall, and Mariana islands. Guam is part of the Marianas.

Polynesia is the largest island region in the Pacific. It includes our fiftieth state, Hawaii. Polynesia consists of a great many high islands, such as Tahiti and Samoa. Dense jungles cover their high volcanic mountains. Along the shores are palm-fringed, sandy beaches. The Tuamotus and Tonga are examples of Polynesia's few low islands and atolls.

Climate, Vegetation, and Natural Resources

The Pacific islands lie in the tropics with warm temperatures year-round. Daytime temperatures reach between the 80s and mid-90s in degrees Fahrenheit (around 32°C) and nighttime temperatures average about 75°F (24°C). The ocean and the winds keep the temperatures from getting too high. The amount of rainfall marks the change from one season to another.

Some Pacific islands have wet and dry seasons. Most islands, however, receive heavy rainfall all year long. In Hawaii, for example, volcanic peaks such as Mauna Kea (MOW nuh KAY uh) receive 100 inches of rain each year, usually in brief, heavy downpours. Some low islands, however, receive only scattered rainfall.

Dangerous Storms

GEOGRAPHY The wet season in the Pacific often brings violent weather. Here, high winds and driving rain bend the coconut palms on Palmerston Atoll in the Cook Islands. **Critical Thinking** The most violent tropical storms occur when the weather is hot. Why do you suppose that is?

Because of high temperatures, much rainfall, and fertile soil, high islands like Papua New Guinea and the Hawaiian Islands have rich vegetation. Tropical rain forests cover the hills and savanna grasses grow in the lowlands. Low islands, on the other hand, have little vegetation. The poor soil supports only palm trees, grasses, and small shrubs.

The Pacific island region has few natural resources. The coconut palm is the most important resource because it provides food, clothing, and shelter. Islanders export dried coconut meat, which is used in margarine, cooking oils, and luxury soaps. Some low islands, like Nauru, have phosphate deposits that can be exported. But the Pacific islands' most valuable resource may be their beauty. Tourism is gaining importance in the region and providing a new source of income.

SECTION 3 ASSESSMENT

AFTER YOU READ

RECALL

1. Identify: (a) Melanesia, (b) Micronesia, (c) Polynesia, (d) Papua New Guinea

COMPREHENSION

2. What are the three main regions of the Pacific islands? Briefly describe the geography of each region.

3. Describe some of the vegetation of the Pacific islands.

CRITICAL THINKING AND WRITING

4. **Exploring the Main Idea** Review the Main Idea statement at the beginning of this section. Then, choose one of the three regions in the Pacific islands. Create a graphic organizer that shows some of its geographic features and natural resources.

5. **Identifying Cause and Effect** Higher islands often have a better standard of living than low islands. Write a paragraph explaining why this is so.

ACTIVITY

6. Suppose you have decided to live on one of the Pacific islands. Write a paragraph explaining why you have decided to move. How will you handle the challenges of island life?

Distinguishing Fact and Opinion

> Kiwis can only be found in New Zealand.

> New Zealand has the most unusual creatures on the Earth.

Learn the Skill

Distinguishing fact from opinion is something you will need to do almost every day of your life, and it is a valuable skill when you read as well. To help you learn the difference between fact and opinion, follow these steps:

A. To determine if a statement is a fact, decide if it can be proven true or false. A fact can always be proven true or false. The first statement above is a fact because you can prove that it is true. You can find evidence to prove that kiwis are not found anywhere else on the Earth other than New Zealand.

B. To determine if a statement is an opinion, decide if it is a belief that cannot be proven true or false. Opinions are often indicated by words and phrases such as "I think," "I believe," "should," or "ought to." An opinion may be based on fact, but it still cannot be proven true or false. The second statement above is an opinion because there is no way to prove that the most unusual creatures on the Earth live on New Zealand. The statement is an expression of the writer's belief.

Practice the Skill

Now distinguish facts from opinions in a real case. First, read the paragraph in the box once or twice until you are sure you understand its meaning. Then, read each sentence one at a time. Ask yourself: Is this a fact that can be proven true or false, or is this an opinion, a belief that cannot be proven true or false? Identify which statements are facts and which are opinions.

Hawaii

Hawaii is a part of the island region in the Pacific called Polynesia. It is also one of the 50 United States. If you want to visit an island in Polynesia, the best island to visit is Hawaii. Its balmy weather is perfect all year. You should avoid the volcanic peaks, though. They receive as much as 100 inches of rain each year. The warm weather and rainfall create lush vegetation, including palm trees, grasses, and shrubs. Hawaii is indeed the most beautiful island in Polynesia.

Apply the Skill

See the Chapter Review and Assessment at the end of this chapter for more questions on distinguishing fact from opinion.

CHAPTER 29 Review and Assessment

Creating a Chapter Summary

On a separate piece of paper, draw a diagram like this one, and include the information that summarizes the first section of the chapter. Then, fill in the remaining boxes with summaries of Sections 2 and 3.

THE PACIFIC REALM: PHYSICAL GEOGRAPHY

Section 1
Australia and New Zealand were formed by the breaking and drifting of the Indo-Australian plate. The movement of that plate resulted in the region's unique plant and animal life.

Section 2

Section 3

Reviewing Key Terms

Match the definitions in Column I with the key terms in Column II.

Column I

a. rocklike material formed by the skeletons of tiny sea creatures

b. animals that carry their young in a body pouch

c. huge piece of the Earth's crust

d. small coral island in the shape of a ring

e. narrow inlet

f. hot spring that shoots scalding water into the air

Column II

1. coral
2. fiord
3. atoll
4. geyser
5. tectonic plate
6. marsupials

Reviewing the Main Ideas

1. How does geographic isolation affect plant and animal life in Australia and New Zealand? (Section 1)

2. What country in the Pacific realm is characterized by diverse physical features such as volcanic mountains, forests, lakes, glaciers, geysers, and fiords? (Section 1)

3. What physical feature would you expect to find on a high island? (Section 1)

4. How does climate affect where people live in Australia? (Section 2)

5. How do New Zealanders use the geysers on North Island? (Section 2)

6. Describe one similarity and one difference between Australia and New Zealand. (Section 2)

7. What geographic factors help determine the climate and vegetation of the Pacific islands? (Section 3)

8. What natural resources are found on the high islands and in coastal areas? (Section 3)

Map Activity

The Pacific Realm

For each place listed below, write the letter from the map that shows its location.

1. Micronesia
2. South Island
3. New Zealand
4. Australia
5. Polynesia
6. Melanesia
7. North Island

 Take It to the NET

Enrichment For more map activities using geography skills, visit the social studies section of **phschool.com.**

Writing Activity

1. **Writing a Travel Itinerary** Choose one country that you read about in this chapter. Then do some research to learn more about it. If you spent a week there, what would you see? Write a list describing the things you would most want to see and do in a week. Then organize your list in a day-by-day plan.

2. **Writing a Book Report** Find and read a traditional story or folk tale from Australia, New Zealand, or the Pacific islands. Think about how the story reflects the geography and culture of the country it comes from. Write a four-or-five-sentence book report similar to one that might be used on a television program like *Reading Rainbow*.

Applying Your Skills

Turn to the Skills for Life activity on p. 561 to complete the following activity.

Using ten note cards, write five facts and five opinions about the Pacific region. On the back of each card, write FACT if you wrote a fact and OPINION if you wrote an opinion. Choose a partner and shuffle your cards. Challenge your partner to identify each statement as a fact or an opinion. For each statement, explain how you decided if it was a fact or an opinion.

Critical Thinking

1. **Recognizing Cause and Effect** How does the shape of New Zealand affect its climate?

2. **Comparing and Contrasting** What are two differences between high islands and low islands? What is one similarity?

 Take It to the NET

Activity Australia, New Zealand, and some of the Pacific islands are collectively known as Australasia. Create a map of Australasia. Include major geographic features, natural resources, and climate. Visit the World Explorer: People, Places, and Cultures section of **phschool.com** for help in completing this activity.

Chapter 29 Self-Test As a final review activity, take the Chapter 29 Self-Test and get instant feedback on your answers. To take the test, visit the Social Studies section of **phschool.com.**

AUSTRALIA, NEW ZEALAND, AND THE PACIFIC ISLANDS:
History, Culture, Economics

Telling the Story of Dreamtime

USING PICTURES

According to Aboriginal tradition, in the "Dreamtime" before humans walked the Earth, mythical ancestors formed the world's mountains, rivers, plants, and animals. Aborigines passed on their traditions orally from generation to generation. Aborigine artists also used carvings and rock paintings like this ancient one in northern Australia, to record stories and history. Aborigines still use such ancient practices to keep their traditions alive.

Writing a Story

Take a close look at the figures in the rock painting. What do you see? What are these figures, and what do you think they symbolize? Write a brief story that might go along with the figures and events shown in this painting.

Making a Rock Painting

If you were to leave behind a drawing to show what life is like at the beginning of the 21st century, what would you draw? Write down several ideas. You might want to brainstorm with a friend. Then, use either a drawing or painting to illustrate an event or activity from life in the 21st century.

Historical and Cultural Traditions

READING FOCUS

1. How did people settle Australia and New Zealand?
2. What groups shaped the cultures of Australia and New Zealand?
3. How have the Pacific island nations been influenced by other cultures?

KEY TERMS

penal colony
station

MAIN IDEA

The strong, unique cultures of the earliest people in Australia, New Zealand, and the Pacific islands were greatly influenced by the arrival of Europeans in the 1700s and 1800s.

NOTE TAKING

Copy the chart below. As you read the section, complete the chart with information about the history and cultures of Australia, New Zealand, and the Pacific islands.

Australia	New Zealand	Pacific Islands
earliest people were Aborigines		

Setting the Scene

Hundreds of giant stone statues dot the landscape of Easter Island. Made of solid volcanic rock, each statue stands 10 to 40 feet (3 to 12 m) tall. Some weigh more than 50 tons (46 metric tons).

Easter Island's statues still impress people. Scientists also wonder how people first came to other parts of the Pacific region.

Early Settlers in Australia and New Zealand

Scientists think that the Aborigines (ab uh RIJ uh neez), the earliest settlers in Australia, came from Asia about 40,000 years ago. For thousands of years, they hunted and gathered food along the coasts and river valleys and learned to live in the Outback.

During this time, the Aboriginal population stayed at a stable, even level. People lived in small family groups that moved from place to place in search of food and water. All had strong religious beliefs about nature and the land. Such beliefs played a key role in their way of life.

Easter Island's Mysterious Statues

CULTURE Eyeless stone giants dot the landscape of Easter Island. No one knows for sure how the ancient islanders carved and erected these statues. **Critical Thinking** Why do you think these huge stone images were built?

Cultural Influences

The Maori of New Zealand   The earliest people in New Zealand were the Maori (MAH oh ree). Their ancestors first traveled from Asia to Polynesia. Then, about 1,000 years ago, the Maori traveled across the ocean to New Zealand and settled in villages, making a living as hunters and farmers. But the Maori also prized fighting and conquering their enemies and used storytelling to pass on their beliefs.

The Arrival of Europeans   European explorers heard about a mysterious continent that lay to the south of Asia and in the 1600s, several ships reached either Australia or New Zealand. In 1769, British captain James Cook explored New Zealand and the next year, the east coast of Australia. He claimed both lands for Britain.

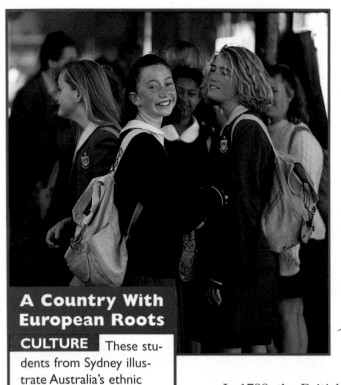

A Country With European Roots

CULTURE   These students from Sydney illustrate Australia's ethnic makeup—95 percent European. **Critical Thinking** What factors account for this ethnic mix?

AS YOU READ

Monitor Your Reading How might the discovery of a resource like gold affect the population of a country?

In 1788, the British founded the first colony in Australia as a **penal colony.** This is a place settled by convicts, or prisoners. Soon, other colonists settled in Australia, some of whom worked for the prison facilities. Others went to find new land. Then, in 1851, gold was discovered, and the population soared. Not long after, Britain stopped sending convicts to Australia. Some 50 years later, in 1901, Australia gained independence.

New Zealand was settled by Europeans at about the same time as Australia and in 1840, the British took control of New Zealand. The colony, with its fine harbors and fertile soil, attracted many British settlers. New Zealand gained independence in 1907.

Present-Day Cultures of Australia and New Zealand

Today, most Australians and New Zealanders are descendants of British settlers. They share British culture, holidays, and customs, and most express pride in their British heritage, especially their parliamentary system of government and belief in freedom and democracy.

However, Australia and New Zealand are not exactly alike. Each has its own unique culture. For example, Australians have added many new words to the language. These include "mate," which means "close friend," and "fair go," which means "equal opportunity." New Zealanders are deeply opposed to nuclear warfare. No ships carrying nuclear arms are allowed to use New Zealand harbors.

The Aborigines Today   Today, about 200,000 Aborigines live in Australia. Since the arrival of Europeans, the Aborigines have suffered great hardships. In the colonial period, settlers forced these native peoples off their lands. Tens of thousands died of European diseases and others were forced to work on sheep and cattle **stations,** which are extremely large ranches. The settlers demanded that the Aborigines adopt European ways. As a result, they began to lose their own customs and traditions. Recently, however, life for Aborigines has begun to improve a little.

The Maori Way of Life   When New Zealand became a British colony, Britain promised to protect Maori land. Settlers, however, broke that promise. For many years, the settlers and the Maori clashed violently. The settlers finally defeated the Maori in 1872.

After their defeat, the Maori were forced to adopt English ways. Maori culture seemed in danger of being destroyed. Slowly, however, Maori leaders gained more power and recovered some traditional lands. New laws now allow the Maori to practice their customs and ceremonies.

Today, there are more than 300,000 Maori in New Zealand. They make up about 9 percent of the country's population. Many Maori now live in cities and work in businesses, factories, and offices. But they still honor their Maori heritage. Many speak both Maori and English. Thanks to their artists, writers, and singers, Maori culture is an important part of the lives of all New Zealanders.

The Cultures of the Pacific Islands

Scientists believe that the first people to inhabit the Pacific islands came from Southeast Asia more than 30,000 years ago. First, these people settled on New Guinea, Melanesia's largest island. Then, over thousands of years, they traveled across the Pacific by canoe to Micronesia and later Polynesia.

A Variety of Cultures   As people settled the Pacific region, they developed many different cultures. Because of the distances between islands, groups could not communicate with each other and each group developed its own language, customs, and religious beliefs. However, the people did have things in common since they lived in an ocean environment. They used the ocean to obtain food and for transportation. Most built their lives around their small villages or farms.

From Colonies to Independence   The arrival of Europeans in the 1800s had a great impact on the Pacific islands. Britain, France, and Germany set up trading posts and naval bases on many islands. Japan and the United States soon joined the race for control of the Pacific region. In the late 1800s, these nations turned the islands into colonies and for the next 100 years, ruled the people of the Pacific.

A Traditional Way of Life

CULTURE   At Rotorua, where many Maori people live, a woman in traditional dress heats her food in the sizzling hot springs. **Critical Thinking** How is this Maori woman making use of a natural resource? What technologies might we use today instead of resources like this?

Life in the Pacific Islands

CULTURE Most of Papua New Guinea's four million residents still farm, fish, and build their houses in the traditional way. **Critical Thinking** Why do you suppose residents of this village build their houses on stilts?

After World War II, most Pacific islands gained independence. By then, traditional island cultures had blended with cultures from Europe, America, and other countries. Most governments were democratic, and most churches were Christian. Many Pacific islanders read and spoke English. Foreign companies operated businesses and large farms here. Since independence, the lives of most island people have improved, but incomes are still low. Many depend on fishing or on growing such crops as taro and yams to make a living.

SECTION 1 ASSESSMENT

AFTER YOU READ

RECALL

1. Define: (a) penal colony, (b) station

COMPREHENSION

2. Where do scientists believe the native peoples of Australia, New Zealand, and the Pacific islands came from?

3. What happened to Native peoples when Europeans arrived in Australia and New Zealand?

CRITICAL THINKING AND WRITING

4. **Exploring the Main Idea** Review the Main Idea statement at the beginning of this section. Then, create a chart that compares the histories of the Aborigines and the Maori. In what ways are they similar? In what ways are they different?

5. **Making Inferences** Why might people who live on an island be able to preserve their culture for a long period of time without change?

ACTIVITY

6. **Making a Timeline** Create a timeline with ten brief entries tracing the history of Australia, New Zealand, and the Pacific islands.

 Take It to the NET

7. **Exploring Aboriginal Culture** Using the information on the web site, choose one aspect of aboriginal culture or history that interests you and create an oral presentation that includes visual aids. Visit the World Explorer: People, Places, and Cultures section of **phschool.com** for help in completing this activity.

Australia and New Zealand

Trade and Agriculture

BEFORE YOU READ

READING FOCUS

1. What are some key aspects of Australia's economy?
2. How does New Zealand's climate influence its economy?

KEY TERMS
artesian well

KEY PLACES
Sydney
Alice Springs

MAIN IDEA
The economies of Australia and New Zealand are dependent upon agriculture and trade, and both countries have close economic ties with Pacific Rim nations.

NOTE TAKING

Copy the table below. As you read the section, complete the table to show some similarities between the economies of Australia and New Zealand.

	Australia	New Zealand
Ranching		
Farming		
Trade with Pacific Rim nations		

Setting the Scene

Michael Chang owns a successful trading company in **Sydney,** Australia's largest city. From his office in a modern glass skyscraper, he sometimes watches Sydney's busy harbor. What interests him most are the large cargo ships.

John Koeyers and his family own a huge cattle ranch in northwest Australia. He uses a Jeep to round up the herds on his ranch. The Koeyers sell most of their cattle to companies that supply fast-food restaurants in Asian nations.

Lyle Sansbury is chairman of the Board of Directors of the Nurungga Farming Company. He is very proud of the farm. It produces barley, wheat, cattle, and sheep. Lyle is full of plans for expanding the company into other activities, such as fish farming. The Nurungga Farm is one of the successful businesses owned and run by Aborigines.

The Sydney Opera House

CULTURE The Sydney Opera House was completed in 1973. The building's white concrete arches look like the sails of a huge ship. **Critical Thinking** How does the architecture of the Opera House relate to its environment?

Australia

COUNTRY · PROFILE

Age Structure (in years)

- Under 15: 22%
- 65 and over: 11%
- 15-64: 67%

Ethnic Groups

- Asian: 4%
- Aboriginal and Other: 1%
- European: 95%

Australia: Economic Activity
KEY

- Hunting and gathering
- Forest products
- Livestock raising
- Commercial farming
- Subsistence farming
- Manufacturing and trade
- Commercial fishing
- Little or no activity

Mercator Projection

Location	The continent of Australia, between the Indian and Pacific oceans
Climate	Dry, with tropical north, subtropical east, and Mediterranean areas south
Terrain	Mostly low plateau with deserts
Population	19.6 million
Major Religion	Christianity
Economy	Agriculture: meat, wool, wheat, barley, sugar cane, fruit, livestock
	Major industries: mining, equipment, food processing, chemicals, steel
Exports	Coal, gold, meat, wool, aluminum oxide, wheat, machinery, transportation equipment
Imports	Machinery, transportation equipment, computers, office machines, petroleum products

GEOGRAPHY The eastern half of the continent receives just enough rain to support the grasses needed to feed the cattle and sheep raised in the area. **Map and Chart Study** In which region of the country does most commercial farming take place? Based on the information on Australia's economy and exports, would you say that livestock raising was an important economic activity? Why or why not?

AS YOU READ

Monitor Your Reading What do all three people have in common? How do they contribute to Australia's economy?

A Trading Economy

Michael Chang, the Koeyers, and Lyle Sansbury are all Australians. The definition of Australian has changed since Australia achieved independence. It is no longer "British." It now reflects the diversity of Australia's people. Today, Australia has close ties with other nations of the Pacific Rim. These nations border the Pacific Ocean. They include Japan, South Korea, China, and Taiwan. The United States is another major Pacific Rim nation. It is one of Australia's key trading partners.

Japan, the United States, and other Pacific Rim nations have invested large amounts of money in Australia's economy. They also have set up banks, insurance companies, and other businesses in Australia. More and more, Australia's economy depends on trade with these Pacific Rim countries.

Michael Chang's trading company is just one of hundreds of companies that do business with Pacific Rim countries. He sends various products to many countries in Asia. John Koeyers is involved in trade, too. Large cargo ships transport his cattle to South Korea and Taiwan. Other cargo ships carry Australian wool, meat, and many other products to foreign markets. And even larger ocean tankers carry Australia's coal, zinc, lead, and other minerals to Japan.

Farming   It seems strange that farm products are an important export, because only about 6 percent of Australia's land is good for farming. Most of this land is in southeastern Australia and along the east coast. The country's few rivers are in those areas. Farmers use the river water to irrigate their crops. Australian farmers raise barley, oats, and sugar cane. However, their most valuable crop is wheat. Australia is one of the world's leading wheat growers and exporters.

Ranching   Ranching is another key part of Australia's economy. Australian sheep and cattle provide lamb, mutton, and beef for export. And Australia is the world's leading wool producer. Most cattle and sheep are raised on large stations. Some of the largest are in the Outback.

For example, the Koeyers' ranch is in a hot, dry area in northwest Australia. It covers 680,000 acres (275,196 hectares). Another Outback station, near **Alice Springs** in the center of Australia, is even larger. It covers 12,000 square miles (31,080 sq km)—about as much

Cattle Round-Up

ECONOMICS

Huge ranches in Australia's hot, dry Outback are ideal for grazing sheep and cattle. Some of these ranches, or stations, are bigger than some American states.

Critical Thinking Why is it necessary for ranchers to use technology, such as the helicopter shown above, on stations such as this one? What other kinds of technology might they use?

Harvesting Wheat

ECONOMICS New Zealand's agricultural productivity is one of the highest in the world. In the picture above, a farmer harvests wheat in Waikari, which is on New Zealand's South Island. **Critical Thinking** Why do you think such a small nation has such high agricultural production?

as the state of Maryland. Even with this much land, the cattle can barely find enough grass for grazing. Fresh water also is scarce. Rain falls rarely, and the region has only a few small streams. To supply water for their cattle, the Koeyers use underground **artesian wells,** holes drilled deep into the Earth to tap porous rock filled with groundwater.

Trade and Agriculture in New Zealand

With favorable climate and conditions, and the widespread use of modern farming methods and machinery, New Zealand has achieved tremendous productivity. Indeed, the agricultural productivity of this small nation is one of the highest in the world.

New Zealand's farmers produce hundreds of thousands of metric tons of cereal crops, including wheat, barley, oats, and maize.

New Zealand's ranchers can raise dairy cows, sheep, and beef cattle relatively cheaply, thanks to the mild climate in which they live. Ranchers do not have to spend money building and maintaining winter livestock shelters.

Foreign Trade Like Australia, New Zealand has close ties with other nations of the Pacific Rim. Its key trading partners include Japan, South Korea, Hong Kong, the United States, and Taiwan. New Zealand also maintains a brisk trade with Australia, the United Kingdom, and Germany.

New Zealand exports more dairy products than any other nation. It also exports more wool than any other nation, except for Australia. Other important exports are cereal crops, kiwi fruit, beef, fish, mutton, and lamb.

SECTION 2 ASSESSMENT

AFTER YOU READ

RECALL

1. Identify: (a) Sydney, (b) Alice Springs

2. Define: (a) artesian well

COMPREHENSION

3. What are some important exports of Australia? Who are Australia's primary trading partners?

4. How is New Zealand's climate suited to ranching?

CRITICAL THINKING AND WRITING

5. **Exploring the Main Idea** Review the Main Idea statement at the beginning of this section. Suppose that you and your family lived on a huge cattle station near Alice Springs. Write a description of what you think your lives would be like. Include economic issues that affect your family.

6. **Drawing Conclusions** Write a brief paragraph explaining why Australia makes a good trading partner for Japan.

ACTIVITY

7. **Write to Learn** You are from New Zealand and setting up your own exporting company. Write a business letter to the owner of a Pacific Rim company explaining the items you plan to export and why he or she should do business with you.

The Pacific Islands
Scarcity of Natural Resources

Setting the Scene

The Pacific Ocean covers nearly one-third of the Earth's surface. About 25,000 islands dot the Pacific. While many of those islands are high islands with fertile soil that allows the people living there to grow crops, other smaller, low islands have poor, sandy soil and little fresh water, which makes it difficult for people to grow crops. Some of these low islands have mineral deposits such as phosphate that can be exported. However, it is the beauty of the Pacific islands that is its top resource, fueling tourism and providing a new source of income for the islands' inhabitants.

A High Island in Polynesia

ECONOMICS

Volcanoes created high islands like the Marquesas Islands in Polynesia. The Pacific islands' stunning beaches and exotic landscapes make them prime tourist attractions and aid in the economy of the region. **Critical Thinking** How do you think these tourist attractions aid in the economy of the region?

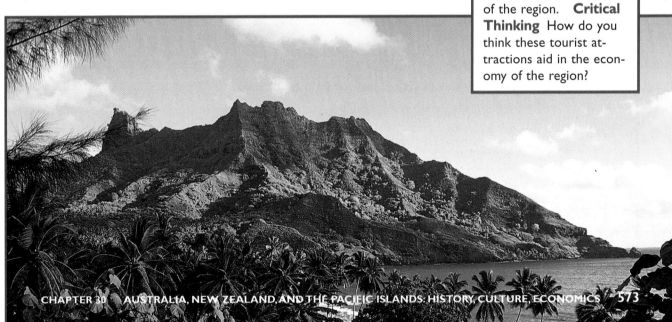

Natural Resource Yields Medicine

Leading coconut-producing nations have joined together in an inter-governmental organization called the Asian and Pacific Coconut Community (APCC). Each year the APCC panel, also called "Co-cotech," holds a meeting in which scientists, researchers, traders, processors, farmers, exporters, and policy makers exchange ideas. In a recent meeting, panelists applauded new research into the potential health and medical benefits of coconut oil. In ongoing clinical tests, researchers are using mono-laurin, a fatty acid found in coconut oil, to treat patients with HIV or AIDS.

Adapting to Life with Few Natural Resources

The whole Pacific island region has few natural resources. The coconut palm is the most important one. It provides food, clothing, and shelter. Islanders export dried coconut meat or **copra,** which is used in margarine, cooking oils, and luxury soaps.

Pacific Island Industries

The economies of the Pacific islands, like those of many developing nations, are based on **primary industries** such as fishing, agriculture, and mining. These industries create or collect raw materials. Most Pacific islanders earn their living by farming or fishing. Many own their own farms, and some farms are owned collectively by entire villages. Besides coconut palm, farmers cultivate other crops that can grow easily in a tropical climate. Sugar cane and bananas are widely grown on the larger islands. Sugar production and export is a key industry on the island of **Fiji,** which also has its share of banana groves. In New Guinea, farmers grow coffee and cocoa for global export.

Mining and forestry employ people on some of the larger islands, including Fiji and Papua New Guinea. Pacific islanders are working hard to develop these other industries. Foreign investment is

Coconut Palm: One Resource, Many Uses

Husk → Copra → charcoal, charcoal, charcoal, charcoal
Husk → Copra → coconut oil, oil cake (cattle feed)
Meat → Coconut Milk
Sap → sugar, vinegar, alcohol
Trunk → construction material, furniture
Dried Leaves → thatch, mats, screens, baskets

ECONOMICS Not only does the coconut palm provide food, clothing, and shelter—it also saves lives. During hurricanes, Pacific islanders can lash themselves to the trunk of the coconut palm to avoid being swept out to sea.

Chart Study Find coconut oil on the chart. (a) From what part of the plant does coconut oil come? (b) Coconut oil is high in lauric acid, which keeps it from spoiling. Why is coconut oil often used in factory-made cookies?

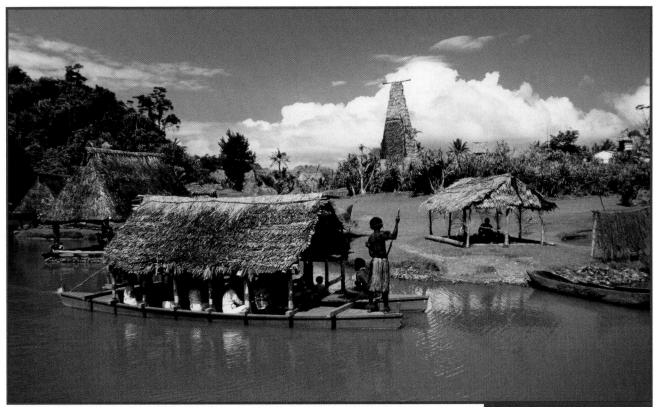

helping to develop one of the world's largest copper mines on the island of Bougainville in Papua New Guinea.

Secondary industries, also known as manufacturing industries, take raw materials (such as sugar) produced by primary industries, and process them into consumer goods (such as candy). Secondary industry is uncommon in the Pacific islands, but there are some exceptions. For example, fishing boats and pleasure craft are built on Fiji. Paint is also manufactured on that island.

Tourism: A Growing Industry

Service industries, also known as **tertiary industries,** do not produce goods, such as cloth or computers, but provide services, such as banking and communications. **Tourism** is the business of providing services for tourists and is a growing tertiary industry in the Pacific islands. Once remote and accessible only by boat or small plane, the Pacific islands became a prime tourist attraction in the 1950s with the availability of jet airplane travel.

More tourists visit Fiji than any other Pacific island nation. In recent years, tourism has outpaced sugar as Fiji's main source of foreign income. French Polynesia—specifically **Tahiti**—is another very popular tourist destination. Many travelers from Japan, the United States, Britain, France, Australia, and New Zealand visit the Pacific islands, reflecting ongoing ties between the region and the countries that once colonized it.

Snorkeling in the Pacific Islands

CULTURE

Surrounded by clear aquablue water and bathed in plenty of sunshine, the Pacific islands offer tourists excellent opportunities to explore the spectacular variety of marine life.

Critical Thinking

What other activities might tourists enjoy on a Pacific island vacation? Do you think tourism is harmful to island and marine ecosystems?

As tourism gains importance in the Pacific islands, it provides a new source of income. Yet tourism has a downside. Most tourist facilities, such as hotels and resorts, are owned not by Pacific islanders but by foreigners. This means that much of the industry's profit leaves the region. Moreover, many jobs in the tourist industry are not open to islanders. Those that are generally require little skill and pay low wages. Finally, many tourist activities can be harmful to the environment. Pacific islanders will need to plan carefully to protect their coral reefs, rain forests, and coastal areas.

SECTION 3 ASSESSMENT

AFTER YOU READ

RECALL

1. Identify: (a) Fiji, (b) Tahiti
2. Define: (a) copra, (b) primary industry, (c) secondary industry, (d) tertiary industry, (e) tourism

COMPREHENSION

3. How are the Pacific islands trying to compensate for a scarcity of natural resources?
4. What are some of the important industries of the Pacific islands?

CRITICAL THINKING AND WRITING

5. **Exploring the Main Idea** Review the Main Idea statement at the beginning of this section. Then, write a short speech in which a Pacific islander explains the value of the coconut palm. Use standard grammar, spelling, sentence structure, and punctuation.
6. **Understanding Cause and Effect** How might the scarcity of natural resources on the Pacific islands affect trade between these nations and other, more industrial nations around the world?

ACTIVITY

7. **Writing a Journal Entry** Suppose you have decided to live on one of the Pacific islands. Write a journal entry explaining your decision to relocate. What are the benefits of island life? What are the drawbacks?

Identifying Frame of Reference

Learn the Skill

William Buckley escaped from a British penal colony in Australia in 1803. While wandering in the bush, he found a broken spear lying on a grave and picked it up. When the Aborigines found Buckley, they welcomed him warmly and took him to live with their tribe. Why did they do this?

To find the answer to this question, you would need to understand Aboriginal culture and the historical period in which this event happened. Doing this will help you understand the frame of reference of the Aborigines. When and where we grow up provides us with certain ways of looking at the world. This frame of reference influences the way a person thinks and behaves. In the case of William Buckley, the people noted that his pale skin was similar to that of their dead, whose skin turned white during cremation. Then, they recognized the spear he was carrying as one that belonged to a relative who had died recently. The Aborigines believed that the land was inhabited by many spirits. They welcomed Buckley because they thought he was their dead relative returning to them.

To identify a frame of reference when you read, follow these steps:

A. Read the information, paying attention to the groups of people or individuals involved and the event that occurs. Write this information on a sheet of paper.

B. Note the place and time in which the event takes place. This information may be revealed directly, but you might also find clues in the language and habits of the people described.

C. Look for evidence of different cultural values, attitudes, and beliefs. Write your evidence on the sheet of paper, being careful not to judge the culture by your own present-day values and attitudes.

D. Use the information you have collected to write a short paragraph describing the frame of reference.

Practice the Skill

Read the following journal entry written by a fictitious character adopted by the Aborigines of Australia. Then, follow the four steps to determine the frame of reference from which it is written.

Living with the Aborigines

I, James Carter, was sent to a penal colony in Australia in 1799 for stealing bread. Two years later I escaped and went to live with the Aborigines in the bush. The following information describes some of my experiences with them:

I arrived at the camp in bad shape, with a bad cut on my leg and a headache from the heat and lack of water. The hunters who found me took me immediately to a shelter. An old woman drew a few green tree ants from a gourd and boiled them to prepare a drink that took my headache away. Another woman examined my leg and then left, only to return a short time later with several large grubs. The grubs, I learned later, were witchety grubs, one of the staple foods of the aborigines. She crushed the worms and used the salve to heal my cut.

After my leg was healed, I attended a moth feast with the aborigines in the Bogong Mountains. Bogong moths covered rock crevices everywhere. The people gathered thousands of these moths and then cooked them in sand and hot ashes to remove their wings and legs. Then the moths were sifted with nets, which removed their heads. I found them to be surprisingly tasty.

Apply the Skill

See the Chapter Review and Assessment at the end of this chapter for more questions on identifying a frame of reference.

Review and Assessment

Creating a Chapter Summary

On a separate piece of paper, draw a chart like this one, and include the information that summarizes the first section of the chapter. Then, complete the chart by summarizing the information in Sections 2 and 3.

	Australia	New Zealand	Pacific Islands
History	• Settled by Aborigines and then by the British	• Settled by Maori and then by the British	
Culture	• Influenced by traditional island and European cultures		
Economics			

Reviewing Key Terms

Read each sentence and decide if the definition is true or false. If it is false, rewrite the definition so that it is correct.

1. A penal colony is a place settled by convicts or prisoners.
2. A station is a very large sheep or cattle ranch.
3. Copra is the dried leaves of the coconut palm.
4. An artesian well is a shallow pool of water.
5. Secondary industries are those industries that manufacture goods and products.

Reviewing the Main Ideas

1. Who were the earliest inhabitants of Australia and New Zealand? (Section 1)
2. What similarities among the Pacific islands are caused by the ocean environment that the islands share? (Section 1)
3. What three important industries contribute to the economies of both Australia and New Zealand? (Section 2)
4. What ties does Australia maintain with other nations of the Pacific region? (Section 2)
5. Why is it difficult for many of the people of the Pacific islands to earn a living? (Section 3)
6. What are four primary industries found in the Pacific islands? (Section 3)

Map Activity

Australia, New Zealand, and the Pacific Islands

For each place listed below, write the letter from the map that shows its location.

1. New Zealand

2. Papua New Guinea

3. Sydney

4. Pacific Ocean

5. Tasmania

 Take It to the NET

Enrichment For more map activities using geography skills, visit the social studies section of **phschool.com.**

Writing Activity

1. Writing a Pamphlet Write a pamphlet explaining how the history and culture of Australia, New Zealand, or the Pacific islands can be seen today. Draw pictures to illustrate your pamphlet, or use pictures clipped from travel brochures or photocopied from reference books or geography magazines. Write a caption for each picture, explaining what it shows and identifying the location shown.

2. Writing an Article Use the information in the Country Profile on page 570 to write an article about Australia for a travel magazine. In your article, provide an overview of the country for people who are planning to visit it.

Critical Thinking

1. Comparing and Contrasting Compare the European influences on Australia, New Zealand, and the Pacific islands. Draw a chart to show similarities and differences.

2. Comparing and Contrasting In American history, Native Americans were forcibly moved to reservations. How does this compare with the history of Aborigines?

Applying Your Skills

Turn to the Skills for Life activity on p. 577 to help you complete the following activity.

Write a brief essay in which you identify and explore some of the influences in your life that might shape your frame of reference.

 Take It to the NET

Activity Read about the region known as Oceania, which includes the Pacific islands. Create a table or chart to organize the information contained in the Web site. Visit the World Explorer: People, Places, and Cultures section of **phschool.com** for help in completing this activity.

Chapter 30 Self-Test As a final review activity, take the Chapter 30 Self-Test and get instant feedback on your answers. To take the test, visit the Social Studies section of **phschool.com.**

TRADE AND INDUSTRY

Without trade and industry, people would have to create everything they needed in order to live. If you wanted a loaf of bread, you would have to grow the wheat, grind it into flour at the mill you built, mix the dough in bowls you carved with tools you made, and bake it in an oven that you built from your own bricks. Industry organizes the production of an item such as bread so that a small number of farmers, millers, bakers, and distributors supply enough bread for everyone. Similar industrial organization is used to supply us with everything we use, from water to automobiles. Trade is the process of buying and selling. Trade helps to supply raw materials to manufacturers and then distribute the goods that are made. Together, trade and industry combine to determine the economics of a nation.

SILK ROAD
Trade between different regions and peoples goes back to ancient times. The Silk Road was one of the earliest and most famous trade routes. Traders led horses and camels along this route between 300 B.C. and A.D. 1600, carrying silk and other goods from China to Europe.

? How do trade and industry influence where and how people live?

A French factory makes the body from British steel.

The engine comes from a factory in Spain.

The transmission is made in Germany.

Final assembly of the car may take place in Spain.

A modern car is so complex that one factory cannot make every part. So, many factories build car components, and an assembly plant puts the behicle together.

STRIP MINING
Australia has huge mineral wealth, and mining is an important industry. The country produces one third of the world's uranium, which is essential for nuclear power. In recent years, iron ore has been excavated in large strip mines where giant digging machines remove entire hills.

MANUFACTURING

The basic form of industry is manufacturing. This means working on materials to make a finished product. Almost everything we use is the product of manufacturing, and most manufacturing takes place in large factories. Some goods go through many stages of manufacturing. For example, workers making cars assemble manufactured parts which, in turn, have been made in many other factories, often in other countries.

FARMING

New Zealand has a warm, moist climate which is ideal for many types of farming. Sheep and cattle ranching are the biggest businesses. There are two cattle and 13 sheep for every human in New Zealand. The country exports more dairy products and lamb than any other nation and is the second largest exporter of wool. Over the past 15 years production of other crops, such as kiwi fruit, oranges, and lemons, has increased. Newly built fishing boats have helped New Zealand's fleet increase its catch, and today the country is a major seafood exporter.

Sheep shearers work very quickly: some can clip a lamb in under a minute.

FACTORIES

Some industry takes place in people's homes, but workers in factories make most of the products that we buy. In a factory each person has a small task in the manufacturing process. He or she may operate a large machine or assemble something by hand. No one person makes an entire product. This process of mass production makes manufacturing cheaper and quicker. Most factories are owned by governments or large companies; a few factories are owned by the people who work in them.

FILMMAKING

The Australian film industry produces a number of important films each year. Some, such as *Picnic at Hanging Rock* (1975), which tells of the mysterious disappearance of a group of Australian schoolgirls, have received international acclaim.

Reference

TABLE OF CONTENTS

Atlas

Central America and the Caribbean

ARCTIC OCEAN

GREENLAND
(DEN.)

ICELAND
Reykjavik

EUROPE

See Inset Below

Moscow

RUSSIA

Astana

ASIA

KAZAKSTAN

Ulan Bator

MONGOLIA

NORTH
KOREA
P'yŏngyang
Seoul
JAPAN
SOUTH
KOREA
Tokyo

GEORGIA
ARMENIA
T'bilisi
Baku
Yerevan
TURKEY
AZERBAIJAN
Algiers
TUNISIA
Rabat
Tripoli
MOROCCO
JORDAN
ISRAEL
Cairo
JORDAN
SYRIA
IRAQ
Baghdad
IRAN
Tehran
AFGHANISTAN
Kabul
Ashkhabad
Dushanbe
Islamabad
PAKISTAN
Bishkek
Tashkent
UZBEKISTAN
TURKMENISTAN
TAJIKISTAN
KYRGYZSTAN

Beijing

CHINA

NEPAL
BHUTAN
New
Delhi
Kathmandu
Dhaka
MYANMAR
(BURMA)
Hanoi

Taipei
TAIWAN
Hong Kong

PACIFIC OCEAN

Tropic of Cancer

NORTHERN MARIANA
ISLANDS (U.S.)

GUAM (U.S.)

MARSHALL
ISLANDS

WESTERN
SAHARA
(MOROCCO)
ALGERIA
LIBYA
EGYPT
KUWAIT
BAHRAIN
QATAR
SAUDI
ARABIA
Riyadh
Abu Dhabi
Muscat
UNITED ARAB
EMIRATES
OMAN

See Inset Below

AFRICA

NIGER
CHAD
Khartoum
SUDAN
Asmara
ERITREA
Sanaa
YEMEN
Djibouti
DJIBOUTI

INDIA
BANGLADESH
Yangon
Bangkok
THAILAND
Vientiane
LAOS
VIETNAM
CAMBODIA
Phnom Penh
BRUNEI

Manila
PHILIPPINES

MICRONESIA

FEDERATED STATES
OF MICRONESIA

Koror
PALAU

Equator

NAURU
KIRIBATI

Niamey
NIGERIA
N'Djamena
Abuja
CENTRAL
AFRICAN REP.
CAMEROON
EQUATORIAL GUINEA
SÃO TOMÉ AND
PRÍNCIPE
Yaoundé
Bangui
Libreville
GABON
Brazzaville
CABINDA
(ANGOLA)
Kinshasa
DEM. REP.
OF THE
CONGO
CONGO
RWANDA
Kampala
UGANDA
KENYA
Nairobi
BURUNDI
TANZANIA
Dar es Salaam
ETHIOPIA
Addis Ababa
SOMALIA
Mogadishu

SRI
LANKA
Colombo
Kuala Lumpur
MALAYSIA
SINGAPORE

Jakarta

INDONESIA

MELANESIA
PAPUA
NEW GUINEA
Port Moresby
SOLOMON
ISLANDS

TUVALU

ATLANTIC
OCEAN

Luanda
ANGOLA
ZAMBIA
Lusaka
MALAWI
Lilongwe
MADAGASCAR
Antananarivo
COMOROS

INDIAN OCEAN

VANUATU
FIJI

NAMIBIA
Windhoek
BOTSWANA
Gaborone
Pretoria
ZIMBABWE
Harare
MOZAMBIQUE
Maputo
SWAZILAND
MAURITIUS
Réunion
(Fr.)

Tropic of Capricorn

AUSTRALIA

NEW CALEDONIA
(Fr.)

Cape Town
SOUTH
AFRICA
LESOTHO

Canberra

NEW
ZEALAND
Wellington

Antarctic Circle

Europe

ANTARCTICA

West Africa

MAURITANIA
Nouakchott

MALI

SENEGAL
THE GAMBIA
Bissau
GUINEA
Conakry
Freetown
SIERRA
LEONE
Monrovia
LIBERIA
Yamoussoukro
CÔTE
D'IVOIRE
BURKINA FASO
Bamako
Ouagadougou
Niamey
NIGER
BENIN
GHANA
TOGO
Accra
Lomé
Porto-
Novo
NIGERIA

ATLANTIC OCEAN

Equator

300   600 mi

300   600 km

FINLAND
NORWAY
SWEDEN
Oslo
Helsinki
Stockholm
Tallinn
ESTONIA
Riga
LATVIA
RUSSIA
IRELAND
Dublin
UNITED
KINGDOM
North
Sea
DENMARK
Copenhagen
LITHUANIA
Vilnius
Minsk
BELARUS
London
The
Hague
NETHERLANDS
Amsterdam
Berlin
Warsaw
POLAND
Kiev
UKRAINE
BELGIUM
Brussels
GERMANY
Prague
CZECH REP.
Paris
LUXEMBOURG
FRANCE
LIECH.
Vienna
Bratislava
SLOVAKIA
Budapest
MOLDOVA
Chişinău
SWITZERLAND
Bern
AUSTRIA
HUNGARY
ROMANIA
SLOVENIA
Ljubljana
Zagreb
CROATIA
Belgrade
Bucharest
GEORGIA
PORTUGAL
Lisbon
Madrid
SPAIN
ANDORRA
MONACO
ITALY
SAN
MARINO
Rome
BOS.
HERZ.
Sarajevo
MONTENEGRO
SERBIA
Sofia
BULGARIA
Black Sea
Tiranë
MACEDONIA
Skopje
ALBANIA
GREECE
GIBRALTAR (U.K.)
Tunis
Athens
TURKEY
Nicosia
CYPRUS
SYRIA
Beirut
LEBANON
Damascus
ISRAEL
Jerusalem
Amman
JORDAN

ATLANTIC
OCEAN

MOROCCO
ALGERIA
TUNISIA
Mediterranean Sea
LIBYA
EGYPT

0   400   800 mi
0   400   800 km

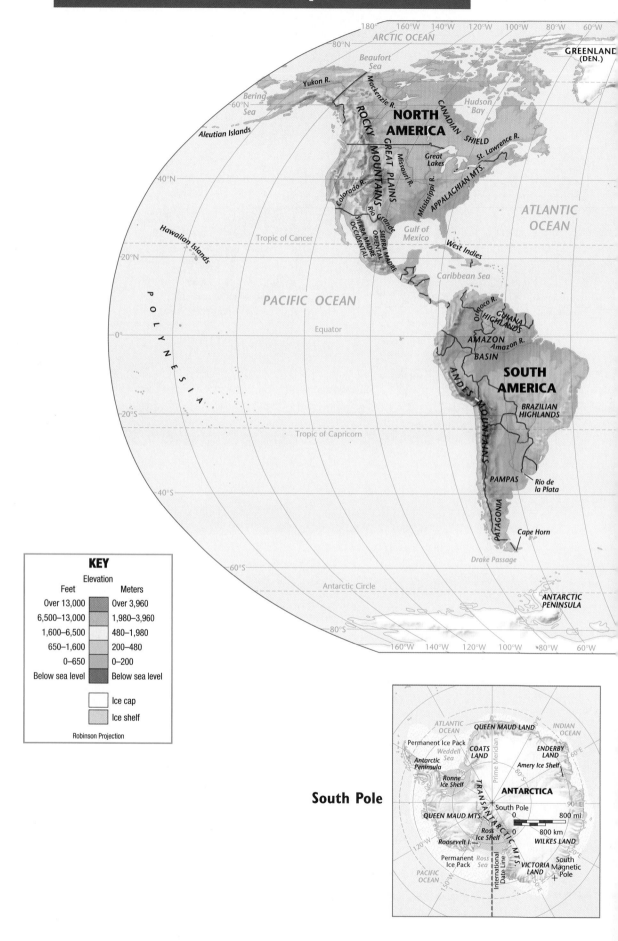

KEY

Elevation

Feet	Meters
Over 13,000	Over 3,960
6,500–13,000	1,980–3,960
1,600–6,500	480–1,980
650–1,600	200–480
0–650	0–200
Below sea level	Below sea level

Ice cap

Ice shelf

Robinson Projection

South Pole

20°W 0° 20°E 40°E 60°E 80°E 100°E 120°E 140°E 160°E 180°

ARCTIC OCEAN

80°N

Arctic Circle

SCANDINAVIAN PEN.

British Isles

North Sea

URAL MTS.

Ob R.

Yenisei R.

SIBERIA

Lena R.

60°N

KOLYMA MTS.

KAMCHATKA PENINSULA

NORTHERN EUROPEAN PLAIN

WEST SIBERIAN PLAIN

EUROPE

ASIA

ALPS

Volga R.

Aral Sea

ALTAI MTS.

L. Baikal

Amur R.

Sea of Japan

40°N

IBERIAN PEN.

BALKAN PEN.

CAUCASUS MTS.

Black Sea

Caspian Sea

TIAN SHAN

GOBI DESERT

NORTH CHINA PLAIN

ATLAS MTS.

Mediterranean Sea

ZAGROS MTS.

HINDU KUSH

KUNLUN SHAN

Huang He

PACIFIC OCEAN

PLATEAU OF IRAN

H I M A L A Y A S

TIBETAN PLATEAU

Yangzi R.

SAHARA

Red Sea

ARABIAN PENINSULA

Persian Gulf

Mt. Everest 29,028 ft. (8,848 m)

Tropic of Cancer

20°N

AFRICA

Nile R.

Arabian Sea

DECCAN PLATEAU

Ganges R.

Bay of Bengal

Philippine Sea

MICRONESIA

NIGER R.

SUDAN

ETHIOPIAN PLATEAU

South China Sea

MELANESIA

Equator

0°

Congo R.

Lake Victoria

INDIAN OCEAN

Sumatra

Borneo

Celebes

East Indies

New Guinea

ATLANTIC OCEAN

Zambezi R.

Madagascar

20°S

KALAHARI

AUSTRALIA

Tropic of Capricorn

Darling R.

GREAT DIVIDING RANGE

Cape of Good Hope

N
W·E
S

0   1,000   2,000 mi

0 1,000 2,000 km

40°S

60°S

Antarctic Circle

80°S

ANTARCTICA

20°W 0° 20°E 40°E 60°E 80°E 100°E 120°E 140°F 160°F

ASIA

TAIMYR PEN.

Laptev Sea

Kara Sea

Severnaya Zemlya

Novaya Zemlya

Barents Sea

New Siberian Islands

Franz Josef Land

East Siberian Sea

Permanent Ice Pack

ARCTIC OCEAN

North Pole

Svalbard (Nor.)

International Date Line

Prime Meridian

Chukchi Sea

0   500 mi

0   500 km

North Magnetic Pole

Ellesmere Island

Queen Elizabeth Islands

Baffin Bay

NORTH AMERICA

North Pole

United States: Political

RUSSIA

ARCTIC OCEAN

Arctic Circle

70°N

70°N

ALASKA

Yukon River

CANADA

60°N

Bering Strait

Anchorage

Bering Sea

Gulf of Alaska

Juneau

0   250   500 mi

0   250   500 km

160°W

140°W

50°N

120°W

110°W

Missouri River

Minot

Columbia River

Seattle

Olympia

WASHINGTON

Spokane

Bismarck

Portland

Salem

Helena

MONTANA

Billings

Sheridan

Pier

OREGON

IDAHO

Boise

Rapid City

Klamath Falls

Snake River

Jackson

Eureka

Twin Falls

WYOMING

40°N

Winnemucca

Great Salt Lake

NEBRASK

Cheyenne

Sacramento

Carson City

Salt Lake City

San Francisco

NEVADA

UTAH

Denver

COLORADO

Grand Junction

Pueblo

Cedar City

Colorado River

Arkar

CALIFORNIA

Las Vegas

PACIFIC

Los Angeles

OCEAN

Santa Fe

Albuquerque

ARIZONA

NEW MEXICO

Phoenix

Rio Grande

San Diego

Roswell

30°N

Tucson

El Paso

160°W

155°W

Honolulu

PACIFIC OCEAN

20°N

HAWAII

20°N

Hilo

0   50   100 mi

0   50   100 km

155°W

MEXICO

120°W

110°W

Tropic of Cancer

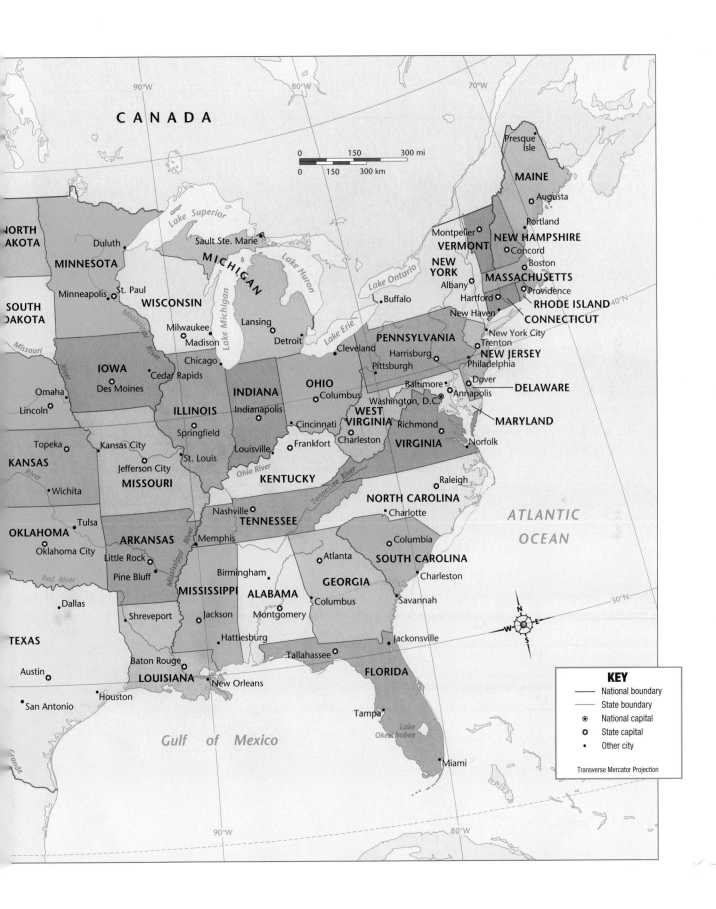

CANADA

NORTH DAKOTA

SOUTH DAKOTA

MINNESOTA
Duluth
Minneapolis • St. Paul

WISCONSIN
Milwaukee
Madison

Lake Superior
Sault Ste. Marie
MICHIGAN
Lake Michigan
Lansing
Detroit

Lake Huron
Lake Ontario
Buffalo

Lake Erie
Cleveland

MAINE
Presque Isle
Augusta
Portland

NEW HAMPSHIRE
Montpelier • Concord
VERMONT
Boston
NEW YORK
Albany
MASSACHUSETTS
Hartford • Providence
RHODE ISLAND
New Haven
CONNECTICUT

IOWA
Omaha
Des Moines
Cedar Rapids
Lincoln

Chicago
ILLINOIS
Springfield

INDIANA
Indianapolis

OHIO
Columbus

PENNSYLVANIA
Harrisburg
Pittsburgh

New York City
Trenton
NEW JERSEY
Philadelphia
Baltimore
Dover
DELAWARE
Annapolis
Washington, D.C.
MARYLAND

Missouri River

KANSAS
Topeka
Wichita

Kansas City
St. Louis
MISSOURI
Jefferson City

Cincinnati
Louisville
Frankfort
KENTUCKY
Ohio River

WEST VIRGINIA
Charleston

VIRGINIA
Richmond
Norfolk

OKLAHOMA
Tulsa
Oklahoma City

ARKANSAS
Little Rock
Pine Bluff
Red River

Nashville
TENNESSEE
Memphis

Mississippi River

Tennessee River

NORTH CAROLINA
Raleigh
Charlotte

Columbia
SOUTH CAROLINA
Charleston

ATLANTIC OCEAN

TEXAS
Dallas
Shreveport
Austin
San Antonio
Houston

MISSISSIPPI
Jackson
Hattiesburg

Birmingham
ALABAMA
Montgomery

Atlanta
GEORGIA
Columbus
Savannah

LOUISIANA
Baton Rouge
New Orleans

Tallahassee
FLORIDA
Jacksonville

30°N

Gulf of Mexico

Tampa
Lake Okeechobee

Miami

90°W   80°W   70°W

40°N

0   150   300 mi
0   150   300 km

N
W   E
S

KEY
— National boundary
— State boundary
⊛ National capital
⊗ State capital
• Other city

Transverse Mercator Projection

North and South America: Political

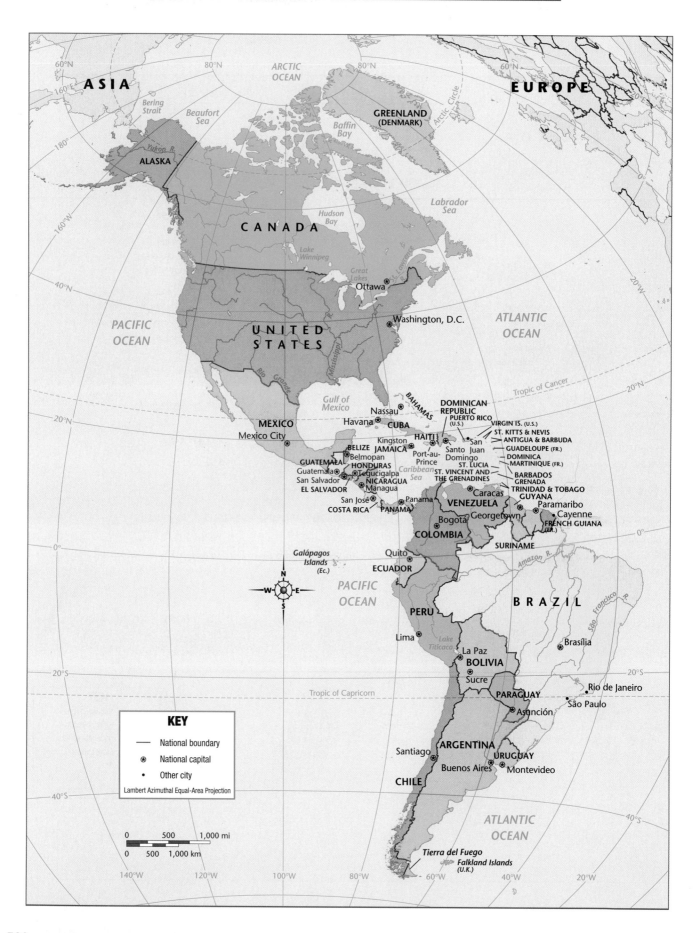

KEY
— National boundary
⊛ National capital
• Other city
Lambert Azimuthal Equal-Area Projection

0   500   1,000 mi
0   500   1,000 km

ASIA

EUROPE

ARCTIC
OCEAN

60°N   80°N   80°N   60°N

160°E

Bering
Strait

Beaufort
Sea

Baffin
Bay

Arctic Circle

180°

Yukon R.

Mackenzie R.

Labrador
Sea

160°W

Hudson
Bay

CANADIAN SHIELD

20°W

40°N

ROCKY MOUNTAINS

GREAT PLAINS

Lake
Winnipeg

Great
Lakes

St. Lawrence R.

CASCADES

Missouri R.

PACIFIC
OCEAN

Great
Salt
Lake

SIERRA NEVADA

Colorado R.

Ohio R.

Mississippi R.

APPALACHIAN MTS.

ATLANTIC
OCEAN

20°W

Tropic of Cancer

20°N

BAJA
CALIFORNIA

SIERRA MADRE OCCIDENTAL

Rio Grande

SIERRA MADRE ORIENTAL

Gulf of
Mexico

YUCATÁN
PENINSULA

Hispaniola

Caribbean Sea

ISTHMUS OF
PANAMA

Orinoco R.

AMAZON
BASIN

Amazon R.

0°

ANDES

Lake
Titicaca

São Francisco R.

BRAZILIAN
HIGHLANDS

ATACAMA
DESERT

MOUNTAINS

Paraguay R.

Paraná R.

20°S

20°S

PACIFIC
OCEAN

KEY

Elevation

Feet	Meters
Over 13,000	Over 3,960
6,500–13,000	1,980–3,960
1,600–6,500	480–1,980
650–1,600	200–480
0–650	0–200
Ice cap	

Lambert Azimuthal Equal-Area Projection

PAMPAS

Tropic of Capricorn

PATAGONIA

ATLANTIC
OCEAN

4°S   40°S

0   500   1,000 mi

0   500   1,000 km

Tierra del Fuego

140°W   120°W   100°W   80°W   60°W   40°W   20°W

KEY

Elevation

Feet	Meters
Over 13,000	Over 3,960
6,500–13,000	1,980–3,960
1,600–6,500	480–1,980
650–1,600	200–480
0–650	0–200
Below sea level	Below sea level
Ice cap	

Lambert Azimuthal Equal-Area Projection

ARCTIC OCEAN

LAPLAND

Norwegian Sea

KJØLEN MTS.

SCANDINAVIAN PENINSULA

Gulf of Bothnia

Lake Ladoga

Faeroe Is. (Den.)

Glittertind 8,110 ft. (2,472 m)

Shetland Is. (U.K.)

ATLANTIC OCEAN

Ben Nevis 4,406 ft (1,343 m)

North Sea

Lake Vänern

JUTLAND PENINSULA

Baltic Sea

Dnieper R.

BRITISH ISLES

NORTHERN EUROPEAN PLAIN

Vistula R.

Thames R.

RUHR VALLEY

Elbe River

Oder River

English Channel

Dniester River

Seine River

CARPATHIAN MTS.

Rhine R.

Danube River

Loire River

Bay of Biscay

Mont Blanc 15,771 ft. (4,807 m)

A L P S

TRANSYLVANIAN ALPS

Po River

MASSIF CENTRAL

Rhône River

Danube River

Garonne R.

DINARIC ALPS

BALKAN MTS.

PYRENEES

Ebro R.

APENNINES

BALKAN PENINSULA

Douro R.

Corsica

Adriatic Sea

MESETA

ITALIAN PENINSULA

PINDUS MTS.

Tagus River

IBERIAN PENINSULA

Sardinia

Black Sea

Bosporus

ASIA

Balearic Is.

Tyrrhenian Sea

Ionian Sea

Aegean Sea

Dardanelles

PELOPONNESE

Strait of Gibraltar

Sicily

Crete

AFRICA

Mediterranean Sea

Arctic Circle

Prime Meridian

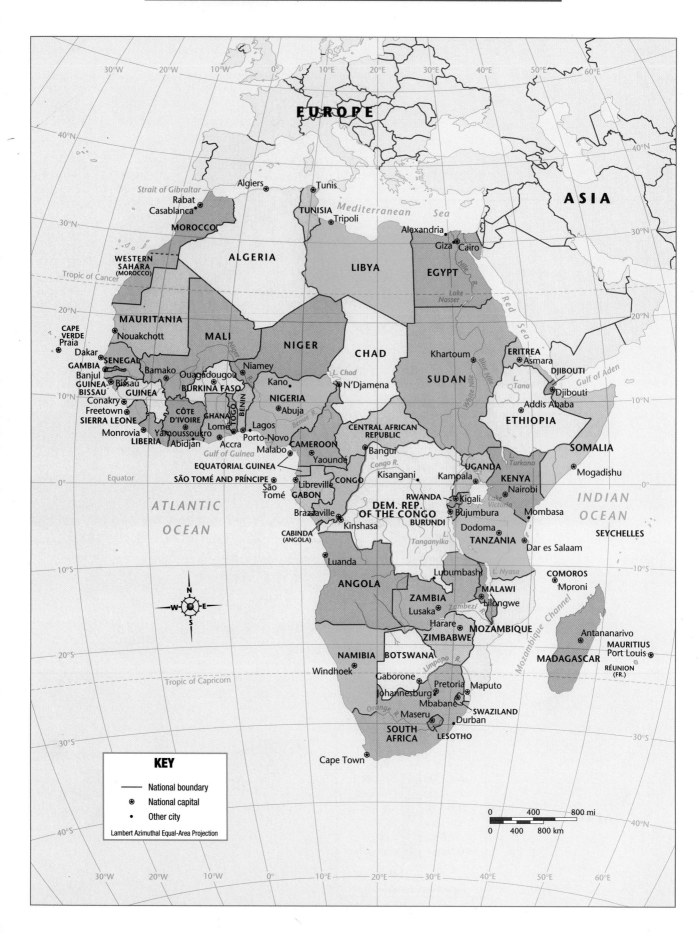

KEY

— National boundary

⊛ National capital

• Other city

Lambert Azimuthal Equal-Area Projection

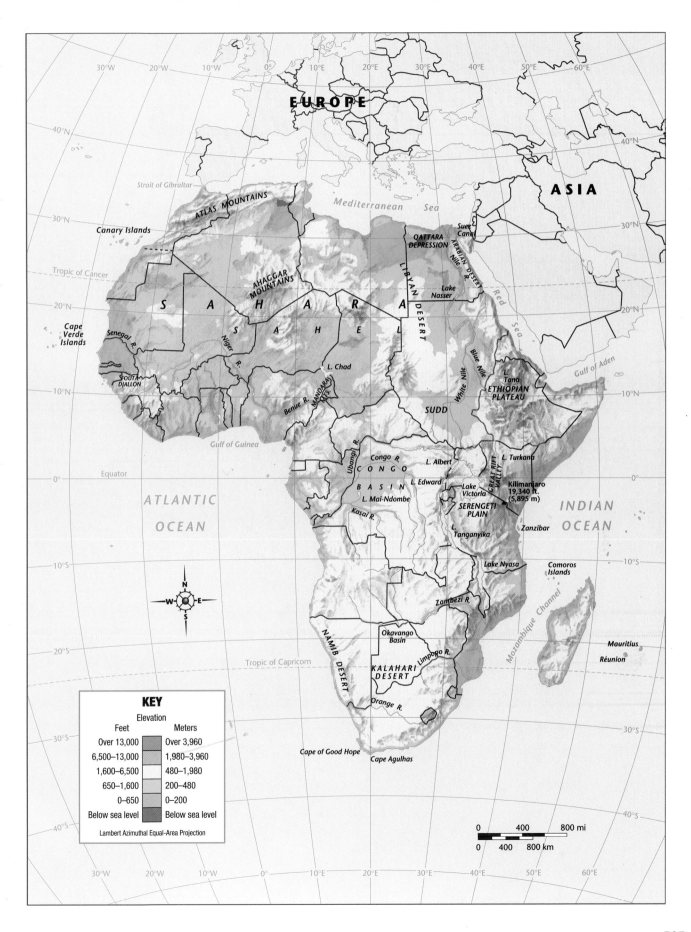

EUROPE

ASIA

Strait of Gibraltar

ATLAS MOUNTAINS

Mediterranean Sea

Canary Islands

QATTARA DEPRESSION

Suez Canal

Tropic of Cancer

AHAGGAR MOUNTAINS

S A H A R A

LIBYAN DESERT

ARABIAN DESERT

Nile R.

Lake Nasser

Red Sea

Cape Verde Islands

Senegal R.

S A H E L

Niger R.

L. Chad

Blue Nile

White Nile

Gulf of Aden

L. Tana

ETHIOPIAN PLATEAU

FOUTA DJALLON

Benue R.

MANDARA MTS.

SUDD

Gulf of Guinea

Ubangi R.

Congo R.

C O N G O

B A S I N

L. Mai-Ndombe

L. Albert

L. Edward

Lake Victoria

L. Turkana

GREAT RIFT VALLEY

Kilimanjaro 19,340 ft. (5,895 m)

Equator

ATLANTIC OCEAN

Kasai R.

SERENGETI PLAIN

Zanzibar

INDIAN OCEAN

L. Tanganyika

Lake Nyasa

Comoros Islands

Zambezi R.

Mozambique Channel

Mauritius

Okavango Basin

Réunion

NAMIB DESERT

Limpopo R.

Tropic of Capricorn

KALAHARI DESERT

Orange R.

Cape of Good Hope

Cape Agulhas

KEY
Elevation
Feet	Meters
Over 13,000	Over 3,960
6,500–13,000	1,980–3,960
1,600–6,500	480–1,980
650–1,600	200–480
0–650	0–200
Below sea level	Below sea level

Lambert Azimuthal Equal-Area Projection

0   400   800 mi

0   400   800 km

Asia: Political

KEY
- National boundary
- ⊛ National capital
- • Other city

Two-Point Equidistant Projection

PACIFIC OCEAN

ARCTIC OCEAN

North Pole

Arctic Circle

Bering Sea

Sea of Okhotsk

Kuril Islands (Russia)

Sakhalin Island

• Verkhoyansk

Sea of Japan

Tokyo ⊛

Vladivostok •

JAPAN

N. KOREA ⊛
P'yŏngyang • Seoul ⊛
S. KOREA

Yellow Sea

East China Sea

Ryukyu Islands

Taipei • TAIWAN

Philippine Sea

Tropic of Cancer

Port Moresby ⊛

PAPUA NEW GUINEA

New Guinea

PALAU ⊛ Koror

Bandar Seri Begawan ⊛

BRUNEI

Celebes

Tanimbar

Timor

I N D O N E S I A

Java Sea

Java

Sumatra

MALAYSIA

SINGAPORE ⊛
Singapore

Kuala Lumpur ⊛

Borneo

Celebes Sea

PHILIPPINES
Manila ⊛

South China Sea

Hong Kong •
Macao •

Fuzhou •

Hanoi ⊛
VIETNAM

LAOS
Vientiane ⊛
THAILAND
Bangkok ⊛
CAMBODIA
Phnom Penh ⊛

Yangon •
MYANMAR (BURMA)

East Siberian Sea

RUSSIA

Lena R.

Lake Baikal

Harbin •

Beijing ⊛

Ulan Bator ⊛
MONGOLIA

Irkutsk •
Bratsk •

Xi'an •

Huang He

CHINA

Yangtze R.

Barents Sea

Ob R.

Yenisei R.

Omsk •

Yekaterinburg •

Samara •

Kharkov •

Moscow ⊛ St. Petersburg •

Riga ⊛ Tallinn ⊛ ESTONIA
LATVIA
LITHUANIA
Vilnius ⊛ Minsk ⊛
BELARUS

UKRAINE
Kiev ⊛

MOLDOVA
Chişinău ⊛

Black Sea

TURKEY
Ankara ⊛

GEORGIA
Tbilisi ⊛
ARMENIA
Yerevan ⊛
AZERBAIJAN
Baku ⊛

Caspian Sea

Astana ⊛
Qaraghandy •
KAZAKSTAN

Aral Sea

Lake Balkhash

UZBEKISTAN
Tashkent ⊛
KYRGYZSTAN
Bishkek ⊛
TAJIKISTAN
Ashkhabad ⊛ Dushanbe ⊛
TURKMENISTAN

Mediterranean Sea

CYPRUS
Nicosia ⊛
LEBANON
Beirut ⊛
SYRIA
Damascus ⊛
ISRAEL Amman ⊛
Jerusalem ⊛ JORDAN
IRAQ
Baghdad ⊛

Tehran ⊛
IRAN
Shiraz •

AFGHANISTAN
Kabul ⊛
PAKISTAN
Islamabad ⊛

Kathmandu ⊛
NEPAL
New Delhi ⊛

BHUTAN
Thimphu ⊛

Dhaka ⊛
BANGLADESH

Ganges R.

INDIA

Mumbai (Bombay) •

Madras •

Bay of Bengal

SRI LANKA
Colombo •

Male •
MALDIVES

INDIAN OCEAN

Arabian Sea

Muscat ⊛
OMAN

Socotra (Yemen)

Abu Dhabi ⊛
UNITED ARAB EMIRATES

Gulf of Oman

Persian Gulf

KUWAIT ⊛
BAHRAIN
QATAR

SAUDI ARABIA
Riyadh ⊛

YEMEN
Sanaa ⊛

Gulf of Aden

Red Sea

Mecca •

A F R I C A

Tropic of Cancer

EUROPE

Equator

1,000 mi

1,000 km

500

500

0

0

ATLAS

596

Asia: Physical

KEY

Elevation

Feet	Meters
Over 13,000	Over 3,960
6,500–13,000	1,980–3,960
1,600–6,500	480–1,980
650–1,600	200–480
0–650	0–200
Below sea level	Below sea level

Two-Point Equidistant Projection

ARCTIC OCEAN

North Pole

PACIFIC OCEAN

EUROPE

AFRICA

INDIAN OCEAN

Mediterranean Sea

Black Sea

Caspian Sea

Red Sea

Gulf of Aden

Arabian Sea

Bay of Bengal

PLATEAU OF ANATOLIA

CAUCASUS MTS.

ZAGROS MTS.

ARABIAN PENINSULA

Socotra (Yemen)

Persian Gulf

URAL MOUNTAINS

Ob R.

Ural R.

Volga R.

Don R.

Yenisei R.

Ob R.

Irtysh R.

Lena R.

Amur R.

Lake Baikal

Lake Balkhash

NORTH SIBERIAN LOWLAND

CENTRAL SIBERIAN PLATEAU

STANOVOI RANGE

KOLYMA MTS.

KAMCHATKA PENINSULA

Bering Sea

East Siberian Sea

Barents Sea

Sea of Okhotsk

Sakhalin Island

Kuril Islands

Sea of Japan

Hokkaido

Honshu

Shikoku

Kyushu

Ryukyu Islands

East China Sea

Yellow Sea

ALTAI MTS.

MONGOLIAN PLATEAU

GOBI DESERT

He

Huang

Yangzi R.

TIAN SHAN

KUNLUN SHAN

PLATEAU OF TIBET

HINDU KUSH

HIMALAYAS

Brahmaputra R.

Ganges R.

Indus R.

INDIAN PENINSULA

DECCAN PLATEAU

WESTERN GHATS

EASTERN GHATS

Irrawaddy R.

Mekong R.

INDOCHINA PENINSULA

MALAY PENINSULA

Sumatra

Borneo

Java

Java Sea

Celebes

Mindanao

Luzon

Philippine Sea

South China Sea

South China Sea

Tanimbar

Timor

New Guinea

Equator

Tropic of Cancer

Tropic of Cancer

Arctic Circle

Equator

Two-Point Equidistant Projection

1,000 mi

1,000 km

500

500

0

0

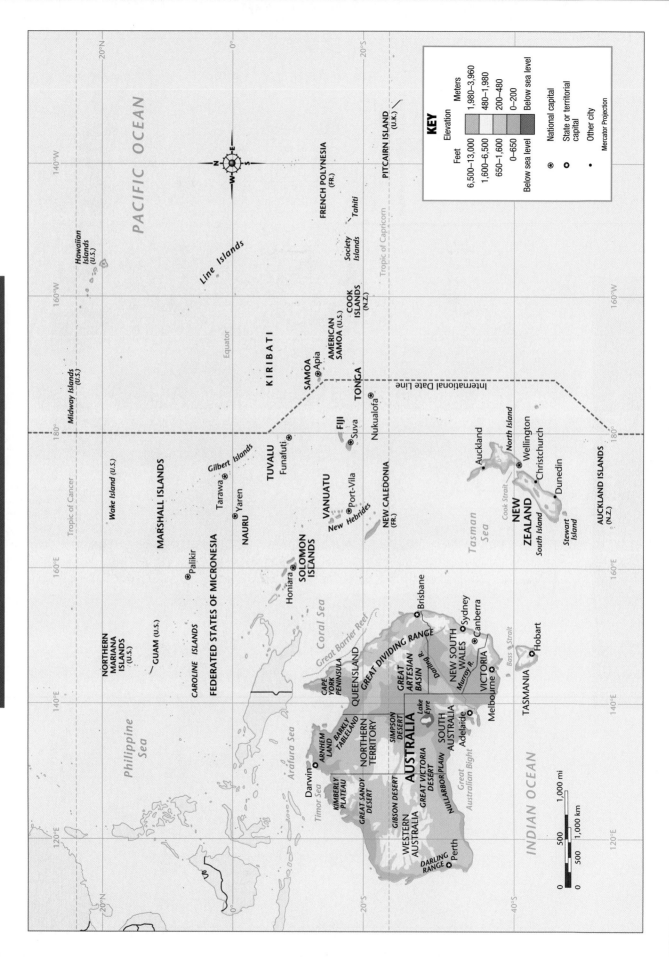

PACIFIC OCEAN

KEY

Elevation

Feet	Meters
6,500–13,000	1,980–3,960
1,600–6,500	480–1,980
650–1,600	200–480
0–650	0–200
Below sea level	Below sea level

⊗ National capital

⊛ State or territorial capital

• Other city

Mercator Projection

Hawaiian Islands (U.S.)

Line Islands

FRENCH POLYNESIA (Fr.)

Society Islands — Tahiti

Tropic of Capricorn

PITCAIRN ISLAND (U.K.)

Midway Islands (U.S.)

Equator

KIRIBATI

COOK ISLANDS (N.Z.)

AMERICAN SAMOA (U.S.)

SAMOA
⊗ Apia

TONGA

International Date Line

Tropic of Cancer

Wake Island (U.S.)

MARSHALL ISLANDS

Gilbert Islands

TUVALU
⊛ Funafuti

FIJI
Suva ⊛

Nukualofa ⊗

NORTHERN MARIANA ISLANDS (U.S.)

GUAM (U.S.)

CAROLINE ISLANDS

FEDERATED STATES OF MICRONESIA

Palikir •

Tarawa ⊗

⊗ Yaren

NAURU

SOLOMON ISLANDS

Honiara ⊗

VANUATU
⊗ Port-Vila

New Hebrides

NEW CALEDONIA (Fr.)

Auckland •

North Island

⊗ Wellington

Christchurch •

Dunedin •

Cook Strait

NEW ZEALAND

South Island

Stewart Island

AUCKLAND ISLANDS (N.Z.)

Tasman Sea

Philippine Sea

Coral Sea

Great Barrier Reef

Brisbane ⊛

GREAT DIVIDING RANGE

Arafura Sea

CAPE YORK PENINSULA

QUEENSLAND

GREAT ARTESIAN BASIN

Darling R.

NEW SOUTH WALES

Sydney •

⊗ Canberra

Melbourne •

VICTORIA

Murray R.

Bass Strait

Hobart ⊛

TASMANIA

Timor Sea

Darwin ⊛

ARNHEM LAND

BARKLY TABLELAND

NORTHERN TERRITORY

SIMPSON DESERT

Lake Eyre

AUSTRALIA

SOUTH AUSTRALIA

Adelaide ⊛

KIMBERLY PLATEAU

GREAT SANDY DESERT

GIBSON DESERT

GREAT VICTORIA DESERT

NULLARBOR PLAIN

Great Australian Bight

WESTERN AUSTRALIA

DARLING RANGE

Perth ⊛

INDIAN OCEAN

1,000 mi

1,000 km

0   500

0   500

The Arctic and Antarctica

The Arctic

Sea of Okhotsk
150°E
60°N
VERKHOYANSKI KHREBET
CHERSKOGO RANGE
Lena R.
ASIA
EUROPE
TAIMYR PEN.
Kara Sea
KOLA PEN.
90°E
Laptev Sea
Severnaya Zemlya
Novaya Zemlya
Barents Sea
SCANDINAVIAN PENINSULA
Baltic Sea
New Siberian Islands
Franz Josef Land
North Cape
KOLYMA MTS.
Arctic Circle
80°N
North Sea
East Siberian Sea
ARCTIC OCEAN
Svalbard (Nor.)
Norwegian Sea
International Date Line
ANADYR RANGE
Wrangel Island
North Pole
0°
Prime Meridian
180°
Bering Sea
CHUKOTSKI PEN.
Chukchi Sea
Permanent Ice Pack
N
80°N
Greenland Sea
Denmark Strait
St. Lawrence Island
Bering Strait
W E
S
ATLANTIC OCEAN
Nunivak Island
Pt. Barrow
70°N
BROOKS RANGE
Yukon R.
Beaufort Sea
North Magnetic Pole
Ellesmere Island
70°N
ALASKA RANGE
Queen Elizabeth Islands
Amundsen Gulf
Banks Island
Baffin Bay
Davis Strait
Arctic Circle
60°N
Kodiak I.
Gulf of Alaska
Mackenzie R.
Victoria Island
Baffin I.
Cape Farewell
30°W
0   250   500 mi
0   250   500 km
NORTH AMERICA

Antarctica

ATLANTIC OCEAN
0°
Antarctic Circle
30°W
30°E
60°S
60°W
70°S
South Shetland Is.
Permanent Ice Pack
Weddell Sea
QUEEN MAUD LAND
Prime Meridian
ENDERBY LAND
SOUTH AMERICA
Antarctic Peninsula
COATS LAND
Filchner Ice Shelf
N
W E
S
Amery Ice Shelf
Alexander I.
Ronne Ice Shelf
Berkner I.
80°S
Bellingshausen Sea
T R A N S A N T A R C T I C   M T S.
ANTARCTICA
INDIAN OCEAN
Vinson Massif 16,066 ft. (4,897 m)
90°W
South Pole
90°E
Amundsen Sea
QUEEN MAUD MTS.
WILKES LAND
Ross Ice Shelf
Roosevelt I.
International Date Line
Permanent Ice Pack
Ross Sea
VICTORIA LAND
PACIFIC OCEAN
120°W
150°W
South Magnetic Pole
150°E
180°
0   400   800 mi
0   400   800 km

KEY

Elevation

Feet		Meters
Over 13,000		Over 3,960
6,500–13,000		1,980–3,960
1,600–6,500		480–1,980
650–1,600		200–480
0–650		0–200

Ice cap

Ice shelf

Orthographic Projection

Regional Database

TABLE OF CONTENTS

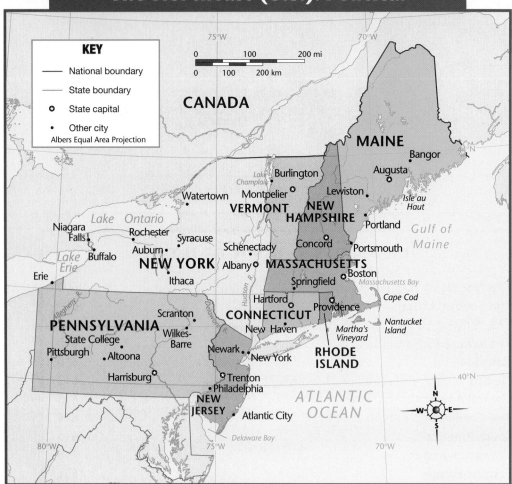

KEY

—— National boundary

—— State boundary

⊙ State capital

• Other city

Albers Equal Area Projection

0 100 200 mi
0 100 200 km

CANADA

MAINE

Bangor

Augusta

Lewiston

Lake Champlain

Burlington

Montpelier

Watertown

VERMONT

NEW HAMPSHIRE

Isle au Haut

Gulf of Maine

Lake Ontario

Niagara Falls

Rochester

Syracuse

Schenectady

Concord

Portland

Portsmouth

Auburn

Buffalo

NEW YORK

Albany

MASSACHUSETTS

Boston

Erie

Lake Erie

Ithaca

Springfield

Massachusetts Bay

Cape Cod

Hudson R.

Hartford

Providence

PENNSYLVANIA

Scranton

CONNECTICUT

New Haven

Martha's Vineyard

Nantucket Island

Allegheny R.

Delaware R.

Wilkes-Barre

Newark

RHODE ISLAND

State College

Pittsburgh

Altoona

Harrisburg

Newark

New York

Trenton

Philadelphia

NEW JERSEY

Atlantic City

ATLANTIC OCEAN

Delaware Bay

40°N

75°W 70°W 80°W 75°W 70°W

N W E S

Connecticut

Capital: Hartford

Area: 5,544 sq mi; 14,359 sq km

Climate: Humid continental; cold winters and long, hot summers

Population: 3.5 million

Agriculture: Mushrooms, vegetables, sweet corn, tobacco, apples, hay; poultry, dairy products, livestock; nursery stock, Christmas trees

Economic Activities: Aircraft engines and parts, submarines, helicopters, machinery and computer equipment, electrical equipment, medical instruments, pharmaceuticals

Maine

Capital: Augusta

Area: 35,387 sq mi; 91,652 sq km

Climate: Humid continental; cold winters and moderate summers; milder along coast

Population: 1.3 million

Agriculture: Potatoes, blueberries, apples; poultry, dairy products; fish; timber

Economic Activities: Pulp and paper, transportation equipment, wood products, food processing, tourism

Massachusetts

Capital: Boston

Area: 10,555 sq mi; 27,337 sq km

Climate: Humid continental; cold winters and long, hot summers; milder along coast

Population: 6.4 million

Agriculture: Cranberries, greenhouse and nursery plants, vegetables; fish

Economic Activities: Electrical, electronic, and industrial equipment, printing and publishing, metal products, food processing

New Hampshire

Capital: Concord

Area: 9,351 sq mi; 24,219 sq km

Climate: Humid continental; long, cold winters and cool summers; severe winters in northern mountains

Population: 1.3 million

Agriculture: Nursery and greenhouse products, hay, vegetables, fruit, maple syrup and sugar products; timber

Economic Activities: Tourism, machinery, electrical and electronic products, plastics

New Jersey

 Capital: Trenton
Area: 8,722 sq mi; 22,590 sq km
Climate: Humid continental; cold, snowy winters and hot, humid summers

Population: 8.6 million

Agriculture: Nursery plants, tomatoes, blueberries, peaches; dairy products; timber

Economic Activities: Chemicals, pharmaceuticals, electronic equipment, food processing, telecommunications, biotechnology, printing and publishing

New York

 Capital: Albany
Area: 54,475 sq mi; 141,090 sq km
Climate: Humid continental; severely cold winters in north; mildest along coast

Population: 19 million

Agriculture: Potatoes, onions, cabbage, sweet corn, grapes, apples, strawberries, pears, maple syrup, hay, wheat, oats, dry beans; dairy products, cattle, poultry; timber

Economic Activities: Printing and publishing, food processing, textiles, pharmaceuticals, machinery, instruments, toys and sporting goods, electronic equipment, automotive and aircraft parts

Pennsylvania

 Capital: Harrisburg
Area: 46,058 sq mi; 119,290 sq km
Climate: Humid continental; fairly wet; harsh winters and short summers in the plateaus and mountains; milder winters and longer summers in the lowlands, valleys, and coastal plain

Population: 12.3 million

Agriculture: Corn, hay, mushrooms, apples, potatoes, winter wheat, oats, vegetables, tobacco, grapes, peaches; dairy products, chickens, cattle, hogs; timber

Economic Activities: Food processing, metal products, industrial machinery and equipment, transportation equipment, rubber and plastics, electronic equipment, chemicals and pharmaceuticals, lumber and wood products, tourism, biotechnology, printing and publishing, mining (coal, limestone)

Rhode Island

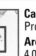 **Capital:** Providence
Area: 1,545 sq mi; 4,002 sq km
Climate: Humid continental (moderated by Atlantic Ocean); fairly wet

Population: 1 million

Agriculture: Greenhouse and nursery products, turf, sweet corn, potatoes; dairy products; fish

Economic Activities: Costume jewelry and silverware, toys, machinery, textiles, electronics

Vermont

 Capital: Montpelier
Area: 9,615 sq mi; 24,903 sq km
Climate: Humid continental; long, cold winters and short, warm summers; heavy snowfall in mountains

Population: 616,000

Agriculture: Apples, maple syrup and sugar; nursery and greenhouse products, vegetables, small fruits, hay; dairy products

Economic Activities: Electrical and electronic equipment, machine tools, furniture, scales, books, food processing, mining (granite, marble, limestone, slate), tourism

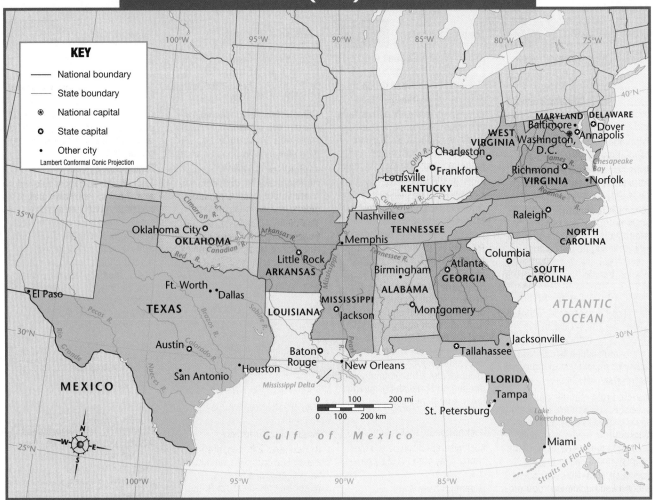

KEY

— National boundary
— State boundary
⊗ National capital
⊙ State capital
• Other city

Lambert Conformal Conic Projection

Alabama

Capital: Montgomery

Area: 52,423 sq mi; 135,775 sq km

Climate: Humid subtropical; short, mild winters and long, hot summers

Population: 4.5 million

Agriculture: Cotton, greenhouse and nursery products, peanuts, sweet potatoes; cattle, chickens; timber

Economic Activities: Pulp and paper, chemicals, electronics, clothing, textiles, mining (iron ore, limestone, coal), lumber and wood products, food processing, iron and steel

Arkansas

Capital: Little Rock

Area: 53,182 sq mi; 137,741 sq km

Climate: Mediterranean; mild, wet winters and long, hot summers; cooler and drier in north and west

Population: 2.7 million

Agriculture: Rice, soybeans, cotton, tomatoes, grapes, apples, peaches, wheat; chickens, cattle, hogs; timber

Economic Activities: Food processing, chemicals, lumber, paper, plastics, electric motors, furniture, auto parts, airplane parts, clothing, machinery, steel, tourism

Delaware

Capital: Dover

Area: 2,489 sq mi; 6,446 sq km

Climate: Humid continental; mild winters and hot, humid summers

Population: 807,000

Agriculture: Soybeans, potatoes, corn, mushrooms, lima beans, green peas, barley, cucumbers, wheat, corn, sorghum, nursery products; chickens, eggs

Economic Activities: Chemicals, tourism, auto assembly, food processing, transportation equipment, clothing

Florida

Capital: Tallahassee

Area: 65,758 sq mi; 170,313 sq km

Climate: Mostly humid subtropical; warm winters, hot summers; tropical in far south

Population: 16.7 million

Agriculture: Citrus fruits, vegetables, melons, nursery products, potatoes, sugarcane; chickens, cattle; fish

Economic Activities: Tourism, electrical, electronic, and transportation equipment, food processing, printing and publishing

Georgia

 Capital: Atlanta
Area: 59,441 sq mi; 153,952 sq km
Climate: Humid subtropical; mild, humid winters and hot, humid summers; cooler in mountains
Population: 8.6 million
Agriculture: Peanuts, cotton, corn, tobacco, hay soybeans; cattle, hogs, chickens; timber
Economic Activities: Textiles, clothing, food processing, pulp and paper, transportation equipment, chemicals, printing and publishing, lumber

Kentucky

 Capital: Frankfort
Area: 40,411 sq mi; 104,664 sq km
Climate: Humid subtropical; cool winters, warm or hot summers
Population: 4.1 million
Agriculture: Tobacco, corn, soybeans, hay; cattle, horses, hogs, chickens
Economic Activities: Transportation and industrial machinery, chemicals, clothing, printing and publishing, food processing, electrical and electronic equipment, mining (coal)

Louisiana

 Capital: Baton Rouge
Area: 51,843 sq mi; 134,273 sq km
Climate: Humid subtropical; short, mild winters and long, hot, humid summers
Population: 4.5 million
Agriculture: Cotton, sugarcane, soybeans, rice, corn, sweet potatoes, pecans, sorghum; cattle; fish; timber
Economic Activities: Tourism, chemicals, food processing, transportation equipment, electronic equipment, petroleum and natural gas, lumber, pulp and paper, construction

Maryland

 Capital: Annapolis
Area: 12,407 sq mi; 32,134 sq km
Climate: Humid subtropical in east; cool winters and hot, humid summers; continental in west, with colder winters and cooler summers
Population: 5.5 million
Agriculture: Greenhouse and nursery products, soybeans, corn, tobacco; chicken, dairy products; timber
Economic Activities: Electrical and electronic equipment, food processing, chemicals, printed materials, tourism, transportation equipment

Mississippi

 Capital: Jackson
Area: 48,434 sq mi; 125,444 sq km
Climate: Humid subtropical; mild winters and long, hot humid summers; cooler in highlands
Population: 2.9 million
Agriculture: Cotton, rice, soybeans, hay, corn; cattle, chickens; timber
Economic Activities: Transportation equipment, chemicals and plastics, food processing, furniture, lumber and wood products, electrical machinery

North Carolina

 Capital: Raleigh
Area: 53,821 sq mi; 139,396 sq km
Climate: Humid subtropical; cool winters, hot summers; colder in mountains
Population: 8.3 million
Agriculture: Tobacco, greenhouse and nursery products, cotton, soybeans, corn, grains, wheat, peanuts, sweet potatoes; turkeys, hogs, chickens, eggs, cattle; fish, timber;
Economic Activities: Food processing, chemicals, textiles, industrial machinery and equipment, electrical and electronic equipment, furniture, tobacco products, pulp and paper, tourism

Oklahoma

Capital: Oklahoma City
Area: 69,903 sq mi; 181,048 sq km
Climate: Mostly humid subtropical; moderate, short winters and very hot, long summers; dry subtropical in west
Population: 3.5 million
Agriculture: Wheat, cotton, hay, peanuts, grain sorghum, soybeans, corn, pecans; cattle, hogs, chickens
Economic Activities: Machinery, transportation equipment, food processing, metal products, mining (coal), petroleum and natural gas, tourism

South Carolina

 Capital: Columbia
Area: 32,007 sq mi; 82,898 sq km
Climate: Humid subtropical; mild winters, hot summers
Population: 4.1 million
Agriculture: Tobacco, greenhouse and nursery products, cotton, soybeans, corn, hay, wheat, peaches, tomatoes; chickens, eggs, turkeys; timber
Economic Activities: Textiles, tourism, chemicals, machinery and other metal products, clothing

Tennessee

Capital: Nashville
Area: 42,146 sq mi; 109,158 sq km
Climate: Humid subtropical; mild winters, hot summers, and abundant rain; colder in mountains
Population: 5.8 million
Agriculture: Tobacco, cotton, soybeans, grain, corn; cattle, chickens, eggs, hogs; timber
Economic Activities: Chemicals, food processing, transportation equipment, industrial machinery and equipment, metal products, rubber and plastic products, pulp and paper, printing and publishing

Texas

 Capital: Austin
Area: 268,601 sq mi; 695,674 sq km
Climate: Varies from humid subtropical in east to semiarid in central area to arid in far west; mostly mild winters and hot summers
Population: 21.8 million
Agriculture: Cotton, wheat and other grains, vegetable, citrus and other fruits, greenhouse and nursery products, pecans, peanuts; cattle, chickens, sheep, hogs, dairy products, eggs; fish; timber
Economic Activities: Industrial machinery and equipment, food processing, electrical and electronic equipment, chemicals, clothing, petroleum and natural gas

Virginia

 Capital: Richmond
Area: 42,769 sq mi; 110,771 sq km
Climate: Humid subtropical; mild, wet winters and hot, mostly humid summers; coldest in northwest
Population: 7.3 million
Agriculture: Tobacco, corn, soybeans, winter wheat, peanuts, cotton; chickens, dairy products, cattle, hogs; fish; timber
Economic Activities: Food processing, transportation equipment, printing, textiles, electrical and electronic equipment, industrial machinery and equipment, lumber and wood products, chemicals, rubber and plastics, furniture

West Virginia

Capital: Charleston
Area: 24,231 sq mi; 62,758 sq km
Climate: Humid continental; cold, humid winters and warm, humid summers
Population: 1.8 million
Agriculture: Apples, peaches, hay, tobacco, corn, wheat, oats; dairy products, eggs, cattle, chickens, turkeys
Economic Activities: Machinery, plastic and hardwood products, metal products, chemicals, aluminum, automotive parts, steel, mining (coal)

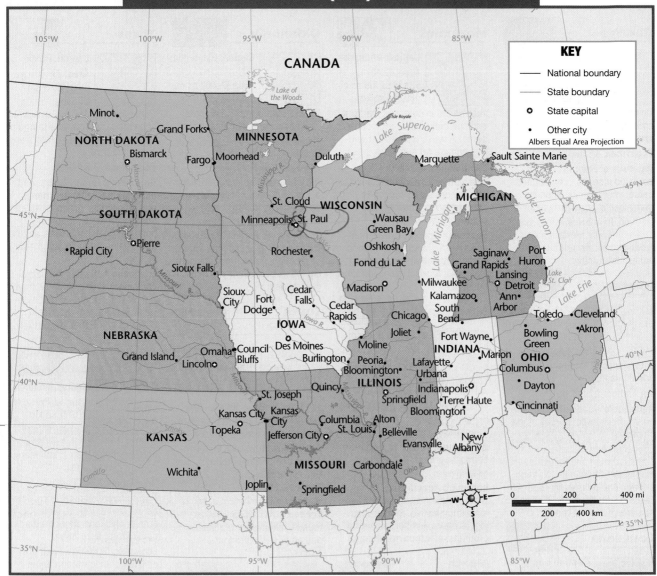

CANADA

KEY
- National boundary
- State boundary
- State capital
- Other city

Albers Equal Area Projection

Lake of the Woods

Isle Royale

Lake Superior

Minot
Grand Forks
NORTH DAKOTA
Bismarck
Fargo · Moorhead
MINNESOTA
Duluth
Marquette
Sault Sainte Marie

St. Cloud
WISCONSIN
MICHIGAN

SOUTH DAKOTA
Pierre
Minneapolis · St. Paul
Wausau
Green Bay

Rapid City
Rochester
Oshkosh
Fond du Lac
Saginaw
Grand Rapids
Port Huron
Lansing
Lake St. Clair

Sioux Falls
Madison
Milwaukee
Detroit
Lake Erie

Sioux City
Fort Dodge
Cedar Falls
Cedar Rapids
Chicago
Kalamazoo
South Bend
Ann Arbor
Toledo · Cleveland
Akron

NEBRASKA
IOWA
Joliet
Fort Wayne
Bowling Green
OHIO

Grand Island
Omaha · Council Bluffs
Des Moines
Moline
INDIANA
Marion
Columbus

Lincoln
Burlington
Peoria
Lafayette
Urbana
Dayton

Bloomington
Indianapolis
Cincinnati

Quincy
ILLINOIS
Springfield · Terre Haute
Bloomington

St. Joseph
Columbia · Alton
St. Louis · Belleville

Kansas City · Kansas City
Jefferson City
Evansville
New Albany

Topeka
KANSAS

Wichita
MISSOURI Carbondale

Joplin
Springfield

0   200   400 mi
0   200   400 km

Illinois

Capital: Springfield

Area: 57,918 sq mi; 150,007 sq km

Climate: Humid continental; cold, snowy winters and hot summers

Population: 12.6 million

Agriculture: Corn, soybeans, wheat, sorghum, hay; hogs, cattle, dairy products, chickens

Economic Activities: Machinery, electrical and electronic equipment, primary metals (steel) and metal products, chemical products, printing and publishing, food processing, construction, mining (coal)

Indiana

Capital: Indianapolis

Area: 36,420 sq mi; 94,327 sq km

Climate: Humid continental; cool winters and long, warm summers; warmer; wetter in far south

Population: 6.2 million

Agriculture: Corn, soybeans, wheat, greenhouse and nursery products, tomatoes and other vegetables, popcorn, fruit, hay, tobacco, mint; hogs, chickens, cattle

Economic Activities: Primary metals (steel), transportation equipment, motor vehicles and equipment, industrial machinery and equipment, food processing, electrical and electronic equipment, pharmaceuticals

---

Iowa

Capital: Des Moines

Area: 56,276 sq mi; 145,754 sq km

Climate: Humid continental; cold winters and warm, moist summers

Population: 2.9 million

Agriculture: Corn, soybeans, oats, hay; hogs, chickens, cattle, dairy products

Economic Activities: Construction, food processing, tires, farm machinery, electronic equipment, appliances, furniture, chemicals, fertilizers, auto parts

---

Kansas

Capital: Topeka

Area: 82,282 sq mi; 213,110 sq km

Climate: Humid continental; cold winters, hot summers; drier in west

Population: 2.7 million

Agriculture: Wheat, sorghum, corn, hay, soybeans, sunflowers; cattle, hogs, dairy products

Economic Activities: Transportation equipment, machinery and computer equipment, food processing, printing and publishing, chemicals, natural gas, rubber and plastic products, clothing

Michigan

Capital: Lansing
Area: 96,810 sq mi; 250,736 sq km
Climate: Humid continental (moderated by Great Lakes); snowy, cold winters and moist, mild to hot summers

Population: 10 million

Agriculture: Corn, wheat, soybeans, dry beans, hay, potatoes, sweet corn, apples, cherries, sugar beets, blueberries, cucumbers, grapes; cattle, hogs, chickens, dairy products

Economic Activities: Automobiles, transportation equipment, machinery, metal products, food processing, plastics, pharmaceuticals, furniture, tourism, cement, mining (iron ore, limestone)

Minnesota

Capital: Saint Paul
Area: 86,943 sq mi; 225,182 sq km
Climate: Humid continental; cold winters, hot summers; dry in far west

Population: 5 million

Agriculture: Corn, soybeans, wheat, sugar beets, hay, barley, potatoes, sunflowers; chickens, turkeys, hogs, cattle, dairy products, eggs

Economic Activities: Mining (iron ore), food processing, chemical and paper products, industrial machinery, electrical and electronic equipment, computers, printing and publishing, scientific and medical instruments, metal products, forest products, tourism

Missouri

Capital: Jefferson City
Area: 69,709 sq mi; 180,546 sq km

Climate: Humid continental; mostly cold winters and hot summers

Population: 5.7 million

Agriculture: Soybeans, corn, wheat, hay, cotton, sorghum; cattle, hogs, dairy products, chickens, turkeys, eggs

Economic Activities: Transportation equipment, food processing, electrical and electronic equipment, chemicals, printing and publishing, tourism

Nebraska

Capital: Lincoln
Area: 77,358 sq mi; 200,356 sq km
Climate: Continental; cold winters, hot summers; dry in northwest

Population: 1.7 million

Agriculture: Corn, sorghum, soybeans, hay, wheat, dry beans, oats, potatoes, sugar beets; cattle, hogs, chickens

Economic Activities: Food processing, industrial machinery, printed materials, electrical and electronic equipment, mining (sand and gravel, limestone), metal products, transportation equipment

North Dakota

 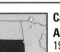

Capital: Bismarck
Area: 70,704 sq mi; 183,123 sq km
Climate: Continental; long, cold winters and hot summers; dry in west

Population: 634,000

Agriculture: Wheat, barley, flaxseed, oats, potatoes, dry beans, honey, soybeans, sugar beets, sunflowers, hay; cattle

Economic Activities: Petroleum and natural gas, mining (coal), food processing, farm equipment, metal products, electronic equipment

Ohio

Capital: Columbus
Area: 44,828 sq mi; 116,104 sq km
Climate: Humid continental; mild to cold winters, warm to hot summers

Population: 11.4 million

Agriculture: Corn, hay, winter wheat, oats, soybeans, greenhouse and nursery products; dairy products, cattle, hogs, chickens

Economic Activities: Transportation equipment, machinery, steel and aluminum, metal products, rubber and plastics, food processing

South Dakota

Capital: Pierre
Area: 77,121 sq mi; 199,743 sq km
Climate: Continental; cold winters, hot summers; low humidity; dry in west

Population: 761,000

Agriculture: Corn, soybeans, oats, wheat, sunflowers, sorghum; cattle, hogs, sheep, dairy products

Economic Activities: Food processing, machinery, electrical and electronic equipment, mining (gold), clothing

Wisconsin

Capital: Madison
Area: 65,503 sq mi; 169,652 sq km
Climate: Humid continental; long, cold winters and short, warm summers (moderated by Great Lakes)

Population: 5.4 million

Agriculture: Corn, hay, soybeans, potatoes, cranberries, sweet corn, peas, oats, snap beans; cattle, dairy products, hogs, chickens

Economic Activities: Food processing, motor vehicles and equipment, paper products, medical instruments and supplies, printing, plastics

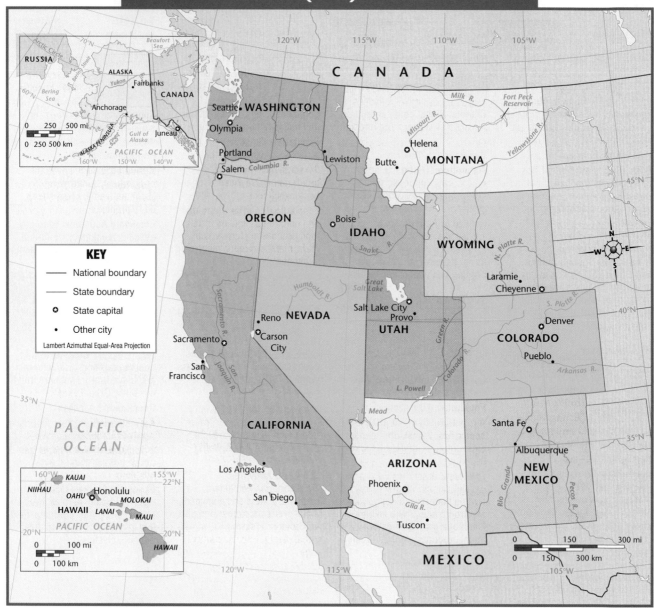

KEY

—— National boundary

—— State boundary

⊛ State capital

• Other city

Lambert Azimuthal Equal-Area Projection

Alaska

Capital: Juneau

Area: 656,425 sq mi; 1,700,134 sq km

Climate: Maritime in southeast and southwest (moist and mild); much colder and drier in west; continental in central area; Arctic in north, with extremely cold winters and cool summers

Population: 644,000

Agriculture: Greenhouse products, barley, oats, hay, potatoes, lettuce; fish

Economic Activities: Petroleum, tourism, fish products, mining (zinc, lead, gold), lumber and pulp, transportation equipment, furs

---

Arizona

Capital: Phoenix

Area: 114,006 sq mi; 295,274 sq km

Climate: Semiarid; mild winters and searing hot summers in south; cold winters and mostly cool summers in the high plateau of the north

Population: 5.5 million

Agriculture: Cotton, lettuce, cantaloupe, cauliflower, broccoli, sorghum, barley, corn, wheat, citrus fruits; cattle

Economic Activities: Electrical and electronic equipment, printing and publishing, food processing, metal products, tourism, mining (copper)

California

Capital: Sacramento

Area: 163,707 sq mi; 423,999

Climate: Marine west coast along northern coast; semiarid in much of south, but extremely arid in desert areas; mostly cool to mild winters and warm to hot summers; cold, snowy winters in mountains

Population: 35.1 million

Agriculture: Grapes, cotton, flowers, citrus fruits, rice, nursery products, hay, tomatoes, lettuce, strawberries, almonds, asparagus; dairy products, cattle, sheep, chickens, eggs; fish; timber

Economic Activities: Tourism, clothing, electrical and electronic equipment, computers, food processing, industrial machinery, transportation equipment and instruments, petroleum

---

Colorado

 Capital: Denver
Area: 104,100 sq mi; 269,618 sq km
Climate: Mostly highlands, with varying temperatures and precipitation; alpine conditions in high mountains; cold, dry winters and hot, dry summers in eastern plains

Population: 4.5 million

Agriculture: Corn, wheat, hay, sugar beets, barley, potatoes, apples, peaches, pears, dry beans, sorghum, onions, oats, sunflowers; cattle, sheep, hogs, chickens

Economic Activities: Computer equipment and instruments, food processing, machinery, aerospace products, construction, tourism, natural gas

Hawaii

 Capital: Honolulu
Area: 10,932 sq mi; 28,314 sq km
Climate: Tropical; rainfall varies greatly; snow on highest peaks in winter

Population: 1.2 million

Agriculture: Sugar cane, pineapples, macadamia nuts, fruits, coffee, vegetables, flowers; cattle; fish

Economic Activities: Tourism, food processing, clothing, printing and publishing

Idaho

 Capital: Boise
Area: 83,574 sq mi; 216,456 sq km
Climate: Semiarid; cold winters, hot summers; cooler and wetter in mountains

Population: 1.3 million

Agriculture: Potatoes, wheat, peas, dry beans, sugar beets, alfalfa seeds, lentils, hops, barley, plums and prunes, mint, onions, corn, cherries, apples, hay; cattle, chickens; timber

Economic Activities: Electronic components, computer equipment, food processing, tourism, lumber and wood products, chemical products, metal products, machinery, mining (phosphate rock, gold)

Montana

 Capital: Helena
Area: 147,046 sq mi; 380,848 sq km
Climate: Mostly dry continental; cold winters, hot summers; milder winters, cooler summers, and more precipitation in west

Population: 909,000

Agriculture: Wheat, barley, sugar beets, hay, oats; cattle, sheep

Economic Activities: Food processing, wood and paper products, mining (copper, gold), printing and publishing, tourism, coal and petroleum

Nevada

 Capital: Carson City
Area: 110,567 sq mi; 286,367 sq km
Climate: Mostly arid; mild winters and extremely hot summers in south; damper and cooler in mountains

Population: 2.2 million

Agriculture: Hay, alfalfa seeds, potatoes, onions, garlic, barley, wheat; cattle, dairy products

Economic Activities: Gaming, tourism, mining (gold, copper, silver), food processing, plastics, chemicals, aerospace products, printing and publishing, irrigation equipment

New Mexico

 Capital: Santa Fe
Area: 121,593 sq mi; 314,925 sq km
Climate: Semiarid; mostly mild, sunny, and dry; cooler and wetter in mountains

Population: 1.9 million

Agriculture: Hay, onions, chiles, greenhouse and nursery products, pecans, cotton; cattle, dairy products, chickens

Economic Activities: Mining (coal, copper), natural gas, petroleum, food processing, machinery, clothing, lumber, printing and publishing, transportation equipment, electronic equipment

Oregon

 Capital: Salem
Area: 98,386 sq mi; 254,819 sq km
Climate: Mostly marine west coast; mild winters and cool summers; highland in mountains, with severe winters; semiarid in east, with cold winters and warm summers

Population: 3.5 million

Agriculture: Greenhouse and nursery products, hay, wheat, grass seed, potatoes, onions, pears, mint; cattle, dairy products, chickens; timber

Economic Activities: Electrical and electronic equipment, lumber and wood products, metals, transportation equipment, food processing, pulp and paper, construction

Utah

 Capital: Salt Lake City
Area: 84,904 sq mi; 219,901 sq km
Climate: Arid; mild, dry winters and hot, dry summers; colder winters in north; wetter and colder in mountains

Population: 2.3 million

Agriculture: Hay, corn, wheat, barley, apples, potatoes, cherries, onions, peaches, pears; cattle, dairy products, poultry, eggs

Economic Activities: Medical instruments, electronic components, food processing, metal products, transportation equipment, steel and copper

Washington

Capital: Olympia
Area: 71,303 sq mi; 184,674 sq km
Climate: Marine west coast in west, with mild, wet winters and cool summers; semiarid in east with cold winters and hot summers

Population: 6 million

Agriculture: Apples, potatoes, wheat, barley, hay, hops, mint, peas, corn; livestock, dairy products; fish; timber

Economic Activities: Transportation equipment, computer software, pulp and paper, lumber and plywood, aluminum, tourism

Wyoming

 Capital: Chayenne
Area: 97,818 sq mi; 253,348 sq km
Climate: Continental; long, cold winters, and warm summers, little precipitation

Population: 499,000

Agriculture: Wheat, beans, barley, oats, sugar beets, hay; cattle, sheep

Economic Activities: Mining (coal), petroleum, natural gas, tourism, chemicals, wood products, food processing

Canada: Political

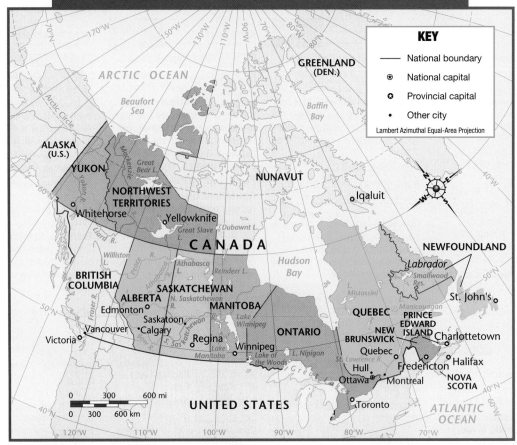

ARCTIC OCEAN

Beaufort
Sea

GREENLAND
(DEN.)

Baffin
Bay

KEY

—— National boundary

⊛ National capital

✪ Provincial capital

• Other city

Lambert Azimuthal Equal-Area Projection

ALASKA
(U.S.)

YUKON

Great
Bear L.

NUNAVUT

Iqaluit

NORTHWEST
TERRITORIES

Whitehorse

Yellowknife

Great Slave

Dubawnt L.

C A N A D A

NEWFOUNDLAND

Labrador

Smallwood
Res.

BRITISH
COLUMBIA

Williston
L.

Athabasca
L.

Reindeer L.

Hudson
Bay

Mistassini

St. John's

ALBERTA

SASKATCHEWAN

N. Saskatchewan

MANITOBA

Edmonton

Saskatoon

Lake
Winnipeg

QUEBEC

Manicouagan

PRINCE
EDWARD
ISLAND

Vancouver

Calgary

Regina

Winnipeg

ONTARIO

NEW
BRUNSWICK

Charlottetown

Victoria

Lake
Manitoba

Lake of
the Woods

L. Nipigon

Quebec

Halifax

Hull

Fredericton

Ottawa

Montreal

NOVA
SCOTIA

0   300   600 mi
0   300   600 km

UNITED STATES

Toronto

ATLANTIC
OCEAN

Alberta

Capital: Edmonton
Area: 255,541 sq mi; 661,848 sq km
Climate: Continental; extremely cold winters and warm summers

Population: 3.1 million

Agriculture: Grains, oilseeds, wheat; cattle, hogs, dairy products, poultry; timber

Economic Activities: Food processing, chemicals, petroleum, refining, construction, paper products, wood products, machinery, metal products, electrical and electronic equipment

British Columbia

Capital: Victoria
Area: 364,764 sq mi; 944,735 sq km
Climate: Mostly continental; colder in mountains; marine west coast along coast, with mild temperatures and much rain

Population: 4.1 million

Agriculture: Peas, tomatoes, apples, cherries, plums, raspberries, strawberries, flowers; dairy products, poultry, cattle; fish, timber;

Economic Activities: Wood processing, pulp and paper, mining (copper, zinc, gold), food processing, tourism, petroleum and coal products, metal products, printed materials, chemicals

Manitoba

Capital: Winnipeg
Area: 250,116 sq mi; 647,797 sq km
Climate: Continental; extremely cold winters, warm summers

Population: 1.2 million

Agriculture: Wheat, canola, flax; hogs, cattle, dairy products

Economic Activities: Food processing, machinery, transportation equipment, printing and publishing, mining (nickel, copper, gold)

New Brunswick

Capital: Fredericton
Area: 28,150 sq mi; 72,908 sq km
Climate: Humid continental; maritime along coasts
Population: 750,000
Agriculture: Potatoes; livestock, poultry, dairy products; fish; timber

Economic Activities: Mining (zinc, lead), paper products, food processing, lumber, metal products

Newfoundland and Labrador

Capital: Saint John's
Area: 156,453 sq mi; 405,212 sq km
Climate: Ranges from subarctic in Labrador to humid continental in Newfoundland; heavy winter snowfalls common
Population: 520,000
Agriculture: Vegetables; dairy products, poultry; fish

Economic Activities: Mining (iron ore), food processing, newsprint

Northwest Territories

Capital: Yellowknife
Area: 519,734 sq mi; 1,346,106 sq km
Climate: Subarctic; extremely cold winters and relatively warm, but short, summers; dry
Population: 42,000
Agriculture: Very limited; some vegetables, dairy products, cattle

Economic Activities: Mining (zinc, gold, lead, silver), petroleum and natural gas, fur trapping

Nova Scotia

Capital: Halifax
Area: 21,345 sq mi; 55,284 sq km
Climate: Humid continental; moderated by cool North Atlantic Ocean
Population: 936,000
Agriculture: Blueberries, vegetables; dairy products, poultry, livestock; fish
Economic Activities: Food processing, pulp and paper products, transportation equipment, iron and steel

Nunavut

Capital: Iqaluit
Area: 808,184 sq mi; 2,093,190 sq km
Climate: Subarctic on mainland, with continuous permafrost; arctic on northernmost islands, with no true summer; dry throughout; polar desert in northwest
Population: 29,000
Agriculture: Fish
Economic Activities: Mining (copper, lead, silver, zinc), tourism, hunting and trapping, arts and crafts products

Ontario

Capital: Toronto
Area: 415,598 sq mi; 1,076,395 sq km
Climate: Humid continental in south; subarctic in far north
Population: 12.2 million
Agriculture: Vegetables, grains, oilseeds; dairy products, livestock, poultry; timber
Economic Activities: Food processing, electrical and electronic equipment, chemicals, mining (nickel, gold, copper, zinc), metal products, transportation equipment, paper products, cement, construction

Prince Edward Island

Capital: Charlottetown
Area: 2,185 sq mi; 5,660 sq km
Climate: Humid continental; moderated by cool North Atlantic Ocean
Population: 138,000
Agriculture: Potatoes, other vegetables, tobacco; diary products, livestock; fish
Economic Activities: Food processing, tourism, fertilizer, commercial printed materials

Quebec

Capital: Quebec
Area: 595,391 sq mi; 1,542,056 sq km
Climate: Mostly continental, with severely cold winters and warm, humid summers; subarctic in north
Population: 7.5 million
Agriculture: Vegetables, grains; dairy products, livestock, poultry; timber
Economic Activities: Pulp and paper, transportation equipment, food processing, mining (gold, copper, zinc, asbestos), electrical and electronic equipment, chemicals, wood products, metal products

Saskatchewan

Capital: Regina
Area: 251,366 sq mi; 651,036 sq km
Climate: Continental; cold winters, warm to hot summers
Population: 995,000
Agriculture: Wheat, barley, oilseeds; cattle, hogs, dairy products
Economic Activities: Food processing, mining (potash, uranium, coal), petroleum, construction, chemicals, machinery, electrical and electronic equipment, printing and publishing, metal products

Yukon Territory

Capital: Whitehorse
Area: 186,272 sq mi; 482,443 sq km
Climate: Mostly subarctic; extremely cold winters and warm summers; dry; arctic in extreme north and mountains
Population: 31,000
Agriculture: Very limited; some potatoes, animal feed crops, and livestock
Economic Activities: Mining (gold, zinc, lead, silver), tourism

Mexico: Political

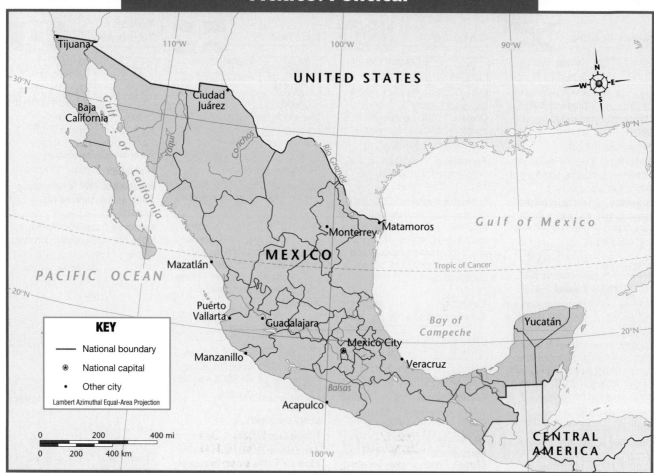

KEY

— National boundary

✳ National capital

• Other city

Lambert Azimuthal Equal-Area Projection

| 0 | 200 | 400 mi |
| 0 | 200 | 400 km |

Mexico

Capital: Mexico City

Area: 761,632 sq mi; 1,972,550 sq km

Climate: Hot and dry north; temperate central; tropical south, with rainy and dry seasons

Population: 103.4 million

Major Ethnic Groups: Mestizo, European, Native American groups

Major Religions: Christianity

Government: Federal Republic

Currency: 1 New Mexican peso (Mex $) = 100 centavos

Leading Exports: Crude oil, oil products, coffee, and silver

Major Languages: Spanish and Mayan dialects

Belize

Capital: Belmopan

Area: 8,865 sq mi; 22,960 sq km

Climate: Subtropical; long rainy season

Population: 263,000

Major Ethnic Groups: African or part African; Native American, mainly Carib and Maya

Major Religions: Christianity

Government: Parliamentary democracy

Currency: 1 Belizean dollar (Bz $) = 100 cents

Leading Exports: Sugar, citrus fruits, bananas, and clothing

Major Languages: English (official), Spanish, Maya, and Garifuna

Costa Rica

Capital: San José

Area: 19,730 sq mi; 51,100 sq km

Climate: Tropical along coast; mild in interior; long rainy season

Population: 3.8 million

Major Ethnic Groups: European, mestizo

Major Religions: Christianity

Government: Democratic republic

Currency: 1 Costa Rican colon (C) = 100 centimos

Leading Exports: Coffee, bananas, textiles, and sugar

Major Languages: Spanish and English

MEXICO

Belmopan
BELIZE

GUATEMALA
Guatemala City
San Salvador
EL SALVADOR

HONDURAS
Tegucigalpa

Caribbean Sea

NICARAGUA
Managua

Panama Canal

COSTA RICA
San José

PACIFIC OCEAN

PANAMA
Panama City

KEY

National boundary

⊛ National capital

Lambert Azimuthal Equal-Area Projection

0   125   250 mi

0   125   250 km

20°N
15°N
10°N
90°W   85°W   80°W

El Salvador

Capital: San Salvador

Area: 8,124 sq mi; 21,040 sq km

Climate: Tropical; very hot along coastal plain but cooler in mountains; rainy summers and dry winters

Population: 6.4 million

Major Ethnic Groups: Mestizo (mix of European with Maya and Nahuatl)

Major Religions: Christianity

Government: Republic

Currency: 1 Salvadoran colon (C) = 100 centavos

Leading Exports: Coffee, sugar cane, and shrimp

Major Languages: Spanish and Nahua

Guatemala

Capital: Guatemala

Area: 42,044 sq mi; 108,890 sq km

Climate: Ranges from hot and humid at coast to cold in mountains; rainy summers and dry winters

Population: 13.3 million

Major Ethnic Groups: Mestizo (mix of European and Native American called Ladino), Maya

Major Religions: Christianity, traditional Mayan

Government: Constitutional democratic republic

Currency: 1 quetzal (Q) = 100 centavos

Leading Exports: Coffee, sugar, bananas, cardamom, and beef

Major Languages: Spanish, Quiche, Cakchiquel, Kekchi, and various languages and dialects

---

Honduras

Capital: Tegucigalpa

Area: 43,280 sq mi; 112,090 sq km

Climate: Tropical; hot, humid coastal lowlands; rainy summers, dry winters

Population: 6.6 million

Major Ethnic Groups: Mestizo

Major Religions: Christianity

Government: Democratic constitutional republic

Currency: 1 lempira (L) = 100 centavos

Leading Exports: Bananas, coffee, shrimp, lobsters, and minerals

Major Languages: Spanish and various dialects

Nicaragua

Capital: Managua

Area: 50,000 sq mi; 129,494 sq km

Climate: Tropical; hottest at coasts; rainy summers

Population: 5 million

Major Ethnic Groups: Mestizo

Major Religions: Christianity

Government: Republic

Currency: 1 gold cordoba (C$) = 100 centavos

Leading Exports: Meat, coffee, cotton, sugar, seafood, and gold

Major Languages: Spanish (official), English, and various languages

Panama

Capital: Panama

Area: 30,194 sq mi; 78,200 sq km

Climate: Tropical; warm and humid

Population: 2.9 million

Major Ethnic Groups: Mestizo, mixed European and African

Major Religions: Christianity

Government: Constitutional democracy

Currency: 1 balboa (B) = 100 centesimos

Leading Exports: Bananas, shrimp, sugar, clothing, and coffee

Major Languages: Spanish (official) and English

UNITED STATES

Nassau ⊛

BAHAMAS

Havana ⊛

CUBA

Turks & Caicos Islands (U.K.)

ATLANTIC OCEAN

Tropic of Cancer

25°N

20°N

DOMINICAN REPUBLIC

Virgin Islands (U.S.)

Virgin Islands (U.K.)

HAITI *Hispaniola*

Port-au-Prince ⊛

Santo Domingo ⊛

Cayman Islands (U.K.)

Kingston ⊛

JAMAICA

G R E A T E R   A N T I L L E S

Puerto Rico (U.S.)

ST. KITTS AND NEVIS

Montserrat (U.K.)

ANTIGUA AND BARBUDA

Guadeloupe (France)

DOMINICA

Martinique (France)

ST. LUCIA

Caribbean Sea

LESSER ANTILLES

15°N

Aruba (Neth.)

Netherlands Antilles

ST. VINCENT AND THE GRENADINES

BARBADOS

GRENADA

TRINIDAD AND TOBAGO

10°N

SOUTH AMERICA

KEY

— National boundary

⊛ National capital

Lambert Azimuthal Equal-Area Projection

0   125   250 mi
0   125   250 km

Antigua and Barbuda

Capital: Saint John's

Area: 170 sq mi; 440 sq km

Climate: Tropical; dry

Population: 67,000

Major Ethnic Groups: African

Major Religions: Christianity

Government: Constitutional monarchy with Westminster-style parliament

Currency: 1 East Caribbean dollar (EC$) = 100 cents

Leading Exports: Petroleum products and manufactures

Major Languages: English (official) and various dialects

Bahamas

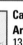

Capital: Nassau

Area: 5,382 sq mi; 13,940 sq km

Climate: Subtropical

Population: 300,000

Major Ethnic Groups: African

Major Religions: Christianity

Government: Constitutional parliamentary democracy

Currency: 1 Bahamian dollar (B$) = 100 cents

Leading Exports: Pharmaceuticals, cement, rum, and crawfish

Major Languages: English and Creole

Barbados

Capital: Bridgetown

Area: 166 sq mi; 430 sq km

Climate: Tropical; rainy season

Population: 275,000

Major Ethnic Groups: African

Major Religions: Christianity

Government: Parliamentary democracy, independent sovereign state within the Commonwealth

Currency: 1 Barbadian dollar (Bds$) = 100 cents

Leading Exports: Sugar and molasses, and rum

Major Languages: English

Cuba

Capital: Havana

Area: 42,805 sq mi; 110,860 sq km

Climate: Semitropical; rainy, hot summers

Population: 11.2 million

Major Ethnic Groups: European, mixed European and African

Major Religions: Christianity

Government: Communist state

Currency: 1 Cuban peso (Cu$) = 100 centavos

Leading Exports: Sugar, nickel, shellfish, and tobacco

Major Languages: Spanish

Dominica

Capital: Roseau
Area: 290 sq mi; 750 sq km
Climate: Tropical; rainy summers and dry winters
Population: 73,000
Major Ethnic Groups: African
Major Religions: Christianity
Government: Parliamentary democracy, republic within the Commonwealth
Currency: 1 East Caribbean dollar (EC$) = 100 cents
Leading Exports: Bananas, soap, bay oil, and vegetables
Major Languages: English and French patois

Dominican Republic

Capital: Santo Domingo
Area: 18,815 sq mi; 48,730 sq km
Climate: Semitropical; warm in lowlands, much cooler and wetter in highlands; rainy season
Population: 8.7 million
Major Ethnic Groups: Mixed European and African
Major Religions: Christianity
Government: Representative democracy
Currency: 1 Dominican peso (RD$) = 100 centavos
Leading Exports: Ferronickel, sugar, gold, coffee, and cocoa
Major Languages: Spanish

Grenada

Capital: Saint George's
Area: 131 sq mi; 340 sq km
Climate: Tropical; rainy season
Population: 89,000
Major Ethnic Groups: African
Major Religions: Christianity
Government: Constitutional monarchy with Westminster-style parliament
Currency: 1 East Caribbean dollar (EC$) = 100 cents
Leading Exports: Bananas, cocoa, and fruits and vegetables
Major Languages: English and French patois

Haiti

Capital: Port-au-Prince
Area: 10,714 sq mi; 27,750 sq km
Climate: Tropical; rainfall heavy in southwest, much lighter in northwest; hot in lowlands, much cooler in highlands
Population: 7.1 million
Major Ethnic Groups: African
Major Religions: Christianity, sometimes combined with African traditional beliefs
Government: Elected government
Currency: 1 gourde (G) = 100 centimes
Leading Exports: Light manufactures and coffee
Major Languages: French and Creole

Jamaica

Capital: Kingston
Area: 4,243 sq mi; 10,990 sq km
Climate: Tropical; hot and humid in coastal lowlands; rain heavy in northeast mountains
Population: 2.7 million
Major Ethnic Groups: African
Major Religions: Christianity
Government: Constitutional parliamentary democracy
Currency: 1 Jamaican dollar (J$) = 100 cents
Leading Exports: Alumina, bauxite, sugar, bananas, and rum
Major Languages: English and Creole

Saint Kitts and Nevis

Capital: Basseterre
Area: 104 sq mi; 269 sq km
Climate: Tropical; rainy season
Population: 39,000
Major Ethnic Groups: African
Major Religions: Christianity
Government: Constitutional monarchy with Westminster-style parliament
Currency: 1 East Caribbean dollar (EC$) = 100 cents
Leading Exports: Machinery, food, and electronics
Major Languages: English

Saint Lucia

Capital: Castries
Area: 239 sq mi; 620 sq km
Climate: Tropical; rainy season
Population: 160,000
Major Ethnic Groups: African
Major Religions: Christianity
Government: Westminster-style parliamentary democracy
Currency: 1 East Caribbean dollar (EC$) = 100 cents
Leading Exports: Bananas, clothing, cocoa, and vegetables
Major Languages: English and French patois

Saint Vincent and the Grenadines

Capital: Kingstown
Area: 150 sq mi; 388 sq km
Climate: Tropical; rainy season
Population: 115,000
Major Ethnic Groups: African
Major Religions: Christianity
Government: Parliamentary democracy, independent sovereign state within the Commonwealth
Currency: 1 East Caribbean dollar (EC$) = 100 cents
Leading Exports: Bananas, and eddoes and dasheen (taro)
Major Languages: English and French patois

Trinidad and Tobago

Capital: Port-of Spain
Area: 1,981 sq mi; 5,130 sq km
Climate: Tropical; rainy season
Population: 1.2 million
Major Ethnic Groups: African, East Indian
Major Religions: Christianity, Hinduism
Government: Parliamentary democracy
Currency: 1 Trinidad and Tobago dollar (TT$) = 100 cents
Leading Exports: Petroleum and petroleum products
Major Languages: English, Hindu, French, and Spanish

South America: Political

Argentina

Capital: Buenos Aires

Area: 1,068,339 sq mi; 2,766,890 sq km

Climate: Mainly temperate; tropical area in northeast; cold in mountains; north wetter than south and west

Population: 37.8 million

Major Ethnic Groups: European

Major Religions: Christianity

Government: Republic

Currency: 1 peso = 100 centavos

Leading Exports: Edible oils, fuels and energy, cereals, feed, motor vehicles

Major Languages: Spanish (official), English, Italian, German, and French

Bolivia

Capital: La Paz

Area: 424,179 sq mi; 1,098,580 sq km

Climate: Varies with elevation, from hot and wet to cold and dry; rainy season

Population: 8.5 million

Major Ethnic Groups: Quechua, Aymara, mestizo

Major Religions: Christianity

Government: Republic

Currency: 1 boliviano ($B) = 100 centavos

Leading Exports: Soybeans, natural gas, zinc, gold, wood

Major Languages: Spanish, Quechua, and Aymara

CARIBBEAN SEA

ATLANTIC OCEAN

Barranquilla · Maracaibo
Cartagena · Barquisimeto · Caracas
Medellín · VENEZUELA
Manizales · Bogotá
Cali · COLOMBIA
Quito
ECUADOR
Guayaquil
Georgetown
GUYANA · Paramaribo
SURINAME · Cayenne
FRENCH GUIANA
Equator
Belém
Manaus
Fortaleza
Trujillo
PERU
Lima
Callao
Lake Titicaca
BOLIVIA
La Paz
Cochabamba
Santa Cruz
Sucre
Tropic of Capricorn
Salta
San Miguel de Tucumán
CHILE
Resistencia
ARGENTINA
Córdoba
Valparaíso · Mendoza · Rosario
Santiago · Buenos Aires · URUGUAY
Concepción · La Plata · Montevideo
Mar del Plata
Temuco · Bahía Blanca
SOUTH PACIFIC OCEAN
Natal
João Pessoa
Recife
Maceió
Aracaju
Salvador
BRAZIL
Brasília
Goiânia
Campo Grande
Ribeirão Preto
Belo Horizonte
Rio de Janeiro
Campinas
Asunción · Londrina · São Paulo
PARAGUAY · Curitiba
Pôrto Alegre
SOUTH ATLANTIC OCEAN
10° N
Equator
10° S
20° S
30° S
40° S
50° S

Strait of Magellan
Tierra del Fuego
Cape Horn
Falkland Islands (U.K.)
South Georgia Island (U.K.)

90° W · 80° W · 70° W · 60° W · 50° W · 40° W · 30° W · 20° W

KEY
— National boundary
⊛ National capital
• Other city

Lambert Azimuthal Equal-Area Projection

0 · 250 · 500 mi
0 · 250 · 500 km

Brazil

Capital: Brasília

Area: 3,286,600 sq mi; 8,511,965 sq km

Climate: Tropical to subtropical; north rainy, hot, and humid all year; central seasonal rains and temperatures; northeast long dry season; south more moderate temperatures and rainfall

Population: 176 million

Major Ethnic Groups: European, mixed European and African

Major Religions: Christianity

Government: Federative republic

Currency: 1 real (R$) = 100 centavos

Leading Exports: Manufactures, iron ore, soybeans, footwear, coffee

Major Languages: Portuguese, Spanish, English, and French

Chile

Capital: Santiago

Area: 292,269 sq mi; 756,950 sq km

Climate: Arid desert in north; mild, dry central; cool, rainy south

Population: 15.5 million

Major Ethnic Groups: Mestizo (mix of Spanish and mainly Araucanian)

Major Religions: Christianity

Government: Republic

Currency: 1 Chilean peso (Ch$) = 100 centavos

Leading Exports: Copper, fish, fruits, paper and pulp, chemicals

Major Languages: Spanish

Colombia

Capital: Bogotá

Area: 439,751 sq mi; 1,138,910 sq km

Climate: Tropical along coasts and river valleys; subtropical to cold in the mountains, rainy and dry periods alternate

Population: 41 million

Major Ethnic Groups: Mestizo, European

Major Religions: Christianity

Government: Republic; executive branch dominates government structure

Currency: 1 Colombian peso (Col$) = 100 centavos

Leading Exports: Petroleum, coffee, coal, and bananas

Major Languages: Spanish

Ecuador

Capital: Quito

Area: 109,487 sq mi; 283,560 sq km

Climate: Tropical along coast; hotter and more humid in rain forest; moderate in central region

Population: 13.5 million

Major Ethnic Groups: Mestizo, Native American

Major Religions: Christianity

Government: Republic

Currency: 1 sucre (S/) = 100 centavos

Leading Exports: Petroleum, bananas, shrimp, and cocoa

Major Languages: Spanish, Quechua, and various languages

French Guiana

Capital: Cayenne
Area: 35,135 sq mi; 91,000 sq km
Climate: Tropical; hot and humid; dry summers, rainy winters
Population: 173,000
Major Ethnic Groups: African or mixed African and European (also known as Creole)
Major Religions: Christianity
Government: Overseas department of France
Currency: 1 French franc (F) = 100 centimes
Leading Exports: Shrimp, timber, gold, rum, rosewood essence, clothing
Major Languages: French

Guyana

Capital: Georgetown
Area: 83,003 sq mi; 214,970 sq km
Climate: Tropical; rainy season
Population: 698,000
Major Ethnic Groups: East Indian, African
Major Religions: Christianity, Hinduism
Government: Republic within the Commonwealth
Currency: 1 Guyanese dollar (G$) = 100 cents
Leading Exports: Sugar, gold, bauxite/alumina, rice and shrimp
Major Languages: English and various dialects

Paraguay

Capital: Asuncion
Area: 157,052 sq mi; 406,750 sq km
Climate: Subtropical; rainy in east; semi-arid in parts of west
Population: 5.9 million
Major Ethnic Groups: Mestizo
Major Religions: Christianity
Government: Constitutional republic
Currency: 1 guarani (G) = 100 centimos
Leading Exports: Soybeans, feed, cotton, meal, edible oils
Major Languages: Spanish (official) and Guarani

Peru

Capital: Lima
Area: 496,243 sq
Climate: Arid along coast; tropical in northeast; temperate to cold in the mountains, where rainfall varies
Population: 28 million
Major Ethnic Groups: Native American, mestizo
Major Religions: Christianity
Government: Constitutional republic
Currency: 1 nuevo sol (S/.) – 100 centimos
Leading Exports: Fish and fish products, copper, zinc, gold
Major Languages: Spanish (official), Quechua (official), and Aymara

Suriname

Capital: Paramaribo
Area: 63,041 sq mi; 163,270 sq km
Climate: Tropical; rainy season
Population: 436,000
Major Ethnic Groups: Asian (mainly from India and Indonesia), mixed African and Native American
Major Religions: Christianity, Hinduism, Islam
Government: Constitutional democracy
Currency: 1 Surinamese guilder, gulden, or florin (Sf.) = 100 cents
Leading Exports: Alumina, Aluminum, crude oil, lumber, shrimp and fish
Major Languages: Dutch (official), English, Sranang, Tongo, Hindustani, and Japanese

Uruguay

Capital: Montevideo
Area: 68,041 sq mi; 176,220 sq km
Climate: Temperate; ample rainfall all year
Population: 3.4 million
Major Ethnic Groups: European
Major Religions: Christianity
Government: Republic
Currency: 1 Uruguayan peso ($Ur) = 100 centesimos
Leading Exports: Meat, rice, leather products, vehicles, dairy products, wool
Major Languages: Spanish and Brazilero

Venezuela

Capital: Caracas
Area: 352,156 sq mi; 912,050 sq km
Climate: Tropical along coast and in grasslands; milder in highlands
Population: 24.3 million
Major Ethnic Groups: Mestizo, European
Major Religions: Christianity
Government: Federal Republic
Currency: 1 bolivar (Bs) = 100 centimos
Leading Exports: Petroleum, bauxite and aluminum, steel
Major Languages: Spanish and various languages

Andorra

Capital: Andorra La Vella

Area: 174 sq mi; 450 sq km

Climate: Temperate; snowy, cold winters and cool, dry summers

Population: 68,000

Major Ethnic Groups: Spanish, Andorran, Portuguese

Major Religions: Christianity

Government: Parliamentary democracy (since March 1993) that retains as its heads of state a coprincipality; the two princes are the president of France and biship of Seo de Urgel, Spain, who are represented locally by coprinces' representatives

Currency: 1 French franc (F) = 100 cenntimes; 1 peseta (Pta) = 100 centimos; the French and Spanish currencies are used

Leading Exports: Tobacco products and furniture

Major Languages: Catalan (official), French, and Castilian

Austria

Capital: Vienna

Area: 32,376 sq mi; 83,850 sq km

Climate: Temperate; cold, often severe winters in valleys; short summers

Population: 8.2 million

Major Ethnic Groups: German

Major Religions: Christianity

Government: Federal republic

Currency: 1 Austrian schilling (AS) = 100 groschen

Leading Exports: Machinery and equipment, and iron and steel, paper and paperboard

Major Languages: German

Map

Reykjavik · ICELAND
Faroe Islands (DENMARK)
Norwegian Sea
Shetland Islands (U.K.)
SWEDEN
FINLAND
Helsinki
NORWAY
Oslo
Stockholm
Baltic Sea
Northern Ireland
North Sea
DENMARK
IRELAND
UNITED KINGDOM
Dublin
Copenhagen
NETH.
Amsterdam
London
Berlin
ATLANTIC OCEAN
English Channel
Brussels
GERMANY
BELG.
Luxembourg
Paris
LUX.
LIECHT.
Vienna
Bay of Biscay
Bern
Vaduz
AUSTRIA
FRANCE
SWITZ.
SAN MARINO
PORTUGAL
ANDORRA
MONACO
Black Sea
Madrid
Corsica (FR.)
ITALY
Bosporus
Lisbon
SPAIN
VATICAN CITY
Rome
Adriatic Sea
Gibraltar
Balearic Is. (SPAIN)
Sardinia (ITALY)
GREECE
GIBRALTAR (U.K.)
Athens
Strait of Gibraltar
Sicily
AFRICA
Valletta · MALTA
Crete
Mediterranean Sea

KEY

—— National boundary

⊛ National capital

Lambert Azimuthal Equal-Area Projection

0   200   400 mi

0 200 400 km

Belgium

Capital: Brussels

Area: 11,780 sq mi; 30,510 sq km

Climate: Temperate; humid and mild at coast; cold winters, hot summers in southeast, with heavy rains, fog, and drizzle common

Population: 10.3 million

Major Ethnic Groups: Fleming, Walloon

Major Religions: Christianity

Government: Federal parliamentary democracy under a constitutional monarch

Currency: 1 Belgian franc (BF) = 100 centimes

Leading Exports: Iron and steel, and transportation equipment, chemicals, diamonds

Major Languages: Dutch, French, and German

Denmark

Capital: Copenhagen

Area: 16,630 sq mi; 43,070 sq km

Climate: Temperate; humid; mild, windy winters and cool summers

Population: 5.4 million

Major Ethnic Groups: Scandinavian, Inuit, Faroese, German

Major Religions: Christianity

Government: Constitutional monarchy

Currency: 1 Danish drone (DKr) = 100 oere

Leading Exports: Machinery and instruments, meat and meat products, and dairy products

Major Languages: Danish, Faroese, Greenlandic, and German

Finland

Capital: Helsinki

Area: 130,132 sq mi; 337,030 sq km

Climate: Cold temperate (moderated by warm North Atlantic Current)

Population: 5.2 million

Major Ethnic Groups: Finn, Swede

Major Religions: Christianity

Government: Republic

Currency: 1 markka (FMk) or Finmark = 100 pennia

Leading Exports: Machinery and equipment, chemicals, metals, timber, paper and pulp

Major Languages: Finnish, Swedish, Lapp, and Russian

France

Capital: Paris

Area: 211,217 sq mi; 547,030 sq km

Climate: Mostly temperate; severe winters and hot summers in interior; more moderate on Atlantic coast; semitropical on Mediterranean coast

Population: 59.8 million

Major Ethnic Groups: French, Celtic

Major Religions: Christianity

Government: Republic

Currency: 1 French franc (F) = 100 centimes

Leading Exports: Machinery and transportation equipment, chemicals, iron and steel products

Major Languages: French and regional dialects and languages

Germany

Capital: Berlin
Area: 137,808 sq mi; 356,910 sq km
Climate: Temperate; cool winters, warm summers; more rainy in south
Population: 83 million
Major Ethnic Groups: German
Major Religions: Christianity
Government: Federal republic
Currency: 1 deutsche mark (DM) = 100 pfennige
Leading Exports: Machines and machine tools, and chemicals, metals and manufactures
Major Languages: German

Greece

Capital: Athens
Area: 50,944 sq mi; 131,940 sq km
Climate: Mediterranean; hot, dry summers; rainy winters on west coast
Population: 10.6 million
Major Ethnic Groups: Greek
Major Religions: Christianity
Government: Parliamentary republic; monarchy rejected by referendum December 8, 1974
Currency: 1 drachma (Dr) = 100 lepta
Leading Exports: Manufactured goods, foodstuffs, fuels, and chemicals
Major Languages: Greek, English, and French

Holy See (Vatican City)

Capital: Vatican City
Area: 0.17 sq mi; 0.44 sq km
Climate: Temperate; mild, rainy winters; hot, dry summers
Population: 900
Major Ethnic Groups: Italian, Swiss, other
Major Religions: Christianity
Government: Monarchical-sacerdotal state
Currency: 1 Vatican lira (Vlit) = 100 centesimi
Leading Exports: None
Major Languages: Italian, Latin, and various languages

Iceland

Capital: Reykjavik
Area: 39,770 sq mi; 103,000 sq km
Climate: Temperate (moderated by North Atlantic Current)
Population: 279,000
Major Ethnic Groups: Mixed Norwegian and Celtic
Major Religions: Christianity
Government: Constitutional republic
Currency: 1 Icelandic krona (Ikr) = 100 aurar
Leading Exports: Fish and fish products, and animal products
Major Languages: Icelandic

Ireland

Capital: Dublin
Area: 27,136 sq mi; 70,280 sq km
Climate: Temperate (moderated by warm North Atlantic Current)
Population: 3.9 million
Major Ethnic Groups: Celtic, English
Major Religions: Christianity
Government: Republic
Currency: 1 Irish pound = 100 pence
Leading Exports: Machinery and equipment, computers, chemicals, pharmaceuticals
Major Languages: English and Irish Gaelic

Italy

Capital: Rome
Area: 116,310 sq mi; 301,230 sq km
Climate: Mediterranean; Alpine in far north; hot, dry in south
Population: 57.7 million
Major Ethnic Groups: Italian
Major Religions: Christianity
Government: Republic
Currency: 1 Italian lira (Lit) = 100 centesimi
Leading Exports: Engineering products, textiles and clothing, production machinery, motor vehicles, transport equipment
Major Languages: Italian, German, French, and Slovene

Liechtenstein

Capital: Vaduz
Area: 62 sq mi; 160 sq km
Climate: Temperate
Population: 33,000
Major Ethnic Groups: Allemanic, Italian, Turkish
Major Religions: Christianity
Government: Hereditary constitutional monarchy
Currency: 1 Swiss franc, franken, or franco (SFR) = 100 centimes, rappen, or centesimi
Leading Exports: Small specialty machinery and dental products
Major Languages: German and Alemannic

Luxembourg

Capital: Luxembourg
Area: 998 sq mi; 2,586 sq km
Climate: Temperate
Population: 449,000
Major Ethnic Groups: Mix of Celtic, French, and German
Major Religions: Christianity
Government: Constitutional monarchy
Currency: 1 Luxembourg franc (LuxF) = 100 centimes
Leading Exports: Finished steel products and chemicals
Major Languages: Luxembourgian, German, French, and English

Malta

Capital: Valletta
Area: 124 sq mi; 320 sq km
Climate: Mediterranean; mild, rainy winters and hot, dry summers
Population: 397,000
Major Ethnic Groups: Maltese (descendants of ancient Carthaginians and Phoenicians, mixed with other Mediterranean groups)
Major Religions: Christianity
Government: Parliamentary democracy
Currency: 1 Maltese lira (LM) = 100 cents
Leading Exports: Machinery and transportation equipment, manufactures
Major Languages: Maltese and English

Monaco

Capital: Monaco
Area: .73 sq mi; 1.9 sq km
Climate: Mediterranean; mild, wet winters and hot, dry summers
Population: 32,000
Major Ethnic Groups: French, Monegasque, Italian
Major Religions: Christianity
Government: Constitutional monarchy
Currency: 1 French franc (F) = 100 centimes
Leading Exports: Exports through France
Major Languages: French (official), English, Italian, and Monegasque

Netherlands

Capital: Amsterdam

Area: 16,036 sq mi; 41,532 sq km

Climate: Temperate; cool summers and mild winters

Population: 16.1 million

Major Ethnic Groups: Dutch

Major Religions: Christianity

Government: Constitutional monarchy

Currency: 1 Netherlands guilder, gulden or florin (f) = 100 cents

Leading Exports: Machinery and equipment, chemicals, fuels, foodstuffs

Major Languages: Dutch

Norway

Capital: Oslo

Area: 125,186 sq mi; 324,220 sq km

Climate: Temperate along coast (moderated by North Atlantic Current); colder inland; subarctic in far north; rainy all year on west coast

Population: 4.5 million

Major Ethnic Groups: Norwegian (Nordic, Alpine, Baltic), Lapps

Major Religions: Christianity

Government: Constitutional monarchy

Currency: 1 Norwegian Krone (NKr) = 100 oere

Leading Exports: Petroleum and petroleum products, machinery and equipment, metals, chemicals

Major Languages: Norwegian (official), Lapp, and Finnish

Portugal

Capital: Lisbon

Area: 35,553 sq mi; 92,080 sq km

Climate: Temperate; cool, rainy in north and warmer, drier in south

Population: 10.1 million

Major Ethnic Groups: Portuguese (mixed Mediterranean)

Major Religions: Christianity

Government: Parliamentary democracy

Currency: 1 Portuguese escudo (Esc) = 100 centavos

Leading Exports: Clothing and footwear, and machinery, chemicals

Major Languages: Portuguese

San Marino

Capital: San Marino

Area: 23 sq mi; 60 sq km

Climate: Mediterranean; mild winters and warm summers

Population: 28,000

Major Ethnic Groups: Sammarinese, Italian

Major Religions: Christianity

Government: Republic

Currency: 1 Italian lira (Lit) = 100 centesimi

Leading Exports: Building stone, lime, wood, and chestnuts

Major Languages: Italian

Spain

Capital: Madrid

Area: 194,892 sq mi; 504,750 sq km

Climate: Temperate; hot, dry summers in central area; cooler, wetter in north; subtropical along Mediterranean coast

Population: 40.1 million

Major Ethnic Groups: Spanish (mixed Mediterranean and Nordic)

Major Religions: Christianity

Government: Parliamentary monarchy

Currency: 1 peseta (Pta) = 100 centimos

Leading Exports: Machinery, motor vehicles, foodstuffs

Major Languages: Spanish, Catalan, Galician, and Basque

Sweden

Capital: Stockholm

Area: 173,738 sq mi; 449,964 sq km

Climate: Temperate in south (moderated by North Atlantic Current); subarctic in north; rainfall low except in higher mountains; heavy snow in north and central regions

Population: 8.9 million

Major Ethnic Groups: Swedish

Major Religions: Christianity

Government: Constitutional monarchy

Currency: 1 Swedish krona (SKr) = 100 oere

Leading Exports: Machinery, motor vehicles, and paper products

Major Languages: Swedish, Lapp, and Finnish

Switzerland

Capital: Bern

Area: 15,943 sq mi; 41,290 sq km

Climate: Temperate on plateau and in lower valleys; moderate rainfall; mountains colder and rainier; with heavy snow in winter

Population: 7.3 million

Major Ethnic Groups: German, French, Italian

Major Religions: Christianity

Government: Federal republic

Currency: 1 Swiss franc, franken, or franco (SFR) = 100 centimes, rappen, or centesimi

Leading Exports: Machinery, chemicals, metals, watches

Major Languages: German, French, Italian, Romansch, and various languages

United Kingdom

Capital: London

Area: 94,529 sq mi; 244,820 sq km

Climate: Temperate; mild, often wet and chilly; cooler, rainier in highlands

Population: 59.8 million

Major Ethnic Groups: English, Scottish, Irish, Welsh

Major Religions: Christianity

Government: Constitutional monarchy

Currency: 1 British pound = 100 pence

Leading Exports: Manufactured goods, fuels, chemicals, food, beverages

Major Languages: English, Welsh, and Scottish Gaelic

Albania

Capital: Tiranë

Area: 11,101 sq mi; 28,750 sq km

Climate: Mediterranean; rainy, mild winters and hot, dry summers at coast; more humid in north; more rainy in mountains

Population: 3.5 million

Major Ethnic Groups: Albanian

Major Religions: Islam, Christianity

Government: Emerging democracy

Currency: 1 lek (L) = 100 qintars

Leading Exports: Asphalt, metals and metallic ores, and electricity

Major Languages: Albanian, Tosk dialect, and Greek

Armenia

Capital: Yerevan

Area: 11,506 sq mi; 29,800 sq km

Climate: Continental; moderate winters and long, hot summers; arid on plains

Population: 3.3 million

Major Ethnic Groups: Armenian

Major Religions: Christianity

Government: Republic

Currency: 1 dram = 100 luma

Leading Exports: Diamonds, scrap metal, machinery and equipment

Major Languages: Armenian and Russian

Azerbaijan

Capital: Baku

Area: 33,438 sq mi; 86,600 sq km

Climate: Dry subtropical, with mild winters and long, hot summers; colder in mountains

Population: 7.8 million

Major Ethnic Groups: Azeri

Major Religions: Islam

Government: Republic

Currency: 1 manat = 100 gopiks

Leading Exports: Oil and gas, machinery, cotton

Major Languages: Azeri, Russian, and Armenian

Belarus

Capital: Minsk

Area: 79,926 sq mi; 207,600 sq km

Climate: Continental; cold winters and cool summers, with high humidity

Population: 10.3 million

Major Ethnic Groups: Belarusian

Major Religions: Christianity

Government: Republic

Currency: Belarusian rubel (BR)

Leading Exports: Machinery and transportation equipment

Major Languages: Byelorussian and Russian

Bosnia and Herzegovina

Capital: Sarajevo

Area: 19,782 sq mi; 51,233 sq km

Climate: Continental; cold winters, hot summers; cooler, harsher in mountains; mild, rainy winters along coast

Population: 4.0 million

Major Ethnic Groups: Serb, Croat

Major Religions: Islam, Christianity

Government: Emerging democracy

Currency: 1 convertible marka (KM) = 100 convertible pfenniga

Leading Exports: None

Major Languages: Croatian, Serbian, Bosnian

Bulgaria

Capital: Sofia

Area: 42,824 sq mi; 110,910 sq km

Climate: Continental; cold winters, hot summers

Population: 7.6 million

Major Ethnic Groups: Bulgarian

Major Religions: Christianity

Government: Parliamentary democracy

Currency: 1 lev (Lv) = 100 stotinki

Leading Exports: Machinery and agricultural products

Major Languages: Bulgarian

Croatia

Capital: Zagreb

Area: 21,830 sq mi; 56,538 sq km

Climate: Continental; cold winters, hot summers; Mediterranean along coast, with mild winters and dry summers

Population: 4.4 million

Major Ethnic Groups: Croat, Serb

Major Religions: Christianity

Government: Presidential parliamentary democracy

Currency: 1 Croatian kuna (HRK) = 100 lipas

Leading Exports: Textiles, chemicals, foodstuffs, fuels

Major Languages: Croatian

Czech Republic

Capital: Prague

Area: 30,388 sq mi; 78,703 sq km

Climate: Temperate; cold, cloudy, humid winters and cool summers

Population: 10.3 million

Major Ethnic Groups: Czech

Major Religions: Christianity

Government: Parliamentary democracy

Currency: 1 koruna (Kc) = 100 haleru

Leading Exports: Machinery and transportation equipment, manufactured goods

Major Languages: Czech and Slovak

Estonia

Capital: Tallinn
Area: 17,414 sq mi; 45,100 sq km
Climate: Maritime; moderate, wet winters and cool summers
Population: 1.4 million
Major Ethnic Groups: Estonian, Russian
Major Religions: Christianity
Government: Parliamentary democracy
Currency: 1 Estonian kroon (EEK) = 100 sents
Leading Exports: Textiles, food products, vehicles, metals
Major Languages: Estonian, Latvian, Lithuanian, and Russian

Georgia

Capital: T'bilisi
Area: 26,912 sq mi; 69,700 sq km
Climate: Continental; cold, wet winters and cool summers in mountains; cold winters, hot summers in far east; subtropical on coast
Population: 5 million
Major Ethnic Groups: Georgian
Major Religions: Christianity
Government: Republic
Currency: 1 lari (GEL) = 100 tetry
Leading Exports: Citrus fruits, tea, and wine
Major Languages: Georgian, Russian, Armenian, Azeri, and various others

Hungary

Capital: Budapest
Area: 35,920 sq mi; 93,030 sq km
Climate: Temperate; cold, humid winters and warm summers
Population: 10.1 million
Major Ethnic Groups: Hungarian
Major Religions: Christianity
Government: Parliamentary democracy
Currency: 1 forint (Ft) = 100 filler
Leading Exports: Machinery and equipment, manufactured goods, fuels and electricity
Major Languages: Hungarian and various others

Latvia

Capital: Riga
Area: 24,750 sq mi; 64,100 sq km
Climate: Maritime; mild winters and cool summers; humid
Population: 2.4 million
Major Ethnic Groups: Latvian, Russian
Major Religions: Christianity
Government: Parliamentary democracy
Currency: 1 Latvian lat (LVL) = 100 santims
Leading Exports: Wood and wood products, machinery and equipment, metals
Major Languages: Lettish, Lithuanian, Russian, and various others

Lithuania

Capital: Vilnius
Area: 25,175 sq mi; 65,200 sq km
Climate: Maritime; mild winters and cool summers
Population: 3.6 million
Major Ethnic Groups: Lithuanian
Major Religions: Christianity
Government: Parliamentary democracy
Currency: 1 Lithuanian litas = 100 centas
Leading Exports: Machinery and equipment, mineral products, textiles and clothing, chemicals, foodstuffs
Major Languages: Lithuanian, Polish, and Russian

Macedonia

Capital: Skopje
Area: 9,781 sq mi; 25,333 sq km
Climate: Continental; cold, snowy winters and hot, dry summers; milder in valleys and river basins
Population: 2.1 million
Major Ethnic Groups: Macedonian Slav, Albanian
Major Religions: Christianity, Islam
Government: Emerging democracy
Currency: 1 Macedonian dinar (MKD) = 100 deni
Leading Exports: Manufactured goods and machinery
Major Languages: Macedonian, Albanian, Turkish, Serb, Gypsy, and various others

Moldova

Capital: Chisinau
Area: 13,012 sq mi; 33,700 sq km
Climate: Continental; mild winters, warm summers; light rainfall
Population: 4.4 million
Major Ethnic Groups: Moldovan, Ukranian, Russian
Major Religions: Christianity
Government: Republic
Currency: Moldovan leu (MLD) (plural lei)
Leading Exports: Foodstuffs, wine, and tobacco
Major Languages: Moldovan (official), Russian, and Gagauz dialect

Poland

Capital: Warsaw
Area: 120,731 sq mi; 312,680 sq km
Climate: Temperate; mild, rainy summers and cold, snowy winters
Population: 38.6 million
Major Ethnic Groups: Polish
Major Religions: Christianity
Government: Republic
Currency: 1 zloty (Zl) = 100 groszy
Leading Exports: Manufactured goods and chemicals, machinery and equipment, food and live animals
Major Languages: Polish

Romania

Capital: Bucharest
Area: 91,702 sq mi; 237,500 sq km
Climate: Temperate; cold, cloudy, snowy winters and warm, sunny summers
Population: 22.3 million
Major Ethnic Groups: Romanian
Major Religions: Christianity
Government: Republic
Currency: 1 leu (L) = 100 bani
Leading Exports: Textiles and footwear, metals and metal products, machinery and equipment, minerals and fuels
Major Languages: Romanian, Hungarian, and German

Serbia and Montenegro

Capital: Belgrade
Area: 39,436 sq mi; 102,350 sq km
Climate: Continental in north and north central region (cold winters and hot, humid summers); Mediterranean in south central region and along coast in south (mild winters and hot, dry summers); colder winters inland
Population: 10.7 million
Major Ethnic Groups: Serbian, Albanian, Montenegrin
Major Religions: Christianity, Islam
Government: Republic
Currency: 1 Yugoslav New Dinar (YD) = 100 paras; Montenegro made the German deutsche mark legal tender alongside the Yugoslav dinar
Leading Exports: Manufactured goods, food and live animals, raw materials
Major Languages: Serbian and Albanian

Slovakia

Capital: Bratislava

Area: 18,860 sq mi; 48,845 sq km

Climate: Temperate; cold winters, hot summers

Population: 5.4 million

Major Ethnic Groups: Slovak, Hungarian

Major Religions: Christianity

Government: Parliamentary democracy

Currency: 1 koruna (SK) = 100 halierov

Leading Exports: Machinery and transportation equipment, manufactured goods, chemicals

Major Languages: Slovak and Hungarian

Slovenia

Capital: Ljubljana

Area: 7,837 sq mi; 20,296 sq km

Climate: Mostly continental; harsh winters, rainy summers in mountains; more moderate in east; Mediterranean along coast

Population: 1.9 million

Major Ethnic Groups: Slovene

Major Religions: Christianity

Government: Parliamentary democratic republic

Currency: 1 tolar (SIT) = 100 stotins

Leading Exports: Manufactured goods, machinery and transportation equipment, chemicals

Major Languages: Slovenian, Serbo-Croatian, and various others

Ukraine

Capital: Kiev

Area: 233,098 sq mi; 603,700 sq km

Climate: Mostly continental; cold winters, warm summers; Mediterranean in far south

Population: 48.4 million

Major Ethnic Groups: Ukrainian, Russian

Major Religions: Christianity

Government: Republic

Currency: 1 hryvna = 100 kopiykas

Leading Exports: Metals, fuel and petroleum products, machinery and transport equipment, food products

Major Languages: Ukranian, Russian, Romanian, Polish, and Hungarian

Russia

Capital: Moscow

Area: 6,952,996 sq mi; 17,075,200 sq km

Climate: Mostly humid continental; long, cold winters and short, cool summers; milder in south; subarctic in north; tundra in far north

Population: 145 million

Major Ethnic Groups: Russian, Tatar, Ukranian

Major Religions: Christianity, Islam

Government: Federation

Currency: 1 ruble (R) = 100 kopeks

Leading Exports: Petroleum and petroleum products, natural gas, wood and wood products

Major Languages: Russian and various languages

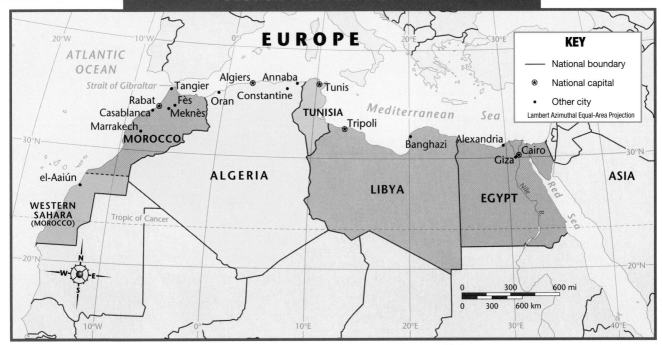

KEY

National boundary

⊛ National capital

• Other city

Lambert Azimuthal Equal-Area Projection

EUROPE

ATLANTIC OCEAN

Strait of Gibraltar
Tangier
Algiers ⊛ Annaba
Constantine
Rabat ⊛ Fès Oran
Casablanca Meknès
Marrakech
MOROCCO

Tunis ⊛
TUNISIA
Tripoli ⊛

Mediterranean Sea

Banghazi Alexandria
Giza ⊛ Cairo

el-Aaiún

ALGERIA

LIBYA

EGYPT

ASIA

Nile R.
Red Sea

WESTERN SAHARA (MOROCCO)

Tropic of Cancer

0   300   600 mi
0   300   600 km

Algeria

Capital: Algiers
Area: 919,626 sq mi; 2,381,740 sq km
Climate: Arid in the Sahara; semiarid along coast; drier with cold winters and hot summers on high plateau
Population: 32.3 million
Major Ethnic Groups: Arab-Berber
Major Religions: Islam
Government: Republic
Currency: 1 Algerian dinar (DA) = 100 centimes
Leading Exports: Petroleum and petroleum products, natural gas
Major Languages: Arabic (official), French, and Berber dialects

Egypt

Capital: Cairo
Area: 386,675 sq mi; 1,001,450 sq km
Climate: Arid
Population: 70.7 million
Major Ethnic Groups: Egyptian, Bedouin, Berber
Major Religions: Islam
Government: Republic
Currency: 1 Egyptian pound = 100 piasters
Leading Exports: Crude oil, petroleum products, cotton, textiles

Major Languages: Arabic, English, and French

Libya

Capital: Tripoli
Area: 679,385 sq mi; 1,759,540 sq km
Climate: Moderate along coast; extremely hot, dry desert interior
Population: 5.4 million
Major Ethnic Groups: Berber, Arab
Major Religions: Islam
Government: Jamahiriya (a state of the masses) in theory, governed by the populace through local councils; in fact, a military dictatorship
Currency: 1 Libyan dinar (LD) = 1,000 dirhams
Leading Exports: Crude oil and refined petroleum products
Major Languages: Arabic, Italian, and English

Morocco

Capital: Rabat
Area: 172,420 sq mi; 446,550 sq km
Climate: Mediterranean; more extreme in interior
Population: 31.2 million
Major Ethnic Groups: Arab-Berber
Major Religions: Islam
Government: Constitutional monarchy
Currency: 1 Morooccan dirham (DH) = 100 centimes
Leading Exports: Phosphates and fertilizers, food and beverages, minerals
Major Languages: Arabic (official), Berber dialects, and French

Tunisia

Capital: Tunis
Area: 63,172 sq mi; 163,610 sq km
Climate: Temperate in north with mild, rainy winters and hot, dry summers; desert in south
Population: 9.8 million
Major Ethnic Groups: Arab
Major Religions: Islam
Government: Republic
Currency: 1 Tunisian dinar (TD) = 1,000 millimes
Leading Exports: Textiles, mechanical goods, phosphates and chemicals, agricultural products
Major Languages: Arabic and French

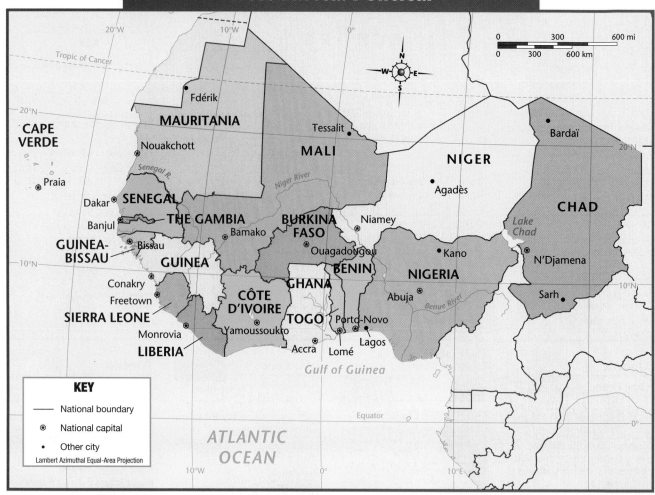

KEY

— National boundary

⊛ National capital

• Other city

Lambert Azimuthal Equal-Area Projection

Benin

Capital: Porto-Novo

Area: 43,484 sq mi; 112,620 sq km

Climate: Tropical; hot, humid in south; semiarid in north

Population: 6.9 million

Major Ethnic Groups: Fon, Adja, Yoruba, Bariba

Major Religions: Traditional African religions

Government: Republic under multiparty democratic rule

Currency: 1 Communaute Financiere Africaine franc (CFAF) = 100 centimes

Leading Exports: Cotton, crude oil, palm products, and cocoa

Major Languages: French (official), Fon, Yoruba, and at least 6 various languages

---

Burkina Faso

Capital: Ouagadougou

Area: 105,873 sq mi; 274,200 sq km

Climate: Tropical; warm, dry winters and hot, wet summers

Population: 12.6 million

Major Ethnic Groups: Mossi, Gurunsi, Senufo, Lobi

Major Religions: Traditional African religions, Islam

Government: Presidential democracy, National assembly

Currency: 1 Communaute Financiere Africaine franc (CFAF) = 100 centimes

Leading Exports: Cotton, gold, and animal products

Major Languages: French (official) and Sudanic languages

Cape Verde

Capital: Praia

Area: 1,556 sq mi; 4,030 sq km

Climate: Tropical; warm, dry summer; little rainfall

Population: 409,000

Major Ethnic Groups: Mixed African and European

Major Religions: Mix of Christianity and traditional African religions

Government: Republic

Currency: 1 Cape Verdean escudo (CVEsc) = 100 centavos

Leading Exports: Fuel, shoes, garments, fish, bananas, hides

Major Languages: Portuguese and Crioulo

Chad

Capital: N'Djamena

Area: 495,772 sq mi; 1,284,000 sq km

Climate: Tropical in south; desert in north

Population: 9 million

Major Ethnic Groups: Arab, Toubou, Hadjerai, Sara, Ngambaye, Mbaye, other indigenous African groups

Major Religions: Islam, Christianity, traditional African religions

Government: Republic

Currency: 1 Communaute Financiere Africaine franc (CFAF) = 100 centimes

Leading Exports: Cotton, cattle, and textiles

Major Languages: French, Arabic, Sara, Sango, and over 100 various languages and dialects

---

Côte D'Ivoire

Capital: Yamoussoukro

Area: 124,507 sq mi; 322,460 sq km

Climate: Tropical along coast, semiarid in far north

Population: 16.8 million

Major Ethnic Groups: Baoule, Bete, Senoufou, Malinke

Major Religions: Islam, Christianity, traditional African religions

Government: Republic; multiparty presidential regime established 1960

Currency: 1 Communaute Financiere Africaine franc (CFAF) = 100 centimes

Leading Exports: Cocoa, coffee, tropical woods, and petroleum

Major Languages: French, Dioula, and 59 other dialects

The Gambia

Capital: Banjul

Area: 4,363 sq mi; 11,300 sq km

Climate: Subtropical; hot, rainy season; cooler, dry season

Population: 1.5 million

Major Ethnic Groups: Mandinka, Fula, Wolof, Jola, Serahuli

Major Religions: Islam

Government: Republic under multiparty democratic rule

Currency: 1 dalasi (D) = 100 butut

Leading Exports: Peanuts and peanut products, and fish

Major Languages: English, Mandinka, Wolof, Fula, and various languages

Ghana

Capital: Accra

Area: 92,104 sq mi; 238,540 sq km

Climate: Tropical; hot, humid in southwest; hot, dry in north; warm, dry along southeast coast

Population: 20.2 million

Major Ethnic Groups: Akan, Moshi-Dagomba, Ewe, Ga

Major Religions: Traditional African religions, Islam, Christianity

Government: Constitutional democracy

Currency: 1 new cedi (C) = 100 pesewas

Leading Exports: Cocoa, gold, timber, tuna, and bauxite

Major Languages: English, Akan, Moshi-Dagomba, Ewe, and Ga

Guinea

Capital: Conakry

Area: 94,930 sq mi; 245,860 sq km

Climate: Mostly hot and humid; monsoonal-type rainy season; dry season

Population: 7.8 million

Major Ethnic Groups: Peuhl, Malinke, Soussou

Major Religions: Islam

Government: Republic

Currency: 1 Guinean franc (FG) = 100 centimes

Leading Exports: Bauxite, alumina, diamonds, gold, and coffee

Major Languages: French and various languages

Guinea-Bissau

Capital: Bissau

Area: 13,946 sq mi; 36,210 sq mi

Climate: Tropical; mostly hot and humid; monsoonal-type rainy season; dry season

Population: 1.4 million

Major Ethnic Groups: Balanta, Fula, Manjaca, Mandinga, Papel

Major Religions: Traditional African religions, Islam

Government: Republic, multiparty since mid-1991

Currency: 1 Communaute Financiere Africaine franc (CFAF) = 100 centimes

Leading Exports: Cashews, shrimp, peanuts, and palm kernels

Major Languages: Portuguese, Crioulo, and various languages

Liberia

Capital: Monrovia

Area: 43,002 sq mi; 111,370 sq km

Climate: Tropical; hot, humid; dry winters; wet, cloudy summers

Population: 3.3 million

Major Ethnic Groups: Kpelle, Bassa, Gio, Kru

Major Religions: Traditional African religions, Christianity, Islam

Government: Republic

Currency: 1 Liberian dollar (L$) = 100 cents

Leading Exports: Diamonds, iron ore, rubber, timber, and coffee

Major Languages: English (official), some 20 ethnic group languages

Mali

Capital: Bamako

Area: 478,783 sq mi; 1,240,000 sq km

Climate: Arid in north, semiarid in south

Population: 11.3 million

Major Ethnic Groups: Bambara, Malinke, Soninke, Peul, Valtaic

Major Religions: Islam

Government: Republic

Currency: 1 Communaute Financiere Africaine franc (CFAF) = 100 centimes

Leading Exports: Cotton, livestock, and gold

Major Languages: French, Bambara, and various languages

Mauritania

Capital: Nouakchott

Area: 397,969 sq mi; 1,030,700 sq km

Climate: Desert, always hot, dry, and dusty

Population: 2.8 million

Major Ethnic Groups: Mixed Maur and indigenous

Major Religions: Islam

Government: Republic

Currency: 1 ouguiya (UM) = 5 khoums

Leading Exports: Iron ore, and fish and fish products

Major Languages: Hasaniya Arabic, Wolof, Pular, and Soninke

Major Languages: English (official), Mende, Temne, and Krio

Niger

Capital: Niamey
Area: 489,208 sq mi; 1,267,000 sq km
Climate: Desert; mostly hot, dry, dusty; tropical in extreme south
Population: 11.3 million
Major Ethnic Groups: Hausa, Djerma
Major Religions: Islam
Government: Republic
Currency: 1 Communaute Financiere Africaine franc (CFAF) = 100 centimes
Leading Exports: Uranium ore and livestock products
Major Languages: French (official), Hausa, and Djerma

Nigeria

Capital: Abuja
Area: 356,682 sq mi; 923,770 sq km
Climate: Tropical; arid in north
Population: 129.9 million
Major Ethnic Groups: Hausa, Fulani, Yoruba, Igbo, Ijaw
Major Religions: Islam, Christianity
Government: Republic transitioning from military to civilian rule
Currency: 1 naira (N) = 100 kobo
Leading Exports: Petroleum and petroleum products
Major Languages: English (official), Hausa, Yoruba, Igbo, and Fulani

Senegal

Capital: Dakar
Area: 75,752 sq mi; 196,190 sq km
Climate: Tropical; hot, humid; rainy season has strong southeast winds; dry season dominated by hot, dry wind
Population: 10.6 million
Major Ethnic Groups: Wolof, Pular, Serer
Major Religions: Islam
Government: Republic under multiparty democratic rule
Currency: 1 Communaute Financiere Africaine franc (CFAF) = 100 centimes
Leading Exports: Fish, ground nuts, and petroleum products
Major Languages: French (official), Wolof, Pulaar, Jola, and Mandinka

Sierra Leone

Capital: Freetown
Area: 27,700 sq mi; 71,740 sq km
Climate: Tropical; hot, humid; summer rainy season; winter dry season
Population: 5.6 million
Major Ethnic Groups: Temne, Mende
Major Religions: Islam, traditional African religions
Government: Constitutional democracy
Currency: 1 leone (Le) = 100 cents
Leading Exports: Diamonds, rutile, cocoa, coffee, and fish
Major Languages: English (official), Mende, Temne, and Krio

Togo

Capital: Lome
Area: 21,927 sq mi; 56,790 sq km
Climate: Tropical; hot, humid in south; semiarid in north
Population: 5.2 million
Major Ethnic Groups: Ewe, Mina, Kabre
Major Religions: Traditional African religions, Christianity
Government: Republic under transition to multiparty democracy
Currency: 1 Communaute Financiere Africaine franc (CFAF) = 100 centimes
Leading Exports: Phosphates, cotton, cocoa, and coffee
Major Languages: French, Ewe and Mina, Dagomba, and Kabye

East Africa: Political

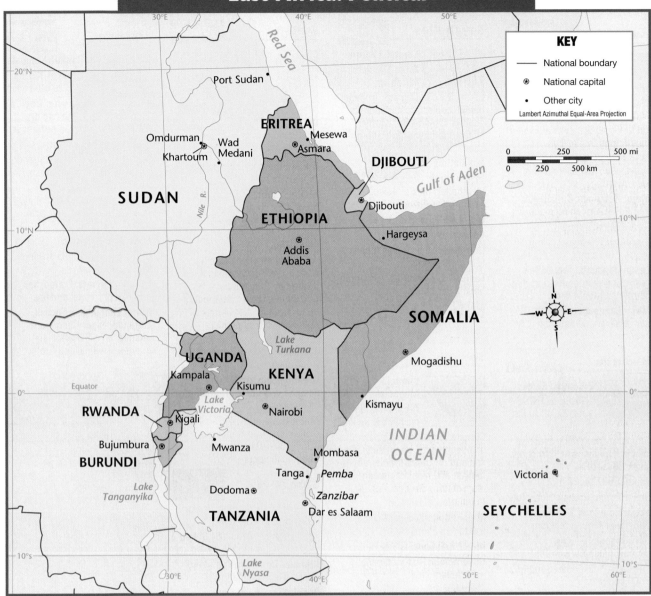

Port Sudan

ERITREA
Mesewa
Asmara ⊛
DJIBOUTI
Omdurman •
Wad
Medani
Khartoum

Gulf of Aden

Djibouti ⊛

SUDAN

ETHIOPIA

10°N

Addis
Ababa ⊛

Hargeysa •

Nile R.

SOMALIA

Lake
Turkana

UGANDA

KENYA
Kampala ⊛
Kisumu •
Mogadishu ⊛

RWANDA
Kigali ⊛
Lake
Victoria
Nairobi •
Kismayu •

Equator
0°

Bujumbura ⊛
Mwanza •
Mombasa •
INDIAN
OCEAN

BURUNDI
Tanga • Pemba
Victoria ⊛

Lake
Tanganyika
Dodoma ⊛
Zanzibar

TANZANIA
Dar es Salaam ⊛
SEYCHELLES

Lake
Nyasa

KEY
— National boundary
⊛ National capital
• Other city
Lambert Azimuthal Equal-Area Projection

0   250   500 mi
0   250   500 km

Burundi

Capital: Bujumbura
Area: 10,746 sq mi; 27,830 sq km

Climate: Tropical; temperature moderated by altitude; wet seasons alternate with dry seasons
Population: 6.4 million
Major Ethnic Groups: Hutu, Tutsi, Twa
Major Religions: Christianity, traditional African religions, Islam
Government: Republic
Currency: 1 Burundi franc (Fbu) = 100 centimes
Leading Exports: Coffee, tea, sugar, cotton, and hides
Major Languages: Kirundi, French, and Swahili

Djibouti

Capital: Djibouti
Area: 8,495 sq mi; 22,000 sq km
Climate: Desert; extremely hot and dry
Population: 473,000
Major Ethnic Groups: Somali, Afar
Major Religions: Islam
Government: Republic
Currency: 1 Djiboutian franc (DF) = 100 centimes
Leading Exports: Hides and skins, and coffee
Major Languages: French, Arabic, Somali, and Afar

Eritrea

Capital: Asmara
Area: 46,844 sq mi; 121,320 sq km
Climate: Hot, dry desert strip along Red Sea coast; cooler and wetter in central highlands; semiarid in western hills and lowlands
Population: 4.5 million
Major Ethnic Groups: Tigrinya, Tigre, and Kunama
Major Religions: Islam, Christianity
Government: Transitional
Currency: 1 nafka = 100 cents
Leading Exports: Livestock, sorghum, textiles, food
Major Languages: Afar, Amharic, Arabic, Tigre, Kunama, Tigrinya and Cushitic dialects

Ethiopia

Capital: Addis Ababa
Area: 435,201 sq mi; 1,127,127 sq km

Climate: Subtropical on central plateau; varies with elevation
Population: 67.7 million
Major Ethnic Groups: Oromo, Amhara, Tigre, Sidamo, Shankella, and Somali
Major Religions: Islam, Christianity
Government: Federal republic
Currency: 1 birr (Br) = 100 cents
Leading Exports: Coffee, leather products, and gold
Major Languages: Amharic, Tigrinya, Orominga, Guaraginga, Somali, Arabic, English, and various languages

Kenya

Capital: Nairobi

Area: 224,970 sq mi; 582,650 sq km

Climate: Humid, wet along coast; dry on plateaus; temperate in highlands

Population: 31.3 million

Major Ethnic Groups: Kikuyu, Luhya, Luo, Kalenjin, Kamba, Kisii, Meru

Major Religions: Christianity, traditional African religions

Government: Republic

Currency: 1 Kenyan shilling (KSh) = 100 cents

Leading Exports: Tea, coffee, horticultural products, and petroleum products

Major Languages: English, Kiswahili, and various languages

Rwanda

Capital: Kigali

Area: 10,170 sq mi; 26,340 sq km

Climate: Temperate; two rainy seasons; mild in mountains with frost and snow possible

Population: 7.4 million

Major Ethnic Groups: Hutu, Tutsi

Major Religions: Christianity, traditional African religions

Government: Republic; presidential, multiparty system

Currency: 1 Rwandan franc (RF) = 100 centimes

Leading Exports: Coffee, tea, hides, and tin ore

Major Languages: Kinyarwanda (official), French (official), English (official), and Kiswahili

Seychelles

Capital: Victoria

Area: 176 sq mi; 455 sq km

Climate: Tropical; humid; cooler season during southeast monsoon; warmer season during northwest monsoon

Population: 80,000

Major Ethnic Groups: Seychellois (mix of Asian, African, and European)

Major Religions: Christianity

Government: Republic

Currency: 1 Seychelles rupee (Sre) = 100 cents

Leading Exports: Fish, cinnamon bark, and copra

Major Languages: English (official), French (official), and Creole

Somalia

Capital: Mogadishu

Area: 246,210 sq mi; 637,660 sq km

Climate: Mostly desert; hot; monsoon winds bring rainy season and dry season; little rainfall, hot and humid between monsoons

Population: 7.8 million

Major Ethnic Groups: Somali, Bantu

Major Religions: Islam

Government: No functioning government

Currency: 1 Somali shilling (SoSh) = 100 cents

Leading Exports: Livestock, bananas, fish, and hides

Major Languages: Somali (official), Arabic, Italian, and English

Sudan

Capital: Khartoum

Area: 967,532 sq mi; 2,505,810 sq km

Climate: Tropical in south; arid desert in north; rainy season

Population: 37.1 million

Major Ethnic Groups: Azande, Dinka, Arab

Major Religions: Islam, traditional African religions

Government: Transitional; note: previously ruling military junta; presidential and National Assembly elections held in March 1996; new constitution drafted by Presidential Committee, went into effect on June 30, 1998 after being approved in nationwide referendum

Currency: 1 Sudanese dinar (SD) = 100 piastres

Leading Exports: Cotton, sesame, livestock, groundnuts, oil, gum arabic

Major Languages: Arabic (official), Nubian, Ta Bedawie, Nilotic, Nilo-Hamitic, and Sudanic dialects

Tanzania

Capital: Dar Es Salaam

Area: 364,914 sq mi; 945,090 sq km

Climate: Tropical wet and dry; temperate in highlands

Population: 37.2 million

Major Ethnic Groups: Bantu

Major Religions: Christianity, Islam, traditional African religions

Government: Republic

Currency: 1 Tanzanian shilling (TSh) = 100 cents

Leading Exports: Coffee, manufactured goods, cotton, cashew nuts, minerals

Major Languages: Kiswahili, Kiunguju, English, Arabic, and various languages

Uganda

Capital: Kampala

Area: 91,139 sq mi; 236,040 sq km

Climate: Tropical; generally rainy with two dry seasons; semiarid in northeast

Population: 24.7 million

Major Ethnic Groups: Baganda, Karamojong, Basogo, Iteso, Langi, Rwanda

Major Religions: Christianity, Islam, traditional African religions

Government: Republic

Currency: 1 Ugandan shilling (Ush) = 100 cents

Leading Exports: Coffee, fish and fish products, and tea

Major Languages: English, Luganda, Niger-Congo languages, Nilo-Saharan languages, Swahili, and Arabic

Cameroon

Capital: Yaounde
Area: 183,574 sq mi; 475,440 sq km
Climate: Varies with terrain, from tropical along coast to semiarid and hot in north; wet in mountains
Population: 16.1 million
Major Ethnic Groups: Cameroon Highlanders, Equatorial Bantu, Kirdi, Fulani
Major Religions: Traditional African religions, Christianity, Islam
Government: Unitary republic; multiparty presidential regime
Currency: 1 Communaute Financiere Africaine franc (CFAF) = 100 centimes
Leading Exports: Crude oil and petroleum products, lumber, cocoa beans, and aluminum
Major Languages: 24 various languages, English, and French

Central African Republic

Capital: Bangui
Area: 240,542 sq mi; 622,980 sq km
Climate: Tropical; hot, dry winters; mild to hot, wet summers
Population: 3.6 million
Major Ethnic Groups: Baya, Banda, Mandjia, Sara
Major Religions: Christianity, traditional African religions, Islam
Government: Republic
Currency: 1 Communaute Financiere Africaine franc (CFAF) = 100 centimes
Leading Exports: Diamonds, timber, cotton, coffee, and tobacco
Major Languages: French, Sangho, Arabic, Hunsa, and Swahili

Congo, Democratic Republic of the

Capital: Kinshasa
Area: 905,599 sq mi; 2,345,410 sq km
Climate: Tropical; very hot and humid; cooler in highlands; rainy seasons north and south
Population: 55.2 million
Major Ethnic Groups: Mongo, Luba, Mangbetu-Azande, Kongo
Major Religions: Christianity, traditional African religions, Islam
Government: Dictatorship; presumably undergoing a transition to representative government
Currency: Congolese franc (CF)
Leading Exports: Diamonds, copper, coffee, cobalt, and crude oil
Major Languages: French, Lingala, Kingwana, Kikongo, and Tshiluba

Congo, Republic of the

Capital: Brazzavile
Area: 132,051 sq mi; 342,000 sq km
Climate: Tropical; rainy and dry seasons; constantly high temperatures and humidity; particularly harsh near Equator
Population: 3.3 million
Major Ethnic Groups: Kongo, Sangha, M'Bochi, Teke
Major Religions: Christianity, traditional African religions
Government: Republic
Currency: 1 Communaute Financiere Africaine franc (CFAF) = 100 centimes
Leading Exports: Petroleum, lumber, plywood, sugar, and cocoa
Major Languages: French, Lingala, Monokutuba, Kikongo, and other languages

Equatorial Guinea

Capital: Malabo
Area: 10,831 sq mi; 28,050 sq km
Climate: Tropical; always hot, humid
Population: 498,000
Major Ethnic Groups: Bubi, Fernandinos, Fang
Major Religions: Christianity, traditional African religions
Government: Republic
Currency: 1 Communaute Financiere Africaine franc (CFAF) = 100 centimes
Leading Exports: Petroleum, timber, and cocoa beans
Major Languages: Spanish, French, pidgin English, Fang, Bubi, and Ibo

Gabon

Capital: Libreville
Area: 103,351 sq mi; 267,670 sq km
Climate: Tropical; always hot, humid; rainy seasons alternate with dry seasons
Population: 1.2 million
Major Ethnic Groups: Fang, Eshira, Bapounou, Bateke
Major Religions: Christianity, traditional African religions
Government: Republic; multiparty presidential regime
Currency: 1 Communaute Financiere Africaine franc (CFAF) = 100 centimes
Leading Exports: Crude oil, timber, manganese, and uranium
Major Languages: French, Fang, Myene, Bateke, Bapounou/Eschira, and Bandjabi

São Tomé and Príncipe

Capital: São Tomé
Area: 371 sq mi; 960 sq km
Climate: Tropical; hot, humid; rainy season
Population: 170,000
Major Ethnic Groups: Mestico (mix of European and Native American), angolares (descendants of Angolan slaves), forros (descendants of freed slaves), servicais (contract laborers from Angola, Mozambique, and Cape Verde), tongas (children of servicais born on the islands)
Major Religions: Christianity
Government: Republic
Currency: 1 dobra (Db) = 100 centimes
Leading Exports: Cocoa, copra, coffee, and palm oil
Major Languages: Portuguese (official)

KEY
National boundary
⊙ National capital
· Other city
Lambert Azimuthal Equal-Area Projection

L. Chad
CHAD
NIGERIA
CENTRAL AFRICAN REPUBLIC
CAMEROON
SUDAN
Douala
Bangui
Malabo
Yaoundé
Edéa
EQUATORIAL GUINEA
São Tomé
Congo R.
L. Albert
São Tomé
Libreville
Kisangani
UGANDA
SÃO TOMÉ AND PRÍNCIPE
GABON
REPUBLIC OF THE CONGO
DEMOCRATIC REPUBLIC OF THE CONGO
L. Edward
RWANDA
Port Gentil
Brazzaville
Bukavu
BURUNDI
ATLANTIC OCEAN
Pointe Noire
Kinshasa
Ilebo
L. Kivu
Matadi
Kananga
Kalemi
TANZANIA
CABINDA (ANGOLA)
Mbuji-Mayi
Tanganyika
ANGOLA
Lubumbashi
Mweru
ZAMBIA

0   200   400 mi
0   200   400 km

Southern Africa: Political

KEY

— National boundary

⊛ National capital

• Other city

Lambert Azimuthal Equal-Area Projection

Angola

Capital: Luanda
Area: 481,370 sq mi; 1,246,700 sq km
Climate: Semiarid in south and along coast to Luanda; tropical in north with a cool, dry season and a hot, rainy season
Population: 10.6 million
Major Ethnic Groups: Ovimbundu, Kimbundu, Bakongo
Major Religions: Traditional African religions, Christianity
Government: Transitional government, nominally a multiparty democracy with a strong presidential system
Currency: 1 kwanza (NKz) = 100 lwei
Leading Exports: Crude oil, diamonds, and refined petroleum products
Major Languages: Portuguese (official), Bantu, and various languages

Botswana

Capital: Gaborone
Area: 231,812 sq mi; 600,370 sq km
Climate: Semiarid; warm winters; hot summers
Population: 1.6 million
Major Ethnic Groups: Batswana
Major Religions: Traditional African religions, Christianity
Government: Parliamentary republic
Currency: 1 pula (P) = 100 thebe
Leading Exports: Diamonds, vehicles, copper and nickel, and meat
Major Languages: English and Setswana

Comoros

Capital: Moroni
Area: 838 sq mi; 2,170 sq km
Climate: Tropical maritime, rainy season
Population: 614,000
Major Ethnic Groups: Antalote, Cafre, Makoa, Oimatsaha, Sakalava
Major Religions: Islam
Government: Independent republic
Currency: 1 Comoran franc (CF) = 100 centimes
Leading Exports: Vanilla, ylang-ylang, cloves, and perfume oil
Major Languages: Arabic, French, and Comoran

Lesotho

Capital: Maseru
Area: 11,719 sq mi; 30,350 sq km
Climate: Temperate; cool to cold, dry winters; hot, wet summers
Population: 2.2 million
Major Ethnic Groups: Sotho
Major Religions: Christianity, traditional African religions
Government: Parliamentary constitutional monarchy
Currency: 1 loti (L) = 100 lisente
Leading Exports: manufactures, wool, mohair, food and live animals
Major Languages: Sesotho, English, Zulu, and Xhosa

Madagascar

Capital: Antananarivo
Area: 226,665 sq mi; 587,040 sq km
Climate: Tropical along coast; temperate inland; arid in south
Population: 16.5 million
Major Ethnic Groups: Merina, Betsileo, Cotiers
Major Religions: Traditional African religions, Christianity
Government: Republic
Currency: 1 Malagasy franc (FMG) = 100 centimes
Leading Exports: Coffee, vanilla, cloves, shellfish, and sugar
Major Languages: French and Malagasy

Malawi

Capital: Lilongwe
Area: 45,747 sq mi; 118,480 sq km
Climate: Tropical; rainy season; cooler in highlands
Population: 10.7 million
Major Ethnic Groups: Chewa, Nyanja, other indigenous African groups
Major Religions: Christianity, Islam
Government: Multiparty democracy
Currency: 1 Malawian kwacha (MK) = 100 tambala
Leading Exports: Tobacco, tea, sugar, coffee, and peanuts
Major Languages: English, Chichewa, and various languages

Mauritius

Capital: Port Louis
Area: 718 sq mi; 1,860 sq km
Climate: Tropical, modified by southeast trade winds; warm, dry winter; hot, wet humid summer
Population: 1.2 million
Major Ethnic Groups: Indo-Mauritian, Creole
Major Religions: Hinduism, Christianity, Islam
Government: Parliamentary democracy
Currency: 1 Mauritian rupee (MauR) = 100 cents
Leading Exports: Clothing, textiles, sugar, cut flowers, and molasses
Major Languages: English (official), Creole, French, Hindi, Urdu, Hakka, and Bojpoori

Mozambique

Capital: Maputo
Area: 309,506 sq mi; 801,590 sq km
Climate: Tropical to subtropical; dry season
Population: 19.6 million
Major Ethnic Groups: Shangaan, Chokwe, Manyika, Sena, Makua
Major Religions: Traditional African religions, Christianity, Islam
Government: Republic
Currency: 1 metical (Mt) = 100 centavos
Leading Exports: Shrimp, cashews, cotton, sugar, copra, and citrus
Major Languages: Portuguese and various dialects

Namibia

Capital: Windhoek
Area: 318,707 sq mi; 825,418 sq km
Climate: Desert; hot, dry; little rainfall
Population: 1.8 million
Major Ethnic Groups: Ovambo, Kavangos
Major Religions: Christianity, traditional African religions
Government: Republic
Currency: 1 Namibian dollar (N$) = 100 cents
Leading Exports: Diamonds, copper, gold, zinc, and lead
Major Languages: English (official), Afrikaans, German, Oshivambo, Herero, Nama

South Africa

Capital: Pretoria
Area: 471,027 sq mi; 1,219,912 sq km
Climate: Temperate; mostly dry; subtropical along eastern coast
Population: 43.6 million
Major Ethnic Groups: Nguni, Caucasian
Major Religions: Christianity, traditional African religions
Government: Republic
Currency: 1 rand (R) = 100 cents
Leading Exports: Gold, diamonds, other minerals and metals
Major Languages: Afrikaans, English, Ndebele, Pedi, Sotho, Swazi, Tsonga, Tswana, Venda, Xhosa, and Zulu (all official)

Swaziland

Capital: Mbabane
Area: 6,641 sq mi; 17,360 sq km
Climate: Mostly temperate; more tropical in east
Population: 1.1 million
Major Ethnic Groups: Swazi
Major Religions: Christianity, traditional African religions
Government: Monarchy, independent member of Commonwealth
Currency: 1 lilangeni (E) = 100 cents
Leading Exports: Sugar, edible concentrates, and wood pulp
Major Languages: English (official), siSwati (official)

Zambia

Capital: Lusaka
Area: 290,594 sq mi; 752,610 sq km
Climate: Subtropical; rainy season
Population: 10.1 million
Major Ethnic Groups: Bemba, Nyanja, Tonga
Major Religions: Christianity, Islam
Government: Republic
Currency: 1 Zambian kwacha (ZK) = 100 ngwee
Leading Exports: Copper, cobalt, electricity, and tobacco
Major Languages: English (official) and about 70 various languages

Zimbabwe

Capital: Harare
Area: 150,809 sq mi; 390,580 sq km
Climate: Tropical; rainy season
Population: 11.3 million
Major Ethnic Groups: Shona, Ndebele
Major Religions: Christian/traditional mix, Christianity, traditional African religions
Government: Parliamentary democracy
Currency: 1 Zimbabwean dollar (Z$) = 100 cents
Leading Exports: Tobacco, gold, ferroalloys, cotton
Major Languages: English, Shona, and Sindebele

China

Capital: Beijing

Area: 3,705,533 sq mi; 9,596,960 sq km

Climate: Mostly continental; varies from tropical in far southeast to subarctic in far north; cold, dry winters and warm summers, with heavy rains along coast

Population: 1.29 billion

Major Ethnic Groups: Han Chinese

Major Religions: Daoism, Buddhism

Government: Communist state

Currency: 1 yuan = 10 jiao

Leading Exports: Textiles, garments, footwear, and toys

Major Languages: Mandarin, Putonghua, Yue, Wu, Minbei, Minnan, Xiang, and Gan and Hakka dialects

Japan

Capital: Tokyo

Area: 145,888 sq mi; 377,835 sq km

Climate: Ranges from subtropical in south to continental in north; mostly mild winters and hot, humid summers; severe, long winters in north

Population: 127 million

Major Ethnic Groups: Japanese

Major Religions: Buddhism, Shintoism

Government: Constitutional monarchy

Currency: yen

Leading Exports: Machinery, motor vehicles, and electronics

Major Languages: Japanese

KEY

— National boundary

⊛ National capital

• Other city

Two-Point Equidistant Projection

Mongolia

Capital: Ulaanbaatar

Area: 604,270 sq mi; 1,565,000 sq km

Climate: Arid; extremely cold winters, mild summers

Population: 2.6 million

Major Ethnic Groups: Halh Mongol

Major Religions: Buddhism

Government: Republic

Currency: 1 tughrik (Tug) = 100 mongos

Leading Exports: Copper, livestock, animal products, and cashmere

Major Languages: Khalkha Mongol, Turkic, Russian, and Chinese

North Korea

Capital: P'yongyang

Area: 46,542 sq mi; 120,540 sq km

Climate: Humid continental; cold winters and wet, hot summers

Population: 22.3 million

Major Ethnic Groups: Korean

Major Religions: Ch'ondogyo (mix of Confucianism and Daoism), Buddhism

Government: Authoritarian socialist, one-man dictatorship

Currency: 1 North Korean won (Wn) = 100 chon

Leading Exports: Minerals and metallurgical products

Major Languages: Korean

South Korea

Capital: Seoul

Area: 38,025 sq mi; 98,480 sq km

Climate: Continental; cold, dry winters and hot, rainy summers

Population: 48.3 million

Major Ethnic Groups: Korean

Major Religions: Christianity, Buddhism

Government: Republic

Currency: 1 South Korean won (W) = 100 chun

Leading Exports: Electronic and electrical equipment

Major Languages: Korean and English

Taiwan

Capital: Taipei

Area: 13,892 sq mi; 35,980 sq km

Climate: Tropical; mild, wet winters and hot, humid summers; cloudy most of year

Population: 22.5 million

Major Ethnic Groups: Han Chinese

Major Religions: Buddhism, Daoism

Government: Multiparty democratic regime headed by popularly elected president

Currency: 1 New Taiwanese dollar (NT$) = 100 cents

Leading Exports: Electrical machinery and electronics

Major Languages: Mandarin Chinese (official), Taiwanese, and Hakka dialects

KEY

— National boundary

⊛ National capital

• Other city

Two-Point Equidistant Projection

0   400   800 mi

0   400   800 km

Brunei

Capital: Bandar Seri Begawan

Area: 2,228 sq mi; 5,770 sq km

Climate: Tropical wet; hot, humid; long rainy season

Population: 351,000

Major Ethnic Groups: Malay, Chinese

Major Religions: Islam

Government: Constitutional sultanate

Currency: 1 Bruneian dollar (B$) = 100 cents

Leading Exports: Crude oil and liquefied natural gas

Major Languages: Malay, English, and Chinese

Cambodia

Capital: Phnom Penh

Area: 69,902 sq mi; 181,040 sq km

Climate: Tropical; hot, humid; rainy season and dry season

Population: 12.8 million

Major Ethnic Groups: Khmer

Major Religions: Buddhism

Government: Multiparty liberal democracy under a constitutional monarchy established in September 1993

Currency: 1 new riel (CR) = 100 sen

Leading Exports: Timber, garements, rubber, rice, fish

Major Languages: Khmer and French

Indonesia

Capital: Jakarta

Area: 741,052 sq mi; 1,919,251 sq km

Climate: Tropical; hot, humid; cooler in upland areas; rainy season and dry season

Population: 231.3 million

Major Ethnic Groups: Javanese, Sundanese

Major Religions: Islam

Government: Republic

Currency: Indonesian rupiah (Rp) = 100 sen

Leading Exports: Oil and gas, plywood, textiles

Major Languages: Bahasa Indonesia, English, Dutch, Javanese, and various dialects

---

Laos

Capital: Vientiane

Area: 91,432 sq mi; 236,800 sq km

Climate: Tropical; cool, dry winters and hot, wet summers

Population: 5.8 million

Major Ethnic Groups: Lao Loum, Lao Theung

Major Religions: Buddhism, traditional beliefs

Government: Communist state

Currency: 1 new kip (NK) = 100 at

Leading Exports: Electricity, wood products, coffee, and tin

Major Languages: Lao, French, English, and various languages

Malaysia

Capital: Kuala Lumpur

Area: 127,322 sq mi; 329,750 sq km

Climate: Tropical; hot, humid, and rainy; cooler and drier in highlands

Population: 22.7 million

Major Ethnic Groups: Malay, Chinese

Major Religions: Islam, Buddhism

Government: Constitutional monarchy

Currency: 1 ringgit (M$) = 100 sen

Leading Exports: Electronic equipment

Major Languages: Malay, English, Mandarin, Tamil, Chinese dialects, and various languages and dialects

Myanmar (Burma)

Capital: Rangoon

Area: 261,979 sq mi; 678,500 sq km

Climate: Tropical; dry, warm winters and rainy, hot, humid summers

Population: 42.2 million

Major Ethnic Groups: Burman

Major Religions: Buddhism

Government: Military regime

Currency: 1 kyat (K) = 100 pyas

Leading Exports: Pulses and beans, prawns, fish, rice; teak

Major Languages: Burmese

Philippines

Capital: Manila

Area: 115,834 sq mi; 300,000 sq km

Climate: Tropical; dry winters and rainy summers

Population: 84.5 million

Major Ethnic Groups: Filipino (Christian Malay)

Major Religions: Christianity

Government: Republic

Currency: 1 Philippine peso (P) = 100 centavos

Leading Exports: Electronics, machinery and transport equipment, textiles, and coconut products

Major Languages: Filipino and English (official)

Singapore

Capital: Singapore

Area: 244 sq mi; 633 sq km

Climate: Tropical; hot, humid, rainy all year

Population: 4.5 million

Major Ethnic Groups: Chinese

Major Religions: Buddhism

Government: Parliamentary republic

Currency: 1 Singapore dollar (S$) = 100 cents

Leading Exports: Machinery and equipment (including electronics

Major Languages: Chinese, Malay, Tamil, and English

Thailand

Capital: Bangkok

Area: 198,456 sq mi; 514,000 sq km

Climate: Tropical; dry, warm winters and hot, wet, summers

Population: 62.5 million

Major Ethnic Groups: Thai

Major Religions: Buddhism

Government: Constitutional monarchy

Currency: 1 baht (B) = 100 satang

Leading Exports: Machinery and manufactures

Major Languages: Thai and English

Vietnam

Capital: Hanoi

Area: 127,248 sq mi; 329,560 sq km

Climate: Mostly tropical; hot, dry winters and hot, rainy summers; cooler winters in North

Population: 81.1 million

Major Ethnic Groups: Vietnamese

Major Religions: Buddhism, Christianity

Government: Communist state

Currency: 1 new dong (D) = 100 xu

Leading Exports: Petroleum, rice, and agricultural products

Major Languages: Vietnamese, French, Chinese, English, Khmer, and various languages

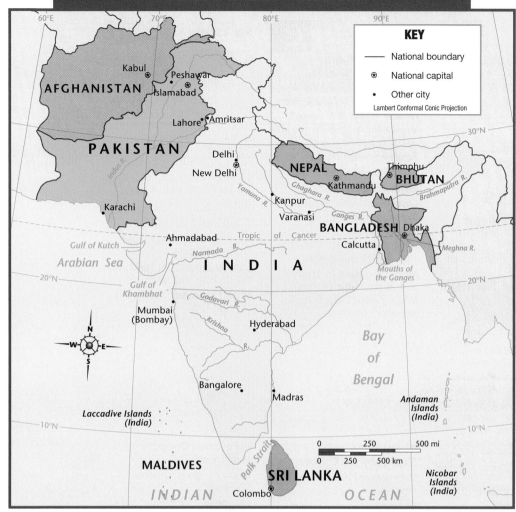

KEY

— National boundary

⊛ National capital

• Other city

Lambert Conformal Conic Projection

Afghanistan

Capital: Kabul
Area: 251,738 sq mi; 652,000 sq km
Climate: Subarctic in mountains; arid in lowlands; cold, dry winters and hot summers
Population: 27.8 million
Major Ethnic Groups: Pashtun, Tajik, Hazara
Major Religions: Islam
Government: No functioning central government, administered by factions
Currency: 1 afghani (AF) = 100 puls
Leading Exports: Fruits and nuts, handwoven carpets, and wool
Major Languages: Pashtu, Afghan Persian, Turkic, and 30 various languages

Bangladesh

Capital: Dhaka
Area: 55,600 sq mi; 144,000 sq km
Climate: Tropical; rainy season
Population: 133.4 million
Major Ethnic Groups: Bengali
Major Religions: Islam
Government: Republic
Currency: 1 taka (TK) = 100 poisha
Leading Exports: Garments, jute and jute goods, and leather
Major Languages: Bangla and English

Bhutan

Capital: Thimphu
Area: 18,147 sq mi; 47,000 sq km
Climate: Subtropical in central valleys, with cool winters and hot summers; hotter and more humid in southern plains; highlands in mountains, with bitterly cold winters and cool summers
Population: 2.1 million
Major Ethnic Groups: Bhutia, Nepali
Major Religions: Buddhism, Hinduism
Government: Monarchy; special treaty relationship with India
Currency: 1 ngultrum (Nu) = 100 chetrum; note – Indian currency is also legal tender
Leading Exports: Cardamon, gypsum, timber and handicrafts
Major Languages: Dzongkha (official), Tibetan dialects, and Nepalese dialects

India

Capital: New Delhi
Area: 1,269,389 sq mi; 3,287,590 sq km
Climate: Mostly tropical in south; mostly subtropical in north; cool, dry winters and hot, dry summers, with heavy rain during monsoon; cold winters and cool summers in mountains; arid in West
Population: 1.05 billion
Major Ethnic Groups: Indo-Aryan, Dravidian
Major Religions: Hinduism
Government: Federal republic
Currency: 1 Indian rupee (Re) = 100 paise
Leading Exports: Clothing, and gems and jewelry
Major Languages: English, Hindi, Bengali, Telugu, Marathi, Tamil, Urdu, Gujarati, Malayam, Kannada, Oriya, Punjabi, Assamese, Kashmiri, Sindhi, Sanskrit, and Hindustani (all official)

Maldives

Capital: Male
Area: 116 sq mi; 300 sq km
Climate: Tropical; hot, humid; rainy season in summer
Population: 320,000
Major Ethnic Groups: mix of Sinhalese, Dravidian, Arabian, and Affrican
Major Religions: Islam
Government: Republic
Currency: 1 rufiyaa (Rf) = 100 laari
Leading Exports: Fish and clothing
Major Languages: Divehi dialect and English

Nepal

Capital: Kathmandu
Area: 54,365 sq mi; 140,800 sq km
Climate: Highlands in North, with cool summers and severe winters; subtropical in south, with hot, wet summers and mild, dry winters
Population: 25.9 million
Major Ethnic Groups: Newars, Indian, Tibetan
Major Religions: Hinduism
Government: Parliamentary democracy
Currency: 1 Nepalese rupee (NR) = 100 paisa
Leading Exports: Carpets, clothing, and leather goods
Major Languages: Nepali (official), and 20 various languages divided into numerous dialects

Pakistan

Capital: Islamabad
Area: 310,414 sq mi; 803,940 sq km
Climate: Mostly arid; cold winters in mountains; extremely hot summers in central valley
Population: 147.7 million
Major Ethnic Groups: Punjabi
Major Religions: Islam
Government: Federal republic
Currency: 1 Pakistani rupee (Pre) = 100 paisa
Leading Exports: Cotton, textiles, clothing, rice, and leather
Major Languages: Urdu (official), English (official), Punjabi, Sindhi, Pashtu, Urdu, Balochi, and other languages

Sri Lanka

Capital: Colombo
Area: 25,333 sq mi; 65,610 sq km
Climate: Tropical; hot, humid; cooler and less humid in mountains; wet in southwest; dry north of mountains
Population: 19.6 million
Major Ethnic Groups: Sinhalese, Tamil
Major Religions: Buddhism
Government: Republic
Currency: 1 Sri Lankan rupee (SLRe) = 100 cents
Leading Exports: Garments and textiles, teas, and diamonds
Major Languages: Sinhala (official) and Tamil

KEY

— National boundary

⊛ National capital

• Other city

Two-Point Equidistant Projection

Black Sea

Istanbul
Izmir
Ankara
GEORGIA Tbilisi
TURKEY
ARMENIA
Yerevan
AZERBAIJAN
Baku
CYPRUS Nicosia
Mediterranean Sea
SYRIA
LEBANON
Beirut
Damascus
Jerusalem
Amman
ISRAEL
JORDAN
IRAQ
Baghdad
Tabriz
Meshed
Tehran
IRAN
Isfahan
KUWAIT
Kuwait
SAUDI
ARABIA
BAHRAIN
Manama
Riyadh
Doha
QATAR
Abu Dhabi
UNITED
ARAB EMIRATES
Muscat
OMAN
OMAN
Jidda
Mecca
Red Sea
Sanaa
Aden
YEMEN
Gulf of Aden
Socotra (Yemen)
Arabian Sea
Persian Gulf
Tropic of Cancer

KAZAKSTAN
Pavlodar
Astana
Semey
Lake Zaysan
Aral Sea
Lake Bolkhash
UZBEKISTAN
Almaty
Bishkek
KYRGYZSTAN
Tashkent
Dushanbe
TAJIKISTAN
TURKMENISTAN
Ashkhabad

0 250 500 mi

0 250 500 km

Armenia

Capital: Yerevan
Area: 11,506 sq mi; 29,800 sq km
Climate: Dry continental, with hot summers and cold winters
Population: 3.3 million
Major Ethnic Groups: Armenian
Major Religions: Christianity
Government: Republic
Currency: 1 dram = 100 luma
Leading Exports: Diamonds, scrap metal, machinery and equipment
Major Languages: Armenian and Russian

Azerbaijan

Capital: Baku
Area: 33,438 sq mi; 86,600 sq km
Climate: Dry to humid subtropical and dry to humid continental; moderate rainfall in south, tundra in mountains of north
Population: 7.8 million
Major Ethnic Groups: Azeri
Major Religions: Islam
Government: Republic
Currency: 1 manat = 100 gopiks
Leading Exports: Oil and gas, machinery, cotton
Major Languages: Azeri, Russian, Armenian

Bahrain

Capital: Manama
Area: 239 sq mi; 620 sq km
Climate: Arid; mild winters and very hot, humid summers
Population: 656,000
Major Ethnic Groups: Bahraini
Major Religions: Islam
Government: Traditional monarchy
Currency: 1 Bahraini dinar (BD) = 1000 fils
Leading Exports: Petroleum and petroleum products
Major Languages: Arabic, English, Farsi, and Urdu

Cyprus

Capital: Nicosia
Area: 3,572 sq mi; 9,250 sq km
Climate: Mediterranean; cool, wet winters and hot, dry summers
Population: 767,000
Major Ethnic Groups: Greek, Turkish
Major Religions: Christianity, Islam
Government: Republic
Currency: Greek Cypriot area: 1 Cypriot pound = 100 cents; Turkish Cypriot area: 1 Turkish lira (TL) = 100 Kurus
Leading Exports: Citrus, potatoes, grapes, wines, and cement
Major Languages: Greek, Turkish, and English

Iran

Capital: Tehran
Area: 636,296 sq mi; 1,648,000 sq km
Climate: Mostly arid or semiarid; extremely hot along southern coast; subtropical along northern coast
Population: 66.6 million
Major Ethnic Groups: Persian, Azerbaijani
Major Religions: Islam
Government: Theocratic republic
Currency: 10 Iranian rials (IR) = 1 toman
Leading Exports: Petroleum, carpets, fruit, nuts, and hides
Major Languages: Persian and Persian dialects, Turkic and Turkic dialects

Iraq

Capital: Baghdad
Area: 168,760 sq mi; 437,072 sq km
Climate: Mostly continental; mild to cool winters with dry, extremely hot summers in central and southern areas; cool summers and cold, often snowy winters in mountains
Population: 24.7 million
Major Ethnic Groups: Arab, Kurdish
Major Religions: Islam
Government: Republic
Currency: 1 Iraqi dinar (ID) = 1,000 fils
Leading Exports: Crude oil
Major Languages: Arabic, Kurdish, Assyrian, and Armenian

Israel

Capital: Jerusalem
Area: 8,019 sq mi; 20,849 sq km
Climate: Mediterranean; cool, rainy winters and warm, dry summers; hot and dry in south and east
Population: 6 million
Major Ethnic Groups: Jewish, Arab
Major Religions: Judaism, Islam
Government: Parliamentary democracy
Currency: 1 New Israeli shekel (NIS) = 100 new agorot
Leading Exports: Machinery and equipment, cut diamonds
Major Languages: Hebrew, Arabic, and English

Jordan

Capital: Amman
Area: 34,447 sq mi; 89,213 sq km
Climate: Mostly arid, rainy season in west
Population: 5.3 million
Major Ethnic Groups: Arab
Major Religions: Islam
Government: Constitutional monarchy
Currency: 1 Jordanian dinar (JD) = 1,000 fils
Leading Exports: Phosphates, fertilizers, and potash
Major Languages: Arabic and English

Kazakstan

Capital: Astana
Area: 1,049,191 sq mi; 2,717,300 sq km
Climate: Continental; ranges from arid to semiarid; cold, snowy winters and hot summers
Population: 16.7 million
Major Ethnic Groups: Kazakh, Russian
Major Religions: Islam, Christianity
Government: Republic
Currency: 1 Kazakhstani tenge = 100 tiyn
Leading Exports: Oil, and ferrous and nonferrous metals
Major Languages: Kazakh and Russian

Kuwait

Capital: Kuwait
Area: 6,881 sq mi; 17,820 sq km
Climate: Arid; intensely hot summers and short, cool winters
Population: 2.8 million
Major Ethnic Groups: Kuwaiti, Arab
Major Religions: Islam
Government: Nominal constitutional monarchy
Currency: 1 Kuwaiti dinar (KD) = 1,000 fils
Leading Exports: Oil
Major Languages: Arabic and English

Kyrgyzstan

Capital: Bishkek
Area: 76,644 sq mi; 198,500 sq km
Climate: Varies from dry continental to polar in mountains; subtropical in southwest
Population: 4.8 million
Major Ethnic Groups: Kyrgyz and Russian
Major Religions: Islam, Christianity
Government: Republic
Currency: 1 Kyrgyzstani som (KGS) = 100 tyiyn
Leading Exports: Wool, meat, cotton, metals, and shoes
Major Languages: Kyrgyz and Russian

Lebanon

Capital: Beirut
Area: 4,016 sq mi; 10,400 sq km
Climate: Mediterranean; mild-to-cool, wet winters and hot, dry summers; snow in mountains
Population: 3.7 million
Major Ethnic Groups: Arab
Major Religions: Islam, Christianity
Government: Republic
Currency: 1 Lebanese pound = 100 piasters
Leading Exports: Agricultural products, chemicals, and textiles
Major Languages: Arabic, French, Armenian, and English

Oman

Capital: Muscat
Area: 82,034 sq mi; 212,460 sq km
Climate: Mostly arid; extremely hot and dry; less dry in mountains; hot and humid along coast
Population: 2.7 million
Major Ethnic Groups: Arab
Major Religions: Islam
Government: Monarchy
Currency: 1 Omani rial (RO) = 1,000 baiza
Leading Exports: Petroleum, re-exports, and fish
Major Languages: Arabic, English, Baluchi, Urdu, and Indian dialects

Qatar

Capital: Doha
Area: 4,247 sq mi; 11,000 sq km
Climate: Arid; extremely hot, dry; humid summers
Population: 793,000
Major Ethnic Groups: Arab, Pakistani, Indian
Major Religions: Islam
Government: Traditional monarchy
Currency: 1 Qatari riyal (QR) = 100 dirhams
Leading Exports: Petroleum products, steel, and fertilizers
Major Languages: Arabic and English

Saudi Arabia

Capital: Riyadh
Area: 757,011 sq mi; 1,960,582 sq km
Climate: Arid; harsh, with warm winters and extremely hot summers; winter frost and snow possible in central area and mountains
Population: 23.5 million
Major Ethnic Groups: Arab
Major Religions: Islam
Government: Monarchy
Currency: 1 Saudi riyal (SR) = 100 halalah
Leading Exports: Petroleum and petroleum products
Major Languages: Arabic

Syria

Capital: Damascus

Area: 71,501 sq mi; 185,180 sq km

Climate: Mostly semiarid; Mediterranean along coast, with mild, rainy winters and hot, dry summers; colder winters in mountains; colder and drier in southeast

Population: 17.2 million

Major Ethnic Groups: Arab

Major Religions: Islam

Government: Republic under military regime since March 1963

Currency: 1 Syrian pound = 100 piastres

Leading Exports: Petroleum, textiles, cotton, and fruits

Major Languages: Arabic, Kurdish, Armenian, Aramaic, Circassian, and French

Tajikistan

Capital: Dushanbe

Area: 55,253 sq mi; 143,100 sq km

Climate: Continental in lowland valleys, with cold winters and hot summers; extremely cold winters and cool summers in eastern mountains

Population: 6.7 million

Major Ethnic Groups: Tajik, Uzbek

Major Religions: Islam

Government: Republic

Currency: Tajikistani ruble (TJR) = 100 tanga

Leading Exports: Cotton, aluminum, fruits, and vegetable oil

Major Languages: Tajik and Russian

Turkey

Capital: Ankara

Area: 301,394 sq mi; 780,580 sq km

Climate: Continental in central region, with cold winters and hot summers; harsher winters in mountains; mild, wet winters near coast

Population: 67.3 million

Major Ethnic Groups: Turkish, Kurdish

Major Religions: Islam

Government: Republican parliamentary democracy

Currency: Turkish lira (TL) = 100 kurus

Leading Exports: Manufactured products and foodstuffs

Major Languages: Turkish, Kurdish, and Arabic

Turkmenistan

Capital: Ashgabat

Area: 188,463 sq mi; 488,100 sq km

Climate: Dry continental; cold winters, very hot summers

Population: 4.7 million

Major Ethnic Groups: Turkmen

Major Religions: Islam

Government: Republic

Currency: 1 Turkmenmanat (TMM) = 100 tenesi

Leading Exports: Natural gas, cotton, and petroleum products

Major Languages: Turkmen, Russian, Uzbek, and various languages

United Arab Emirates

Capital: Abu Dhabi

Area: 32,000 sq mi; 82,880 sq km

Climate: Arid; mild winters, extremely hot summers; cooler in mountains

Population: 2.4 million

Major Ethnic Groups: South Asian, Emiri (native Arab peoples)

Major Religions: Islam

Government: Federation with specified powers delegated to the UAE federal governments and other powers reserved to member emirates

Currency: 1 Emirian dirham (Dh) = 100 fils

Leading Exports: Crude oil, natural gas, re-exports, and dried fish

Major Languages: Arabic, Persian, English, Hindi, and Urdu

Uzbekistan

Capital: Tashkent

Area: 172,748 sq mi; 447,400 sq km

Climate: Harsh continental; mild winters and long hot summers; arid in north central desert region; semiarid in east

Population: 25.5 million

Major Ethnic Groups: Uzbek

Major Religions: Islam

Government: Republic; effectively authoritarian presidential rule, with little power outside the executive branch; executive power concentrated in the presidency

Currency: Uzbekistani som (UKS)

Leading Exports: Cotton, gold, natural gas, and minerals

Major Languages: Uzbek, Russian, Tajik, various languages

Yemen

Capital: Sanaa

Area: 203,857 sq mi; 527,970 sq km

Climate: Mostly arid; hot and humid along coast; milder in highlands; extraordinarily hot, dry, harsh in east

Population: 18.7 million

Major Ethnic Groups: Arab

Major Religions: Islam

Government: Republic

Currency: Yemeni rial (YER) = 100 fils

Leading Exports: Crude oil, cotton, coffee

Major Languages: Arabic

Antarctica

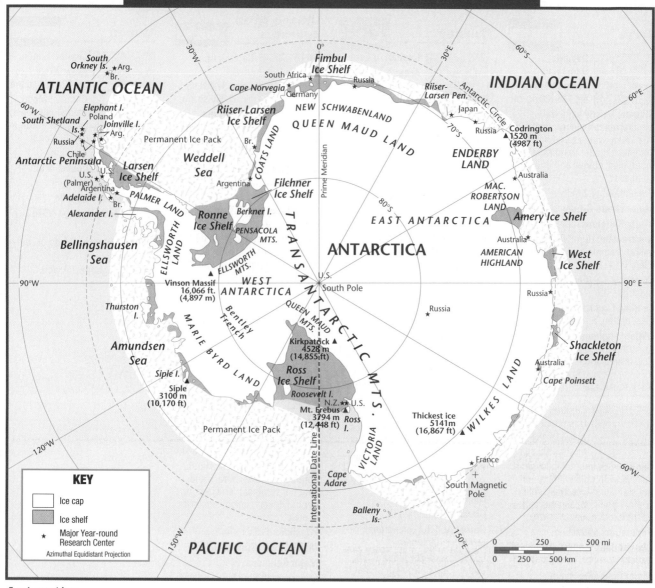

Antarctica

Capital: None

Area: 5,400,000 sq mi; 14,000,000 sq km

Climate: Ice Cap; dry, windy, extremely cold; coldest in the interior, where winter low temperature falls below −110°F (-80°C); warmest along coast of Antarctic Peninsula, where summer high temperature rises just above freezing

Population: (Staff of research stations) About 4,115 people in summer, about 1,046 in winter

Major Ethnic Groups: None

Major Religions: None

Government: Antarctic Treaty

Currency: None

Leading Exports: None

Major Languages: None

Australia and New Zealand: Political

KEY

— National boundary
— Provincial boundary
⊛ National capital
⊘ Provincial capital
• Other city

Mercator Projection

Australia

Capital: Canberra
Area: 2,968,010 sq mi; 7,686,850 sq km
Climate: Mostly arid to semiarid; tropical in north, with warm, dry winters and hot, wet summers; cool winters and warm summers in south and east
Population: 19.6 million
Major Ethnic Groups: European (British, Irish ancestry)
Major Religions: Christianity
Government: Democratic, federal-state system recognizing the British Monarch as Soverign
Currency: 1 Australian dollar ($A) = 100 cents
Leading Exports: Coal, gold, meat, wool, and alumina
Major Languages: English and various languages

New Zealand

Capital: Wellington
Area: 103,741 sq mi; 268,680 sq km
Climate: mostly temperate; generally mild all year, with moderate to abundant rainfall; warmest in far north; coldest in mountains of southwest
Population: 3.8 million
Major Ethnic Groups: European (British ancestry), Maori
Major Religions: Christianity
Government: Parliamentary democracy
Currency: 1 New Zealand dollar (NZ$) = 100 cents
Leading Exports: Wool, lamb, muton, beef, fish, and cheese
Major Languages: English and Maori

KEY

— National boundary

⊛ National capital

• Other city

Mercator Projection

140°E   160°E   Midway Is. (U.S.)   160°W   140°W

Tropic of Cancer

Hawaiian Is.

20°N

NORTHERN MARIANA IS. (U.S.)   Wake Island (U.S.)   HAWAII (U.S.)

GUAM (U.S.)   MARSHALL ISLANDS   PACIFIC   OCEAN

Koror   ⊛ Majuro

PALAU   ⊛ Palikir

FEDERATED STATES OF MICRONESIA   Line Islands

Tarawa ⊛   Marquesas Is.

Wewak   ⊛ Yaren District   KIRIBATI   0°

INDONESIA   NAURU

PAPUA NEW GUINEA   SOLOMON IS. Funafuti ⊛   TOKELAU (N.Z.)

⊛ Port Moresby   Honiara ⊛   TUVALU   SAMOA   Society Is.   Tuamotu Archipelago

WALLIS AND FUTUNA (FR.)   Apia ⊛   AMERICAN SAMOA (U.S.)   Tahiti

VANUATU   ⊛ Port-Vila   TONGA   NIUE (N.Z.)   COOK ISLANDS (N.Z.)

20°S   NEW CALEDONIA (FR.)   Suva ⊛ FIJI   Nuku'alofa   FRENCH POLYNESIA (FR.)   20°S

AUSTRALIA   PITCAIRN ISLAND (U.K.)   Easter Island (Chile)

Tropic of Capricorn

Tasman Sea

N W E S

40°S   NEW ZEALAND   40°S

0   750   1,500 mi
0   750   1,500 km

140°E   160°E   180°   160°W   140°W

Federated States of Micronesia

Capital: Palikir

Area: 271 sq mi; 702 sq km

Climate: Tropical; hot and humid, with heavy rainfall all year

Population: 136,000

Major Ethnic Groups: Micronesian

Major Religions: Christianity

Government: Constitutional government in free Association with the US; the Compact of Free Association entered into force November 3, 1986

Currency: 1 United States dollar (US$) = 100 cents

Leading Exports: Fish, copra, bananas, and black pepper

Major Languages: English, Turkese, Pohnpeian, Yapese, and Kosrean

Fiji

Capital: Suva

Area: 7,054 sq mi; 18,270 sq km

Climate: Tropical; hottest, wettest in summer

Population: 856,000

Major Ethnic Groups: Fijian, Indian

Major Religions: Christianity, Hinduism

Government: Republic

Currency: 1 Fijian dollar (F$) = 100 cents

Leading Exports: Sugar, clothing, gold, processed fish, and lumber

Major Languages: English, Fijian, and Hindustani

Kiribati

Capital: Tarawa

Area: 277 sq mi; 717 sq km

Climate: Tropical; hot, humid (moderated by trade winds)

Population: 96,000

Major Ethnic Groups: Micronesian

Major Religions: Christianity

Government: Republic

Currency: 1 Australian dollar ($A) = 100 cents

Leading Exports: Copra, seaweed, and fish

Major Languages: English and Gilbertese

Marshall Islands

Capital: Majuro

Area: 70 sq mi; 181.3 sq km

Climate: Tropical; hot, humid; rainy season

Population: 73,000

Major Ethnic Groups: Micronesian

Major Religions: Christianity

Government: Constitutional government in free Association with the US; the Compact of Free Association entered into force October 21, 1986

Currency: 1 United States dollar (US$) = 100 cents

Leading Exports: Coconut oil, fish, live animals, and trichus shells

Major Languages: English, Marshallese dialects, and Japanese

Nauru

Capital: Government offices in Yaren District

Area: 8 sq mi; 21 sq km

Climate: Tropical; hot, humid; rainy season

Population: 12,000

Major Ethnic Groups: Nauruan, other Pacific Islander

Major Religions: Christianity

Government: Republic

Currency: 1 Australian dollar ($A) = 100 cents

Leading Exports: Phosphates

Major Languages: Nauruan and English

Palau

Capital: Koror – note: a new capital is being built about 20 km northeast of Koror

Area: 177 sq mi; 458 sq km

Climate: Tropical; hot, humid; rainy season

Population: 19,000

Major Ethnic Groups: Palauan (mix of Polynesian, Malayan, and Melanesian)

Major Religions: Christianity, Modekngei (traditional Palauan religion)

Government: Constitutional government in free Association with the US; the Compact of Free Association entered into force October 1, 1994

Currency: 1 United States dollar (US$) = 100 cents

Leading Exports: Trochus, tuna, copra, and handicrafts

Major Languages: English (official), Sonsorolese, Angaur, Japanese, Tobi, and Palauan

Papua New Guinea

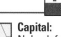

Capital: Port Moresby

Area: 178,704 sq mi; 462,840 sq km

Climate: Tropical; hot and humid in lowlands; cooler in mountains; heavy rain in most areas all year

Population: 5.2 million

Major Ethnic Groups: Melanesian, Papuan

Major Religions: Christianity, mix of Christian and traditional beliefs

Government: Parliamentary democracy

Currency: 1 kina (K) = 100 toea

Leading Exports: Gold, copper ore, oil, logs, and palm oil

Major Languages: English, pidgin English, and Motu

Samoa

Capital: Apia

Area: 1,104 sq mi; 2,860 sq km

Climate: Tropical; hot, humid; rainy season

Population: 179,000

Major Ethnic Groups: Samoan

Major Religions: Christianity

Government: Constitutional monarchy under native chief

Currency: 1 tala (WS$) = 100 sene

Leading Exports: Coconut oil and cream, taro, copra, and cocoa

Major Languages: Samoan and English

Solomon Islands

Capital: Honiara

Area: 10,985 sq mi; 28,450 sq km

Climate: Tropical; hot, humid

Population: 495,000

Major Ethnic Groups: Melanesian

Major Religions: Christianity

Government: Parliamentary democracy

Currency: 1 Solomon Islands dollar (SI$) = 100 cents

Leading Exports: Fish, timber, palm oil, cocoa, and copra

Major Languages: Melanesian pidgin and English

Tonga

Capital: Nukualofa

Area: 289 sq mi; 748 sq km

Climate: Tropical; (modified by trade winds); very humid; warm season and cool season

Population: 106,000

Major Ethnic Groups: Polynesian

Major Religions: Christianity

Government: Hereditary constitutional monarchy

Currency: 1 pa'anga (T$) = 100 seniti

Leading Exports: Squash, vanilla, fish, root crops, and coconut oil

Major Languages: Tongan and English

Tuvalu

Capital: Fongafale, on Funafuti atoll

Area: 10 sq mi; 26 sq km

Climate: Tropical; warm, humid all year (moderated by trade winds); heavy summer rains

Population: 11,000

Major Ethnic Groups: Polynesian

Major Religions: Christianity

Government: Constitutional monarchy with a parliamentary democracy, began debating republic status in 1992

Currency: 1 Tuvaluan dollar ($T) or 1 Australian dollar ($A) = 100 cents

Leading Exports: Copra

Major Languages: Tuvaluan and English

Vanuatu

Capital: Port-Vila

Area: 5,699 sq mi; 14,760 sq km

Climate: Tropical; hot, humid (moderated by winter trade winds); wettest in northern islands

Population: 196,000

Major Ethnic Groups: Melanesian

Major Religions: Christianity

Government: Republic

Currency: 1 vatu (VT) = 100 centimes

Leading Exports: Copra, beef, cocoa, timber, and coffee

Major Languages: English, French, pidgin, and Bislama

Glossary of Basic Geographic Terms

basin
a depression in the surface of the land; some basins are filled with water

bay
a part of a sea or lake that extends into the land

butte
a small raised area of land with steep sides

▲ butte

canyon
a deep, narrow valley with steep sides; often has a stream flowing through it

cataract
a large waterfall; any strong flood or rush of water

◀ cataract

delta
a triangular-shaped plain at the mouth of a river, formed when sediment is deposited by flowing water

flood plain
a broad plain on either side of a river, formed when sediment settles on the riverbanks

glacier
a huge, slow-moving mass of snow and ice

hill
an area that rises above surrounding land and has a rounded top; lower and usually less steep than a mountain

island
an area of land completely surrounded by water

isthmus
a narrow strip of land that connects two larger areas of land

mesa
a high, flat-topped landform with cliff-like sides; larger than a butte

mountain
an area that rises steeply at least 2,000 feet (610 m) above surrounding land; usually wide at the bottom and rising to a narrow peak or ridge

▶ glacier

◀ delta

mountain pass
a gap between mountains

peninsula
an area of land almost completely surrounded by water and connected to the mainland by an isthmus

plain
a large area of flat or gently rolling land

plateau
a large, flat area that rises above the surrounding land; at least one side has a steep slope

river mouth
the point where a river enters a lake or sea

strait
a narrow stretch of water that connects two larger bodies of water

tributary
a river or stream that flows into a larger river

volcano
an opening in the Earth's surface through which molten rock, ashes, and gasses from the Earth's interior escape

▶ volcano

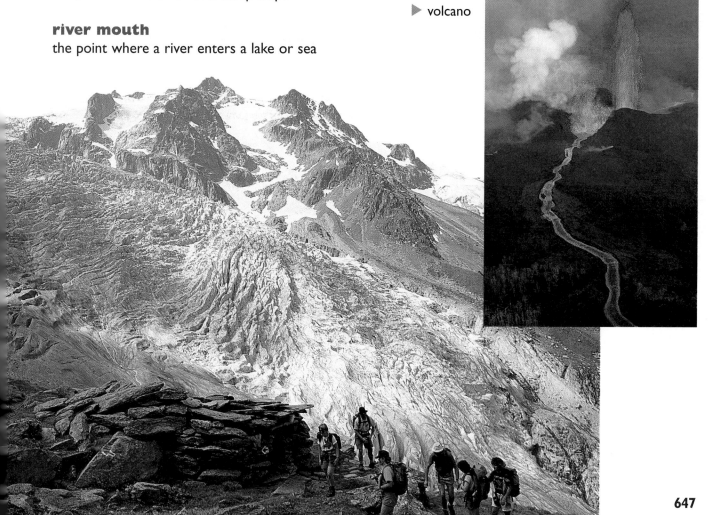

Gazetteer

A

Abuja (9°N, 7°E) the federal capital of Nigeria, p. 408

Aix-en-Provence (43.32°N, 5.26°E) a city in the south of France, p. 319

Aksum an ancient city in northern Ethiopia, a powerful kingdom and trade center from about A.D. 200 to A.D. 600, p. 374

Alice Springs (23°S, 133°E) a town in Northern Territory, Australia, p. 571

Amazonian rain forest a large tropical rain forest occupying the drainage basin of the Amazon River in northern South America and covering an area of 2,700,000 square miles, p. 175

Amsterdam (52.22°N, 4.53°E) a major financial center of the Netherlands, p. 314

Andes Mountains (13°S, 75°W) a mountain system extending along the western coast of South America, pp. 175, 206

Angkor Wat (13°N, 103°E) an archaeological site in present-day Angkor, in northwest Cambodia; the world's largest religious temple complex, p. 469

Antarctic Circle (66°S) line of latitude around the Earth near the South Pole, p. 14

Appalachian Mountains a mountain system in eastern North America, p. 74

Arctic Circle (66°N) line of latitude around the Earth near the North Pole, p. 14

Atacama Desert (23.5°S, 69°W) a desert in Chile, South America; the driest place on the Earth, p. 175

Athens (38°N, 23.38°E) the capital city of modern Greece; the world's most powerful cultural center in the 400s B.C., p. 275

Atlanta (33°N, 84°W) the capital of the state of Georgia, p. 125

B

Balkans a region located south of the Danube River made up of several countries, including the former Yugoslavia, that gets its name from the Turkish word for "mountain," p. 330

Barcelona (41.25°N, 2.08°E) a city and seaport in northeastern Spain, p. 265

Berlin (51.31°N, 13.28°E) the capital city of Germany; divided into East Berlin and West Berlin between 1949 and 1989, pp. 291, 315

Bethlehem (31.43°N, 35.12°E) a town outside of Jerusalem considered to be holy by Christians as the town where Jesus was born, p. 495

Bosnia a Balkan country in which Croatian, Serbian, and Bosnian are spoken, and Muslim, Orthodox, and Roman Catholic faiths are practiced, p. 331

Boston (42°N, 71°W) the capital of the state of Massachusetts, p. 123

Brasilia (15.49°S, 47.39°W) the capital city of Brazil, p. 236

Brazil (9°S, 53°W) the largest country in South America, p. 177

Brunei a small kingdom on the northwestern coast of the island of Borneo with large deposits of oil, p. 489

Brussels (50°N, 4.22°E) capital of Belgium, p. 313

Buenos Aires (34.35°S, 58.22°W), capital of Argentina, p. 241

C

Cairo (30°N, 31°E) the capital of Egypt and most populous city in Africa, p. 403

Canal Zone a 10-mile strip of land along the Panama Canal, stretching from the Atlantic Ocean to the Pacific Ocean, p. 224

Cape Town (33°S, 18°E) the legislative capital of the Republic of South Africa; the capital of Cape Province, p. 431

Caracas (10.3°N, 66.58°W) the capital city of Venezuela, p. 240

Caribbean (14.3°N, 75.3°W) a part of the southern Atlantic Ocean, p. 169

Central America (10.45°N, 87.15°W) the part of Latin America that includes the seven republics of Guatemala, Honduras, El Salvador, Nicaragua, Costa Rica, Panama, and Belize, p. 171

Chicago (41°N, 87°W) a major city in the state of Illinois, on Lake Michigan, p. 132

Colombia (3.3°N, 72.3°W) a country in South America, p. 177

Congo River a river in Central Africa that flows into the Atlantic Ocean, p. 359

Copán (14.5°N, 89.1°W) a ruined ancient Mayan city in western Honduras, p. 183

Cuba (22°N, 79°W) the largest island country in the Caribbean Sea, p. 44, 204

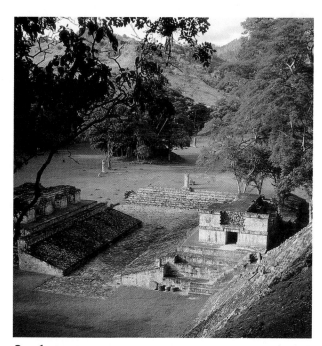

Copán

Cuzco (13.36°S, 71.52°W) a city in Peru; capital of the Incan empire, p. 184

Czech Republic (50°N, 15°E) a country in Eastern Europe, p. 297

D

Death Valley (36°N, 117°W) the hottest, driest region of North America, located in southeastern California, p. 74

Detroit (42°N, 83°W) a city in the state of Michigan, p. 132

E

Egypt (26°S, 27°E) a country in North Africa, officially Arab Republic of Egypt, p. 372

Equator an imaginary line that circles the globe at its widest point (halfway between the North and South poles), dividing the Earth into two halves called hemispheres; used as a reference point from which north and south latitudes are measured, p. 13

Euphrates River a river that flows south from Turkey through Syria and Iraq; the ancient civilizations of Babylon and Ur were situated near its banks, p. 453

Eurasia the landmass that includes the European and Asian continents, p. 261

Europe (50°N, 15°E) the world's second-smallest continent; a peninsula of the Eurasian landmass bounded by the Arctic Ocean, the Atlantic Ocean, the Mediterranean Sea, and Asia; p. 261

F

Fiji a Pacific island nation popular with tourists, p. 575

Flanders region in north Belgium, p. 313

Fraser River a major river of western North America along the border between British Columbia and Alberta, p. 151

Himalaya Mountains

G

Ganges River a river in India and Bangladesh flowing from the Himalaya Mountains to the Bay of Bengal; considered by Hindus to be the most holy river in India, p. 453

Ghana (8°N, 2°W) a country in West Africa, officially Republic of Ghana, p. 375

Grand Coulee Dam (47°N, 119°W) a dam on the Columbia River in the state of Washington, p. 81

Great Dividing Range a series of plateaus and mountain ranges in eastern Australia, p. 555

Great Lakes a group of five large lakes in central North America: Lakes Superior, Michigan, Huron, Erie, and Ontario, p. 75

Great Rift Valley the major branch of the East African Rift System, p. 359

Greece an important civilization in the classical era; currently a modern country in Europe on the Mediterranean Sea, p. 275

Guatemala (15.45°N, 91.45°W) a country in Central America, p. 217

H

Himalaya Mountains the Central Asian mountain range extending along the India-Tibet border, through Pakistan, Nepal, and Bhutan, and containing the world's highest peaks, p. 451

Ho Chi Minh City (10°N, 106°E) the largest city in Vietnam, named for the President of North Vietnam; formerly Saigon, p. 514

Honduras a rural country in Central America, p. 200

Huang He the second-longest river in China; it flows across northern China to the Yellow Sea; also known as the Yellow River, p. 452

I

Iceland a geographically isolated island nation near the Arctic Circle, p. 266

Indus River a river rising in Tibet and flowing through India and Pakistan into the Arabian Sea, p. 453

Irkutsk (ihr KOOTSK) (52.16°N, 104°E) a city in east-central Russia, on the Central Siberian Plateau, p. 265

J

Jakarta (6°S, 106°E) the capital and largest city of the Republic of Indonesia, p. 46

Jamaica (17.45°N, 78°W) a tropical island country in the Caribbean Sea; pp. 177, 203

Jamestown the first permanent British settlement in North America, located in present-day Virginia; now a site of historic preservation, p. 88

Jerusalem (31.47°N, 35°E) the capital of Israel; a holy city for Christians, Jews, and Muslims, p. 495

K

Kano (12°N, 8°E) a city and the capital of Kano state in northern Nigeria; a historic kingdom in northern Nigeria, p. 409

Kashmir (39°N, 75°E) a disputed territory in northwest India, parts of which have been claimed by India, Pakistan, and China since 1947, p. 519

Kemerovo (55.31°N, 86.05°E) a city in south-central Russia, p. 338

Kilwa late tenth-century Islamic city-state located on an island off the coast of present-day Tanzania, p. 376

Kosovo the site of fighting in 1999 when Serbs fought against Albanians seeking independence, p. 333

L

Lagos (6°N, 3°E) a city and chief Atlantic port of Nigeria; a state in Nigeria, p. 408

Locorotondo (40.45°N, 17.20°E) a town located in southern Italy, p. 322

London (51.3°N, .07°W) the capital city of the United Kingdom, p. 291

M

Madrid (40.26°N, 3.42°W) the capital city of Spain, p. 291

Mali (15°N, 0.15°W) an early African empire; a present-day country in West Africa, officially Republic of Mali, p. 375

Mecca (21°N, 39°E) a city in western Saudi Arabia; birthplace of the prophet Muhammad and most holy city for Islamic people, pp. 496, 527

Mecca

Melanesia (13°S, 164°E) the most populous of the three groups of Pacific islands; includes Fiji, Papua New Guinea, and others, p. 559

Mesopotamia a historic region in western Asia between the Tigris and Euphrates rivers; one of the cradles of civilization, p. 476

Mexico (23.45°N, 104°W) a country in North America, p. 170

Mexico City (19.28°N, 99.09°W) the capital of and largest city in Mexico; one of the largest urban areas in the world, pp. 198, 213

Micronesia one of the three groups of Pacific islands; includes Guam, the Marshall Islands, and others, p. 559

Milan (45.27°N, 9.17°E) a city in northern Italy known for its fashion industry, p. 322

Mississippi River a large river in the central United States flowing south from Minnesota to the Gulf of Mexico, p. 76

Montreal (45°N, 73°W) the largest city in the province of Quebec, Canada, p. 142

Moscow (55.45°N, 37.37°E) the capital city of modern Russia; one of the largest cities in the world; the home of the czars, p. 339

Mount Kenya (0.10°S, 37°E) a volcano in central Kenya, p. 423

N

Nairobi (1°S, 36°E) the capital of Kenya, p. 425

Negev Desert a triangular, arid region in southwest Israel, touching the Gulf of Aquaba, p. 531

New York City (40°N, 73°W) a large city and port at the mouth of the Hudson River in the state of New York, p. 124

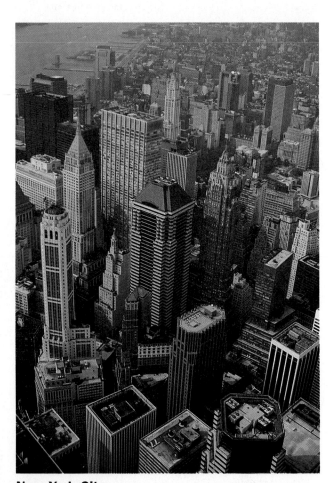

New York City

Nicaragua the largest country in Central America in area, but not the largest in population, p. 219

Niger River the river in West Africa that flows from Guinea into the Gulf of Guinea, p. 359

Nile River the longest river in the world, flows through northeastern Africa into the Mediterranean Sea, p. 359

Northern Ireland the largely Protestant region of Ireland governed by Great Britain, p. 319

North Sea (56.09°N, 3.16°E) an arm of the Atlantic Ocean between Great Britain and the European mainland, p. 269

Norway country in northwestern Europe occupying the western part of the Scandinavian peninsula, pp. 265–266

Nubia an ancient region in North Africa, p. 372

Nunavut a Canadian territory with its own government, p. 114

O

Ontario (50°N, 88°W) the second-largest province in Canada, p. 99

Ottawa (45.24°N, 75.43°W) national capital of Canada, p. 147

Outback in general, a remote area with few people; specifically, the arid inland region of Australia, p. 556

P

Pacific Northwest the region in the northwestern United States that includes Oregon, Washington, and part of Idaho, p. 135

Pacific Rim the countries bordering on the Pacific Ocean, p. 152

Palestine (31°N, 35°E) a historical region at the east end of the Mediterranean Sea, now divided between Israel and Jordan, pp. 276, 477

Pampas [PAHM puhs] a vast, flat grassland similar to the Great Plains in the United States, p. 241

Panama (9°N, 80°W) a country in Central America, p. 221

Panama Canal (9.2°N, 79.55°W) an important shipping canal across the Isthmus of Panama, linking the Caribbean Sea (and the Atlantic Ocean) to the Pacific Ocean, p. 221

Pangaea according to scientific theory, a single landmass that broke apart to form today's separate continents; thought to have existed about 180 million years ago, p. 28

Papua New Guinea (7°S, 142°E) an island country in the southwest Pacific; the eastern half of New Guinea, officially the Independent State of Papua New Guinea, p. 559

Papua New Guinea

Paris (48.51°N, 2.2°E) the capital city of France, p. 291

Patagonia (46.45°S, 69.3°W) desert in southern Argentina; the largest desert in the Americas, p. 174

Pennsylvania Colony a colony in America founded in 1680 by William Penn, who purchased land from the Native Americans, p. 88

Philadelphia (40°N, 75°W) a city and port in Pennsylvania on the Delaware River, p. 123

Polynesia largest of the three groups of Pacific islands, includes New Zealand, Hawaii, Easter, and Tahiti islands, p. 559

Portland (45°N, 122°W) the largest city in the state of Oregon, p. 136

Q

Quebec (51°N, 70°W) a province in southeastern Canada, p. 99

Quebec City (46°N, 71°W) the capital city of the province of Quebec, Canada, p. 141

R

Republic of South Africa (28°S, 24°E) southernmost country in Africa, p. 394

Rio de Janeiro (22.5°S, 43.2°W) a major city in Brazil, p. 236

Riyadh (24°N, 46°E) the capital of Saudi Arabia, p. 528

Rocky Mountains the major mountain range in western North America, extending south from Alberta, Canada, through the western United States to Mexico, p. 74

Rome (41.52°N, 12.37°E) the capital of modern Italy; one of the world's greatest ancient empires (753 B.C.–A.D. 476), p. 276

Ruhr Valley (51.18°N, 8.17°E) an area along a river in the major industrial region in western Germany, p. 269

Russia (61°N, 60°E) a country in northern Eurasia, p. 261

S

St. Lawrence Lowlands a major agricultural region in eastern Canada, p. 82

St. Lawrence River a river in eastern North America; the third-longest river in Canada, p. 76

St. Louis (38°N, 90°W) a major city in Missouri, on the Mississippi River, p. 132

St. Petersburg (59.57°N, 30.2°E) the second-largest city in Russia (previous names Petrograd, Leningrad), located on the Baltic Sea; founded by Peter the Great, p. 301

Sahara largest desert in the world, covers almost all of North Africa, p. 357

São Paulo (23°S, 46°W) the largest city in Brazil, p. 46

San Jose (37°N, 121°W) a city in western California, p. 136

Santiago (33.26°S, 70.4°W) the capital city of Chile, p. 238

Sarajevo (43.5°N, 18.26°E) the capital city of Bosnia-Herzegovina, p. 333

Saskatchewan (50.12°N, 100.4°W) province in central Canada, p. 152

Shaba [SHAB uh] a southern province in Zaire, p. 427

Siberia [Sy BIHR ee uh] (57°N, 97°E) a resource-rich region of Russia, extending east across northern Asia from the Ural Mountains to the Pacific Coast, p. 261

Sierra Nevada a mountain range in California in the western United States, p. 135

Silesia [sy LEE shuh] (50.58°N, 16.53°E) a historic region located in today's southwest Poland, p. 269

Slovakia (48.5°N, 20°E) a country in Eastern Europe, pp. 296, 335

Songhai an empire and trading state in West Africa founded in the 1400s, p. 375

South America (15°S, 60°W) the world's fourth-largest continent, bounded by the Caribbean Sea, the Atlantic Ocean, and the Pacific Ocean, and linked to North America by the Isthmus of Panama, p. 171

Stockholm (59.20°N, 18.03°E) capital of Sweden, p. 291

Sydney (33°S, 151°E) the capital of New South Wales, on the southeastern coast of Australia, p. 569

T

Tahiti a popular tourist destination in the Pacific islands, p. 575

Taiwan (23°N, 122°E) a large island country off the southeast coast of mainland China, formerly Formosa; since 1949, the Nationalist Republic of China, p. 504

Tenochtitlán Aztec capital city covering more than five square miles on a series of islands in Lake Texcoco; Spanish conquerors destroyed the city and built modern Mexico City atop its ruins, p. 184

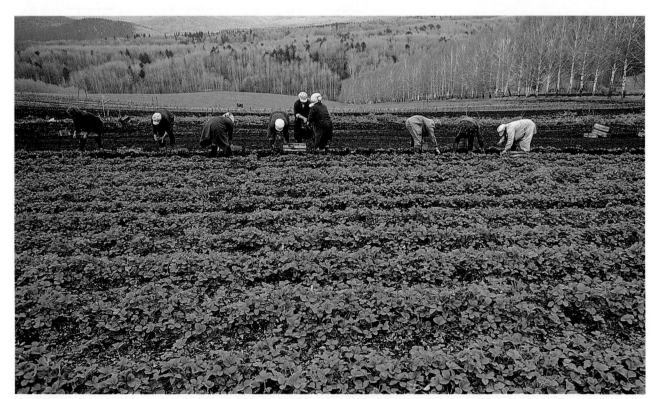

Siberia

Tigris River a river that flows through Turkey, Iraq, and Iran to the Persian Gulf; the ancient civilizations of Nineveh and Ur were situated near its banks, p. 453

Tombouctou (16°N, 3°W) city in Mali near the Niger River; in the past an important center of Islamic education and a trans-Saharan caravan stop (also spelled Timbuktu), p. 375

Toronto (43.39°N, 79.23°W) capital of Ontario, p. 147

Trinidad and Tobago (11°N, 61°W) republic of the West Indies, on the two islands called Trinidad and Tobago, p. 205

Tropic of Cancer (23.5°N) the northern boundary of the tropics, or the band of Earth that receives the most direct light and heat energy from the sun; such a region lies on both sides of the Equator; p. 13

Tropic of Capricorn (23.5°S) the southern boundary of the tropics; see above, p. 13

U

Ukraine [yoo KRAYN] an independent country in Eastern Europe, formerly part of the Soviet Union, p. 269

Ural [YOOR uhl] **Mountains** (56.28°N, 58.13°E) a mountain system in northern Eurasia forming part of the border between Europe and Asia, p. 261

V

Valley of Mexico the area in Mexico where Lake Texcoco, Tenochtitlán, and modern Mexico City are located, p. 184

Vancouver (49°N, 123°W) a city in southwestern British Columbia, Canada, p. 149

Vatican an independent city-state located in Italy that is the world headquarters of the Roman Catholic Church, p. 321

Venezuela (8°N, 65°W) a country in South America, p. 177

Vatican

W

Wallonia region in southern Belgium, p. 313

Washington, D.C. (38°N, 77°W) the capital city of the United States, located between Maryland and Virginia on the Potomac River, pp. 128

Y

Yangzi the longest river in Asia, flowing through China to the East China Sea, p. 452

Z

Zambezi River a river in Central and Southern Africa that flows into the Indian Ocean, p. 360

Glossary

A

abolitionist a person who believed that enslaving people was wrong and who wanted to end the practice, p. 92

alliance a mutual agreement between countries to protect and defend each other, p. 283

alluvial relating to the fertile topsoil left by rivers after a flood, p. 80

apartheid [uh PAHR tayt] the South African system in which racial groups were separated and racial discrimination was legal, p. 433

aquaculture a cultivation of the sea; common crops are shrimp and oysters, p. 459

aqueduct a pipe or channel used to carry water from a distant source to dry areas, p. 185

arable land land that can produce crops, p. 456

aristocrats people who are in the minority but are considered a privileged, upper class, p. 421

artesian well a deep well drilled into the Earth to tap groundwater in porous rock, p. 572

atmosphere the multilayered band of gases that surrounds the Earth, p. 27

atoll [A tawl] a group of small coral islands in the shape of a ring that encloses a lagoon, p. 554

authoritarian controlled by one person or a small group, p. 429

axis an imaginary line around which a planet turns; the Earth turns around an axis which runs between its North and South poles, p.12

B

bazaar a traditional open-air market with rows of shops or stalls, p. 403

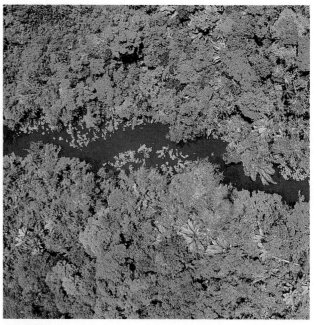
canopy

bilingual speaking two languages; having two official languages, p. 100

birthrate the number of live births each year per 1,000 people, p. 43

bolas [BOH lahs] a set of leather cords and three iron balls or stones thrown at the legs of animals to capture them, p. 244

boom a period of increased prosperity during which more of a product is produced and sold, p. 240

boomtown a settlement that springs up quickly, often to serve the needs of miners, p. 151

boycott a refusal to buy or use goods and services, pp. 89, 379

C

campesinos [kahm peh SEE nohs] landless peasants and poor farmers, pp. 198, 233

canopy a dense mass of leaves forming the top layer of a forest, p. 234

capital money used to expand a business, p. 131

capitalism an economic system in which people and privately owned companies own both basic and nonbasic businesses and industries, p. 53

cardinal direction one of the four compass points: north, south, east, and west, p. 21

Carnival an annual celebration in Latin America with music, dances, and parades, p. 205

casbah an old, crowded section of a North African city, p. 407

cash crop a crop raised to be sold for money on the world market, pp. 365, 459

caste a class of people in India, p. 473

cataract a rock-filled rapid, p. 359

caudillo [kow DEE yoh] a military officer who rules strictly, p. 191

census a count of the people in a country, p. 410

city-state a loose organization of people that has its own government and controls much of the surrounding land, p. 376

civilization a society with cities, a central government, social classes, and, usually, writing, art, and architecture, p. 372, 465

civil rights movement a large group of people who worked together in the United States beginning in the 1960s to end the segregation of African Americans and support equal rights for all minorities, p. 97

Civil War the war between the northern and southern states in the United States, which began in 1861 and ended in 1865, p. 93

clan a group of families who claim a common ancestor, pp. 389, 466

climate the weather patterns that an area typically experiences over a long period of time, p. 34

Cold War a period of great tension between the United States and the former Soviet Union, which lasted for more than 40 years after World War II, pp. 97, 286

colonize to settle an area and take over or create a government, p. 378

colony a territory ruled by another nation, usually one far away, p. 474

command economy an economy in which economic decisions are made by the government, p. 53

commonwealth a self-governing political unit with strong ties to a particular country, p. 232

commune a community in which land is held in common and where members live and work together, p. 484

Communism a theory of government in which property such as farms and factories is owned by the government for the benefit of all citizens; a political system in which the central government controls all aspects of citizens' lives, pp. 97, 285

commute to travel regularly to and from a place, particularly to and from a job, p. 121

compass rose a map feature that usually shows the four cardinal directions, p. 21

compass rose

Confederacy the Confederate States of America; a group of Southern states that seceded from the United States following Abraham Lincoln's 1860 election, p. 93

coniferous [koh NIF ur us] pertaining to cone-bearing trees, p. 267

conquistador [kon KEES ta dor] 16th-century conquerors working for the Spanish government who were in charge of gaining land and wealth in the Americas, p. 187

constitution a statement of a country's basic laws and values, pp. 55, 232

Constitution the document written in 1787 and approved in 1789 that established three branches of American government and protected the rights of individual citizens, p. 89

constitutional monarchy a government in which a king or queen is the head of state but has limited powers; for example, the present government of Great Britain, p. 308

consumer a person who buys goods and services, p. 52

Continental Divide the boundary that separates rivers flowing toward opposite sides of a continent; in North America, in the Rocky Mountains, p. 74

copra dried coconut meat used in margarine, cooking oils, and luxury soaps, p. 574

coral a rock-like substance formed from the skeletons of tiny sea animals, pp. 171, 554

corporate farm a large farm run by a corporation; may consist of many smaller farms once owned by families, p. 131

cosmopolitan characterized by ethnic or cultural diversity and sophistication, p. 241

coup [koo] the takeover of a government, often done by military force, p. 414

Creole a person, often of European and African descent, born in the Caribbean or other parts of the Americas, whose culture has strong French and African influence; a dialect spoken by Creoles, p. 219

coral

criollo [kree OH yoh] a person born of Spanish parents born outside Spain; often among the best-educated and wealthiest people in the Spanish colonies, p. 190

cultural diffusion a spreading of ideas and practices from one culture to another, pp. 387, 467

cultural diversity a wide variety of cultures, pp. 105, 388

cultural exchange a process in which different cultures share ideas and ways of doing things, p. 105

cultural landscape a landscape that has been changed by human beings and that reflects their culture, p. 48

cultural trait a behavioral characteristic of a people, such as a language, skill, or custom, passed from one generation to another, p. 48

culture language, religious beliefs, values, customs, and other ways of life shared by a group of people, p. 48, 385

culture region an area in which people share the same cultural traits, p. 48

czar [ZAR] title of Russian emperors before the formation of the Soviet Union, p. 285

D

death rate the number of deaths each year per 1,000 people, p. 43

deciduous [duh SID joo us] pertaining to trees that lose their leaves, p. 267

Declaration of Independence the document written by Thomas Jefferson in 1776 that explained American colonists' reasons for rejecting British rule; representatives from each of the thirteen colonies showed their for independence by signing the document, p. 89

degree a unit of measure used to determine absolute location; on globes and maps, latitude and longitude ar measured in degrees, p. 16

demilitarized zone a border area between countries in which no weapons are allowed; in the Koreas, it is the zone between South and North Korea, p. 509

democracy [dih MAHK ruh see] government of the people, by the people, pp. 55, 275

demographer a scientist who studies human populations, including their size; growth; density; distribution; and rates of births, marriages, and deaths, p. 41

dialect a version of a language found only in certain regions, p. 485

dictator a ruler of a country who has complete power, pp. 231, 286

dictatorship a government in which one person, a dictator, governs, p. 56

direct democracy a system of government in which the people participate directly in decision-making, p. 55

discriminate to treat people unfairly based on race, religion, or gender, p. 433

discrimination unfair treatment, often based on race or gender, p. 508

distortion a misrepresentation of the true shape; each map projection used by a cartographer produces some distortion, p. 20

diversify to add variety; to expand, pp. 178, 511

diversity variety, p. 201

domesticate to adapt wild plants and animals for human use, p. 372

dominion a self-governing area subject to Great Britain, for example, Canada prior to 1939, p. 99

drought a long period without rain, p. 519

Duma a Russian congress established by Czar Nicholas whose members were elected by the people, p. 285

dynasty a series of rulers from the same family; Chinese history is described by dynasties, p. 466

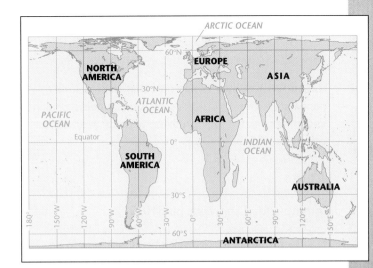

distortion

E

economy the ways that goods and services are produced and made available to people; pp. 52, 192

elevation height of land above sea level; pp. 174, 358

emigrate to move out of one country into another, p. 199, 319

emperor a ruler of widespread lands, p. 466

empire a large collection of people and lands ruled by a single government, p. 276

environment all of the surroundings and conditions that affect living things, such as water, soil, and air, p. 11

erosion a process by which water, wind, or ice wears away landforms and carries the material to another place, p. 29

escarpment a high, steep slope or cliff at the edge of a plateau or mountain range, p. 359

estancias [eh STAHN see yahs] estates owned privately by individuals, p. 242

ethics the standards or code of moral behavior that distinguishes between right and wrong for a particular person, religion, group, profession, and so on, p. 50

ethnic group a group of people who share the same ancestors, culture, language, or religion, pp. 106, 204, 296, 373

extended family a family unit that may include parents, children, grandparents, aunts, uncles, cousins, and other relatives, often living with or near each other, pp. 49, 389

F

famine a food shortage, pp. 310, 511

fellaheen peasants or agricultural workers in an Arab country, p. 404

fertile containing substances that plants need in order to grow well, pp. 359, 372

feudalism [FYOOD ul iz um] a kind of society in which people worked and sometimes fought for a local lord in return for protection and the use of land, p. 277

fiord [fyord] a narrow bay or inlet from the sea bordered by steep cliffs, p. 553

Flemish Dutch the language spoken by the people of Flanders in northern Belgium, p. 313

forty-niner one of the first miners of the California Gold Rush of 1849, p. 135

fossil fuel any one of several nonrenewable resources such as coal, oil, or natural gas, created from the remains of plants and animals, pp. 32, 268

Francophone a person who speaks French as his or her first language, p. 143

free enterprise an economic system in which individuals can start and run their own businesses, pp. 53, 327, 503

G

ganwa princes or lords, p. 421

gauchos [GOW chohz] nomadic cowboys of the mid-18th century who roamed the Pampas and later became hired farmhand on private estates, pp. 241–242

genocide deliberate murder of a racial, political, or ethnic group, p. 317

geography the study of the Earth's surface and the processes that shape it, the connections between places, and the relationships between people and their environment, p. 15

geyser [GY zur] a hot spring that shoots scalding water into the air, p. 553

glacier a huge, slow-moving sheet of ice that fills valleys between mountains, p. 74

globe a round model of the Earth that shows the continents and oceans in their true shapes, p. 19

Golden Horseshoe a manufacturing region in Ontario that includes the Toronto metropolitan area, p. 147

goods products that are made to be sold; cars, baskets, computers, and paper are all examples of goods, p. 52

government the system that establishes and enforces the laws and institutions of a society; some governments are controlled by a few people, and others are controlled by many, p. 54

Green Revolution changes in agriculture since the 1950s that have greatly increased the world's food supply; the Green Revolution's reliance on costly technologies and dangerous pesticides can be both financially and environmentally damaging to nations, p. 43

glacier

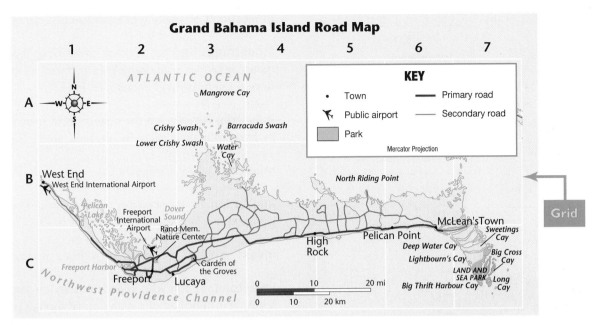

Grand Bahama Island Road Map

grid

grid a system used on maps to help locate places; some are based on longitude and latitude, while others are composed of letters and numbers, p. 22

griot [GREE oh] an African storyteller, p. 389

Group of Seven a group of Canadian painters in the 1920s and 1930s who developed bold techniques in their landscape works, p. 111

guerilla a person who takes part in irregular warfare as a member of an independent group, p. 220

hacienda [hah see EN duh] plantation owned by the Spanish settlers or the Catholic Church in Spanish America, p. 188

hajj the pilgrimage made by Muslims to Mecca, p. 527

harambee the Swahili word for "let's pull together"; the campaign in Kenya begun by President Jomo Kenyatta in 1963, after the country became independent, p. 425

heritage the customs and practices passed from one generation to the next, p. 299

hieroglyphics a system of writing using signs and symbols, used by the Maya and other cultures, p. 184

high latitudes the regions between the Arctic Circle and the North Pole and the Antarctic Circle and the South Pole, p. 14

hill a landform that rises above the surrounding land and that has a rounded top; a hill is lower and usually less steep than a mountain, p. 27

Holocaust the execution of 6 million Jews by German Nazis during World War II, pp. 96, 317

homeland South African lands where blacks were forced to live during apartheid; driest and least fertile parts of the country, p. 433

Homestead Act a law passed in 1862 giving 160 acres (65 hectares) of land on the Midwestern plains to any adult willing to live on and farm it for five years, p. 95

homogeneous having similar members, in reference to a group, p. 486

humanism an approach to knowledge that focused on worldly rather than religious values, p. 279

hunter-gatherer person who gathers wild food and hunts animals to survive, p. 371

hydroelectricity electric power produced by moving water, usually generated by releasing water from a dam across a river, pp. 81, 177

Map Key

KEY

Tropical Climates
- Tropical wet and dry

Mild Climates
- Humid subtropical
- ⊛ National capital
- • Other city

Lambert Azimuthal Equal-Area Projection

Map labels: Gulf of Mexico, FLORIDA, Lake Okeechobee, Miami, Key West, Florida Keys, Straits of Florida, Nassau, BAHAMAS, Andros Island, Tropic of Cancer, Havana, Cárdenas, Cienfuegos, CUBA, Caribbean Sea, ATLANTIC OCEAN, Guantánamo, Guantanamo Bay

key

hydroelectric power the power generated by water-driven turbines, p. 270

I

immigrant a person who moves to a new country in order to settle there, pp. 44, 91

immunity a natural resistance to disease, p. 150

imperialism the control by one country of the political and economic life of another country or region, p. 282

import to bring products into one country from another to sell, p. 208

improvisation an element in jazz in which musicians spontaneously create music, p. 110

incentive a benefit often used by large companies to attract workers and keep them happy, p. 507

indentured servant a person who, in exchange for benefits received, must work for a period of years to gain freedom, p. 88

indigenous originating in a certain place, p. 114, 150

industrialization the process of building new industries in an area dominated by farming; the development of large industries, p. 127

Industrial Revolution the change from making goods by hand to making them by machine, pp. 91, 281

injustice lack of fairness, p. 201

institution an important practice, relationship, or organization in a society or culture, p. 49

invest to spend money to earn more money, p. 192

investor a person who spends money on improving a business in hopes of making more money, p. 339

irrigate to artifically water crops, p. 362

isthmus narrow strip of land that has water on both sides and joins two larger bodies of land, p. 171

K

key the section of a map that explains the symbols for the map features; also called a legend, p. 22

kibbutz a cooperative settlement found in Israel, p. 533

kinship a family relationship, p. 389

L

labor force the supply of workers, p. 95

ladino [lah DEE noh] in Guatemala, a mestizo, or descendant of Native Americans and Spaniards, p. 217

landform an area of the Earth's surface with a definite shape; mountains and hills are examples of landforms, p. 27

latitude an imaginary line, also called a parallel, that circles the Earth parallel to the Equator; used to measure a distance north or south of the Equator in degrees, p. 13

life expectancy the number of years that a person may be expected, on average, to live, p. 43

lineage a group of families with a common ancestor, p. 389

Line of Demarcation an imaginary line from the North Pole to the South Pole (at about 50° longitude) set forth in the 1494 Treaty of Tordesillas; Spain had the right to settle and trade west of the line and Portugal had the right to settle and trade east of the line, p. 187

lock a section of waterway in which ships are raised or lowered by adjusting the water level, p. 221

loess [LOH ess] a type of rich, dustlike soil found on the North European Plain, p. 270

longitude an imaginary line, also called a meridian, that runs north and south from one pole to another; used to measure a distance east or west of the Prime Meridian in degrees, p. 16

Louisiana Purchase the sale of land in 1803 by France to the United States; all the land between the Mississippi River and the eastern slope of the Rocky Mountains, p. 90

low latitudes the region between the Tropic of Cancer and the Tropic of Capricorn, p. 13

M

maize both the plant and the kernel of corn, p. 184

manufacturing the process of turning raw materials into a finished product, p. 319

market economy an economy in which most businesses are privately owned, p. 53

marsupial an animal, such as the kangaroo or the koala, that carries its young in a body pouch, p. 551

maquiladora [ma kee la DOR a] a factory, often near the U.S.-Mexico border, that assembles goods for export, p. 199

mass transit a system of subways, buses, and commuter trains used to transport large numbers of people to and from urban areas, p. 136

megalopolis a number of cities and suburbs that blend into one very large urban area, p. 121

meridian an imaginary line that circles the globe from north to south and runs through both the North and South poles; the lines of longitude on maps or globes are meridians, p. 16

mestizo a person of mixed Spanish and Native American ancestry, p. 188

Middle Ages the period in European history between ancient and modern times; approximately A.D. 500–1500, p. 277

middle class a group of people that included traders, merchants, and others who were economically between the poor and the very rich, p. 279

middle latitudes the regions between the Tropic of Cancer and the Arctic Circle and the Tropic of Capricorn and the Antarctic Circle, p. 14

migrant farmworker a laborer who travels from one area to another, picking crops that are in season, p. 213

migrant worker a person who moves from place to place to find work, p. 396

migrate to move from one place to another, p. 373

migration a movement from place to place, pp. 44, 295, 466

minaret a high tower attached to a mosque, with one or more balconies, p. 494

minaret

mixed-crop farm a farm that grows several different kinds of crops, p. 130

monarch the ruler of a kingdom or empire, such as a king or queen, p. 279

monarchy a system of authoritarian government headed by a monarch—usually a king or a queen—who inherits the throne by birth, p. 55

monsoons the winds that blow across East Asia at certain times of the year; in summer, they are very wet; in winter, they are generally dry unless they have crossed warm ocean currents, p. 456

moshavim small farming villages in Israel, p. 532

mountain usually, a landform that rises more than 2000 ft (610m) above sea level and is wide at the bottom and narrow at the peak, p. 27

mountain

muezzin [moo EZ in] a person who summons Muslims to pray by chanting, p. 494

multicultural influenced by many cultures, p. 293

multiethnic containing many ethnic groups, p. 408

mwami king, p. 421

N

nationalism a feeling of pride in one's own homeland; a group's identiy as members of a nation, pp. 283, 379

nationalist a person who is devoted to the interests of his or her country, p. 468

nationalize to put a once-private industry under national control, p. 429

natural resource any useful material found in the environment, p. 31

navigable [NAV ih guh bul] wide enough and deep enough for ships to travel through, p. 263

nonrenewable resource a resource that cannot be replaced once it is used; nonrenewable resources include fossil fuels such as coal and oil, and minerals such as iron, copper, and gold, pp. 32, 268

nomad a person who moves around to make a living, usually by herding animals, trading, hunting, or gathering food, pp. 363, 486

nuclear family a family unit that includes a mother, father, and their children, pp. 49, 389

O

oasis a fertile place in a desert where there is water and vegetation, p. 362

one-crop economy an economy in which only one crop provides a majority of a country's income, p. 230

orbit the path followed by an object in space as it moves around another, such as that of Earth as it moves around the sun, p. 12

P

Pan-Africanism a movement that stressed unity among all Africans, p. 379

parallel in geography, any of the imaginary lines that circle Earth parallel to the Equator; a latitude line, p. 16

parliament a lawmaking body, p. 525

Parliament a group of elected officials in Great Britain who help govern by deciding about taxes and other laws, pp. 280, 308

partition division, p. 475

partitioned divided, p. 309

prairie

Pax Romana Roman peace; a 200-year period of peace that began when Augustus, the first emperor of Rome, took power in 27 B.C., p. 276

penal colony a place settled by convicts or prisoners; the British founded the first colony in Australia as a penal colony, p. 566

peninsula land nearly surrounded by water, p. 264

permafrost permanently frozen layer of ground below the top layer of soil, pp. 79, 267

persecution harassment, often based on religious or ethnic intolerance, p. 310

petrochemical a substance, such as plastic, paint, or asphalt, that is made from petroleum, p. 127

photosynthesis [foht oh SIN thuh sis] the process by which green plants and trees produce their own food using water, carbon dioxide, and sunlight; oxygen is released as a result of photosynthesis, p. 234

pilgrimage a religious journey; for Muslims, the journey to Mecca, p. 375

plain a large area of flat or gently rolling land usually without many trees, p. 27

plantation a large, one-crop farm with many workers, common in the Southern United States before the Civil War, pp. 88, 393

plate in geography, a huge section of Earth's crust, p. 28

plate tectonics the theory that the Earth's crust is made of huge, slowly moving slabs of rock called plates, p. 28

plateau [pla TOH] a large, mostly flat area that rises above the surrounding land; at least one side has a steep slope; pp. 27, 170, 262, 358

polders new pieces of land reclaimed from the sea; in the Netherlands, land created by building dikes and draining water, p. 311

policies methods and plans governments use to do their work, p. 275

political movement a large group of people who work together to defend their rights or to change the leaders in power, p. 219

population the people living in a particular region; especially, the total number of people in an area, p. 41

population density the average number of people living in an area, pp. 42

population distribution how a population is spread over an area, p. 41

porteños Europeans who settled in and around Buenos Aires to trade, p. 243

prairie a region of flat or rolling land covered with tall grasses, pp. 79, 267

precipitation all the forms of water, such as rain, sleet, hail, and snow, that fall to the ground from the atmosphere, p. 34

primary industry the part of the economy that produces raw materials; examples include agriculture, fishing, mining, and forestry, pp. 52, 574

Prime Meridian an imaginary line of longitude, or meridian, that runs from the North Pole to the South Pole through Greenwich, England; it is designated 0° longitude and is used as a reference point from which east and west lines of longitude are measured, p. 16

privatization the return of businesses to private ownership and management, pp. 240, 336

producer a person who makes products that are used by other people, p. 52

projection a representation of the Earth's rounded surface on a flat piece of paper, p. 20

propaganda the spread of ideas designed to promote a specific cause, p. 299

"push-pull" theory a theory of migration that says people migrate because certain things in their lives "push" them to leave, and certain things in a new place "pull" them, p.45

Q

quaternary industry information technologies, including industries that provide Internet services, computer software, cable, and telephone service, p. 52

Quran [koo rahn] the holy book of the religion of Islam, p. 375

Quebecois literature French Canadian literature, p. 110

Quiet Revolution a peaceful change in the government of Quebec, Canada, in which the Parti Québécois won control of the legislature and made French the official language, p. 143

quota a certain portion of something, such as jobs, set aside for a group, pp. 55, 116

R

radical extreme, p. 502

rain shadow an area on the side of a mountain away from the wind that receives little rainfall, p. 78

refugees

The Ramayana an ancient Hindu epic poem that Hindus believe was revealed to its author by Brahma, the god of creation, pp. 487–488

raw material a material or resource that is still in its natural state, before being processed or manufactured into a useful product, p. 32

recession a downturn in business activity and economic prosperity, not as severe as a depression, p. 131

Reconstruction United States plan for rebuilding the nation after the Civil War, included a period when the South was governed by the United States Army, p. 93

recyclable resource a resource that cycles through natural processes in the environment; water, nitrogen, and carbon are recyclable resources, p. 32

referendum a ballot or vote in which voters decide for or against a particular issue, p. 143

refugees people who seek safety in another country, pp. 421, 514

religious diversity a variety of religious faiths coexisting in a single region, p. 107

Renaissance a period of European history that included a rebirth of interest in learning and art, peaking in the 1500s, p. 279

renewable resource a natural resource that the environment continues to supply or replace as it is used; trees, water, and wind are renewable resources, p. 32

repress to put down, keep from acting, p. 300

representative a person who represents, or stands for, a group of people, usually in government, p. 308

representative government a system of government in which the people elect representatives to run the affairs of the country, p. 55

reservation land set aside for a specific purpose, as by the Canadian government for indigenous peoples, p. 113

reunification the process of becoming unified again, p. 318

revolution one complete orbit of the Earth around the sun; the Earth completes one revolution every 365 days, or one year, p. 12

revolution a political movement in which people overthrow the existing government and set up another, pp. 189, 280

Revolutionary War the war in which the American colonies won their independence from Britain, fought from 1775–1781, p. 89

rift a deep crack in the Earth's surface, p. 359

robot a computer-driven machine that does tasks once done by humans, p. 505

rotation the spinning motion of Earth, like a top on its axis; Earth takes about 24 hours to rotate one time, p. 12

rural having to do with the countryside, p. 198

rural area an area with low population density, such as a village or the countryside, p. 46

S

savanna region of tall grasses, p. 363

scale the size of an area on a map as compared with the area's actual size, p. 19

scarce resource a resource that does not exist in sufficient quantities to satisfy all desires to use it, p. 456

Scientific Revolution a movement that took place during the 1600s and 1700s, when scientists began to base their study of the world on observable facts rather than on beliefs, p. 280

secondary industry manufacturing businesses that take materials from primary industries and other secondary industries and make them into goods, pp. 52, 575

savanna

segregate to set apart and force to use separate schools, housing, parks, and so on because of race and religion, p. 93

serf a person who lived on and farmed a lord's land in feudal times; he or she did not own land and depended on the lord for protection, p. 277

services work done or duties performed for other people, such as the work of a doctor or of a television repair person, p. 52

settlement house a community center for poor immigrants to the United States, p. 95

silt fine-grained sediment deposited by rivers, p. 359

social structure the relationships within a society (or a large group of people) that form a basis for interaction among members of that society, p. 49

souq an open-air marketplace, p. 407

sovereignty [SAHV run tee] political independence, p. 413

squatter a person who settles on someone else's land without permission, p. 214

standard of living the material quality of life, p. 460

station in Australia, a very large sheep or cattle ranch, p. 567

steppes mostly treeless plains; in Russia, the steppes are grasslands of fertile soil suitable for farming, p. 267

strike work stoppage; a refusal to continue to work until certain demands of workers are met, p. 219

subcontinent a large landmass that is a major part of a continent; for example, the Indian subcontinent, p. 451

subsidize to economically support; some governments subsidize certain industries, p. 507

subsistence farmer one who grows just enough food to support one's family, p. 207

subsistence farming raising just enough crops to support one's family, p. 364

Sun Belt area of the United States stretching from the southern Atlantic Coast to the coast of California; known for its warm weather, p. 128

surplus more than is needed, p. 372

Swahili an African language that includes some Arabic words, p. 376

T

taiga [TY guh] an enormous Russian forest, covering more than four million square miles, p. 267

tariff a fee or tax that a government charges for goods entering the country, p. 294

technology tools and the skills that people need to use them; the practical use of scientific skills, especially in industry, p. 48

tectonic plate a large piece of the Earth's crust, p. 552

temperature the degree of hotness or coldness of something, such as water or air, usually measured with a thermometer, p. 34

terrace a platform cut into the side of a mountain, used for growing crops in steep places, p. 406

tertiary industry service activities such as banking, transportation, health care, and police protection, pp. 52, 575

terrace

textiles cloth products, p. 281

totem poles a tall, carved wooden pole containing symbols, found among Native Americans of the Pacific Northwest, p. 150

tourism the business of providing services for tourists, or visitors, to a region, p. 575

traditional economy an economy in which producing, buying, and selling goods operates by the customs, traditions, and habits of the group, pp. 52–53

transportation barrier physical features that make it difficult to travel or transport goods from one region to another, p. 359

transportation corridors routes through which people can travel by foot, vehicle, rail, ship, or airplane; pp. 76, 222

treaty an agreement in writing made between two or more countries, p. 187

Treaty of Tordesillas [tor day SEE yas] the 1494 treaty setting up the Line of Demarcation, giving Spain the right to settle and trade west of the line and Portugal the same rights east of the line, p. 187

tributary (TRIB yoo tehr ee) a stream that flows into a larger river or body of water, pp. 76, 172, 263, 360

tropics the area on Earth between the 23°N and 23°S lines of latitude, where the climate is almost always hot, p. 78

tundra a cold, dry region covered with snow for more than half the year; a vast, treeless plain where the subsoil is always frozen, p. 79, 267

turbines large spinning machines, often powered by water, that can generate electricity, p. 270

U

United Empire Loyalists American colonists loyal to Great Britain who relocated to Canada after the American Revolution, p. 145

vegetation

United Nations an organization of countries established in 1945 that works for peace and cooperation around the world, p. 333

urban having to do with the city, p. 198

urban area an area with a high population density; a city or a town, p. 46

urbanization the movement of populations toward cities and the resulting city growth, pp. 45, 292

V

vassals servants, p. 421

vegetation the plants in an area, p. 36

W

weather the condition of the bottom layer of the Earth's atmosphere in one place over a short period of time, p. 34

weathering the breaking down of rocks by wind, rain, or ice, p. 29

Spanish Glossary

A

abolitionist/abolicionista persona que consideraba a la esclavitud como un error y quería terminar con esta costumbre, p. 92

alliance/alianza acuerdo mutuo entre países para protegerse y defenderse uno al otro, p. 283

alluvial/aluvión relativo al suelo superficial fértil que dejan los ríos después de una inundación, p. 80

apartheid/apartheid sistema sudafricano en el que la población estaba separada por raza, y la discriminación racial era legal, p. 433

aquaculture/acuicultura cultivo marítimo; los cultivos más comunes son los de camarón y de ostras, p. 459

aqueduct/acueducto tubería o canal que sirve para transportar agua desde una fuente distante hasta regiones áridas, p. 185

arable land/tierras de cultivo terreno que puede producir cosechas, p. 456

aristocrats/aristócratas personas que son minoría, pero que se consideran una clase privilegiada y alta, p. 421

artesian well/pozo artesiano pozo profundo perforado en la roca porosa de la superficie terrestre para obtener el agua subterránea, p. 572

atmosphere/atmósfera franja de varias capas de gases que rodea a la Tierra, p. 27

atoll/atolón grupo de pequeñas islas de coral con forma de anillo que encierra a una laguna, p. 554

authoritarian/autoritario controlado por una persona o un pequeño grupo, p. 429

axis/eje línea imaginaria en torno a la cual gira un planeta; la Tierra gira en su propio eje, que va del Polo Norte al Polo Sur, p. 12

B

bazaar/bazar mercado tradicional al aire libre con hileras de tiendas o puestos, p. 403

bilingual/bilingüe que habla dos idiomas; que tiene dos idiomas oficiales, p. 100

birthrate/tasa de natalidad porcentaje por año de nacimientos con vida por cada 1,000 habitantes, p. 43

bolas/boleadoras conjunto de cordeles de cuero y tres esferas de hierro o piedras que se lanzan a las patas de los animales para capturarlos, p. 244

boom/auge periodo de prosperidad en aumento en el que se produce y se vende una mayor cantidad de cierto producto, p. 240

boomtown/pueblo en auge población que tiene un rápido crecimiento, con frecuencia para satisfacer las necesidades de los mineros, p. 151

boycott/boicoteo renuencia a comprar o usar bienes y servicios, pp. 89, 379

C

campesinos/campesinos aldeanos sin tierras y agricultores de pocos recursos, pp. 198, 233

canopy/dosel masa densa de hojas que forma la capa superior de un bosque, p. 234

capital/capital dinero que sirve para expandir un negocio, p. 131

capitalism/capitalismo sistema económico en que las personas y las compañías privadas son propietarias de negocios e industrias básicos y no básicos, p. 53

cardinal direction/punto cardinal uno de los cuatro puntos de la brújula: norte, sur, este y oeste, p. 21

Carnival/carnaval celebración anual en América Latina que se lleva a cabo con música, danzas y desfiles, p. 205

casbah/casbah barrio antiguo y muy poblado de las ciudades de África del Norte, p. 407

cash crop/cultivo para la venta producto de cultivo que se cosecha para cambiarlo por dinero en el mercado mundial, pp. 365, 459

caste/casta una clase de personas en la India, p. 473

cataract/catarata rápido que corre sobre un lecho de rocas, p. 359

caudillo/caudillo oficial militar que gobierna estrictamente, p. 191

census/censo recuento de la población de un país, p. 410

city-state/ciudad-estado forma de organización en que las poblaciones tienen su propio gobierno y controlan gran parte del territorio que las rodea, p. 376

civilization/civilización sociedad con ciudades, un gobierno central, clases sociales y, por lo general, escritura, arte y arquitectura, pp. 372, 465

civil rights movement/movimiento por los derechos civiles grupo numeroso de personas que se unieron en Estados Unidos desde principios de la década de 1960 para acabar con la discriminación de los afroestadounidenses y para apoyar la igualdad de derechos para los grupos minoritarios, p. 97

Civil War/Guerra Civil guerra entre los estados del norte y del sur de Estados Unidos que empezó en 1861 y terminó en 1865, p. 93

clan/clan grupo de familias que mantienen un antecesor común, pp. 389, 466

climate/clima pautas atmosféricas típicas que experimenta una región durante un largo periodo, p. 34

Cold War/Guerra Fría periodo de gran tensión entre Estados Unidos y la antigua Unión Soviética, que duró más de 40 años después de la Segunda Guerra Mundial, pp. 97, 286

colonize/colonizar establecerse en un área y crear o apoderarse de un gobierno, p. 378

colony/colonia territorio gobernado por otra nación, por lo general lejana, p. 474

command economy/economía dirigida economía en que las decisiones económicas las toma el gobierno, p. 53

commonwealth/mancomunidad unidad política autogobernada y con fuertes lazos hacia un país en particular, p. 232

commune/comuna comunidad donde las tierras son comunes y los miembros viven y trabajan juntos, p. 484

Communism/comunismo teoría de gobierno en que las propiedades como las granjas y las fábricas son propiedad del gobierno para el beneficio de todos los ciudadanos; sistema político en que el gobierno central controla todos los aspectos de la vida de los ciudadanos, pp. 97, 285

commute/viajar a diario ir y regresar regularmente de un lugar a otro, particularmente de la casa al trabajo, p. 121

compass rose/rosa de los vientos figura de un mapa que por lo común muestra los cuatro puntos cardinales, p. 21

Confederacy/Confederación los Estados Confederados; conjunto de estados del sur que se separó de Estados Unidos después de la elección de Abraham Lincoln en 1860, p. 93

coniferous/coníferas pertenecientes a los árboles con frutos en forma de cono, p. 267

conquistador/conquistador soldado del siglo XVI que al mando del gobierno español tenía la misión de obtener tierras y riquezas en el continente americano, p. 187

constitution/constitución declaración de las leyes y los valores básicos de un país, pp. 55, 232

Constitution/Constitución documento escrito en 1787 y aprobado en 1789 que estableció los tres poderes del gobierno estadounidense y protegió los derechos individuales de los ciudadanos, p. 89

constitutional monarchy/mornarquía constitucional gobierno en el que un rey o reina dirige el estado, pero que tiene poderes limitados; por ejemplo, el gobierno actual de Gran Bretaña, p. 308

consumer/consumidor persona que compra bienes y servicios, p. 52

Continental Divide/divisoria continental límite que separa a los ríos de un continente que corren en direcciones opuestas; en América del Norte, en las montañas Rocosas, p. 74

copra/copra pulpa de coco deshidratada que se usa para hacer margarina, aceites de cocina y jabones finos, p. 574

coral/coral sustancia que parece roca y está formada de esqueletos de pequeños animales marinos, pp. 171, 554

corporate farm/granja corporativa granja muy grande dirigida por una corporación; puede estar formada por varias granjas más pequeñas que alguna vez fueron propiedades familiares, p. 131

cosmopolitan/cosmopolita caracterizado por diversidad étnica o cultural y sofisticación, p. 241

coup/golpe de estado toma de un gobierno, generalmente por parte de las fuerzas militares, p. 414

Creole/*Creole* persona nacida en el Caribe o en otra parte de América, por lo general de descendientes europeos y africanos, cuya cultura tiene fuertes influencias francesas y africanas; dialecto que hablan los criollos, p. 219

criollo/criollo persona de padres españoles nacida fuera de España; por lo general perteneciente a la clase adinerada y mejor educada en las colonias españolas, p. 190

cultural diffusion/difusión cultural diseminación de ideas y costumbres de una cultura para otra, pp. 387, 467

cultural diversity/diversidad cultural extensa variedad de culturas, pp. 105, 388

cultural exchange/intercambio cultural proceso en el que culturas diferentes comparten ideas y formas de hacer las cosas, p. 105

cultural landscape/paisaje cultural paisaje modificado por los seres humanos y que refleja su cultura, p. 48

cultural trait/rasgo cultural comportamiento particular de una población, tales como idioma, destrezas y costumbres, que pasan de una generación a otra, p. 48

culture/cultura idioma, creencias religiosas, valores, costumbres y demás formas de vida que comparte un grupo de personas, pp. 48, 385

culture region/región cultural área donde las personas comparten los mismos rasgos culturales, p. 48

czar/zar título de los emperadores rusos antes de la formación de la Unión Soviética, p. 285

D

death rate/tasa de mortalidad número de muertes por año por cada 1,000 personas, p. 43

deciduous/caducifolio perteneciente a los árboles que pierden sus hojas, p. 267

Declaration of Independence/Declaración de Independencia documento escrito por Thomas Jefferson en 1776 que expuso las razones de los colonos estadounidenses para rechazar al gobierno británico; los representantes de cada una de las trece colonias firmaron el documento para mostrar su postura en favor de la independencia, p. 89

degree/grado unidad de medida para determinar la ubicación precisa; en globos terráqueos y mapas, la latitud y la longitud se miden en grados, p. 16

demilitarized zone/zona de tolerancia área de la frontera entre países donde no se permite el uso de armas; en Corea, es la zona entre Corea del Norte y Corea del Sur, p. 509

democracy/democracia gobierno del pueblo por el pueblo, pp. 55, 275

demographer/demógrafo científico que estudia las características de las poblaciones humanas, como su tamaño, crecimiento, densidad y distribución, así como sus tasas de nacimiento, matrimonios y mortandad, p. 41

dialect/dialecto versión de un idioma que se habla sólo en ciertas regiones, p. 485

dictator/dictador gobernante de un país que tiene todo el poder, pp. 231, 286

dictatorship/dictadura gobierno dirigido por una persona, por un dictador, p. 56

direct democracy/democracia directa sistema de gobierno en que el pueblo participa directamente en la toma de decisiones, p. 55

discriminate/discriminar tratar con injusticia a las personas por su raza, religión o género, p. 433

discrimination/discriminación trato injusto a menudo a causa de la raza o el género, p. 508

distortion/distorsión representación falsa de una forma verdadera; los mapas de proyección (planisferios) que usan los cartógrafos generan cierta distorsión, p. 20

diversify/diversificar variar; expandir, aumentar, pp. 178, 511

diversity/diversidad variedad, p. 201

domesticate/domesticar adaptar plantas silvestres y animales salvajes para el uso humano, p. 372

dominion/dominio zona de autogobierno sujeta a Gran Bretaña, por ejemplo, Canadá antes de 1939, p. 99

drought/sequía periodo largo sin lluvia, p. 519

Duma/Duma congreso ruso, establecido por el zar Nicolás, a cuyos miembros los elegía el pueblo, p. 285

dynasty/dinastía serie de gobernantes pertenecientes a la misma familia; la historia china se describe por medio de sus dinastías, p. 466

E

economy/economía manera de producir y poner al alcance del pueblo los bienes y servicios en un país, pp. 52, 192

elevation/altitud elevación del terreno sobre el nivel del mar, pp. 174, 358

emigrate/emigrar irse a vivir de un país a otro, p. 199, 319

emperor/emperador gobernante de un extenso territorio, p. 466

empire/imperio extenso grupo de personas y tierras regidas por un solo gobernante, p. 276

environment/medio ambiente todo el medio y las condiciones que afectan a los seres vivos, por ejemplo, el agua, el suelo y el aire, p. 11

erosion/erosión proceso mediante el cual el agua, el viento o el hielo desgasta el relieve del suelo y transporta la materia a otro sitio, p. 29

escarpment/escarpadura acantilado escarpado al borde de una meseta o cordillera, p. 359

estancias/estancias haciendas o fincas que son propiedad particular de un individuo, p. 242

ethics/ética estándares o código de comportamiento moral de una persona, una religión, un grupo, una profesión, etcétera, que permite distinguir entre el bien y el mal, p. 50

ethnic group/grupo étnico grupo de personas cuyos antepasados, cultura, idioma y religión les son comunes, pp. 106, 204, 296, 373

extended family/familia extendida unidad familiar que abarca padres, hijos, abuelos, tías, tíos, primos y demás parientes, que por lo general viven bajo el mismo techo o muy cerca uno de otro, pp. 49, 389

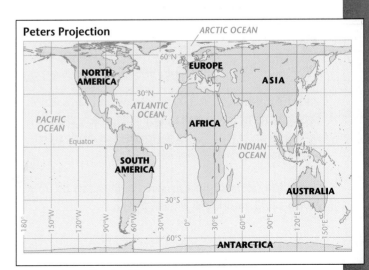

distortion/distorsión

F

famine/hambruna insuficiencia de alimentos, pp. 310, 511

fellaheen/felá campesino o labrador agrícola de los países árabes, p. 404

fertile/fértil se dice del suelo que contiene las sustancias que las plantas necesitan para crecer bien, pp. 359, 372

feudalism/feudalismo clase de organización social en donde las personas trabajaban e incluso peleaban para un señor a cambio de protección y de permiso para usar la tierra , p. 277

fiord/fiordo bahía estrecha o entrada del mar, rodeado de acantilados escarpados, p. 553

Flemish Dutch/holandés flamenco idioma que se habla en Flandes, región del norte de Bélgica, p. 313

forty-niner/*forty-niner* uno de los primeros mineros de la Fiebre del Oro en 1849, p. 135

fossil fuel/combustible fósil cualquiera de los recursos no renovables como el carbón, el petróleo o el gas natural, que se formaron a partir de los restos de plantas y animales, pp. 32, 268

Francophone/francófono persona que habla el francés como primera lengua, p. 143

free enterprise/libre empresa sistema económico en el que los individuos establecen y dirigen su propio negocio, pp. 53, 327, 503

G

ganwa/ganwa príncipes o lores, p. 421

gaucho/gauchos vaqueros nómadas de mediados del siglo XVIII que vagaban por la Pampa y después se volvieron trabajadores agrícolas asalariados en propiedades privadas, pp. 241–242

genocide/genocidio asesinato deliberado de un grupo racial, político o étnico, p. 317

geography/geografía estudio de la superficie de la Tierra y de sus procesos de formación, las conexiones entre lugares y las relaciones entre las personas y su medio ambiente, p. 15

geyser/géiser manantial caliente que lanza agua hirviente al aire, p. 553

glacier/glaciar bloque de hielo enorme, de movimiento muy lento, que ocupa un valle entre dos montañas, p. 74

globe/globo terráqueo modelo redondo de la Tierra que muestra los continentes y océanos en sus formas reales, p. 19

Golden Horseshoe/*Golden Horseshoe* región manufacturera de Ontario que abarca el área metropolitana de Toronto, p. 147

goods/bienes de consumo productos que se fabrican para su venta; autos, cestos, computadoras y papel son ejemplos de bienes, p. 52

government/gobierno sistema que establece y hace cumplir las leyes e instituciones de una sociedad; algunos gobiernos están controlados por pocas personas y otros por muchas personas, p. 54

Green Revolution/Revolución verde cambios en la agricultura desde la década de 1950 que han aumentado en gran medida el abastecimiento de alimentos en el mundo; la sustentación de la Revolución verde en tecnología costosa y pesticidas peligrosos puede perjudicar tanto el medio ambiente como a las finanzas de las naciones, p. 43

grid/cuadrícula sistema para localizar lugares en los mapas; algunas se basan en la longitud y la latitud, y otras usan números y letras, p. 22

griot/griot contador de cuentos africano, p. 389

Group of Seven/Grupo de los Siete grupo de pintores canadienses en las décadas de 1920 y 1930 que desarrollaron técnicas audaces en sus obras paisajistas, p. 111

guerilla/guerrillero persona que participa en una guerra irregular como miembro de un grupo independiente, p. 220

H

hacienda/hacienda plantación de colonos españoles o de la Iglesia católica en la América hispana, p. 188

hajj/hajj peregrinación que hacen los musulmanes a la Meca, p. 527

harambee/harambi palabra suajili que significa "hagámoslo juntos"; campaña en Kenya que inició el presidente Jomo Kenyatta en 1963, después de que el país se independizó, p. 425

heritage/herencia hábitos y costumbres que pasan de una generación a otra, p. 299

hieroglyphics/jeroglíficos sistema de escritura con signos y símbolos que usaron los mayas y otras culturas, p. 184

high latitudes/latitudes altas regiones entre el círculo polar Ártico y el polo Norte y el círculo polar Antártico y el polo Sur, p. 14

hill/colina formación del suelo más alta que el terreno que la rodea, con una cima redondeada; por lo general una colina es más baja y menos empinada que una montaña, p. 27

Holocaust/Holocausto ejecución de 6 millones de judíos por los nazis alemanes durante la Segunda Guerra Mundial, pp. 96, 317

homeland/tierra natal tierras de Sudáfrica donde eran forzadas a vivir las personas de raza negra durante el apartheid; zonas más áridas y menos fértiles del país, p. 433

Homestead Act/ley de colonización ley aprobada en 1862 que otorgaba 160 acres (65 hectáreas) de tierra de las llanuras del Medio Oeste a todo adulto que quisiera vivir en ella y cultivarla durante 5 años, p. 95

homogeneous/homogéneo que tiene elementos similares en relación con un grupo, p. 486

humanism/humanismo aproximación del conocimiento que se enfocó en los valores materiales más que en los valores religiosos, p. 279

hunter-gatherer/cazador-recolector persona que recolectaba alimentos silvestres y cazaba animales para sobrevivir, p. 371

hydroelectricity/hidroelectricidad energía eléctrica producida por agua en movimiento, por lo común es la que se genera al soltar el agua de una presa, pp. 81, 177

hydroelectric power/energía hidroeléctrica energía generada por turbinas impulsadas por agua, p. 270

I

immigrant/inmigrante persona que se muda a otro país para establecerse en él, pp. 44, 91

immunity/inmunidad resistencia natural a la enfermedad, p. 150

imperialism/imperialismo control que ejerce un país en la vida política y económica de otro país o región, p. 282

import/importar introducir productos de un país a otro para venderlos, p. 208

improvisation/improvisación recurso del jazz donde los músicos crean música espontáneamente, p. 110

incentive/incentivo prestación que las grandes empresas usan para atraer a sus empleados y mantenerlos contentos, p. 507

indentured servant/sirviente por contrato persona que, a cambio de un beneficio, trabaja por un periodo de años para liberarse, p. 88

indigenous/autóctono originario de cierto lugar, p. 114, 150

industrialization/industrialización proceso de establecimiento de nuevas industrias en una región donde predomina la agricultura; desarrollo de grandes industrias, p. 127

Industrial Revolution/Revolución Industrial cambio de elaborar productos a mano para producirlos con máquinas, pp. 91, 281

injustice/injusticia falta de equidad, p. 201

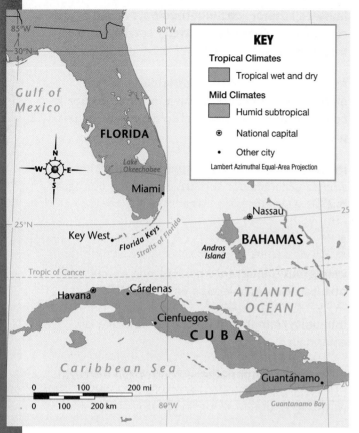

key/clave

institution/institución organización, relación o costumbre importante en una sociedad o cultura, p. 49

invest/invertir usar el dinero para obtener más dinero, p. 192

investor/inversionista persona que gasta dinero para mejorar un negocio con la esperanza de obtener más dinero, p. 339

irrigate/regar regar los cultivos de manera artificial, p. 362

isthmus/istmo franja estrecha de tierra con agua en ambos lados y unida a dos masas de tierra más grandes, p. 171

K

key/clave parte del mapa que explica la simbología de las características del mapa; también se llama leyenda, p. 22

kibbutz/kibutz asentamiento cooperativo que se encuentra en Israel, p. 533

kinship/parentesco relación familiar, p. 389

L

labor force/fuerza laboral trabajadores con que se cuenta, p. 95

ladino/ladino en Guatemala, mestizo o descendiente de indígenas americanos y de españoles, p. 217

landform/accidente geográfico área de la superficie terrestre con forma definida; las montañas y las colinas son ejemplos de accidentes geográficos, p. 27

latitude/latitud línea imaginaria, también llamada paralelo, que rodea a la Tierra y es paralela al ecuador; sirve para medir distancias en grados al norte y al sur del ecuador, p. 13

life expectancy/expectativa de vida cantidad de años que se espera que viva en promedio una persona, p. 43

lineage/linaje grupo de familias con un antepasado común, p. 389

Line of Demarcation/línea de demarcación línea imaginaria del polo Norte al polo Sur (aproximadamente a 50° de longitud) establecida en 1494 en el Tratado de Tordesillas; España tenía el derecho de colonizar y comerciar al oeste de la línea y Portugal al este de la línea, p. 187

lock/esclusa sección de vía marítima donde se eleva o se baja a los barcos ajustando el nivel del agua, p. 221

loess/loes clase de suelo nutritivo, de grano fino, que se encuentra en las planicies del norte de Europa, p. 270

longitude/longitud línea imaginaria, también llamada meridiano, que va de norte a sur, de un polo a otro; sirve para medir en grados la distancia de este a oeste del primer meridiano, p. 16

Louisiana Purchase/Compra de Luisiana venta de tierra en 1803 de Francia a Estados Unidos; todo el terreno entre el río Mississippi y la ladera este de las montañas Rocosas, p. 90

low latitudes/latitudes bajas región entre el trópico de Cáncer y el trópico de Capricornio, p. 13

M

maize/maíz planta y grano del maíz, p. 184

manufacturing/manufactura proceso de convertir materia prima en productos terminados, p. 319

market economy/economía de mercado economía en la que la mayoría de los negocios son de propiedad privada, p. 53

marsupial/marsupial animal que, como el canguro o el koala, lleva a su cría en una bolsa de su cuerpo, p. 551

maquiladora/maquiladora fábrica de montaje de productos para la exportación, frecuentemente ubicada cerca de la frontera entre México y E.E. U.U., p. 199

mass transit/transporte masivo sistema de trenes subterráneos, autobuses y ferrocarriles de viaje por abono que transporta una gran cantidad de personas desde y hacia las áreas urbanas, p. 136

megalopolis/megalópolis conjunto de ciudades y de suburbios que mezclan en una gran área urbana, p. 121

meridian/meridiano línea imaginaria que rodea a la Tierra de norte a sur, y que pasa por los polos; las líneas de longitud en los mapas o globos terráqueos son los meridianos, p. 16

mestizo/mestizo persona que desciende de la mezcla entre españoles e indígenas americanos, p. 188

Middle Ages/Edad Media periodo de la historia europea entre la antigüedad y la era moderna; aproximadamente de los años 500 a 1500 D.C., p. 277

middle class/clase media grupo de personas, entre las que había comerciantes y mercaderes, que económicamente estaban entre los pobres y los muy ricos, p. 279

middle latitudes/latitudes medias regiones entre el trópico de Cáncer y el círculo polar Ártico, y el trópico de Capricornio y el círculo polar Antártico, p. 14

migrant worker/trabajador migratorio persona que se traslada de un lugar a otro para encontrar trabajo, p. 396

migrate/emigrar ir de un lugar a otro, p. 373

migration/migración trasladarse de un lugar a otro, pp. 44, 295, 466

minaret/minarete torre alta unida a una mezquita, con uno o más balcones, p. 494

mixed-crop farm/granja de cultivo mixto granja que produce diferentes clases de cultivo, p. 130

monarch/monarca gobernante de un reino o imperio, que puede ser un rey o una reina, p. 279

monarchy/monarquía sistema de gobierno autoritario encabezado por un monarca –por lo general un rey o una reina—que hereda el trono de nacimiento, p. 55

monsoons/monzón vientos que soplan por el este de Asia en ciertas épocas del año; en verano son muy húmedos; en invierno por lo general son secos, a menos que hayan cruzado las corrientes oceánicas cálidas, p. 456

moshavim/moshavim pequeñas aldeas de cultivo en Israel, p. 532

mountain/montaña por lo general, accidente geográfico que alcanza más de 2000 pies (610 m) por encima del nivel del mar, y es ancho en su base y angosto en su cima, p. 27

muezzin/muecín persona que convoca a los musulmanes por medio de cantos a orar, p. 494

multicultural/multicultural influido por varias culturas, p. 293

multiethnic/multiétnico que contiene varios grupos étnicos, p. 408

mwami/mwami rey, p. 421

N

nationalism/nacionalismo sentimiento de orgullo hacia la tierra natal propia; identidad de un grupo como miembros de una nación, pp. 283, 379

nationalist/nacionalista persona dedicada a los intereses de su país, p. 468

nationalize/nacionalizar poner la industria que alguna vez fue privada bajo el control de la nación, p. 429

natural resource/recurso natural cualquier materia útil que se encuentre en el medio ambiente, p. 31

navigable/navegable lo suficientemente ancho y profundo para que los barcos lo puedan recorrer, p. 263

nonrenewable resource/recurso no renovable recurso que no puede reemplazarse después de usarse; algunos recursos no renovables son los combustibles fósiles como el carbón y el petróleo, y los minerales como el hierro, el cobre y el oro, pp. 32, 268

nomad/nómada persona que se traslada constantemente para ganarse la vida, casi siempre mediante el pastoreo de animales, el comercio, la caza y la recolección de alimentos, pp. 363, 486

nuclear family/familia nuclear unidad familiar formada por un padre, una madre y sus hijos, pp. 49, 389

O

oasis/oasis lugar fértil del desierto, donde hay agua y vegetación, p. 362

one-crop economy/economía de un solo cultivo economía en que un solo cultivo proporciona la mayor parte de los ingresos de un país, p. 230

orbit/órbita trayectoria que sigue un objeto en el espacio cuando se mueve alrededor de otro, como la Tierra que se mueve alrededor del Sol, p. 12

P

Pan-Africanism/panafricanismo movimiento que acentuó la unidad entre todos los africanos, p. 379

parallel/paralelo en geografía, cualquiera de las líneas imaginarias paralelas al ecuador que rodean la Tierra; cualquier línea de latitud, p. 16

parliament/parlamento organismo que hace las leyes, p. 525

Parliament/Parlamento grupo de funcionarios electos en Gran Bretaña que ayudan al gobierno a determinar los impuestos y a emitir otras leyes, pp. 280, 308

partition/separación división, p. 475

partitioned/separado dividido, p. 309

Pax Romana/Pax Romana paz romana; periodo de 200 años de paz que empezó cuando Augusto, el primer emperador romano, tomó el poder en al año 27 A.C., p. 276

penal colony/colonia penitenciaria lugar establecido por convictos o prisioneros; los británicos fundaron la primera colonia en Australia como colonia penitenciaria, p. 566

peninsula/península tierra rodeada por agua casi por completo, p. 264

permafrost/permafrost capa de tierra permanentemente congelada bajo la capa superior del suelo, pp. 79, 267

persecution/persecución acosamiento, con frecuencia basado en intolerancia religiosa o étnica, p. 310

petrochemical/producto petroquímico sustancia que se deriva del petróleo, como plástico, pintura o asfalto, p. 127

photosynthesis/fotosíntesis proceso por el que las plantas y los árboles verdes producen su propio alimento por medio de agua, dióxido de carbono y luz solar; el oxígeno se libera como consecuencia de la fotosíntesis, p. 234

pilgrimage/peregrinación recorrido religioso; para los musulmanes, viaje a La Meca, p. 375

plain/llanura región grande de tierras llanas o ligeramente ondulantes sin muchos árboles, p. 27

plantation/plantación granja muy grande de un solo cultivo con muchos trabajadores, común en el sur de Estados Unidos antes de la Guerra Civil, pp. 88, 393

plate/placa en geografía, sección grande de corteza terrestre, p. 28

plate tectonics/placas tectónicas teoría de que la corteza terrestre está formada por enormes porciones de roca, de lento movimiento, llamadas placas, p. 28

plateau/meseta región grande, la mayor parte plana, que sobresale del terreno que la rodea; tiene al menos un lado de cuesta empinada, pp. 27, 170, 262, 358

polders/pólder terreno nuevo que se ha ganado al mar; en los Países Bajos, terreno que se forma al construir diques y drenar el agua del mar, p. 311

policies/políticas métodos y planes que usan los gobiernos para realizar sus proyectos, p. 275

political movement/movimiento político grupo grande de personas que trabajan juntas para defender sus derechos o cambiar a los líderes que están en el poder, p. 219

population/población personas que viven en una región particular; en especial la cantidad total de personas en una región, p. 41

population density/densidad de población cantidad promedio de personas que viven en una área, p. 42

population distribution/distribución de la población forma en que la población de una región está repartida, p. 41

porteños/porteños europeos que se establecieron en Buenos Aires y sus alrededores para comerciar, p. 243

prairie/pradera región de terreno plano u ondulante cubierto con pastos altos, pp. 79, 267

precipitation/precipitación todas las formas del agua, como lluvia, aguanieve, granizo y nieve, que cae de la atmósfera a la Tierra, p. 34

primary industry/industria primaria parte de la economía que produce materia prima; ejemplos de ella son la agricultura, la pesca, la minería y la silvicultura, pp. 52, 574

Prime Meridian/primer meridiano línea imaginaria de longitud, o meridiano, que va del polo Norte al polo Sur y pasa por Greenwich, Inglaterra; tiene designado el grado cero de longitud y se usa como punto de referencia para que puedan medirse las líneas de longitud del este y del oeste, p. 16

privatization/privatización restitución de los negocios a la propiedad y la administración privadas, pp. 240, 336

producer/productor persona que fabrica productos que usan otras personas, p. 52

projection/proyección representación de la superficie redonda de la Tierra en la superficie plana de un papel, p. 20

propaganda/propaganda difusión de ideas para promover una causa específica, p. 299

"push-pull" theory/teoría de "atracción y rechazo" teoría migratoria que afirma que las personas emigran por el rechazo a ciertas cosas en su vida y la atracción hacia ciertas cosas de un nuevo lugar, p. 45

quaternary industry/industria cuaternaria tecnología de información, abarca las industrias que proveen servicios de Internet, software para computadoras, y servicios de cable y telefonía, p. 52

Quran/Corán libro sagrado de la religión islámica, p. 375

Quebecois literature/literatura de Quebec literatura canadiense en lengua francesa, p. 110

refugees/refugiados

Quiet Revolution/Revolución silenciosa cambio pacífico del gobierno de Quebec, Canadá, en el que el Parti Québécois tomó el control de la legislatura e hizo del francés el idioma oficial, p. 143

quota/cuota cierta parte de algo, como un trabajo, que se reserva para un grupo, pp. 55, 116

R

radical/radical extremo, p. 502

rain shadow/sombra de lluvia área sin viento en un lado de la montaña, donde cae una lluvia ligera, p. 78

The Ramayana/el Ramayana poema épico hindú antiguo que los hindúes consideran una revelación de Brahma, el dios de la creación, para su autor, pp. 487–488

raw material/materia prima materia o recurso que aún se encuentra en su estado natural, antes de procesarse o manufacturarse como producto útil, p. 32

recession/recesión una baja en la actividad de los negocios y el crecimiento económico, no tan grave como una depresión, p. 131

Reconstruction/Reconstrucción plan de Estados Unidos para reconstruir la nación después de la Guerra Civil, abarca el periodo en que el ejército de Estados Unidos gobernó los estados del Sur, p. 93

recyclable resource/recurso cíclico recurso con un proceso cíclico natural en el medio ambiente; entre ellos el agua, el nitrógeno y el carbono, p. 32

referendum/referéndum boleta o voto con el que los votantes deciden a favor o en contra de un asunto en particular, p. 143

refugees/refugiados personas que buscan seguridad en otro país, pp. 421, 514

religious diversity/diversidad religiosa variedad de creencias religiosas que existen al mismo tiempo en una región, p. 107

Renaissance/Renacimiento periodo de la historia europea en el que surgió un nuevo interés en la enseñanza y el arte; culminó en el siglo XVI, p. 279

renewable resource/recurso renovable recurso natural que el medio ambiente continúa suministrando o que reemplaza al usarlo; los árboles, el agua y el viento son recursos renovables, p. 32

repress/reprimir sofocar, abstenerse de actuar, p. 300

representative/representante persona que representa o defiende a un grupo de personas, por lo general en el gobierno, p. 308

representative government/gobierno representativo sistema de gobierno en el que las personas eligen a sus representantes para que resuelvan los asuntos del país, p. 55

reservation/reservación terreno que se reserva para un propósito específico, como lo hizo el gobierno de Canadá con los pueblos indígenas, p. 113

reunification/reunificación proceso de volver a unirse, p. 318

revolution/traslación vuelta completa de la Tierra alrededor del Sol; la Tierra completa una revolución cada 365 días o cada año, p. 12

revolution/revolución movimiento político en el que el pueblo derroca el gobierno existente y establece otro, pp. 189, 280

Revolutionary War/Guerra de Independencia guerra entre los años 1775–1781 en que las colonias estadounidenses lograron su independencia de Gran Bretaña, p. 89

rift/grieta hendidura profunda en la superficie terrestre, p. 359

robot/robot máquina dirigida por computadora que realiza tareas que antes hacían los seres humanos, p. 505

rotation/rotación movimiento giratorio de la Tierra, como un trompo en su eje; la Tierra tarda 24 horas para hacer una rotación, p. 12

rural/rural relativo al campo, p. 198

rural area/área rural región con una densidad de población baja, como una villa o el campo, p. 46

S

savanna/sabana región de pastos altos, p. 363

scale/escala tamaño de una región en un mapa en relación con su tamaño real, p. 19

scarce resource/recurso escaso un recurso con insuficiente cantidad para satisfacer los deseos de todos, p. 456

Scientific Revolution/Revolución científica movimiento que tuvo lugar durante los siglos XVII y XVIII, cuando los científicos basaron sus estudios sobre el mundo en hechos observables más que en creencias, p. 280

secondary industry/industria secundaria empresas de manufactura que elaboran productos con materiales de la industria primaria y de otras industrias secundarias, pp. 52, 575

segregate/segregar apartar y obligar a usar otras escuelas, casas, parques, etc., por la raza o la religión, p. 93

serf/siervo persona que vivió y trabajó las tierras de un señor feudal; no era propietaria de las tierras y dependía de la protección del señor feudal, p. 277

services/servicios trabajo o tarea que se realiza para otra persona, como la atención de un médico o la reparación del televisor por parte de otra persona, p. 52

settlement house/casa de establecimiento centro comunitario para inmigrantes pobres en Estados Unidos, p. 95

silt/cieno sedimento de grano fino depositado por los ríos, p. 359

social structure/estructura social conjunto de relaciones que fomentan la interacción entre miembros de una sociedad (o grupo importante de personas), p. 49

savanna/sabana

souq/souq mercado al aire libre, p. 407

sovereignty/soberanía independencia política, p. 413

squatter/ocupante ilegal persona que se establece en el terreno de otro sin su permiso, p. 214

standard of living/estándar de vida calidad de vida material, p. 460

station/dehesa en Australia, un rancho muy grande de ovejas o ganado, p. 567

steppes/estepas llanuras en su mayor parte sin árboles; en Rusia, las estepas son praderas de suelo fértil apto para la agricultura, p. 267

strike/huelga interrupción del trabajo; renuncia a seguir trabajando hasta que se satisfagan ciertas demandas de los trabajadores, p. 219

subcontinent/subcontinente gran masa de tierra que forma la mayor parte de un continente; por ejemplo, el subcontinente de la India, p. 451

subsidize/subsidiar apoyar económicamente; algunos gobiernos subsidian ciertas industrias, p. 507

subsistence farmer/agricultor de subsistencia agricultor que produce sólo lo necesario para mantener a su familia, p. 207

subsistence farming/agricultura de subsistencia cultivar solo las cosechas suficientes para mantener a la familia, p. 364

Sun Belt/*Sun Belt* (franja del sol) región de Estados Unidos que se extiende desde el sur de la costa del Atlántico hasta la costa de California; zona conocida por su clima cálido, p. 128

surplus/excedente más de lo necesario, p. 372

Swahili/suajili idioma africano que contiene algunas palabras árabes, p. 376

T

taiga/taiga en Rusia, bosque enorme que cubre más de cuatro millones de millas cuadradas, p. 267

tariff/arancel derecho o impuesto que un gobierno cobra por introducir productos en el país, p. 294

technology/tecnología herramientas y destrezas que las personas necesitan usar; uso práctico de las destrezas científicas, especialmente en la industria, p. 48

tectonic plate/placa tectónica porción grande de la corteza terrestre, p. 552

temperature/temperatura grado de calentamiento o enfriamiento de algo, como el agua o el aire; por lo general se mide con un termómetro, p. 34

terrace/terraza plataforma recortada en la ladera de una montaña; se usa para hacer cultivos escalonados en lugares empinados, p. 406

tertiary industry/industria terciaria industrias de servicio como bancos, transportes, cuidado de la salud y protección policiaca, pp. 52, 575

textiles/textiles productos de tela, p. 281

totem pole/poste totémico poste alto de madera tallado con símbolos; se encuentra entre los indígenas estadounidenses de la costa noroeste del Pacífico, p. 150

tourism/turismo negocios que dan servicio a los turistas o visitantes de una región, p. 575

traditional economy/economía tradicional economía en que se producen, se compran y se venden bienes de acuerdo con las costumbres, las tradiciones y los hábitos del grupo, pp. 52–53

transportation barrier/barrera de transportación características físicas que impiden viajar o transportar productos de una región o otra, p. 359

transportation corridors/corredores de transportación rutas por las que se puede viajar a pie, en vehículo, en tren, en barco o en avión, pp. 76, 222

treaty/tratado acuerdo por escrito entre dos o más países, p. 187

Treaty of Tordesillas/Tratado de Tordesillas
tratado de 1494 que establece la Línea de
demarcación, que da a España el derecho de poblar
y comerciar al oeste de la línea y a Portugal los
mismos derechos al este de la línea, p. 187

tributary/tributario corriente de agua que fluye
hacia un gran río o a un depósito de agua mayor, pp.
76, 172, 263, 360

tropics/trópico región de la Tierra entre las líneas
de latitud 23° N y 23° S, cuyo clima casi siempre es
caluroso, p. 78

tundra/tundra región fría y seca cubierta de
nieve más de la mitad del año; gran planicie sin
árboles donde el subsuelo siempre está congelado,
pp. 79, 267

turbines/turbinas enormes máquinas con hélices
por lo general impulsadas por agua y que generan
electricidad, p. 270

U

**United Empire Loyalists/United Empire
Loyalists** (Unión de Colonos Leales al Imperio)
colonos estadounidenses leales a Gran Bretaña que
se trasladaron a Canadá después de la Guerra de
Independencia, p. 145

**United Nations/Organización de las Naciones
Unidas** organización de países establecida en 1945,
que actúa a favor de la paz y la cooperación entre
los países, p. 333

urban/urbano relativo o referente a la ciudad,
p. 198

urban area/área urbana zona densamente
poblada; una ciudad o un pueblo, p. 46

urbanization/urbanización crecimiento de las
ciudades como consecuencia del flujo de personas
hacia ellas, pp. 45, 292

vegetation/vegetación

V

vassals/vasallos sirvientes, p. 421

vegetation/vegetación conjunto de plantas de
una zona, p. 36

W

weather/tiempo condiciones de la capa inferior
de la atmósfera terrestre en un lugar durante un
periodo corto, p. 34

weathering/desgaste desintegración de las rocas
producida por el viento, la lluvia o el hielo, p. 29

Index

The *italicized* letters preceding page numbers refer to maps (*m*), charts (*c*), pictures (*p*), tables (*t*), or graphs (*g*).

megalopolis, 121, m123, 663
Melanesia, 559, 567, 650
Melville, Herman, 110
Mengoni, Giuseppe, p322
Mercator, Gerhardus, 20
Mercator projection, 20, m20
meridians, 16, 663
Meroë, 372
mesa, 646
Mesopotamia, 476, 495, 650
mestizos, 188, 201, 207, 238, 243, 663
Mexico, 169, 650
  Aztec civilization in, 184
  country profile of, c198, m198
  cultures of, 197–199, p197, m198, p199
  earthquakes in, m214
  farming in, 199, p199
  independence in, 190, p190
  landforms of, 170–171
  language of, 197
  migration in, 213–216
  natural resources of, 176–177
  petroleum in, 33, 178
  population of, 198–199, m199
  poverty in, 198–199, 214
  regional database, 612, m612
  religion in, 197
  United States and, 199
  volcanoes in, m214
Mexico City, Mexico, 184, 188, 198–199, 213–216, p213, m215, p216, 651
Miami, Florida, 128
Michelangelo, 344
Michigan
  regional database, 607
Micronesia, 559, 567, 651
  regional database, 644
Middle Ages, 277, 290, 663
Middle America. See Central America; Mexico

middle class, 279, 339–340, 663
Middle Kingdom, 466
middle latitudes, 14, 663
Midwest, U.S.,
  regional database, m606
  regional profile of, c130, m130
migrant farmworkers, 213, 396, 663
migration, 44–45, 295, 663
Milan, Italy, 322, 651
Milky Way, 11
minaret, 494, p494, 663
mineral resources, 81, 82
mining, 427, p427, 580
Minnesota
  regional database, 607
Miskito people, 219
Missionaries of Charity, 526
Mississippi, 125, 126
  regional database, 605
Mississippi River, 76, p76, 80, 651
Missouri
  regional database, 607
Missouri River, 18, 76, 80
Mistry, Roda, 526
mixed-crop farm, 130, 664
Moctezuma, 187, p187
models, using, 415
moderate climate, 36
Mohenjo-Daro, 472, p472
Moldova
  regional database, 622
Mombasa, 376
Monaco
  regional database, 619
monarchs, 279, 438, 664
Monet, Claude, 345
Mongolia
  regional database, 634
Mongols, 284–285, p284
monsoon forests, 558

monsoons, m447, 456, 457, 521, 664
Montana
  regional database, 608
Montenegro, 298, 331, c331
  regional database, 622
Montgomery, Lucy Maud, 110
Montreal, Quebec, 142, 651
Montserrat, 204
Moore, Annie, 124
Morocco, 385, p385, 386
  regional database, 625
Moscow, Russia, 284–285, 339–340, p340, 651
moshavim, 532, 664
mosques, p386, 402, p489, p494
mosquitoes, 223
Mother Jones, 95
Mother Teresa, 526
Mount Cook, 553, p556
Mount Everest, 452, 557
Mount Kenya, 423, 651
Mount Kilimanjaro, 358
Mount Logan, 75
Mount McKinley, 73, p73
Mount Vesuvius, 276
mountains, 27, 647, 664
mountain pass, 647
movement, 18
Mozambique, 360, 365, 392
  regional database, 633
muezzin, 494, p494, 644
Mughal Empire, 474
Muhammad (prophet), 375, 474, 496
Muir Woods National Monument, p80
multiculturalism, 293, 644
multiethnic, 408, 644
Mumbai, India, g457
Munro, Alice, 110
Murray River, 555

Acknowledgments

Cover Design
Pearson Educational Development Group

Cover Photo
Top right, clockwise: Harald Sund/Image Bank; SuperStock; SuperStock; SuperStock; SuperStock; José Fuste Raga/Corbis StockMarket; David Hiser/Stone; Cartesia/Photodisc; McDaniel Woolf/Photodisc; Travelpix/FPG; **Center image:** Robert Everts/Stone; **Silouette figure with binoculars:** Ken Karp Photography.

Maps
38, 78, 122 T, 126 T, 130 T, 134 T, 146 T, 146 B, 218 T, 242 T, 242 B, 247, 266, 269, 276, 312 T, 312 B, 335 T, 335 B, 367 L, 367 R, 417, 420 T, 420 B, 444, 452, 463, 537, 544 T, 544 B, 561, 579, 613 T, 614 T, 616 T, 618 T, 621 T, Ortelius Design, Inc.; all other maps by MapQuest.com, Inc.

Map information sources: Columbia Encyclopedia, Encyclopaedia Britannica, Microsoft® Encarta®, National Geographic Atlas of the world, Rand McNally Commerical Atlas, The Times Atlas of the World.

Staff Credits
Joyce Barisano, Carolyn Casey, Clare Courtney, Stephen Flanagan, Kathryn Fox, **Mary Hanisco, Catherine Holder, Estelle Needleman, Kirsten Richert, Miriam Rodriquez, Peter Sacks,** Betsy Sawyer-Melodia, and the **Pearson Education Development Group.**

Additional Credits
Design, Art, and Production: Pronto Design, Inc.

Text
11, Excerpt from *North American Indian Mythology* by Cottie Burland. Copyright © 1965 by Cottie Burland. Reproduced by permission of The Hamlyn Publishing Group Limited. **87,** Excerpt from *The Crown of Columbus* by Michael Dorris and Louise Erdrich. Copyright © 1991 by Michael Dorris and Louise Erdrich. Reproduced by permission of Harper-Collins Publishers. **94,** Excerpt from *How the Other Half Lives* by Jacob Riis. Copyright © 1971 by Dover Publications, Inc. Reproduced by permission of Dover Publications, Inc. **109,** Excerpt from *Obscure Destinies* by Willa Cather. Copyright © 1930 by Willa Cather. Copyright © renewed 1932 by Willa Cather. Reproduced by permission of Alfred A. Knopf. **120,** Excerpt from *America, the Beautiful* by Katherine Lee Bates. Copyright © 1993 by Neil Waldman. Reproduced by permission of Macmillan Publishing Company. **196,** "Wind and Water and Stone" by Octavio Paz. Copyright © 1979 by The New Yorker Magazine. Reproduced by permission of New Directions Publishing Corporation. **290,** Excerpt from *Pearl in the Egg* by Dorothy Van Woerkom. Copyright © 1980 by Dorothy Van Woerkom. Reproduced by permission of Thomas Y. Crowell. **326,** Excerpt from *Zlata's Diary* by Zlata Filipovic. Copyright © 1994 by Fixot et editions Robert Laffont. Reproduced by permission of Viking. **418,** Excerpt from *Mandela: An Illustrated Autobiography* by Nelson Mandela. Copyright © 1994, 1996 by Nelson Rolihlahla Mandela. Reproduced by permission of Little, Brown and Company. **464,** Excerpt from *Selected Works of Jawaharlal Nehru.* Copyright © 1987. Reproduced by permission of Oxford University Press. **477,** Excerpt from *Voices from Kurdistan,* edited by Rachel Warner. Copyright © 1991 by the Minority Rights Group. Reproduced by permission of the Minority Rights Group. **482,** Excerpt from *Sadako and the Thousand Paper Cranes* by Eleanor Coerr. Copyright © 1977 by Eleanor Coerr. Reproduced by permission of G.P. Putnam's Sons.

Illustration
9, 71, 167, 259, 355 BR, 449, 549 Michael Digiorgio

Photos
DK Dorling Kindersley 60 C, 60 BL, 61 T, 61 C, 248 BL, 249 TR, 438 TR, 538 BR, 539, 580 C, 581 TL

Table of Contents vi, Sami Sarkis/Photodisc; **vii T,** Larry Chiger/SuperStock; **vii B,** Bettman/Corbis; **viii,** Aubrey Diem/Valan Photos; **ix T,** Thomas Kitchin/Tom Stack & Associates; **ix B,** Art Wolfe/Getty Images; **x,** Alex Irvin/Alex Irvin Photography; **xi,** Wolfgang Kaehler/Liaison Agency, Inc.; **xii,** Stephen Johnson/Getty Images; **xiii,** Wolfgang Kaehler/ Wolfgang Kaehler Photography; **xiv,** M. & E. Bernheim/Woodfin Camp & Associates; **xv,** Frans Lanting/Minden Pictures; **xvi,** Jerry Alexander/Getty Images; **xvii T,** Janette Ostier Gallery, Paris, France/SuperStock; **xvii B,** Matthew Neal McVay/Getty Images; **xviii,** Ahreim Land, Northern Territory, Australia, Explorer SuperStock; **xix T,** Philip & Karen Smith/Getty Images; **xix B,** Wolfgang Kaehler/Wolfgang Kaehler Photography; **Special Features** xx, Christie's Images, London, UK/Bridgeman Art Library; **Unit I** xxxviii BL, Radhinka Chalasani/Getty Image; **xxxviii BC,** Ted Streshinsky/Corbis; **xxxviii BR,** Adam Woolfitt/Corbis; **1 TL,** Andrew Errington/Getty Images; **1 TR,** Andy Sacks/Getty Images; **1 BR,** Andy Sacks/Getty Images; **1 B,** © Victor Englebert/Photo Researchers Inc.; **2 TR,** Philip & Karen Smith/ Getty Images; **2 BL,** Corbis; **2 BR,** Don Smetzer/Getty Images; **3 TR,** Larry Chiger/SuperStock; **3 B,** Bettmann/Corbis; **4 T,** Ken Graham/Getty Images; **4 B,** Robert Frerck/Odyssey/Chicago; **5 TL,** Alan Abramowitz/Getty Images; **5 TR,** Peter Carmichael/Getty Images; **Chapter I** 10 T, Mike Agliolo/Corbis; **10 B,** Jeremy Woodhouse/PhotoDisc, Inc.; **11,** Stocktrek/PhotoDisc, Inc.; **14,** Sami Sarkis/PhotoDisc; **15,** Kevin Kelley/Getty Images; **19,** British Museum; **Chapter 2** 26, ESA/TSADOD/Tom Stack & Associates; **27,** © James A. Sugar/Corbis; **31,** Larry Chiger SuperStock; **34,** David Falconer/Getty Images; **36,** Rod Planck/Tom Stack & Associates; **Chapter 3** 40, The Granger Collection; **41,** Paul Chesley/Getty Images; **42,** Ken Fisher/Getty Images; **44,** © Bill Gentile/Corbis; **46,** Donna DeCesare; **47,** Paul Conklin/PhotoEdit; **48,** Don Smetzer/Getty Images; **49,** Donna DeCesare; **51,** Julia Vindasius/Vindasius; **53,** AP/Wide World Photos; **54,** © Bettmann/Corbis; **55,** Adam Woolfitt/Corbis; **56,** Hulton Deutsch Collection/Corbis; **Unit I** **DK** 60 TL, Jeff Divine/FPG International by Getty Images; **60 C,** Dorling Kindersley; **60 BL,** Dorling Kindersley; **61 T,** Dorling Kindersley; **61 C,** Dorling Kindersley; **61 B,** Mary Evans/Mary Evans Picture Library; **Unit 2** 62 T, Charles Sykes/Visuals Unlimited; **62 BL,** Bruce Forster/Getty Images; **62 BR,** J. Eastcott/Yva Momatiuk/Valan Photos; **63 TL,** Alan Klehr/Getty Images; **63 TR,** Robin Smith/Getty Images; **63 BL,** Corbis-Bettmann; **63 BR,** John Edwards/Getty Images; **64 TR,** Gordon Fisher/Getty Images; **64 BL,** John Trumball/The Granger Collection; **64 BR,** Lawrence Migdale/Getty Images; **65 T,** Thomas Kitchin/Tom Stack & Associates; **65 B,** Celestica, Inc.; **Chapter 4** 72, John Edwards/Getty Images; **73,** Olaf Soot/Getty Images; **75,** Thomas Kitchin/Tom Stack & Associates; **76,** Science VU/Visuals Unlimited; **77,** Donald Nausbaum/Getty Images; **79,** © Lowell Georgia/Corbis; **80,** Harold Sund/Getty Images; **81,** H. Armstrong Roberts; **82,** Vince Streano/Getty Images; **Chapter 5** 86 TL, Corbis Sygma; **86 TR,** Stock Trec/PhotoDisc, Inc; **86 B,** Eric Long/NASA/Smithsonian Inst.; **87,** Steve McCutcheon/Visuals Unlimited; **90,** The Granger Collection; **91,** The Granger Collection; **93,** Corbis; **94,** The Granger Collection; **95,** The Granger Collection; **96,** Library of Congress; **97,** Hutton/Archive

Photos; **98,** John D. Cunningham/Visuals Unlimited; **99,** Library of Congress; **Chapter 6 104 T,** Thomas Kitchin/Tom Stack & Associates; **104 B,** Bob Thomason/Getty Images; **105,** Lawrence Migdale/Getty Images; **108,** T. Phillibrown/Library of Congress; **109,** AP/Wide World Photos; **110,** Archive Photos; **111,** J. Eastcott/Yva Momatïuk/Valan Photography; **112,** Corbis/Stock Market; **113,** Dave G. Houser/Houser Stock, Inc.; **115,** Reuters/Corbis-Bettmann; **116,** Hutton/Archive Photos; **Chapter 7 120 T,** Jeremy Woodhouse/PhotoDisc, Inc.; **120 B,** McDaniel Woolf/PhotoDisc, Inc.; **121,** Wayne Eastep/Getty Images; **125,** AFP/Corbis; **127,** Bob Thomason/Getty Images; **129,** Inga Spence/Tom Stack & Associates; **132,** Gurmankin/Morina/Visuals Unlimited; **133,** Rosemary Calvert/Getty Images; **135,** Art Wolfe/Getty Images; **Chapter 8 140 T,** Glen Allison/Getty Images; **140 B,** Aubrey Diem/Valan Photos; **141,** Jean Bruneau/Valan Photos; **143,** Reuters/Corbis-Bettmann; **144,** John Edwards/Getty Images; **145,** ™ and © by Queen's Printer for Ontario 2001, reproduced with permission; **147,** © Cosmo Condina/Getty Images; **148,** © Michael S. Yamashita/Corbis; **149,** Hulton/Getty Images; **150,** Glen Allison/Getty Images; **Unit 2 DK 156 TR,** Corbis; **156 BL,** David G. Houser/Corbis; **156 BR,** Corbis-Bettmann; **157 TL,** Josef Scaylea/Corbis; **157 TR,** Brian Stablyk/Getty Images; **157 BL,** Corbis-Bettmann; **157 BR,** Sandy Felsenthal/Corbis; **Unit 3 158 T,** Ed Simpson/Getty Images; **158 BL,** Ed Simpson/Getty Images; **158 BR,** Robert Frerck/ Odyssey/Chicago; **159 TL,** D.E. Cox/Getty Images; **159 TR,** Mark Segal/Getty Images; **159 BL,** © Neil Beer/Corbis; **159 BR,** Corbis-Bettmann; **160 T,** Jaques Jangoux/Getty Images; **160 BR,** D.E. Cox/Getty Images; **160 BL,** Robert Frerck/Odyssey/Chicago; **161 T,** Chip & Rosa María de la Cueva Peterson; **161 B,** Robert Frerck/Odyssey/Chicago; **Chapter 9 168 T,** Chip & Rosa María de la Cueva Peterson; **168 B,** Robert Frerck/Odyssey/Chicago; **169,** Will & Deni McIntyre/Getty Images; **171,** Bryan Parsley/Getty Images; **173,** Robert Frerck/Odyssey/Chicago; **175,** Wolfgang Kaehler/Wolfgang Kaehler Photography; **176,** Erik Svenson/Getty Images; **177,** Robert Frerck/Odyssey/Chicago; **178,** Chip & Rosa María de la Cueva Peterson; **Chapter 10 182,** Ed Simpson/Getty Images; **183,** Chip & Rosa María de la Cueva Peterson; **184,** Chip & Rosa María de la Cueva Peterson; **185,** Chip & Rosa María de la Cueva Peterson; **186,** Daniel Aubry/Odyssey/Chicago; **187,** Stock Montage; **188,** Archivo Iconografico, S.A/Corbis; **189,** North Wind Picture Archives; **190,** Robert Frerck/Odyssey/Chicago; **191,** Robert Frerck/Odyssey/Chicago; **192,** Mark Segal/Getty Images; **Chapter 11 196 T,** Phillipe Columbi/PhotoDisc; **196 B,** Robert Frerck/Odyssey/Chicago; **197,** Demetrio Carrasco/Getty Images; **199,** Chip & Rosa María de la Cueva Peterson; **199 B,** David R. Frazier/Getty Images; **200,** Elizabeth Harris/Getty Images; **201,** Sheryl McNee/Getty Images; **201 BR,** Sheryl McNee/Getty Images; **202,** Robery E. Daemmrich/Getty Images; **203,** Jason Laure'/ Laure' Communications; **204,** SuperStock; **205,** Doug Armand/ Getty Images; **206,** Alex Irvin/Alex Irvin Photography; **207,** Ed Simpson/Getty Images; **209,** Sheryl McNee/Getty Images; **Chapter 12 212 T,** Jose Diego Maria Rivera, "Sugar Cane," 1931. Fresco. 57 1/8 x 94 1/8 in. (145.1cm x 239.1 cm). Philadelphia Museum of Art. Gift of Mr. and Mrs. Herbert Cameron Morris. 1943–46–2. (C) Banco de Mexico Diego Rivera Museum Trust; **212 B,** James Nelson/Getty Images; **213,** David R. Frazier/Getty Images; **216,** Robert Frerck/Odyssey/Chicago; **217,** Robert Frerck/Odyssey/Chicago; **220,** © Bill Gentile/Corbis; **221,** Chip & Rosa María de la Cueva Peterson; **224,** Robert Freck/ Odyssey/Chicago; **Chapter 13 228,** Doug Armand/Getty Images; **229,** © Jeff Greenberg/Omni-Photo Communications, Inc.; **231,** Corbis-Bettmann; **232,** Suzane L. Murphy/D.D. Bryant Photography; **233,** Chip & Rosa María de la Cueva Peterson; **235,** Sylvain Grandadam/Getty Images; **236,** Ary Diesendruck/Getty Images; **237,** Rhonda Klevansky/Getty Images; **238,** Charles Phillip/Photri-Microstock; **241,** Liaison Agency Inc./© Wolfgang Kaehler; **244,** Pan American Airways Corp.; **Unit 3 DK 248 TR,** Chiapas State, Mexico/Index/Bridgeman Art Library; **248 BL, 249 TR,** Dorling Kindersley; **249 BL,** Mary Evans/Mary Evans Picture Library; **249 BR,** Tony Morrison/South American Pictures; **Unit 4**

250 T, SIPA Press; **250 BR,** Michael Rosenfeld/Getty Images; **250 BL,** SuperStock; **251 TL,** Reuters Newsmedia, Inc./Corbis; **251 TR,** SuperStock; **251 BL,** David Barnes/Stock Market; **251 BR,** N. Ray/Art Directors/TRIP; **252 TR,** Julian Calder/Getty Images; **252 BL,** AP/Wide World Photos; **252 BR,** AP/Wide World Photos; **253,** AP/Wide World Photos; **Chapter 14 260,** W. Jacobs/Art Directors/TRIP; **261,** M. Feeney/Art Directors/TRIP; **263,** James Balog/Getty Images; **265,** D. MacDonald/Art Directors/TRIP; **267,** © Len Rue/Photo Researchers, Inc.; **268,** Arnulf Husmo/Getty Images; **Chapter 15 274 TL,** Stock Montage; **274 TR,** Bettmann/Corbis; **274 B,** Erich Lessing/Art Resource; **275,** SuperStock; **277,** Marte Ueda/Getty Images; **278,** The Granger Collection; **279,** Biblioteca Reale, Turin Italy/SuperStock; **281,** North Wind Picture Archives; **283,** AP/Wide World Photos; **284,** Victoria & Albert Museum, London, NY/Bridgeman Art Library/Art Resource; **285,** Historical Museum, Moscow, Russia/SuperStock; **286,** Novosti/Corbis-Bettmann; **Chapter 16 290 T,** Philip Webb, The Red House, Bexley Heath, UK, 1859. Photo by Charlotte Wood; **290 B,** Dewitt Jones/Getty Images; **291,** SuperStock; **292,** Stephen Johnson/Getty Images; **293,** Joseph Okwesa/Art Directors/TRIP; **294,** Michael Rosenfeld/Getty Images; **295,** North Wind Picture Archives; **297,** Ibrahim/Art Directors/TRIP; **298,** AP/ Wide World Photos; **299,** SuperStock; **300,** A. Kuznetsov/Art Directors/TRIP; **301,** Alexandra Avakian/Woodfin Camp & Associates; **302,** Wolfgang Kaehler/ Wolfgang Kaehler Photography; **303,** The Forbes Collection, New York; **Chapter 17 306 T,** Erich Lessing/Art Resource; **306 B,** EKA/Eureka Slide; **307,** John Drysdale/Woodfin Camp & Associates; **308,** AP/Wide World Photos; **311,** B. & C. Alexander/Bryan and Cherry Alexander Photography; **313,** © Paul Almasy/Corbis; **314,** Ian Murphy/Getty Images; **315,** AP/Wide World Photos; **317,** AP/Wide World Photos; **318,** Corbis-Bettmann; **319,** Chad Ehlers/Getty Images; **321,** Jean Pragen/Getty Images; **322,** Peter Timmermans/ Getty Images; **Chapter 18 326 T,** Jellybean Photographic and Imaging; **326 B,** B & C Alexander/Bryan & Cherry Alexander Photography; **327,** Henryk T. Kaiser/Envision; **330,** SuperStock; **333,** AP/Wide World Photos; **334,** AP/Wide world Photos; **336,** © Richard Oliver/Corbis; **337,** SIPA Press; **339,** Wolfgang Kaehler/Wolfgang Kaehler Photography; **340,** B. Turner/Art Directors/TRIP; **Unit 4 DK 344 T,** National Archaeological Museum, Athens, Greece/Ancient Art & Architecture Collection Ltd/Bridgeman Art Library; **344 L,** Biblioteque Nationale, Paris, France/Bridgeman Art Library; **344 R,** Vatican Museums and Galleries, Vatican City, Italy/Bridgeman Art Library; **344 B,** National Gallery, London; **345 TL,** Wallace Collection, London, UK/Bridgeman Art Library; **345 TR,** Musee d'Orsay, Paris, France/ Bridgeman art Library; **345 BL,** Hulton Archive/Getty images; **345 BR,** Los Angeles County Museum of Art,CA, USA/Bridgeman Art Library; **Unit 5 346 T,** Reuters/Corbis-Bettmann; **346 BL,** M. & E. Bernheim/Woodfin Camp & Associates; **346 BR,** Jason Laure'/Laure' Communications; **347 TL,** AP/Wide World Photos; **347 TR,** Jason Laure'/Laure' Communications; **347 BL,** Tim Davis/Getty Images; **347 BR,** Betty Press/Woodfin Camp & Associates; **348,** © John Conrad/Corbis; **348 BL,** Corbis Images Royalty Free; **348 BR,** Miguel Raurich/Getty Images; **349,** Ian Murphy/Getty Images; **349 B,** Paula Bronstein; **Chapter 19 356,** Victor Englebert/Victor Englebert Photography; **357,** Penny Tweedle/Getty Images; **358,** G. Winters/Art Directors/TRIP; **361,** Frans Lanting/Minden Pictures; **364,** Victor Englebert/Victor Englebert Photography; **364 BR,** Cabisco/Visuals Unlimited; **Chapter 20 370,** Jason Laure'/Laure' Communications; **371,** The Granger Collection; **372,** Boltin Picture Library; **373, 374,** SuperStock; **375,** The Granger Collection; **377,** Erich Lessing/Art Resource; **378,** Robert Frerck/Odyssey/Chicago; **379,** AP/Wide World Photos; **380,** Wolfgang Kaehler/Wolfgang Kaehler Photography; **Chapter 21 384 T,** M. & E. Bernheim/ Woodfin Camp & Associates; **384 B,** M. & E. Bernheim/ Woodfin Camp & Associates; **385,** Glen Allison/Getty Images; **386,** Lorne Resnick/Getty Images; **388,** Wolfgang Kaehler/Wolfgang Kaehler Photography; **389,** Wolfgang Kaehler/Wolfgang Kaehler Photography; **390,** M. & E. Bernheim/ Woodfin Camp & Associates;

391, Robert Frerck/Odyssey/Chicago; 392, Boyd Norton/Boyd Norton Photography; 393, P. Joynson-Hicks/Art Directors/TRIP; 394, Jason Laure'/Laure' Communications; 395, Jason Laure'/Laure' Communications; **Chapter 22 400 T,** Roland & Sabrina Michaud/Woodfin Camp & Associates; **400 B,** Lawrence Manning/Getty Images; 401, P. Mitchell/Art Directors/TRIP; 403, Israel Talby/ Woodfin Camp & Associates; 404, Don Smetzer/Getty Images; 405, Sylvain Grandadam/Getty Images; 408, Robert Frerck/Odyssey/Chicago; 411, AP/Wide World Photos; 413, Tim Beddow/Getty Images; 414, AP/Wide World Photos; 415, David Young-Wolff/PhotoEdit; **Chapter 23 418 T,** Dekeerle/ © Liaison Agency, Inc.; **418 B,** B. Mnguni/Art Directors/TRIP; 419, © Tom Mchugh/Photo Researchers; 421, AP/Wide World Photos; 422, Agence France © AFB/Corbis; 423, M. & E. Bernheim/Woodfin Camp & Associates; 426, Victor Englebert/Victor Englebert Photography; 427, Jason Laure'/Laure' Communications; 429, M. Jelliffe/Art Directors/TRIP; 430, AP/Wide World Photos; 431, Jason Laure'/Laure' Communications; 433, Paula Bronstein; **Unit 5 DK 438 TR,** Dorling KIndersley; **438 BL,** AP/Wide World Photos; **438 BR,** Mary Evans/Mary Evans Picture Library; **439 TL,** Richard T. Nowitz/Corbis; **439 TR,** Christie's Images, London, UK/Bridgeman Art Library; **439 BL,** Peter Dejong/AP/Wide World Photos; **439 BR,** Liaison Agency; **Unit 6 440 T,** Blaise Musau/AP/Wide World Photos; **440 BL,** Wendy Chan/Getty Images; **440 BR,** Wolfgang Kaehler/Wolfgang Kaehler Photography; **441 TL,** Al Stephenson/Woodfin Camp & Associates; **441 TR,** Karen Kasmauski/Woodfin Camp and Associates; **441 BL,** Kim Newton/Woodfin Camp &Association; **441 BR,** Cary Wolinsky/Getty Images; **442 TR,** Charles Preitner/Visuals Unlimited; **442 BL,** Jerry Alexander/Getty Images; **442 BR,** Andrea Booher/Getty Images; 443, Natalie Fobes/Getty Images; **443 B,** UPI/Corbis-Bettmann; **Chapter 24 450 T,** Howard Sochurek/Woodfin Camp & Associates; **450 B,** Art Wolfe/Getty Images; 451, D. Jenkin/Tropix Photographic Library; 454, Getty Images; 455, Wayland Publishers Limited/Wayland Publishers Limited; 456, Reuters/Will Burgess/Getty Images; 458, Robert Frerck/ Woodfin Camp & Associates; 461, Janette Ostier Gallery, Paris, France/SuperStock; **Chapter 25 464 T,** © Hulton Getty/Liaison Agency, Inc.; **464 B,** Cameramann International; 465, Vanni/Art Resource; 467, Scala/Art Resource; 469, Jerry Alexander/Getty Images; 472, Dilip Mehta/Woodfin Camp & Associates; 474, Wolfgang Kaehler/Wolfgang Kaehler Photography; 475, SuperStock/Culver Pictures, Inc.; 476, Erich Lessing/Art Resource; 478, Al Stephenson/ Woodfin Camp & Associates; **Chapter 26 482 T,** Pearson Education; **482 B,** Matthew Neal McVay/Getty Images; 483, A. Ramey/Woodfin Camp & Associates; 484, Cary Wolinsky/Getty Images; 486, Hulton Getty/Liaison Agency; 487, Wolfgang Kaehler/Wolfgang Kaehler Photography; 488, Jack Novak/SuperStock; 489, Robin Smith/Getty Images; 490, Andrea Booher/Getty Images; **491 T,** Cameramann International; **491 B,** M.M.N./Dinodia Picture Library; 492, Jason Laure'/Laure' Communications; 494, Zeynep Sumen/Getty Images; 495, A. Ramey/Woodfin Camp & Associates; 496, AFP/Corbis-Bettmann; **Chapter 27 500 T,** Yann Layma/ Getty Images; **500 B,** Ettagale Blauer/Laure' Communications; 501, D.E. Cox/Getty Images; 504, © Liu Liqun/ Corbis; 505, Karen Kasmauski/Woodfin Camp & Associates; 507, AP/Wide World Photos; 508, Cameramann International; 509, SuperStock; 511, Kim Newton/Woodfin Camp & Associates; 512, Natalie Fobes/Getty Images; **Chapter 28 518 T,** Wolfgang Kaehler/ Wolfgang Kaehler Photography; **518 B,** Barry Iverson/Woodfin Camp & Associates; 519, SuperStock; 521, Charles Prietner/Visuals Unlimited; 522, Photri-Microstock; 523, Ann & Bury Peerless/Ann & Bury Peerless Picture Library; **525 TL,** Steve Vidler/Getty Images; **525 TR,** Joel Simon/Getty Images; 527, Nabeel Turner/Getty Images; **529 TR,** Jane Lewis/Getty Images; **529 TL,** Barry Iverson/Woodfin Camp & Associates; 531, A. Ramsey/Woodfin Camp & Associates; **533 TL,** Cameramann International Limited; **533 TR,** Israel/Talby/Woodfin Camp & Associates; 534, Richard T. Nowitz/Corbis; **Unit 6 DK 538 TR,** Richard Anthony/Photo Researchers; **538 BL,** Astrid & Hans Frieder Michler/Science Source/Photo Researchers; **538 BR,** Dorling Kindersley; 539, Dorling Kindersley; **Unit 7 540 T,** AP/Wide World; **540 BL,** Wolfgang Kaehler/Wolfgang Kaehler Photography; **540 BR,** SuperStock; **541 TL,** Wolfgang Kaehler/Wolfgang Kaehler Photography; **541 TR,** Doug Armand/Getty Images; **541 BL,** Kurt Scholtz/SuperStock; **541 BR,** Zigy Kaluzney/Getty Images; 542, Wolfgang Kaehler/Wolfgang Kaehler Photography; **542 BL,** Wolfgang Kaehler/Wolfgang Kaehler Photography; **542 BR,** Robert Frerck/Getty Images; 543, Philip & Karen Smith/Getty Images; **543 B,** SuperStock; **Chapter 29 550,** Joseph Green Life File/PhotoDisc, Inc.; 551, SuperStock; 555, Patrick Ward/Getty Images; 556, Philip & Karen Smith/Getty Images; **556 B,** Doug Armand/Getty Images; 558, B & C Alexander/Bryan & Cherry Alexander Photography; 559, Roger Ressmeyer/Corbis; 560, Wolfgang Kaehler/Wolfgang Kaehler Photography; **Chapter 30 564 T,** Ahrem Land, Northern Territory, Australia/Explorer, SuperStock; **564 B,** Robert Frerck/Getty Images; 565, Wolfgang Kaehler/Wolfgang Kaehler Photography; 566, Zigy Kaluzney/Getty Images; 567, Getty Images; 568, Wolfgang Kaehler/Wolfgang Kaehler Photography; 569, Randy Wells/Getty Images; 571, SuperStock; 572, © James L. Amos/Corbis; 573, Wolfgang Kaehler/Wolfgang Kaehler Photography; 575, Dave Hiser/Getty Images; 576, Oliver Strewe/ Getty Images; **Unit 7 DK 580 TR,** Mary Evans/Mary Evans Picture Library; **580 C,** Dorling Kindersley; **580 BL,** Geoscience Features Picture Library; **580 BR,** Ed Lallo/Index Stock Photography; **581 TL,** Dorling Kindersley; **581 C,** Jeff Sherman/Getty Images; **581 BR,** The Kobal Collection; **Reference 582-583,** Kaz Chiba/PhotoDisc, Inc; **Regional Database 600-601,** Adam Crowley/PhotoDisc, Inc; **Glossary of Basic Geographic Terms 646 TL,** A & L Sinibaldi/Getty Images; **646 BL,** John Beatty/Getty Images; **647 TL,** Hans Strand/ Getty Images; **647 BL,** Spencer Swanger/Tom Stack & Associates; **647 BR,** Paul Chesley/Getty Images; **Gazetteer 649,** Chip & Rosa María de la Cueva Peterson; **650,** D. Jenkin/Tropix Photographic Library; 651, Nabeel Turner/Getty Images; 652, Charles Sykes/Visuals Unlimited; 653, Wolfgang Kaehler/Wolfgang Kaehler Photography; 654, James Balog/Getty Images; 655, Jean Pragen/Getty Images; **Glossary 656,** Jacques Jangoux/Getty Images; 658, Tammy Pelusol/Tom Stack & Associates; 660, Spencer Swanger/Tom Stack & Associates; 663, Nabeel Turner/Getty Images; 664, D. Jenkin/Tropix Photographic Library; 665, The Granger Collection; 666, SuperStock; 667, Nicholas Parfitt/Getty Images; 668, Don Smetzer/Getty Images; 669, Rod Planck/Tom Stack & Associates; **Spanish Glossary 680,** AP/Wide World Photos; 681, Nicholas Parfitt/Getty Images; 683, Rod Planck/Tom Stack & Associates.

Fabric Borders Unit 1, Japack Company/Corbis; **Unit 2,** Lowe Museum of Art, University of Miami/SuperStock; **Unit 3,** Kevin Schafer/Stone; **Unit 4,** State Hermitage Museum, St. Petersburg, Russia/Corbis; **Unit 5,** PEDG; **Unit 6,** Collection of the Newark Museum, Gift of Jacob E. Henegar, 1986/Art Resource; **Unit 7,** Ralph A. Clevenger/Corbis.